1 MONTH OF
FREE
READING

at
www.ForgottenBooks.com

By purchasing this book you are eligible for one month membership to ForgottenBooks.com, giving you unlimited access to our entire collection of over 1,000,000 titles via our web site and mobile apps.

To claim your free month visit:
www.forgottenbooks.com/free1116647

ISBN 978-0-331-38932-6
PIBN 11116647

Forgotten Books is a registered trademark of FB &c Ltd.
Copyright © 2018 FB &c Ltd.
FB &c Ltd, Dalton House, 60 Windsor Avenue, London, SW19 2RR.
Company number 08720141. Registered in England and Wales.

For support please visit www.forgottenbooks.com

HE·ARCHITECT
~AND·ENGINEER~
·OF·CALIFORNIA·

· JANUARY · 1917 ·

PVBLISHED·IN·SAN·FRANCISCO
TWENTY·FIVE·CENTS·THE·NVMBER

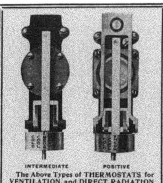
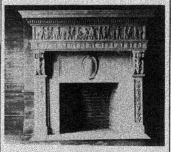
When writing to Advertisers please mention this magazine.

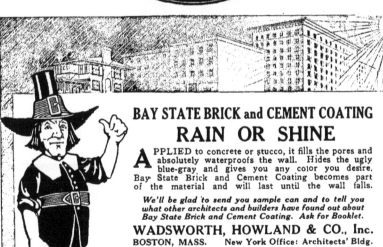

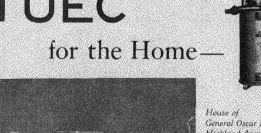

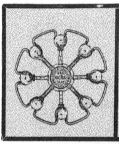

Architects' Specification Index

(For Index to Advertisements, see next page)

An Index to the Advertisements

ARCHITECTS' SPECIFICATION INDEX—*Continued*

CEMENT EXTERIOR FINISH
Bay State Brick and Cement Coating, made by Wadsworth, Howland & Co. (See list of Distributing Agents in adv.)
Concreta, sold by W. P. Fuller & Co., all principal Coast cities.
Glidden's Liquid Cement and Liquid Cement Enamel, sold on Pacific Coast by Whittier, Coburn Company, San Francisco.
Medusa White Portland Cement, California Agents, the Building Material Co., Inc., 587 Monadnock Bldg., San Francisco.
Samuel Cabot Mfg. Co., Boston, Mass., agencies in San Francisco, Oakland, Los Angeles, Portland, Tacoma and Spokane.
"Technola," manufactured and sold by C. Roman Co., 55 New Montgomery street, San Francisco.

CEMENT FLOOR COATING
Bay State Brick and Cement Coating, made by Wadsworth, Howland & Co. (See list of Distributing Agents in adv.)
Fuller's Concrete Floor Enamel, made by W. P. Fuller & Co., San Francisco.
Glidden's Concrete Floor Dressing, sold on Pacific Coast by Whittier, Coburn Company, San Francisco.

CEMENT HARDENER
J. L. Goffette Corporation, 227 San Bruno Ave., San Francisco.

CEMENT TESTS—CHEMICAL ENGINEERS
Robert W. Hunt & Co., 251 Kearny St., San Francisco.

CHURCH INTERIORS
Fink & Schindler, 218 13th St., San Francisco.

CHUTES—SPIRAL
Haslett Warehouse Co., 310 California St., San Francisco.

CLOCKS—TOWER—STREET—PROGRAM
E. Howard Clock Co., Boston. Pacific Coast Agents, The Albert S. Samuels Co., 895 Market St., San Francisco. Joseph Mayer & Bro., Seattle, Wash.

COLD STORAGE PLANTS
T. P. Jarvis Crude Oil Burning Co., 275 Connecticut St., San Francisco.

COMPOSITION FLOORING
Germanwood Floor Co., 1621 Eddy St., San Francisco.
Malott & Peterson, Monadnock Bldg., San Francisco.
"Vitrolite," Vitrolite Construction Co., 34 Davis St., San Francisco.

COMPRESSED AIR MACHINERY
General Machinery & Supply Co., 39 Stevenson St., San Francisco.

COMPRESSED AIR CLEANERS
Spencer Turbine Cleaner. Sold by Hughson & Merton, 530 Golden Gate Ave., San Francisco.
Tuec, mfrd. by United Electric Company, 556 Sutter St., San Francisco, and 724 S. Broadway, Los Angeles.

CONCRETE CONSTRUCTION
American Concrete Co., Humboldt Bank Bldg., San Francisco.
Clinton Construction Co., 140 Townsend street, San Francisco.
Barrett & Hilp, Sharon Bldg., San Francisco.
Palmer & Peterson, Monadnock Bldg., San Francisco.
Pacific Coast Steel Company, Rialto Bldg., San Francisco.

CONCRETE MIXERS
Austin Improved Cube Mixer. J. H. Hansen & Co., California agents, 508 Balboa Bldg., San Francisco.
Foote Mixers. Sold by Edw. R. Bacon, 40 Natoma St., San Francisco.

CONCRETE REINFORCEMENT
United States Steel Products Co., San Francisco, Los Angeles, Portland and Seattle.
Twisted Bars. Sold by Woods, Huddart & Gunn, 444 Market St., San Francisco.
Pacific Coast Steel Company, Rialto Bldg., San Francisco.
Southern California Iron and Steel Company, Fourth and Mateo Sts., Los Angeles.
Triangle Mesh Fabric. Sales agents, Pacific Building Materials Co., 523 Market St., San Francisco.

CONCRETE SURFACING
"Concreta." Sold by W. P. Fuller & Co., San Francisco.
Wadsworth, Howland & Co.'s Bay State Brick and Cement Coating. Sold by Jas. Hambly Co., Pacific Bldg., San Francisco, and Los Angeles.
Glidden Liquid Cement, manufactured by Glidden Varnish Co., Whittier, Coburn Co., San Francisco.

CONTRACTOR'S BONDS
Bonding Company of America, Kohl Bldg., San Francisco.
Globe Indemnity Co., 120 Leidesdorff St., San Francisco.
Fred H. Boggs, Foxcroft Bldg., San Francisco.
Fidelity & Deposit Co. of Maryland, Insurance Exchange, San Francisco.
J. T. Costello Co., 216 Pine St., San Francisco.

CONTRACTORS, GENERAL
Arthur Arlett, New Call Bldg., San Francisco.
Farrell & Reed, Gunst Bldg., San Francisco.
American Concrete Co., Humboldt Bank Bldg., San Francisco.
Barrett & Hilp, Sharon Bldg., San Francisco.
Carnahan & Mulford, 45 Kearny St., San Francisco.
Houghton Construction Co., Hooker & Lent Bldg., San Francisco.
W. T. & W. E. Commary, Crocker Bank Bldg., San Francisco.
Geo. H. Bos, Hearst Bldg., San Francisco.
Larsen, Sampson & Co., Crocker Bldg., San Francisco.
J. D. Hannah, 725 Chronicle Bldg., San Francisco.
Clinton Construction Company, 140 Townsend St., San Francisco.
Dioguardi & Terranova, Westbank Bldg., San Francisco.
Wm. A. Larkins, 1024 Hearst Bldg., San Francisco.
Teichert & Ambrose, Ochsner Bldg., Sacramento.
L. G. Bergren & Son, Call Bldg., San Francisco.
Grace & Bernieri, Claus Spreckels Bldg., San Francisco.
Geo. W. Boxton & Son, Hearst Bldg., San Francisco.
W. C. Duncan & Co., 526 Sharon Bldg., San Francisco.
A. P. Brady, Humboldt Bank Bldg., San Francisco.
Cameron & Disston, 831 Hearst Bldg., San Francisco.
Howard S. Williams, Hearst Bldg., San Francisco.
Kerr & McLean, General Contractors Ass'n, San Francisco.
Harvey A. Klyce, Sheldon Bldg., San Francisco.
Knowles & Mathewson, Call Bldg., San Francisco.
Lange & Bergstrom, Sharon Bldg., San Francisco.

WHIT'TIER - COBURN CO.

MANUFACTURERS
WHITTIER QUALITY PAINTS
Distributors
GLIDDEN CONCRETE PAINTS   BRIDGEPORT STANDARD STAINS
Sales Office :: Howard and Beale Streets, San Francisco, Cal.

ARCHITECTS' SPECIFICATION INDEX—*Continued*

CONTRACTORS, GENERAL—Continued
Masow & Morrison, 518 Monadnock Bldg., San Francisco.
McLeran & Peterson, Sharon Bldg., San Francisco.
Monson Bros., 1907 Bryant St., San Francisco.
Seabury B. Peterson Co., 46 Kearny St., San Francisco.
J. M. Dougan Co., Hearst Bldg., San Francisco.
Palmer & Peterson, Monadnock Bldg., San Francisco.
Robert Trost, Twenty-sixth and Howard Sts., San Francisco.
John Monk, Sheldon Bldg., San Francisco.
Ward & Goodwin, 110 Jessie St., San Francisco.
Williams Bros. & Henderson, 381 Tenth St., San Francisco.

CONVEYING MACHINERY
Meese & Gottfried, San Francisco, Los Angeles, Portland and Seattle.

CORK TILING, FLOORING, ETC.
Beaver Cork Tile. Sold by W. L. Eaton & Co., 812 Santa Marina Bldg., San Francisco.

CORNER BEAD
Capitol Sheet Metal Works, 1827 Market St., San Francisco.
United States Metal Products Co., 525 Market St., San Francisco; 750 Keller St., San Francisco.

CRUSHED ROCK
Grant Gravel Co., Flatiron Bldg., San Francisco.
California Building Material Company, new Call Bldg., San Francisco.
Niles Sand, Gravel & Rock Co., Mutual Bank Bldg., San Francisco.
Pratt Building Material Co., Hearst Bldg., San Francisco.
Niles Canyon Stone Products Co., Niles, Cal.

DAMP-PROOFING COMPOUND
Glidden's Liquid Rubber, sold on Pacific Coast by Whittier, Coburn Company, San Francisco.
Armorite Damp Resisting Paint, made by W. P. Fuller & Co., San Francisco.
Imperial Co., 183 Stevenson St., San Francisco.
"Pabco" Damp-Proofing Compound, sold by Paraffine Paint Co., 34 First St., San Francisco.
Wadsworth, Howland & Co., Inc., 84 Washington St., Boston. (See Adv. for Coast agencies.)

DOOR HANGERS
McCabe Hanger Mfg. Co., New York, N. Y.
Pitcher Hanger, sold by National Lumber Co., 326 Market St., San Francisco.
Reliance Hanger, sold by Sartorius Co., San Francisco; D. F. Fryer & Co., B. V. Collins, Los Angeles, and Columbia Wire & Iron Works, Portland, Ore.

DRAIN BOARDS, SINK BACKS, ETC.
Germanwood Floor Co., 1621 Eddy St., San Francisco.

DRINKING FOUNTAINS
Haws Sanitary Fountain, 1808 Harmon St., Berkeley, and C. F. Weber & Co., San Francisco and Los Angeles.
Crane Company, San Francisco, Oakland, and Los Angeles.
Pacific Porcelain Ware Co., 67 New Montgomery St., San Francisco.

DUMB WAITERS
Spencer Elevator Company, 173 Beale St., San Francisco.
M. E. Hammond, Humboldt Bank Bldg., San Francisco.

ELECTRICAL CONTRACTORS
Butte Engineering Co., 683 Howard St., San Francisco.
NePage, McKenny Co., 149 New Montgomery St., San Francisco.
Newbery Electrical Co., 413 Lick Bldg., San Francisco.
Pacific Fire Extinguisher Co., 507 Montgomery St., San Francisco.
H. S. Tittle, 245 Minna St., San Francisco.
Rex Electric and Construction Co., Inc., 1174 Sutter St., San Francisco.
Standard Electrical Construction Company, 60 Natoma St., San Francisco.

ELECTRICAL ENGINEERS
Chas. T. Phillips, Pacific Bldg., San Francisco.

ELECTRIC PLATE WARMER·
The Prometheus Electric Plate Warmer for residences, clubs, hotels, etc. Sold by M. E. Hammond, Humboldt Bank Bldg., San Francisco.

ELEVATORS
Otis Elevator Company, Stockton and North Point, San Francisco.
Spencer Elevator Company, 126 Beale St., San Francisco.
Van Emon Elevator Co., 54 Natoma St., San Francisco.

ELEVATOR ENCLOSURES
Dahlstrom Metallic Door Company, Jamestown, N. Y. (See advertisement for Coast representatives.)

ENGINEERS
Chas. T. Phillips, Pacific Bldg., San Francisco.
Hunter & Hudson, Rialto Bldg., San Francisco.

FIRE EXIT DEVICES, DOORS, ETC.
Dahlstrom Metallic Door Company, Jamestown, N. Y.

FIRE ESCAPES
Palm Iron & Bridge Works, Sacramento.
Western Iron Works, 141 Beale St., San Francisco. .

FIRE EXTINGUISHERS
Scott Company, 243 Minna St., San Francisco
Pacific Fire Extinguisher Co., 507 Montgomery St., San Francisco.

ARCHITECTS' SPECIFICATION INDEX—*Continued*

FIREPROOFING AND PARTITIONS
Gladding, McBean & Co., Crocker Bldg., San Francisco.
Keyhold Lath Co., Monadnock Bldg., San Francisco.
Los Angeles Pressed Brick Co., Frost Bldg., Los Angeles.

FIXTURES—BANK, OFFICE, STORE. ETC.
T. H. Meek & Co., 1130 Mission St., San Francisco.
Mullen Manufacturing Co., 20th and Harrison Sts., San Francisco.
The Fink & Schindler Co., 218 13th St., San Francisco.
A. J. Forbes & Son, 1530 Filbert St., San Francisco.
C. F. Weber & Co., 365 Market St., San Francisco, and 210 N. Main St., Los Angeles, Cal.

FLAG POLE TOPS
Bolander & Son, 270 First St., San Francisco.

FLOOR TILE
New York Belting and Packing Company, 519 Mission St., San Francisco.
W. L. Eaton & Co., 112 Market St., San Francisco.

FLOOR VARNISH
Bass-Hueter and San Francisco Pioneer Varnish Works, 816 Mission St., San Francisco.
Fifteen for Floors, made by W. P. Fuller & Co., San Francisco.
Standard Varnish Works, Chicago, New York and San Francisco.
Glidden Products, sold by Whittier, Coburn Co., San Francisco.
R. N. Nason & Co., San Francisco and Los Angeles.

FLOORS—COMPOSITION
"Vitrolite," for any structure, room or bath. Vitrolite Construction Co., 1490 Mission St., San Francisco.
Malott & Peterson, Inc., Monadnock Bldg., San Francisco.
Germanwood Floor Co., 1621 Eddy St., San Francisco.

FLOORS—HARDWOOD
Oak Flooring Bureau, Conway Bldg., Chicago, Ill.
Strable Mfg. Co., 511 First St., Oakland.

FLUMES
California Corrugated Culvert Co., West Berkeley, Cal.

GAS FURNACES
Cole Gas Furnace, Cole Heater Sales Co., Lick Bdg., San Francisco, 1764 Broadway, Oakland.

GARAGE EQUIPMENT
Bowser Gasoline Tanks and Outfit, Bowser & Co., 612 Howard St., San Francisco.

GLASS
W. P. Fuller & Company, all principal Coast cities.
Whittier, Coburn Co., Howard and Beale Sts., San Francisco.

GRANITE
California Granite Co., Sharon Bldg., San Francisco.
McGilvray-Raymond Granite Co., 634 Townsend St., San Francisco.
Raymond Granite Co., Potrero Ave. and Division St., San Francisco.

GRAVEL AND SAND
California Building Material Co., new Call Bldg., San Francisco.
Del Monte White Sand, sold by Pacific Improvement Co., Crocker Bldg., San Francisco.
Pratt Building Material Co., Hearst Bldg., San Francisco.
Grant Gravel Co., Flatiron Bldg., San Francisco.
Grant Rock & Gravel Co., Cory Bldg., Fresno.
Niles Sand, Gravel & Rock Co., Mutual Savings Bank Bldg., 704 Market St., San Francisco.
Niles Canyon Stone Products Co., Niles, Cal.

HARDWALL PLASTER
Henry Cowell Lime & Cement Co., San Francisco.

HARDWARE
Pacific Hardware & Steel Company, representing Lockwood Hardware Co., San Francisco.
Sargent's Hardware, sold by Bennett Bros., 514 Market St., San Francisco.

HARDWOOD LUMBER—FLOORING. ETC.
Dieckmann Hardwood Co., Beach and Taylor Sts., San Francisco.
Parrott & Co., 320 California St., San Francisco.
White Bros., cor. Fifth and Brannan Sts., San Francisco.
Strable Mfg. Co., 511 First St., Oakland.

HEATERS—AUTOMATIC
Pittsburg Water Heater Co., 478 Sutter St., San Francisco.

HEATING AND VENTILATING
Gilley-Schmid Company, 198 Otis St., San Francisco.
Mangrum & Otter, Inc., 507 Mission St., San Francisco.
Charles T. Phillips, Pacific Bldg., San Francisco.
J. C. Hurley Co., 509 Sixth St., San Francisco.
William F. Wilson Co., 328 Mason St., San Francisco.
Pacific Fire Extinguisher Co., 507 Montgomery St., San Francisco.
Scott Company, 243 Minna St., San Francisco.
Thermic Engineering Company, Claus Spreckels Bldg., San Francisco.
C. A. Dunham Co., Wells Fargo Bldg., San Francisco.

McELHINNEY TILE CO.

Contractors for
FLOOR, WALL AND MANTEL TILE

1097 Mission Street, San Francisco   Park 6986

ARCHITECTS' SPECIFICATION INDEX—*Continued*

HEAT REGULATION
Johnson Service Company, 149 Fifth St., San Francisco.

HOLLOW BLOCKS
Denison ·Hollow Interlocking Blocks, Forum Bldg., Sacramento, and Chamber of Commerce Bldg., Portland.
Gladding, McBean & Co., San Francisco, Los Angeles, Oakland and Sacramento.
Pratt Building Material Co., Hearst Bldg., San Francisco.

HOLLOW METAL DOORS AND TRIM
Dahlstrom Metallic Door Company, Jamestown, N. Y.
Edwin C. Dehn, 301 Hearst Bldg., San Francisco, representing Interior Metal Mfg. Co., Jamestown, N. Y.

HOSPITAL FIXTURES
J. L. Mott Iron Works, 135 Kearny St., San Francisco.

HOTELS
St. Francis Hotel, Union Square, San Francisco.

INGOT IRON
"Armco" brand, manufactured by American Rolling Mill Company, Middletown, Ohio, and Monadnock Bldg., San Francisco.

INSPECTIONS AND TESTS
Robert W. Hunt & Co., 251 Kearny St., San Francisco.

INTERIOR DECORATORS
Mrs. H. C. McAfee, 504 Sutter St., San Francisco.
Albert S. Bigley, 344 Geary St., San Francisco.
A. Falvy, 323 Sutter St., San Francisco.
The Tormey Co., 681 Geary St., San Francisco.
Fick Bros., 475 Haight St., San Francisco.
O'Hara & Livermore, Sutter St., San Francisco.

IRONING BOARDS
Noack Disappearing Ironing Board Co., Humboldt Bank Bldg., San Francisco, and 324 Broadway, Oakland.
Western Equipment Co., Building Material Exhibit, 77 O'Farrell St., San Francisco.

KITCHEN CABINETS
Western Equipment Co., Building Material Exhibit, 77 O'Farrell St., San Francisco.
Hoosier Cabinets, branch 1067 Market St., San Francisco.

LIGHTING FIXTURES
"The Crystal Light," manufactured by Modern Appliance Co., 128 Sutter St., San Francisco.

LAMP POSTS, ELECTROLIERS, ETC.
J. L. Mott Iron Works, 135 Kearny St., San Francisco.
Ralston Iron Works, 20th and Indiana Sts., San Francisco.

LANDSCAPE GARDENERS
MacRorie-McLaren Co., 141 Powell St., San Francisco.

LATHING MATERIAL
"Buttonlath," manufactured and sold by Pioneer Paper Company, Los Angeles and San Francisco.
Keyhold Lath Co., Monadnock Bldg., San Francisco.

LIGHT, HEAT AND POWER
Pacific Gas & Elec. Co., 445 Sutter St., San Francisco.

LIME
Henry Cowell Lime & Cement Co., 2 Market St., San Francisco.

LINOLEUM
D. N. & E. Walter & Co., O'Farrell and Stockton Sts., San Francisco.

LOCKS—KEYLESS
Nydia Bank Lock Co., 52 Main St., San Francisco.

LUMBER
Dudfield Lumber Co., Palo Alto, Cal.
Hooper Lumber Co., Seventeenth and Illinois Sts., San Francisco.
Sunset Lumber Co., Oakland, Cal.
Santa Fe Lumber Co., Seventeenth and De Haro Sts., San Francisco.
Pacific Manufacturing Company, San Francisco, Oakland and Santa Clara.
Pacific Mill and Timber Co., First National Bank Bldg., San Francisco.
United Lumber Company, 687 Market St., San Francisco.

MASTIC FLOORING
Malott & Peterson, Monadnock Bldg., San Francisco.

MAIL CHUTES
Cutler Mail Chute Co., Rochester, N. Y. (See adv. on page 30 for Coast representatives.)
American Mailing Device Corp., represented on Pacific Coast by U. S. Metal Products Co., 525 Market St., San Francisco.

MANTELS
Mangrum & Otter, 561 Mission St., San Francisco.
Oakland Mantel Co., 2148 Telegraph Ave., Oakland.

MARBLE
Joseph Musto Sons, Keenan Co., 535 N. Point St., San Francisco.
Sculptors' Workshop. S. Miletin & Co., 1705 Harrison St., San Francisco.

METAL CEILINGS
San Francisco Metal Stamping & Corrugating Co., 2269 Folsom St., San Francisco.

METAL DOORS AND WINDOWS
Dahlstrom Metallic Door Company, Jamestown, N. Y. (See advertisement for Coast Representatives.)
U. S. Metal Products Co., 525 Market St., San Francisco.
Capitol Sheet Metal Works, 1927 Market St., San Francisco.

METAL FURNITURE
Capitol Sheet Metal Works, 1927 Market St., San Francisco.
Ralston Iron Works, Twentieth and Indiana Sts., San Francisco.
Edwin C. Dehn, Manufacturer's Agent, Hearst Bldg., San Francisco.

METAL SHINGLES
San Francisco Metal Stamping & Corrugating Co., 2269 Folsom St., San Francisco.

MILL WORK
Dudfield Lumber Co., Palo Alto, Cal.
Pacific Manufacturing Company, San Francisco, Oakland and Santa Clara.
National Mill and Lumber Co., San Francisco and Oakland.
The Fink & Schindler Co., 218 13th St., San Francisco.

OIL BURNERS
S. T. Johnson Co., 1337 Mission St., San Francisco.
T. P. Jarvis Crude Oil Burner Co., 275 Connecticut St., San Francisco.
Fess System, 220 Natoma St., San Francisco.
W. S. Ray Mfg. Co., 218 Market St., San Francisco.

ORNAMENTAL IRON AND BRONZE
American Art Metal Works, 13 Grace St., San Francisco.
California Artistic Metal and Wire Co., 349 Seventh St., San Francisco.
Brode Iron Works, 31-37 Hawthorne St., San Francisco.

ARCHITECTS' SPECIFICATION INDEX—*Continued*

ORNAMENTAL IRON AND BRONZE—Con't.
Palm Iron & Bridge Works, Sacramento.
Ralston Iron Works, 20th and Indiana Sts., San Francisco.
J. L. Mott Iron Works, 135 Kearny St., San Francisco.
C. J. Hillard Company, Inc., 19th and Minnesota Sts., San Francisco.
Schreiber & Sons Co., represented by Western Builders Supply Co., San Francisco.
Sims, Gray & Sauter Iron Works, 156 Main St., San Francisco.
Schrader Iron Works, Inc., 1247 Harrison St., San Francisco.
West Coast Wire & Iron Works, 861-863 Howard St., San Francisco.

PAINT FOR CEMENT
Bay State Brick and Cement Coating, made by Wadsworth, Howland & Co. (Inc.) (See adv. in this issue for Pacific Coast agents.)
Fuller's Concreta for Cement, made by W. P. Fuller & Co., San Francisco.
Samuel Cabot Mfg. Co., Boston, Mass., agencies in San Francisco, Oakland, Los Angeles, Portland, Tacoma and Spokane.
C. Roman Co., 55 New Montgomery St., San Francisco.

PAINT FOR STEEL STRUCTURES, BRIDGES, ETC.
Glidden's Acid Proof Coating, sold on Pacific Coast by Whittier, Coburn Company, San Francisco.
Paraffine Paint Co., 34 First St., San Francisco.
Premier Graphite Paint and Pioneer Brand Red Lead, made by W. P. Fuller & Co., San Francisco.

PAINTING, TINTING, ETC.
I. R. Kissel, 1747 Sacramento St., San Francisco.
D. Zelinsky & Sons, San Francisco and Los Angeles.
Fick Bros., 475 Haight St., San Francisco.

PAINTS, OILS, ETC.
The Brininstool Co., Los Angeles, the Haslett Warehouse, 310 California St., San Francisco.
Bass-Hueter Paint Co., Mission, near Fourth St., San Francisco.
C. Roman Co., 55 New Montgomery St., San Francisco.
Whittier, Coburn Co., Howard and Beale Sts., San Francisco.
Magner Bros., 419-421 Jackson St., San Francisco.
R. N. Nason & Company, San Francisco, Los Angeles, Portland and Seattle.
W. P. Fuller & Co., all principal Coast cities.
Standard Varnish Works, 55 Stevenson St., San Francisco.

PANELS AND VENEER
White Bros., Fifth and Brannan Sts., San Francisco.

PIPE—VITRIFIED SALT GLAZED TERRA COTTA
Gladding, McBean & Co., Crocker Bldg., San Francisco.
Pratt Building Material Co., Hearst Bldg., San Francisco.
Steiger Terra Cotta and Pottery Works, Mills Bldg., San Francisco.
G. Weissbaum & Co. Pipe Works, 127 Eleventh St., San Francisco.

PLASTER CONTRACTORS
C. C. Morehouse, Crocker Bldg., San Francisco.
MacGruer & Co., 180 Jessie St., San Francisco.

PLASTER EXTERIORS
"Kellastone," an imperishable stucco. Blake Plaster Co., Bacon Block, Oakland.
Keyhold Lath Co., Monadnock Bldg., San Francisco.
Buttonlath, for exterior and interior plastering, Pioneer Paper Co., San Francisco and Los Angeles.

PLUMBING CONTRACTORS
Alex Coleman, 706 Ellis St., San Francisco.
A. Lettich, 365 Fell St., San Francisco.
Gilley-Schmid Company, 198 Otis St., San Francisco.
Scott Co., Inc., 243 Minna St., San Francisco.
Wm. F. Wilson Co., 328 Mason St., San Francisco.

PLUMBING FIXTURES, MATERIALS, ETC.
Crane Co., San Francisco and Oakland.
California Steam Plumbing Supply Co., 671 Fifth St., San Francisco.
Gilley-Schmid Company, 198 Otis St., San Francisco.
Glauber Brass Manufacturing Company, 1107 Mission St., San Francisco.
Improved Sanitary Fixture Co., 632 Metropolitan Bldg., Los Angeles.
J. L. Mott Iron Works, D. H. Gulick, selling agent, 135 Kearny St., San Francisco.
Haines, Jones & Cadbury Co., 857 Folsom St., San Francisco.
H. Mueller Manufacturing Co., Pacific Coast branch, 589 Mission St., San Francisco.
Pacific Sanitary Manufacturing Co., 67 New Montgomery St., San Francisco.
Wm. F. Wilson Co., 328 Mason St., San Francisco.
C. A. Dunham Co., Wells Fargo Bldg., San Francisco.

POTTERY
Gladding, McBean & Co., San Francisco, Los Angeles, Oakland and Sacramento.
Steiger Terra Cotta and Pottery Works, Mills Bldg., San Francisco.

POWER TRANSMITTING MACHINERY
Meese & Gottfried, San Francisco, Los Angeles, Portland, Ore., and Seattle, Wash.

PUMPS
Simonds Machinery Co., 117 New Montgomery St., San Francisco.

RAILROADS
Southern Pacific Company, Flood Bldg., San Francisco.

REFRIGERATORS
McCray Refrigerators, sold by Nathan Dohrmann Co., Geary and Stockton Sts., San Francisco.

REVERSIBLE WINDOWS
Hauser Reversible Window Company, Balboa Bldg., San Francisco.
Whitney Windows, represented by Richard Spencer, 801-3 Hearst Bldg., San Francisco.

REVOLVING DOORS
Van Kennel Doors, sold by U. S. Metal Products Co., 525 Market St., San Francisco.

ROLLING DOORS, SHUTTERS, PARTITIONS, ETC.
Pacific Building Materials Co., 523 Market St., San Francisco.
C. F. Weber & Co., 365 Market St., S. F.
Kinnear Steel Rolling Doors, W. W. Thurston, agent, Rialto Bldg., San Francisco.
Wilson's Steel Rolling Doors, U. S. Metal Products Co., San Francisco and Los Angeles.

'ARCHITECTS' SPECIFICATION INDEX—Continued

ROOFING AND ROOFING MATERIALS
Grant Gravel Co., Flatiron Bldg., San Francisco.
H. W. Johns-Manville Co., Second and Howard Sts., San Francisco.
Malott & Peterson, Inc., Monadnock Bldg., San Francisco.
Niles Sand, Gravel and Rock Co., Mutual Bank Bldg., San Francisco.
"Malthoid" and "Kuberoid," manufactured by Paraffine Paint Co., San Francisco. .
Pioneer Roofing, manufactured by Pioneer Paper Co., 513 Hearst Bldg., San Francisco.
United Materials Co., Crossley Bldg., San Francisco.
RUBBER TILING
Goodyear Rubber Company, 587 Market St., San Francisco.
New York Belting & Rubber Company, 519 Mission St., San Francisco.
SAFETY TREADS
"Sanitread," sold by Richard Spencer, 801-3 Hearst Bldg., San Francisco.
SANITARY DRINKING FOUNTAINS
J. L. Mott Iron Works, 135 Kearny St., San Francisco.
Haws' Sanitary Drinking Faucet Co., 1808 Harmon St., Berkeley.
SCENIC PAINTING—DROP CURTAINS, ETC.
The Edwin H. Flagg Scenic Co., 1638 Long Beach Ave., Los Angeles.
SCHOOL FURNITURE AND SUPPLIES
C. F. Weber & Co., 365 Market St., San Francisco; 512 S. Broadway, Los Angeles.
SCREENS
Hipolito Flyout Screens, sold by Simpson & Stewart, Dalziel Bldg., Oakland.
Watson Metal Frame Screens, sold by Richard Spencer, 801-3 Hearst Bldg., San Francisco.
SEEDS
California Seed Company, 151 Market St., San Francisco.
SHEATHING AND SOUND DEADENING
Samuel Cabot Mfg. Co., Boston, Mass., agencies in San Francisco, Oakland, Los Angeles, Portland, Tacoma and Spokane.
Paraffine Paint Co., 34 First St., San Francisco.
SHEET METAL WORK, SKYLIGHTS, ETC.
Capitol Sheet Metal Works, 1927 Market St., San Francisco.
U. S. Metal Products Co., 525 Market St., San Francisco.
SHINGLE STAINS
Cabot's Creosote Stains, sold by Pacific Building Materials Co., Underwood Bldg., San Francisco.
Fuller's Pioneer Shingle Stains, made by W. P. Fuller & Co., San Francisco.
SIDEWALK LIGHTS
P. H. Jackson & Co., 237-47 First St., San Francisco.
STEEL AND IRON—STRUCTURAL
Central Iron Works, 621 Florida St., San Francisco.
Dyer Bros., 17th and Kansas Sts., San Francisco.
Brode Iron Works, 31 Hawthorne St., San Francisco.

STEEL AND IRON—STRUCTURAL—Con't.
Golden Gate Iron Works, 1541 Howard St., San Francisco.
Judson Manufacturing Co., 819 Folsom St., San Francisco.
Mortenson Construction Co., 19th and Indiana Sts., San Francisco.
Pacific Rolling Mills, 17th and Mississippi Sts., San Francisco.
Palm Iron & Bridge Works, Sacramento.
Ralston Iron Works, Twentieth and Indiana Sts., San Francisco.
U. S. Steel Products Co., Rialto Bldg., San Francisco.
Sims, Gray & Sauter, 156 Main St., San Francisco.
Schrader Iron Works, Inc., 1247 Harrison St., San Francisco.
Southern California Iron and Steel Co., Fourth and Mateo Sts., Los Angeles.
Western Iron Works, 141 Beale St., San Francisco.
STEEL PRESERVATIVES
Bay State Steel Protective Coating. (See adv. for coast agencies.)
Paraffine Paint Co., 34 First St., San Francisco.
STEEL MOULDINGS FOR STORE FRONTS
Dahlstrom Metallic Door Company, Jamestown, N. Y. (See advertisement for Coast Representatives.)
STEEL FIREPROOF WINDOWS
United States Metal Products Co., San Francisco.
STEEL REINFORCING
Pacific Coast Steel Company, Rialto Bldg., San Francisco.
Southern California Iron & Steel Company, Fourth and Mateo Sts., Los Angeles.
Woods, Huddart & Gunn, 444 Market St., San Francisco.
STEEL ROLLING DOORS
Kinnear Steel Rolling Door Co., W. W. Thurston, Rialto Bldg., San Francisco.
STEEL SASH
"Fenestra," solid steel sash, manufactured by Detroit Steel Products Company, Detroit, Mich.
STEEL WHEELBARROWS
Champion and California steel brands, made by Western Iron Works, 141 Beale St., San Francisco.
STONE
California Granite Co., 518 Sharon Bldg., San Francisco.
McGilvray Stone Company, 634 Townsend St., San Francisco.
STORAGE SYSTEMS—GASOLINE, OIL, ETC.
S. F. Bowser & Co., 612 Howard St., San Francisco.
STORE FRONTS
Kawneer Manufacturing Co., Berkeley, Cal.
TEMPERATURE REGULATION
Johnson Service Company, 149 Fifth St., San Francisco.
THEATER AND OPERA CHAIRS
C. F. Weber & Co., 365 Market St., San Francisco.

ARCHITECTS' SPECIFICATION INDEX—*Continued*

TILES, MOSAICS, MANTELS, ETC.
California Tile Contracting Company, Sheldon Bldg., San Francisco.
Mangrum & Otter, 561 Mission St., San Francisco.
Oakland Mantel Co., 2148 Telegraph Ave., Oakland.
McElhinney Tile Co., 1097 Mission St., San Francisco.
TILE FOR ROOFING
Gladding, McBean & Co., Crocker Bldg., San Francisco.
United Materials Co., Crossley Bldg., San Francisco.
TILE WALLS—INTERLOCKING
Denison Hollow Interlocking Blocks, Forum Bldg., Sacramento.
Gladding, McBean & Co., San Francisco, Los Angeles, Oakland and Sacramento.
Pratt Building Material Co., Hearst Bldg., San Francisco.
TREES
California Seed Company, 151 Market St., San Francisco.
VACUUM CLEANERS
"Tuec" Air Cleaner, manufactured by United Electric Co. Coast agencies, 556 Sutter St., San Francisco, and 724 S. Broadway, Los Angeles.
Spencer Turbine Cleaner, sold by Hughson & Merton, 530 Golden Gate Ave., San Francisco.
VALVES
Sloan Royal Flush Valves. T. R. Burke, Pacific Coast agent, Wells Fargo Bldg., San Francisco.
Crane Radiator Valves., manufactured by Crane Co., Second and Brannan Sts., San Francisco.
VALVE PACKING
N. H. Cook Belting Co., 317 Howard St., San Francisco.
VARNISHES
W. P. Fuller Co., all principal Coast cities.
Glidden Varnish Co., Cleveland, O., represented on the Pacific Coast by Whittier, Coburn Co., San Francisco.
R. N. Nason & Co., San Francisco, Los Angeles, Portland and Seattle.
Standard Varnish Works, San Francisco.
S. F. Pioneer Varnish Works, 816 Mission St., San Francisco.
VENETIAN BLINDS, AWNINGS, ETC.
Burlington Venetian Blinds, Burlington, Vt., and C. F. Weber & Co., 365 Market St., San Francisco.
Western Blind & Screen Co., 2702 Long Beach Ave., Los Angeles.
VITREOUS CHINAWARE
Pacific Porcelain Ware Company, 67 New Montgomery St., San Francisco.
WALL BEDS, SEATS, ETC.
Lachman Wall Bed Co., 2019 Mission St., San Francisco.
Marshall & Stearns Co., 1154 Phelan Bldg., San Francisco.
Peek's Wall Beds, sold by Western Equipment Co., 72 Fremont St., San Francisco.
Perfection Disappearing Bed Co., 737 Mission St., San Francisco.

WALL BEDS, SEATS, ETC.—Continued
Noack Disappearing Ironing Board Co., Sherman Kimball Co., selling agents, 199 First St., San Francisco.
WALL PAINT
Nason's Opaque Flat Finish, manufactured by R. N. Nason & Co., San Francisco, Portland and Los Angeles.
San-A-Cote and Vel--va-Cote, manufactured by the Brininstool Co., Los Angeles; Marion D. Cohn Co., Hansford Bldg., San Francisco, distributor.
WALL BOARD
"Amiwud" Wall Board, manufactured by Paraffine Paint Co., 34 First St., San Francisco.
WATER HEATERS—AUTOMATIC
Pittsburg Water Heater Co. of California, 478 Sutter St., San Francisco, and Thirteenth and Clay Sts., Oakland.
Cole Heater Company, Lick Bldg., San Francisco.
WATERPROOFING FOR CONCRETE, BRICK, ETC.
Armorite Damp Resisting Paint, made by W. P. Fuller & Co., San Francisco.
J. L. Goffette Corporation, 227 San Bruno Ave., San Francisco.
Hill, Hubbell & Co., 1 Drumm St., San Francisco.
H. W. Johns-Manville Co., San Francisco.
Glidden's Concrete Floor Dressing and Liquid Cement Enamel, sold on Pacific Coast by Whittier, Coburn Company, San Francisco.
Imperial Co., 183 Stevenson St., San Francisco.
Samuel Cabot Mfg. Co., Boston, Mass., agencies in San Francisco, Oakland, Los Angeles, Portland, Tacoma and Spokane.
Wadsworth, Howland & Co., Inc. (See adv. for Coast agencies.)
WATER SUPPLY SYSTEMS
Kewanee Water Supply System—Simonds Machinery Co., agents, 117 New Montgomery St., San Francisco.
WHEELBARROWS—STEEL
Western Iron Works, Beale and Main Sts., San Francisco.
WHITE ENAMEL FINISH
"Gold Seal," manufactured and sold by Bass-Hueter Paint Company. All principal Coast cities.
"Silkenwhite," made by W. P. Fuller & Co., San Francisco.
"Satinette," Standard Varnish Works, 113 Front St., San Francisco.
WINDOWS—REVERSIBLE, CASEMENT, ETC.
Whitney Window, represented by Richard Spencer, Hearst Bldg., San Francisco.
Hauser Reversible Window Co., Balboa Bldg., San Francisco.
International Casement Co., represented by Edwin C. Dehn, Hearst Bldg., San Francisco.
WIRE FABRIC
U. S. Steel Products Co., Rialto Bldg., San Francisco.
WOOD MANTELS
Fink & Schindler, 218 13th St., San Francisco.
Mangrum & Otter, 561 Mission St., San Francisco.

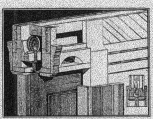

When writing to Advertisers please mention this magazine.

When writing to Advertisers please mention this magazine.

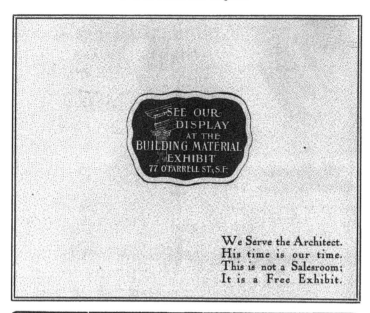
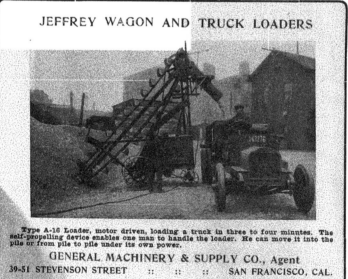

When writing to Advertisers please mention this magazine.

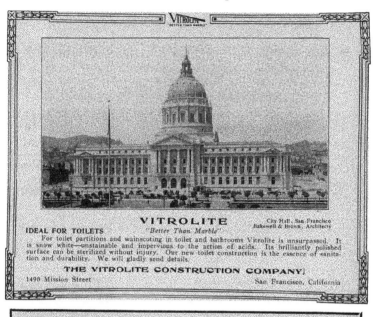
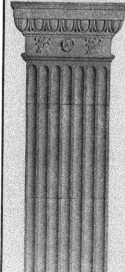

SANTA MONICA GARAGE, SANTA MONICA, CALIFORNIA

A. S. HEINEMAN, ARCHITECT

FACED WITH

GOLDEN RUFFLED BRICK

and

IVORY ENAMEL TRIM

Small Mission Roofing Tile

MANUFACTURED BY

Los Angeles Pressed Brick Company

LOS ANGELES

UNITED MATERIALS COMPANY

CROSSLEY BUILDING, SAN FRANCISCO

Distributers for Northern California

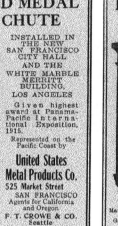

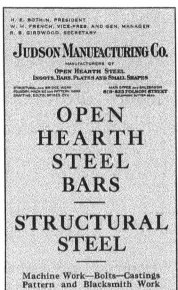

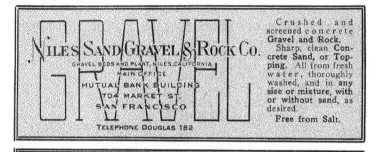

THE ARCHITECT & ENGINEER

25c Copy,　　　　OF CALIFORNIA　　　Vol. XLVIII.
$1.50 a Year.　　　　　　　　　　　　　Number 1.

Issued monthly in the interest of Architects, Structural Engineers, Contractors and the Allied Trades of the Pacific Coast.

Entered at San Francisco Post Office as Second Class Matter.

CONTENTS FOR JANUARY, 1917

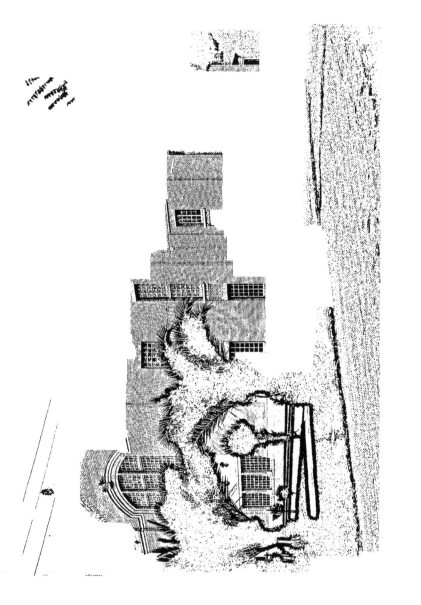

THE

Architect and Engineer

Of California

VOL. XLVIII.   JANUARY, 1917   No. 1.

The Second Church of Christ, Scientist, Oakland, California

By WILLIAM ARTHUR NEWMAN, Architect.

SECOND CHURCH OF CHRIST, SCIENTIST, of Oakland, at Thirty-fourth street, near Telegraph avenue, illustrated in this issue, furnishes an interesting and unusual experience in co-operative church building, instructive to the building community, whether Christian Scientists or not.

This church, composed of a small body of earnest individuals of very limited means, and with no financial standing, has had the courage and ability to initiate and bring to a successful conclusion a building project involving more than $100,000.

In the fall of 1914 the architect was instructed by the unanimous vote of the church membership to prepare necessary drawings for an edifice to cost not less than $75,000. The membership then numbered less than seventy-five.

The following spring, with about $600 in the treasury, two contracts were awarded for a brick and terra cotta edifice with steel frame—the auditorium seating 1,200 and Sunday-school room half that number. One contract was for general construction, the other for heating, etc., these contracts totaling $67,000.

This action seemed extraordinary from a conservative business standpoint, taken at a period of general business depression, with a great war in progress, but the church met the payments, in one way or another, so promptly that the contractors were never called upon to "slow up" with the work, and several thousand dollars' worth of betterments were added to the original plans. In addition, a fine organ, costing $10,000, was installed, and sufficient means found available to entirely carpet the auditorium, and purchase special oak furniture and pews. Sunday 10 Sept 1916 opened

The edifice was occupied September last, and the ease with which the task was accomplished seems little short of marvelous, when it is known that no one was requested to contribute to the building fund.

The general style of architecture is Modern Renaissance. The exterior is faced with light cream pressed brick and terra cotta. Steps and buttresses are of grey granite. The columns are Indiana limestone.

Polychrome terra cotta is used in soft, harmonious tones, with a new sanded finish recently developed by the manufacturers.

Heavy steel trusses in clear spans of nearly one hundred feet support the slate roof, and permit dispensing with obstructing columns in the auditorium.

Incised in the terra cotta over one of the three main entrance doorways are the words "Let there be light," and this thought has been carried out, as far as possible for a church, throughout the interior.

Passing the entrance portico and vestibule into a main foyer, with check rooms and retiring rooms adjacent, the visitor is ushered directly into the

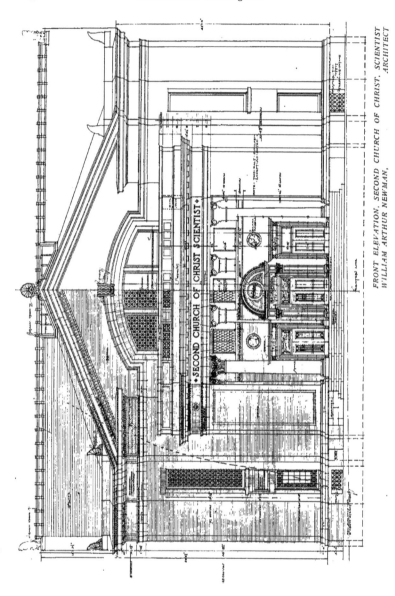

FRONT ELEVATION, SECOND CHURCH OF CHRIST, SCIENTIST
WILLIAM ARTHUR NEWMAN, ARCHITECT

COLONNADE, SECOND CHURCH OF CHRIST, SCIENTIST
William Arthur Newman, Architect

auditorium, or by other stairways to an upper foyer, with library and offices of the church officials on one side and the auditorium opposite.

This auditorium is especially free from the usual treatment of church interiors. The effort has been to avoid ornamentation of an elaborate type, tending to distract the attention of auditors from the sermon and yet not lacking the refinement of the desired atmosphere—a soft, rich, restful, peaceful quiet pervading the whole interior. It is the feeling of comfort and repose which is most conducive to receptive thought.

After an experience of three months, the acoustics have been pronounced perfect and have called forth a great deal of favorable comment. This

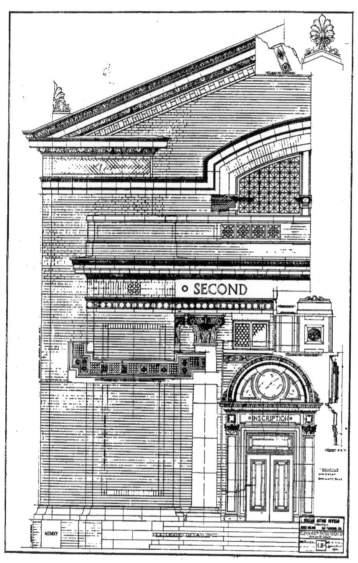

DETAIL OF FRONT, SECOND CHURCH OF CHRIST, SCIENTIST, OAKLAND
WILLIAM ARTHUR NEWMAN,   ARCHITECT

ENTRANCE VESTIBULE, SECOND CHURCH OF CHRIST, SCIENTIST

VIEW FROM AUDITORIUM FOYER, SECOND CHURCH OF CHRIST, SCIENTIST
William Arthur Newman, Architect

AUDITORIUM, SECOND CHURCH OF CHRIST, SCIENTIST
William Arthur Newman, Architect

ROSTRUM AND ORGAN SCREEN, SECOND CHURCH OF CHRIST, SCIENTIST
William Arthur Newman, Architect

matter was the subject of the most careful planning in design and furnishings, and the results forecasted have been actually demonstrated. A large light Sunday-school room has been placed under the auditorium.

The materials employed have been of the most substantial kinds, oak being largely used for interior finish, and in the lightest tones.

An improved oil burner simplifies the heating problem, while the ventilating apparatus supplies 23,000 cubic feet of fresh air per minute, at the desired temperature, in the auditorium, evenly distributed by the mushroom system. All of this air is filtered and screened of dust particles before entering the building.

By the use of new electrical devices, the indirect system of lighting is giving excellent results in even, quiet, light tones, at a minimum of cost.

In the preparation of these drawings a careful study was made of the arrangement of several hundred Christian Science church edifices. Many of these indicate a decided tendency toward independence from the traditional denominational designs.

From the democratic character of the organization of this denomination, it is seen that there will never be an exclusive style of architecture adopted for these church edifices, as independent action of each organization is provided for in building matters. The membership is the most cosmopolitan—composed of those formerly affiliated with all of the orthodox, unorthodox and Jewish churches, and of no church whatever—native Americans and those from foreign shores. These varied elements mingling, with their differing ideas of architectural style, indicate that the architecture will vary to meet such conditions.

In a settled New England community like Concord, N. H., it is easy to understand the appeal of a beautiful Gothic church, such as that designed for the Scientists by Messrs. Allen & Collens—or the original Mother Church in Boston, in the Romanesque, constructed twenty-two years ago. The present edifice, erected twelve years ago at a cost of $2,000,000, has Renaissance details.

In New York and Philadelphia Messrs. Carrere & Hastings used similar motifs for the Science churches they designed.

In Chicago the eight or ten edifices of this denomination show a freedom in their solutions in plan and elevation which have resulted in increased efficiency in the church work and the consequent large memberships.

Many of the older and more experienced Scientists consider that a gallery in a Christian Science church is a sad mistake, on account of the separation, and obstruction to sight and hearing at the weekly testimonial meetings. This also applies to columns in the auditorium which hinder a full view of all present.

Poor acoustics have decreased the efficiency of many an otherwise acceptable structure.

Improperly placed stairways, inadequate for the needs, are most objectionable. Damp and dark Sunday-school rooms are altogether too common and should by all means be avoided. Lighting, heating and ventilation are subjects which have hitherto been largely overlooked—but should have the most careful study.

Heavy plaster ornament, figured mural decorations and elaborate designs in art glass in the auditorium are undesirable where they divert the attention.

A foyer sufficient to accommodate fifty per cent of the seating capacity is not too large. A small foyer is an inefficient misfit in a church of this denomination.

REAR OF AUDITORIUM, SECOND CHURCH OF CHRIST, SCIENTIST
William Arthur Newman, Architect

A library is desirable for the circulation of literature, as requested by the trustees under the will of Mary Baker Eddy.

Check rooms, where damp clothing and umbrellas can be deposited, are provided in the Mother Church and found most convenient and necessary.

From a brief analysis, it is apparent that strict adherence to an architectural style which expresses a condition of thought outgrown is unthinkable. A religion offering freedom from the mental and physical bondage of the ages is not expressed within the confines of architectural styles founded on such limitations.

The very youth of this movement accounts in a measure for many architectural inconsistencies in plan and design, found in costly Christian Science edifices, all of which tend to hamper proper growth and efficiency.

Better solutions of these problems, more in harmony with the actual requirements, are being demanded, and through the wise selection of architects will be forthcoming in the future.

The Beauty of Humble Gardens

THE sense of the beautiful is a gift shared alike by those of low as well as of high degree, as are all the other finest experiences of life, such as love, happiness, joy of motion, delight of perfume and sweet sounds. Therefore there is no reason at all why humble little gardens should not be owned by every one. They breathe as exquisite a spirit and show forth as perfect a form as those of nobler magnitude, because they are made by people who want them very much indeed, writes Mrs. Alex. Caldwell in The Craftsman.

As a matter of fact, unassuming little gardens are often far more pleasing, more adorable and altogether to be desired than pretentious ones, for they are fashioned by intuition, inspired by love instead of created at the arrogant command of some one who does not understand their ways at all, but desires them because he sees other people have them. Gardens as individuals are like flowers themselves, that is, some are queenly like the rose, some splendid of color, but for which we feel no attachment such as the dahlia; some delightfully winsome like the pansy. There are formal aristocratic gardens, flawless in culture and breeding, and there are wild gypsy gardens, brimming over with gaiety, scorning law and restraint; there are modest little gardens that like violets, mignonettes and wild roses, exhale so sweet a fragrance that they steal into our hearts and win everlasting place in our memory.

The humblest cottage is often glorified by a rose vine a king might envy or a flowering tree that has been tenderly cared for as if it were a member of the family through many generations. An old flag man that I know tends a row of gay and wonderful hollyhocks that stand beside his mite of a station, because they make him happy and because, as he said, "they give pleasure to all the folks who goes by 'em." Such brilliant display only costs but a few cents, so it is easy for everybody to have beauty in their doorways who really want it.

Humble gardens should never be prim and precise and look as though set in their ways. They should instead appear unstudied, unconscious, bright and sprightly as little children. No deep lore of hybridizing, grafting or of landscape composition is required to create a little garden; nothing save the love and interest that suggests what to do. Inexpensive old-fashioned flowers instead of the latest creations, simple hedges of privet instead of box; arches, benches and arbors of rustic rather than of expensively turned columns, compose the humble garden furniture. Hardy plants, bulbs, perennials and flowering shrubs that increase and multiply of themselves should be favored, while native shrubs and trees, such as hydrangeas, azaleas, dogwood, redbud, holly, hemlock, pine and cedars are suitable and to be had for the trouble of transplanting. Honeysuckle, gourd vine and moon-flowers, marigolds, zinnias, petunias and many kinds of lilies will return to the garden year after year if once given a support.

* * *

Apparatus for Testing Fireproofness

The United States Bureau of Standards has installed a very complete apparatus for testing the resistance of structures and materials to fire, especially as regards walls and partitions. From the results of the tests it is possible to determine whether a fire will be confined to one room of a building long enough to permit firemen to reach the same and attack it with their appliances, or whether it will spread rapidly through the building and to adjoining structures.

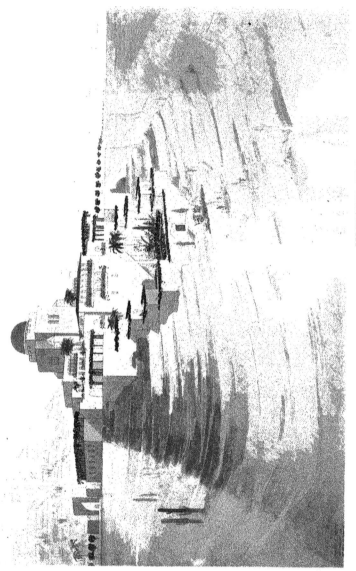

PERSPECTIVE, PRINCIPAL GROUP OF A MINING TOWN
LE BRUN TRAVELING SCHOLARSHIP COMPETITION
THIRD MENTION   ERNEST E. WEIHE

WINNING DESIGN, LE BRUN TRAVELING SCHOLARSHIP COMPETITION
Austin Whittlesey

Le Brun Traveling Scholarship

By JOHN BAKEWELL, JR.

THE third biennial competition for the Le Brun Traveling Scholarship, which was recently held, was won by Mr. Austin Whittlesey of New York, son of Charles F. Whittlesey, architect, of San Francisco. One of our San Francisco draughtsmen, Mr. Ernest Weihe, was placed third. As there were forty competitors, and as all of them represented the most clever young draughtsmen throughout the United States, this honor which Mr. Weihe has received is a noteworthy one.

The subject of the competition was a settlement to be erected in connection with a large gold and silver mine in the Southwest. It was stated in the

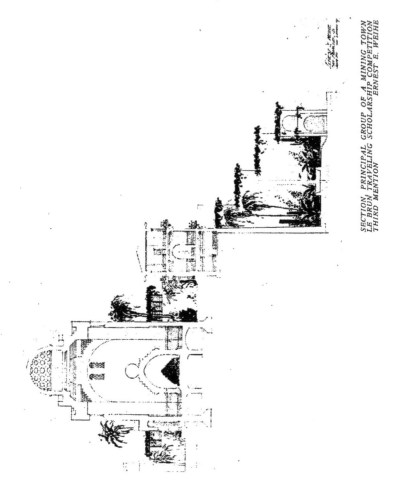

SECTION. PRINCIPAL GROUP OF A MINING TOWN
LE BRUN TRAVELING SCHOLARSHIP COMPETITION
THIRD MENTION   ERNEST E. WEIHE

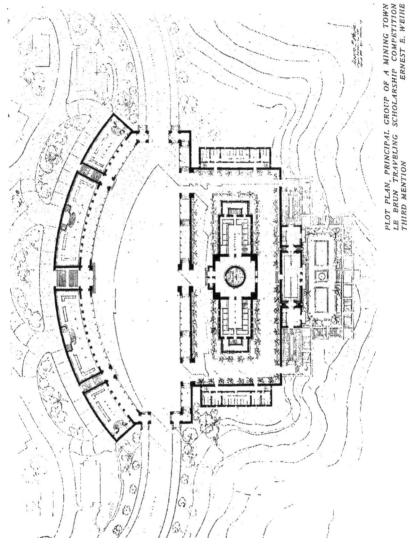

program that the architecture of the settlement should suggest the ethnic history of the surroundings, in other words, to recall the fact that the country had been traversed by the Spaniards and before that had been inhabited by the Pueblo Indians. It was suggested that the work of the Moors in Africa might also be taken as an example of an architecture well adapted to the arid and desert nature of the site.

Mr. Weihe's design shows that he had a very clear perception of the requirements of the program, and he has solved it in a very pleasing manner. While holding rigidly to the simple and massively crude character of the architecture chosen, he has so varied his masses and so studied his proportions as to produce a very interesting design.

There is a conscious effort in Mr. Weihe's design to avoid archeological composition, but rather to seize and interpret the spirit of the desert architecture.

Mr. Whittlesey's perspective is very ably and beautifully rendered in water color, showing not only the building that formed the problem itself, but also a very considerable amount of the surroundings. It is interesting to know that Mr. Whittlesey's life has been spent in the West, which accounts for the fidelity of his rendering of the sun-baked and shrub-spotted mountains and canyons of the Southwest.

*   *   *

Colonial Architecture

A LECTURE on "Colonial Architecture and Colonial Architects," delivered by Professor Fiske Kimball, of the University of Michigan, before the Pennsylvania Society of the Archeological Society of America, reviews a number of interesting facts relating to the earlier phases of American architecture. Professor Kimball is quoted as saying:

"The Colonial period in the United States closed, of course, with the Declaration of Independence, yet many of the finest buildings which are called Colonial came after the Revolution. Among these are the famous designs of Bulfinch, of Boston, and of McIntire, of Salem, as well as the tall-columned houses of the Piedmont region in Virginia.

"Three periods may, indeed, be distinguished in 'Colonial architecture.' The work of the seventeenth century was an offshoot of the medieval cottage architecture of the various medieval countries of the colonists—simple, informal, rudimentary as the struggle with the wilderness. The work of the eighteenth century, down to the Revolution, shows the adoption of the Renaissance forms of detail, the striving to conform to the style of Sir Christopher Wren in England.

"On the resumption of building after the Revolution began an effort to make buildings more monumental and more classical, to make them national in character rather than provincial. During this 'Early Republican' period contrast between the conservatives and the radicals was marked. One group clung to the old traditions and produced works which may well be called 'post-Colonial.' The other group tried to give American buildings that Roman or Greek magnificence which was the aim of the contemporary 'classical revival' abroad.

"The men who designed our early buildings are by no means all nameless and forgotten craftsmen. At first, to be sure, men had to build their own houses, and later many a masterpiece of beautiful simplicity was raised without drawings by obscure carpenters imbued with the fine traditions of their craft. From early in the eighteenth century, however, in the case of important buildings, an effort was made to obtain more elaborate design, and we find men whom we may designate as architects whose personality is of much interest.

"The first of those to attempt to bring our buildings into accordance with European standards were cultivated amateurs like Governor Francis Bernard, of Massachusetts; Andrew Hamilton and Dr. John Kearsley, of Philadelphia, and, later, Thomas Jefferson. They derived their knowledge largely from the numerous architectural books of the period. Two of the best known of the early architects, Charles Bulfinch and William Thornton, were thus self-trained, and they remained amateurs in spirit, even though they took money for their services.

"By similar study there arose, from the craftsmen, a group of carpenter-architects, who both designed their buildings and helped construct them. Among these were such gifted men as McIntire and Samuel Rhoads, of Philadelphia. Finally there began to come to this country architects of regular professional training. Some believe the pioneer of these to have been Peter Harrison, of Newport, author of a series of exceptional designs. The French engineer officers, like L'Enfant, had some architectural training and a fund of foreign observation:

"With the establishment of the Federal Government appeared men like Stephen Hallet, Benjamin H. Latrobe and Joseph Mangin, men of the highest experience and talents, who brought our Colonial style to a close, and established the early architecture of the nation on monumental lines worthy of a new republic."

* * *

Joint Meeting of the State Boards of Architecture

A joint meeting of the State Boards of Architecture of the Southern and Northern Jurisdictions of California, together with the committee on legislation of the Southern California Chapter of the American Institute of Architects, was held January 6th at Santa Barbara. The purpose of the meeting was to consider proposed amendments to the State law governing the practice of architecture to make the act more effective and practical. Those who attended the session were: Messrs. Octavius Morgan, Sumner P. Hunt, Frederick L. Roehrig, John P. Krempel and W. S. Hebbard, members of the State Board of Architecture for the Southern District; Sylvain Schnaittacher and John Bakewell, members of the State Board of Architecture of the Northern District, and J. E. Allison, John C. Austin and Edwin Bergstrom of the Southern California Chapter.

* * *

Lumber by the Mile

The following letter received by a lumber company in the West and published in the Chicago Tribune, is likely to draw a smile to the reader:

Dear Gentlemen: In your letter to me quoting prices on lumber, let me know what you mean by M., feet of lumber. Does that mean one mile of lumber? And do you lay it out and measure how much is in a mile of lumber? You know the place I want to build should not reach a mile, but should be only a little house for chickens. Be sure to let me know right away how much is in a mile of lumber. Yours very respectable.

TIM ———, Ottumwa, Ia.

HOUSE OF L. A. REDMAN, ESQ., PIEDMONT
LOUIS M. UPTON, ARCHITECT

House of Lander A. Redman, Esq.

THE house here illustrated was designed by Louis M. Upton, a San Francisco architect, for Lander A. Redman, Esq. It occupies a hillside eminence of nearly two acres in Piedmont, Alameda county. The house is designed in the Italian Renaissance, which period has also been followed in the garden scheme and for the smaller buildings on the estate. Approach to the house is through a rather pretentious pair of ornamental iron gates, leading to winding drives, mid terraced gardens and cultivated greenery.

Back of the house there is a Japanese garden with inviting pool, bubbling water fall and tea arbor, suggestive of the Nippon feeling. The stucco exterior of the house is painted a dull grey, topped with Monterey sand. The living porch or solarium is a feature of the home. It measures 15 by 40 feet and from the windows of this and the living and dining rooms one may enjoy a wonderful view of San Francisco bay and the distant mountains.

The popularity of the out-of-doors living room, a feature of the home long enjoyed by Californians, has spread to the East, and today few houses are designed without the livable porch. A decorator who can create a wonderful interior must also be able nowadays to take care of the out-of-doors living room. It used to be that the piazza was the last and least thing to consider. The modern porch must be the go-between of the indoors and the flowering garden. Allied to each as to color, fitness and accommodations, the porch carries out the spirit of both.

One is rather apt in furnishing porches to be content with odds and ends or else whatever the stores offer. For years the stores have offered willow furniture, Gloucester hammocks, green denim and turkey red. How many of us can remember when our piazzas were even furnished from the wagon of the traveling woodenware man! From that we went on to wicker, and from that we come to a porch furnished with a mingling of linens and reed and plants and wrought iron. The room may be painted an unusual color and the rugs toned to match. It is this exclusive individual touch that makes the porch the envy of the outsider and the joy of the possessor.

To return to the Redman home. The entrance vestibule, finished in mahogany with floor of Italian marble, leads to a spacious reception hall with turned and fluted columns and quartered oak panels to the ceiling. The living room is 20 by 40 feet and is finished in dull mahogany. There is a strikingly beautiful hand-carved mantel in this room, with Levanto marble hearth and facing. The walls are covered with old gold Italian brocade, which coloring is carried out in the lighting fixtures and hardware.

The general color scheme of dining room is silver and gray, relieved with a touch of old rose and mahogany furniture. The dining room has a low wood-wainscot with panels extending to the ceiling and covered with two-toned gray silk. All woodwork is finished a French gray.

On the ground floor is also a billiard room finished with fumed quartered oak, six feet paneled wainscoting. Spanish leather is used above the wainscoting to the ceiling, the latter being quite ornamental.

There is also a cosy breakfast room with stained wood paneling and cornice.

The bed rooms are all finished in old ivory, with daintily papered walls.

SIDE VIEW, HOUSE OF L. A. REDMAN, ESQ.
LOUIS M. UPTON, ARCHITECT

DETAIL OF ENTRANCE, HOUSE OF L. A. REDMAN, ESQ.
Louis M. Upton, Architect

LIVING PORCH, HOUSE OF L. A. REDMAN, ESQ.
Louis M. Upton, Architect

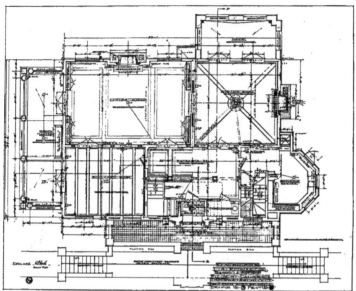

FIRST FLOOR PLAN, HOUSE OF L. A. REDMAN, ESQ.
Louis M. Upton, Architect

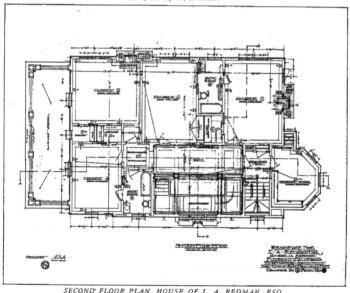

SECOND FLOOR PLAN, HOUSE OF L. A. REDMAN, ESQ.
Louis M. Upton, Architect

GARDEN, HOUSE OF L. A. REDMAN, ESQ.
Louis M. Upton, Architect

JAPANESE TEA GARDEN, HOUSE OF L. A. REDMAN, ESQ.
Louis M. Upton, Architect

RECEPTION HALL, HOUSE OF L. A. REDMAN, ESQ.
* Louis M. Upton, Architect

Coast Architects Honored by Institute

TWO Pacific Coast architects were honored by the American Institute of Architects at the recent annual convention held in Minneapolis. Mr. W. R. B. Willcox, of Willcox & Sayward of Seattle, Wash., was elected second vice-president, and W. B. Faville, of Bliss & Faville, San Francisco, was elected a director.

The delegates from the coast report a very enjoyable trip and are united in praising President John Lawrence Mauran's splendid utterances on "The Altruistic Ideals and Services of the American Institute of Architects." Mr. Mauran said in part:

"The American Institute of Architects is not an organization for the moment. It has been developing for about sixty years, and perhaps centuries from now it will still be in existence. I venture to say that the day is not far

DETAIL OF HALL, HOUSE OF L. A. REDMAN, ESQ.
Louis M. Upton, Architect

distant when the prerequisites for practice in the United States will not be a registration or license law, but the basic one of membership in the A. I. A.

"I venture to say the day is not far distant when all the members of the Institute, as well, perhaps, as those still on the outside, will accept the fact that respect for the profession by our clients will never come until we ourselves have shown a proper respect for the dignity of our profession; when we will cease to offer and urge that we be allowed to give something for nothing. Do you know any doctor or lawyer who would permit a number of patients or clients to come to him and ask for a prescription in competition or a submission of briefs to determine which doctor or lawyer he could select? It is absurd that we should lower our dignity to offer to make sketches when we are not asked. It is a thing hard to realize, because it is not hard to make sketches. You go to a doctor because you believe in him; you go to a lawyer because you know he is upright and has the brains to pull you through; why don't we stand on the same pinnacle? Aren't we entitled to it? I found that it pays to stand on that ground; it pays more in self-respect than it does in dollars at first, but ultimately it pays in dollars and you have the self-respect unimpaired. Some day, and I believe it is not far distant, the truism will strike home that each 'job' can ultimately go to but one architect.

"Architecture is considered more or less a luxury. You remember when hard times came some three years ago, when our architects with twenty or thirty or forty 'jobs' were cut down to one and two, or perhaps none. Architecture is a luxury that they do first without. With us it is a case of 'feast or famine,' and in times of stress, in what we call famine times, there is something about the moral fibre which causes it to loosen and become lax. In bad times the weak man goes under.

"Where would the profession of architecture be in times of stress were it not for the American Institute of Architects? There would be chaos. The influence which gives a broader view point than the close view of problems and trials permits, is governed by membership in the Institute.

"Do you know, any of you, of the lawyer who is not a member of the bar association, or the doctor who is not a member of the medical association? Wouldn't you be a little inclined to question his standing? That always struck me as a peculiar thing in regard to the A. I. A. I haven't always thought that way, but I do now. I think you would question his standing when you stopped to think and so it is through all the professions which have ethical strength down to the workingman's protective league, the labor union. It is used sometimes as a club; nevertheless that was not its original purpose. That purpose was to gain the strength that comes from unity. What would the state be if it stood alone? Chaos would exist if the states were not welded into the United States. The state standing alone is similar to the non-organized profession. A great many thoughtful men in the profession fail to see their duty as I failed to see mine a good many years ago.

"When I first went to St. Louis I found out of the entire profession there but one firm of architects who lived what I thought an ethical life and when I was asked to join the St. Louis chapter I said I saw nothing in it. I retained that position for over a year until someone came to me and said, 'I understand it is useless to ask you to join the chapter because the members don't live an ethical life; what business have you to stand on the outside and criticise? Why don't you get in and help us?' I said, 'I never thought of that before.' So I joined the chapter and very shortly after joined the Institute, and I think you know I have been with the Institute heart and soul ever since."

A resolution that future conventions be held in the spring instead of in December as at present received the approval of the Institute, and the convention concurred in the resolution by a unanimous vote. It was pointed out that at present the period for committee work is too short. It must practically be done during the month of October, after the summer vacation season. By holding conventions in the spring the committees will be able to do much of their work in the winter. Mr. Mauran pointed out that the only objection to this plan lies in the contention that spring is the architects' busy season, but that in conversation with other members of the institute, they concurred in the thought that spring "used to be" the architects' busy season, but falling thermometers do not stop construction work now as they did in the past, and that the architects' work is more evenly distributed throughout the year. [This is especially so in California.]

The plan of reorganization which has been under consideration by the institute for several years was adopted. Under the new regulations the membership in the chapters will consist of the institute members and associate members on probation, the latter to become institute members within a stated period or retire from the chapter. Heretofore, the chapters have been composed of institute and chapter members, there being no limitation on the terms of the chapter membership. The result was that the chapter members out-numbered the institute members in many chapters and controlled the chapter activities and enjoyed practically all the benefits of institute membership.

* * *

The officers elected for the ensuing year were: John Lawrence Mauran, St. Louis, president; C. Grant La Farge, New York, first vice-president; W. R. B. Willcox, Seattle, second vice-president; W. Stanley Parker, Boston, secretary, succeeding Burt L. Fenner, New York; D. Everett Waid, New York, treasurer; W. B. Faville, San Francisco; Thomas R. Kimball, Omaha, and Burt L. Fenner, New York, directors.

Washington, D. C., was named as the meeting place of the next annual convention.

*

* ❧

Tunneling Under San Francisco Bay

THE proposition to tunnel San Francisco bay, discussed somewhat seriously by engineers and others a number of years ago, has been revived. Parties, said to be responsible, have applied to the government authorities for permission to construct the tube. The government, however, declines to interest itself in the project until it has received the approval of the people of San Francisco and Oakland. In other words, Uncle Sam wants to know "public sentiment" before going on record. Just what the tunnel scheme is has not been made public. The idea of building a tube beneath the waters of San Francisco bay as a means of better transportation, however, is not a new one. A plan was described in this magazine as early as August, 1909, by Mr. F. W. Fitzpatrick of Washington, D. C. The article is reprinted here by request:

The article on this subject by Mr. F. T. Newberry in a recent issue of The Architect and Engineer was most interesting, and particularly to me because it is a revival of a project that was set afoot some years ago and with which I had much to do. Some water company there in California was back of the affair, but it couldn't raise the capital or something or other happened. Anyway, the matter was dropped and I had not thought of it again until I saw Mr. Newberry's paper.

It seems to me, however, that that gentleman is a wee bit off in his estimates. If he can build five miles of an excavated tunnel for $2,500,000 he will accomplish something that has never yet been done. In tunnel work there are always contingencies arising that never confront one in ordinary construction, and you Californians will be lucky indeed if you ever get a tunnel, as badly as you need one, for twice what Mr. Newberry calculates.

The scheme we contemplated was based upon American patents that I control and for a system of tunneling that is being considered now in St. Louis and several other American points, but that has not yet been actually installed here, though it is in successful operation under the Seine at Paris. Leading engineers, however, concede that while novel, almost revolutionary, it is absolutely practicable and is the least costly of subaqueous construction, much less costly than excavated or shield work tunneling.

Briefly described, the tunnel is really a subaqueous bridge. It was fully illustrated in the Engineering News and the Scientific American a couple of years ago and attracted much attention in engineering circles. I plan to build square tubes of reinforced concrete, tubes 26 feet wide and 20 feet high and 100 feet long. It is unnecessary to go into the reinforcing system, but the sides are virtually great trusses 100 feet long, of about 24-inch thick concrete, thoroughly embedding the reinforcement and completely covered with waterproofing and properly lined with damp repellant furring. These tubes to be made at any convenient point on land, the ends temporarily bulkheaded and the tube towed out in calm weather to about its proper position. There the bulkheads are removed, the tube filled with water and sinks. The bottom of the stream or bay or river is previously prepared, either simply smoothed off or trenched by means of the ordinary dredge. Guide piles are driven and after the section of the tube is properly placed on the bottom, a jointing caisson is towed to its end, covers the end and its juncture is made with the land portion of the tunnel or with a previously laid section of tube. A new section is towed out and jointed to this last in the same manner and so on until the whole is completed. The joints are bolted and fastened together and then concreted with a great mass of concrete just about in the same fashion as street car rails used to be welded together in place a few years ago. All the excavation or dredging that is necessary is in shallow places so as to insure that the top of the tunnel is well below navigation. Apart from that one consideration of leaving free way for vessels, the tubes are virtually laid upon the bed of the stream or bay. When the entire length of tube is laid and joins the land's ends or open cuts the water is pumped out and there's the whole thing complete and ready for laying of rails, installation of syphon drains, ventilation, electric lights and so on.

It is simplicity itself and the one in Paris was built and completed in a most extraordinarily short time. I got my notion of this from the building of the old "whaleback" vessels on Lake Superior some fifteen years or so ago, another scheme in which I took a deep interest and that was called by the over-conservatives a wild-eyed dream, though it has proven itself a splendid reality.

This species of submarine bridge is a complete entity in each double-track run. If traffic increases, all there is to do is to lay another tube alongside of the old one and so on ad infinitum. Unlike other bridges, there is no stopping of traffic to make the necessary additions, changes, etc.

The details of reinforcement, stresses and all that sort of thing were worked out by Mr. F. W. Lepper, C. E., a well-known U. S. Government engineer now in charge of the government work in Cleveland and who was with me and did all the figuring and engineering work on the steel framing of the huge government building at Chicago.

Incidentally this scheme was suggested by me to the Pennsylvania Railway people for their tunnels at New York. They had already gotten too far along with their plans for the bored, shield system, however, and deemed this too revolutionary to try here. They have encountered great difficulty in their boring and the work has cost enormously and. I have heard upon very good authority that the powers that be are kicking themselves now that they didn't adopt the scheme that was presented to them then; in this case I think I am far enough in the van that you San Francisco people need not have to say later on that they wished they had known about it before.

The Carrere Memorial

The memorial to the late John M. Carrere, famous New York architect, has just been completed in New York city. The memorial takes the form of an exedra and staircase leading from the level of Riverside Drive and Ninety-eighth street to the park between the drive and the river. The memorial was designed by Thomas Hastings, of Carrere & Hastings, and is built of pink Milford granite with platforms and steps of bluestone. The delays in the building of this memorial have been occasioned by the question of location and scheme. It was first decided to place the stone at Riverside Drive and Ninety-second street, but it was found that the Joan of Arc monument had been located at Ninety-third street and Riverside Drive, and it was thought the two monuments would be too close together.

COMPLETED SECTION OF OCEAN BEACH ESPLANADE, SAN FRANCISCO

The Ocean Beach Esplanade and Protective Parapet at San Francisco

By RUDOLPH W. VAN NORDEN,
Mem. Am. Soc. Civil Eng'rs, Fellow Am. Inst. Elect. Eng'rs.*

WITHIN the last five years the city of San Francisco has been singularly fortunate in acquiring permanent civic improvements of many kinds which, architecturally and from the standpoint of engineering excellence, place its name in the front rank of cities not only in the United States but of the world. The people themselves, probably in general, little realize the multiplicity of efforts and the vast amount of thought and work, much of it original and daring, which has been and is being accomplished in the even and serene progress of the present administration, and more particularly of the City Engineer and his organization.

There are not many San Franciscans, or few visitors in the never-ending stream of tourists and sightseers, who are not familiar with that section of San Francisco, the ocean beach, and who have, perhaps, at some time or other, been inspired by the relentless power of the breakers during an unusually high tide or a storm. But these magnificent displays have long been the cause of much uneasiness and speculation as to the ultimate effect upon the Great Highway which skirts the beach and which is built on the drifted sands of ages and which has been periodically threatened with annihilation by the underwashing action of the sea. From time to time local attempts have been made to repair such damage and prevent it, and many abortive plans have been advanced. But these have never been permanent,

*Rialto building, San Francisco.

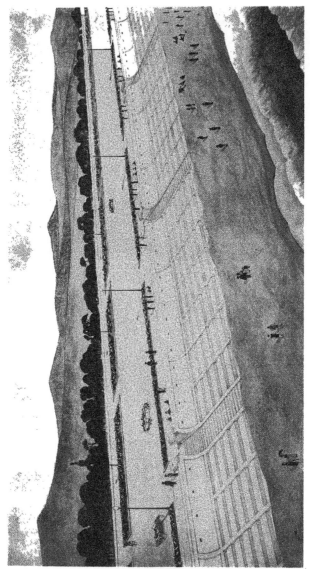

SECTION OF OCEAN BEACH ESPLANADE AS IT WILL APPEAR WHEN COMPLETED

and have always taken from the natural beauty of the ocean front and led away, rather than toward, the cherished desire of every San Franciscan, to make the highway one in reality and the ocean front a thing of architectural beauty which shall blend with the magnificent natural setting, to be one of the beauty spots known around the world.

It has remained for the City Engineering Department to work out the solution of this problem and at the same time the salvation of this famous boulevard. How it has been done is the subject of this description. Nothing has ever been done like it before and the daring in its conception, the cleverness and thoroughness in design where an exceedingly difficult group of conditions were to be contended with is, from the engineer's point of view, most satisfactory, while the final effect as an architectural finish which will add rather than detract from the natural beauty is like a coinciding inspiration. Not the least interesting, however, especially to the engineer, are the methods of construction and works management employed by the builder in pulling through to successful completion this novel structure, so entirely untried and difficult to approach from the estimator's standpoint, but so satisfactorily completed.

Of course the esplanade is not entirely completed; there are three miles of ocean front which must be so improved to carry out the parking plan contemplated, while, so far, but two sections, or 670 feet, of the esplanade is finished. But in these two sections the problem of design and methods of construction have been solved. San Francisco can have a parkway in accordance with its most cherished plans, free from the fear of the ocean's reaching it with any destructive force. It will take only the money required to do it, and as rapidly as this money is available it will be well spent.

General Description:

The ocean beach at San Francisco is an almost straight stretch lying north and south, for a distance of over three miles, between two rocky promontories. At the northern end is "Sutro Heights," at whose extremity is placed the famous "Cliff House." From this point south for a distance of 2.8 miles the beach is paralleled by a wide roadway, known as "The Great Highway." This highway forms the western boundary of Golden Gate Park and the park area is extended along the highway to its terminus and embraces it. The highway has a width of 207 feet, not including the beach proper. The beach has a width of about 200 feet and a gradual slope of 3 feet per 100 feet. The highway has an elevation of 113 feet above a datum, taken as 100 feet below the city base, and which is, in turn, 6.5 feet above mean high tide. The beach roughly terminates in an embankment, or more or less abrupt rise of about 12 feet, to the level of the highway. The southern two miles of the highway is further protected by a natural dune, or levee, which has from time to time been widened and improved and on which an elevated roadway has been built. Between the northern extremity and the commencement of the natural dune, a distance of about one mile, there has heretofore been no protection of the highway from the action of extreme tides and storms, except abortive attempts to build bulkheads, at points where damage to the highway has already occurred. This section, therefore, is the part of the highway which has been the cause for the most concern.

In order that a permanent protection might be afforded, the City Engineer approached the problem, not as an experiment to be made, and which might succeed in the ultimate attainment, but rather after a careful study of the conditions to be met, analyses of the necessary requirements and applica-

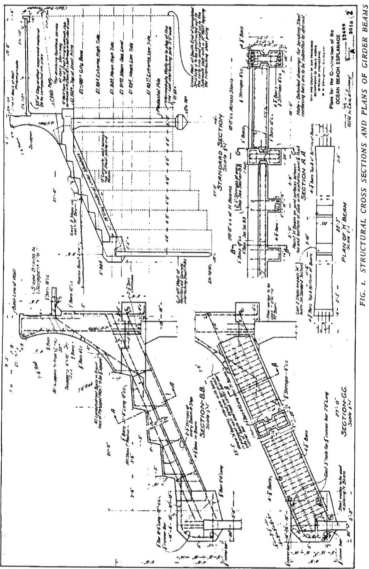

FIG. 1. STRUCTURAL CROSS SECTIONS AND PLANS OF GIRDER BEAMS

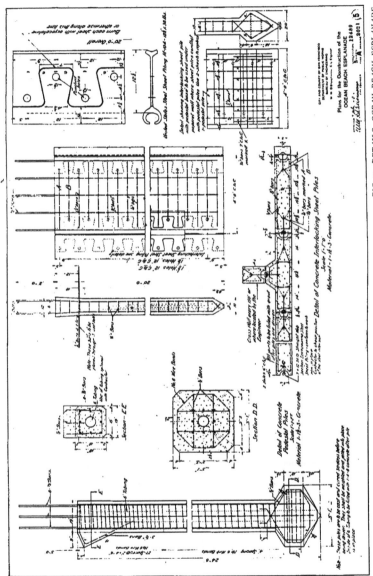

FIG. 2. DETAILS, OCEAN BEACH ESPLANADE

tion of the laws of hydraulics, has created a proper design to meet these conditions.

As already stated, the beach has a considerable width and a fairly gentle slope. Ordinary high tide brings the sea to the edge of the beach at the foot of the twelve-foot embankment which limits the highway. During the extra high spring tides and storms giant breakers have an unimpeded rollway and expend their force against the unprotected highway, often flooding the roadway and throwing the spray, at times, entirely across it. The problem, then, at the outset is, first, to protect the roadway and its embankment from the disintegrating effect of the force of the sea, and, next, to prevent all further travel of the water, either in the form of a break-over, or of spray, which might injure the roadway directly or indirectly by the undermining effect from the wetting or seeping action of the water, and also which would inconvenience the users of the highway. The foundation available for any form of protection is sand, which extends for a depth of 200 feet beneath the roadway, and which is entirely pervious and unstable except where it has or may be retained. The solution of the problem therefore resolves itself into four main requirements; a structure of such stability as will at all times resist the direct action of the sea; that shall by its form prevent the possibility of any undercutting, or undermining action, either from the direct force of the waves or from the ebbing action of the water in carrying back the beach sand; from the hydrostatic instability due to seepage through the sand under the structure at low tide; resistance to the overturning action due to the hydrostatic pressure from behind the structure, whose head may be equal to the height of the roadway; and finally, to lessen the velocity of the oncoming waves, gradually changing the direction of action until the moving water is entirely reversed in direction and will expend its remaining force against the succeeding wave to assist in the reduction of the unspent energy therein contained.

The first requirement necessitates a structure which, by its composition, shall at all times resist any possible disintegrating action of its surface. Experience has shown that modern concrete fulfills this requirement. The structure must, through its weight, or its structural strength, possess stability against direct force. Here the problem is somewhat different from that of a dam, where the hydrostatic pressure is continuous and determinable, because the pressure exerted is not continuous and for the greater part of the time may be negative, but when it does occur is in the form of a blow, the force of which is variable and within narrow limits may be considered as an unknown quantity. It is, then, at this point where an analysis of the action is necessary and where care in design can produce a form which will, through its inherent strength and the correct manipulation of the forces to be neutralized, use a part of that force to increase its stability. Instead, therefore, of building a straight vertical wall which would receive the direct force of the water, such a wall is divided into a series of low walls, or steps, each one receiving the direct action of the oncoming force, causing an abrupt stopping and turning action which, by the formation of eddies and air pockets still further assists in neutralization, while the position of the steps on a slope absorbs force by the lifting effect, and hence, from its reaction, causes a downward resultant force against the structure which is in turn resisted by the confined foundation. By this design a large part of the structure's stability is produced by the action of the sea itself and relieves the necessity of structural weight to produce the necessary stability. So far, then, the designer is allowed to produce a structure of weight only sufficient to contain the amount of material for the necessary internal tensile and compressive strains which may be imposed upon the structure. But there are two other possible causes of instability, because while the direct force of the wave is somewhat broken and retarded, it must be finally reversed upon itself, which reversal must necessarily be accomplished at the highest point and at the rear of the lift. Here again energy is expended, the resultant action against the structure being in a horizontal plane. This action must be rigidly resisted, either from the rear, or through the integrity of the structure. For the former the solid embankment behind the structure might suffice, but being at the surface, and consisting of sand which may be saturated, might be unstable. The horizontal force of the turning wall acts as a cantilever against the main structure, tending to overturn it. This overturning effect, as already stated, is resisted both by the weight of the oncoming water and by the weight of the structure, while the weight of the sheet piling which is integral with the structure further acts as the other side of a couple against this turning moment. The designer is therefore confronted with not only a structural strength to resist the bending strains as on a deck, or floor, but the additional angle strains due to the cantilever action of the final turning wall.

So far the design of the structure resists direct action. From the rear, the possibility of hydrostatic action is always present, i. e., water which has seeped through from the ocean to which is added water which may have seeped under the roadway, will when there becomes a difference between its level and that of the sea, cause an uplift under the structure and a further tendency to shove the structure toward the ocean, because, while this difference in head may be but a few feet, the aggregate pressure may be tremendous, amounting to 1600 lbs. per square foot. Under ordinary conditions, the dead weight of the structure would be sufficient to overcome such an uplift, while the sheet piling on the ocean side is of sufficient depth below the point of shifting sand to withstand any sliding effect, but for a maximum pressure condition an added precaution is made by the designer. While the weight of the structure might be carried by the underlying sand foundation, and is so supported in part, this is in reality calculated to be supported on piling. The sheet piling extends along the front and is integral with the deck sections and is a supporting wall for the sea side of the structure as well as a cut-off wall from any undersurface flow action. The rear of the structure is supported on reinforced concrete bulb piles. The weight of these, in part, prevents the uplift, but to insure the prevention of any possible pressure from causing uplift, the bulb, at the bottom of the pile resists any pulling out effect, because, to lift the pile and bulb would necessitate the lifting of a cone of sand whose weight is much greater than any possible lifting force.

The remaining features of the design are for accommodation only, such as flights of steps spaced at convenient intervals. The face of the structure where it is made up of succeeding steps, forms a series of "bleachers," where, a great part of the time, the many thousands of visitors and sightseers may find convenient seats overlooking the breakers. The steps make a break in the turning wall, or top of the parapet where high water might go through. But behind the parapet is a sidewalk 20 feet wide, bounded by a curb, while in the parapet proper, are placed steeply sloping scuppers, so that any water falling over onto the sidewalk will flow rapidly back to the parapet and discharge through the scuppers.

Construction:

The total length of the present esplanade is 670 feet, having been built in two sections, of which the first is 500 feet. As the result of the experience in the construction of the first section, some slight changes in design, for the purpose of simplifying the construction work in the second section, were made. These will be noted later.

The cut-off wall which forms the front foundation of the structure and an impervious barrier between the movement of the ocean and the beach sands and the underlying sand fill and backfill is a line of specially designed and precast reinforced interlocking concrete piles. These are rectangular in cross-section, 10 inches thick and 4 feet wide. A reinforced concrete wall was desired in order to give the necessary supporting strength in compression and to enable a continuation of the reinforcement into the deck sections, but for interlocking purposes, sheet steel piling was desirable. In order to embrace both features, sheet steel piles were used which were cast into the concrete pile. In the first section, one piece of Lackawanna, 7 inches, 12.5 pounds per foot sheet pile was embedded in either edge of each pile. (See Fig. 1), a groove of trapezoidal section being cast into the pile, leaving the exposed lock flush with the edge of the pile. The reinforcing consists of ten vertical $\frac{1}{2}$-inch deformed bars, the horizontal bars being $\frac{1}{4}$ inch. In the second section a change was made in the lock sheet piling, in that but one piece of sheet piling was used for each pile. This sheet piling was United States, $12\frac{1}{2}$ inches wide, weighing 38 pounds per foot. Before placing in the mold, the sheet piling was split through the web. This was done by the aid of an oxy-acetylene flame, the cut being made in a zigzag interlocking pattern which may be better understood by reference to Fig. 2. The two halves of the sheet pile were then cast into the opposite edges of each pile, the zigzag edge of the web forming a strong hold in the concrete, and the transverse reinforcement of the pile being threaded through holes punched in each tooth of the web.

The front piles were of three varieties, the first being the body pile, as described above. A second style of the same width and thickness was provided with an outlet fillet into whose edge was embedded a steel sheet piling. These were to provide for an interlocking bond between the front piling wall and the transverse piling walls, of which there is one every 150 feet. The third type were similar to the first with the exception of their being one foot wider, and were required for spacers to bring the cross and end wall piles at the proper positions.

The piles were driven in progression, each interlock being formed as the pile was placed in position. After the piles were in place and before the cap was poured, the recesses, or grooves which, coming face to face, after the piles were in place, formed eight-sided openings around the interlocks, were filled with concrete grout, thus making a wall mechanically continuous and impervious to the passage of water.

The length of the piles is 20 feet and they were driven until the tops were at elevation 92.75, or about 16 feet below the mean sea level. The jetting method of driving these piles was used to the point where the top of the pile was level with the sand, and from there down until the pile was in place, a steam hammer was employed.

Water under pressure was obtained from the system of the Olympic Salt Water Company, nearby. This was led through a 6-inch iron pipe to a point near where it was to be used. This pipe terminated in a 6-inch tee, the two straight ends of which were bushed to 3 inches. From each of these led in order, a nipple, tee, nipple and elbow, and from the tees and elbows, four 2-inch outlets, each equipped with a gate valve. From these valves, four 2-inch high-pressure hoses, about 40 feet long led to return elbows at the tops

BUILDING SECTION B PREPARATORY TO PLACING H-BEAM GIRDERS. SHEET PILING
IN PLACE

SECTION B OF ESPLANADE. H-BEAM GIRDERS AND REINFORCEMENT FOR BLEACHER
SLABS IN PLACE

of the four jetting pipes. The jetting pipes were arranged in pairs and so fastened, a pair being placed on each side of the pile. The pipes extending slightly below the lower extremity of the pile terminated in a nozzle in the end of which was a ¾-inch opening. The normal operating pressure was 130 pounds, although this increased at times, while the water company's pumps were operating, to 160 pounds static. It was found that with the lower static pressure, and four nozzles in operation, the pressure in the nozzle dropped to 94 pounds, while with the higher pressure the terminal pressure was 109 pounds. It was found that with the higher pressure, the results were much more rapid than with the lower and which appeared to be in greater proportion in effectiveness than the difference in the pressures would indicate. The average time for jetting a pile was 3 minutes, while the final drive with the steam hammer required five to eight minutes The steam hammer used was of conventional type and was swung into position 'from the boom of a stiff-leg steam derrick equipped with a 100-foot boom. This derrick was mounted on wheels and moved on a track. Angle iron extensions were made from the bottom of the hammer frame and these were bound together by a steel ring, all in such a manner as to fit snugly over the head of the pile. In driving, an ironbark wood follower was inserted on the top of the pile to prevent crushing, or chipping, from the force of the hammer blow. In driving the piles for Sec. B., the steam hammer was not used, but, instead, the sand on either side of the piling was excavated to the desired depth of 8 feet, and a cofferdam of timber sheet piling was built to hold the excavation. This prevented the sand from caving against the piles which were jetted to their final position in one operation.

The bulb piles are 24 feet 6 inches long, the body of the piles for Sec. A being 18 inches square, while those for Sec. B are 19 inches square, the corners in both cases being champfered. The bulb at the bottom of the pile has a total height of 26 inches, and is 3 feet 1 inch square. This also has champfered corners. These piles are reinforced with eight ⅞-inch deformed bars which are bound together with No. 6 iron wire bands. The tops of the Sec. A piles are plain, but the tops of the Sec. B piles have a shoulder cast on one side and reinforced integral with the pile, while the bulb is reinforced for upward strain as well as lateral stresses. (See Fig. 1.)

The difference in size between the piles for the first section and those for the second was made on account of difficulties encountered in construction which were overcome by the change in size. Also, in section "B" piles a shoulder was cast to carry and align the "H" beam girders, thereby saving much time for the contractor. The pedestal piles are placed 10 feet c. to c., and were jetted into position in a manner similar to that used with the sheet piles.

The "H" beams, or girders which support the deck of the structure, like the piles, were precast. These are 29 feet 2 inches long over all, 3 feet 7 inches deep and have a width, top and bottom, of 20 inches, while the web or center section is 10 inches thick. The object of the "H" form is to provide deep grooves along each side of the beam into which the deck or bleacher floor may lock and be supported. The beams are reinforced longitudinally with four ⅞-inch bars, top and bottom, these bars protruding from the ends to tie into the other sections of the structure. The stirrups are ⅜-inch bars spaced 6 inches c. to c. One end of the beam is recessed to give bearing on the top of the sheet piling wall. The girder beams were lifted from the casting floor into position by a heavy derrick provided with a 115-foot boom.

After all sheet piling, cross walls and pedestal piles were in position and the H-beam girders placed and aligned, the remainder of the structure was poured. This work commenced with the coping over the sheet piling making the tie with the girders. This coping was cast with a shoulder to carry the bleacher floor. To prevent water either from drainage or seepage from the ocean interfering with this work, an 8-inch terra cotta drain pipe was laid in crushed rock under the coping within the line of piles. This was loosely calked and led to a sump from which the drainage water was pumped by a 6-inch motor-driven centrifugal pump.

The bleacher structure was next poured. This was a work requiring great care and considerable ingenuity. This is a slab supported by the girders on either side, the coping over the sheet piles at the lower side and longitudinal beams cast integral with the slab and supported on the heads of the pedestal piles, at the upper side. Two transverse beams are also cast integral with the slab. The slab is reinforced for pressures from either side. The surface of the slab, as already stated, is made into a series of steps, or bleachers. In order to form the steps it was necessary to use a covering form, and this in the first section was made continuous between the H-beams. In this form, at the center of each step and spaced evenly between the H-beams was an opening in the form through which the concrete could be tamped and puddled. It was found, however, that, due to the shrinking of the surface, it was difficult to give a smooth surface, shallow wrinkles and curious markings being left in the surface. To remedy this defect in the second section of the structure, the tread forms were divided into five sections each, which would lift out between the holding studs which consisted of two pieces of 2-inch by 4-inch lumber nailed together. Two hours after the slab had been poured, these step sections were removed and the surface of the step was floated and troweled to as smooth a finish as could be made without plastering.

The parapet wall required the more intricate form work to provide an even and correct curve in the face. To provide for expansion joints, the parapet was poured in alternate sections, 20 feet long, that course being a requirement in specification. It was found difficult in following this method to maintain absolutely perfect alignment of the parapet and accounts for a slight unevenness which, however, is not noticeable, except from close scrutiny.

Before laying the sidewalk back of the parapet, it was necessary to backfill the structure with beach sand. This was done by means of a Krogh 6-inch centrifugal sand pump, the fill being hydraulicked into place and allowed to become thoroughly compacted. The average consistency was found to be 30 per cent sand and 70 per cent water. The results were very satisfactory when proper agitation was given with ample water. To agitate two water jets were used, one tied to the end of the suction pipe and the other in the direction of suction.

This sidewalk has a width of 20 feet. On the parapet side it is keyed into a shoulder cast in the parapet wall and on the highway side it rests in a recessed concrete curb. Before the slab was laid, there was placed a layer of thoroughly compacted clay. The slab is 6 inches thick, which includes a ½-inch top. The highway side of the slab is at elevation 113, and there is a surface slope of 12 inches in the 20-foot width. The reinforcement consists of ½-inch rods both placed longitudinally and ⅜-inch bars placed transversely, the former being 12 inches c. to c. and the latter 18 inches c. to c. The slabs were carefully marked diagonally, the longitudinal and transverse spacing of the diagonal markings being 5 feet apart. Expansion joints were placed in the older section, every 30 feet, and in the newer section every 20 feet. These expansion joints followed the markings and are hence on the bias. In construction, the one side of the joint is vertical, while the other is also vertical, but the slab is extended below and under the other slab, a distance of 6 inches, the slab extension being also 6 inches thick. In making the joint, building paper was placed on the slip, and "Elastite" between the vertical section of the joints. This material was also used in the expansion joints in the parapet. In Sec. A, of the sidewalk, the steel reinforcement is continuous. This was found to give unsatisfactory results and prevent the proper movement of the joints. In the second section the reinforcement was cut at the joint. In all other parts of the structure the reinforcement is continuous.

As much of this work as was possible was precast, this included all sheet-piling and bulb piles, and the H-beam girders. The remainder of the work was poured in the ordinary manner. For the fabrication of the precast members, a platform was constructed. The sheet-piles were cast on their sides and after the platform was covered with poured piles, another layer was built resting on the first layer and separated therefrom by a cheap tar building paper. As the tops of the sheet-piles flare, the second layer was cast in the opposite direction, the flaring ends extending over the pointed ends of the lower layer. This method of pouring continued with alternate layers in opposite directions until there were seven layers in place. The sheet-piles were seasoned for 40 days. Test pieces were made at the time of casting the piles, and these, after 28 days, showed a tensile strength of 2800 pounds per square inch. The H-beam girders were poured upside down due to the two small step projections on the upper side of the beam.

In all of the precast work, the mix was 1:1½:3; Santa Cruz Portland cement was used. For the sand content, the beach sand was found to be satisfactory. This was scraped and stored, care being taken to gather both fine and coarse sand, keeping the two grades separate. No screening was necessary, and the sand was mixed in the ratio of 1:1. The cost of gathering and storing the sand was 50 cents per cubic yard. Healy-Tibbits crushed rock was used in sizes No. 3 and No. 4 and in the proportions of 1/3:2/3.

The total amount of concrete in the precast work for Sec. A was 681 cubic yards, or 1.36 cubic yards per running foot of structure.

The poured concrete was mixed to the proportions of 1:2:4, the proportions in the sand and rock, running as in the precast mix.

The yardage per running foot of structure for the various sections of the work is as follows:

Piles and girders .... 1.36 cu. yd. per running ft. structure
Bleacher panels .... 2.27 cu. yd. per running ft. structure
Stairways .... 2.38 cu. yd. per running ft. structure
Parapet and rollway .... 1.28 cu. yd. per running ft. structure
Sidewalk .... .39 cu. yd. per running ft. structure

	Run. ft. Struc.	Total
Total yardage, Sec. "A"	5.32 cu. yd.	2658.5 cu. yd.
Total weight, Sec. "A"	11.47 tons	5730.0 tons
Weight of steel, Sec. "A"	648.0 lb.	324000.0 lb. (162 tons)

Following are unit quantities and weights of materials in the precast members:

	Concrete		Steel Reinforcing Bars					
			¼ in.		⅜ in.		½ in.	
	Cu. Yd.	Wt. lb.	No. pcs.	Wt. lb.	No. pcs.	Wt. lb.	No. pcs.	Wt. lb.
Sheet Piles, Standard...	2.45	9922.5	360.	75.6	......	......	176.	149.6
Sheet Piles, Cross Wls...	3.06	12412.5	540.	113.4	......	......	220.	187.0
Sheet Tie Piles.........	2.90	11835.0	531.	109.8	......	......	220.	187.0
Spec. Sheet Bulb Piles...	2.57	10420.5	368.	77.3	176.	149.6	......	......
Pedestal Piles.........	2.26	9142.5	......	......	......	......	35.	29.75
H-Beam Girders........	5.25	21244.5	......	......	1990.36	465.47	......	......

	⅛ in.		No. 6 Iron Wire		Lagging		Total
	No. Ft.	Wt. lb.	No. Ft.	Wt. lb.	No. Ft.	Wt. lb.	Weight
Sheet Piles, Standard......	......	......	......	......	40.	500.	10647.7
Sheet Piles, Cross Wls......	......	......	......	......	40.	500.	13212.9
Sheet Tie Piles..........	......	......	......	......	60.	750.	12881.8
Spec. Sheet Bulb Piles......	......	......	......	......	40.	500.	11165.9
Pedestal Piles............	213.25	550.26	440.	17.6	......	......	9740.11
H-Beam Girders...........	267.68	690.6	......	......	......	......	22400.58

Both sections of the structure have been built by contract, the contractor in each case being J. D. Hannah. Throughout, the work has been under the close supervision of the City Engineer, Mr. M. M. O'Shaughnessy and the City Engineering Department, and more especially under the direct inspection of Mr. C. N. Taylor, who has co-operated closely with the contractor. Much credit is due to the contractor for the rapid and satisfactory completion of the work and the high class of workmanship, and to the Engineering Department of the city for the sound engineering expressed in the design of the structure and a most satisfactory solution of a difficult problem of long standing.

* * *

City-Plan Commission Advocated at Los Angeles

DEFINITE steps for the appointment of a city planning commission in Los Angeles were taken at the January meeting of the Southern California Chapter of the American Institute of Architects. A number of city officials, together with representatives of the leading civic associations of the city, were present as guests of the Chapter and pledged their co-operation in furthering the movement.

The first speaker of the evening was Henry F. Withey, who read a paper on "City Planning" and submitted a draft of a proposed ordinance providing for the creation of a city planning commission. The ordinance was prepared by the City Planning Association working jointly with committees from the Chapter of Architects, Municipal League and City Club.

The ordinance, as drawn up, was read and explained by Mr. Withey, who was followed by J. E. Allison, president of the Chapter, who presided at the meeting.

Others who spoke in favor of the ordinance were S. H. V. Lewis, president of the Federated Improvement Association; Siegfried Goetz, Sumner P. Hunt, Wilbur D. Cook, A. F. Rosenheim, president of the Municipal Art Commission, and A. H. Koebig, president of the Architects' and Engineers' Association.

The Engineer After the War

THE post-bellum period is bound to bring its problems and difficulties. That the warring nations realize this is evidenced by the very efficient preparations that the entente allies are making for the struggle that will be an aftermath of the present war—a struggle for commercial superiority and prestige, a struggle that has been characterized as the "bloodless war of the future." Economic recuperation will be a momentous problem that will require our greatest energies and our most influential efforts. But these commercial rearrangements will be largely external; they affect only our relations with outside nations and outside affairs. . Readjustments, as great or greater, must be expected in the internal conditions of our nation. New situations must be prepared for and internal readjustments must be admitted if the plans for the Allies' collaboration and mutual assistance after the war are to hold. Internal disarrangements must not be allowed to render abortive the efforts that are being put forth for allied co-operation.

*   *   *

One great problem that will affect our country, and that is fully and clearly recognized, will be the disposal of the men back from the front. That the matter is of serious concern is realized by the efforts that our governments, our commissions, our societies and organizations, and our public men are putting forth to effect a solution. Even now, with the end of the war not yet in view, they are making preparations and urging broad schemes and suggestions. On cessation of hostilities there will be available hundreds of thousands of men of hardy physique, accustomed to open-air life and endowed with virility and eagerness. That the majority of these men will be available for hard physical work of an outdoor character is evident. The openings which these men will seek can be supplied by engineering works, by opening up railroads, roadways, and other transportation lines, by erecting buildings, and by promoting our natural resources and riches.

The financial situation will undoubtedly contribute some difficulty. Our governments will be more anxious to recuperate than to spend, but they must realize a responsibility to provide for those who have served their country. Our contemporary, Engineering, covered the point well when it stated some time ago that "the government must afford assistance on the principle that it is better to advance loans to municipal authorities and to public corporations for the prosecution of work of a profit-yielding character than to organize benevolent schemes for the help of men and their families who are unable at once to find employment."

It is here that the engineer will have his opportunity. A broad scheme of readjustment embracing copious engineering achievements will bring the engineer into prominence as nothing else ever could. This problem of employing the skilled and unskilled labor that the battlefield and the munition factory will release will require his greatest efforts and his greatest ingenuity. The situation will be acute, no doubt, but in adjusting the country to it, it will be the engineer who will be the controlling factor. Not only in this, but in the larger plans of international co-operation which the Entente nations have formulated, opportunities are presented for the engineer to show his abilities. Much is being spoken and written today about the engineer's place in political life and in our governmental organizations. It has been felt that he has kept aloof too long. It is gratifying to observe that efforts are now being made to have the engineer's status recognized and to have his efforts and achievements not rendered subservient to any man. Now is the time to begin preparations for capturing the wider and more influential field that awaits the engineer after the war.—Contract Record, Toronto, Canada.

DROP CURTAIN, RAMONA CONVENT

Some Practical Suggestions for the Design and Equipment of Theatre and School Stages

By EDWIN H. FLAGG.

IN planning a theatre or school auditorium the principal requisites are: vantage points from which the auditors can best view and hear the entertainment and an arrangement of the stage to best accommodate the regulation paraphernalia that use and custom have proven necessary.

Usually the first and what is erroneously considered the most important requisite is the auditorium portion. This includes the main and balcony floors, lobby and foyers, seating, etc., and is more commonly understood than the second and most vitally important matter of stage arrangement, such as rigging loft, fly gallery, dressing rooms and stage lighting.

To consider the spectator's comfort before giving the entertainers a proper place to work is like planning a residence with a beautiful dining room and elaborate furnishings, and then incorporating in the same house a kitchen of dwarflike proportions and void of equipment.

The auditorium is your dining room.

The stage is your kitchen.

The owner is your host and the actor your cook with the stage hands as assistants, pantry men, waiters, etc. The technical name of the floor of the rigging loft is the "gridiron," and it is as important to your cup of entertainment as the range in the kitchen is necessary to your plate of food.

Is it not of more importance to have a convenient kitchen properly equipped and a simple plain dining room, even though incomplete, than an inadequate kitchen and perfect dining room?

It is exactly the same with a stage and auditorium.

Of course, where means will allow, make the dining room—your auditorium—as elaborate as possible—but not at the expense of the kitchen—your stage.

You don't plaster the bare cement or brick walls of your stage—you paint them white. That saves light bills and is cleaner and more cheerful, and there are many more important reasons. Every theatre or school auditorium stage that has been plastered, and many foolishly have been, is a glaring example of the mistake. Architects experienced in building metropolitan stages will smile at some of the errors herein cautioned to avoid. But they would be more surprised to see how many prominent architects do continually, through ignorance, make these same errors.

The mistake that architects most commonly make in school stages is placing a wall almost even with each side of the proscenium arch from the front to the back of the stage, either at right angles with the front and back walls or obliquely toward the center of the back of the stage. All the Berkeley school stages are arranged this way, but the worst example is the Polytechnic High School in San Francisco. Here, without any excuse, what should have been the entire stage, is divided into three parts at a considerable expense and the stage is absolutely ruined.

Going back to the kitchen simile, it is the same as if you took a fine large kitchen and ran two walls across it and put a small door in each.

It would have saved the taxpayers thousands of dollars and have given the school a satisfactory and perfectly efficient stage if the requirements had been more thoroughly looked into before building. That stage has been practically useless since it was built and will be until sufficient money has been spent to remodel it.

The usual post mortem excuse for a stage like this is that school stages are not intended to be practical. That, "they are not intended to be used like theatre stages." That, "the community has no money to spend to build or equip a stage so that plays can be produced." Or that, "they would have liked to have built and equipped it properly, but that there was not money enough." The facts are that a school stage can be properly built and equipped with an outfit of scenery, lights and all necessary paraphernalia sufficient to produce almost any play a class would attempt, and this can be done for less money than has been spent in ceiling and plastering and butchering many school stages.

The Manual Arts High School in Los Angeles sets the highest example of efficiency in dramatic work of any public school in America.

The history of its struggle for a practical stage is typical.

The architects evidently thought they were planning perfection, because they were unhampered with either lack of money or space. They built an auditorium seating over two thousand people. The stage in width and depth was equal to a metropolitan theatre. The proscenium arch is much larger than that of most metropolitan theatres. While they had sufficient loft space to allow drops to fly straight up out of sight, as is absolutely necessary— they evidently saw no reason for utilizing this, so they put in an additional lower ceiling, cutting off the loft, and then proceeded to lath and plaster the entire interior of the stage.

The principal, Dr. Wilson, sent for the writer to figure on building and installing the necessary scenic equipment. Had the scenery been built and installed as the building was arranged the original installation would have cost a thousand dollars more than it would otherwise and it would have given trouble and every piece of scenery that was used there thereafter would have had to have been built especially for that stage. But, of most importance, it would have been utterly impossible for them to have staged the productions they have put on since with wonderful artistic and financial success. They produced with correct scenic investiture "The Bluebird," a production that taxes the capacity of the largest theatres.

DROP CURTAIN IN ORPHEUM THEATRE, LOS ANGELES

DROP CURTAIN IN EMPRESS THEATRE, SAN FRANCISCO

First we tried to get them to make the necessary alterations, but the school board having already spent so much money on the stage, refused to appropriate any more. We then asked the contractors if they would tear out what they had done if we gave them the material and released them from the lathing and plastering of the stage. This they finally consented to do, thereby leaving a perfect stage.

Outside of a gridiron it isn't so much what is put on a stage as what is left out that counts.

Being constantly engaged in studying stages, after comparing thousands of them all over America and Europe, covering a period of over twenty years, and noting many of them that were altered, some changed several times, I am convinced that certain rules can be laid down that will accomplish satisfactory results.

A good size for a metropolitan proscenium arch is 24 feet high by 36 feet wide, and not less than 18 feet by 30 feet for a small theatre. The footlight trough should be straight and between two and three feet from and parallel with the drop curtain line. The lights should be so placed that the center of the light is on a level with the stage floor. The trough should be wired in three circuits, half of the total on one circuit—white and quarter red and quarter blue—placed alternately W R W B W R W B. A light shield just sufficient to cut off this light from the highest seat in the auditorium, must extend across the front of the footlight trough. This should be 2¾ inches above the level of the stage in ordinary school stages and more in theatres or where there are balconies or galleries. The width of the stage should take up the space available between side walls of building, and dressing rooms should be built under the stage if possible, or back of the stage, but not at the sides unless you have over 60 feet in width.

The height of the stage to the gridiron must be between two to five feet more than double the height of the proscenium arch, unless the arch is over 20 feet in height, on small stages, or over 24 feet in height on large stages. This space must be clear of beams or trusses.

The gridiron hangs from the roof and is supported by the walls, leaving sufficient room in which a man can walk around between the gridiron and the roof. The gridiron is usually made of 2-inch by 10-inch joists (lighter if the span is short) placed at right angles with the footlights from front to back wall on 12-inch centers and floored with 1-inch by 4-inch or 2-inch by 4-inch flat on 8-inch centers.

Four open slots each occupying the space between two joists, viz.: 10 inches wide extending from the front to the back wall as follows: One over the center of the proscenium arch, two at equal distances from the center and about one foot inside of each side of the proscenium arch. The fourth slot 16 inches wide extends from front to back wall and is situated exactly over the pin rail.

The pin rail, made of 6-inch by 4-inch Oregon pine, should be attached to the fly gallery and seated in the front and back walls to hold down the weight of several tons pulling up. One and one-eighth inch (1⅛″) holes should be bored through the 4-inch side vertically on 8-inch centers its entire length for belaying pins, which should be supplied by scenic contractor. The bottom of the pin rail should be 3 feet from the fly gallery floor.

The fly gallery should be between 4 feet and 6 feet in width, with a solid floor something over 18 feet 6 inches in the clear from the stage floor and reached from the stage by a ladder fastened to the side wall as near to the switchboard as possible and located on the right side of the stage looking toward the audience.

All stage directions are given looking toward the audience. Auditorium directions are given looking toward the stage. Down stage is toward the footlights and up stage is toward the back wall, off stage is either R or L. from the center. The proscenium walls should be made with offsets allowing for the flare of the arch. Into the right offset, parallel with the footlights, place the switchboard, not closer than two feet from the edge of the proscenium opening. Allow plenty space back of board to work on buss-bars. As the space in the corner back of a line drawn on a 45 degree angle from the proscenium arch to the side wall of auditorium is useless as far as the auditorium is concerned, include it in the stage and use the triangular room thus gained on the right for an electrical room and the one on the left for a property room. Or in certain cases these can be used for dressing rooms, others added above each other, reached by stairs on the side walls.

The switchboard should be equipped with switches for three footlight circuits, three or four border lights of three circuits each (wired the same as the footlights), switches for floor pockets, orchestra, fly gallery, rigging loft, basement and dressing room lights and some extra switches for emergency. This number in addition to the switches controlling the auditorium lights. Dimmers should be provided for the auditorium as well as the stage lights, if means will allow.

The conduits for the circuits from the switchboard to the border lights should be carried either to the right wall or fly gallery floor, then up stage, stopping the first border light three feet from the front wall and each one of all additional border light circuits, five or six feet up stage, depending on depth of the stage. Equip each end of conduit with an outlet. Connect the border light to the outlet with a flexible, fire and water proof cable, of sufficient length to allow the border light to be lowered to within six feet of the stage floor. The border lights should be made of any accepted design, preferably a rectangular trough made of No. 20 to No. 28 gauge galvanized iron 9 inches high on the side, furled on the bottom, by 4 inches top by 2½ inches deep on back. Into this set another piece 4 inches wide, into which 1⅜-inch holes have been punched on 6-inch centers or closer if required. One-half-inch edges on this piece are turned at right angles with the 4-inch part on each side, making this 4 inches in the clear out of 5-inch wide piece of iron. Into this 4-inch piece screw No. 001 G. E. or similar, sign receptacles and wire them in three circuits before enclosing in the trough.

Both the trough and the ½-inch flange of the wired piece should have holes drilled in them so that when held together with ⅛-inch stove bolts, with the nuts on the inside of the flange, but on the open side of the trough, just so the flange is seated flush with the 2½-inch back edge of the trough.

The wiring should be done as follows: Make the first socket on one circuit, white, the next socket red, the next white and the next blue, the next white, next red, next white and the next blue, and so on for as many sockets as you have. This gives the most satisfactory distribution of the light that is needed on any stage.

The number of lights is a matter of opinion and requirement. Orpheum theatres and houses of that class use between two and three hundred lights to a border. Small school stages and halls from thirty up. In a thirty-light border light wired as above, 15 would be white, 8 red and 7 blue. Forty or 60 watt tungsten or nitrogen lamps give the best satisfaction. The length of the trough should be about two feet less than the width of the proscenium opening.

This same trough, with slight modifications, answers for a footlight trough.

For economy of space and initial expense, straight footlight troughs, parallel to the curtain line, with as small an apron as the law will, allow, are advocated by all theatre architects.

Dimmer plates mounted either in bank construction and controlled by both separate and master levers are necessary for regular theatres. Where not so many plates are required, where the capacity is small, and where it is not required that small sections be operated separately, plates can be mounted at right angles to the wall, separately, and must be operated separately. Where not over four plates are required they can be mounted flat against the wall. The bank construction costs about twice as much as the angle construction, and the flat construction about 15 per cent less than the angle.

In suspending a border light it must hang from six points, from iron loops around border light, distributed to even the load, each three pairs of loops, suspended from a cable bridle, which is hung from a line, hanging from each of the three sheave slots in the gridiron. These three lines extend up through the gridiron, over six-inch pulleys, or loft blocks of special construction, over to the right, to the slot directly over the pin rail, through a triple pulley, or head block, straight down to the pin rail, where they are either tied off or attached to a counterweight, and equipped with an endless line to either raise or lower the borderlight.

Practically this same arrangement applies to all of the lines on the stage with which all the different drops and borders are operated. The correct installation of this arrangement, although of the utmost simplicity, is the most important item in the practical and economical operation of a stage.

Put no lights around the face of the proscenium arch, but a strip light and reflector can be inserted on the stage side of the proscenium arch, so as not to interfere with the raising or lowering of the front curtain, at an angle to throw all the light possible toward the down stage or curtain line portion of the stage. This reflector trough should be about twelve feet high, made out of No. 20 gauge galvanized iron, painted flat white, equipped with sockets to hold 100 watt nitrogen lamps, vertically.

As to the amount of scenery necessary to equip a stage.

The stage of a school, a hall or a theatre, requires the same essential items. The number of pieces to each scene, the variety of scenes in the same class, the completeness in which they are assembled and the size of the scenes are the only differences.

For instance, on a school stage an adequate drawing room scene could consist of a large arch, two practical doors, in door wings, and four regular wings or boxing pieces, set up to conform to the sides and angles of an ordinary room, the top of the set being "masked" or closed in with the plain blue borders that give the appearance of a blue ceiling. These same borders appear as the sky used with the side foliage or "wood wings," and a landscape drop at the rear of the stage, producing a non-committal outdoor setting. All scenes in plays being either laid indoors or outdoors, any play written could be staged with these two sets.

This outfit being too meagre for regular usage, the following list of scenes, with the front drop curtain, "valance" or first border, "grand drapery," or second border, "teaser," or, working border, which with the "tormentors" or front wings, allow the stage to be made smaller or larger, and the necessary borders, backings, etc., for each scene, can advantageously be added and are given in the order of their relative importance: plain chamber scene, garden scene, library setting, horizon, set house, set rocks, set bridge, thick wood, palace, kitchen, ancient street, prison, corridor, set tree, conservatory, set cottage, Gothic interior, Louis XV drawing room, rocky pass, cut wood, etc.

Interchangeable with different sets would be borders, ceilings, fireplaces, alcove and French windows, balustrades, mantels, steps, platforms, etc.

In executing the above scenes artists excel in certain lines. In scene painting studios having sufficient volume of business to employ many artists, each artist does only that in which he excels, which further develops his specialty until his ability along certain lines is greatly superior to those who have not had the benefit of this individualizing.

The stage floor must be level, three feet nine inches above the auditorium floor level, and five feet above the level of the orchestra pit.

Placing the seats in the auditorium on a forty-foot radius, and the footlight trough being placed parallel with, and the outer edge three feet distant from, the curtain line, the orchestra pit will be properly deeper in the center.

The proper elevation to give the auditorium floor so that every seat gives an equally good view of the stage, is as follows: Allowing that the seats are placed thirty-two inches from back to back, as they generally are, have the first six rows level, give the next six rows an elevation of nine inches, the next six rows an elevation of fifteen inches, the next, eighteen inches, increasing the slope three inches every sixteen feet, which would in an auditorium of one hundred feet in length give an elevation of seven feet; allowing for a foyer in the rear.

For the slope of the balcony and galleries, if any, take a line from the last row in the balcony to a point six feet below where the curtain touches the stage.

A point in the construction of auditoriums about which there has been considerable controversy between the owner, the architect, and the lessee, is the line of vision from the rear seats on the ground floor to the stage. Some claim that the entire proscenium arch should be visible from the rear seats. From an experience in designing and operating theatres, and from observing practically all theatres, all that is necessary is a view from the rear seats of the lower half of the proscenium arch. This is based on the loss of seats and the added cost to give the occasional back seater a view of the upper half of the drop curtain, because as the line of vision slants upwards, a full view of a stage setting is seen anyway, when only half of the proscenium arch is in view.

* * *

Went With the Load

An Irishman, having arrived in New York a few days ago, got employment with a lumber merchant. Later he was ordered to take a load of lumber some distance away. Having gone half his journey he came to a steep hill, and while the horses were struggling to get to the top his boss happened to meet him, and, seeing the horses in such a difficulty, and Pat sitting on top of the load, he stopped him and exclaimed:

"Do you think the horses haven't got enough to do without hauling you up this hill?"

Pat, fixing himself more comfortably on top of the load, said:

"Is that what you stopped me for?"

Then, with a crack of the whip, Pat concluded:

"Get up; it's a poor ship that can't carry the captain."

Too Many Middlemen

WHEN one stops and thinks of the vast numbers, whether in the cities or going to and fro between the cities and the places where things are actually produced, one may realize what a deal of money has to be added to the cost of the primary products to pay the living of all the middlemen who are engaged in handling them.

Of course these middlemen are entitled to a living, that is, as many of them as are necessary for the work of transportation, manufacture and marketing. But the question is, may there not be too many of them?

What if every single man were paid wages proportionate to, say the railway men's wages that they objected to recently as being too low? What if every single one of them had a job? Can't you imagine that the cost of things now high would be higher still? Flour was up to $12.50 per barrel a few days before this was written, and yet at that very time many a man in New York City was in despair because he couldn't make both ends meet on the wages he was earning, and they were hardly more than half what the lowest paid railway hand objected to and demanded should be increased.

A little deliberate thought might convince anybody that there are too many people in the cities; the country does not produce enough to keep them all going in the luxury that they are entitled to, and the poor devils are obliged to live off one another.

It's a great game, this, living off the other fellow. It's been going on since the time of Adam and will go on till the Resurrection Day no doubt; but people have a way of refusing to give up—of refusing to be resigned to it just the same, and democracy has done, oh, such a lot to distribute the load, as the engineers say.

The game is going on now in one of its most interesting phases. They call it the elimination of the middleman. They should call it the reduction of the number of middlemen, and, taking a humane view of it, if it is not to be actual death or the poorhouse for the unneeded portion of the strugglers, there should be an accompanying movement to increase the number of producers.

One of the things that makes life interesting nowadays is the union—men banded together to get a bigger share of the product of toil than their fellows who may not be banded together. You know that for every man that gets more there must be some one to get less, and the more the few get the greater the number of those who must take less.

We're beginning to see what unionism really means since the railway men succeeded—or did they succeed?—with their recent coup. But that really is beside the question that I am interested in.

Building has been unionized to an extraordinary extent and the share of the public's money that goes for that necessary element of our modern life has been disproportionate to the amount left for other activities. It has caused two things,—one excessive competition in that branch of industry, and, two, emulation on the part of all other branches of industry, which will lead to all being unionized or, at any rate, all being raised. When everybody is raised we will be just the same as we were before, but our money will buy only a half or a third as much as it did "before the war."

For this war is like the war in Europe. It is a struggle for more room in the sun, and while this is bloodless and may remain so, it is going to result, as the one in Europe has resulted, in a lot of vacancies.

There are too many middlemen, indeed, but not too many kinds.

One might here venture to speak on that delicate subject, the relation of architects and master builders to society. It would be easier to say architects and builders but I mean now the managing builders, men who supervise and direct the whole work, as distinguished from the "subs" who do the different parts of building, each as a specialist.

One of the interesting phases of this question was the appearance of "construction companies," as they were called, which were widely heralded by the old-style builders as institutions that were intended to eliminate the architect. It was really the old-style builders that the "construction companies" threatened, and with characteristic cunning—if it could be called cunning—those who were threatened managed to work up a great fear in the minds of architects. The fear was largely an imaginary one, conjured up as a rule in the brain of the narrow-minded architect whose conscience may have pricked him or, worse, may have been so burdened by the thoughts of pet "subs" to whom he was under obligations that he imagined the devil himself would be better than a business-like organization to manage things and keep the grafting down. Some folks that ought to know better have really thought that one or the other—that is, the architect or the builder—could or should be eliminated, and I don't know any that have been so scared about it as one or two of the leading architects of a few years back right here in New York.

It is true that ordinary business shows a merging under one head of the two functions which are performed by the architect on the one hand and the builder on the other, but that is like speculative building where the goods are manufactured and then offered for sale, just as they are in the case of furniture or clothes or shoes or what not.

Building, considered as the production for a third party, the owner, of an object that must be designed for that owner in advance of its making, is not within the confines of the merchant's or manufacturer's functions. That is a truth that should some day sink into the consciousness of some folks, and it will, too.

It all grows out of the well-known human quality of hating to see anybody profit at your expense. It starts with the owner, or is played up to the owner to win his favor. The architect is entitled to a living. If he does his work properly he should have ten per cent. The builder is entitled to ten per cent. "Whew!" says the owner, "twenty per cent! I can't stand that." And if he is a "good business man"—what does he do? Well, if he is a real business man and uses judgment in the selection of his "help" he does pay both architect and builder a good profit and gets his affairs carefully administered.

But human nature and the presence of too many middlemen makes it hard for the money-maker to see go by an opportunity to take a pound or two of somebody's flesh. Here is a chance to make a killing, says the money-maker, and alas! it is too often true.

One of the favorite games of this modern bloodless war is the setting of architect against builder and the attempt to make the architect perform both his own work and the work of the other without paying him for the other man's work.

Some architects professedly eliminate the master builder, announce their performance of his work and charge accordingly.

Others—architects, I mean—are driven by the pressure from the owner to attempt the two-man job at the one man's pay. The conscientious performance of this task is a heart-breaking and ruinous thing. It makes the architect work for practically nothing. If the architect is not wonderfully capable there is danger of the thing resolving itself into a piece of business that is full of drummer's overcoats.

You've heard that story, haven't you? Let me tell it, my way. The drummer put into an expense account the cost of an overcoat, and the boss cut it out. Next time the expense account had no overcoat and the boss said, "I see you didn't put in the overcoat this time." The drummer replied, "I didn't put it in, but it's there just the same."

What an honest fellow the drummer was, by the way!

The middlemen must go; that is, some of them must go, but the builder will stay and some day it is to be hoped he will get a square deal. And the architect—of course he must have his square deal, too.—Theodore Starrett in Architecture and Building.

* * *

The Story of San Francisco

By JAMES A. EMERY*

General Counsel, National Council for Industrial Defense.

SAN FRANCISCO is writing a new page of civic and industrial history. Long reputed to be a stronghold of class control in politics and government, she has entered upon a civic revival of the first order. Best of all, her reform is inspired and led from within. No external suggestion or leadership has been required. She has gone about setting her industrial house in order with the same spontaneity and determination that marked her miraculous reconstruction after the fire, or her contribution of the world's greatest exposition spectacle.

The circumstances which aroused her citizens were as sudden and dramatic as the results which have flowed from their newly organized action. A water front strike extending through the months of June and July, a gross violation of an agreement between the water front employers and the longshoremen, paralyzed the commerce of the port and was marked by circumstances of violence and disorder, tolerated by the mayor and ultimating in a control over the loading and unloading of shipping so autocratic and exclusive that the minted coin of the Government moved past the pickets of the union to its steamship destination under written permission of the strike leaders. The Secretary of Labor, without effect, condemned the union's violation of its contracts, and appealed for their observance.

Under these circumstances the Chamber of Commerce, under the leadership of its president, Frederick Koster, a man of exceptional courage, ability and balance, asserted the sanctity of contracts, the necessity for the preservation of law and order, the right of employer and employee to pursue their occupation without molestation. The Chamber established a Law and Order Committee fortified with voluntary contributions of a million dollars, to vindicate these principles through the courts, administrative authority and public opinion.

The Chamber first appealed to the business community and added 5000 recruits to its ranks upon the issue raised, making itself the largest Chamber of Commerce in the United States. Its purpose is thus significantly approved. The Chamber's committee, through its legal staff, proceeded to give practical protection to employer and employee against illegal interference and intimidation. In eighty-seven injunction suits, it swept that public nuisance, the intimidating and disorderly picket, from the city sidewalks, and in a series of damage suits is bringing home to the thoughtful and right-minded

*Abstract of address delivered at Convention of National Founders' Association, New York, November 15, 1916.

trade unionist his joint responsibility for the acts of the reckless and criminal with whom he associates and over whom he must therefore exert rational control or become financially responsible for the illegal acts of their common agents. Recognizing the complete right of the worker to organize, the Chamber has conducted a campaign of education to make the unionist and the community distinguish between the use and abuse of collective action, and is impressing upon every class that no section of the municipality can or should be permitted to advance its special interest at the expense of all, or injure the reputation or retard the development of a great city.

Supporting no candidate, it has urged by every practical device at its disposal the duty of the citizen to register and vote at this election, and to permanently abate the public nuisance of picketing, in which the courts have justified its effort.

San Francisco has supplied the final evidence of the proposition which this election has demonstrated—the American electorate cannot be organized and delivered in racial, religious or class groups. The leaders of organized labor undertook to commit their followers not merely to a national ticket but to Congressional candidates who were presumed to represent a dominant trade union interest. The returns offer a conclusive proof that the effort has been as unsuccessful in the present as it has been in the past. The national vote gives no testimony of the separable delivery of organized labor's ballots to a Presidential candidate. The Congressional returns reinforce this conclusion. If it be said that the vote of San Francisco which decided the election in California was brought about through the political dominance of organized labor in that city, the idea is refuted by the fact that the electorate which carried that city for the President gave a majority of 5000 against an anti-picketing ordinance.

*

*   *

About Old Buildings

In buying old buildings the costs of repairs to bring them up to a fair living condition should always be considered, and if extensive alterations are desired the cost of these should be figured out approximately and added to the purchasing price before the question of cheapness can be decided. There are many frame houses in this country that are more than a century old, and they may last for a long time to come, but if they are in any kind of livable condition it is due to the good materials and workmanship of the builders or to splendid care and intelligent upkeep through the years of their usefulness. It is estimated by experts of the United States government that a frame building occupied by the owner depreciates from two to two and a half per cent a year, and from two and a half to three per cent when occupied by a tenant.

According to these figures, a frame house occupied by tenants will not last much more than forty years. That is the approximate age of its usefulness, but if occupied by the owner, who gives good care to it, it may not be old at fifty or sixty years. By proper maintenance and constant repairs, the building may be practically made over in every twenty or thirty years. That is, all except certain parts of it. The shingles of a roof may be renewed, but hardly the rafters and roof beams except at an abnormal cost. The inside plastering and sheathing may be torn down and replaced, but not the studding and wall girders except at a ruinous cost. A new floor may be laid, but not floor joists unless you want to go to great expense.—Exchange.

SWIMMING POOL FOR GEO. POPE ESTATE
WILLIS POLK & COMPANY. ARCHITECTS

RUSTIC COTTAGE CONTAINING DRESSING ROOMS AND RECTANGULAR POOL

Municipal and Private Outdoor Swimming Pools

THE private swimming pool is growing more and more popular, and no country estate is now considered complete without it. Small cities, too, are building public pools, and compared with the municipal bath houses of ten years ago they are as far advanced in refinement and conveniences as the modern electrically lighted home eclipses the old-fashioned lamp-lighted house.

To many persons outdoor bathing is one of the most enjoyable of recreations. Indulgence in this sport is, however, often limited by lack of opportunity in the form of a natural body of water or swimming pool. Of late years park improvements in many cities have included outdoor concrete swimming pools, and their popularity has had much to do with the spread of the swimming pool idea, even as an adjunct of the private home grounds, where the family can indulge in outdoor swimming often regardless of the season of the year.

An examination of the illustrations will impress one with the wide range of cost that may govern in the construction of a swimming pool, and will also suggest that such a structure may be simple and therefore of moderate cost.

In selecting a site for the outdoor swimming pool, a location should be chosen where natural drainage of the soil is good. Careful thought to the subject of location will suggest the many ways in which such a pool may be made to bear a harmonious relation to other structures or landscape details of the home grounds. Often considerable architectural adornment in the form of a pergola or departures from a plain, square or rectangular plan may be made features of the work. These, while often pleasing, do not, however, add to the utility of the pool, and might represent an expense that to some would be a bar to undertaking the construction.

POOL AND PERGOLA, A MENLO PARK ESTATE
Chas. Peter Weeks, Architect

Concrete construction is deemed by many an ideal material for swimming pools. It insures strength, watertightness, freedom from expensive upkeep, and permanence when properly designed and performed. The prime essential of a swimming pool is that it shall be watertight. This can be attained with concrete by using properly proportioned mixtures, carefully placed, and protecting the concrete after placing until it has hardened sufficiently to permit use. The utmost possible degree of sanitation is also desirable in a swimming pool. Well made concrete is dense and impervious, hence a concrete swimming pool can readily be kept in sanitary condition. Although no surface finish other than that secured by spreading the concrete carefully next to the face of well-made, smooth forms, nevertheless if another surface finish is desired, it can readily be obtained in a number of ways.

It may be necessary to arrange for dressing room facilities in connection with the outdoor pool. A shelter for this purpose may be a part of the architectural plan of the pool and its location, or may be a separate feature. The swimming pool itself requires few and simple furnishings or appointments. There should be a springboard at one end. Usually handrails or handholds are placed around the inside of the pool, slightly above water level.

The season during which the outdoor pool may be used can be materially lengthened by providing facilities for heating the water. Steam coils may be placed along one or more sides of the pool, hot water or steam being circulated from a hot-water boiler or steam plant. Exhaust steam where available is often sufficient to warm the water to the desired temperature.

WADING POOL IN PUBLIC PARK, WISCONSIN

PRIVATE CONCRETE POOL, FITTING NICELY INTO THE LANDSCAPE

A GOOD ILLUSTRATION OF THE SWIMMING POOL AND PERGOLA COMBINED

ANOTHER COMBINATION POOL AND PERGOLA

A MUNICIPAL BATHING POOL

A PLAIN, RECTANGULAR OUTDOOR POOL.

SALT WATER PUBLIC POOL, ALLENHURST, N. J.

ANOTHER VIEW OF THE ALLENHURST POOL
The water is drawn into this pool from the ocean through a sand filter ten or twelve feet thick.

A GLASS-ENCLOSED POOL

CIRCULAR WADING POOL FOR CHILDREN

CIRCULAR CONCRETE WADING POOL SIMILAR TO THAT SHOWN IN DESIGN

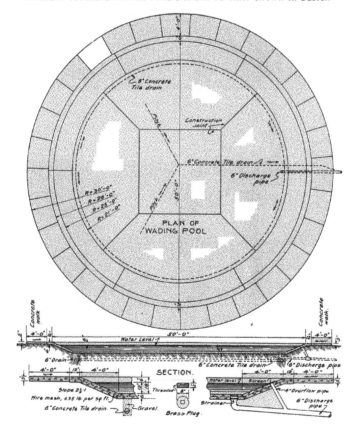

FOUNTAIN AND POOL IN GANESHA PARK, POMONA, CALIFORNIA

Probably the simplest method of warming water is to circulate it through a hot water boiler. In such a case it is necessary that the boiler be set low enough in relation to the water in the pool so that the water will return to the boiler by gravity.

Overflow and discharge pipes should be provided for. It is particularly necessary that for inexpensive operation the facilities for filling and emptying the pool be as simple as possible to arrange. The pool should be located so that gravity flow will empty it when necessary to change the water for cleaning the pool or for other reasons.

Unless the water supply is from a source that furnishes pure clear water, it is desirable to arrange to filter the water before passing it into the pool. Sparkling cleanliness of the water contributes much to the pleasure of bathing in the outdoor pool and to the feeling of security when diving.

Some who have constructed swimming pools for private use have made such structures a source of actual profit. In the East a properly designed and constructed concrete swimming pool may be allowed to freeze over in winter and then will provide a private skating rink, or if one is so situated

AN OUTDOOR SWIMMING POOL, ST. LOUIS PARK DEPARTMENT

that the home supply of ice can be harvested and stored, the profit from the construction comes from utilizing it in this manner.

The following estimate will enable one to determine the probable cost of the average size pool:

```
Portland cement .............................301 barrels
Sand ........................................90 cubic yards
Pebbles or broken stone ....................135 cubic yards
Reinforcement ..............................9,280 pounds
```

If lumber must be purchased solely for this work, about 6,000 feet board measure will be required. Hardware, such as nails, and miscellaneous tools, etc., are estimated at approximately $125. All concrete pools should be waterproofed and a glazed or enamel tile has been found to be a very satisfactory lining.

Although many outdoor swimming pools, especially those which are planned with a view to public or semi-public use, are so designed as to include the possibility of being used as a wading pool also, nevertheless the depth of water at the shallow end of such pools is often greater than is safe for small children who cannot swim.

Many public parks have added to their free-for-all enjoyment features a wading pool in which small children can splash at will and race their miniature yachts. The maximum depth of water in such pools is uniformly 12 inches. This maximum can be decreased, if desirable, by placing the outlet lower, thus lowering the water level correspondingly. This pool has an over-all diameter of 50 feet. A sloping pavement permits easy entrance to the water. The construction throughout should be of 1:2:3 concrete.

* * *

Standardization of Schoolhouse Design and Construction

THE Committee on Standardization of School-house Design and Construction appointed by the Department of School Administration of the National Education Association has begun work by making public a statement of the reasons for its own existence and for the study which it is to undertake. The statement reads as follows:

In the United States over one hundred millions of dollars are spent each year for new school buildings, the plans of which have been chiefly selected on the basis of the personal preference of architects, educators and members of school boards, rather than from fitness and economy of arrangement ascertained by the application of tests.

Up to the present time no data have been collected for establishing national standards by which to judge the skill that has been exercised in working up the plan or to check the plan as to economy of erection.

This has caused great variation in the plans of school buildings of the same type and number of rooms and probably leads to a great waste of public money.

A study of published plans shows many of these variations to be of primary importance in school-house design; and results obtained by investigations into the cost of school buildings (such as the investigations by the Cleveland Board of Survey) show an apparent waste of public money.

Any comparison of a number of school buildings of the same type, the same number of rooms, and the same general construction, exposed unwarranted difference in their cost.

The situation therefore demands an investigation to determine whether the money appropriated is being spent to best advantage and how to eliminate waste.

that the horse supply of ice can be harvested and stored, the profit from the excavation comes from utilizing it in this manner.

The following estimate will enable one to determine the probable cost of the average size pool:

Portland cement	............................90½ barrels
Sand	.................................90 cubic yards
Pebbles or broken stone	.................135 cubic yards
Reinforcement	............................9,280 pounds

If lumber must be purchased solely for this work, about 6,000 feet board measure will be required. Hardware, such as nails, and miscellaneous tools, etc., are estimated at approximately $125. All concrete pools should be waterproofed and a glazed or enamel tile has been found to be a very satisfactory lining.

Although many employ swimming pools, especially those which are planned with a view to public or semi-public use, are so designed as to include the possibility of being used also as a wading pool also, nevertheless the depth of water at the shallow end of such pools is often greater than is safe for small children who cannot swim.

Many public parks have added to their free-for-all enjoyment features a wading pool in which small children can splash at will and race their miniature yachts. The maximum depth of water in such pools is uniformly 12 inches. This maximum depth can be decreased, if desirable, by placing the outlet lower, thus lowering the water level correspondingly. This pool has an overall diameter of 30 feet. A sloping pavement permits easy entrance to the water. The construction throughout should be of 1:2:3 concrete.

* * *
Standardization of Schoolhouse Design and Construction

THE Committee on Standardization of School-house Design and Construction appointed by the Department of School Administration of the National Education Association has begun work by making public a statement of its reasons for its own existence and for the study which it is to undertake. The statement reads as follows:

In the United States over one hundred millions of dollars are spent each year for new school buildings, the plans of which have been chiefly selected on the basis of the personal preference of architects, educators and members of school boards, rather than from fitness and economy of arrangement ascertained by the application of tests.

Up to the present time no data have been collected for establishing national standards by which to judge the skill that has been exercised in working up the plan or to check the plan as to economy of erection.

This has caused great variation in the plans of school buildings of the same type and number of rooms and probably leads to a great waste of public money.

A study of published plans shows how many of these variations to be of primary importance in schoolhouse design, and results obtained by investigations into the cost of school buildings (such as the investigations by the Cleveland Board of Survey) show an apparent waste of public money.

Any comparison of a number of school buildings of the same type, the same number of rooms, and the same general construction, exposed unwarranted difference in their cost.

The situation therefore demands an investigation to determine whether the money appropriated is being spent to best advantage and how to eliminate waste.

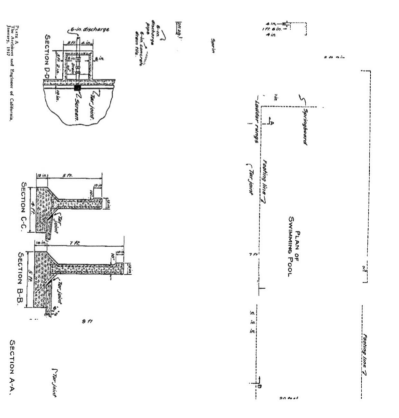

PLAN OF SWIMMING POOL

SECTION A-A.

SECTION B-B.

SECTION C-C.

SECTION D-D.

that the home supply of ice can be harvested and st ed, the profit from the construction comes from utilizing it in this manner

The following estimate will enable one to determine the probable cos of the average size pool:

Portland cement ....'....301, barrels
Sand ....90 cubic yards
Pebbles or broken stone .... 135 cubic yards
Reinforcement ....9,280 pounds

If lumber must be purchased solely for this worl about 6,000 feet boa measure will be required. Hardware, such as nails, id miscellaneous tor etc., are estimated at approximately $125. All c crete pools should waterproofed and a glazed or enamel tile has been fund to be a very sat factory lining.

Although many outdoor swimming pools, espcially those which planned with a view to public or semi-public use, a so designed as to clude the possibility of being used as a wading po also, nevertheless depth of water at the shallow end of such pools is o en greater than is for small children who cannot swim.

Many public parks have added to their free-for-il enjoyment featur wading pool in which small children can splash and vil and race their m ture yachts. The maximum depth of water in suc pools is uniform inches. This maximum can be decreased, if desirab, by placing the c lower, thus lowering the water level correspondigly. This pool h over-all diameter of 50 feet. A sloping pavement irmits easy entra the water. The construction throughout should be 1 :2 :3 concrete.

*   *

Standardization of Schoolhous(Design and Construction

THE Committee on Standardization of School-bore Design and Cc tion appointed by the Department of School Administration of t tional Education Association has begun wok by making p statement of the reasons for its own existence and or the study whi to undertake. The statement reads as follows:

In the United States over one hundred millions f dollars are spe year for new school buildings, the plans of which hav been chiefly sel the basis of the personal preference of architects, educators and mer school boards, rather than from fitness and econon of arrangemer tained by the application of tests.

Up to the present time no data have been collected for establishing standards by which to judge the skill that has been exercised in workir plan or to check the plan as to economy of erection.

This has caused great variation in the plans of school building same type and number of rooms and probably leads a great waste money.

A study of published plans shows many of these vriations to be o importance in school-house design; and results obtained by investiga the cost of school buildings (such as the investigation by the Clevela of Survey) show an apparent waste of public mone.

Any comparison of a number of school building of the same same number of rooms, and the same general construction, expose ranted difference in their cost.

The situation therefore demands an investigation o determine money appropriated is being spent to best advantage and how waste.

Suggested Design

for

Concrete

Swimming Pool

The investigation should also furnish data by means of which officials and committees could judge the economy and suitability of plans for school buildings when submitted to them.

The Department of School Administration of the National Education Association considered this situation at the New York Convention (July, 1916) and appointed a committee to investigate the subject of school architecture. The committee included Frank Irving Cooper, architect, Boston, chairman; Mr. S. A. Challman, Commissioner of School Buildings of Minnesota; Mr. C. E. Chadsey, Superintendent of Schools, Detroit; Dr. Louis M. Terman, professor of hygiene, Stanford University, and Dr. Leonard P. Ayres, director, Department of Education, Russell Sage Foundation.

The immediate business of the committee will be an endeavor to determine a definite basis for its work and may be separated into three divisions:

First: To select from those standards the details in construction pertaining to school architecture which have been already determined upon by the various states and which are in general use by various trade organizations.

Second: To select from standard details those usually accepted by educational authorities.

Third: To fix standards of school planning.

The first and second parts of this work call for correspondence with authorities on existing standards and it is hoped that school boards and school officials will furnish the committee with such information as may be called for from time to time, and also furnish opportunities for investigation by the committee or its representatives.

The third part means original research analyzing the architectural plans of floor arrangements of school buildings, to determine relative areas set apart for different uses and to form such scientific standards as may be applied, by persons unskilled in the intricacies of the architectural profession in order to enable them to test plans submitted to them.

Plans and cost sheets of buildings already erected will afford a basis for study which will be very much appreciated.

General findings only will become public property for the use of all who have to do with the school buildings of the United States.

* * *

Time Required for Mixing Concrete

The chief engineer of the Pennsylvania State Highway Department reports that his practice is to mix every batch of concrete for a period of 1½ minutes, the reason for this being that a number of experiments made by him indicated that the maximum strength commensurate with economy in cost of mixing was obtained from mixtures of this timing.

The following are the results given by the experiments in question, all the results being based on tests at the age of eight days:

Time of Mixing Minutes	No. of Revo- lutions	Compressive Strength of Concrete lb. per sq. in.
½	9	1400
1	17	1587
1½	26	1926
2	36	1661
3	51	1673

Opinions as to the most advantageous period that should be allowed for machine mixing are apt to differ. The point, however, is one that could readily be settled by a series of simple tests.

The Concrete Superintendent*
Qualifications That are Essential to His Success
By L. C. WASON

THE very first step which a contractor must take in starting the execution of a job is selecting a general superintendent to handle the work. The type that is hired for a single job, and discharged at its completion, is not worth having. The really desirable superintendent is a development from experience, the one survival from many tried; and, when once obtained, a firm cannot afford to lose him. Some owners and engineers appreciate the value of personality so much that they have given the writer's company contracts under condition that a certain superintendent be put in charge.

Frederick W. Taylor, in his excellent paper entitled "Shop Management," specifies nine different qualifications which go to make up a well-rounded man, namely: "Brains, education; special or technical knowledge; manual dexterity or strength; tact; energy; grit; honesty; judgment or common sense; and good health." He states that there are plenty of men to be found who embody three of these qualifications. Four make a higher-priced man. A man combining five is quite hard to get; and one combining six, seven, or eight is almost impossible.

If a building superintendent is to be successful, he must combine at least seven of these qualities. He must have brains, special and technical knowledge of both direct contract and sub-contract work, tact, energy, honesty, judgment, and good health. He must have a personality which drives to activity several hundred originally unorganized men who are without special interest in the company they work for or in the result accomplished, and with such tact and judgment as to weld them into a harmonious working force, cheerful and self-respecting, with high morale, and ultimately with enthusiasm for the work in hand. He carries a care so great that he builds in full size, with permanent materials, the intricacies of design which trouble the engineer's drafting room to show clearly on paper; with an honor so fine that the company is ready to leave its reputation in his hands, to trust him with funds; and with special experience so trained that dangerous operations are carried on as a matter of routine, without worry to himself or the company, yet with a constant oversight of a thousand chances for accident or perhaps death which may occur to the men in his charge; with a forethought so great that he sees ahead and provides for the problems, which are to come up perhaps months later; with a temper so good that he never loses self-control under the most provoking circumstances, and is able to take with the best of grace changes in his plans from the office, and to work in the close co-operation with the company which is so necessary to make it an effective contracting organization.

Such men have a temperament that responds quickly to criticism or praise. Praise comes sparingly, even when deserved, while criticism is freely meted out. Superintendents in the employ of the company have recalled to memory words of appreciation from an owner or an engineer long after the job has faded from the writer's memory, and he has seen a man's work improve in quality and cost purely through praise for some detail of the work which was ably handled or some difficulty which was ingeniously overcome. The company, including its superintendent, feels as much pride in the jobs it does as do the engineers

* From a paper, "The Problems of the Contractor," read before the Boston Society of Civil Engineers.

who have designed these structures. The members of the executive force on any job which is sharply criticized, will try to avoid criticism by refusing the slightest responsibility beyond what they believe to be clearly their own. A company sharply criticized by an engineer is likely to do precisely the same thing, and will throw onto the engineer every bit of responsibility which it can possibly avoid. The attitude of the engineer in this respect is reflected in the execution of the work. One engineer may call attention to a mistake with a letter that is harsh and ends with a sting, which leaves the feeling of injustice and soreness in the recipient. Another in calling attention to a similar matter, ends his letter with some expression like the following: "We appreciate your wish to make this work as satisfactory as possible, and recognize that this occurred through failure to understand my exact requirements." In response to such a letter as the first, the tendency is to do just as little as will satisfy the engineer, and take your own time about it. But as the writer knows from personal experience, in response to the second letter, you jump to correct the trouble cheerfully, quickly, and without comment, and also sometimes do more than was asked for.

The problem in selecting the superintendent which the contractor must consider, is whether in the particular location he will be able to handle the difficulties which arise. Perhaps the owner and engineer desire an exceptionally fine appearance in the finished mill. One superintendent is especially good at this. Perhaps finish is of no great moment, and business ability is, on account of the job being isolated so that the superintendent is left alone for some days at a time. Perhaps the local conditions may demand a great deal of tact in the handling of labor. The following illustration shows what tact is required. When the writer's company executed its first contract in Buffalo, it was for a firm which had had considerable trouble with labor, and it was anticipated that there would be a strike before the job was very far advanced. This firm had been marked by the local labor organizations as their natural prey, and these organizations were also prejudiced against outside firms coming into their territory. The carpenters there have a strong organization. During the early stages of this job, while there were but a few carpenters, the superintendent could give them considerable personal attention, and things went smoothly; but as soon as work began on the second floor, where they could not be so easily seen and the superintendent was too busy with other matters to watch them closely, unit costs began to climb day by day. The superintendent studied the situation to find the cause. By the time form work was starting on the third story, he became convinced that the union steward of the job was to blame and was holding the men back from doing their best. The natural impulse would have been to discharge him immediately, but that would have made hard feeling with the union. The superintendent took this man aside, confided to him his troubles, and then made this man sub-foreman with entire charge of erecting forms for the columns, which was the particular item that showed the highest cost. Immediately the costs came down, and on the fourth story were the lowest on the whole job. The result was saving a thoroughly first-class workman and keeping in the good graces of the local organization.

These various questions must be weighed and settled before a start is made. Experience has shown that after a job has once started with a given organization, a change in the superintendent is the cause of much disturbance to its satisfactory completion and economy in the handling of labor. It is of the most vital importance that this question be settled rightly once for all.

THE

Architect and Engineer
OF CALIFORNIA

Founded in 1905 by E. M. C. WHITNEY

A. I. WHITNEY　-　-　-　　*Manager*
T. C. KIERULFF　-　-　-　　*Legal Points*
FREDERICK W. JONES　-　-　　*Editor*

Published Monthly in the Interests of the
Architects, Structural Engineers, Contract-
ors and the Allied Trades of the Pacific
Coast by the Architect and Engineer.

BUSINESS OFFICE AND EDITORIAL ROOMS
627-629 Foxcroft Building, San Francisco
Telephone Douglas 1828

The publishers disclaim any responsibility for statements
made in the advertisements of this magazine.

TERMS OF SUBSCRIPTION
(Including postage) to all parts of the United States $1.50
per annum; to Canada 50c additional; to all Foreign points
$1 additional.

VOL. XLVIII.　JAN., 1917　NO. 1

"Little Houses in Brick and Stucco" is the title of a paper in the October *Craftsman* that presents a number of shrewdly reasoned observations on the subject of what might be called the architectural verities. To quote:

COMBINING BEAUTY WITH UTILITY IN DOMESTIC ARCHITECTURE

Reasonableness and imagination, says the writer, recognized by the medieval builders as the underlying principles of all great architecture, should be as inseparably united in the small home of today as they were in the great cathedrals of old. For the little house is an expression of thought, though a very different kind of one, as well as a cathedral. It is also an expression of art—if beauty be combined with usefulness. Art was born, as has often been pointed out, when useful things were accurately and beautifully made, were formed with vision. A square box strengthened with iron bands was a useful thing. When the bands were made in graceful forms and the box carved, then it became beautiful —a work of art. A house staunchly made to defy enemies and shut out the rains was a satisfactory shelter, but it came not under the head of architecture until it was made shapely as well as stout, when doors and windows were set in symmetrical relation and the roof pitched to a pleasing angle. Common sense must go hand in hand with beauty, or as Michaelangelo says it: "Beauty must rest on necessities. The line of beauty is the result of perfect economy." Beauty must be organic, said the old architects. Outside embellishment can easily become a deformity unless introduced in the most sympathetic of ways. This truth seems especially obvious in the small house. Large houses carry adornment better than the small ones, but even they reach to highest dignity when left free from what is generally termed ornament. The very word ornament, Pater points out, indicates that it is non-essential. The small house depends almost entirely upon structural symmetry for its beauty. A little home built upon a common sense floor plan with a simple exterior in which a delicate imagination and sense of proportion is expressed is one of the pleasantest objects to be seen in the whole world.

Worth quoting that, comments the *Builder's Guide*. And for the young man in architecture, worth memorizing. The philosophy of it is not only sound. It is stimulating. It is tonic. It states, in little space, so much that ought to enable the young designer to avoid what is fundamentally bad in his art.

Every so often we read in the technical press an answer to the query:

SHOULD ARCHITECTS READ ADVERTISEMENTS? "Should architects read advertisements?" It is a fact that a great many architects find their time too closely occupied to permit of reading magazine advertisements. Others, with a false conception of ethics, decline to lower their dignity by perusing the advertising pages further than to hurriedly skim through them. It is not an uncommon sight to see an architect rip every advertising page out of his architectural book and then file the pictures and reading pages.

The following editorial in Building Management has the right ring to it:

The man today who would advance with the rapid development of his profession should keep in touch with what the manufacturers of products he uses are doing. Good advertising today no longer savors of the old-style circus methods of misstatements and exaggerated claims. The publicity of the progressive manufacturer is educational, and full of valuable and useful information.

Particularly are these conditions true in the building field. Improvements in construction, equipment and finishing of buildings are appearing with such rapidity that the architect, engineer and contractor must keep in touch with what the manufacturers of building products are doing. The manufacturer, on his part, is anxious to present his information in the way that will be most satisfactory to the man who specifies and uses his product. Printed announcements are published in magazines and catalogs and circulars are distributed; yet, unfortunately, a large percentage of these efforts is wasted.

The aloofness of technical and professional men to all things savoring of publicity should stop. They ought to co-operate with the manufacturer just as the manufacturer is trying in every way to co-operate with them. Successful building demands the co-working of all the forces entering into it. The architect, the engineer, the contractor, the owner and the manufacturer—all are important factors in securing perfect results. Each one should sincerely work with the others, and not assume an attitude of suspicion and distrust.

There is another important reason why the architect and builder should co-operate with the progressive manufacturer who is conducting publicity campaigns in magazines. These publications are read by the general public who could not be reached directly to any great extent by professional men. This educational advertising is a powerful influence in the development of improved methods of building. Thus, the manufacturer is educating the public to better standards of building and is promoting the same ideals as the leaders in the architectural and construction field.

Many progressive architects and builders have appreciated these facts and have profited by the improved methods developed by commercial institutions. Let us have, however, a universal co-operation on all sides, an open-mindedness on the part of the architect to receive useful information, and a sincere effort on the part of the manufacturer to provide really educational publicity.

Review of Recent Books

MY GROWING GARDEN. By J. Horace McFarland. 52 illus. MacMillan, N. Y. $2.00.

The joy of making one's own garden, and the individuality thus obtained impresses itself keenly on the reader of this refreshing narrative. We have had a surfeit of garden books on formal gardens which the owner had no part in. This describes the development during a half dozen years of a notable two-acre garden, on a modest yet inspiring and artistic scale. The enthusiasm of the owner is imparted through every chapter, so that one comes to know him and be fond of him, as well as of his plants and the simple but effective landscape architecture he has so charmingly described. His friendly consultations with an expert in landscape design are productive of interesting results in hedges, borders, walks and vistas. But above all he shows that he has caught the value of the right placing of the big and important masses of shrubbery, etc., to produce something of real art. After this intimate view of Mr. McFarland's real and enthusiasm at home, it is not difficult to understand why he has been such an effective president of the American Civic Association for the last several years.

<hr>

Books Received—To Be Reviewed Later

Napoleon in His Own Words. H. E. Law and C. J. Rhodes, A. C. McClurg & Co. $1.00.

Matching Granite in an Old Building

The old National Bank building at Spokane, Wash., is being enlarged and remodelled to accommodate the Union Trust and Savings Bank. It is desired to keep everything in harmony with the existing work, so that unusual precautions are being made. A portion of the iron grill has been shipped to Chicago in order that it may be copied, as the original maker went into bankruptcy and the patterns were lost. In the same way a section of the mahogany desks used by the officers was shipped to Milwaukee so that the color, grain and finish could be matched. Additional granite will be needed for the exterior. It was impossible to send a sample of the granite used to the quarries in Barre, Vt., where the granite originally was cut. The process has been reversed and the Barre firm is sending samples to Spokane to be matched with the existing base. From the sample that matches, the new granite blocks will be cut and shipped to Spokane. The work of remodelling is being done under the direction of Graham, Burnham & Co., of Chicago, who designed the original building.

Superiority of American Oak

A remarkable point in the hardwood situation is the reversion of demand from the soft foreign imported oaks to our American domestic oak which is, as a matter of fact, superior in every way to all the other oaks in the world. Architects and builders are everywhere recognizing that our American wood is the best to use on account of its durability, liveliness of tone, lasting and wearing qualities. The good old-fashioned oak of our ancestors is still supreme today.

Sacramento Factory

E. C. Hemmings is completing plans for a one-story hollow tile factory to be erected in North Sacramento for the Essex Lumber Company.

American Institute of Architects
(ORGANIZED 1857)
OFFICERS FOR 1916-17

PRESIDENT.....JOHN LAWRENCE MAURAN, St. Louis
FIRST VICE-PRESIDENT......C. GRANT LA FARGE, New York
SECOND VICE-PRESIDENT....W. R. B. WILLCOX, Seattle, Wash.
SECRETARY....W. STANLEY PARKER, Boston, Mass.
TREASURER..........D. EVERETT WAID, New York

Board of Directors

For One Year—W. R. B. Willcox, Seattle, Wash.; Octavius Morgan, Los Angeles; Walter Cook, New York.

For Two Years—Edwin H. Brown, Minneapolis; B. J. Lubschez, Kansas City, Mo.; Horace Wells Sellers, Philadelphia.

For Three Years—Burt L. Fenner, New York; Thos R. Kimball, Omaha; W. B. Faville, San Francisco.

San Francisco Chapter

PRESIDENT...................EDGAR A. MATHEWS
VICE-PRESIDENT.........SYLVAIN SCHNAITTACHER
SECRETARY AND TREASURER........MORRIS BRUCE
TRUSTEES......................{ W. B. FAVILLE
                              { G. A. WRIGHT

Southern California Chapter

PRESIDENT......................J. E. ALLISON
VICE-PRESIDENT................J. J. BACKUS
SECRETARY.......................A. R. WALKER
TREASURER.............AUGUST WACKERBARTH
Board of Directors
ROBT. D. FARQUHAR   PERCY A. EISEN
            S. B. MARSTON

Portland, Ore., Chapter

PRESIDENT...................JOSEPH JACOBBERGER
VICE-PRESIDENT................J. A. FOUILHOUX
SECRETARY....................W. C. KNIGHTON
TREASURER....................FOLGER JOHNSON
TRUSTEES.....................{ ION LEWIS
                            { M. H. WHITEHOUSE

Washington State Chapter

PRESIDENT.............CHARLES H. BEBB, Seattle
1ST VICE-PRES....DANIEL R. HUNTINGTON, Seattle
2D VICE-PRESIDENT.........GEORGE GOVE, Tacoma
3D VICE-PRESIDENT.........L. L. RAND, Spokane
SECRETARY...............JOSEPH S. COTE, Seattle
TREASURER..........ELLSWORTH STOREY, Seattle
COUNCIL..............{ JAMES STEPHEN, Seattle
                     { JAMES H. SCHACK, Seattle
                     { CHARLES H. ALDEN, Seattle

California State Board of Architecture
NORTHERN DISTRICT.

PRESIDENT....................EDGAR A. MATHEWS
SECRETARY-TREASURER.....SYLVAIN SCHNAITTACHER
Members
JOHN BAKEWELL, JR.   J. CATHER NEWSOM

SOUTHERN DISTRICT.

PRESIDENT....................JOHN P. KREMPEL
SECRETARY-TREASURER..........FRED H. ROEHRIG
                          { OCTAVIUS MORGAN
MEMBERS...................{ SUMNER P. HUNT
                          { WM. S. HEBBARD

San Francisco Architectural Club
OFFICERS FOR 1916

PRESIDENT ....CHAS. PETER WEEKS
VICE-PRESIDENT ....A. WILLIAMS
SECRETARY ....JOHN F. BEUTTLER
TREASURER ....WILLIAM HELM

San Francisco Society of Architects

PRESIDENT.................CHARLES PETER WEEKS
VICE-PRESIDENT.............GEORGE W. KELHAM
SECRETARY AND TREASURER.....WARREN C. PERRY
DIRECTORS..................{ ERNEST COXHEAD
                           { FREDERICK H. MEYER

Engineers and Architects Association of Los Angeles

PRESIDENT......................A. H. KOEBIG
FIRST VICE-PRESIDENT...............A. S. BENT
SECOND VICE-PRESIDENT..........IRA H. FRANCIS
Directors
H. L. SMITH, J. J. BACKUS, G. P. ROBINSON
               A. C. MARTIN.

San Diego Architectural Association

PRESIDENT..................CHARLES CRESSEY
VICE-PRESIDENT........W. TEMPLETON JOHNSON
SECRETARY...................ROBT. HALLEY, JR.
TREASURER.....................G. A. HAUSSEN

San Joaquin Valley Ass'n of Architects

PRESIDENT....................JOSEPH LOSEKANN
VICE-PRESIDENT.................L. S. STONE
SECRETARY-TREASURER.........FRANK V. MAYO

With the Architects

Building Reports and Personal Mention of Interest to the Profession

Winners of Cover Design Competition

On January 4th the jury named to select a cover design for The Architect and Engineer of California met in the rooms of the Building Material Exhibit, 77 O'Farrell street, San Francisco, and awarded first prize to Edward L. Frick of 1375 California street, San Francisco; second prize to Ernest E. Weihe of 251 Kearny street, San Francisco, and third prize to M. J. Rist, with C. E. Gottschalk, Phelan building, San Francisco. Special mention was given Arthur O. Johnson, head draftsman for Henry H. Meyers. The jury was composed of Frederick H. Meyer, Arthur Brown, Jr., and Charles Peter Weeks. After the judgment the designs were placed on exhibition at the Building Material Exhibit and were viewed by a large number of interested visitors. The winning design will be used for the February cover.

Honor for J. J. Donovan

John J. Donovan, architect for the city of Oakland, has been appointed by the Department of School Administration of the National Education Association to serve as a member of the Committee on the Standardization of the Planning and Construction of School Buildings.

Among the other architects serving on the committee are William B. Ittner, city architect for St. Louis, and C. B. J. Snyder, architect for the city of New York.

Donovan will collect data on the best schools of the Pacific Coast and later will meet with the committee to tabulate the information obtained from all the great cities of the United States.

$85,000 Elks Building

Bids will be called for this month for constructing the new Elks' Home at Visalia. The building will be three stories in height and will contain a store room on the first floor, club rooms above and lodge hall on the third floor. The estimated cost is $85,000. Swartz & Swartz, of Fresno, are the architects.

Protests Holding Competition

Mr. Ernest Newton, the president of the Royal Institute of British Architects, has sent to the High Commissioner for Australia a strong protest against the resumption at the present time of the competition to select an architect for the Australian Federal Parliament House, which Mr. Walter B. Griffin has announced as being open until January 31, 1917. Mr. Newton points out that under present conditions the competition is practically confined to neutral countries, whose architects would have preponderating advantage over those of the empire and its allies. Sir John J. Burnet, the British assessor, has protested against the competition being held, and has withdrawn his name as assessor. Eight prizes are being offered, aggregating £6,000, in addition to commission for service.

To Exhibit Plans of State Building

The competitive plans for the million-dollar State building for the San Francisco Civic Center are to be displayed in the rooms of the Building Material Exhibit at 77 O'Farrell street, San Francisco, as soon as the jury of award selects the winning design after February 15.

The eight architects and architectural firms chosen among the fifty-three exhibitors at the first exhibition for having the eight best designs are working on their final drawings, which will include elevations, sections and floor plans.

Four-Story Oakland Building

William Knowles, Hearst building, San Francisco, is preparing plans for a four-story Class "C" building to be erected in the city of Oakland for a client. The building will be put up by day labor.

Mr. Knowles is completing plans for a two-story Swiss chalet to be built in Redwood Highlands, at Redwood City, for Mrs. W. T. Kellogg, daughter of John A. Britton of the Pacific Gas and Electric Company.

Proposed Architects' Law

Both the Oregon and the Washington State Chapters of the American Institute of Architects are endeavoring to have enacted at the coming session of the legislature, a law to regulate the use of the title architect. It must be understood, however, that the chapters do not seek to prevent an owner, or engineer, or draftsman, or designer from making drawings for buildings and structures. They are not presuming to legislate any one now practicing out of business and would not preclude any one from practicing who can and will show that he is qualified, by passing such examination as the state board of examiners may deem necessary to prove such qualifications.

The proposed law provides that only those who are entitled through experience and training to call themselves architects, shall be permitted the use of the title on plans, stationery or other mediums. It would permit those who now use the professional title to file their names with a state board before a certain date. After this date those who have not registered in the state as architects would be compelled to go through an examination conducted by a state board if they desired to use the title "Architect."

The Washington State Chapter is seeking to enlist the endeavors of the architects of the state in behalf of the measure and has addressed a letter to them with this end in view.

The Oregon Chapter of the American Institute of Architects, of which W. C. Knighton, Portland, is secretary, is preparing a bill for the licensing of architects to practice in that state; also the Oregon Society of Architects, of which Harrison A. Whitney, of Portland, is president. The bill which the former is preparing provides for a board of five men, named by the governor, serving without pay, to attend to registration and issuing of certificates to all practicing architects; making a charge of $20 for initial registration and an annual fee of $5 thereafter. The bill being prepared by the Oregon Society of Architects provides that the examination of architects shall be under the supervision of the regents of the University of Oregon. Under this bill the provisions of the proposed law do not apply to architects now practicing in the state.

Given Certificates to Practice

At a recent meeting of the State Board of Architecture, Southern District, Edward A. Strong, 1347 Sycamore avenue, and B. G. Horton, 750 East Colorado street, Pasadena, and Arthur J. Kooken, 502 West First street, Los Angeles, were granted certificates to practice architecture in the State of California.

News from Professor Cret

Though Professor Paul. P. Cret has been engaged with the French troops in the Somme drive, he is "still in possession of all his members," and is in high spirits, according to a letter written on November 5 to his business associate, Albert Kelsey, of Philadelphia.

"I am sensible of the good opinion that you have, in common with your compatriots, of the effectiveness of our work here. It is a crisis which leaves but few unaffected and which, unfortunately, will not cease with the ending of hostilities," he writes. Professor Cret left the University of Pennsylvania when the war began and comments on a clipping which referred to him as "Dr. Cret," saying: "When I was a 'Doc' seems long ago."

Professor Cret has seen all sorts of service, and when not in the trenches he is engaged in drawing military maps. These are made from aeroplane photos, which show how the country has been honeycombed by the craters made by big shells.

Want More Drastic State Law

At the December meeting of the Southern California Chapter, A. I. A., Edwin Bergstrom, for the committee of permanent legislation, stated that progress was being made in framing a measure to present to the next state legislature respecting the practice of architecture in California. A draft of the proposed act was read at the November meeting of the chapter, since which time the committee to which it was referred has been endeavoring to frame a measure which will be satisfactory to all and which will in its opinion be more certain of passage by the state legislature. Changes were suggested to make the law more of a public safety measure and to omit the limitation as to cost of buildings for which plans may be prepared by unlicensed architects.

Architects Move

Alfred Kuhn announces the removal of his office from the Phelan building to 958 Pacific building, San Francisco. Mr. Kuhn has recently let a contract to J. P. W. Jensen to erect a four-story slow-burning factory building at First and Folsom streets, for the Catherine Dunn Company.

Harry Skidmore has moved his office from the Hearst building to the new Call building, San Francisco.

Messrs. Heiman-Schwartz have moved from the Nevada Bank building, San Francisco, to 212 Stockton street.

William Wilde, Oakland architect, has moved to offices in the Maskey building, San Francisco.

Mercantile Houses Expand

A number of the large retail houses in San Francisco plan to materially increase their floor space this year. The White House will occupy as an annex the building at Post street and Grant avenue, now being vacated by the Hastings Clothing Company. The Emporium is building a one-story addition to its main building and a six-story annex, from plans by Morris M. Bruce. Magnin & Son will build a two-story addition to its home at Geary street and Grant avenue, for which plans have been completed by Architect Frederick H. Meyer. The same architect also has plans for a one-story addition to the Bankers Investment building on Market street. The City of Paris building at the southeast corner of Geary and Stockton streets, San Francisco, has been sold to John A. Hooper for $1,-200,000, which is the same price paid for the lot at the southeast corner of Market and Fourth streets. The property has an area of 137½ by 137½ feet and comprises a six-story steel frame store and office building. It is understood the offices will be torn out to give additional floor space for the City of Paris.

Engineer Wins Suit for Services

The city of East San Diego will be compelled to pay a judgment of $4937 obtained in the superior court last summer by D. L. Bissell, former city engineer, on an account for engineering work done in connection with street improvements. An appeal was taken by city attorney, F. G. Blood, for the city, but on application of attorney for Bissell, the state Supreme Court at a hearing in San Francisco dismissed the appeal on account of defects in the procedure. Before filing suit Bissell offered twice to make settlement with the city for half the amount which was allowed him by the court. Each time his claim was turned down by the then city officials. It was alleged at the time that Bissell was indebted to the city instead of the city owing him. Several months after his claim was rejected Bissell filed suit against the city.

Milton Lichtenstein Busy

Milton Lichtenstein, 111 Ellis street, San Francisco, has prepared plans for a reinforced concrete factory building to be erected in the Mission district for the manufacture of chemicals. The same architect has made plans for a hollow tile addition of one story to the reinforced concrete factory building of S. & G. Gump, Co., on Clay street, near Stockton, San Francisco.

Mr. Lichtenstein has taken bids for the erection of a three-story and basement brick rooming house for Chin Yuey on property on Clay street, near Powell.

Wm. Binder to Build

William Binder, a San Jose architect, who erected a fine two-story business building for himself last year, has prepared plans for a second building to be erected on his property on South First street, San Jose. It will be a two-story structure of brick and concrete and will cost $20,000.

Mr. Binder expects that work will be started this year on a three-story store and apartment building at First and San Carlos streets, and another building at Second and San Antonio streets, in San Jose, for Messrs. Anderson, Twohy and Montgomery.

Mr. Binder has revised the plans for the addition to the Hotel Montgomery. The building is to be three stories instead of two, of reinforced concrete and will cost approximately $35,000.

Waterfront Improvements

Improvements to the San Francisco waterfront are going ahead and it is gratifying to know that the state of California is planning to spend several million dollars on new piers and slips the present year. Pier No. 3 will be constructed at the foot of Jackson street at a cost of $350,000. It will be built on concrete piles and will have a cement deck with asphalt surface. Other work will include a wharf shed on Pier No. 29 and a wharf building for the United States Naval Training Station on Pier No. 14.

Mills Building

Benjamin G. McDougall, Sheldon building, San Francisco, is preparing working drawings for a six-story Class "A" store and office building to be erected on Pine street, adjoining the United States Subtreasury building, for the Mills Estate. Part of the building has been leased by the Aetna Fire Insurance Company. The estimated cost of the improvement is from $300,000 to $500,000.

Oakland Cotton Mills

A. C. Grienauck, with the Engineering Department of the State Harbor Commission, San Francisco, has designed the new factory building which the California Cotton Mills will build at its East Oakland plant. Considerable common brick will be used and possibly a tapestry brick will be adopted for exterior finish. The steel sash already has been ordered. Separate bids will be taken for the plumbing, automatic sprinkler system and masonry work. Building will be 200 by 126 feet, and will cost in the neighborhood of $100,000.

Arizona Mining Building

The plans of J. B. Lyman of San Diego, for the mining building of the University of Arizona, the same architect whose plans for the agricultural building were accepted, were voted by the board of regents to be the best and Mr. Lyman probably will be commissioned to ·do the work.

The architect will be required to give a bond that the building can be constructed for the estimated amount, $150,000, or, with changes, perhaps a few thousand dollars more, and he will be required to personally supervise the construction.

Plans were submitted in competition by seventeen other architects.

Six-story Concrete Building

The regents of the University of California have. decided to improve their property on the east side of First street, between Market and 'Mission streets, San Francisco, with a six-story and basement reinforced concrete factory, which has been leased to Buckingham & Hecht, wholesale shoe merchants. The plans were prepared by Architects Bakewell & Browne, and the contract has been let to the Clinton Construction Company for $120,000.

Electric Wiring Changes

The Los Angeles City Council has adopted the recommendation of City Electrician R. H. Manahan for certain changes in the manner of installing electric wiring in buildings. The new requirements will compel the placing of wires in all buildings in either conduit or armored cable. The old ordinance permitted the installation of exposed wiring in dwellings of five rooms or less and for certain alteration work. The new law will not become effective until April 1st.

Factory and Apartments

Henry Shermund, Mills building, San Francisco, has completed plans for a four-story Class C factory to be erected at Fifteenth and Vermont streets, San Francisco.

Mr. Shermund has also prepared revised drawings for the construction of an apartment house for B. F. Meyer on the south side of California street, 80 feet east of Third avenue, San Francisco.

Napa Theatre and School ·

L. M. Turton, the Napa architect, is preparing plans for a $30,000 moving picture theatre. Mr. Turton has completed plans and taken bids for a one-story concrete school house for the Carneros School District.

Iowa Chapter Offers Advice to Clients

In a circular of information and suggestion to persons contemplating building. The Iowa State Chapter of the American Institute of Architects offers the following advice:

After your architect· is chosen rely upon him. Do not appeal to the contractor or journeyman. Do not be stampeded by neighborly critics and advisers.

Make up your mind what you must have, then take the architect into your confidence as to the amount you are willing or able to expend; be perfectly frank with him; either take what your money will pay for, or do not build.

Do not hurry; be satisfied with the sketches before working drawings and specifications are made; and then make no changes without careful consideration and for good reason.

Arrange every step beforehand in writing; pay fair prices; value for value the world over—you will get no more for your money than you pay for.

Do business only with a suitable and honest contractor; "you cannot get blood out of a turnip."

Watch the work but do all business through your confidential adviser and supervisor, the architect, who is the master-builder;' he alone should give orders to workmen.

The contractor who comes to you with suggestions or to call your attention to real or fancied errors in the plans and specifications should be referred to the architect, to whom he should have gone in the first place. Make use of the architect's advice and avoid the chance of marring the whole with incongruous furnishings within and environments without; the mind that designed the building should be manifest throughout.

If you follow these few hints, in all that they might imply, there is no reason why your structure should cost you a cent beyond the estimated price, or why it should cause you more worry than buying a new suit of clothes.

A. G. Headman Has Much Work

One of the busy San Francisco architects since the first of the year is August G. Headman, formerly of Righetti & Headman. The new work in Mr. Headman's office includes a $100,000 building for Van Ness avenue; a $20,000 garage for the J. Allec Cleaning and Dyeing Works; a $7,000 Berkeley residence; a $20,000 fireproof machine shop and extensive alterations to the Castro Street Moving Picture Theatre.

French Apartments

J. F. Dunn, formerly of Dunn & Kearns, San Francisco architects, has completed plans for a $25,000 three-story and basement frame apartment house for Mrs. A. Willson. It will be erected on the north side of Pine street, west of Leavenworth, and will be designed in the French Renaissance style.

$200,000 Ice Plant

The Pacific Fruit Express, an adjunct of the Southern Pacific Company, will erect a $200,000 cold storage and ice manufacturing plant at Sparks, Nevada. By using this plant the Southern Pacific will be able to save thirty minutes in transporting fruit and perishable freight to Eastern points. The ice plant at present is at Truckee.

Electrical Department

Domestic Lamp Socket Heating Devices
By E. A. Wilcox, in Journal of Electricity, Power and Gas.

(In this article the author treats of certain electric heating devices that may be attached to the wiring system of the ordinary household without readjusting the wiring fixtures.)

WHEN we look back and think of how the housewife of the past was hampered in the performance of her duties, and compare these difficulties with her present-day opportunities of making housework an enjoyable pastime, we naturally wonder whether it is possible for the future to bring forth conditions which will be any more ideal.

The various household labor-saving devices which have so enormously transformed economic conditions are here classified, as well as possible, to set forth their chief points of superiority. Although a single device may produce only a small revenue, taken collectively these devices are of ever-increasing importance in the production of profitable central station incomes.

Electric irons were the first heating devices to come into universal use. They are now manufactured in many sizes, shapes and capacities and sold in greater quantities than any other electrically heated device known.

The principal advantages of the electric iron over the old-fashioned sad iron are saving in time and steps, even heat distribution, freedom from smoke, grease and soot, absence of excessive heat, and ease with which it may be used in any part of the house. Irons varying in weight from 3 pounds to 9 pounds and in capacities from 200 watts to 675 watts are available for domestic uses.

Electric Stoves.—Both the disc and open coil type are manufactured in various sizes and capacities. The disc stove has a metallic heating surface and delivers heat to the utensil by conduction. The open coil stove gives off radiant heat from exposed coils which are usually imbedded in grooves of porcelain or mounted above metallic reflectors.

Electric stoves are useful for many household purposes in place of gas or alcohol burners. They are suitable for heating water for various purposes, or for doing light cooking. They are safe, convenient and durable. For domestic lamp socket use they are seldom larger than six inches in diameter and 600 watts in capacity.

Toaster Stoves.—Two distinct types are made—horizontal and vertical. Toast made on the horizontal type will be produced quickly but will not be toasted through so well unless the bread be dry. Toast made below radiant coils or in the vertical type toasters will be produced slowly but will be toasted thoroughly. Vertical toasters are usually provided with a warming shelf on top to keep the toast or other food warm.

One great advantage of electric toasters is that they may be used on the dining room table instead of in the kitchen. From 400 to 600 watts are usually required for operating toasters.

Chafing Dishes.—These frequently have an outer pan in addition to the food pan for use as double boilers. The food pans are made in two and three-pint sizes. The capacities vary from 250 to 600 watts. A wide variety of styles and ornamental types are available.

Electric chafing dishes are obviously safer to operate than alcohol or other flame types, and furthermore they give off no disagreeable odors or fumes.

Coffee Percolators.—Coffee made in an electric percolator is rich in flavor, free from grounds, and contains less caffein and other harmful elements than boiled coffee. Starting with cold water, strong coffee may be prepared in from ten to fifteen minutes.

Electric percolators in all styles, shapes

and character of ornamentation and in sizes varying from four to nine cups are available. They usually require from 450 to 600 watts. They are ideal for use on the dining room table because they are attractive in appearance and also keep the coffee hot with practically no attention.

Tea Samovars.— The housewife who prides herself on her tea-making is pleased with a device where the tea-ball may be drawn up when the infusion is just right and a beverage served of fine flavor, and free from the bitter tannic acid taste that results from boiling tea leaves in an ordinary pot. It is especially desirable for the afternoon tea because it can be operated in the living room. It furthermore does away with the disagreeable odors, fumes and dangers of alcohol or other fuel types.

Tea Samovars are usually made in five, six and seven-cup sizes and in capacities varying from 400 to 500 watts.

Tea Kettles.—Two and three pint sizes are usually made, requiring from 400 to 550 watts for operation. They are convenient and dainty for heating water for the tea service. They make an attractive addition to the table and possess the charm of a modern household luxury.

Table Cooking Outfits. — Single disc stoves supplied with a variety of hollow-ware utensils are called unit-sets, dining room sets or combination stoves. Coffee percolators, tea samovars, chafing dishes, nursery milk warmers, frying pans, tea kettles, griddle plates, and other utensils are included in the various sets.

These devices bring electric cookery within reach of all. For the hostess who does her own cooking the table cooking outfits are ideal. They are an ornament to any sideboard or table.

The Electric Range in Apartment Houses

The electric range seems to be peculiarly adapted for use in apartment houses. The character of construction of the buildings, the mode of living of the tenants, and the many recognized advantages of the electric range make it much superior to the fuel burning stove. A resume of the most essential qualifications of this type of apparatus and the better conditions that may be brought about where it is installed for apartment house cooking service should not be out of place here.

In the design of the modern apartment house every foot of space is valuable and the architect must plan to utilize it to the best advantage. His efforts in this direction seem to have resulted in the laying out of very small kitchens which are often stuffy and poorly ventilated. The electric range is best fitted to meet these recognized conditions for several reasons: It is compact in construction, and as the exterior never becomes hot

enough to burn the woodwork it may be placed against the wall and thereby take up less space. The unbearable heat of a fuel range in a small kitchen is eliminated. There is no combustion in the electric range and it neither throws off poisonous fumes nor takes up the life-giving oxygen from the air.

The initial outlay required for the installation of chimneys and gas plumbing may be entirely eliminated. When the building is once occupied the periodical expenditures incident to repainting, re-tinting and repapering may be cut in half. The very nature of the electric range, which creates no products of combustion, and which overcomes the smoke, moisture and grease nuisances peculiar to the fuel range, makes the frequent refinishing of interiors unnecessary.

Where fuel stoves are used there is constant danger of fire. Gas offers the menace of asphyxiation and explosion. The careless opening of a valve, a temporary cut-off of the main supply, or a little mistake of the cook or housewife may result disastrously. In as much as the electric range produces no flame, and neither utilizes nor gives off any explosive or poisonous gas, its use does away with all danger of loss of life or property.

Water Softening by Electricity

Water softening by electricity, especially as regards boiler feed water, is attracting the close attention of American engineers. After the softening compound has been added to the water it is circulated past parallel electrodes which are placed close together in order that as much of the water as possible may be brought in contact with the surface of the plates. The ionising properties of electricity separate the compounds into their components, thereby hastening the recombination to form precipitates, which are easily removed. Ten million gallons of water per day, it is stated, may be treated with only 480 watts per million gallons.

Many Lighting Customers

There are 5,800,000 electrical lighting customers in the United States. This means the central stations send out 70,-000,000 bills per annum. The cost is about 15 cents per average bill, including meter reading. This means an expenditure of $10,500,000 a year for accounting.

Nine Million Electrical Appliances

Report of eighty-four manufacturers shows that over 9,000,000 electrical household appliances, such as irons, toasters, grills, etc., have been manufactured and sold since this industry started.

Variety—The Spice of Lighting

By M. LUCKIESH.

MANY observations have led the writer to subscribe to the somewhat paradoxical title of this brief comment. Of all lighting systems, Nature's lighting is the least monotonous and it appears this is due largely to the perpetual changeableness of the distribution and color of light. When Nature's lighting is restricted in distribution and color as it is indoors by the artificial shackles constructed by man, its variety is suppressed and it often becomes monotonous and even unsatisfactory. However, in the great outdoors where Nature is unhampered by man, the lighting varies continually throughout a given day as well as from day to day and from season to season. It presents the extremes of variation in light distribution on overcast and sunny days and in the latter cases the shadows are continually shifting with the sun's altitude. The color aspect varies throughout the day from sunrise to sunset and no sunrise, sunset, or landscape ever present identical appearances. If a certain landscape be studied throughout the day usually it will be most interesting during early morning and late afternoon on a clear day because of the presence of variety due to long shadows. Nature's scenes lose much of their interest on overcast days owing to the less variety due to absence of long, well-defined shadows. In many interiors, symmetry is a keynote and in such cases, symmetrical lighting effects harmonize with the whole. But in a great many interiors, such as living rooms, restaurants, and lounging rooms, symmetrical lighting effects are unnecessary and are often monotonous and even obtrusive.

On viewing an art exhibition with a great artist where daylight quality of light had been simulated by artificial lighting units placed above a slight diffusing skylight, the artist remarked that the quality of light was excellent and that the light was evenly distributed but that daylighting in a broad sense had not been entirely imitated. Something was missing which upon further discussion proved to be a degree of directedness or lack of symmetry required by the artist's fine sensibility which had often communed with Nature.

Let us take the same case to the home. On entering the living room and pressing the switch a central lighting unit is lighted. How monotonous this symmetrical and invariable distribution of light becomes! Table lamps and brackets lend variety which pleases the finer sensibilities and such units provide means for adapting the lighting to the mood or occasion.

The bigness of Nature is great enough to play an important role in the making of a human mood. However, the latter usually desires to dominate the artificial setting and therefore means should be provided for adjusting the lighting in harmony with the mood. This is brought about by variations in light, shade and color. Lighting units are appearing on the market which are designed to satisfy this desire for variety to a limited degree at least. The so-called direct-indirect units make it possible to alter the distribution from a concentration of light in a small area, leaving the remainder of the room in twilight, to a flood of light over the entire room when the mood or occasion demands it. Portable units and brackets, asymmetrically located, carry this idea further so that it is readily possible to obtain the desired distribution of light and shade.

To obtain variety in color these units can be equipped with shades of various colors. A fixture can be wired with several circuits controlled by separate switches, and tinted lamps can be installed so that by using these separately or in combinations, a variety of delicate tints can be obtained.

Monotony in lighting can only be avoided by varying the distribution and quality of light. Fixtures of today are generally too simple in wiring and design

to give artificial lighting an even chance with Nature's lighting outdoors in gaining the favor of the finer human sensibilities. The advent of lighting units designed to furnish a degree of variety of light, shade and color is perhaps an indication of a recognition of this aesthetic demand but the work has barely begun. It is believed that when the full import of variety in lighting has been appreciated by lighting experts and light users, the procedure of lighting a great many classes of interiors will be altered considerably.—Lighting Journal.

Something New in Lighting Fixtures

Something comparatively new in artificial illumination has been brought out by the Western Art Glass & Shade Works, Claude W. Jolly, sales manager, with show rooms and factory at 105 Turk street, San Francisco. The fixture is called crystalite and its rays are so nearly like the true daylight colors that it is difficult to realize you are working or moving about beneath an artificial light. It is considered by many an ideal office fixture because all light is diffused before it strikes the eye.

All panels or reflectors are spaced apart, allowing constant circulation of air around the lamp to prevent so much heat, which will increase the life of a 500-Watt lamp from 700 to 1000 hours; ventilation is one of the big items necessary.

Architects and Electrical Specifications

ONE of the chief needs of the electrical contractor has been closer cooperation with the architect. The architect is the planner, the contractor the doer. Upon their co-ordinated efforts depends the satisfaction of the owner. Heretofore both contractor and architect have been too far apart in their ideas to insure that the owner will also be pleased, says the Journal of Electricity, Power and Gas.

In the first place, it is a lamentable fact that the electrical equipment is too often the first to be curtailed when consideration is given to cutting the cost of a proposed building. The number of outlets is minimized, baseboard receptacles are omitted and adequate provision for electrical conveniences is neglected. As a result the average house has barely enough lighting fixtures, and no opportunity for utilizing electric heat and power in the home or office. Considering the well-nigh universal use of the electric iron, the large number of washing machines and vacuum cleaners and the serious limitations of lamp-socket circuits on all heating appliances, it is high time to wire every home for electric heat and power utilization as well as for lighting.

Then, again, even when the architect provides for these electrical conveniences, he is sometimes at a loss in preparing the specifications. With so many highly specialized branches of construction—mechanical, electrical and sani-

LOADING SAND FROM YUBA RIVER AT MARYSVILLE

tary—it is too much to expect an architect to be an expert in every line. The specifications are therefore frequently hazy regarding important details and their interpretation causes needless friction.

For the contractor to furnish specifications is an unfair burden for him to bear, and likely to prove unsatisfactory to the owner.

The first step in the solution of this problem is for the architect to employ an electrical engineer to prepare the specifications. The architect thus protects his reputation and his client, the contractor is enabled to make an intelligent bid and the owner is assured a good job.

But, as time goes on, it is found that many jobs are so similar that only minor changes are necessary to adapt the specifications for one installation to another. It becomes possible to use standard specifications.

Recognizing this fact, several manufacturers have served the architect by supplying him with specifications to meet required conditions. But because of the suspicion that certain makes of material will be specified to the exclusion of other, meritorious brands, this practice does not always meet with favor.

Consequently the standard specifications prepared for the use of Los Angeles contractors and architects by Mr. H. Conger Bowers, and which will be printed in full in the February Architect and Engineer, will undoubtedly be found of considerable value. They allow a wide latitude in the choice of approved materials. Emphasis is placed upon quality rather than upon the manufacturer. The architect is greatly assisted by their use and every branch of the industry is benefited.

Mr. Friesleben Returns

Mr. H. M. Friesleben, sales manager of the Pacific Sanitary Manufacturing Company, has returned from the Orient, with his order book well filled. He established agencies throughout Japan, China and the Philippines. He found the Pacific Sanitary fixtures already installed in Shanghai, Tietsin, and other cities, and giving such perfect satisfaction that the architects throughout the Orient are specifying them in new structures. Building operations, especially in China, are reported as large, and Mr. Friesleben has optimistic views regarding the extent of their future trade in the Orient.

Johns-Manville Gives Employes Bonus

Every employe of the H. W. Johns-Manville Company of California who has been with the company a year or more was gladdened by the receipt of a Christmas greeting signed by President T. F. Manville, announcing the board of direc-

tors' decision to give a bonus equal to 10 per cent of the year's salary.

Keyless Combination Burglar-proof Lock

THE latest fixture in hardware which is commanding the attention of San Francisco architects and owners is a keyless combination door lock operated by the sense of touch. From a standpoint of convenience and protection this lock is really a revelation. It is manufactured by The Nydia Bank Lock Co. of Cincinnati, Ohio, recognized experts in their line, and is known as the Nydia Combination Door Lock.

This lock requires no keys. If tenants leave, you have no keys to bother with. You simply change the combination in about one minute's time and you have a new lock on the door. This eliminates the cost of new keys, which at times is quite an item of expense, and also protects the owner's interests against dishonesty and the expense of new equipment. For absolute protection or where privacy is desired, this lock cannot be too highly recommended. It is absolutely impervious to manipulation or tampering and as an additional protection part of the equipment consists of a patent kiefer and strike plate, which entirely covers the bolt, rendering the forcing of a door next to impossible.

Any kind of a fixture can be made to harmonize with the type of house or style of architecture. Both outside and inside doors can be equipped with the lock. Builders of high-class residences will find it much easier to dispose of their property with outside doors supplied with this up-to-date combination lock. The Nydia lock is equal in construction to the locks used in the very best bank vaults. Combinations can be operated in the dark as well as in the light and in less time than you can get keys for the ordinary lock out of your pocket. You have no keys to bother with, no lockouts to experience and no keys to get into the hands of unauthorized persons. Quite a number of these fixtures already have been sold in San Francisco to business houses and to owners of private homes.

Mr. Edwin R. Barth has been appointed general agent for Northern California, Oregon and Washington, with headquarters at 52 Main street, San Francisco. Mr. Barth has a complete line of working models and will be glad to explain the operation and advantages of the lock to architects and others interested upon receipt of word from them. The company carries a stock on hand and is in a position to supply orders on short notice.

The Contractor

HIS TROUBLES AND SOME OTHER THINGS

A Woman Concrete Contractor

CARELESSLY propped up against a fence at the end of a blind street in Silver City, New Mexico, is a huge sign in black and white that reads:

MRS. O. S. WARREN

GENERAL CONTRACTOR AND BUILDER

CONCRETE WORK A SPECIALTY

Down on Bullard street, which is to say Broadway, is a severely plain one-story building of gray pebbledash with a large plate glass window on which sedate gold letters announce:

THE WARREN AGENCY

INSURANCE

Back of the two signs, you will find a gray-haired woman of fifty-six, only a few inches over five feet in height, with alert brown eyes behind strong glasses, her dress sometimes spattered with paint and mortar, notes a writer in the American Magazine.

This woman was for twenty-five years the leading insurance agent in the Southwest, and today she is the largest general contractor in Silver City and the surrounding Grant county, that prosperous hunting-ground of miners, ranchers and "lungers." Of German parentage (her father was exiled after the failure of the revolution in '48 and he came over to America with Carl Schurz), she married Orange S. Warren in 1874 and with him traveled from her home in Brooklyn. At different times they set up their household goods in Little Rock, San Francisco and Walla Walla. In 1881 they came with their three children to Silver City, several years before the branch line was built which connects it with the world and the Southern Pacific at Deming.

Silver City was young when Mr. Warren opened an insurance office there, but he was unusually successful in writing policies. Four years later he died with tragic suddenness of heart failure. Mrs. Warren had centuries of precedent to guide the course of her widowhood. She could go home with her children to her husband's relatives or her own, and find out by experience how steep are the stairs in other people's houses; or, seeking independence, she could do plain sewing or teach school to supplement her income. Instead, she took over the management of her husband's insurance business.

She built a combination house and office on what was then the main business street of Silver. Usually she had a cook and a clerk, but there were times when she ran the office and the kitchen and the nursery quite unaided, and apparently without neglecting any of them.

From 1885 until 1910, when she sold her insurance business because of the pressure of other interests, Mrs. Warren wrote more policies than any other recording agent in the Southwest, El Paso not excluded. When she was asked at a convention of insurance agents what obstacles she had encountered on account of her sex, she answered with characteristic humor:

"None, except the lack of proper pockets."

In 1906 the Solons of Silver City empowered a civil engineer to draw red lines hither and yon over the city map, and ordered the owners of such property as the red lines touched to lay sidewalks. Mrs. Warren, who in the course of twenty years had acquired many scattered blocks of town property, was horrified to find that the red lines bordered almost every one of her buildings. She sent to El Paso and Albuquerque for bids on the work. The Albuquerque contractor refused to consider it; a man from the El Paso firm came up to look over the materials at hand, but would not undertake the contract because the only sand obtainable was useless on account of the silt in it. He had seen one small pile of the right grade, but it had been carted to the land of a man who was in California and no one knew where it had come from.

But the pavements had to be laid. Mrs. Warren talked over the dilemma with Miss M. R. Koehler, the principal of the Silver City schools, whose brother had been a cement contractor. As Miss Koehler had acquired some of the lore of cement making, Mrs. Warren decided to engage her as a foreman, get a practical workman in concrete from El Paso, set up a stone crusher on a porphyritic granite ledge in the heart of town, which she happened to own, and lay her own sidewalks. She brought the sand up to the required standard by washing the silt out of it in washtubs.

By the time the first few hundred feet of pavement had been laid, Mrs. Warren discovered that she herself owned the arroyo from which the one good pile of sand in Silver City had come. That lucky chance, and the insistent clamor of her fellow citizens for sidewalks as good as those she had laid along her property, established Mrs. Warren first as a concrete maker and, by a natural sequence, as a general contractor and builder. Now she plans and builds from start to finish anything from a frame lean-to to a fireproof vault. She plasters, papers, paints and plumbs, with Miss Koehler as her efficient foreman.

The genius for "making over" the useless and ugly into the useful and beautiful, that in most women is dissipated in bouts with clothing and furnishings, is turned by Mrs. Warren to the remodeling of old houses. She has planned, built or built over more than fifty of the best houses in Silver in the past six years. One of her most picturesque pieces of work was the transformation of an old adobe barn into a two-story cement house, all gray pebble-dash and white paint, with simple lines, a big fireplace and long narrow windows under the eaves.

The most impressive piece of work that Mrs. Warren and Miss Koehler have put through is of a type hitherto universally conceded to the male of the species. It is a wall five hundred feet long, five feet thick, and from twenty to forty feet high, built of solid masonry and reaching down to bed rock, along the side of an arroyo whose turbulent waters at the rainy season threatened to undermine the business portion of Silver City. Mrs. Warren was her own engineer for this monumental piece of masonry. She cut from her own quarries the huge rocks used. She hauled lumber for the forms from her own sawmill. She installed steam derricks, steam shovels and steam pumps. She and Miss Koehler worked many a twenty-four-hour stretch, superintending relays of Mexicans, fighting the rising water to give the cement time to dry. There were over three hundred Mexicans on her pay rolls in those days, but only Miss Koehler on the skilled workman list.

Expert engineers have examined that wall since and found not the tiniest crack in the cement cap along the top. This proved that in more than fifty thousand cubic feet of construction a uniform mixture was obtained. And so the engineers marveled. But not Silver City! It would have been mightily surprised at any other result when Mrs. Warren was the builder.

"Pacific" Department Heads Banquet

The second organization banquet of the department heads of the "Pacific" Plumbing Fixtures Companies showed conclusively the reason for the success of their products.

Co-operation is undoubtedly the largest single factor in any manufacturing line and was heartily expressed by everyone present. It was not merely talk, as each man's words were backed by his actions during the past year.

M. E. Wangenheim presided as toastmaster. N. W. Stern spoke on "Organization." C. V. Cameron told of the improvements made in the product of the enameled iron ware plant. H. M. Friesleben related some of the interesting experiences of his recent trip through the Orient, where he established the "Pacific" brand. W. A. Potter spoke of the improvements made in the product of the potteries. G. F. Duffey, in his speech, "Looking Towards 1917," prophesied that the demand for "Pacific"

would increase even faster in 1917 than in the past year. C. B. Noyes told of how the harmony between the producing and selling forces had helped their progress. L. R. Brown read a clever poem which strongly emphasized the appreciation of the co-operation of the various departments.

Those present shown in the picture are, seated at the speaker's table from left to right: H. M. Friesleben, foreign manager; C. V. Cameron, superintendent enameled iron ware plant; N. W. Stern, general manager; W. A. Potter, superintendent potteries; C. B. Noyes, sales manager; John Paglerio, superintendent of pottery No. 2. The others, reading from left to right, are: E. Dunhoff, C. E. Bredhoff, G. F. Duffey, L. J. Waldear, M. E. Wangenheim, manager service department; W. A. Tenney, L. F. Wolff, B. F. Gable, R. H. Roemer, L. R. Brown, office manager; J. E. Deasey, G. Bosq, A. Wagle, J. D. Coleman, S. E. Ramsey, M. Heise, heads of the various departments.

THE BRAIN RESIDENCE AT SPRINGFIELD. OHIO. ARMCO IRON SPIRAL LATH EMPLOYED AS BASE FOR STUCCO

Modern architects and engineers in ever increasing numbers specify ARMCO IRON. The sheet and plate metal portions of thousands of twentieth century structures are of this durable material. True economy requires its employment for Roofs, Pipes, Gutters, Cornices, Window Frames, Fire-Proof Doors, Heating and Ventilating Systems, Boiler Tubes, Storage Tanks and Fencing. Metal Lath affords a protection against fire in partitions and ceilings which is beyond all price — but its material should be **lasting**.

ARMCO IRON
Resists Rust

and gives long and faithful service.

Armco Iron's rust-resistance is a result of its unequalled purity and of the scientific care which characterizes every phase of its production.

Herringbone "Armco" Iron Lath Manufactured by General Fireproofing Company, Youngstown, Ohio

Write for the booklet "The Story of Armco Iron." It affords full information as to the qualities and uses of a remarkable product.

The trade mark ARMCO carries the assurance that iron bearing that mark is manufactured by The American Rolling Mill Company with the skill, intelligence and fidelity associated with its products, and hence can be depended upon to possess in the highest degree the merit claimed for it.

THE AMERICAN ROLLING MILL COMPANY
MIDDLETOWN, OHIO

Licensed Manufacturers under Patents granted to the International Metal Products Company

Armco Iron Sheets, Plates, Roofing, Pipe, Gutter and Metal Lath

Pacific Coast Sales Office—Monadnock Building, San Francisco: Other Branch Offices in New York, Chicago, Pittsburgh, Cleveland, Detroit, St. Louis, Cincinnati and Atlanta.

An Ample Stock of Armco Iron Is Carried At San Francisco

The Building Outlook for 1917

ARCHITECTS of San Francisco and the Bay cities predict a good year, if prospects are any criterion. Construction will be especially heavy in industrial plants. Following is a forecast of work promised from a number of San Francisco, Oakland and Berkeley offices.

WILLIAM H. WEEKS, 75 Post street, San Francisco.

Class "A" theatre, 8th avenue and Clement street, San Francisco, for J. R. Saul...............$ 85,000
Union High school, Colusa....... 85,000
High school building, Salinas.... 100,000
Class "C" loft and store building, 21st street and Broadway, Oakland 30,000

WASHINGTON J. MILLER, Lachman building, San Francisco.

Cannery buildings, warehouses, etc., near Walnut Grove, Sacramento county, California, for Libbey, McNeill & Libbey..... 100,000
Residence — owner's name withheld 7,500

G. A. LANSBURGH, Gunst building, San Francisco.

Two-story reinforced concrete warehouse and factory, San Francisco, for Ogden· Packing Company 30,000
Auditorium and alterations to building on Haight street for Y. M. H. A. Society............. 18,000
New Orpheum, New Orleans..... 300,000
Alterations to Livingston Bros., Geary and Grant avenue...... 12,000
Branch Carnegie Library, 18th and Irving streets, San Francisco 42,000

AUGUST G. HEADMAN, New Call building, San Francisco.

One-story reinforced concrete machine shop, Golden Gate avenue and Gough street, San Francisco, for Gihrecke & Kuner estate 20,000
Reinforced concrete garage, Folsom street, for J. Allec Cleaning Works ..·.................... 20,000
Alterations to Haight Street theatre 5,000
Four-story reinforced concrete automobile sales building, Van Ness avenue, San Francisco... 75,000
Residence in Berkeley for Mrs. B. Whiteside 7,000

DICKEY & DONOVAN, Perry building, Oakland.

Group of school buildings, Elko, Nevada 130,000
Class "C" bank building, Elko, Nevada 30,000
New buildings for Mills College, East Oakland 200,000
Two branch library buildings, Oakland 60,000
Prospective work in Honolulu... 100,000

MILTON LICHTENSTEIN, 111 Ellis street, San Francisco.

Three-story and basement brick rooming house, on Clay street, San Francisco, for Chin Yuey..$ 10,000
Two-story reinforced concrete loft building, Mission street, San Francisco 20,000
One-story addition to S. &. G. Gump warehouse 10,000

LEWIS P. HOBART, Crocker building, San Francisco.

Five-story steel frame Class "C" Y. W. C. A. building, Sutter street, San Francisco......... 130,000
Two-story basement and attic residence and garage, Atherton, for Chas. R. McCormick...... 20,000
Residence for Dr. C. Chidester, San Mateo 16,000

WILLIAM KNOWLES, Hearst building, San Francisco.

Four-story Class "C" store and loft building, Oakland........ 40,000
Residence for Mrs. W. T. Kellogg, Redwood City 10,000

FREDERICK H. MEYER, Bankers Investment building, San Francisco.

Six-story steel frame Class "C" store and office building, for Pope Estate, Montgomery street, San Francisco 100,000
Two-story addition to I. Magnin mercantile building, Geary street and Grant avenue, San Francisco 100,000
One-story Class "A" addition to Bankers Investment building, Market street, San Francisco... 60,000

LOUIS C. MULLGARDT, Chronicle building, San Francisco.

Country residence and landscape work, foot of Mt. Diablo, for Ansel Mills Easton of Hillsborough 100,000
Residence for President of Stanford University, Palo Alto..... 90,000
Museum building, Golden Gate Park 100,000

WARD & BLOHME, Alaska Commercial building, San Francisco.

Alterations and additions to Armsby building, Davis and California streets, San Francisco 10,000
Building for H. N. Cook Belting Company, Folsom and Fremont streets, San Francisco........ 35,000
Fire house for city of San Francisco 35,000

WALTER D. REED, Oakland
Bank of Savings building,
Oakland.
Two-story Class "C" garage for
Taft & Pennoyer.............$ 20,000
Office building for the Hutchinson
Company 30,000
BENJAMIN G. McDOUGALL,
Sheldon building, San Francisco.
Class "A" store and office building
for Mills Estate, Pine. street,
San Francisco 250,000
Factory for Briscoe Automobile.. 100,000
Swimming bath house, A¡ameda.. 60,000
Apartment building on Haight
street for Nightingale Estate... 100,000
JOHN R. MILLER, Lick building,
San Francisco.
Two-story semi-fireproof resi-
dence, Los Altos, Cal., for Dr.
Morris Herzstein of San Fran-
cisco 30,000
Alterations to Spreckels building,
Market and Fremont streets,
San Francisco .... 25,000.
Residence in Alameda for Chas.
Page 15,000
BAKEWELL & BROWNE, 251
Kearny street, San Francisco.
Six-story reinforced c o n c r e t e
warehouse and factory, First
street near Market, for Regents
of the University of California. 120,000
Class "A" library building for
Stanford University, Palo Alto,
California 500,000
Alterations and additions to Bur-
lingame Club building......... 75,000
THOS. M. EDWARDS, Bank build-
ing, Burlingame.
Reinforced concrete building for
the Bank of South San Fran-
cisco 30,000
Residence in San Mateo Park for
Mrs. D. F. Walker............ 8,000
Residence in San Mateo Park for
Mr. Ruton S. Smoot.......... 6,000
Apartment house at San Mateo
for Mr. Canepa 10,000
Residence in San Mateo Park for
Mr. O. Olsen 9,000
Residence at Easton, San Mateo
county, for Mr. Chas. Finger... 4,200
Residence at Easton for Mr. Ed-
ward McRoskey 4,000
Residence at Palo Alto for Mr.
Jos. Torber 10,000
Residence in El Cerrito Park, San
Mateo county, Cal., for Mr.
Samuel Goslinsky 8,000
Brick store building at Easton,
San Mateo county, for Mr. C. S.
Crary 10,000
Residence in San Mateo Park for
Mr. J. W. Wolf.............. 9,000
M o t o r speedway, grandstand,
bleachers, etc. 200,000

GEORGE W. KELHAM, Sharon
building, San Francisco.
Ten-story Class "A" building for
American National Bank, Cali-
fornia and Montgomery streets,
San Francisco (P. J. Walker,
contractor) $600,000
Woman's dormitory, Stanford
University, Palo Alto 100,000
Three-story frame country club
building near Lake Merced, San
Mateo county 75,000
WILLIS POLK & COMPANY,
Hobart building, San Francisco.
Class "A" addition to Hobart
building, facing Sutter street,
San Francisco, for Hobart
Estate 600,000
Three-story reinforced concrete
office building, northeast corner
Montgomery and Pine streets,
San Francisco, for McCreary
Estate 50,000
Two residences, names withheld
for present 40,000
Completion of W. B. Bourn
country residence in San
Mateo county 200,000
Completion of residence for Mrs.
Andrew Welch, San Francisco. 100,000
Completion of Blaney country
home near Los Gatos.......... 75,000
Completion of garage for Wal-
lace Estate on Van Ness ave-
nue, San Francisco........... 40,000
FABRE & BEARWALD, Mer-
chants National Bank building,
San Francisco.
Four-story reinforced concrete
loft building 40,000
Three-story brick store and apart-
ment building 30,000
Frame apartment house, in the
Mission, San Francisco........ 20,000
F. HOLBERG-REIMERS, Ache-
son building, Berkeley.
Three-story 25-room addition to
Oakland hotel 35,000
Apartment house on College ave-
nue, Berkeley 30,000
Two-story frame and plaster resi-
dence for J. S. Roberts, Clare-
mont court, Berkeley 6,000
One-story and basement Class "C"
addition to store and hall build-
ing for A. M. Harvey, Berkeley 7.500
Three-story reinforced concrete
warehouse, Berkeley 45,000
Two-story and attic, Fraternity
house, for the Sigma Nu Society
at Stanford University, Palo
Alto 30,000
WILLIAM E. SPINK, 2127 University avenue, Berkeley.
Two-story and basement frame
Colonial residence for C. A.
Park on 40th street, Oakland. 12,000

BERNARD R. MAYBECK, Lick building, San Francisco.

Class "C" moving picture theatre..$ 60,000

RICHARDSON & BURRELL, Albany building, Oakland.

Four-story Class "C" store and Hotel building, Oakland...... 50,000

Six-Story Class "B" store and apartment house, 90x240 feet, Oakland 210,000

Masonic Temple, San Joaquin Valley 35,000

Two-story Class "C" market and loft building, 9th street, near Webster, Oakland, California.. 10,000

MORAN'S CO.'S PRIVATE ENGINEER.

Group of buildings in South San Francisco, for Moran Packing Company 500,000

JOHN HUDSON THOMAS, 1st National Bank building, Berkeley.

Two-story and basement frame and plaster residence at Rock Ridge, Oakland 15,000

Two-story and basement brick veneer residence, Berkeley..... 12,000

Mr. Thomas also has several small residences, further details will be given later on.

SMITH O'BRIEN, Humboldt Bank building, San Francisco.

Reinforced concrete church for the Catholic Diocese of Monterey 75,000

Four-story Class "C" apartment house 50,000

HERMAN BARTH, 12 Geary street, San Francisco.

Three-story brick factory, southwest corner Front and Pacific streets, for Frye & Co........ 50,000
(Figured but no contract let.)

Two-story and basement brick veneer residence, for a client whose name is withheld for the present 10,000

JAMES W. PLACHEK, Acheson building, Berkeley.

Completion of Class "C" moving picture theatre, University avenue, Berkeley 100,000

Two-story Venetian style store and apartment building, Berkeley 12,000

Completion of brick and steel laundry, 22d and Chestnut streets, Oakland, for Crystal Laundry 10,000

New church in Oakland........ 15,000

Assembling plant for Ford Automobile Company in San Joaquin Valley 30,000

CHAS. W. McCALL, Central Bank building, Oakland

Four-story Class· "A" hospital, Oakland, for Dr. M. M. Enos..$ 75,000

WELSH & CAREY, Merchants National Bank building, San Francisco.

Class "C" garage, Market and Church streets, for Sunset Realty Company 30,000

Roman Catholic Chinese Mission, Jackson street, San Francisco.. 40,000

Addition of one story to Class "B" warehouse, Sheriff Whelan, owner 5,000

Residence, Burlingame, for E. P. Sullivan 8,000

Store building for Orosi Farms Company, Tulare county....... 5,000

O. R. THAYER, 240 Montgomery street, San Francisco.

Class "C" apartment house, Madison street, Oakland.......... 54,000

Frame apartment house, Walsworth street, Oakland 24,000

Store and flat building, 42d avenue, San Francisco........... 9,500

Residence, Merritt Terrace, San Francisco 3,700

Residence, Merritt Terrace, San Francisco 4,800

Residence, Stockton, Cal........ 6,500

Lodge building, Vallejo, Cal.... 32,000

ROUSSEAU & ROUSSEAU, French Bank building, San Francisco.

Six-story and basement steel frame apartment house and store building, southwest corner Geary and Leavenworth streets, San Francisco 135,000

Six-story steel frame apartment house and store building, northwest corner Eddy and Hyde streets, San Francisco........ 85,000

Four-story and basement Class "C" store and apartment house, southeast corner Post and Hyde streets, San Francisco, for the Gerard Investment Company.. 85,000

Three-story and basement frame apartment house, 14th avenue, between "A" and Geary streets, San Francisco, for Dr. Geo. H. Bluhm 15,000

Group of twelve, one-story frame residences, in Westwood Park, San Francisco 24,000

Group of four, two-story frame and plaster residences, St. Francis Wood, San Francisco, each.. 8,500

Three two-story frame and plaster residences, 24th avenue, near Fulton street, San Francisco, each 6,500

JOHN REID, JR., 1st National Bank building, San Francisco.
Two-story and basement steel frame, "Fairmount School," Chenery street, San Francisco .$140,000

O'BRIEN BROS., 240 Montgomery street, San Francisco.
Three-story Class "C" apartment house, Devisadero street and Duboce avenue, San Francisco, for J. J. Flynn 35,000

HENRY SHERMUND, Mills building, San Francisco.
Three-story and basement frame apartment house, California street, near 3d avenue, San Francisco, for B. F. Meyer.... 27,000
Four-story mill and brick construction factory building, 15th and Vermont streets, for C. R. Peterson, San Francisco....... 100,000
Residence flat building, 5th avenue near Lake street, San Francisco, for Nathan Delbanco.... 22,000
One, two and three-story Class "C" factory, on the peninsula.. 60,000

KENNETH McDONALD, JR., Holbrook building, San Francisco.
Completion of seven-story reinforced concrete store and loft building, for George A. Hooper, Sansome, near California street, San Francisco 200,000
Three-story reinforced concrete barracks and armory for the U. S. Volunteer Officers League of America, 17th street, San Francisco 100,000

HENRY C. SMITH, Humboldt Bank building, San Francisco.
Two-story reinforced concrete high school building, Yreka, Cal. 75,000
Reinforced concrete community apartment house, Green and Taylor streets, San Francisco.. 200,000

E. H. DENKE, 1317 Hyde street, San Francisco.
Three-story and basement frame apartment house, Green street, near Van Ness avenue, for J. Pasqualetti. (Building will contain nine apartments and four garages.) Sub-bids are now being taken 20,000

MACDONALD & KAHN, Rialto building, San Francisco.
Eight-story reinforced concrete office building 200,000
Three-story reinforced concrete automobile sales building, Pine and Franklin streets, San Francisco 40,000
Three-story Class "C" store and loft building, Sansome street, for Lawrence Meyers.......... 50,000

C. A. MEUSSDORFFER, Humboldt Bank building, San Francisco.
Seven-story Class "B" apartment house, Jackson and Franklin streets, San Francisco, for Meyer Wood $110,000
Eight-story Class "B" apartment house, Jackson street near Franklin, San Francisco....... 105,000
Completion of three-story frame apartment house, Pacific avenue, and Franklin, San Francisco, for Messrs. Green & Saalfield 36,000

C. H. MILLER, First Savings building, Oakland, California.
Three-story and basement frame apartment house, Lakeside district, Oakland 35,000
Two-story brick garage 20,000

CARL WERNER, Phelan building, San Francisco.
Masonic Temple, Fresno...... 80,000
Completion of Scottish Rite Temple, Sacramento 100,000

SHEA & LOFQUIST, Bankers Investment building, San Francisco.
One and two-story reinforced concrete school building, Sacramento 150,000
Completion of Italian Church, San Francisco 100,000

ALFRED I. COFFEY, Humboldt Bank building, San Francisco.
Six-story steel frame Class "C" physicians' building, Bush street, San Francisco.... 100,000
Five-story addition to St. Francis Hospital, Bush and Hyde streets, San Francisco. 75,000

HELMAN - SCHWARTZ, 212 Stockton street, San Francisco.
Two-story and basement frame residence for J. J. Guill, Claremont Court.... 8,500
Seven-story Class "B" apartment house (name of owner and location withheld for present) 90,000
Two-story Class "C" garage, Geary street, near Larkin, San Francisco 25,000

JOHN D. HATCH, Humboldt Bank building, San Francisco.
Three-story Class "C" Masonic Temple, Vallejo........ 100,000

ALLISON & ALLISON, Hibernian building, Los Angeles.
Reinforced concrete high school group, Merced......... 150,000
Reinforced concrete and hollow tile school buildings, Palo Alto 100,000

MAURICE C. COUCHOT, C. E., French Bank building, San Francisco.

Five-story reinforced concrete factory building, Eighth and Brannan streets, for the American Ever-Ready Dry Battery Company. (Contract to be let this week)........$200,000

Reinforced concrete buildings, Vallejo, for Sperry Flour Company. (Contract let to the Dinwiddie Construction Company, Crocker building, San Francisco) 500,000

WEEKS & DAY, Phelan building, San Francisco.

Four-story reinforced concrete apartment house . (Name of owner and location withheld for the present) 150,000

Class "A" theater............ 100,000

Residence at Woodside for Richard Girvan 15,000

Residence at Piedmont......... 25,000

Reinforced concrete bridges in various counties 100,000

Additional building at Alameda County Infirmary, Oakland 100,000

REID BROS., California Pacific building, San Francisco.

Ten-story Class "A" store and office building for Matson Navigation Company, Market and Main streets, San Francisco 500,000

(This firm has some other good work in prospect, but it is too early yet to be specific.)

A. C. GRIENWANK, State Engineering Department, Ferry building, San Francisco.

Four-story brick addition to California Cotton Mills, East Oakland. (Now being figured) 100,000

Christian Science Church

William Arthur Newman has been commissioned to prepare plans for a $40,000 Christian Science church for the First Church of Christ, Scientist, Honolulu. The edifice will be designed in the American Renaissance and will have a pressed brick exterior. There will be a pipe organ, stained glass windows, and ventilating system. All preliminary drawings have been approved and working plans are now under way.

Cowell Company Retains Its Name

The right to do business under the corporate name of Henry Cowell Lime and Cement Company has been granted by Superior Judge Seawell to the company which was incorporated here under that name thirty years ago, and which has been in active operation since. The decision defeats the claim of Charles B. Blessing, J. H. Smith and M. G. Clark, who organized a company in San Francisco on May 1 of last year under the identical name of the old company.

Acting on the fact that the old company had failed to pay its corporation tax on schedule time, Blessing and his associates formed a corporation with the same name and applied to the Superior Court for an injunction preventing the use of the name by the old company. The corporation tax was later paid and accepted by the state, and Judge Seawell holds that the court cannot deprive the company of its name.

The decision carries with it an injunction preventing Blessing's company from using the name.

Houghton Construction Company

Shirley Houghton, who has formerly operated under the name of Van Sant, Houghton & Co., of which he was sole proprietor, has changed the name of his concern to the Houghton Construction Co.—not incorporated. Mr. Houghton will, as before, make specialties of reinforced concrete buildings of the industrial type, in addition to railway structures. The offices remain in the Hooker & Lent (now Cunard) building, San Francisco, and Century building, Denver.

Terra Cotta for S. P. Building

Gladding, McBean & Co. is busy manufacturing the terra cotta for the Southern Pacific building being erected in San Francisco. Some very high-class terra cotta features will be embodied in the decorative scheme.

Big Ornamental Iron Contract

Edwin R. Jackson, of P. H. Jackson & Co., San Francisco, who is Pacific Coast agent for the Hecla Iron Works of Brooklyn, New York, the largest ornamental iron and bronze works in this country, recently secured the contract for all the ornamental iron work on the new Portland (Oregon) post office building, Lewis P. Hobart, architect, and Grant Fee, general contractor. The iron contract amounts to $106,000.

P. H. Jackson & Co. are the pioneers in the manufacture of sidewalk lights, doors, patent sidewalks, and other sidewalk specialties, having begun business in San Francisco in 1877, although the antecedents of the firm made sidewalk lights in New York as early as 1853. They are the owners of more than two hundred patents covering every feature of sidewalk lights, roof lights, basement ventilators, and "No Leak" sidewalk doors.

They have persevered in their efforts to overcome many of the obstacles for making sidewalk lights both durable and waterproof. Perhaps no other part of building construction is subject to so much wear, abuse and unjust criticism as sidewalk lights. It was found by actual count that in front of one Market street building in San Francisco, between the hours of 8 a. m. and 5 p. m. of a single day, approximately 74,000 persons walked upon the sidewalk lights. Then, too, heavy car service, and motor trucking causes excessive vibration which is a destructive factor not known in earlier days. These causes together with the expansion and contraction due to temperature changes lead to many difficult problems which the sidewalk light manufacturer has to solve. He must build for permanency, often encountering light beams and thin sidewalk slabs built by others which of necessity makes constant repairing of sidewalk lights necessary, a condition for which the sidewalk

When writing to Advertisers please mention this magazine.

light manufacturer is usually blamed. Economy means disaster.

P. H. Jackson & Co. report a very good year just passed, with many large and notable installations, including the following:

Southern Pacific building, San Francisco;

The Langley & Michaels Co.'s building, First and Stevenson streets;

Somers building, Mission street between Fourth and Fifth streets;

Robert White Company's building;

Hughes building, Palo Alto, Cal.;

Wheeler hall, University of California;

Engine House No. 4, Howard, near Third street, San Francisco;

San Francisco Public Library, Civic Center;

San Mateo County Jail, Redwood City, Cal.;

T. & D. Theatre, erected by the Moffitt Estate Building Company, Oakland, Cal.;

Charles Jurgens & Co.'s, Inc., building, Oakland, Cal.;

Piedmont Terminal building, Oakland, Cal.

P. H. Jackson & Company are represented in Portland, Oregon, by the John McCraken Co.; in Seattle and Tacoma, by F. T. Crowe & Co.; in Los Angeles, by Gus Odemar; in San Diego, by the Frost Hardwood Lumber Company, and in the Territory of Hawaii, by the Von-Hamm Young Company, Ltd.

Another Pottery Plant?

H. T. Epperson, San Francisco, has been seeking to develop a clay deposit, said to be valuable, which he has discovered at Forest Knolls near San Rafael. Several prominent parties are making a careful study of the proposition, among these being E. T. Bell of San Francisco. The plan is to organize a company and start an art pottery plant on a fairly large scale. Specimen pottery made of the clay is certainly very beautiful. It is proposed to call the product "Redwood Art Pottery."

Plans Model Settlement

The Los Angeles Pressed Brick Company, whose No. 4 plant has been completed at Alberhill, near Elsinore, is planning to erect a model settlement for the workers near the factory. Attractive little bungalows of hollow tile construction are being built. Fifty men are now employed at the plant, but fully three hundred are expected to be needed by next summer.

New Displays at Building Material Exhibit

Architects are manifesting more interest daily in the permanent Building Material Exhibit at 77 O'Farrell street, San Francisco. A few of the new exhibits recently installed and on display are as follows:

Rector System Gas Heating.
"Pacific Heater," manufactured by C. H. Sharp Mfg. Company, Los Angeles.
"Peerless" Gas Radiator and Humphrey Hot Water Heater, by the Pacific Gas Appliance Company.
"Radiantfire" Gas Grate, by the General Gas Light Company.
Keyhold Lath Company, showing the latest construction in patent lath.
"Kellastone" composition for flooring, as well as exterior finish. Blake Plaster Company, distributors.
Be-ver Cork Tiling, represented by W. L. Eaton & Company.
Red Cedar Bungalow, showing the kind of wood that is used in lining cedar closets and making cedar chests by White Bros. Company.
Kitchen Sink Combination, with one-piece apron sink and drain board, by Kohler Company.
Builtin Soap Holders, manufactured by the Fairfax Company, New York, and represented by Wm. Horn Company.

Fee Awarded $25,000 Claim

Grant Fee, formerly a director and vice-president of the San Francisco General Contractors Association, has recovered $25,000 as compensation for services rendered by him some years ago to the McPhee Company. The case had been pending for some years and was recently decided in Mr. Fee's favor and the money paid over.

Personal

Donald B. Parkinson, son of John Parkinson, Los Angeles architect, who is attending the Massachusetts Institute of Technology at Boston, has been selected as a member of the university's swimming team. Young Parkinson is finishing a course in architecture and after graduation will engage in business with his father.

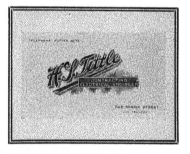

When writing to Advertisers please mention this magazine.

When writing to Advertisers please mention this magazine.

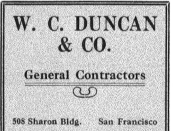
When writing to Advertisers please mention this magazine.

When writing to Advertisers please mention this magazine.

When writing to Advertisers please mention this magazine.

E ARCHITECT
D ENGINEER
CALIFORNIA

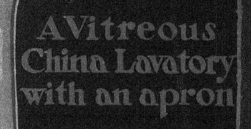

AVitreous China Lavatory with an apron

The Del Monte is the first Vitreous China Lavatory ever made with a straight apron in one piece.

This has heretofore been considered an impossible achievement.

The Del Monte Lavatory is devoid of all ornamentation and is beautiful in its very simplicity. It is so unusually attractive that it will lend an artistic tone to the bathrooms you plan.

"Pacific"
PLUMBING FIXTURES
For sale by all jobbers

Main Office and Showroom,
67 New Montgomery St.,
San Francisco, Cal.

Factories,
Richmond,
California

RESIDENCE OF MR. E. C. DUNCAN, FOREST HILL, SAN FRANCISCO
Heiman-Schwartz, Architects

EXTERIOR OF

Medusa White Portland Cement

SOLD BY

The Building Material Co.

Incorporated

MONADNOCK BUILDING,

SAN FRANCISCO   Phone, Kearny 621

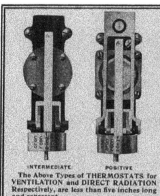

When writing to Advertisers please mention this magazine.

Architects' Specification Index

(For Index to Advertisements, see next page)

ACOUSTICAL·CORRECTION
H. W. Johns-Manville Co., Second and Howard Sts., San Francisco.

ARBUR CULTURE
S. P. McClenahan, 738 Merchants Exchange B'dg., San Francisco.

ARCHITECTURAL SCULPTORS, MODELING, ETC.
G. Rognier & Co., 233 R. R. Ave., San Mateo.
Sculptors' Workshop. S. Miletin & Co., 1705 Harrison St., San Francisco.
A. F. Swoboda, modeler, 204 Second St., San Francisco.

ARCHITECTURAL TERRA COTTA
Gladding, McBean & Company, Crocker Bldg., San Francisco.
Steiger Terra Cotta and Pottery Works, Mills Bldg., San Francisco.

ASBESTOS ROOFING
H. W. Johns-Manville Company, San Francisco, Los Angeles, San Diego, Sacramento.

AUTOMATIC SPRINKLERS
Scott Company, 243 Minna St., San Francisco.
Pacific Fire Extinguisher Co., 507 Montgomery St., San Francisco.

BANK FIXTURES AND INTERIORS
Fink & Schindler, 218 13th St., San Francisco.
A. J. Forbes & Son, 1530 Filbert St., San Francisco.
C. F. Weber & Co., 365 Market St., San Francisco.
Home Mfg. Co., 543 Brannan St., San Francisco.
T. H. Meek Co., 1130 Mission St,. San Francisco.
Mullen Manufacturing Co., 20th and Harrison Sts., San Francisco.

BLACKBOARDS
C. F. Weber & Co., 365 Market St., San Francisco.

BONDS FOR CONTRACTORS
Fidelity & Casualty Co. of New York, Merchants Exchange Bldg., San Francisco.
Robertson & Hall, First National Bank Bldg., San Francisco.
Fred H. Boggs, Foxcroft Bldg., San Francisco.
Casualty Company of America, Kohl Bldg., San Francisco.
J. T. Costello Co., 216 Pine St., San Francisco.
California Casualty Co., Merchants' Exchange Building, San Francisco.
Fidelity & Deposit Co. of Maryland, 701 Insurance Exchange, San Francisco.
Globe Indemnity Co., Insurance Exchange Bldg., San Francisco.
Edw. M. Jones, Merchants Exchange Bldg., San Francisco.

BOOK BINDERS AND PRINTERS
Hicks-Judd Company, 51-65 First St., San Francisco.

BRASS GOODS, CASTINGS, ETC.
H. Mueller Manufacturing Co., 589 Mission St., San Francisco.

BRICK—PRESSED, PAVING, ETC.
Gladding, McBean & Company, Crocker Bldg., San Francisco.
Los Angeles Pressed Brick Co., Frost Bldg., Los Angeles.
Livermore Brick Company, pressed, glazed and enameled, etc., Livermore, Cal.
Steiger Terra Cotta & Pottery Works, Mills Bldg., San Francisco.
United Materials Co., Crossley Bldg., San Francisco.

BRICK AND CEMENT COATING
Armorite and Concreta, manufactured by W. P. Fuller & Co., all principal Coast cities.
Wadsworth, Howland & Co., Inc. (See Adv. for Pacific Coast Agents.)
Glidden Products, sold by Whittier, Coburn Co., Howard and Beale Sts., San Francisco; California Glass & Paint Company, Los Angeles.
Paraffine Paint Co., 34 First St., San Francisco.
R. N. Nason & Co., 151 Potrero Ave., San Francisco.

BRICK STAINS
Samuel Cabot Mfg. Co., Boston, Mass., agencies in San Francisco, Oakland, Los Angeles, Portland, Tacoma and Spokane.
Armorite and Concreta, manufactured by W. P. Fuller & Co., all principal Coast cities.

BUILDERS' HARDWARE
Bennett Bros., agents for Sargent Hardware, 514 Market St., San Francisco.
Pacific Hardware & Steel Company, San Francisco, Oakland, Berkeley, and Los Angeles.

BUILDING MATERIAL, SUPPLIES, ETC.
Pacific Building Materials Co., 523 Market St., San Francisco.
C. Jorgensen, Crossley Bldg., San Francisco.
Richard Spencer, Hearst Bldg., San Francisco.

CEMENT
Mt. Diablo, sold by Henry Cowell Lime & Cement Co., 2 Market street, San Francisco.
Medusa White Portland Cement, sold by Building Material Co., Inc., Monadnock Bldg., San Francisco.

CEMENT EXTERIOR WATERPROOF PAINT
Bay State Brick and Cement Coating, made by Wadsworth, Howland & Co. (See distributing agents in advertisement.)
Glidden's Liquid Cement and Liquid Cement Enamel, sold on Pacific Coast by Whittier, Coburn Co., San Francisco.
Armorite, sold by W. P. Fuller & Co., all principal Coast cities.
Imperial Waterproofing, manufactured by Imperial Co., 183 Stevenson St., San Francisco.
Paraffine Paint Co., 34 First St., San Francisco.

CEMENT EXTERIOR FINISH
Bay State Brick and Cement Coating, made by Wadsworth, Howland & Co. (See list of Distributing Agents in adv.)
Concreta, sold by W. P. Fuller & Co., all principal Coast cities.

An Index to the Advertisements

ARCHITECTS' SPECIFICATION INDEX—*Continued*

CEMENT EXTERIOR FINISH—Continued
Glidden's Liquid Cement and Liquid Cement Enamel, sold on Pacific Coast by Whittier, Coburn Company, San Francisco.
Medusa White Portland Cement, California Agents, the Building Material Co., Inc., 587 Monadnock Bldg., San Francisco.
Samuel Cabot Mfg. Co., Boston, Mass.; agencies in San Francisco, Oakland, Los Angeles, Portland, Tacoma and Spokane.
"Technola," manufactured and sold by C. Roman Co., 55 New Montgomery street, San Francisco.

CEMENT FLOOR COATING
Bay State Brick and Cement Coating, made by Wadsworth, Howland & Co. (See list of Distributing Agents in adv.)
Fuller's Concrete Floor Enamel, made by W. P. Fuller & Co., San Francisco.
Glidden's Concrete Floor Dressing, sold on Pacific Coast by Whittier, Coburn Company, San Francisco.

CEMENT HARDENER
J. L. Goffette Corporation, 227 San Bruno Ave., San Francisco.

CEMENT TESTS—CHEMICAL ENGINEERS
Robert W. Hunt & Co., 251 Kearny St., San Francisco.

CHURCH INTERIORS
Fink & Schindler, 218 13th St., San Francisco.

CHUTES—SPIRAL
Haslett Warehouse Co., 310 California St., San Francisco.

CLOCKS—TOWER—STREET—PROGRAM
E. Howard Clock Co., Boston. Pacific Coast Agents, The Albert S. Samuels Co., 895 Market St., San Francisco. Joseph Mayer & Bro., Seattle, Wash.

COLD STORAGE PLANTS
T. P. Jarvis Crude Oil Burning Co., 275 Connecticut St., San Francisco.

COMPOSITION FLOORING
Germanwood Floor Co., 1621 Eddy St., San Francisco.
Malott & Peterson, Monadnock Bldg., San Francisco.
"Vitrolite," Vitrolite Construction Co., 34 Davis St., San Francisco.

COMPRESSED AIR MACHINERY
General Machinery & Supply Co., 39 Stevenson St., San Francisco.

COMPRESSED AIR CLEANERS
Spencer Turbine Cleaner. Sold by Hughson & Merton, 530 Golden Gate Ave., San Francisco.
Tuec, mfrd. by United Electric Company, 397 Sutter St., San Francisco, and 724 S. Broadway, Los Angeles.
Western Vacuum Supply Co., 1125 Market St., San Francisco.

CONCRETE CONSTRUCTION
American Concrete Co., Humboldt Bank Bldg., San Francisco.
Clinton Construction Co., 140 Townsend street, San Francisco.
Barrett & Hilp, Sharon Bldg., San Francisco.
Palmer & Peterson, Monadnock Bldg., San Francisco.
Pacific Coast Steel Company, Rialto Bldg., San Francisco.

CONCRETE HARDNER
Master Builders Method, represented in San Francisco by C. Roman, Sharon Bldg.

CONCRETE MIXERS
Austin Improved Cube Mixer. J. H. Hansen & Co., California agents, 508 Balboa Bldg., San Francisco.
Foote Mixers. Sold by Edw. R. Bacon, 40 Natoma St., San Francisco.

CONCRETE REINFORCEMENT
United States Steel Products Co., San Francisco, Los Angeles, Portland and Seattle.
Twisted Bars. Sold by Woods, Huddart & Gunn, 444 Market St., San Francisco.
Pacific Coast Steel Company, Rialto Bldg., San Francisco.
Southern California Iron and Steel Company, Fourth and Mateo Sts., Los Angeles.
Triangle Mesh Fabric. Sales agents, Pacific Building Materials Co., 523 Market St., San Francisco.

CONCRETE SURFACING
"Concreta." Sold by W. P. Fuller & Co., San Francisco.
Wadsworth, Howland & Co.'s Bay State Brick and Cement Coating. Sold by Jas. Hambly Co., Pacific Bldg., San Francisco, and Los Angeles.
Glidden Liquid Cement, manufactured by Glidden Varnish Co., Whittier, Coburn Co., San Francisco.

CONTRACTOR'S BONDS
Bonding Company of America, Kohl Bldg., San Francisco.
Globe Indemnity Co., 120 Leidesdorff St., San Francisco.
Fred H. Boggs, Foxcroft Bldg., San Francisco.
Fidelity & Casualty Co. of New York, Merchants Exchange Bldg., San Francisco.
Fidelity & Deposit Co. of Maryland, Insurance Exchange, San Francisco.
J. T. Costello Co., 216 Pine St., San Francisco.
Robertson & Hall, First National Bank Bldg., San Francisco.
Edwin M. Jones, 723 Merchants Exchange Bldg., San Francisco.

CONTRACTORS, GENERAL
Arthur Arlett, New Call Bldg., San Francisco.
Farrell & Reed, Gunst Bldg., San Francisco.
American Concrete Co., Humboldt Bank Bldg., San Francisco.
Barrett & Hilp, Sharon Bldg., San Francisco.
Carnahan & Mulford, 45 Kearny St., San Francisco.
Houghton Construction Co., Hooker & Lent Bldg., San Francisco.
W. T. & W. E. Commary, Crocker Bank Bldg., San Francisco.
Geo. H. Bos, Hearst Bldg., San Francisco.
Larsen, Sampson & Co., Crocker Bldg., San Francisco.
J. D. Hannah, 725 Chronicle Bldg., San Francisco.
Clinton Construction Company, 140 Townsend St., San Francisco.
Dioguardi & Terranova, Westbank Bldg., San Francisco.
Wm. A. Larkins, 1024 Hearst Bldg., San Francisco.
Teichert & Ambrose, Ochsner Bldg., Sacramento.
L. G. Bergren & Son, Call Bldg., San Francisco.
Grace & Bernieri, Claus Spreckels Bldg., San Francisco.
Geo. W. Boxton & Son, Hearst Bldg., San Francisco.
W. C. Duncan & Co., 526 Sharon Bldg., San Francisco.
A. P. Brady, Humboldt Bank Bldg., San Francisco.
Cameron & Disston, 831 Hearst Bldg., San Francisco.
Howard S. Williams, Hearst Bldg., San Francisco.
Kerr & McLean, General Contractors Ass'n, San Francisco.

WHITTIER - COBURN CO.

MANUFACTURERS

WHITTIER QUALITY PAINTS

Distributors

GLIDDEN CONCRETE PAINTS   BRIDGEPORT STANDARD STAINS

Sales Office   ::   Howard and Beale Streets, San Francisco, Cal.

ARCHITECTS' SPECIFICATION INDEX—Continued

CONTRACTORS, GENERAL—Continued
Harvey A. Klyce, Sheldon Bldg., San Francisco.
Knowles & Mathewson, Call Bldg., San Francisco.
Lange & Bergstrom, Sharon Bldg., San Francisco.
Foster Vogt Co., 411 Sharon Bldg., San Francisco.
Thos. Elam & Son, Builders Exchange, San Francisco.
Masow & Morrison, 518 Monadnock Bldg., San Francisco.
McLeran & Peterson, Sharon Bldg., San Francisco.
Monson Bros., 1907 Bryant St., San Francisco.
J. M. Dougan Co., Hearst Bldg., San Francisco.
Palmer & Peterson, Monadnock Bldg., San Francisco.
Robert Trost, Twenty-sixth and Howard Sts., San Francisco.
John Monk, Sheldon Bldg., San Francisco.
Ward & Goodwin, 110 Jessie St., San Francisco.
Williams Bros. & Henderson, 381 Tenth St., San Francisco.

CONVEYING MACHINERY
Meese & Gottfried, San Francisco, Los Angeles, Portland and Seattle.

CORK TILING, FLOORING, ETC.
David Kennedy, Inc., Sharon Bldg., San Francisco.
Bever Cork Tile. Sold by W. L. Eaton & Co., 812 Santa Marina Bldg., San Francisco.

CORNER BEAD
Capitol Sheet Metal Works, 1827 Market St., San Francisco.
United States Metal Products Co., 525 Market St., San Francisco; 750 Keller St., San Francisco.

CRUSHED ROCK
Grant Gravel Co., Flatiron Bldg., San Francisco.
California Building Material Company, new Call Bldg., San Francisco.
Niles Sand, Gravel & Rock Co., Mutual Bank Bldg., San Francisco.
Pratt Building Material Co., Hearst Bldg., San Francisco.

DAMP-PROOFING COMPOUND
Glidden's Liquid Rubber, sold on Pacific Coast by Whittier, Coburn Company, San Francisco.
Armorite Damp Resisting Paint, made by W. P. Fuller & Co., San Francisco.
Imperial Co., 183 Stevenson St., San Francisco.
"Pabco" Damp-Proofing Compound, sold by Paraffine Paint Co., 34 First St., San Francisco.
Wadsworth, Howland & Co., Inc., 84 Washington St., Boston. (See Adv. for Coast agencies.)

DOOR HANGERS
McCabe Hanger Mfg. Co., New York, N. Y.
Pitcher Hanger, sold by National Lumber Co., 326 Market St., San Francisco.
Reliance Hanger, sold by Sartorius Co., San Francisco; D. F. Fryer & Co., B. V. Collins, Los Angeles, and Columbia Wire & Iron Works, Portland, Ore.

DRAIN BOARDS, SINK BACKS, ETC.
Germanwood Floor Co., 1621 Eddy St., San Francisco.

DRINKING FOUNTAINS
Haws Sanitary Fountain, 1808 Harmon St., Berkeley, and C. F. Weber & Co., San Francisco and Los Angeles.
Crane Company, San Francisco, Oakland, and Los Angeles.
Pacific Porcelain Ware Co., 67 New Montgomery St., San Francisco.

DUMB WAITERS
Spencer Elevator Company, 173 Beale St., San Francisco.
M. E. Hammond, Humboldt Bank Bldg., San Francisco.

ELECTRICAL CONTRACTORS
Butte Engineering Co., 683 Howard St., San Francisco.
Goold & Johns, 113 S. California St., Stockton, Cal.
NePage, McKenny Co., 149 New Montgomery St., San Francisco.
Newbery Electrical Co., 413 Lick Bldg., San Francisco.
Pacific Fire Extinguisher Co., 507 Montgomery St., San Francisco.
H. S. Tittle, 245 Minna St., San Francisco.
Rex Electric and Construction Co., Inc., 1174 Sutter St., San Francisco.
Standard Electrical Construction Company, 60 Natoma St., San Francisco.

ELECTRICAL ENGINEERS
Chas. T. Phillips, Pacific Bldg., San Francisco.

ELECTRIC PLATE WARMER
The Prometheus Electric Plate Warmer for residences, clubs, hotels, etc. Sold by M. E. Hammond, Humboldt Bank Bldg., San Francisco.

ELEVATORS
Otis Elevator Company, Stockton and North Point, San Francisco.
Spencer Elevator Company, 126 Beale St., San Francisco.
Van Emon Elevator Co., 54 Natoma St., San Francisco.

ENGINEERS
Chas. T. Phillips, Pacific Bldg., San Francisco.
Hunter & Hudson, Rialto Bldg., San Francisco.

FIRE ESCAPES
Palm Iron & Bridge Works, Sacramento.
Western Iron Works, 141 Beale St., San Francisco.

FIRE EXTINGUISHERS
Scott Company, 243 Minna St., San Francisco
Pacific Fire Extinguisher Co., 507 Montgomery St., San Francisco.

ARCHITECTS' SPECIFICATION INDEX—*Continued*

FIREPROOFING AND PARTITIONS
Gladding, McBean & Co., Crocker Bldg., San Francisco.
Keyhold Lath Co., Monadnock Bldg., San Francisco.
Los Angeles Pressed Brick Co., Frost Bldg., Los Angeles.

FIXTURES—BANK, OFFICE, STORE, ETC.
T. H. Meek & Co., 1130 Mission St., San Francisco.
Mullen Manufacturing Co., 20th and Harrison Sts., San Francisco.
The Fink & Schindler Co., 218 13th St., San Francisco.
A. J. Forbes & Son, 1530 Filbert St., San Francisco.
C. F. Weber & Co., 365 Market St., San Francisco, and 210 N. Main St., Los Angeles, Cal.

FLAG POLE TOPS
Bolander & Son, 270 First St., San Francisco.

FLOOR TILE
New York Belting and Packing Company, 519 Mission St., San Francisco.
W. L. Eaton & Co., 112 Market St., San Francisco.

FLOOR VARNISH
Bass-Hueter and San Francisco Pioneer Varnish Works, 816 Mission St., San Francisco.
Fifteen for Floors, made by W. P. Fuller & Co., San Francisco.
Standard Varnish Works, Chicago, New York and San Francisco.
Glidden Products, sold by Whittier, Coburn Co., San Francisco.
R. N. Nason & Co., San Francisco and Los Angeles.

FLOORS—COMPOSITION
"Vitrolite," for any structure, room or bath. Vitrolite Construction Co., 1490 Mission St., San Francisco.
Malott & Peterson, Inc., Monadnock Bldg., San Francisco.
Germanwood Floor Co., 1621 Eddy St., San Francisco.

FLOORS—HARDWOOD
Oak Flooring Bureau, Conway Bldg., Chicago, Ill.
Strahle Mfg. Co., 511 First St., Oakland.

FLUMES
California Corrugated Culvert Co., West Berkeley, Cal.

GAS FURNACES
Cole Gas Furnace, Cole Heater Sales Co., Lick Bldg., San Francisco, 1764 Broadway, Oakland.

GAS GRATES
General Gas Light Co., 768 Mission St., San Francisco.

GARAGE EQUIPMENT
Bowser Gasoline Tanks and Outfit, Bowser & Co., 612 Howard St., San Francisco.
Rix Compressed Air and Drill Company, First and Howard Sts., San Francisco.

GLASS
W. P. Fuller & Company, all principal Coast cities.
Whittier, Coburn Co., Howard and Beale Sts., San Francisco.

GRANITE
California Granite Co., Sharon Bldg., San Francisco.
McGilvray-Raymond Granite Co., 634 Townsend St., San Francisco.
Raymond Granite Co., Potrero Ave. and Division St., San Francisco.

GRAVEL AND SAND
California Building Material Co., new Call Bldg., San Francisco.
Del Monte White Sand, sold by Pacific Improvement Co., Crocker Bldg., San Francisco.
Pratt Building Material Co., Hearst Bldg., San Francisco.
Grant Gravel Co., Flatiron Bldg., San Francisco.
Grant Rock & Gravel Co., Cory Bldg., Fresno.
Niles Sand, Gravel & Rock Co., Mutual Savings Bank Bldg., 704 Market St., San Francisco.

HARDWALL PLASTER
Henry Cowell Lime & Cement Co., San Francisco.

HARDWARE
Pacific Hardware & Steel Company, representing Lockwood Hardware Co., San Francisco.
Sargent's Hardware, sold by Bennett Bros., 514 Market St., San Francisco.

HARDWOOD LUMBER—FLOORING, ETC.
Dieckmann Hardwood Co., Beach and Taylor Sts., San Francisco.
Parrott & Co., 320 California St., San Francisco.
White Bros., cor. Fifth and Brannan Sts., San Francisco.
Strahle Mfg. Co., 511 First St., Oakland.

HEATERS—AUTOMATIC
Pittsburg Water Heater Co., 478 Sutter St., San Francisco.

HEATING AND VENTILATING
Gilley-Schmid Company, 198 Otis St., San Francisco.
Mangrum & Otter, Inc., 507 Mission St., San Francisco.
Charles T. Phillips, Pacific Bldg., San Francisco.
J. C. Hurley Co., 509 Sixth St., San Francisco.
Illinois Engineering Co., 563 Pacific Bldg., San Francisco.
William F. Wilson Co., 328 Mason St., San Francisco.
Pacific Fire Extinguisher Co., 507 Montgomery St., San Francisco.
Scott Company, 243 Minna St., San Francisco.
Thermic Engineering Company, Claus Spreckels Bldg., San Francisco.
C. A. Dunham Co., Wells Fargo Bldg., San Francisco.

McELHINNEY TILE CO.
Contractors for
FLOOR, WALL AND MANTEL TILE
1097 Mission Street, San Francisco   Park 6986

ARCHITECTS' SPECIFICATION INDEX—Continued

HEAT REGULATION
Johnson Service Company, 149 Fifth St., San Francisco.

HOLLOW BLOCKS
Denison Hollow Interlocking Blocks, Forum Bldg., Sacramento, and Chamber of Commerce Bldg., Portland.
Gladding, McBean & Co., San Francisco, Los Angeles, Oakland and Sacramento.
Pratt Building Material Co., Hearst Bldg., San Francisco.

HOLLOW METAL DOORS AND TRIM
Dahlstrom Metallic Door Company, Jamestown, N. Y.
Edwin C. Dehn, 301 Hearst Bldg., San Francisco, representing Interior Metal Mfg. Co., Jamestown, N. Y.

HOSPITAL FIXTURES
J. L. Mott Iron Works, 135 Kearny St., San Francisco.

HOTELS
St. Francis Hotel, Union Square, San Francisco.

INGOT IRON
"Armco" brand, manufactured by American Rolling Mill Company, Middletown, Ohio, and Monadnock Bldg., San Francisco.

INSPECTIONS AND TESTS
Robert W. Hunt & Co., 251 Kearny St., San Francisco.

INTERIOR DECORATORS
Mrs. H. C. McAfee, 504 Sutter St., San Francisco.
Albert S. Bigley, 344 Geary St., San Francisco.
A. Falvy, 323 Sutter St., San Francisco.
The Tormey Co., 681 Geary St., San Francisco.
Fick Bros., 475 Haight St., San Francisco.
O'Hara & Livermore, Sutter St., San Francisco.

IRONING BOARDS
Noack Disappearing Ironing Board Co., Humboldt Bank Bldg., San Francisco, and 324 Broadway, Oakland.
Western Equipment Co., Building Material Exhibit, 77 O'Farrell St., San Francisco.

KITCHEN CABINETS
Western Equipment Co., Building Material Exhibit, 77 O'Farrell St., San Francisco.
Hoosier Cabinets, branch 1067 Market St., San Francisco.

LIGHTING FIXTURES
"The Crystal Light," manufactured by Modern Appliance Co., 128 Sutter St., San Francisco.

LAMP POSTS, ELECTROLIERS, ETC.
J. L. Mott Iron Works, 135 Kearny St., San Francisco.
Ralston Iron Works, 20th and Indiana Sts., San Francisco.

LANDSCAPE GARDENERS
MacRorie-McLaren Co., 141 Powell St., San Francisco.

LATHING MATERIAL
"Buttonlath," manufactured and sold by Pioneer Paper Company, Los Angeles and San Francisco.
Keybold Lath Co., Monadnock Bldg., San Francisco.

LIGHT, HEAT AND POWER
Pacific Gas & Elec. Co., 445 Sutter St., San Francisco.

LIME
Henry Cowell Lime & Cement Co., 2 Market St., San Francisco.

LINOLEUM
D. N. & E. Walter & Co., O'Farrell and Stockton Sts., San Francisco.

LOCKS—KEYLESS
Nydia Bank Lock Co., 52 Main St., San Francisco.

LUMBER
Dudfield Lumber Co., Palo Alto, Cal.
Hooper Lumber Co., Seventeenth and Illinois Sts., San Francisco.
Sunset Lumber Co., Oakland, Cal.
Santa Fe Lumber Co., Seventeenth and De Haro Sts., San Francisco.
Pacific Manufacturing Company, San Francisco, Oakland and Santa Clara.
Pacific Mill and Timber Co., First National Bank Bldg., San Francisco.
Pope & Talbot, foot of Third St., San Francisco.
United Lumber Company, 687 Market St., San Francisco.

MASTIC FLOORING
Malott & Peterson, Monadnock Bldg., San Francisco.

MAIL CHUTES
Cutler Mail Chute Co., Rochester, N. Y. (See adv. on page 30 for Coast representatives.)
American Mailing Device Corp.,' represented on Pacific Coast by U. S. Metal Products Co., 525 Market St., San Francisco.

MANTELS
Mangrum & Otter, 561 Mission St., San Francisco.
Oakland Mantel Co., 2148 Telegraph Ave., Oakland.

MARBLE
Joseph Musto Sons, Keenan Co., 535 N. Point St., San Francisco.
Sculptors' Workshop. S. Miletin & Co., 1705 Harrison St., San Francisco.

METAL CEILINGS
San Francisco Metal Stamping & Corrugating Co., 2269 Folsom St., San Francisco.

METAL DOORS AND WINDOWS
Dahlstrom Metallic Door Company, Jamestown, N. Y. (See advertisement for Coast Representatives.)
U. S. Metal Products Co., 525 Market St., San Francisco.
Capitol Sheet Metal Works, 1927 Market St., San Francisco.

METAL FURNITURE
Capitol Sheet Metal Works, 1927 Market St., San Francisco.
Ralston Iron Works, Twentieth and Indiana Sts., San Francisco.
Edwin C. Dehn, Manufacturer's Agent, Hearst Bldg., San Francisco.

METAL SHINGLES
San Francisco Metal Stamping & Corrugating Co., 2269 Folsom St., San Francisco.

MILL WORK
Dudfield Lumber Co., Palo Alto, Cal.
Pacific Manufacturing Company, San Francisco, Oakland and Santa Clara.
National Mill and Lumber Co., San Francisco and Oakland.
The Fink & Schindler Co., 218 13th St., San Francisco.

OIL BURNERS
American Standard Oil Burner Company, Seventh and Cedar Sts., Oakland.
S. T. Johnson Co., 1337 Mission St., San Francisco.
T. P. Jarvis Crude Oil Burner Co., 275 Connecticut St., San Francisco.
Fess System, 220 Natoma St., San Francisco.
W. S. Ray Mfg. Co., 218 Market St., San Francisco.

ORNAMENTAL IRON AND BRONZE
American Art Metal Works, 13 Grace St., San Francisco.
California Artistic Metal and Wire Co., 349 Seventh St., San Francisco.
Brode Iron Works, 31-37 Hawthorne St., San Francisco.

ARCHITECTS' SPECIFICATION INDEX—*Continued*

ORNAMENTAL IRON AND BRONZE—Con't.
Palm Iron & Bridge Works, Sacramento.
Ralston Iron Works, 20th and Indiana Sts., San Francisco.
J. L. Mott Iron Works, 135 Kearny St., San Francisco.
C. J. Hillard Company, Inc., 19th and Minnesota Sts., San Francisco.
Schreiber & Sons Co., represented by Western Builders Supply Co., San Francisco.
Sims, Gray & Sauter Iron Works, 156 Main St., San Francisco.
Schrader Iron Works, Inc., 1247 Harrison St., San Francisco.
West Coast Wire & Iron Works, 861-863 Howard St., San Francisco.

PAINT FOR CEMENT
Bay State Brick and Cement Coating, made by Wadsworth, Howland & Co. (Inc.) (See adv. in this issue for Pacific Coast agents.)
Fuller's Concreta for Cement, made by W. P. Fuller & Co., San Francisco.
Samuel Cabot Mfg. Co., Boston, Mass., agencies in San Francisco, Oakland, Los Angeles, Portland, Tacoma and Spokane.
C. Roman Co., 55 New Montgomery St., San Francisco.

PAINT FOR STEEL STRUCTURES, BRIDGES, ETC.
Glidden's Acid Proof Coating, sold on Pacific Coast by Whittier, Coburn Co., San Francisco.
Paraffine Paint Co., 34 First St., San Francisco.
Premier Graphite Paint and Pioneer Brand Red Lead, made by W. P. Fuller & Co., San Francisco.

PAINTING, TINTING, ETC.
I. R. Kissel, 1747 Sacramento St., San Francisco.
D. Zelinsky & Sons, San Francisco and Los Angeles.
Fick Bros., 475 Haight St., San Francisco.

PAINTS, OILS, ETC.
The Brininstool Co., Los Angeles, the Haslett Warehouse, 310 California St., San Francisco.
Bass-Hueter Paint Co., Mission, near Fourth St., San Francisco.
C. Roman Co., 55 New Montgomery St., San Francisco.
Whittier, Coburn Co., Howard and Beale Sts., San Francisco.
Magner Bros., 419-421 Jackson St., San Francisco.
R. N. Nason & Company, San Francisco, Los Angeles, Portland and Seattle.
W. P. Fuller & Co., all principal Coast cities.
Standard Varnish Works, 55 Stevenson St., San Francisco.

PANELS AND VENEER
White Bros., Fifth and Brannan Sts., San Francisco.

PIPE—VITRIFIED SALT GLAZED TERRA COTTA
Gladding, McBean & Co., Crocker Bldg., San Francisco.
Pratt Building Material Co., Hearst Bldg., San Francisco.
Steiger Terra Cotta and Pottery Works, Mills Bldg., San Francisco.
G. Weissbaum & Co. Pipe Works, 127 Eleventh St., San Francisco.

PLASTER CONTRACTORS
C. C. Morehouse, Crocker Bldg., San Francisco.
MacGruer & Co., 180 Jessie St., San Francisco.

PLASTER EXTERIORS
"Kellastone," an imperishable stucco. Blake Plaster Co., Bacon Block, Oakland.
Keyhold Lath Co., Monadnock Bldg., San Francisco.
Buttonlath, for exterior and interior plastering, Pioneer Paper Co., San Francisco and Los Angeles.

PLUMBING CONTRACTORS
Alex Coleman, 706 Ellis St., San Francisco.
A. Lettich, 365 Fell St., San Francisco.
Gilley-Schmid Company, 198 Otis St., San Francisco.
Scott Co., Inc., 243 Minna St., San Francisco.
Wm. F. Wilson Co., 328 Mason St., San Francisco.

PLUMBING FIXTURES. MATERIALS. ETC.
Crane Co., San Francisco and Oakland.
California Steam Plumbing Supply Co., 671 Fifth St., San Francisco.
Gilley-Schmid Company, 198 Otis St., San Francisco.
Glauber Brass Manufacturing Company, 1107 Mission St., San Francisco.
Improved Sanitary Fixture Co., 632 Metropolitan Bldg., Los Angeles.
J. L. Mott Iron Works, D. H. Gulick, selling agent, 135 Kearny St., San Francisco.
Haines, Jones & Cadbury Co., 857 Folsom St., San Francisco.
H. Mueller Manufacturing Co., Pacific Coast branch, 589 Mission St., San Francisco.
Pacific Sanitary Manufacturing Co., 67 New Montgomery St., San Francisco.
Wm. F. Wilson Co., 328 Mason St., San Francisco.
C. A. Dunham Co., Wells Fargo Bldg., San Francisco.

POTTERY
Gladding, McBean & Co., San Francisco, Los Angeles, Oakland and Sacramento.
Steiger Terra Cotta and Pottery Works, Mills Bldg., San Francisco.

POWER TRANSMITTING MACHINERY
Meese & Gottfried, San Francisco, Los Angeles, Portland, Ore., and Seattle, Wash.

PUMPS
Simonds Machinery Co., 117 New Montgomery St., San Francisco.

RAILROADS
Southern Pacific Company, Flood Bldg., San Francisco.
Western Pacific Company, Mills Bldg., San Francisco.

REFRIGERATORS
McCray Refrigerators, sold by Nathan Dohrmann Co., Geary and Stockton Sts., San Francisco.

REVERSIBLE WINDOWS
Hauser Reversible Window Company, Balboa Bldg., San Francisco.
Whitney Windows, represented by Richard Spencer, 801-3 Hearst Bldg., San Francisco.

REVOLVING DOORS
Van Kennel Doors, sold by U. S. Metal Products Co., 525 Market St., San Francisco.

ROLLING DOORS, SHUTTERS, PARTITIONS, ETC.
Pacific Building Materials Co., 523 Market St., San Francisco.
C. F. Weber & Co., 365 Market St., S. F.
Kinnear Steel Rolling Doors. W. W. Thurston, agent, Rialto Bldg., San Francisco.
Wilson's Steel Rolling Doors, U. S. Metal Products Co., San Francisco and Los Angeles.

ARCHITECTS' SPECIFICATION INDEX—Continued

ROOFING AND ROOFING MATERIALS
Grant Gravel Co., Flatiron Bldg., San Francisco.
H. W. Johns-Manville Co., Second and Howard Sts.. San Francisco.
Malott & Peterson, Inc., Monadnock Bldg., San Francisco.
Niles Sand, Gravel and Rock Co., Mutual Bank Bldg., San Francisco.
"Malthoid" and "Ruberoid," manufactured by Paraffine Paint Co., San Francisco.
Pioneer Roofing, manufactured by Pioneer Paper Co., 513 Hearst Bldg., San Francisco.
United Materials Co., Crossley Bldg., San Francisco.

RUBBER TILING
Goodyear Rubber Company, 587 Market St., San Francisco.
New York Belting & Rubber Company, 519 Mission St., San Francisco.

SAFETY TREADS
"Sanitread," sold by Richard Spencer, 801-3 Hearst Bldg. San Francisco.

SANITARY DRINKING FOUNTAINS
J. L. Mott Iron Works, 135 Kearny St., San Francisco.
Haws' Sanitary Drinking Faucet Co., 1808 Harmon St., Berkeley.

SCENIC PAINTING—DROP CURTAINS, ETC.
The Edwin H. Flagg Scenic Co., 1638 Long Beach Ave., Los Angeles.

SCHOOL FURNITURE AND SUPPLIES
C. F. Weber & Co., 365 Market St., San Francisco; 512 S. Broadway, Los Angeles.

SCREENS
Hipolito Flyout Screens, sold by Simpson & Stewart, Dalziel Bldg., Oakland.
Watson Metal Frame Screens, sold by Richard Spencer, 801-3 Hearst Bldg., San Francisco.

SEEDS
California Seed Company, 151 Market St., San Francisco.

SHEATHING AND SOUND DEADENING
Samuel Cabot Mfg. Co., Boston, Mass., agencies in San Francisco, Oakland, Los Angeles, Portland, Tacoma and Spokane.
Paraffine Paint Co., 34 First St., San Francisco.

SHEET METAL WORK, SKYLIGHTS, ETC.
Capitol Sheet Metal Works, 1927 Market St., San Francisco.
U. S. Metal Products Co., 525 Market St., San Francisco.

SHINGLE STAINS
Cabot's Creosote Stains, sold by Pacific Building Materials Co., Underwood Bldg., San Francisco
Fuller's Pioneer Shingle Stains, made by W. P. Fuller & Co., San Francisco.

SIDEWALK LIGHTS
P. H. Jackson & Co., 237-47 First St., San Francisco.

STEEL AND IRON—STRUCTURAL
Central Iron Works, 621 Florida St., San Francisco.
Dyer Bros., 17th and Kansas Sts., San Francisco.
Brode Iron Works, 31 Hawthorne St., San Francisco.

STEEL AND IRON—STRUCTURAL—Con't.
Golden Gate Iron Works, 1541 Howard St., San Francisco.
Judson Manufacturing Co., 819 Folsom St., San Francisco.
Mortenson Construction Co., 19th and Indiana Sts., San Francisco.
Pacific Rolling Mills, 17th and Mississippi Sts., San Francisco.
Palm Iron & Bridge Works, Sacramento.
Ralston Iron Works, Twentieth and Indiana Sts., San Francisco.
U. S. Steel Products Co., Rialto Bldg., San Francisco.
Sims, Gray & Sauter, 156 Main St., San Francisco.
Schrader Iron Works, Inc., 1247 Harrison St., San Francisco..
Southern California Iron and Steel Co., Fourth and Mateo Sts., Los Angeles.
Western Iron Works, 141 Beale St., San Francisco.

STEEL PRESERVATIVES
Bay State Steel Protective Coating. (See adv. for coast agencies.)
Paraffine Paint Co., 34 First St., San Francisco.

STEEL FIREPROOF WINDOWS
United States Metal Products Co., San Francisco and Los Angeles.

STEEL REINFORCING
Pacific Coast Steel Company, Rialto Bldg., San Francisco.
Southern California Iron & Steel Company, Fourth and Mateo Sts., Los Angeles.
Woods, Huddart & Gunn, 444 Market St., San Francisco.

STEEL ROLLING DOORS
Kinnear Steel Rolling Door Co., W. W. Thurston, Rialto Bldg., San Francisco.

STEEL SASH
"Fenestra," solid steel sash, manufactured by Detroit Steel Products Company, Detroit, Mich.

STEEL WHEELBARROWS
Champion and California steel brands, made by Western Iron Works, 141 Beale St., San Francisco.

STONE
California Granite Co., 518 Sharon Bldg., San Francisco.
McGilvray Stone Company, 634 Townsend St., San Francisco.

STORAGE SYSTEMS—GASOLINE, OIL, ETC.
S. F. Bowser & Co., 612 Howard St., San Francisco.
Rix Compressed Air and Drill Co., First and Howard Sts., San Francisco.

STORE FRONTS
Kawneer Manufacturing Co., Berkeley, Cal.

TEMPERATURE REGULATION
Johnson Service Company, 149 Fifth St., San Francisco.

THEATER AND OPERA CHAIRS
C. F. Weber & Co., 365 Market St., San Francisco.

When writing to Advertisers please mention this magazine.

The Most Up=to=Date WALL BEDS

2019 MISSION ST.
NEAR 16TU
SAN FRANCISCO

Perfect Concealment	Simple Installation
Economy of Space	Most Inexpensive
Only 16″ in depth required	Strong and Durable

ARCHITECTS' SPECIFICATION INDEX—Continued

TILES, MOSAICS, MANTELS, ETC.
Rigney Tile Company, Sheldon Bldg., San Francisco.
Mangrum & Otter, 561 Mission St., San Francisco.
McElhinney Tile Co., 1097 Mission St., San Francisco.

TILE FOR ROOFING
Gladding, McBean & Co., Crocker Bldg., San Francisco.
United Materials Co., Crossley Bldg., San Francisco.

TILE WALLS—INTERLOCKING
Denison Hollow Interlocking Blocks, Forum Bldg., Sacramento.
Gladding, McBean & Co., San Francisco, Los Angeles, Oakland and Sacramento.

TREES
California Seed Company, 151 Market St., San Francisco.

VACUUM CLEANERS
"Tuec" Air Cleaner, manufactured by United Electric Co. Coast agencies, 556 Sutter St., San Francisco, and 724 S. Broadway, Los Angeles.
Palm Vacuum Cleaners, sold by Western Vacuum Supply Co., 1125 Market St., San Francisco.
Spencer Turbine Cleaner, sold by Hughson & Merton, 530 Golden Gate Ave., San Francisco.

VALVES
Sloan Royal Flush Valves. T. R. Burke, Pacific Coast agent, Wells Fargo Bldg., San Francisco.
Crane Radiator Valves., manufactured by Crane Co.. Second and Brannan Sts., San Francisco.

VALVE PACKING
N. H. Cook Belting Co., 317 Howard St., San Francisco.

VARNISHES
W. P. Fuller Co., all principal Coast cities.
Glidden Varnish Co., Cleveland, O., represented on the Pacific Coast by Whittier, Coburn Co., San Francisco.
R. N. Nason & Co., San Francisco, Los Angeles, Portland and Seattle.
Standard Varnish Works, San Francisco.
S. F. Pioneer Varnish Works, 816 Mission St., San Francisco.

VENETIAN BLINDS, AWNINGS, ETC.
Burlington Venetian Blinds, Burlington, Vt., and C. F. Weber & Co., 365 Market St., San Francisco.
Western Blind & Screen Co., 2702 Long Beach Ave., Los Angeles.

VITREOUS CHINAWARE
Pacific Porcelain Ware Company, 67 New Montgomery St., San Francisco.

WALL BEDS, SEATS, ETC.
Lachman Wall Bed Co., 2019 Mission St., San Francisco.
Marshall & Stearns Co., 1154 Phelan Bldg., San Francisco.
Peek's Wall Beds, sold by Western Equipment Co., 72 Fremont St., San Francisco.
Perfection Disappearing Bed Co., 737 Mission St., San Francisco.
Noack Disappearing Ironing Board Co., Sherman Kimball Co., selling agents, 109 First St., San Francisco.

WALL PAINT
Nason's Opaque Flat Finish, manufactured by R. N. Nason & Co., San Francisco, Portland and Los Angeles.
San-A-Cote and Vel--va-Cote, manufactured by the Brininstool Co., Los Angeles; Marion D. Cohn Co., Hansford Bldg., San Francisco, distributor.

WALL BOARD
"Amiwud" Wall Board, manufactured by Paraffine Paint Co., 34 First St., San Francisco.

WALL PAPER
Uhl Bros., 38 O'Farrell St., San Francisco.

WATER HEATERS—AUTOMATIC
Pittsburg Water Heater Co. of California, 478 Sutter St., San Francisco, and Thirteenth and Clay Sts., Oakland.
Cole Heater Company, Lick Bldg., San Francisco.

WATERPROOFING FOR CONCRETE, BRICK, ETC.
Armorite Damp Resisting Paint, made by W. P. Fuller & Co., San Francisco.
J. L. Goffette Corporation, 227 San Bruno Ave., San Francisco.
Hill, Hubbell & Co., 1 Drumm St., San Francisco.
H. W. Johns-Manville Co., San Francisco and principal Coast cities.
Glidden's Concrete Floor Dressing and Liquid Cement Enamel, sold on Pacific Coast by Whittier, Coburn Company, San Francisco.
Imperial Co., 183 Stevenson St., San Francisco.
Samuel Cabot Mfg. Co., Boston, Mass., agencies in San Francisco, Oakland, Los Angeles, Portland, Tacoma and Spokane.
Wadsworth, Howland & Co., Inc. (See adv. for Coast agencies.)

WATER SUPPLY SYSTEMS
Kewanee Water Supply System—Simonds Machinery Co., agents, 117 New Montgomery St., San Francisco.

WHEELBARROWS—STEEL
Western Iron Works, Beale and Main Sts., San Francisco.

WHITE ENAMEL FINISH
"Gold Seal," manufactured and sold by Bass-Hueter Paint Company. All principal Coast cities.
"Silkenwhite," made by W. P. Fuller & Co., San Francisco.
"Satinette," Standard Varnish Works, 113 Front St., San Francisco.

WINDOWS—REVERSIBLE, CASEMENT, ETC.
Whitney Window, represented by Richard Spencer, Hearst Bldg., San Francisco.
Hauser Reversible Window Co., Balboa Bldg., San Francisco.
International Casement Co., represented by Edwin C. Dehn, Hearst Bldg., San Francisco.

WIRE FABRIC
U. S. Steel Products Co., Rialto Bldg., San Francisco.

WOOD MANTELS
Fink & Schindler, 218 13th St., San Francisco.
Mangrum & Otter, 561 Mission St., San Francisco.

Time for Planting is close at hand. Lay out your Country Place with the best
the market affords in

TREES · SEEDS · BULBS
California Seed Company

AL. J. NEVRAUMONT, Manager
Phone Douglas 5895

151 Market Street, San Francisco

When writing to Advertisers please mention this magazine.

When writing to Advertisers please mention this magazine.

When writing to Advertisers please mention this magazine.

VITROLITE

City Hall, San Francisco
Bakewell & Brown, Architects

IDEAL FOR TOILETS   *"Better Than Marble"*

For toilet partitions and wainscoting in toilet and bathrooms Vitrolite is unsurpassed. It is snow white—unstainable and impervious to the action of acids. Its brilliantly polished surface can be sterilized without injury. Our new toilet construction is the essence of sanitation and durability. We will gladly send details.

THE VITROLITE CONSTRUCTION COMPANY

1490 Mission Street   San Francisco, California

BUILDING FOR H. R. BOYNTON CO., LOS ANGELES, CALIFORNIA

W. J. DODD, ARCHITECT

When writing to Advertisers please mention this magazine.

When writing to Advertisers please mention this magazine.

THE ARCHITECT & ENGINEER

25c Copy
$1.50 a Year.

OF CALIFORNIA

Volume XLVIII
Number 2

Issued monthly in the interest of Architects, Structural Engineers, Contractors and
the Allied Trades of the Pacific Coast.
Entered at San Francisco Post Office as Second Class Matter.

CONTENTS FOR FEBRUARY, 1917

Frontispiece
The Architect and Engineer
of California
for February, 1917

RANDOLPH APARTMENTS, SAN FRANCISCO
WOOD & SIMPSON.   ARCHITECTS

THE
Architect and Engineer
Of California

VOL. XLVIII.   FEBRUARY, 1917   No. 2.

An Apartment House Designed in the Colonial Type

THE design of apartment houses in San Francisco has followed a certain general type for so long that fear is frequently expressed that the city may be drifting into a "rut." This tendency has been aggravated, in some respects, by the state housing laws; not through any inherent fault of the laws, but solely because of the habit of regarding them as express directions instead of minimum restrictions.

It is, therefore, refreshing to see such a radical departure from the traditional routine, as the new "Randolph Apartments" at Larkin and Post streets. The architects, in solving the problem presented, considered it from the standpoint of the occupants as well as from that of the owner, and the result has been a building covering less than one-half of the lot and having the rear apartments equally as well lighted as those in front. Every kitchen has direct outside light and ventilation, baths are ventilated by courts double the size required by the "Burnett Law," one-half of the dressing rooms also are so ventilated although this is not required by the law, and in spite of these liberal accommodations and the fact that the living rooms are fully 20 per cent over the legal minimum, the cost of the building was so low on account of the compact type of plan, that the property is an exceedingly good investment. The compactness also produces a great saving in janitor service, cost of carpeting, depreciation, etc. In the design of the building the architects aimed to produce a building which should suggest a home rather than a hotel; it being their fixed conviction that the lack of the domestic quality is one of the most lamentable failings of the average apartment house.

The type of architecture follows, in a general way, the so-called "Colonial style" which prevailed in the American colonies in the eighteenth century. The exterior is of red brick with white stone trim and is embellished with a portico and fence of white painted wood. The vestibule is panelled and painted white; main lobby panelled in Southern red gum, and elsewhere through the building the finish is of white or light grey enamel, producing a very cheerful and homelike effect.

A noteworthy feature is a garden in the rear, attractively planted with grass and ornamental shrubs and with brick paved walks.

The idea of covering approximately one-half of the lot of what might almost be called downtown property was at first most definitely rejected by the owner, but an estimate of the cost and rentals demonstrated that a considerably better return would be realized from this scheme than from any others which utilized the ground up to the limits of the Tenement House Act. The practicability of the scheme has been demonstrated conclusively by the fact that there has been so much demand for these apartments that the owner has felt justified in increasing the rental. The space left vacant has by its treatment enhanced the appearance not only of the property to which it belongs but also of the adjoining property. A treatment of this kind carried out throughout the apartment house district would most certainly improve the locality and add a certain tone to the city which it has always lacked on account of the absence of foliage and verdure.

Messrs. Wood and Simpson are the architects.

PERSPECTIVE, RANDOLPH APARTMENTS, SAN FRANCISCO
WOOD & SIMPSON,   ARCHITECTS

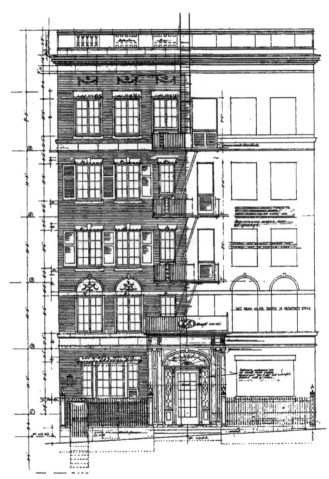

FRONT ELEVATION, RANDOLPH APARTMENTS, SAN FRANCISCO
WOOD & SIMPSON,   ARCHITECTS

PERSPECTIVE, RANDOLPH APARTMENTS, SAN FRANCISCO
WOOD & SIMPSON,   ARCHITECTS

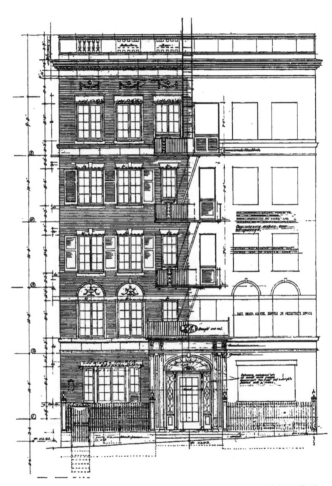

FRONT ELEVATION, RANDOLPH APARTMENTS, SAN FRANCISCO
WOOD & SIMPSON,   ARCHITECTS

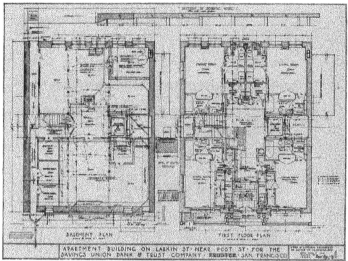

FLOOR PLAN, RANDOLPH APARTMENTS, SAN FRANCISCO
Wood & Simpson, Architects

ENTRANCE HALL, RANDOLPH APARTMENTS, SAN FRANCISCO
Wood & Simpson, Architects

THIRD STREET ELEVATION, SOUTHERN PACIFIC RAILROAD STATION, SAN FRANCISCO

Some California Railroad Stations*

By FREDERICK JENNINGS

WHEN the Central and Southern Pacific railroads were constructed the first depots to be erected were combined freight and passenger stations, known as Standard Depot No. 22. These served the passenger and freight business and also provided living quarters on the second floor for the agent or operator. Most of these structures have now been displaced by newer and better forms of construction, but at various places the original buildings still stand and are ample for the volume of business transacted, the company having always had in mind the future growth of the community, building well and with an eye to the development of the surrounding country. At many places, however, towns have grown up into cities and the need has been felt for improved station facilities, and at these places the old frame structures have been moved to new locations, remodeled and enlarged to handle freight traffic only; the station grounds have been enlarged, paved, and provided with electroliers, and at many places parks have been installed.

The new stations have been planned to meet the requirements of the surrounding country for many years to come, and, contrary to the former practice, no two stations are alike, but at each location the stations are designed to represent the progressiveness of the community. In each case the stations have been of modern construction—cement exterior or brick prevailing, with either slate or clay tile roofs. The structures have been designed to correspond with the character of the locality and climatic conditions, the Mission type, typifying the early Spanish architecture portrayed by the various Old Missions, prevailing. The California climate has made open waiting rooms a favored arrangement, and in addition to this feature, arcades have been used in some instances.

*Editor's Note.—The depots selected to illustrate Mr. Jennings' article are undoubtedly among the best the Southern Pacific Company has built along its California lines in recent years. They are not shown necessarily to convey our judgment of what constitutes an ideal architectural treatment, but more to emphasize the trend of the times to build better buildings and to beautify the space surrounding these buildings, making the stations a delight to the weary passenger instead of an eyesore.

CLOISTERS AND TOWER, THIRD AND TOWNSEND STREET STATION, SAN FRANCISCO
DESIGNED BY ARCHITECTURAL BUREAU,   SOUTHERN PACIFIC COMPANY

The floors are generally of cement or tile, woodwork of weathered oak finish. Sanitary plumbing throughout, with ice-cooled bubbling drinking fountains are prominent features in the new stations. Large photo panels depicting various scenic attractions, resorts, etc., are arranged around the interior· walls of the waiting rooms. Vitreous tile floors, marble stalls and glazed tile wainscoting are used throughout in the toilet rooms. Heating is usually accomplished by means of low-pressure steam or by circulating hot water systems; at some places electric fans are provided in the office and waiting rooms. Telegraph wires enter the building through underground cables instead of overhead, as formerly. The floor arrangement provides for either separate waiting rooms for men and women or for a large. general waiting room with separate women's retiring room and men's smoking room. Among the stations recently constructed, the following are good examples:

San Francisco, Third street	Berkeley, University avenue	
Los Angeles	Santa Barbara	Visalia
Davis	Porterville	Modesto
Richmond	Turlock	Los Altos

The Third street station in San Francisco is of "Mission" architecture, brick construction, with imposing elevations at· Third and Townsend streets. The exterior is of light gray cement stucco, with granite base and red Mission tile roof. The building is "L" shape in plan, with the following over-all dimensions: 115x265 feet on Third street and 35x275 feet on Townsend street. Wide arcades stretch along on both frontages and under a spacious marquise passengers may be discharged from automobiles. either on Third street or Townsend street, and be under cover at all times.

All platforms are under cover full length, extending to Fourth street. The construction of these train sheds is of reinforced concrete of the "Butterfly" type, the Southern Pacific Company being the first to adopt this form of construction.

The outbound and inbound travel has been entirely. separated. While the principal entrance may be designated at Third street, near Townsend street, and also on Townsend street, the exit is near King street, where a large area for auto parking has been provided.

The general waiting room is 64 by 110 feet, with an arched ceiling 45 feet high. Passengers may enter from here direct into women's waiting and men's waiting rooms, also restaurant. Light enters from three sides, and in order to diffuse such light, amber Moss glass was used, giving the room a warm and cozy atmosphere.

The ticket office is centrally located, and, adjoining the concourse, it is on the natural line of travel, no matter at which side passengers enter. Special ticket openings are provided towards concourse should extraordinary occasion demand. A special feature of the ticket office is the absence of the usual counter grille and ticket case. The counter is entirely open. Information may be had or tickets purchased from the ticket agent without having him turn around or make unnecessary steps. A revolving ticket drum in the counter holds the card-board stock, from which any ticket may be drawn.

Interior finish of the station is of oak. The floor of the general waiting room is of California marble with "Tavernelle" marble wainscoting 7 feet high on verde-antique marble base. Walls above and the arched ceiling are in Caen stone finish.

THIRD AND TOWNSEND STREET STATION, SAN FRANCISCO
DESIGNED BY ARCHITECTURAL BUREAU, SOUTHERN PACIFIC COMPANY

GENERAL WAITING ROOM, SOUTHERN PACIFIC THIRD AND TOWNSEND STREET
STATION, SAN FRANCISCO

The women's waiting room is finished in old ivory, with tile floor, and is tastefully furnished with rugs, drapery and lounging chairs.

Passengers find the baggage room conveniently located off the concourse, where parcels may be checked before entering gates to the train platforms.

In each and every room is an electrically controlled clock. In connection with this system are chimes located in the attic which ring the quarter, half and full hour Westminster chimes.

A ventilating system changes the air in the rooms and the electric lighting is of the indirect system, making for good illumination without the glare of lamps.

* * *

The new Los Angeles station replaced the old structure commonly known as the "Arcade Station" and was designed by Messrs. Parkinson & Bergstrom of that city. The governing features of the design were:

1. Separation of pedestrian grades and track grades.
2. Separation of incoming and outgoing passengers.
3. Conveniences and comforts for waiting passengers.
4. Baggage handling for enormous tourist traffic.
5. A ticket office of maximum selling efficiency and convenience to passengers.
6. An information bureau of service directly to arriving as well as departing passengers, in which all public telephone and telegraph facilities are centered.
7. Power plant, modern kitchen and dining room, ventilation, office room, general lighting, service piping, private car yards, express facilities, all carefully studied and worked out.

SOUTHERN PACIFIC STATION. LOS ANGELES
PARKINSON & BERGSTRØM, ARCHITECTS

GENERAL WAITING ROOM, CENTRAL STATION, LOS ANGELES
Parkinson & Bergstrom, Architects

UMBRELLA SHEDS AND TRACKS, CENTRAL STATION, LOS ANGELES

DEPOT AT VISALIA, CALIFORNIA
Designed by Architectural Bureau, Southern Pacific Company

DEPOT AT PORTERVILLE, CALIFORNIA
Designed by Architectural Bureau, Southern Pacific Company

DEPOT AT DAVIS, CALIFORNIA
Designed by Architectural Bureau, Southern Pacific Company

DEPOT AT BERKELEY, CALIFORNIA
Designed by Architectural Bureau, Southern Pacific Company .

DEPOT AT LOS ALTOS, CALIFORNIA
Designed by Architectural Bureau, Southern Pacific Company

DEPOT AT RICHMOND, CALIFORNIA
Designed by Architectural Bureau, Southern Pacific Company

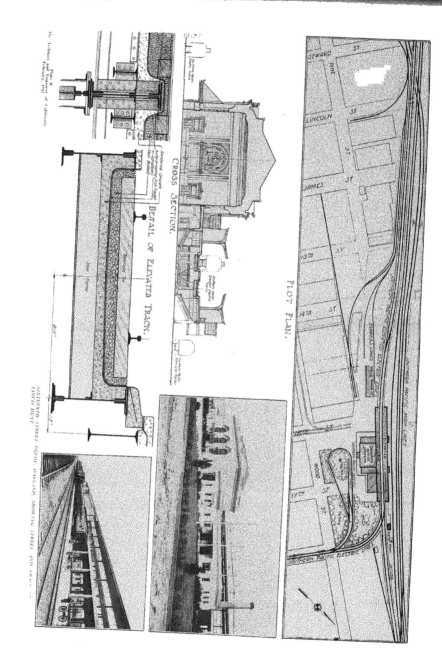

CROSS SECTION.

DETAIL OF ELEVATED TRACK.

PLOT PLAN.

Plate B
The Architect and Engineer of California
February, 1917

SIXTEENTH STREET DEPOT, OAKLAND, SHOWING STREET AND TRACKS

DEPOT AT TURLOCK, CALIFORNIA
Designed by Architectural Bureau, Southern Pacific Company

The central portion of the building, 208x70 feet, is the main waiting room. To the north a wing 225x60 feet contains baggage room on first and second, floors, connected by freight elevators and a chute for returning baggage to the lower floor.

The third floor carries office quarters conveniently arranged for the use of the local division organization.

To the south a wing 136x70 feet contains the exit concourse and the head of the exit incline from the underground passage from train platforms. This room is 45x60 feet and is joined on the south by a large and modern dining and lunch room, with attendant kitchen, the latter operated by the Southern Pacific Company's dining car department. The second floor of this wing corresponds in height to the third floor of the north wing and is finished in the large, and provided with plumbing for future subdivision, now held as reserve office space.

Outgoing passengers are passed by gatemen through doors in the east wall of the waiting room to an enclosure on the same level, from which a 15 per cent. ramp leads down parallel with the building to the level of a subway, which in turn leads to all station tracks, ten in number.

The ticket office presents a new departure in that no grille is used, the counter being designed for free business intercourse between purchaser and seller. The arrangement of ticket cases is unique, all coupon forms being in drawers under the counter, while all card tickets are held in two horizontal revolving cases set into the counter.

The construction is of brick and steel on concrete foundations. The exterior is finished with white cement stucco to carry out modern Renaissance designs.

The interior wood finish is of oak, with tile floor and 7-foot high Alaska marble wainscoting in the general waiting room.

Besides its Southern Pacific brick passenger station of Colonial design at First and Broadway, Oakland has the distinction of possessing the only elevated railroad station west of the Rocky mountains—the Sixteenth street station.

It serves passengers for main line trains at grade and local passengers for elevated electric train service for Oakland, Alameda and Berkeley.

The elevated structure is about. 4,000 feet long and was built to eliminate dangerous grade crossings at Eleventh and Fourteenth streets and also pedestrians' grade crossing at the station platform. The entire building foundation is on special concrete piles. The construction is Class A, with brick walls, terra cotta facing (tool-marked to represent granite), steel trusses and tile roof.

Umbrella sheds on the elevated platform are the "Butterfly type' of steel construction. The interior is finished in Flemish oak, with Alaska marble floor and wainscoting.

The central portion contains the main waiting room, 60x116 feet, with ticket office, telegraph, telephone and news service.

The wings contain at one end women's retiring room, men's smoking room and also toilet facilities; the other wing baggage and boiler room. Various other features are shown in the illustrations.

* * *

Dangerous Structures

THERE is as much profit in studying failures in any branch of work as in considering only the great successes. We must learn what to avoid as well as what to imitate. W. G. Perkins, district surveyor, recently read before a meeting of the Concrete Institute in London a practical paper on "Dangerous Structures."

Amongst the causes of a dangerous structure are the following:—(a) faulty construction; (b) faulty materials; (c) faulty design; (d) decay and fatigue; (e) overloading; (f) removal of extraneous support; (g) wind pressure, shock, etc.; (h) fire and explosion, bombs, says Mr. Perkins. "I propose to enumerate a number of cases where failures have resulted from one or more of these causes; particularly (a), (b) and (c).

"Perhaps few of us have had any experience with failures arising from faulty design and materials in modern structures, as a sufficient period has not elapsed for time to have done its work, but there are numerous instances in buildings erected by former generations. We moderns are often called to account for the supposed inferior manner in which we build, being told that our buildings are not solid like those erected in 'the good old times,' that we have lost the art of making good mortar, etc. People who make such remarks have, I fear, only an acquaintance with the jerry-builder of the very bad type. The majority of buildings erected in London 100 to 200 years ago were constructed in a most inferior manner. The mortar appears to have been compounded with a fat lime, dry slaked, and, judging from the nodules of loam it contains, mixed with a good deal of the 'top spit' of the field. Naturally such stuff has, and had, no binding qualities, and to this day is only so much dusty rubbish. The bricks were badly shaped and easily broken, so much so that in taking down old walls one finds course after course of what appeared to be headers to be only 'bats.'

"In many old buildings the main beams of the floors are placed diagonally and the loads from the roof and four stories are imposed upon a pier of brickwork about 14 inches square. Needless to say, such piers have crushed. Strangely enough, this kind of brick work is always stronger in damp positions, the moisture having enabled the lime to a certain extent to set. Workmen refer to this state as being 'water bound.'

"Failures have occurred by using unsuitable materials in the composition of concrete. There was the case of a reservoir where blast furnace slag was used as the aggregate for its concrete walls. The water affected the concrete so that it became quite soft and rotten, and the walls had to be rebuilt.

"Concrete made with breeze is a dangerous material. It is one of the materials specified in the London Building Acts as a fire-resisting material, and as a district surveyor I have, much against my better knowledge, to pass it. This stuff was used for the floors of sculleries in the first stories of a row of houses built under my official supervision. In every house this stuff expanded, pushing out the walls, some of which had to be rebuilt. In another district I had to inspect a block of residential flats, the walls of which were bulged at every floor level, owing to the expansion of the breeze concrete.

"The term 'foundation' is sometimes used in a very indefinite manner, and may mean the actual base upon which the superstructure is reared or the soil itself. It has been suggested that the proper meaning of the word is the artificial arrangement or construction prepared or made to support the base of a superstructure; whilst the soil beneath should be termed the foundation bed. Foundations are important, as when defective or insufficient they will lead sooner or later to a dangerous structure.

"In dealing with structures rendered dangerous by settlement owing to the insufficient bearing capacity of the soil, I prefer, wherever there is an underlying stratum of firm material, to sink down to it, even though it should be at a considerable depth. The sinking should be in the form of pits (the area of which would be determined by the loading and the bearing capacity of the firm material), filled up with good mass concrete. Then from pier to pier either construct beams of reinforced concrete or fix rolled steel joists encased in a rich and well-graded concrete and turn arches.

"I am not an advocate of raft foundations, for unless your structure can be symmetrically disposed about the raft or its center of gravity be made to coincide therewith—a very difficult thing to do except in a symmetrical building—the pressure on the soil will be unequal, the raft will tilt and throw your structure out of the perpendicular. The same thing will happen if the soft soil is not of even consistency and bearing value all over."

* * *

The Santa Fe Building, San Francisco

RAPID progress is being made on the new Santa Fe building at the corner of Second and Market streets, and within a few weeks enough work will be in place to give a fair idea of the completed appearance of the building. The structure is of steel frame construction, with concrete floors, walls of especially made red brick, with white terra cotta trim, and first two floors of white marble, bronze and glass.

The conflict between art and economy, which is always present in a commercial building, was particularly acute in this case, but by careful study and by reason of certain innovations in construction the architects were able to produce what gives promise of being a distinguished and convenient building, while keeping the cost at a very low figure. The Santa Fe Railroad Company has leased the first four floors and will fit them up for its use in the most complete fashion, using to a large extent imported marbles, hardwood and ornamental plaster. The remaining eight floors will be subdivided for offices in the usual manner.

SANTA FE BUILDING, SAN FRANCISCO
WOOD & SIMPSON,   ARCHITECTS

SANTA FE BUILDING, SAN FRANCISCO
Steel frame completed by Dyer Bros. November 12, 1916. *Lower plate shows
progress picture taken January 27, 1917*
Wood & Simpson, Architects

Advantages and Disadvantages of Reinforced Concrete

By PERCY J. WALDRAM.

CONCRETE is a material which has received, during the last few years, a considerable amount of very skillful and successful advertising. The effect of this has been enhanced by the intricate nature of the mathematics and formulae by means of which it is commonly supposed to be calculated, and it is popularly regarded as a mysterious and wonderful material, which is superior to the natural laws of structural mechanics— enormously strong, extremely cheap, and eminently suitable to almost every possible form of construction from a factory to a stationary cabinet. It is, in fact, far too frequently credited with the almost miraculous powers with which electricity was popularly invested some years ago, before its physical and economic limitations became generally known. In many ways electricity has exceeded the expectations which were formed of it, but we still use a little coal and oil for various purposes. Reinforced concrete has possibly similar unexpected triumphs awaiting it, but steel, wood, brick, and stone are by no means obsolete yet. It would appear to be essentially the province of surveyors to form a fair and businesslike estimation of its advantages, because without going into intricate calculations it is possible to arrive at a sufficient and correct opinion of its general physical character and of the conditions essential to its proper production, and when these are clearly grasped the problem resolves itself into a matter of ordinary valuation. The general ·physical properties of the material are fairly summed up in its title. It is concrete reinforced. The steel bones and tendons which we supply to the concrete flesh enable it to overcome that want of tensile strength which previously restricted its use to situations in which it could act in compression only—as in arches, arching floors, walls, footings, etc. But the presence of reinforcement does not make any very great difference to the nature of the concrete itself. The latter still remains an active partner in the firm, and the steel must work pari passu with it or dissolve partnership; and unless the steel reinforcement is made capable of carrying on the whole of the work, with the concrete acting merely as fireproofing material, dissolution of partnership means ruin. Hence even in beams which are reinforced in compression we are constantly hampered in design by the capabilities of the concrete, which unfortunately are not very high; and in spite of all the important structural advantages resulting from the monolithic form of construction in which the strength of each part of a structure enhances that of its neighbors, reinforced concrete is necessarily heavy and weak for its size as compared with steel or wood. This disadvantage is partially balanced by its almost perfect durability, which enables us to utilize a greater proportion of its ultimate strength than is the case with more perishable materials. But in all cases where severe stresses and the dead weight of long spans are involved, it is useless to expect from it the same strength that we obtain from wood or steel at the same cost. There are, however, situations where it would, for other reasons, pay to use the weaker material. When properly designed and properly made in situations where it is suitable, it is rotproof, verminproof, fire-resisting, almost waterproof, and grows stronger with age instead of decaying. It can also be readily moulded to any given form, and in entire structures it is wonderfully monolithic, a very considerable advantage in bad foundations. But at the same time it is not a material to be used without accurate knowledge of its limitations.

It must be designed with skill, made with more than customary care, painstakingly nursed during infancy, and protected during the whole of its lifetime from agencies which are deleterious to cement such as impermeating oils and acids. In some cases these disadvantages are immaterial, and it is the peculiar province of the surveyor to estimate them. In all situations where plain concrete, brick work, or masonry would customarily be employed it can be expected to do the same work with far less bulk of material. But on the other hand, its use invariably entails extra expenditure in casing, which may or may not outweigh the saving of material.

A retaining wall, for instance, in reinforced concrete will do the same work as a solid brick or concrete gravity wall at a fraction of the cost; but in ordinary dwelling-house solid walls, where there is not much thickness which can properly be saved, reinforced concrete and its casing must be expected to prove more expensive than brick or stone. On account of the great difference between the stiffness of steel and concrete, as well as between their respective strengths, it is a matter of no small mathematical difficulty to devise formulae which will tell us accurately how such an ill-matched team are going to pull together upon any given load, and what work we can safely entrust to them without running the risk of the too willing steel being overworked, or setting a pace which the concrete cannot keep up with. Even at the present time, after engineering scientists all over the world have been engaged for years upon the subject, there are still problems which no textbooks meet. Many minds are, however, at work, endeavoring on the one hand to complete and standardize our knowledge, and on the other to simplify the mathematics involved.

Reinforced concrete suffers, and suffers badly, from the incubus of tedious and intricate calculations, and it is gratifying to be able to say that the results given by all formulae can be plotted to curves. When these are drawn to large scale the slightest inaccuracy in calculating them is seen in some irregularity in the sweep of the curve. When they are used instead of the formulae, the designer's task is reduced to that of selecting values from a set of diagrams. In my own office we have almost completely eliminated the necessity for using the long standard formulae, having plotted them all on diagrams. The saving of time and trouble effected by their use is enormous, but what is far more important is the notable gain in accuracy. If a draughtsman has a long and intricate formula to work to, the chances of error are far greater than if he has merely to take a value from a plotted curve. Another important and unexpected advantage which results from the substitution of curves for tedious mathematics is the rapidity with which the designer can grasp the possibilities of a problem, can compare reinforced concrete with other materials, and, if it is found suitable, select the particular form in which it will give the results which combine efficiency and economy. In a material which has a high ratio of dead weight to strength it is frequently only possible to secure a proper factor of safety by eliminating all superfluous bulk.

The subject of design in reinforced concrete is being extensively taught in technical institutions and it is to be hoped that as the supply of skilled designers increases the disadvantages of excessive mathematics will disappear. The necessity for skilled labor in construction is often considered to discount the use of reinforced concrete in remote country districts, where it would never pay to send down specialist workmen. I would suggest, however, that it is rather a matter of the skilful supervision of the structural ability which is to be found in country and private estate workmen. The more remote a district is from large centers of population the more multifarious are the demands made upon the intelligence and ability of the local workmen. Opinions probably differ on the point, but personally I have always found country workmen remarkably intelligent, and can see no reason why the average mason should not very quickly be taught all that is required to make, or to supervise the making of good reinforced concrete. If he is given good materials and clear drawings, all that is required is a somewhat unusually rigid attention to comparatively simple rules, which can easily be typed on a page or two of foolscap, or stated in his specification. Any man who is capable of mixing and making really good concrete, who can read, understand, and carry out drawings intelligently, and who can be trusted loyally to adhere to instructions without varying them according to his own ideas, possesses all the necessary capabilities; but he cannot be expected to turn out good work in a material with regard to which he has no previous knowledge or traditional skill unless his preliminary instructions are clear, definite, and complete.

* * *

Cracked Plaster Work

Cracks in plaster work are due to various causes. They may act individually or in combination. Cracks are often caused by settlement of the building. These cracks may be easily discerned by their breadth, depth and length. They also arise from the shrinkage of bad or unseasoned lumber used in the construction or framing of the building, which may cause displacement in the joists or lath. Other causes are the too sudden drying of the work; strong winds or heat; the laying of one coat of mortar on another coat before the first has sufficiently dried, or on walls that have a strong suction, which absorbs the moisture or "life" of the coat being laid, when it becomes short, or crumbly, scaly and apt to peel or fall off. In this last case it does not set, but only dries and shrinks, which gives rise to cracks, and eventually falls or crumbles away. The use of bad materials, insufficient use of lime and hair, or skimping of labor is often followed by cracks. Insufficient labor and unskilled workmanship in the application of materials is a great source of trouble; but it will be understood that the best quality of labor will not make bad materials good and strong; and, on the other hand, the best materials will not compensate for bad labor. It is only by judicious selection of materials and their skilled manipulations that a high and enduring class of work can be obtained.—Rock Products.

* * *

The Value of Courtesy

One of the best assets a business can have is courtesy. Discourtesy breeds ill will and ill will is probably the most deadly little business killer at large. Common courtesy costs nothing; a little extra courtesy takes but little more time. But its dividends are surprisingly large. It is one of our most captivating little builder-uppers of business. Everybody likes it. It pays.

Factory Construction in America and Abroad

By PERCIVAL M. FRASER, A. R. I. B. A.*

IT is now generally recognized that a well-equipped series of shops is an absolutely essential factor in a successful industrial concern. It is as important as the machinery and plant and the site. It is not difficult to prove that these will be crippled by being housed in unsuitable buildings where the first must be limited in efficiency, underdriven, and wastefully or harmfully worked, and the second so badly utilized as to counteract its peculiar merits. To be completely efficient, it is necessary to be as thoroughly up to date in the buildings as in the plant, for to be up to date means to have taken advantage of every development and improvement in machinery and organization, and, other things being equal, indirectly it is the most important factor in success.

It must be admitted that English factory buildings, whether in reinforced concrete or otherwise, cannot bear comparison with similar buildings abroad, especially in America. That English factory buildings, even with the most enterprising and successful firms, are often disgraceful, no one who has had any experience in our great manufacturing centers can deny. The American will frankly admit that he does not build his factories for posterity but is content if they last a couple of generations. I do not suggest that we are incapable in England of erecting efficient ranges of factories, and I trust that we shall never erect buildings which will depreciate a hundred per cent in fifty years, but there is a happy medium of design and expenditure in regard to factory construction which we should endeavor to seek.

It is often found that a factory manager will dabble in building construction, so that in addition to his onerous and complex technical and commercial duties he lightly undertakes the combined work of several professions and trades, with more or less indifferent results.

It is my experience that the engineer who knows his mind on the development of his works will always be ready to admit that building construction, with its scores of allied trades, and, further, the duties of an architect and of a civil engineer, are not what he is paid for, nor are they things for which his training has fitted him. He will therefore content himself with an intelligent collaboration with a professional man.

The relations of the architect and the engineer who is dealing with the lay-out of the plan or who is running the process of manufacture should be very close and sympathetic. Periodical consultations between these parties result in a considerable saving of labor, and only a complete *entente* between both parties will permit of all considerations and requirements being harmoniously collated.

In this connection I would mention the somewhat common custom of the factory owner, after negotiating for a site, being inveigled by the land agent into entrusting the design of the factory into his hands. This is a common and growing practice, and it is inconceivable to me how a levelheaded business man can enter upon such an arrangement. He will eventually have to pay for professional services in one form or another, and it is obvious that he should have the first-hand services of an experienced professional adviser on so vital a point.

There is another aspect which I cannot forbear to touch on in this connection—viz., that some of the reinforced concrete specialists make a point

---

*Extract of a paper read at the forty-second general meeting of the Concrete Institute, Westminster, S. W.

of preparing complete designs for factories and other buildings, concerning which they can have absolutely no experience or knowledge, and this is a further prolific source of ill-designed and inefficient factory premises.

The governing principle in the design of industrial works is to provide efficient buildings at the lowest cost. A certain operation takes place in each department, and these processes are components of the finished article for the manufacture of which the buildings are erected. Each building unit, therefore, must be designed to allow its particular process to be carried out under the best conditions and without restrictions, and the buildings as a whole must be schemed to allow the various processes to pass through them in the most direct manner without loss of time or waste in any shape or form. To achieve this ideal lay-out requires detailed and sympathetic collaboration of the architect and engineer. The engineer embodies the special knowledge of the technical heads of the various departments, whilst the architect collates all problems connected with the building and design. The complete scheme should be looked upon as one single, if complicated, piece of machinery which can be operated by the factory manager; and the more harmoniously the units work together the greater the facility with which the manager handles the business, and the more likely it is to be profitable. The scheme should be conceived on what the Americans call "broad-gauge lines." Economy in one department may entail extravagance in all the other departments. The difficulties and restrictions of a building site must be courageously dealt with, and are frequently put to valuable use; such as, for instance, difficulties in the levels of a building site may be frequently utilized to convey the material by gravitation through the various departments and thus reduce handling and power consumption. and again will often enable loading stages to be formed at convenient heights.

The effect of well-constructed, light, and healthy buildings on the health and spirits of the workpeople is an important factor. A draughty, dark, cold, and badly ventilated workshop will in time dispel the enthusiasm of the best workmen; the lack of decent sanitary accommodation will destroy his self-respect, and his health must suffer from working in ill-designed and insanitary buildings. In this connection I would suggest that portions of factory sites not utilized for buildings should be planted with trees and shrubs so as to make the factory premises a little less of a work-house to the workpeople, and it is my experience that where the workpeople are afforded opportunities of recreation in the meal-hours at the expense of the building owners, the results have always been satisfactory, and the workpeople are made thereby physically and mentally more decent.

Among the questions which frequently come before an architect in designing industrial buildings is the following: Whether the building as a whole should be one story or more in height. This question is often automatically disposed of by the cost of land, the amount of labor to be accommodated, and the nature of the machinery. Unless the foundations are likely to prove abnormally expensive it will generally be found, however, that the one-story building can be constructed the more cheaply.

A second important detail which practically always arises is the question of eliminating columns or reducing their number and planning their positions to the best effect. When the engineer does not object to columns, be sure he has evil designs on them, and ample strength should be provided accordingly.

Other questions which must infallibly arise are the nature of the lighting, which must, for many manufactures, be from the roof. In two-story buildings the width of the building is determined hereby, but it is an advantage to make the upper floor with the roof light. Too much daylight, unlike artificial light, cannot be provided, but the increase of window space will add to cost and complicate heating and ventilation. The north or sawtooth roof is always an advantage, but is not always worth the expense, costing as it does 10 per cent more than an ordinary pitched roof in steel or 20 per cent more than a flat roof in reinforced concrete.

With regard to the clear height of workrooms, a margin should be allowed over the bare necessity, as it is comparatively cheap to add to the height of a floor, and a lofty room conduces greatly to its general utility.

The number and disposition of floor beams is often dictated by the needs of economical design, but frequently one has to provide floor slabs free from beams to increase headroom or for other reasons. A disposition of beams not in itself economical may save an expensive multiplication of nozzles in a sprinkler system. Hollow floors or roof slabs may be occasionally introduced with advantage.

An eminent member of my profession said to me recently: "I have heard enough about the advantages of reinforced concrete; tell me some of its disadvantages."

There are, of course, three attributes of every marketable commodity—namely, goodness, badness, and indifference; let us therefore first approach the question with indifference. A casual examination will show that ferro-concrete will be adaptable and suitable for factory construction. We have, therefore, to weigh the special advantages that it possesses with the disadvantages, and decide whether the advantages are such that it is as good as other methods of construction at the same or less cost.

The serious competitors of reinforced concrete which are at present before the building world are as follows:—

Brick, steel and cast-iron, wood, sheet-iron and metal lathing and plastering, tiling, terra-cotta or similar slabbing and casing, and a number of patent forms of construction too numerous to mention and most difficult to classify, most of which, however, come within the scope of reinforced concrete in one or more respects.

It is exceedingly difficult, if not impossible, to definitely pronounce on the comparative economies of the foregoing materials, and we can only take specific instances and endeavor to generalize from these. I am able to give a case where competitive prices were obtained for a building, which is of a fair size, straightforward, and a really useful one for this comparison. In this case alternative schemes were prepared in the fullest detail and competitive prices obtained. The results were as follows:—

Per Cent

1. For a steel-frame building with brick walls, corrugated iron roof (two-thirds north light), wood joists and boards on steel bearers to galleries, and patent glazing to roofs, the cost was.......... 100
2. For a reinforced concrete building with roofs as last............. 92
3. As last, but with concrete roofs, part flat, part with north lantern lights, but with brick panel walls 89
4. As No. 1, but with corrugated iron walls....................... 89
5. Wholly in reinforced concrete 88

The building was actually carried out in reinforced concrete, including the gutters, down pipes, roofs, walls, foundations, and every detail where it was possible for this material to be used. I may say that in this case there were no special circumstances whatsoever in favor of reinforced concrete; indeed, the question of the supply of aggregate was a very difficult one, as it had to be brought from twenty-five to thirty miles by rail. In my experience I have found that the foregoing figures will apply to all cases of ordinary buildings costing more than, say, £2000. A building of less cost will, generally speaking, be found cheaper in some other form of construction, and I believe walls will nearly always be found cheaper in brick panels than in concrete slabs.

The freedom of concrete from deterioration permits of savings in maintenance charges. These are exceedingly great in large series of factory buildings, and can never be shown on paper. Maintenance means more than merely guarding against the ravages of time. The necessity for maintenance implies decay; the maintenance costs are a dead loss, and maintenance is in itself a thankless job owing to the fact that it is simply patched-up work, merely staving off the inevitable, which every year becomes at once more onerous and more useless.

Perhaps the unique merit of reinforced concrete lies in its extraordinary adaptability. There is no other building material which can be put to such extraordinarily diverse uses without unwarrantable eccentricity or expense. I am able to give illustrations which emphasize this claim in a conclusive manner. The value of a material which can be used for practically any purpose which may arise in the construction of the wide variety of buildings comprised in industrial works need hardly be dilated upon. The practical economy of such a material is also evident. Provided there are no insurmountable difficulties in getting on to the site steel rods, timber, gravel, and cement, we have at hand constituents which are capable of being moulded into any shape and resisting any strain and fulfill purposes which collectively would require the use of a large number of different materials. In the ingredients of reinforced concrete there is nothing which cannot be readily obtained in the most remote locality of the kingdom.

. Following on the adaptability of reinforced concrete is the speed with which construction can go forward. If a contractor will lay down a well-considered and efficient plant, the rapidity with which a concrete job can go forward is remarkable. A larger number of workmen (mostly unskilled labor) can be usefully employed, and the building as a whole can be proceeded with uniformly and in a manner which simplifies supervision. Should it be found desirable in a steel or iron construction to make alterations, time is lost in waiting for the various revised members to be delivered. With reinforced concrete such deviations can readily be made.

An objection which is often urged against concrete buildings, which does not apply to brickwork or the usual form of construction, is that it is by nature unsightly. If appearance is an object in a reinforced concrete building, I do not hesitate for a moment to say that a very agreeable effect can be obtained by perfectly legitimate and economical means. In the case of one high factory building the actual appearance is far better owing to the selection of a good-colored facing brick and the effect of the shadows, without which the façade, of course, looks lifeless and uninteresting. The cost of the decorative work on this building represents .02 per cent of the total cost of the building, and this is showing a deference to public feelings at a very cheap rate.

Another objection which may be held against reinforced concrete, especially for factory construction, is the great difficulty of making alterations which may be found necessary for various reasons, such as an expansion of business; but in the first place a successful factory owner should be able to see so far ahead that possible extensions can be provided for at the outset; secondly, that the practice of installing departments into buildings not intended for their use always produces inefficiency and undue expense; and thirdly, that, assuming the building has to be altered owing to circumstances which no brain could have foreseen, such extensions and alterations are not impossible. Even if the expense of same is abnormal, it is one of those factors which every shrewd business man will be prepared for; for in the same way he has frequently to throw on the scrap-heap a valuable machine which has been supplanted by something which saves more time or labor in output.

In this connection the American will frequently tell you that if he builds a factory which will last without undue maintenance a couple of generations, he has more than done his duty by posterity. We, personally, can hardly appreciate this point of view, but that the American is certainly willing to raze to the ground any building which he considers is out of date is evidenced by the fact that one of the New York skyscrapers is being taken down because after a few years' existence it is found to be inconvenient.

· It cannot be denied that concrete, when it has settled down, is an exceedingly tough material, but the great strength to which this material attains should hardly be urged as an objection to its use.

The inherent strength of a building constructed entirely of reinforced concrete compares favorably with a building in any other material or combination of materials. Much has been said about the monolithic nature of reinforced concrete. We should not, however, forget that although a building is monolithic it is not monoferric (if such a word be allowable)— that is to say, that the steelwork consists of a multitude of small members held together by the concrete, but the external adhesion of concrete to steelwork makes a well-designed structure in practice a jointless one. Thus, an eccentric load on one portion of the building is disseminated over a large area of the surrounding structural members, and the local tendency of a building to spread or settle is resisted, not by the members locally affected but by the structure as a whole.

In conclusion, factory buildings are liable to be grossly overloaded, the costs are always reduced to the utmost farthing, and the buildings are not usually treated with such care as domestic or public buildings, and, as mentioned before, are liable to be severely mutilated and subjected to the deleterious effects of steam, vapors, fumes, acids, oils and undue vibration, etc., and consequently the factor of safety in design should never be reduced below four. It is also advisable to construct certain portions with even an increased factor, as, for instance, flat roofs which will with certainty be used for storage, and walls, beams, slabs, and columns, which are generally subjected to the suspension of shafting, motors, and other live loads without consideration of the purpose for which they have been actually designed.

I think that in view of the enormous extent in which reinforced concrete has been used for buildings of this class during the past few years that it has been comparatively immune from failure.

RESIDENCE OF MR. JAMES L. FLOOD, SAN FRANCISCO
BLISS & FAVILLE.   ARCHITECTS

A "HOUSE OF STEPS" IN PARIS

*This method of apartment house building gives the occupants all the advantages of a
hillside dwelling—light, air, and view—and a balcony as fine as the suburbanite's
porch. Each family, moreover, owns its own apartment.*

Unique Apartment House Architecture

A FIRM of architects in Paris recently completed a somewhat fantastic
seven-story apartment house that might be copied to good advantage by San Francisco architects in search of something different for
the North Point hills. The Paris house has been appropriately termed
the **maison** à gradius or "house of steps." Each floor is set back several
feet from the one below, thereby giving the front of the apartment a
decided slope. Describing this building in the American City, Charles J.
Storey writes:

"Paris, in spite of its many wide streets and its splendid system of
boulevards and frequent squares and parks, has a large number of ancient,
narrow streets, and it is in these that the architects expect their scheme
of building to be of great use.

"Each floor above the third is set back some eight feet, and the space
thus left open is converted into a balcony or terrace. By means of an
ingenious arrangement of the overhang, the privacy of the occupant below
is secured, for, although an unobstructed view of the street is given, the

terrace below cannot be seen. In the finished house the terrace has a row of plants along the edge, and the green, viewed from the street, has a most pleasing effect. An ornamental iron railing protects the edge of the terrace and provides an open-air playground.

"This style of building, if constructed on both sides of a street, will give almost as much light to the lower stories as to the top ones. Actually, the apartment on the Rue Vavin gains an hour more of sunlight a day than do houses of ordinary construction situated on the same side of the same street.

"Although the building covers more ground than an ordinary one, the increased cost of land is made up by the increased height to which the building can be raised without interfering with the light of the lower floors or of those across the street. This is especially advantageous in Paris, where the building code does not permit a building on a street, say 27 feet wide, to be more than 50 feet high on the building-line. Above this height it must recede. By the plan of Sauvage and Sarazin, the architects of this innovation, ten stories may be built conforming to the spirit and the letter of the law where only six main and two inferior floors could be constructed under the usual design.

"All rooms in the model apartment have direct light either from the street or from the court at the rear. Central heat does away with the innumerable chimneys common to Paris—one for each fireplace in each room—and the architects claim a substantial saving from this one item.

"The façade of the building is finished in white-glazed brick with a simple and pleasing decorative motive in bright-blue bricks, which well set off the green flower-gardens on the terraces. The rooms are painted in quiet colors, and, unlike many French houses, are devoid of plaster decoration, having only a picture-molding. This, of course, has reduced the cost of the building, as has also the simple exterior treatment.

"Another point of interest is the ownership of the building. The house has been constructed by a company formed of persons who were willing to live together, and each shareholder owns his own apartment. This co-operative plan insures each member of the corporation the full or partial ownership of his home, according to the amount invested. For example, if a man has subscribed $10,000 he will have a reduction in his rent of, say, $500 a year. He will in reality have his apartment rent free and also receive a dividend on his investment if the venture proves as profitable as is anticipated."

Los Angeles Architectural Exhibit

The annual architectural exhibit under the auspices of the Southern California Chapter of the American Institute of Architects will be held in the Metropolitan building, opening Thursday, March 1st, and continuing two weeks. The following committee of architects, appointed by President J. E. Allison of the Southern California Chapter, will have charge of the exhibit: Myron Hunt, chairman; A. F. Rosenheim, S. Tilden Norton, John C. Austin, and S. B. Marston. Space for the exhibit will be provided on the sixth floor of the Metropolitan building.

Mr. William L. Woollett's Criticism of the San Francisco City Hall

By B. J. S. CAHILL, Architect

IN the September number of The Architect and Engineer Mr. Woollett contributed some notes apropos of my description of the City Hall in the number preceding.

Mr. Woollett's criticisms obviously did not purport to be understood very literally, nor, from the tone of his article, do I imagine he meant his censures to be taken as seriously as some of his readers took them. Mr. Woollett objected to my article because it found no fault with the building, whereupon he dwells a moment on its defects. But some of his readers, quite ignoring Mr. Woollett's substantial tribute to the building's qualities, have rather gleefully seized on the censures while they have passed over the praise. Mr. Woollett admits that "this building is beautiful" and "conscientiously seconds the splendid compliments of Mr. Cahill."

Those who gloated over the censure, I fear, did it not from any sort of wistful regret that Art had not been adequately served. They rather rejoiced in the hope that a rival had been adequately "knocked."

And this is the danger and mischief of this type of offhand "criticism" made when "criticism" (in the sense of censure) can be of little practical value.

Mr. Woollett seems to regret "the unalloyed praise of this skillful paper" and thinks that a "truly critical article might be acceptable."

The right time to "criticise," if by criticism we mean fault finding (which is not the correct meaning of the word), is when the building plans are agreed upon but not carried out. In writing of the original competition (Architect and Engineer, July, 1912), I said:

"Those of us who imagined that such an enticing appeal to the talent of a town would bring out local characteristics or new tendencies were woefully disappointed." But "for work to be done in a hurry and municipal work at that, no doubt it is wise to choose 'the regular thing.' Even in work where time is not such an important element, there are good arguments in favor of adopting some familiar form or feature that has been done well and done often rather than risk failure in attempted creations of our own. The leading architectural firm of the country has shown how successfully this can be done. The progressives in the profession who lament the chosen design might take consolation in the fact, too, that public work must almost necessarily be behind the general line of march. It indicates the architectural status of the community *en masse* rather than the standard of the advanced few. A city hall design should express the people rather than the profession. It should express the voters' idea of architecture rather than the ideas of the votaries of architecture. And perhaps, after all, this community judgment is the best of all judgments in the long run."

This point, of course, was made touching the general and familiar lines of the City Hall design as shown on small scale competition sketches, but has no bearing on the degree of excellence possible by developing the detail intensively within the lines of the familiar and rather conventional looking cadre.

In concluding I pointed out several questionable features. For example: "The scale of the four interior great piers, it will be noted, is actually bigger than anything on the exterior façade." On the working

drawings this big order was actually reduced fifty per cent by the introduction of a base course.

"A plaster model," I predicted, "will probably call for a more stilted
dome." And a model was made and the dome was stilted and broadened, too.

Regarding the scale of the exterior, I wrote: "As an example of the
fickleness of fashion in building as in dress, it will be noted that 'the big
column' did not win. Neither did the long colonnade. Whether this indicates a reaction or whether the smaller interrupted order was dictated
by the needs of the composition is a difficult matter to determine. Personally I incline to the latter view. Either the big column or the big
dome must dominate. In this case I seem to feel that the dome is the
important thing and that its vertical expression was a paramount need."

It will serve our purpose to quote another paragraph, this time from
the October issue:

"A public building like the City Hall, selected in a competition wherein
over ninety trained architects—the best we have—take an eager part
is, *ipso facto*, an elaborate final judgment that this plan now chosen, which
this firm of architects has prepared on paper, is the best that our elaborate
and expensive machinery of selection can hit upon. If still further judgment (i. e., criticism) is to be rendered on top of this, it must necessarily
be in the nature of further endorsement or explanation, with perhaps
some well-considered suggestions where improvements in minor matters
seem to be within reason. This sort of criticism serves a definite, useful
purpose, whereas a belated wail, when the structure is finished, that it is
all wrong, serves no purpose but to provoke a snicker among the ground-
ling, tickle the controvertialists of the hostile camp" (and there are, of
course, different schools or viewpoints in all the arts) "and arouse the
instincts of those more keen for the lower contentiousness than for the
higher criticism. * * *

"If radical objection is made to the whole spirit and character of any
important building representing the genius of the time and place so completely as does the new City Hall of San Francisco, objections can only
have value that include also all other buildings done at the same period
and in the same spirit."

Mr. Woollett bewails the lack of local spirit and local history in the
City Hall design and finds it tame, unheroic and altogether too nice and
urbane to express the hardy pioneers, the big-souled fighting men of the
West, Mackay, Fair, Flood, O'Brien and the rest.

Now all this is perfectly obvious to most of us, more especially to
those of us who do not belong here and are not part of this picturesque
pioneering. We all think these things, but on second thought we all
abandon any attempt to express them, for the excellent reason that any
flavor of the primordial heroic and abysmal thing is exactly what a community in that phase of its existence wants to forget and get away from.

Nothing in the whole psychology of national art is more firmly established than this. The very last thing that a rather raw and new community wishes is to be reminded, no matter how magnificently, of its all
too conscious rudeness and crudeness. The one thing a pioneer settlement most devoutly desires is to be considered urbane and refined. And
it is in strange confirmation of this principle, which, of course, works
both ways, that Mr. Woollett took his example of an heroic scale building, the School of Technology, not from Chicago or Salt Lake, but from
the most civilized and sophisticated city in the country, Boston!

Our highly refined, exquisite City Hall exactly suits the temper of a town which so hotly resents being called "Frisco"—a name by which it is affectionately known over the whole wide world!

George Bernard Shaw relates an amusing custom of a certain great European statesman whose difficult task was to select the right kind of men for very varied purposes. In his reception room he had the wall of one side covered with pictures of battles, sieges and sackings of towns; scenes of riot and bloodshed. On the opposite wall were hung pastoral idyls, pictures of domestic peace, family life and rural serenity. The men he found absorbed in the admiration of scenes of blood and violence he put to tasks calling for patience, sympathy and kindliness. Those who turned to the other wall and were attracted to scenes of gentleness and peace he allotted to positions demanding pugnacity and truculence.

In other words, men enjoy an environment that is in contrast and not in harmony with their habitual mental complexes. Your real artist paints in a dingy, mussed-up workroom, while your money magnate sits in a bower of beauty. No one likes home comforts like a soldier or a ship master, and no one reads murder trials and other police horrors quite so assiduously as do mild old ladies who habitually attend church. It is the barkeeper who tries to act like a gentleman and the college man who dresses like a tough.

* * * * *

In my article on the City Hall I tried to show why American taste in architecture, literature and art ran to refinement and "delicatesse" and I showed that it was largely because we are still in the trail-making period of our culture. I might have added that Massachusetts, being on the oldest edge of the continent, and California on the newest, we might infer that their architectural expression would contrast with their spirit in an inverse ratio; sedate and scholarly Boston producing the heroic Tech and heroic San Francisco producing our scholarly and sedate City Hall.

So much for the larger argument.

When we come to matters of technique and detail we see why for many reasons a big scale building would have been impossible. To begin with, the new "Tech" building at Cambridge spreads over a very much larger area than our City Hall, which, as Mr. Woollett says, "the giants who live in such buildings could pick up and carry under their arms through the main portal."

This is a figure of speech and, of course, not in the least bit literally true. But it IS literally true that if the Parthenon could be moved horizontally off the Acropolis a few hundred yards it could have been dropped bodily into the later Roman temple of Jupiter Olympus—and when this was done the Erectheum, the Propylæa, the temple of Nike Apteros and a dozen other of the marvels of this supreme spot on all earth could have been dumped in, too. And still from the exterior no one would know what had happened, so big was this late Roman monster compared to all the glories of Athens built before it!

Now I want to ask what architect thinks about this Roman Corinthian temple when Athens is mentioned? In comparison with the priceless art treasures of the Acropolis this huge temple is of little more value than a pile of rock. If anyone thinks of the Corinthian order even at all in connection with Athens of old, it is merely of its budding prototype in the monument of Lysicrates, the drum, cornice, finial, podium and all of which could have been carved out of a section of one of the great columns of this temple! But architecturally the little monument showing the beginning of the Corinthian ·order has more claim to respect than the giant one which foretells its end. The first was great, the second was only big. Old-fashioned alienists used to call the passion for big things "the folly of grandeurs" and as a matter of fact big scale is really more a mania than a merit—megalomania is the precise word for it.

And it is, in reality, rather a vulgar obsession. What Gothic enthusiast would place the noble perfection of Amiens cathedral above the commonplace colossus of Cologne? Devout young pilgrims to Rome may stand literally petrified by the sight of Saint Peters, which was made overwhelming for this particular purpose, but the more masterly minds detached from the bias of religion will soon sense the gulf that separates what is really precious from what is merely pretentious—and will pass on to smaller and better things.

Mr. Woollett's diction is not without signs of a carelessness rather inexcusable in sounding this note of deliberate censure, however much this censure may be subsequently qualified and ·nullified. For instance, he says: "On account of the small scale of the buildings San Francisco's Civic Center is not 'heroic'; it is not 'grand'; it is not 'sublime'; it is not 'classic.' * * * "

If we are to understand that classic is more or less synonymous with what is heroic, grand and sublime, why, then, Mr. Woollett attaches no definite meaning to this word. Indeed, he does much worse; he attaches a meaning to the word by implication which is not only indefinite but quite false, as though he should say that blood was green or sheep were goats. And in this Mr. Woollett seems to speak as a painter or writer rather than as an architect. The term classic is rightly applied to any work of art conceived in perfect sanity, executed with perfect technique and so free from the bias of time and place that it is never out of date and of course as a consequence eternally fit to teach in schools and classes. Classic art is normal art and it follows that it is essentially free from over emphasis, exaggeration, fashion, bias, passion or any form of passing mode or mania.

From this it follows that classic excellence is a matter of balance, proportion, restraint, sobriety and calmness, as distinguished from the more temporal and temperamental forms of art that grow out of violence of feeling from within the soul or disturbing conditions from without—passion and fashion.

In architecture we use the term classic much as in literature, to designate the eternal masterpieces of the antique world where this perfection was first attained. The word has this historical period meaning. It also has a wider meaning, to denote a work in any art or any period down to the last minute. And the word is even carried outside the domain of art into sport, athletics, etc.

The appeal of classic art, with its perfection of form and suppression of undue emphasis in any one direction, naturally excludes all that is sensational, mordant or moody. In personal deportment the classic quality becomes poise, or what the the French call "tenue" and the English "good form." Lessing pointed out that Greek sculptures show no trace of feeling on the faces even of warriors engaged in deadliest combat. Thus, while it delights in heroes, it abhors heroics. It is essentially aristocratic and represents the highest of human ideals. So lofty is the classic spirit, indeed, that it is impossible that it should pervade and animate our ordinary needs and deeds exclusively.

·A wholly antithetical school of expression must serve to express the problems and crises that develop from day to day. This mode may be roughly termed the Romantic. It is the mode for strife and adventure of each period of a person or a people. All art or literature in this mode runs into extremes. It expresses what is abnormal—and consequently of brief and passing duration, but quite obviously of more biting human interest. The classic mode is for the ages and historic periods, the Romantic and others for the passing moment. The one lives in the exalted region of typical and abstract ideas, the other dwells with and serves us from day to day.

The classic spirit is therefore not the heroic; quite otherwise. It does not delight in hugeness of scale nor any other form of emphasis or exaggeration. Its most persistent spirit seeks invariably the middle way. Nor is the classic spirit concerned at all, except quite incidentally, with commemoration of local or historical episodes. This is the supreme glory of the classic spirit, the very characteristic that makes it immortal—above time and independent of place. How on earth could any art be local and commemorative and at the same time be universal and for all time? A classic masterpiece in its essence is not even national.

In thinking along these lines and in a score of other directions that will crowd the reader's mind, it becomes clear that Mr. Woollett's demand in our City Hall for big scale, for the heroic mood, for sculptural annals of our forty-niners, for some expression of our "naif bohemianism," are all of them quite out of key with the classic spirit. The City Hall is, first of all, an office building on rather a restricted area. A huge scale order on the exterior might give a sensational thrill, but it would be at the sacrifice of more practical needs. It would necessitate larger bays, quite embarrassing in a small roomed structure, as contrasted with a museum or art gallery. It would mean a very high entablature of dead wall where light is needed; it would in addition quite misrepresent the interior.

As a matter of fact, the classic spirit does not and never did depend on "features." Its excellence is and always has been based on intensive and not extensive development. Size and scale have nothing to do with classic excellence whose lines are perfectly simple and unexciting. The merit is in the delicacy and balance of one part with another, in harmony, proportion, finish and a certain detachableness that characterizes animal organisms. Also, like animal organism, a classic structure develops symmetry from side to side and variety from end to end. And also, as with animal organisms, no part can be added without producing monstrosity and no part taken away without inflicting mutilation.

The demand for mere bigness in classic structures seems immature and childish. It is a popular and human failing, but, as we have seen, classic perfection is not really and never was for the sensation-loving public, which, it seems to me, too often includes artists and authors.

As to sculptural ornament depicting the doughty deeds of Flood, O'Brien & Co., surely Mr. Woollett is getting a little satirical!

If we had sculptors, and time permitted, no one could object to pictorial annals, but it is and always has been the art that counted and was worth while, and not the story. Who, outside of archaeologists and antiquaries, cares a rap what the procession of the peplum was all about? The art and technique of these masterful reliefs are what posterity values. The sculptors of the Parthenon knew this evidently and out of all stirring subjects that might have been put upon these friezes they chose a religious ritual for its pictorial value mainly. Of all futile expenditures of human brains and ingenuity I have always thought that the allegorical frescoes and friezes and groups on public buildings of this or any other country really yielded the very smallest returns. I speak of their local and historical value quite apart from their artistic merits. Personally I have looked at miles of frescoes and whole communities of stone and marble statues. Conscientious tourists of thrifty instincts, with guide book in hand, will often insist on deciphering the precise meaning of these cryptic representations, with an eye to getting their money's worth. They do not care much for the picture or the group unless they know exactly what each is all about. To people with tireless energy and abundant time there must be a fine sense of conquest in this performance.

But for my part I can enjoy these things immensely as Art, but as Allegory they are simply tiresome.

Now I have no doubt that Messrs. Bakewell & Brown could have crowded the City Hall with emblems of our origin, our civic history and our gorgeous destiny and other fine things of that kind, if time had permitted. But one can easily see that the difficulties to be overcome in organizing and controlling the large operations of so important a building would not have yielded time to go into these delicate and difficult enterprises. They have shown far more wisdom in not risking failure than by attempting something not only at variance with the spirit of classic design but something for which no adequate machinery of production is ready to hand. In these times, when everybody can read and buildings are no longer sculptured bibles, all the tendencies flow away from and not towards symbolism in detail, fables in frescoe or stories in stone.

And much the same arguments can be urged against attempts at optical refinements and artificial perspective, the alleged utter absence of which so worries Mr. Woollett.

In our day of organized labor, stone cutting machinery, and with our artisans in the main lacking in enthusiasm for their crafts as individuals, it is extremely difficult to secure intelligent co-operation in practice so at variance with the perfunctory routine of the average stone yard. I know it can be done and I have several times done it myself in small work over which complete personal control is possible.

Now the widening in plan of the end bays of a colonnade or an arcade involves no difficulties and the inclination of columns in a ring under a dome is simple enough and is habitually done (I believe it is actually done in our City Hall dome). But it is by no means so easy to incline exterior columns worked in granite. Interior plaster or exterior cement lend themselves better to these niceties. In granite work they involve many special drawings and special processes fatally disconcerting to the practice and methods of the average stone working contractor. One only has to consider for a moment the hand work involved in giving a slight curvature to the corona on a large pediment. It would call for infinitesimal variations on the jointing planes and arrises of each separate stone. A slight curvature in plan to achieve the same optical results would be just as complicated. And all this raises the question as to how much importance we actually attach to these refinements. Mr. Woollett unwittingly furnishes an admirable answer. He says in effect that we are so little sensitive to the intensive excellencies of form in plain work in the classic mode that we must stimulate interest in our architecture by the popular appeal of what is huge in scale and heroic in sentiment. And the entire argument rests finally on this one fact. If we have the fine sensitiveness of the absolutely normal "mens sana in corpore sano," the prime conditions for creating and enjoying classic architecture, we do not need the more vulgar stimulant of mere size in our scale or sentiment in our stone work.

As a matter of fact, Mr. Woollett and those who think with him are not merely finding fault with the design of our City Hall, but are entering a protest against the spirit and scope of all classic architecture in favor of some other school in which form is subordinated to feeling. His criticism deploring the absence of the latter element is absolutely inconsistent with the fault he finds with the lack of refinement in the former.

And here we are up against the fallacy of too indiscriminate eclecticism. We want, too often, to marry the detached excellences of one style with those of another which is neither as simple nor as easy as it sounds. In this we are reminded of that enthusiastic eugenist who succeeded in making a match between a very homely but exceedingly brainy man and a magnificent looking but quite stupid woman. When, instead of the superman expected of this alliance, the issue was a blend of the ugliness of one parent with brainlessness of the other!

In conclusion I wish to applaud the editor of this magazine for encouraging this sort of discussion, and I would like also to add that I am quite at one with Mr. Woollett in his implied regrets that we haven't a little more of keen interest in these controversies that obtained in the days of that old scaramouch, Cellini.

*   *   *

New State Bill Endorsed

An adjourned meeting of the San Francisco Chapter of the American Institute of Architects was held on Saturday, January 20th, to consider the proposed new bill regulating the practice of architecture. Mr. Selby, the attorney for the State Board of Architecture, was present and gave a synopsis and opinion as to the new legislation.

It was moved and seconded that the amendments to the present act, regulating the practice of architecture, prepared by the State Board of Architecture, be recommended by the Chapter and that the proposed new law to govern the safety of buildings prepared by the Southern California Chapter be not opposed.

At a special meeting held on Tuesday, January 23d, it was voted to endorse the general intent of the law proposed by the Southern California Chapter to govern the safety of buildings and the legislative committee of the Chapter was authorized to consult with the committee of the Southern California Chapter, with full power to act.

*   *   *

New Theatre to Seat 6,000

Messrs. Cunningham & Politeo have been commissioned to prepare plans for a new moving picture theatre to be erected on the Central Park site at Eighth and Market streets, San Francisco. It will be the largest theatre west of Chicago, seating 6,000 persons and costing $350,000. There will be no galleries. The project has been financed by the McCreery Estate.

*   *   *

$100,000 Dormitory Planned

Messrs. Bakewell & Brown of San Francisco have been commissioned to prepare plans for a new girls' dormitory at Mills College. The building will be designed in the Mission type and will cost $100,000.

APARTMENT HOUSE FOR MR. F. NELSON, OAKLAND
C. H. Miller, Architect

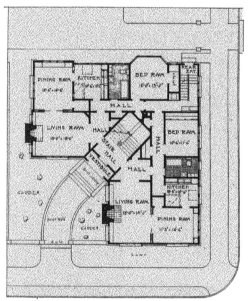

FIRST FLOOR AND PLOT PLAN

FLOOR PLAN, APARTMENT HOUSE FOR MR. F. NELSON, OAKLAND
C. H. Miller, Architect

GLEN GARRY APARTMENTS, BERKELEY
W. H. Ratcliff, Jr., Architect

Apartment Houses

THE apartment is no longer essentially the dwelling for the poor, the working and the middle classes—it is the home of the rich, the multi-millionaire—twenty-seven rooms and nine baths, a palace on a floor, cleverly designed, wonderfully wrought—rent $30,000 a year.

The development of the apartment house throughout the country is a striking feature in our modern American life. It is the modernity that brings the rents. The owner who is alive to the demands and the architect who is able to give him the best plans and equipment meets with success.

In other cities than New York there are a few large apartment houses, but New York is where they greatly flourish. The Record and Guide of New York recently had this to say of the situation:

"An examination of the national income tax figures may tend toward an explanation of the success which has attended the construction of high-class apartment houses and private residences the last year. The demand for residential accommodations has been unprecedented, and the call for space ranging in rental from $3000 to $25,000 a year has been so insistent that the efforts of builders directed toward meeting this demand have been in practically every instance well rewarded. A few years ago renting from the plans was unheard of, yet 1916 has witnessed, as a common experience, leases closed almost over the architects' working boards. Numerous cases may be cited where buildings have been entirely rented from the plans before a single tenant was in possession."

ANGELUS APARTMENTS, SAN FRANCISCO
RIGHETTI & HEADMAN,   · ARCHITECTS

. DETAIL ENTRANCE, ANGELUS APARTMENTS
RIGHETTI & HEADMAN,   ARCHITECTS

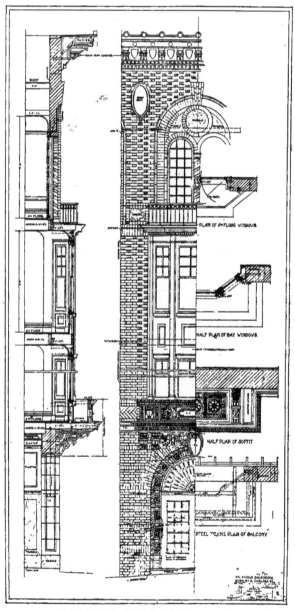

SCALE DETAIL, ANGELUS APARTMENTS, SAN FRANCISCO
RIGHETTI & HEADMAN,   ARCHITECTS

Detail Top Story,
Angelus Apartments

Righetti & Headman,
Architects

OAK LODGE APARTMENTS, OAKLAND
Chas. W. McCall, Architect

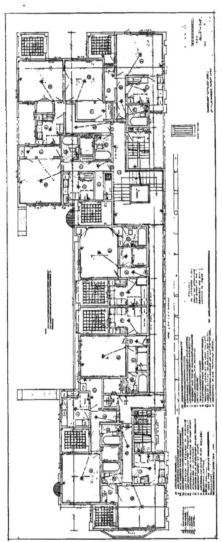

TYPICAL FLOOR PLAN, OAK LODGE APARTMENTS
CHAS. W. McCALL,
ARCHITECT

RIVERSIDE APARTMENTS, SAN FRANCISCO
C. A. MEUSDORFFER,   ARCHITECT

McKENZIE APARTMENTS, VAN NESS AVENUE AND BUSH STREET, SAN FRANCISCO

Unique Feature of Chicago Apartments

A rather unusual apartment house is planned for Chicago, Ill., the feature consisting in the fact that, although the building is to be fully six stories high, it will contain no more than four apartments. The first floor is to be devoted to an entrance hall, entertainment room, retiring rooms, service kitchen, storerooms, janitor's flat, chauffeurs' rooms and garage. The top floor will contain a roof garden, guest rooms, outside sleeping quarters and baths. Each of the apartments is to contain thirteen rooms and four baths. The building will occupy a lot 60 x 170, but will cover only a depth of 157 feet. It will be of reinforced concrete and cost $175,000.

"The Outlook and Inlook Architectural"*

By JOHN GALEN HOWARD, F. A. I. A.

" A S the twig is bent the tree is inclined." The die was cast, for the distinctive character of American architecture, for all time, I guess, when a certain Pilgrim first set an old-world foot on Plymouth Rock and found it—good building material; a trifle hard and therefore difficult to work, doubtless, with some few fractures, or at all events distinctly noticeable stratifications or lines of cleavage, and with not a few rough edges; but, on the whole, sound, as rocks go, and firmly fixed in ancient world-tradition. Strong stuff was Plymouth Rock; but it held its own not merely by reason of its strength, but by virtue of the sort of strength it had. An architecture is determined neither by material alone nor by the mind that moulds it, but by both together, inseparable and interactive. No mere cart-horse kind of power was the force which fashioned Plymouth Rock; kinship in mettle to the Arabian thoroughbred gave it aptness to the desert task, with its long thirsts and hungers, its utter isolations, its lonesome yearnings. Not mere strength, but refined strength, was its property. For Refinement—that sort which is a thing of eliminations rather than of delicacies and determined about equally by temperament (coldness of temperament, agreed, in this case) and by means too straitened for much kicking over the traces even had the blood been hotter; Refinement was one, if not the, salient characteristic of the architecture which became in those old days out of arduously shapen Plymouth Rock; and in spite of all the kicking over the traces in which our people have indulged in more recent times, Refinement, even though it be of another stripe, is still a dominant characteristic of the American style. There is, I suppose, little room for disagreement as to the old work—look at the delicate, thin treatment everywhere, the paucity of ornament, the dryness of surface, the amenity (not inconsistent with a degree of vigor either) of the whole—above all the total absence of anything remotely resembling "splurge." These points witness a psychological tendency quite independent in a way of the particular forms used—of the "styles" in which it found its tongue. One thinks of the pure beauty of the Greek work: of the grandeur of the Roman: Byzantine spells splendor: the mediæval cathedrals voice daring aspiration—so our Colonial work connotes essentially that not very large, perhaps, but at any rate (so far as it goes) admirable quality which I have named—and, of that quality, the phase in which almost ascetic restraint plays the major part. Granted. But is it as readily evident that that same quality runs through, and indeed informs our characteristic architecture of today—with its wide range of "styles," its genuine eclecticism, from the point of view of the field as a whole, however "correct," within their own choice of style, individual practitioners may be; is it clear that this note of refinement is dominant? Does the point need some discussion? That may be.

Suppose, to start with, we look back over the way we have come.

"Cut out passion!" not "Make passion lovely!" was the law—unwritten— of early cis-Atlantic effort in the way of art, as of life; of art, what there was of it, doubtless because of life. Yet, after all, he who sets himself consciously to cut out passion lets his cat out of the bag—there must have been the passion to cut out; and the chances are that, sooner or later, if he seeks to cut out passion by putting it in a bag, he will bring about all the more viciously mordant scratchings, and, in the end, if the cat is really

*An address before the National Institute of Arts and Letters, New York.

there, and a cat, with the customary complement of lives, and all the more
tempestuous felinity of escape, by way of rugged rent instead of by way of
neatly hemstitched placket. We have sometimes been privileged to observe
the cat in the act of issuing from the bag, and by that issue—as indeed by
all self-respecting cats—there hangs, if you will permit the expression, a
tale: and, in this case, what is more, a tale of passion—which proves reas-
suringly that the cat was there anyway. As the saying is, "A muffled
cat is no good mouser." Open bags make more successful nests than do
tied bags prisons—for the architect they make capital warm nests in fact,
as "styles," while as prisons "styles" are apt to be either too strong, in
which case they inhibit action, or else they are too flimsy and invite dis-
respect. If at times our cat has been too closely muffled, the escapes, not
to say the escapades, have restored, or tended to restore a fair average.
As a whole our architecture can hardly be said to be too "correct"!

Half a century or more ago we saw the cat of the English Gothic
revival, poor creature though it were, and worse for water-wear (which
all cats hate), scratch out the eyes of our Colonial tradition, and leave it
nigh to death, with "none so mean to do him reverence." The purest
poetic justice was done when, reversing the ancient course of architectural
history, Gothic was transmogrified into Romanesque. The most anemic of
all lack-cap stocks begot the fullest blooded of all sports. There was
passion for you! and not in a bag at that! But is this a cat I see? Nay,
a very lion in the way, a king of cats, 'twould seem, who can consent no
further than to hold a bag to be a convenient nest or lair of refuge, when desired, but never, never, never such a pitiful thing as a prison. "In truth, the
prison, unto which we doom ourselves, no prison is," and styles may be comforts to the creative mind, but only on condition that they have no drawing
strings. So, at all events, Richardson regarded his Romanesque; its sounding name was as an open sesame to consideration,—a big stick of resonant
"authority" if you like,—but, you may rest well assured, not for a moment
a limitation to the activities of his imagination. And that may be one
reason why his "style" was not found to serve in the long run. It was too
personal, it operated on too narrow a margin of common consent, in spite
of all its own robust splendor. Being so personal, the range of vision, for
other workers, was too close—there was not room enough in it for more
than that one great personality which informed and filled it and made it in
certain ways, and in certain very important ways, too, big with promise.

All this time poor little Colonius lay stripped of his raiment and wounded
by the way. Priest in the gown of Gothic, and Levite with Provencal
scrip, had not so much as looked on him, but passed by on the other side.
"But a certain Samaritan, as he journeyed, came where he was; and when
he saw him, he had compassion on him." On the face of things, Colonius
Redivivus owed his oil and wine to the insight, taste and wisdom of McKim
and White, and others of their group: (I should say particularly Mead,
but for the manner of Anthologies, which omit the living names lest their
owners blush becomingly, no doubt): but he owed his resuscitation fundamentally to his Americanism. McKim, Mead and White were the active
instrument of a latent movement larger than themselves. The Colonial
revival succeeded, not because that kind of architecture was the best conceivable, or because it was in such refreshing contrast with the preceding
fashion, or because of the personal power of those who reintroduced it,
great as that power was, or for any other reason whatsoever, but that it
was in real harmony with the American instinct, taste and ideal. And it
had the further advantage of being a worthy tradition, all the stronger

and more acceptable for having been neglected for a time. Penitence pointed our return. Convalescence gave a fillip to what might otherwise have seemed insipid. Plymouth Rock too, under these circumstances, was found to have a sparkle. We felt as if we had got back home from hospital and had a reasoning sense of knowing where we were. Very likely we struck out too blindly in our new health against the spell that just now bound us. We hated Romanesque so cordially that we could not fairly focus the compelling genius that loomed behind and above the smoke of our temporary aberration. In the new joy of finding a working system of architectural hygiene to which we were all equally heritors,—discovered to us, and interpreted, by masters, it is true, but ours just as much as theirs, after all,—we became possessed of a sense of well-being and of mastery which was most agreeable. And it was a habit well worth while acquiring, to be sure,—that using of a style whose limits we well know, and were pleased to accept. It induced a frame of mind which enabled us later to turn to other closely related, more monumental not to say more fundamental styles (styles which had all the while underlain the Colonial), and work in them with something flatteringly resembling the ease of mastery; with no small degree of archeological dryness, at times, we must concede, but with a "correctness" which, for the time being, was in itself a valuable quality, providing the tendency were not carried too far. Architecture has, like other growing phenomena, to go to school before it can wisely be emancipated. It is a distinctly promising sign of future power, for a young people and for a young art as for a young man, feeling his oats, looking upon his individuality and finding it good, conscious of original power, to forget self for the time being in the quiet, assiduous acquisition of knowledge already established by others. The time for fresh personal expression will come later. But get the schooling first,—and, of course, as early as may be; for the blade of creative originality may lose its edge if it keep scabbard too long.

I have spoken of the succession of architectural styles among us. That is merely a convenient way of alluding to the several phases through which this art, and perhaps other arts as well, have passed in these latter decades. But I don't wish to lay too much stress on these phrases as "styles." In fact I do not take much stock in 'styles' anyway. What I do take stock in, all I can get, and have the money to pay for, and I pray for more, is Style. The Gothic revival in this country in the middle of the last century was not really a revival of Gothic at all. The fact that pointed arches "came in," the pointeder the better, had nothing to do with it. The pointed arch was a fashion in architectural dress merely, like the crinoline or the poke bonnet; but gracious me! did you ever think for one minute that the lady inside the crinoline was that shape?—No more, then, the architecture that wore pointed arches was that kind inwardly. I adore the real thing too devotedly to let it be supposed that I mean what I say when I call that sort of thing Gothic; but one can't always tack across the page a dozen times to make port. One must go as the crow flies, especially if there's but twenty minutes headway or so. Take the old word for the new thought, and let's get on. Just as the Gothic revival wasn't Gothic, neither was the Romanesque Romanesque. They were both little more than the manifestation of phrases of our national life—ante-bellum and post-bellum. The former was the expression of a life gone to seed, dried up, finished, the last leaf dropped—short of a new sowing. Then was "the winter of our discontent";—the "glorious summer" followed with all the exuberance of new life, and its expression in architecture was more exuberant even than itself, because of the overwhelming exuberance of the man responsible for the architecture. Of course in this we have to reckon with the wholly extraordinary Richardson. Without him and his personal passion for Romanesque, we should have had some other exuberance. He, like all other great men, have happened at just the right moment. Those not on our list have happened at the wrong moment: though, of course, the great moment tends to enlarge all its men, and make its great ones greater. That's what happened to Richardson; he was the great personality of the art of his time,—the period of reconstruction, of the laying in of the foundations of our real national existence; and the architecture of that period was determined almost solely by him. The artist and his period, his community, grew more exuberant hand in hand, each on its own account, and each the more for the other.

And, quite contrary to what it is now the fashion to maintain, the influence of Richardson has not proved ephemeral in its larger character and significance. The art of our own time is different and larger, for his foundation work. Whether we anathematize his art or admire from afar off (for there are few or none nowadays who venture to come nigh unto it), it must be recognized that because of him, because of his breaking ground, and making big and solid and sound when we began all over again, on a firmer footing, to try to be a nation, the building that came after was bigger and solider and sounder that it would otherwise have been. Can it be thought for one instant that McKim and White, to whom we so largely owe the turning back to the classic manner, came under Richardson's intimate influence without being touched by it? Richardson's sort of radioactivity has a way of making indelible marks. He was a great man in being; they were great men in embryo, young and impressionable. They had their own point of view, and they adhered to it with the tenacity which is an attribute of the finest type of genius; but their ideas were enlarged, their views clarified and fixed, and their ideals enriched by association with their great master. And with all the daintiness of their detail, more especially at first, they took abroad with them, when they embarked with Mead on their own career, a generous measure of the Discoverer. "Vogue la Galere!"—Undoubtedly as time went on Richardson's influence, not consciously as his influence, but as the development within themselves of seeds he had wakened and nourished, though they had been sown in their very being, became more and more manifest in increased largeness of conception and organic simplicity of handling. And it is for those qualities for which we are ever more indebted to McKim, Mead and White (I speak now of the, I hope, permanent Institution, eliminating personalities) than we are for their exquisite detail, incomparable as that is. The detail was a part of our heritage,—the largeness was a needed contribution, offered in the first instance by Richardson, continued by them, and complexed with the fineness which was from of old inbred in our architectural sense. And in both these respects, of largeness and of exquisiteness alike, let me recur again for a moment to the personal note, in recognizing the ever potent influence of Mead. He had had no direct or at any rate no close association with Richardson,—he simply did not escape, and being big himself was all the readier to accept, what no one in this country has wholly escaped, whether he would or not,—the contagious largeness of that personality; to maintain which is no derogation from the original power of each member of the great firm, the permanent institution, as I have called it. It only goes to prove, what I began with, that Style in the great sense has little or nothing to do with the "style" (in the small sense) in which a given architect may be working. It is Style in the great sense that McKim, Mead and White and all others who follow the true faith of architectural development in this country have in common, difficult as it often is to put one's finger on its elements. Style overlies and includes, or may include, a multitude of "styles." And we have now right at hand an example of this,—which brings me fairly to the second stage of my discussion.

There is, I think all will be disposed to agree, a closer affinity, somehow, between the "Gothic" work of Cram, Goodhue and Ferguson (and by the way don't mix up their lovely work with the earlier "Gothic Revival" already alluded to), and the "Classic" work of McKim, Mead and White, than there is between the latter and the work of, say, Palmer and Hornbostel, for example; yet these last, too, are working mostly in a modified classic style,—even more "modified," to use Mr. Cram's word (I think it is his) than his own "modified" Gothic. Of course the truth of the matter is that neither of them is either Gothic or Classic, unless you much emphasize the "modified." Of course they both have to be modified, to meet modern conditions. I am not unfavorably criticising but rather praising them, from my own point of view, when I insist on the "modified," as both Mr. Cram and Mr. Hornbostel would surely wish me to do. I take it they use the words "Gothic" and "Classic" as I do, as short cuts. If they don't, I beg their pardon. But I must ask the privilege just the same for the purpose of the present analysis. On Gothic read Moore, and you may be convinced—though I am not, wholly, I must confess, by that particular reasoning; as for Classic, he who runs may read. But after all, this is more or less a haggling over terms.

In spite of my original intention to avoid all personal allusions in this paper, I have ventured to mention three firms; this is merely a short-cut method like my "Gothic" and "Classic"; there are many other names that might have answered my purpose almost equally well, and certainly many others that deserve admiring tributes (or the reverse) were this a piece of praise and blame; but I am merely trying to bring out the general characteristics of our architecture at this time, and its trend. I have quite inevitably named McKim, Mead and White because they stand in a peculiarly representative relation to our art. It is hardly too much to say that we have two lists of Architects—those who are McKim, Mead and White men and those who are not,—and the latter list is the smaller. But of course in the former category are included many who have not actually worked with the great firm as well as all of those who have. The list of their lineal descendants, now running into several generations of pupilage, is astonishingly long, and includes many names in the first rank of achievement. And the penumbra of that pupilage is even larger, and quite as distinguished. In the camp of that tradition is vital solidarity nowadays, pretty much, as to essentials. In the other is schism,—nay confusion worse confounded. But I seem to see two main groups here, among the minority who are not McKim, Mead and White men, which for the purposes of this discussion may be identified by the mention of the other two firms I have named. I have, then, mentioned these three firms as each representing a phase of our art now; the first stands for the simple straightforward dignity and beauty of architectural art typified in classic or renaissance feeling, as nearly as may be in an ancient manner; Palmer and Hornbostel represent indeed a pseudo-classic-renaissance type, generally taking the old Roman or Greek forms as a basis, but using them in a well-nigh wholly free and individual way, even mingled with elements from other styles, especially in ornament, which to the taste of the purist are inharmonious with the general architectonic scheme and even a superfetation upon it; while Cram, Goodhue and Ferguson represent the Gothic manner, not indeed at all punctiliously as regards archeological correctness, but yet far more so than Palmer and Hornbostel their classic: while less so perhaps than McKim, Mead and White theirs.

I am not a Gothicist by any manner of means, if to be a Gothicist means to advocate the use of pointed forms in our modern work, for general purposes, though I yield to none in admiration for the old 13th century masterpieces. Except for certain special uses such as, for instance, those churchly types to which Cram, Goodhue and Ferguson for the most part confine them, those forms seem to me not naturally expressive of our modern needs and in most cases quite out of key with our life. And yet, for all that, I feel in the psychology of Cram, Goodhue and Ferguson's work a something which in spite of the forms in which it is expressed breathes the genuine American spirit in a striking degree. Perhaps I feel the psychological quality of it all the more keenly for a certain detachment. It has a—what shall I say?—a something catholic about it, even though it be Anglican catholic, and perhaps too pointedly Anglican at that;—but if Anglican, why not, by an easy tradition, American?—that is, in fact, precisely what I am trying to identify,—the American catholic in architecture. I am seeking to ignore mere forms, in order to get at the spirit behind them. The "style" may go,—character must remain. So any work, no matter what "style" it is in, which manages to express broadly enough our national spirit, is American catholic.

Well, then, if I am right in sensing a real kinship betwixt McKim, Mead and White's work and Cram, Goodhue and Ferguson's it is interesting to ask whether the qualities they have in common can be identified. If they can I take it that we shall be in the way of identifying the dominant quality of our architecture,—the quality which a wholly disinterested observer, say five centuries hence, might see to be characteristic of our age, just as we fix on the essential note of Greek, of Roman, of Byzantine, of Mediæval work. For undoubtedly these two firms, with their adherents, not only represent two of the most vital forces in our architecture at the present time, but they represent the extremes of divergent choice as to style. Classic and Gothic,—the fight is on between these two, as between no others. If their special champions have something vital in common, it must be something very American indeed, and more important, for the purposes of the critic, even than their very "styles" themselves. All the more will this be true if we find the same something in the notable workers of strongly marked individualistic tendencies who belong to neither of these schools, if one may call them such, nor in fact to any school, since they stand practically alone—men like Sullivan, for instance, or the Ponds—but there aren't so very many of them.

To begin with, Classicists, Gothicists, Byzantinists, Eclecticists—they all despise the coarse thing, the over-done thing, like poison. Anything like a "shocker" they would avoid assiduously; they are afraid of it as with a religious fear. They would be as ashamed of a lewd architectural thought as an old maid. Refined taste is the thing. And if we are to judge of architectural tendencies by professional successes this tendency has of late become even more accentuated than ever. I suppose the work which has received the most general approval, built within these last few years, is a certain Washington house of Pope's in the Adams' manner, which carries refinement one point beyond anything else we have. Walk past it almost any day or any hour of the day and you will find some admirer on his knees (figuratively speaking) before it. I admire it heartily myself, but I mention it here merely to point my argument, without attempting to estimate its value as a milestone, or rather as a stepping-stone, to further progress. It is the dernier cri of a tendency which is practically universal among our representative architects,—refinement first, last, and all the time. Here we see the colonial tradition more powerful than ever. Character, indeed, as the Greeks held, is Fate. Plymouth Rock is still our backbone. But, you say, how about those others who are using classic as a base, yet who are farther from the representative classicists than are the Gothicists themselves?—Ah! they are perhaps the exception that proves the rule!

But, now, that word Refinement—it is an extremely "refined" word. I have used it to fix a notable quality, good or bad—good and bad—which seems to distinguish American architecture from that of most other countries nowadays. I don't wholly like the word—it has connotations somewhat too feminine. I have used it, perhaps, often enough. It has carried us far; let us not force a willing horse. If we could only find a more robust word—for a greater thing.

And any way it isn't only one quality we are looking for,—it takes more than one thing to make up the American Catholic. Surely in addition to the restrained delicacy which was so characteristic of the colonial work and which, to the extent (and more) that the original stock still colors our civilization, we must recognize as an equally universal property of American architecture that freedom which is traditionally identified with our national life,—partly a thing of origins, partly an ever renewed contribution from the newcomers,—and which is, I take it, a fundamental, actually as well as traditionally, of our character. And then again we cannot fail to acknowledge a law-abidingness, a sane and persistent respect for precedent, which is wholly consonant with that high type of intellectual courage, the courage to be wholly one's self even in acknowledgment of indebtedness to forerunners. The small type of original dares not place himself alongside the elder great; he strives therefore for a new kind, and ends as like as not, in mere eccentricity. The larger original, and especially the greatest, is not afraid to stand with the elders, fully aware that his own mind will at the same time gain from close relationship with theirs and yet all the more clearly separate itself and hold its own against them as a background. Many of our best men have that kind of courage; perhaps none deserves to be called best who does not possess it. In any case I feel that it has been a distinguishing quality of all our work best worth remembering and treasuring, and that it is and must in the nature of things be a quality inherent in all permanent art.

I was seeking for a word to group these qualities under. Refinement, freedom, respect for precedent, courage—these, I think, make up as aggregates the mere parts of that particular kind of reinforced concrete which I have called the American Catholic. They are all aristocratic virtues, and they deserve an aristocratic name. What better one is there than—Distinction? Distinction, is after all, what we are all after. In all the wholly successful American work, that, we feel, is the representative beauty, which we all recognize the value of and which we struggle consciously or unconsciously to attain in our work, however far short individual achievement may fall. Here in America, just where, a priori, you might least expect to find precisely that ideal, you find it most securely horsed and off for the crusade. Compare the representative American work of today with corresponding work abroad. You will find here a tireless and persistent search for the fine thing as the keynote of design, as against the venturing into new fields over there, especially on the Continent. I know, there are reasons, sound reasons, for this; they have their fine old examples, they are tired of imitating them, they want to try their wings, and they often go far afield to do it; but the fact remains as I have said that we are on the whole the conservatives, they are the free lances. L'Art Nouveau, that iconoclastic socialism, not to say anarchy, of art, has gone like wild-fire from end to end of Europe these last years, while we are on the still hunt for aristocratic Distinction. I'm not saying that we always bag the game or that we have all the advantage in this comparison by any means. I dare say Europe may in some ways be in advance on the trail to the future, and may have that to offer even in the Art Nouveau which we must needs take over if we are to join the world movement onward. They seem to be already in the aeroplane age of architecture, while we are still content with automobiling. But, as a prejudiced observer, I may be permitted, I hope, to express the conviction that on the whole we are on the surer ground,—on the ground, I should say, instead of in the air. With painting it is much the same. Europe is tired of saying and doing the same old things, and bursts with desire to get on; America distrusts and hates more and more the crudities and anxieties of revolt and yearns for the halcyon peace of establishment. We could almost stand a State religion, I sometimes think (providing it were catholic enough), and we are actually within gun-shot of a State architecture. Faguet brings out capitally the necessity of incorporating the aristocratic principle in democracy, just as Croly does in another way; believe me, it is even more vital in architecture.

"Nuns fret not at their convent's narrow room,"—In the midst of freedom, "Form, give us form!" we cry,—and too often we get—mere Standardization. There is our Scylla over against the Charybdis of License. After all, we must steer a mean course, keep midchannel, if our ship is to come in. And there is no rule for sailing a ship except—to sail it. Above all, keep on deck!

* * *

Grouped Buildings for High Schools

THE idea of utilizing a number of buildings, each suited to a specific department of high-school instruction—the whole forming a complete school plant—is rapidly growing in favor in California and other far-Western States. Usually the group consists of a central unit, housing the academic classes, the administration offices and the assembly hall, and separate units for manual training, domestic science and physical instruction. There is much to commend in this "group plan," both from the standpoint of economy and educational efficiency.

It has been the experience of growing communities that the group plan permits the erection of a central unit to house the entire initial enrollment of the high school, adding further units as the community grows and the scope of the school is broadened. Each building is complete in itself, and the size of the site is practically the only limit to the expansion of the school.

Architecturally, the scheme has much merit. The central structure can be planned to express its importance and each of the auxiliary structures can express the exact purpose for which they are used. The whole group may be so arranged as to form a most interesting educational and civic center. Each building can be a complete architectural whole from the beginning so that there will be no inartistic lack of balance.

Educationally, the group buildings have been found especially advantageous in segregating the noisy and dusty wood and metal shops and the noisy gymnasium from the academic class-rooms which depend upon absolute quiet for much of their success. Believers in the segregation of the sexes have found that practically all of the advantages of entirely separate institutions can be obtained without a duplication of special facilities and with just enough desirable contact between boys and girls.

The departmental organization of the high school seems to work out far better in that the heads of the several divisions of the school are practically principals of their own buildings and are better able to organize and specialize in their branches.

To school boards, the economy of arrangement will appeal most strongly in group buildings for high schools. The experience of the California cities leads to the conclusion that in the long run this type of plant is far more economical. safe against fire and panic, and durable than the enormous buildings now being erected in the large cities.—School Journal.

*

*   *

The Steel Market and Concrete Construction

THE soaring price of steel is affecting the concrete industry from numerous angles. The high price and the impossibility of securing structural steel are turning the attention of many designers to reinforced concrete for relief. This is particularly true in the case of long girders and roof trusses. ..

Reinforcing bars have advanced sharply and, while some manufacturers of fabricated reinforcement are having difficulty in securing sufficient supplies to care for their demands, others report their ability to make prompt deliveries where traffic conditions permit.

Wire reinforcement and expanded metal are naturally advancing in sympathy with the advance of raw material, with prospects of further increase. Deliveries are reported as being fairly prompt at the present time.

A. I. Findley, editor of The Iron Age, writes:

Architects have reported recently an increasing number of their clients who have abandoned building projects requiring structural steel or are attempting to work out designs in reinforced concrete, yet there is a good volume of structural steel work before the trade. Railroad bridge work has been of more consequence lately and there is an unusual amount of industrial construction. The steel companies in particular are building considerable additions and this is true in various lines of manufacture for which rolled steel is the raw material. There has been an exceptional demand for bars for reinforcing purposes and the turning of so much mild steel into war channels has increased the call for high carbon bars for reinforcing. In a number of cases bars rolled from rails have been accepted for work usually let under soft steel specifications. The fabricating works are having difficulty in getting full shipments under their contracts and in some cases are having to eke out by paying stiff prices for shapes from warehouse stocks. Whatever the number of building projects put aside on account of high cost of steel, such action has made no impression on prices. The tendency is still upward where early deliveries are involved, and from present indications it will be a good many months before high prices will cause any loosening up in the situation at structural mills.

The condition of the steel market is reflected in equipment. A number of mixer manufacturers have found it necessary to advance prices and undoubtedly other advances will follow. While a good proportion of mixer manufacturers state their ability to deliver promptly at the present time there is every reason to believe that late mixer buyers will have trouble in securing delivery.—Concrete.

FORMAL GARDENS, COUNTRY ESTATE OF MR. C. TEMPLETON CROCKER, HILLSBOROUGH, CALIFORNIA

The Particular Building For That Peculiar Lot

By F. W. FITZPATRICK

EVERY lot, I don't care how misshapen it may be, presents an interesting problem to the capable designer.

Stores, loft buildings and that sort of business can be accommodated on pretty nearly any kind of a lot provided some light is gotten into the building and you can get the requisite floor area. In an office building it is different. There are fundamental facts that most people ignore. For instance, it is only in certain lines of business that very deep offices are of any use. Normally, office space more than fifteen feet from a window is practically valueless for clerical purposes. A room twenty feet deep may look very imposing, but you are not going to get any more rent for it than if it were fifteen feet deep. And about as shallow a room as you can well rent is ten feet deep. Less than that a fellow feels cramped up. Corridors four feet wide serve a practical purpose. Six feet is better, but much beyond that becomes a luxury, more or less extravagant. Not so with light courts. The wider you can get them the better, and six feet ought to be as narrow as the law allows.

And that very matter of light courts deserves a paragraph all its own. Diagram "K" shows the least desirable light space. It is all enclosed; it abuts another man's property that you cannot control and the rooms facing that court are at the mercy of the neighbor in regard to what's going on on his property as well as in regard to fire. Your windows have to be particularly well protected on such a court and it is always more or less gloomy anyway. "J" is open to much the same criticism, but is infinitely better than "K" as far as light and air are concerned, because it is opened into an alley or a back street where there is a current of air and from which an added volume of light sifts into the court. "L," "M," and "N" are simply variations of light courts upon your own property. You control the outlook and the surroundings; every office in those courts virtually looks out upon the street; there is immunity from fire save that occurring on your own premises, and you get the advantage of the whole width of the street in both light and air.

As to light courts, the matter of height is a very great factor. In a light court, such as "J" or "K," six feet wide may get you enough light so as to make the offices rentable in a four or five-story building at most, but if you go up ten or twelve at the bottom of the well might just as well be without windows. It is a chasm and just about as light as one of those "dark, dank" things is. Every foot that's added to the height of a building should have a compensating number of inches, or rather fractions thereof added to the width of the light court and then everything done to make it as light as possible, cream enameled brick, sash painted white, white blinds, all those things help a little bit.

Now let's get back to the best "buys" in lots for office buildings. Assuming that the property is divided into rectangular lots and that the depth is always the greater of the unit dimensions I have established several minimums. The depth of the lot is a more or less negligible quantity. It's merely a matter of so many offices deep on a hundred-foot lot, and so many more on a hundred and fifty-foot depth. The widths on the street front are the great factors in cost. Now, diagrams "A," "B," "C," and "D" are arranged on the supposition that the desired lot is a corner one with light on front and one side, a blank wall on the other.

Diagram "A" shows that sixteen feet is about the minimum width one can afford to buy to get the best returns on his square footage of office space. The ground floor arrangement, of course, is another matter. Every inch of store room in width is valuable, but I am writing now about office space. This width allows for ten-foot rooms and a four-foot passageway. You get some increased rental for every foot you add to those offices in depth up to fifteen feet and it would be very nice to make the corridor six feet, and since twenty-five feet is about the average normal width of lot unit, offices eighteen feet deep and a corridor six feet wide would ·be very nice, but the building costs more and your ground area costs more, and while I wouldn't build on less than 16 feet I wouldn't give a snap for a one-tier office building of much over twenty feet wide.

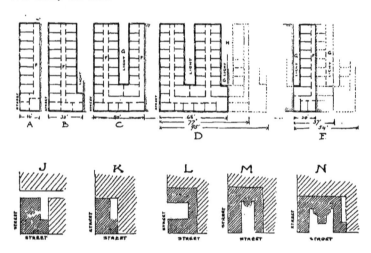

Of course, I haven't taken into account in these diagrams the stairs, elevators, toilets and all that sort of detail. Those matters don't affect the problem a bit as far as widths are concerned. My next best purchase would be a thirty-three-foot lot ("B"), two rows of ten-foot offices, a four-foot corridor, and a six-foot light court—I mean, my most economical purchase. A lot a bit wider that would allow for twelve or fifteen-foot rooms and a six-foot corridor, an eight-foot light court would be better, but more than that for a two-tier building isn't desirable. Naturally, if you can get· your neighbor to allow the same width of light court on his side as you have on your side, you and he are that much ahead of the game. And also bear in mind that' if you ·go above four or five stories you have to have more than six feet of light court.

My next best used lot is fifty feet front, two tiers of offices ten feet deep, a four-foot corridor, an eight-foot light court, another tier of ten-foot rooms and another corridor against your neighbor, your light on your own premises. Some argument in this as in the other cases; increase that lot so that you get fifteen-foot rooms, six-foot corridors, and ten-foot court, and you have a sumptuous arrangement—luxury. Above or beyond that is waste and the fifty-foot is the minimum. So much for diagram "C." "D" presents a new arrangement whose minimum is sixty-eight feet wide, four tiers of ten-foot offices, two four-foot corridors, one eight-foot light court and one six-foot one against the neighbor. If you can get him to also make a light court and have one in common as at "H" so much the better. Then let us note diagram "D." Same argument for depth of offices. Sixty-eight feet the minimum and everything above that to rooms fifteen feet deep just that much nearer luxury but with hardly a commensurate increase in rental returns.

The next minimum is seventy-seven feet, which is simply adding another row of offices and a corridor to the sixty-eight feet. And the next best minimum is ninety-five feet. You already have a corridor, so you but add the offices and the light court. Increase all your widths to accommodate deeper offices up to fifteen feet if you wish, but these diagrams show you the minimum of good rental returns. Considering the cost of building today and the high cost of real estate, or land rather, and the keen competition in office buildings, I'd be tempted to say that the very best widths of lots are mighty near these minimums.

You get into an entirely different problem when you strike inside lots ("E"). Less than twenty-five feet wide is practically worthless. On that width you can get a six-foot light court, ten-foot rooms and a four-foot corridor. The same argument holds good in this case as in the corner building as far as depth of rooms and width of corridor is concerned. The wider the light court you get the better will the lower rooms be; and, of course, your every effort should be to get the neighbor to make a similar light court. The next minimum lot would be a thirty-seven-foot one, light each side and two rooms of offices with a corridor between. You get your corridor on the twenty-foot arrangement, therefore a thirty-seven-foot purchase is just that much of an improvement over twenty feet. The next minimum is fifty-four feet, or perhaps by squeezing the light court every inch possible we might say that we could manage three tiers of offices on a fifty-foot lot, the arrangement indicated at "E"; seventeen feet added to that would give you four rows of offices and so on in similar multiples.

The point I want to emphasize is, take this diagram "E" for instance, that a lot twenty feet wide is the smallest thing I'd buy to build offices upon. Twenty-five feet would give me more desirable rooms and better light, but not extraordinarily so. And unless I was simply a public benefactor and I didn't care to squeeze every penny out of my investment that I could possibly extract I wouldn't give a whoop for a lot over twenty-five feet wide unless it was at least thirty-seven feet when I could slap on another row of offices and squeeze that much more rent out of it. And there you are.

*　　*　　*

Concrete, Anyhow!

One morning in school the teacher asked for a definition of a concrete noun. A little boy in the back raised his hand frantically and said: "A concrete noun is a noun that is made out of cement."

*　　*　　*

Doubtful!

"I ran across an old friend of yours today," remarked the chauffeur. "Will he recover?" inquired the architect.

"CAROLANDS," FRENCH CHATEAU OF MR. FRANCIS CAROLAN, HILLSBOROUGH
E. SANSON, ARCHITECT   A. DUCHÈNE, LANDSCAPE AND GARDEN ARCHITECT
WILLIS POLK & CO., STRUCTURAL DESIGNERS AND MANAGERS OF CONSTRUCTION

Lace Treatments in Decoration

By ALBERT S. BIGLEY

IT is useless to deny that there is a prejudice against lace curtains, and that the average decorator, especially in the West, discourages their use. It is my wish to show that curtains and panels properly designed and proportioned, are an art deserving of due consideration, and should be a part of the decorations of all homes. That they are not always given a prominent place in the schemes of the majority of decorators is due to a lack of knowledge of the real art involved in the execution of laces and motifs, and the beautiful and pleasing effects that can be obtained in the correct assembling of laces for window decorations. Is there anything so charming as lace; anything so graceful and softening in effect, as filmy ruffles and delicate webs of flaxen thread?

Real laces are a constant study, and show the skill and artistic ability of the maker, and if good taste is used in their selection and arrangement, the resulting product must have charm and a distinctive character all its own. Arguments are often advanced when laces are effeminate when used in decoration, and the truth of this has to be admitted—but what is more a part of the real home than a woman, and is it unreasonable to try and make the surroundings reflect her delightful qualities—especially when the use of laces cannot help but add to the charm and grace of artistic window treatments, and express something of the spirit with which everything that is really beautiful is endowed? Too often in this age the thought of a sale influences us to suggest things which are not always a credit to our work, and again, lacking knowledge of the artistic results possible from judicious usage of laces, the decorator and salesman too often are eager to suggest the ordinary piece of scrim or net for windows, thereby losing the opportunity of not only adding to the beauty of their decorative scheme but also losing many hundred dollars additional to their sales.

A leading decorator recently stated to me that his reason for using casement cloth, plain nets and scrims in preference to lace curtains was that he wished at all times to use the newest things, and that his idea was to treat windows as simply as possible. It is to be regretted that the majority of the public and some decorators' sole knowledge is gained from the simplicity idea advanced by some of our leading fashion magazines, which no doubt are authority for the latest in style and fashion, but have no right to expect their advice to be accepted in matters pertaining to interior decoration.

There will always be simple curtains used, and places where any other kind would be considered out of place—but the very fact that the bed room and dressing room windows are treated along simple lines, should be argument for the better curtains in our drawing rooms and library. One would not think of using the same style furniture, rugs or even draperies in the lower part of the home that have been used in the upstairs scheme. This being the case, why the indiscriminate use of plain nets and scrims throughout the entire home, yes, even to the extent of using the same material in drawing rooms that is used in kitchen and pantry?

This certainly shows a lamentable lack of knowledge of the artistic possibilities of window treatments, and still it is often seen in some of the supposedly best decorated homes.

Due consideration should be given to the outside treatment of a window, as well as the interior, and nothing adds more to the exterior beauty than a properly curtained window. Nothing presents a colder or less auspicious window than the blank expressionless family-away look of uncurtained glass. Undoubtedly the improper arrangement of laces, with no thought

FRENCH DOOR TREATMENTS—FILET, POINT VENISE AND EMBROIDERY
By Albert S. Bigley

ENTRANCE HALL TREATMENT—POINT VENISE, EMBROIDERY AND FILET LACE
Designed and executed by Albert S. Bigley

LACE PANEL TREATMENT FOR ENTRANCE HALL
Door is divided into three openings, design being arranged so that outside appearance presents
three separate panels while inside effect is of one complete design
Design by Albert S. Bigley

of design or material is deplorable, but comparisons of correct treatments, with crude, gaudy, overdressed, or uncurtained windows, will soon convince even the most skeptical that laces should have a prominent place in all decorative schemes for homes, and architects and decorators who will take the time to investigate the possibilities of the improvements resulting from the correct usage of laces properly proportioned and designed to meet the requirements of the particular window for which they are intended, will gradually realize that they have neglected one of the most essential parts of decorative art.

It is not fair to condemn the use of lace curtains, because a great many of them are lacking in taste and refinement. It should be a question of selection and discernment, and good understanding of correct usage. Material and patterns should be selected so that in daylight the entire beauty of the outside surroundings will not be blotted out, and at night time, add a more pleasing effect than the ordinary shade. Soft creme tints are advisable, and white should rarely ever be used except in bed rooms. It is easy to see the mistakes all around us. Architects design so many styles and sizes of doors and windows, and it is no wonder that there is a hesitancy in the indiscriminate use of curtains, but if each opening is carefully considered with regard to its own particular demand and needs, these spaces can all be beautified, and the finished scheme will offer a more beautiful picture for having been curtained along pleasing lines.

Following these suggestions certainly we may hope for a result not wholly unworthy of graceful architectural setting.

Student Training in an Architect's Office

By EDWARD G. GARDEN, Architect

IN the year 1890 I entered the office of Mr. William Channing Whitney, F. A. I. A., in Minneapolis, Minn., as a student. In other words, Mr. Whitney furnished me with a place to work, with access to his library, with materials, tools, paper and especially instruction. While it is true that Mr. Whitney, in addition to the foregoing benefits, did not pay me any

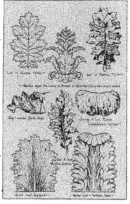

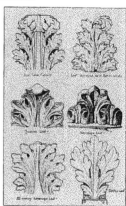

PLATE ONE

money, I felt that I was receiving so much and giving so little that the obligation has always remained with me. All that I was able to do for my patron for many months was to get there in the morning early and say that he was out, to dust his desk, to answer the telephone and run such errands as he might require. All of this service could have been readily obtained from an office boy for $3 per week.

To begin with, Mr. Whitney, who was a graduate of the M. I. T., gave me to study his own copy of Vignola on the orders and I drew them all in plate form. He also set me the task of reproducing a set of plans at one-fourth inch scale of a Colonial residence designed by himself, and these drawings were executed in ink and color on Whatman's paper, complete, including dimensions.

By this time I was able to do real work on working drawings and so was put on the pay roll with a regular weekly wage.

Leaving Mr. Whitney, I went East and after working as a draughtsman for about nine years I finally entered independent practice in the year 1900 as a member of a firm in which my particular duties were as one in charge of draughting and design.

PLATE TWO

PLATE THREE

During all this time as a draughtsman and head draughtsman in various offices and as architect I had had charge of many beginners and, remembering my own start, taught and will continue to teach those whom I think "have the vocation," as I was myself instructed by Mr. Whitney.

Since my removal of residence to California I have had several students, all of whom have graduated and are now earning their living as draughtsmen, but this article is written to show what, after an experience as teacher of over twenty years, has become my established practice.

When a young man applies to me for an opportunity to "learn the business," I first inquire as to his general education, and if he is not at least a graduate of a high school no encouragement is given. If this condition is met with, I ask for samples of the drawing which he has accomplished in his course and also for such free-hand sketches as he may have made from time to time, because if a man does not love to draw or illustrate his impressions of objects or life as he sees them it is useless for him to contemplate a career as an architect. I have no time to spend on a man whose capabilities will not permit him to go farther than an ordinary "hack draughtsman," and no man is ever taken on by me as a student unless I think, by reason of education, character and studiousness, he is one who can go farther and eventually qualify as an architect.

I have made many mistakes in judgment so far in this programme in the past, but I have never graduated a man from the office who has not been at least a qualified assistant to some other architect, while some of my students have gone very far.

The illustrations accompanying this, represent the work done by one student during his probationary course of six months.

Plate One—This was an enlargement of a plate from Meyer's Handbook of Or-

PLATE FOUR

nament and w a s given as a test of the student's sense of free-hand drawing. I had previously been shown a number of high school plates demonstrating his ability as a mechanical draughtsman a n d was satisfied that he knew the use of the instruments, the scale and the protractor. Had he not been able to make a satisfactory drawing of this subject, the instruction w o u l d have ceased immediately.

PLATE FIVE

Plate Two—Line drawing of the Doric order enlarged from Vignola. This demonstrated his love for and ability to conceive the three dimensions.

Plate Three—Study of the Ionic order in the form of a façade for a city bank. This study included the arch, and also the detail of the doorway and the sash, etc., also the rendering of same, and was practically his own conception, supplemented by numerous visits to local buildings of a similar character.

Many previous studies of washes and rendering were made before this plate was completed, but it represents the student's first essay in design and presentation.

Plates Four, Five and Six—Study of the Corinthian Order. This study includes the first plan problem and was given to the student in written form for his own solution.

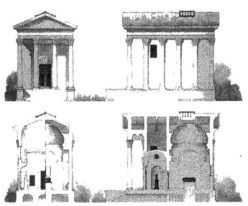

PLATE SIX

The project is for a mausoleum in the Corinthian order and is illustrated by plan, section, elevation and perspective, all of which presentations involved much work on the part of the student. After his preliminary studies were completed and approved, the entire theory and practice of perspective had to be mastered, and before the rendering of this drawing was accomplished many sketching trips to familiarize the student with the use of water color were undertaken, and the results show for themselves. This was the big problem and kept the student busy during working hours for about two months.

All of the above-mentioned work, (more not illustrated) and study were accomplished in a period of about six months and in addition the student not only performed the ordinary duties of office boy but progressed far enough to be useful as a tracer in the latter weeks of this period.

He is now a draughtsman earning his own keep and is also a member and an earnest student of the Atelier of the San Francisco Architectural Club—and if he studies in the future as hard as he has in the past will undoubtedly be heard from in the profession.

Reading—During this six months' probationary period the student has read and studied Ferguson, Sturgis History of Architecture, Ruskin, Violett Le Duc, and has also asked eight million questions, many of which his preceptor has had to sidestep. Having an inquiring mind, he is never satisfied with generalizations, but runs things down to their root or idea, and this is what has inspired the writing and illustrations of this article.

The pleasure one derives from imparting the seed of knowledge from his own experience to a receptive mind and seeing it not only germinate but develop, is akin to the satisfaction which the parent sees in his progeny. I like to feel that I am returning in part at least my debt to my preceptors, and when a student especially worthy comes under my notice I like to tell about it. Hence this article.

Frank L. Schultz is the name of the student in question.

In conclusion, the author wishes to say that out of many who started well and did not finish—out of some who started slower and finished better, and out of many who through circumstances not under their own control started when they should not—one earnest student is a recompense to the teacher for the many who will not work.

* * *

How to Build a Bungalow

A correspondent of Building Age, who evidently has a humorous streak in his make-up, sends that publication the following recipe for building a "bungalow":

There is probably no one in this world who has not at some period in his career desired to own a bungalow. A bungalow is a long, low, rakish-looking house, with a porch in front and an ash can behind. You get into it by going on your hands and knees, and you crawl out backward, for there generally isn't room inside to turn around without upsetting two or three hundred dollars' worth of furniture.

One way to build a bungalow is to follow the advice of the enthusiasts. According to them, you can build a bungalow for any price from $4.50 up to $3,000,000, and you can go a little higher than the last-named figure if you want to have plumbing in it. The usual recipe for a $4.50 bungalow is about as follows:

Lumber	$1.01	Tin work	.65
Brick	.39	Heating	.39
Paint	.10	Extras	.29
Carpenter work	.71		
Plastering	.96	Total	$4.50

Of course it can be done a little cheaper by leaving off the roof and side walls, but it seems as though any one ought to be able to afford a bungalow at the figure named. We have a friend who is building one of the $4.50 variety after one of these recipes. Up to date, it has cost him only $8,796.53, and it is nearly half done.

The last paragraph may be based on the writer's personal experience, and in that event it would be interesting to know the name of his architect. Off hand, we should say he's a victim of the carpenter-designer, and it will probably cost him double $8,796.53 before his bungalow is finished.—Editor.

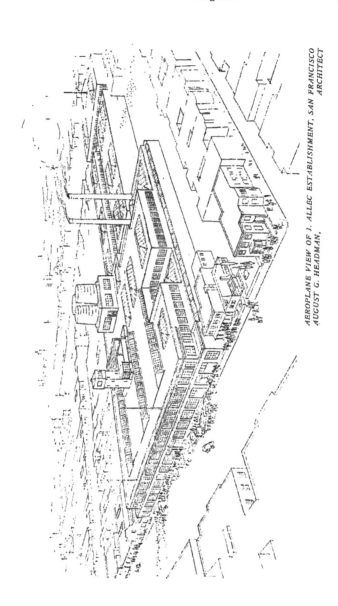

AEROPLANE VIEW OF J. ALLEC ESTABLISHMENT, SAN FRANCISCO
AUGUST G. HEADMAN, ARCHITECT

Winner of Scholarship Writes of His Work

THE following series of letters from P. J. Weber, telling of his progress in the School of Architecture at the University of Pennsylvania, will doubtless interest those who contributed to the scholarship offered by the Architectural League of the Pacific Coast, and which scholarship was awarded to young Weber for his excellent work in the San Francisco Architectural Club Atelier, John Baur, patron. Weber was awarded a $1000 traveling scholarship, but on account of the war, he decided to remain in the United States and take a two years course in the University of Pennsylvania. Following are a number of his letters, addressed to Mr. August G. Headman, who was formerly secretary-treasurer of the Architectural League of the Pacific Coast:

Before I begin to tell you of my trip to Philadelphia and my first two months at college I must apologize for not writing and letting you know that I arrived and was admitted to the university. I made the trip up the Sacramento Valley to Seattle, then to Vancouver, through the Canadian Rockies to St. Paul and Chicago, where I stopped three days at my cousin's house. From Chicago I went straight through to Philadelphia, stopping about two hours at Niagara Falls, as my ticket was limited.

I shall never regret the trip through the Canadian Rockies; it was certainly wonderful, although it was a little cloudy during that day. The evening of the day I arrived in Philadelphia I met Wm. Gunnison and Earl Giberson at the address Tom Bendell had given me. It was the place he stayed while here.

So we three now have a large front room on the third floor at 3613 Locust street. The next day we met Roger Blaine, an Oakland boy, and a member of the S. F. A. C., so he took the room adjoining ours. The day after that Fred Chapman, also a member of the S. F. A. C., came on and shared the room which Blaine had taken.

On the floor above us, Clyde Payne, a San Francisco boy, Eugene Gilbert from Oakland, and William Creighton from Los Angeles, have their rooms, so we have really a California house.

As the lights were not in the new Architectural Building, which was the Dental Department, we made an atelier out of our room, and we had some spirit, too, as is shown by our success in the first projet.

We all got advanced standing in design on presenting our drawings. William Gunnison was placed in Grade VI, Chapman in Grade V, Blaine, Giberson and I in Grade IV.

In the judgment of our first projet Gunnison got second mention, there being no first mentions awarded. Chapman, Blaine and I got first mentions and Giberson second mention.

As I was looking through the plates in the library, the other day, I happened to come across a mounted post-card which you had sent one of the professors while you were in Italy.

A letter dated Philadelphia, Pa., April 4, 1916, reads:

Since I last wrote you, a number of interesting things have happened. Tom Bendell arrived last Thursday and is going to work in the office of John T. Windrim all summer. He has taken the room over us and we will therefore be constantly under his influence, which I think will help us all a great deal. Tom is an enthusiastic, systematic worker, and I am afraid that our work lacks system.

We have just finished the sixth charette of the year and there are three more problems to do, an extra one having been added to help the Seniors get enough points for graduation.

In the last judgment, that is Problem Five, Chapman received a second mention in Grade VI, Gunnison a check in the same grade, Blaine a second mention in Grade V, and Giberson and I first mentions in Grade V. This judgment put me in Grade VI, the first problem in that grade being just finished, but the judgment, however, has not been made.

William Gunnison left us about a month ago, to go back to work for Rousseau and Rousseau for $50 per week. His eyes troubled him while he was here. He was a month in the hospital, so when he received this offer he thought he would go back home, because the work would be easier on his eyes.

The Byzantine ball, which came off last month, was a great success, especially the decorations. These were done under the direction of Lancelot Suckert, a second-year partial student, who had worked in San Francisco and Oakland for about six years previous to coming to Pennsylvania. He was also in the office of Bakewell and Brown and worked on the City Hall while there.

Earl Giberson received a letter about a month ago from a friend of his in a New York office. The letter says that things are bright there, which encourages my idea of working there for the summer.

I think it will have a good influence to work and live in the grand Metropolis. The environment of all that refined work cannot fail to have its effect.

Another letter dated May 22, 1916, reads in part:

This afternoon I was surprised to find a letter awaiting me in which was enclosed your check. All the boys enjoyed the (busy man's) letter very much.

Everything here has the appearance of closing time. The Seniors have begun to wear their caps and gowns and everybody is studying for final exams.

Earl Giberson and I are going up to New York to look around and see if we can get located. Blaine will go with us and continue on to Boston on a sight-seeing trip.

Yesterday there was an advertisement in the Ledger for some draftsmen at the office of Paul A. Davis, who is one of the professors on the Design Staff. Earl and I thought that it would be a good opportunity to work in a first-class office, so we applied, but some of his former men had offered to return and he said he would let us know definitely tomorrow.

Things are very prosperous here, according to all reports, and I hope they will become better in the West.

Kindly extend my appreciation and thanks to the League for the completion of my first year at Pennsylvania.

The following letter was written by Weber on November 3, 1916:

Many things have happened since I last wrote you, and, indeed, I should have written before now, or at least before returning to school, when I had more time.

As business was very prosperous this spring, instead of working here, I decided to move to New York, where I was working for Alfred Hopkins at a salary of twenty dollars per week.

Mr. Hopkins makes a specialty of farm buildings; he has written a book on the subject, but he also has been doing a number of banks and is now working on a penitentiary, for Westchester county, at White Plains.

In the evenings after work, I spent most of my time, at the Beaux Arts Society studio, in ornament modelling. For the first six weeks instruction was provided, Mr. Lloyd Warren acting as critic, and a professional modeler as instructor. Every Monday evening, as a part of our study of ornament, we made drawings in charcoal from flowers. The course in modelling takes up about nine months of each year, one month being given to the study of each style. The plates, which the society has a fine collection of, are brought out, that is all those in the particular style being studied, and every one selects a piece to copy. Four or five pieces are completed by each man during the month and at the end there is a judgment.

The other boys from California all separated, each going his own way. Chapman made a tour of Canada and New England with his folks, for the first two months of the summer and then he came to New York and worked for Herbert Lucas, the architect. We two boarded together for the rest of the vacation. Earl Giberson worked for John T. Windrim here in Philadelphia, and Blaine went home to work for McCall in Oakland. However, we all met again and are living at the same old place, just the same as when we left.

Our roster is a little heavier this term than at any other time during the course. Tomorrow we take the esquisse for our first Beaux Arts problem, which will go to New York to be judged. Professor Van Pelt has resigned from the Design Staff, and his place is now being held by Mr. Wynkoop of Squires and Wynkoop of New York City. He comes down here to criticize three times a week, and all four of us have him as our patron.

Tom Bendell still lives with us, but for how much longer we do not know.

Business is still very prosperous here and in New York, and from all indications it will continue so. I hope that the West is beginning to get its share of prosperity.

As I saved a little money in New York, I do not need any for a month or two.

Hoping you are getting along well and with best regards to the other members of the League, I am,

Very respectfully yours,

PETER J. WEBER.

THE "PATH OF GOLD" ON MARKET STREET, SAN FRANCISCO
(See text on page 111)

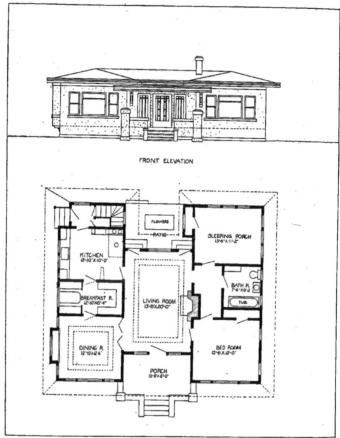

FRONT ELEVATION

PRIZE PLAN FOR A BUNGALOW IN ALAMEDA

Alameda School has Architectural Class

IT may interest architects to know that the old Sharp tract of land, lying between High street and Ferndale avenue, Alameda, recently purchased by Dr. C. P. Pond, president of the Alameda Chamber of Commerce, was once owned by Augustus Lauer, the architect of San Francisco's old City Hall. Dr. Pond has cut a road through this tract and is putting up forty bungalows for sale on the installment plan.

Prizes were offered for the best designs submitted by the class in architecture of the Alameda High school. The five plans selected were made by the following pupils: Verena Ford, Helen Knight, Edwin Greaves, Edward Bayliss and Alvin Montgomery.

In order to determine the best of these five plans, Dr. George Thompson, principal of the Alameda High school, called in the assistance of Architect B. J. S. Cahill, who awarded the first prize to Alvin Montgomery, which is here illustrated. The teachers in the class of architectural drawing are Mr. Carpenter, assisted by Mr. Chourré.

THE
Architect and Engineer
OF CALIFORNIA

Founded in 1905 by E. M. C. WHITNEY

A. I. WHITNEY - - - *Manager*
T. C. KIERULFF - - - *Legal Points*
FREDERICK W. JONES - - *Editor*

Published Monthly in the interests of the Architects, Structural Engineers, Contractors and the Allied Trades of the Pacific Coast by the Architect and Engineer.

BUSINESS OFFICE AND EDITORIAL ROOMS
627-629 Foxcroft Building, San Francisco
Telephone Douglas 1828

The publishers disclaim any responsibility for statements made in the advertisements of this magazine.

TERMS OF SUBSCRIPTION

(Including postage) to all parts of the United States $1.50 per annum; to Canada 50c additional; to all Foreign points $1 additional.

VOL. XLVIII.   FEB., 1917   No. 2

"Is it worth while: this thing of externals?" said the secretary of a large real estate firm recently.

COMPULSORY STANDARDS FOR GOOD ARCHITECTURE "Two men came into my office the other day to see me. Both men were of the same build, equally good looking, and equally well trained in their profession. One was dressed in an East Side sweatshop suit worth about $10, and the other had on a suit made by a competent tailor. The materials were very much the same. I granted time to the man with the good looking suit, but I passed the other one by. Why? Because the one man had enough respect for himself to spend a little time and a little money on his personal appearance.

"The same thing applies to the building of a suburban house. Architecture is not a reckless, tasteless layman's job. I have seen a house, the plans for which were prepared in the office of some competent architect, built by the side of one, the plans for which had been thrown together by a novice. The materials were the same, just the same number of square feet of timber were used in one as in the other, just the same number of rooms of the same size appeared in both houses. But one actually profited its owner on being sold, a handsome sum; the other one is still for sale. Perhaps only an architect, or a shrewd real estate man could tell why one sold and the other did not!

"The restriction of residential building sites has become a practice with several of the large real estate firms who control residential developments and in this way they set a compulsory standard for good architecture which has many points in its favor. Many plot-buyers feel that the provision reserving the right to approve of the plans, specifications and color scheme of houses to be erected, is a vicious one and unfair to the purchaser. But it is right and proper to reserve this privilege. It is not a matter of espionage. It is not criticism of where a man's kitchen shall be (on the front or the back) or where his living-room shall be. These are matters of personal taste, and his domestic menage is his own:—but we will not allow a man to build an atrocity, so far as exterior architecture is concerned.

"In many cases we find that a purchaser has incurred the expense of his plans and procured his loan before the sketches were submitted to us for approval. In one or two such cases we have had to do something that we dislike very much to do, that is, to withhold our consent until changes are made. This could have been easily avoided had the owner submitted the sketches to us in the beginning. He may have tried to economize by doing without. an architect—a short-sighted and bad policy!

"I firmly believe that if appropriate architecture itself be given thought, it ought to be a part of the value of a house, as much as the kitchen range, or the electric fixtures! Again, I think that the very fact that we have this right to approve the plans gives the man who has already 'gone through the mill' and has built his house with our approval, a feeling of safety and protection. He knows that we are going to be just as skeptical with his neighbor who builds, and his neighbor's neighbor, so that the proximity of ugly houses will not cheapen his, and the result, in the end, is that the district is developed with attractive and harmonious homes."

In a recent editorial the Saturday Evening Post sapiently remarks:

A WORLD'S CENTRE A customs union embracing the twenty-odd states that now compose the German Empire was a precursor of the empire. Teutonic advices indicate that a customs union including Germany and Austria-Hungary is coming. It may well prove the forerunner of a closer political bond between the two empires. Mutual tariff arrangements for England, France, Russia and Italy are discussed. That also may bring more extensive federation.

At first, of course, the two great tariff combinations would confront each other hostilely. But the moment peace is signed war hatreds will begin to cool before the civilizing desire for trade. Trade has been the great civilizer, breaking the barriers and opening the roads between nations. It will play its beneficent part

again. One can imagine a time when the states of Europe will sit down together to discuss tariff—and then other things.

If that imagining should come true, what will the United States be doing? We believe finally in a more or less closely articulated world federation; in a coming time when a man will put no more emphasis on his citizenship in France, as against citizenship in England or Germany, than a man now puts on citizenship in Minnesota as against citizenship in Texas. Certainly he will be a Frenchman, with French culture, ideals, modes of thought and feeling, producing French art and philosophy. But he will have complete respect for the English, German, and Russian men; he will not want to set up invidious comparisons and animosities against them; he will be content to be French, yet cooperate fully with them in many large common interests.

In other serious journals, in Congress, in colleges and societies, wherever thinking men assemble or express themselves you'll find similar tendencies toward internationalism, suggestions of an international court, the abolition of national militarism and the substitution of an international police force, inviolable freedom of the seas, etc., etc. The great war seems to have centered the world's attention upon internationalism as the salve nearest to a panacea it can think of for the ills that so sorely afflict it today.

All this brings to mind the oldest and most advanced scheme of all in the field of nationalism, the movement started many years ago to establish at some central point a great World's Centre, a World's Capital City, really an international clearing-house for all matters of state, things scientific, financial, educational and sociological, etc., etc., the creation of a world library, a world university and perhaps a world market, a project that may appear visionary but that is most practical, sane and feasible.

A society with branches in every European country has been established. Good work has already been done, but strangely enough, less of it here—the land of its birth—than in any other country. The king of Italy is the president of that society, King George, Emperor William, the Czar and President Poincare have taken, and though some of them are not now exactly on speaking terms, they are severally taking a very lively interest in the matter and all the great national societies of Europe are working at it with renewed vigor. It may seem a bit paradoxical perhaps, but the war has really advanced the project farther than it could have traveled in twenty years of peace.

San Francisco Building for 1916

The record for the year 1916 shows a total of building operations entered into of $19,545,357. This is an increase of nearly $1,000,000 over the figures for the year 1915, when the building operations reached a total of $18,626,199. The figures include not only the private building contracts, but also the contracts let by the municipal government, the State of California and the United States government. These latter items were inconsiderable in amount during the year just closed. The following table gives the total yearly building record in San Francisco since 1895:

Year	Amount
1895	$5,639,942
1896	5,621,442
1897	4,203,900
1898	3,490,603
1899	4,732,748
1900	6,390,705
1901	7,437,562
1902	14,289,938
1903	14,984,514
1904	16,916,118
1905	20,111,861
1906	39,254,467
1907	50,499,499
1908	35,128,549
1909	30,411,196
1910	22,873,942 .
1911	24,495,168
1912	26,269,006
1913	32,797,259
1914	30,468,457
1915	18,626,199
1916	19,545,357

In connection with the yearly figures as shown in the above table, it is noted that the immense building impetus beginning with 1905 reached its climax in 1907, and that it has gradually decreased until it can be said that the building operations of the past five years are practically down to normal.

American Institute of Architects
(ORGANIZED 1857)
OFFICERS FOR 1916-17
PRESIDENT.....JOHN LAWRENCE MAURAN, St. Louis
FIRST VICE-PRESIDENT......C. GRANT LA FARGE, New York
SECOND VICE-PRESIDENT....W. R. B. WILLCOX, Seattle, Wash.
SECRETARY....W. STANLEY PARKER, Boston, Mass.
TREASURER.........D. EVERETT WAID, New York

San Francisco Chapter
PRESIDENT...................EDGAR A. MATHEWS
VICE-PRESIDENT.........SYLVAIN SCHNAITTACHER
SECRETARY AND TREASURER........MORRIS BRUCE
TRUSTEES...................{ W. B. FAVILLE
                            { G. A. WRIGHT

Southern California Chapter
PRESIDENT.....................J. E. ALLISON
VICE-PRESIDENT................J. J. BACKUS
SECRETARY.....................A. R. WALKER
TREASURER.............AUGUST WACKERBARTH
Board of Directors
ROBT. D. FARQUHAR   PERCY A. EISEN
           S. B. MARSTON

Portland, Ore., Chapter
PRESIDENT................JOSEPH JACOBBERGER
VICE-PRESIDENT...............J. A. FOUILHOUX
SECRETARY..................W. C. KNIGHTON
TREASURER..................FOLGER JOHNSON
TRUSTEES.................{ ION LEWIS
                         { M. H. WHITEHOUSE

Washington State Chapter
PRESIDENT............CHARLES H. BEBB, Seattle
1ST VICE-PRES....DANIEL R. HUNTINGTON, Seattle
2D VICE-PRESIDENT.......GEORGE GOVE, Tacoma
3D VICE-PRESIDENT........L. L. RAND, Spokane
SECRETARY...........JOSEPH S. COTE, Seattle
TREASURER..........ELLSWORTH STOREY, Seattle
                  { JAMES STEPHEN, Seattle
COUNCIL...........{ JAMES H. SCHACK, Seattle
                  { CHARLES H. ALDEN, Seattle

California State Board of Architecture
NORTHERN DISTRICT.
PRESIDENT..................EDGAR A. MATHEWS
SECRETARY-TREASURER....SYLVAIN SCHNAITTACHER
Members
JOHN BAKEWELL, JR.   J. CATHER NEWSOM
SOUTHERN DISTRICT.
PRESIDENT..................JOHN P. KREMPEL
SECRETARY-TREASURER..........FRED H. ROEHRIG
                  { OCTAVIUS MORGAN
MEMBERS.................{ SUMNER P. HUNT
                  { WM. S. HEBBARD

San Francisco Architectural Club
OFFICERS FOR 1917
PRESIDENT ....CHAS. PETER WEEKS
VICE-PRESIDENT ....A. WILLIAMS
SECRETARY ....JOHN F. BEUTTLER
TREASURER ....WILLIAM HELM

San Francisco Society of Architects
PRESIDENT............CHARLES PETER WEEKS
VICE-PRESIDENT.........GEORGE W. KELHAM
SECRETARY AND TREASURER.....WARREN C. PERRY
                  { ERNEST COXHEAD
DIRECTORS...........{ FREDERICK H. MEYER

Engineers and Architects Association of Los Angeles
PRESIDENT.................A. H. KOEBIG, SR.
FIRST VICE-PRESIDENT.............A. S. BENT
SECOND VICE-PRESIDENT..........IRA J. FRANCIS
Directors
J. J. BACKUS, GEO. P. ROBINSON, ALBERT C. MARTIN, H. L. SMITH

San Diego Architectural Association
PRESIDENT...................CHARLES CRESSEY
VICE-PRESIDENT.........W. TEMPLETON JOHNSON
SECRETARY.................ROBT. HALLEY, JR.
TREASURER..................G. A. HAUSSEN

San Joaquin Valley Ass'n of Architects
PRESIDENT....................W. J. WRIGHT
VICE-PRESIDENT..................E. B. BROWN
SECRETARY-TREASURER.........FRANK V. MAYO

With the Architects

Building Reports and Personal Mention of Interest to the Profession

Stockton Architects Active

The San Joaquin Architects Association held their annual meeting at the Hotel Stockton January 21st. The association is doing splendid work in its efforts to educate the public into making use of an architect's services instead of employing a carpenter or irresponsible contractor to prepare building plans. The members receive a percentage of not less than 5 per cent for their services. They are not affiliated with the Institute. The society has appointed a committee to work with the Stockton city authorities in the preparation of a new building ordinance. The members are also deeply interested in a city planning movement, a safety first programme and a city of good sanitation and public health. The following officers have been elected for the year 1917:

President, W. J. Wright; vice-president, E. B. Brown; secretary, Frank V. Mayo.

Additions to Diablo Park

Arthur B. Benton, 114 North Spring street, Los Angeles, is preparing plans for some extensive improvements at Mt. Diablo park. He is planning an assembly hall and an amusement center, also a group of individual apartments as an annex to the Inn. These apartments will contain sleeping porches, dressing rooms and baths, and will be reached from the Inn by an artistic covered bridge. Another building will contain a dining hall and sleeping apartments.

Southern Pacific Building

Good progress is being made on the new Southern Pacific office building, San Francisco, which is to house the 2000 or more employees now occupying five floors in the James Flood building. The new structure will be ready, the contractors predict, early next fall. Rumors are rife as to what will become of the extensive floor space in the Flood building when the S. P. moves. There is a report that the John Wanamaker Department store of Chicago will lease part of the building.

Geo. W. Kelham Busy

One of the busiest architects in San Francisco is George W. Kelham, Sharon building. The new San Francisco Carnegie Library has just been completed from plans by Mr. Kelham, and a new ten-story bank building is under construction in Stockton from his design. Plans are being completed for a girls' dormitory at Stanford University to cost $100,000, a $500,000 ten-story bank building for the American National Bank at Montgomery and California streets, San Francisco, a $75,000 club building in the English type, for the San Francisco Golf Club, and a $20,000 store and office building in San Francisco for the Sharon Estate, and which is to be occupied by the Keuffel & Esser Company.

$100,000 Easton Home

Louis C. Mullgardt, whom it was announced last month is designing the new country home at Diablo for Ansel Mills Easton, states that the house is to be a mixture of Spanish and California architecture. Construction will be frame, with stucco walls and clay tile roof. There will be two wings and a large patio, with sleeping apartments leading off of the latter. The improvements will also include the construction of a number of farm buildings, several concrete bridges, an irrigating plant, and extensive landscape gardening.

John Reid, Jr., to Design Club House

John-Reid, Jr., First National Bank building, San Francisco, has been commissioned by the Lakeside Country Club to prepare plans for a $50,000 club house to be built near Lake Merced at the San Mateo county line. The building will be a two-story attic and basement frame structure, designed in the English type of architecture.

Los Angeles Architects Selected

The school board of Modesto has commissioned Messrs. De Remer & Hewitt, 624 Title Insurance building, Los Angeles, who designed the grammar school in Modesto, to prepare plans for the new high school. The building is to cost $125,000, and will probably be of hollow tile construction, with stucco exterior.

Washington State Chapter, A. I. A., Indignant

In view of the proposal of the State Capitol Commission of Washington to abandon the adopted group plan of state buildings at Olympia and the request for new legislation on the subject, the Washington State Chapter of the American Institute of Architects has adopted by unanimous vote the following resolutions:

Whereas, Under due authority of an Act of Legislature approved in 1909 and amended in 1911, the then existing State Capitol Commission, realizing that the co-operation of departments rather than individual sufficiency typified the evolution of State government, and cognizant of the fact that a single building for State Capitol purposes was entirely inadequate according to the experiences of other and older states, in the exercise of its proper functions instituted a competition among the architects of the United States for a grouping system of buildings and drawings for a Temple of Justice to meet the most urgent demands of that section of the government; and

Whereas, In response to the Invitation of the State Capitol Commission, thirty-one firms of architects from various sections of the country submitted plans, and after careful study and consideration architects were selected under the terms of the competition; and

Whereas, After six months of most careful consideration; study on the ground, and proper preparation, the architects selected submitted final drawings for the group plans, and said group plans were adopted as the group plans for the State Capitol buildings, and a Temple of Justice was constructed so far as the money appropriated for the purpose by the Legislature would permit; and

Whereas, We are informed that the present State Capitol Commission proposes to now abandon the duly adopted group plan and request new legislation along, generally speaking, the following lines: For the purposes of completing the Temple of Justice, paying off all indebtedness and erecting a State Capitol building to cost approximately $1,700,000, to invest the entire Industrial Insurance Reserve Funds, amounting to $2,000,000, in bonds secured by the Capitol Grant, to dispose of a further bond issue of $2,000,000 to outside investors secured by the Capitol Grant, the new building to face east and to be located to the west of the Temple of Justice, to be built according to sketch plans prepared by other architects contrary to the group plans originally adopted by the Legislature and now in force;

Now, therefore, The Washington State Chapter of the A. I. A., in the firm belief that the only way the State can hope to have worthy and coherent work on the Capitol grounds and buildings accomplished is to carry out the plans so excellently prepared, already adopted and paid for by the State; and

Further, The State Capitol building itself will be the greatest building the State will erect, not a temporary building erected for the immediate present but looking far into the future. The citizens of the State of Washington have a right to expect and to demand the highest order of building, not only from prideworthy sentiments, but as typifying the intelligence of the community and the majesty and dignity of its government; and in view of the facts above set forth we hereby protest against the abandonment of the adopted group plans now in possession of the State, and further, in the event that the present Legislature approve an Act making the construction of a Capitol building possible, that the State Capitol Commission, following the prevailing custom that has proved successful in other States, institute a competition similar thereto for the selection of an architect, and that the building when constructed be located according to the group plans already adopted and now in force. Be it further

Resolved, That a copy of the above resolutions be forwarded to all State Government officials and to each member of the House and Senate, to the daily press, and such civic bodies and other organizations as the Chapter may determine.

Ark'-i-tekt and Kon-trakt'-or.

(From Southwest Contractor)

At the last meeting of Los Angeles Chapter, A. I. A., some of the members were called to task by their fellows for mispronouncing the word "contractor." So rarely does one hear it pronounced correctly that the incorrect pronunciation, by common usage, may perhaps be considered permissible. In fact, probably the majority of contractors, if they were called "Mr. Kon-trakt'-or," with the accent on the second syllable, might think the one addressing them were speaking in irony or calling them names in derision of their honorable calling. Pronouncing "contractor" with the accent on the first syllable, as one almost universally hears it, is not recognized by the good dictionaries.

"Murdering" English is not confined, however, to the word "contractor." Even worse is the too common mispronunciation of the word "architect." The contractors in this are the worst offenders. One frequently hears "R'-chi-tect," or 'R'-shi-tect," and the well-intentioned contractor does not know he is a "murderer." And sometimes we have heard "R'-ti-teck." A good architect should be called "Mr. Ark'-i-tekt."

Million Dollar Hotel Addition

John Parkinson, who designed the New Rosslyn Hotel at Fifth and Main streets, Los Angeles, for Hart Bros., has been commissioned to make plans for a million dollar addition to the building on the Main street side. The Rosslyn is a twelve-story and basement steel frame structure faced with ruffled brick and terra cotta. It contains about 800 rooms. The addition will correspond in design and construction to the original building.

New Church for Tracy

H. M. Patterson, 324 O. T. Johnson building, Los Angeles, has been commissioned to prepare plans for a new church for the Presbyterian Society, Tracy. It will be of frame construction, one story and will seat 250 persons.

New Architects' Organization

Washington State Society of Architects has been formed with A. Warren Gould, Seattle, president; William J. Jones, secretary, and Harry H. James, R. Hamilton Rowe and C. Alfred Breitung, trustees.

State Buildings Planned

· The California State Board of Control has asked the Legislature now in session to appropriate money for the following new buildings:

Site and buildings for a new home for the feeble-minded in the southern portion of the state, $250,000.

Completion of the building programme and plant of the new Norwalk State hospital, $246,700.

Further progress in reconstruction of the Whittier Boys' school, $127,000.

Completion of the building programme of the new school for girls at Ventura, $123,200.

Replacement of pavilion at the State Fair grounds, destroyed by fire, $300,000.

Buildings for the new Humboldt Normal school, $230,000.

Construction of necessary buildings at the Davis Farm school, $140,000.

Completion of buildings at the Citrus Experiment Station at Riverside, $50,000.

Construction of a new state printing office, $100,000.

Purchase of a ranch necessary to the maintenance of the Stockton State hospital, $60,000.

Construction of training school, San Jose Normal school to replace buildings destroyed by fire, $53,000.

Co-operation with the United States Government in a project of controlling the Sacramento river, $500,000.

Stockton Architects Busy

Messrs. Stone and Wright of Stockton are preparing plans for a one-story $25,000 addition to St. Joseph's hospital in Stockton. They have drawings complete for a Japanese theatre to cost $16,000.

Frank V. Mayo has completed plans for a $15,000 apartment house and contracts have been let for a municipal building at Tracy which will cost $9,000. Mr. Mayo's associate, Peter L. Sala, has been quite ill.

Frank P. Morrell has a club building and a dozen or more cottages for the Spreckels Sugar Refinery at Manteca. Mr. Morrell also has a number of residences, stores and apartments to be built in Lathrop, and an apartment flat building for Turlock.

Joseph Losekann has plans practically completed for a two-story detention home for the San Joaquin county supervisors. The work will be figured shortly. Estimated cost, $20,000.

$30,000 Piedmont Home

Plans have been completed by Albert Farr, Foxcroft building, San Francisco, for a $30,000 French chateau to be built at Piedmont for Frank Proctor of the Union Savings bank, Oakland. Construction will be frame and stucco with slate hip roof.

Residence for Dr. Majors

John Hudson Thomas, First National Bank building, Berkeley, is preparing plans for a handsome Spanish frame and plaster home to be built at Rockridge in Alameda county, for Dr. Ergo A. Majors of Oakland. The house will cost approximately $15,000.

Mr. Thomas also has plans on the boards for a $10,000 shingle house at Rockridge for Ralph Fageol of the Fageol Motor Sales Company.

Designing Many Residences

Messrs. Falch & Knoll, Hearst building, San Francisco, are designing a large number of high-class residences for St. Francis Wood and Forest Hill. Among those who will build in these popular residence tracts from plans by this firm are Charles Dixon, A. Perry, A. Schlief, R. S. Runge, the Newell-Murdock Company and Theodore E. Rulfs. Houses will range in cost from $6500 to $12,000.

Alterations to White House

Morris Bruce, who succeeded to the practice of Albert Pissis, Flood building, San Francisco, is preparing plans for alterations and additions to the White House building, and also to an adjoining building formerly occupied by the Hastings Clothing Company. The decorative work will be in charge of Messrs. Bakewell & Browne.

Martinez Office Buildings

A. A. Cantin of San Francisco, has prepared plans for a one-story concrete office building to be erected at Martinez for the Contra Costa Abstract and Title Company. In the same town the Martinez Abstract and Title Company will build a one-story Class "C" office building, from plans by James T. Narbett of Richmond.

Seven-Story Concrete Building

O'Brien Bros., Inc., San Francisco, have completed plans for a seven-story reinforced concrete store and office building to be erected at Pine and Front streets, San Francisco, for Dr. Wheeler, at an estimated cost of $80,000.

The same architects have made plans for a two-story brick duplex flat building for A. L. O'Brien. It will cost $8500.

Los Almos Bank Building

Perseo Righetti, Phelan building, San Francisco, has prepared plans for a $12,000 one-story bank building for the First National Bank of Los Almos.

Carson City Jail

F. J. DeLongchamps, Nixon building, Reno, Nevada, is preparing plans for a new jail building to be erected at Carson City at an estimated cost of $200,000.

Pasadena Architect Has Place of Honor

(From the Pasadena Star-News)

Thirty-five pages in The Architect and Engineer for December, 1916, are devoted to the work of Elmer Grey, architect of this city, with handsome photogravures showing homes and buildings planned by him. His work in conjunction with Myron Hunt is also shown in pictures of Throop College, the beautiful home of Henry E. Huntington and the gardens at the home of G. W. Wattles at Hollywood.

Mr. Grey's own home is also shown, as well as the Beverly Hills Hotel, which he designed. Other smaller structures and homes also come in for consideration. Mr. Grey was the architect for a number of Christian Science churches, one at Palo Alto being particularly interesting; another, the First Church of Christ, Scientist, Los Angeles, being unique in design and admirably arranged within. In the article accompanying, Mr. Grey outlines the history of church architecture from the year 1 A. D., and shows how the practical side of Christian Science finds expression in its church edifices.

Mr. Grey has pointed out in his first article in the magazine, "What a Home Should Mean in California," the benefits of living in California, the opportunities for pleasures which were impossible "back home," and the joy of having the home conform to conditions as they are found in this State. This article, profusely illustrated, is quite pleasing and instructive.

Architect Is Recovering

Leonard A. Cooke, formerly a Pasadena architect, with offices in the Braley building, and recently reported killed in action while serving in the British army, has been heard from in a communication from Mr. Cooke and Dr. Edna Hatcher. Mr. Cooke has been wounded and is now recovering in a Liverpool hospital, and states he will rejoin his regiment on his release, taking the office of first lieutenant in the Royal Hussars.

Residence and Ranch Buildings

Messrs. Mayberry & Parker, 472 Pacific Electric building, Los Angeles, have been commissioned to prepare plans and specifications for a residence, fireproof warehouse, together with bridges, dams and an irrigation system to improve a ranch property near Fallbrook, San Diego county, for an Eastern capitalist. The total cost of the work will be approximately $150,000. The construction work will be done by Guy S. Bliss.

Eureka Architect Goes East

Edmund J. Burke, who has been practicing architecture in Eureka, Humboldt county, California, for a number of years, has left for Detroit, and is succeeded by Fay R. Spangler, a San Francisco architect.

During his stay in Eureka Mr. Burke handled many of the larger building projects, including a number of buildings for the Cottage Gardens Nurseries.

Another Oakland Factory

The Valveless Rotary Pump Company will erect a plant costing $75,000 to $100,000 in Oakland. The company is understood to have an option on two or three very desirable sites. It is proposed to put up a group of one and two-story manufacturing buildings.

Piedmont Residence

B. G. McDougall, Sheldon building, San Francisco, is preparing plans for a $20,000 frame and plaster residence and garage to be erected at Piedmont for H. K. Fletcher, of the Standard Oil Company.

The same architect has completed plans for a five-story reinforced concrete office building to be erected on Pine street, between Montgomery and Sansome streets, San Francisco, for the Mills Estate. The building will cost $125,000, and will be constructed by J. S. Bogart.

Apartment House and Garage

Chas. E. J. Rogers, Phelan building, San Francisco, has prepared plans for a three-story and basement Class "C" apartment house to be erected at Turk and Webster streets, San Francisco, for the Ketler Estate Company, Inc. The plan is "L" shape and there will be fifty apartments of two and three rooms each. The estimated cost is $135,000. The plans also include a $15,000 garage.

C. C. Moore to Build

C. C. Moore of San Francisco, who was president of the Panama-Pacific International Exposition, has purchased a lot 90x150 feet at the northwest corner of Grand avenue and Eleventh street, Los Angeles, and will improve it with a four-story Class "A" building, with foundations heavy enough to carry additional stories.

More About Cloverdale School

Ernest Norberg, Bank building, Burlingame, states that work on the plans for the Cloverdale Intermediate school is progressing satisfactorily. The building will be one-story, of reinforced concrete and will have tar and crushed brick roof. There will be seven class rooms, auditorium, teachers' room, library, lavatories, etc. A plenium hot air heating system will be installed.

Fresno Office Building

P. A. Palmer of San Francisco and Emmett Riggins of Fresno have been awarded a contract by Architect Eugene Mathewson of that city to erect a six-story Class "A" store and office building in the Raisin City, for Mrs. Nellie Mason. Amount of contract is $151,000, exclusive of plumbing, heating and elevators.

Los Angeles Building

Messrs. F. Pierpont Davis and Walter S. Davis are preparing plans for a Class A building to be erected at the northeast corner of Sixth and Broadway for the O. H. Churchill Company and George D. Rowan estate. The building will be 72x120 feet, four or six stories in height, with basement.

Electrical Department

San Francisco's New "Path of Gold"
By WALTER D'ARCY RYAN

THE local effect of the Panama-Pacific International Exposition lighting resulted in a determination on the part of the people of San Francisco to perpetuate the illumination in so far as possible by lighting the main business streets of the city, largely by the use of. the high-current luminous arc lamps which were used extensively for facade and avenue lighting at the exposition.

The new lighting·system for San Francisco is divided into three groups, according to the type of standard employed:

1. Market street and the Ferry Plaza.
2. Downtown retail business district.
3. Union ·Square and the Civic Center.

The inauguration of the lighting of the first group, designated as the "Path of Gold," was celebrated by an illumination carnival on ·October 4th and 5th. The city of San Francisco prepared unusual decorations for the streets, building fronts and show windows, and many novel features to entertain the thousands of visitors during the celebration, which was of·the Mardi Gras order. The principal features were the lighting of Market street, and the Ferry Plaza, the illumination of the Ferry tower and new City hall, an illumination parade with floats depicting the ·history of lighting from the cave days to the present time, dancing and general carnival in the street, the firing of time flares for the taking of moving pictures, a special fireworks display, an illumination ball at the Civic Auditorium, and a fashion show.

The initial ·Market street installation extends from· the Ferry building to Seventh street, a distance of approximately one and one-half miles, including the Ferry Plaza of the Embarcadero.

The system which was replaced consisted of one direct-current inclosed arc lamp on the top of iron trolley poles. These poles were ,designed by Willis Polk, chairman of the architectural commission of the Panama-Pacific International Exposition, and modeled by Arthur Putnam, a sculptor of international fame. It was decided to utilize these poles with a tri-unit top, which was designed by Willis Polk and modeled by Leo Lentelli, one of the noted sculptors of the Exposition. One hundred and forty-three poles were converted. The over-all dimensions of the new standard is 32 feet, and the average distance between poles 110 feet. Each of these is surmounted by three General Electric ornamental luminous arc lamps, which were taken from the exposition and modified ·by the addition of a new sectional globe with special "San Francisco Gold Carrara" glassware. These lamps are grouped in the form of a triangle, with its plane transverse to the street. The poles are painted in imitation bronze, with a strong Verd-antique finish, which blends happily with the golden color of the glassware. The general effect is very pleasing, and adds materially to the dignified appearance of the street ·by day as well as by night.

The glassware was made by the Gleason-Tiebout Company in collaboration with the writer, and is very much less insistent than the ordinary white or opal glassware commonly used. The absorption is practically the same as white Carrara of the same diffusing quality.

It was decided to depart from the usual title, "White Way," and call this installation "Path of Gold," more on account of the ·day appearance. The effect of the light by night is a warm white, and far removed from the broken red-yellow color of the flame arc. It is also whiter and of a different character than the Mazda light. This, however, still maintains a good contrast with the window lighting and the street signs, which, of course, are much warmer in tone.

The Board of Harbor Commissioners has installed eighteen lamps on six three-light standards in front of the Ferry building, and also has improved the lighting of the Ferry tower.

The initial installation consists of 411 lamps on Market street, eighteen lamps in front of the Ferry building, making a total of 429 lamps.

The Pacific Gas & Electric Company assumed the entire cost of the installation, including lamps, cable and underground system, modification of the poles, station equipment. etc., at a cost of approximately $100,000. Owing to the city charter, which does not permit of a street lighting contract extending for a period of more than one year, and since it was necessary for the Pacific Gas & Electric Company to have a guarantee

for at least three years, a contract was arranged with the Downtown Merchants' Association, which was instrumental in the promotion of the system, to assume all financial obligations for the merchants and property owners, thereby making it unnecessary for the Pacific Gas & Electric Company to deal with individuals. While the contract was arranged on a three-year basis, the cost was predicated over a longer period, on the natural assumption that the system would be in operation at least from seven to eight years before improvements in the art would be sufficient to warrant a change. A separate contract has been arranged with the Harbor Commission on a five-year basis.

The United Railroads has incorporated in its franchise with the city an agreement to maintain one lamp on each pole on Market street at a cost of $48 per

CLOSE VIEW OF ORNAMENTAL TOP AND LAMPS
Note size by comparison with man alongside

year. This amount has been applied with the Downtown Merchants' Association fund for the maintenance of the two side lamps which burn until midnight. The city maintains the center lamp on all-night service. The rate for the all-night lamp is $96.73 each per year, and the midnight lamp $78.48 per lamp per year, making a total for merchants, property owners and the United Railroads of $21,503.52 per annum, the city $13,252.01, the Harbor Commissioners and the Palace Hotel approximately $2,700.

The illumination of the triangle section of the downtown business district, bounded by Powell, Post and Market streets, will probably be completed very soon. At the present time there are in use five-light clusters with one 40-watt lamp in each of the bracket globes and two 25-watt lamps in the center globe. These will be replaced by a new standard designed by J. W. Gosling, of the Illuminating Engineering Laboratory of the General Electric Company. In character it is very similar to the Market street standard, except that it is 21 feet over all, and carries one 6.6-amp. luminous arc in the center, with the gold Carrara sectional globe, the same as on Market street. This unit will be maintained by the merchants and property owners at a cost of $110 per lamp per year, on midnight service. The standard also carries two 100-watt Mazda "C" upright bracket lamps, each inclosed by an oval-shaped gold Carrara globe, 14 in. in diameter. . The city will maintain these lamps at a cost of $54.75 per standard per year on all-night service. It is interesting to note that this is probably the first time that arc and incandescent lamps have been artistically combined on a single standard for street illumination.

The present lighting standards are spaced approximately one to each 80 linear feet of street, arranged in staggered formation. With the new system some advantage would be gained by relocating certain poles, but for economic reasons, existing locations will be maintained so that the present distribution system can be used for the incandescent lamps without modification. This system will be supplemented by underground series arc circuits.

The initial installation will include approximately 110 standards, and will probably be extended in the near future. The Pacific Gas & Electric Company has made practically the same arrangements with the Downtown Merchants' Association as for the Market street lighting, except that the contract is on a five-year basis.

Briefly, the combination of the trolley poles and lighting standards is the principal feature of the lighting system by day. They are of a dignified, artistic design, free from obtrusiveness, and add greatly to the character of the streets. At night this economical combination of utilitarian and display lighting floods the building facades as well as the streets with a warm, pleasing illumination. A slight suggestion of the carnival is produced by the tone of the glassware, the grouping of the lamps and the artistic treatment of the standards. This gives Market street, particularly, a distinctive character, and should result in a general tendency toward better and more esthetic commercial street lighting.—News Letter.

Steel Frames for Class A Buildings

Shroder Iron Works report a gratifying volume of business during the past year, with splendid prospects for 1917. For the past twelve months this firm has carried out some very substantial contracts in structural iron. Among the jobs undertaken are the following:

Washington School, Alameda, Henry H. Meyers, architect.

Porter School, Alameda, Rogers & Werner, architects.

New theatre, Franklin and Thirteenth streets, Oakland, E. T. Foulkes, architect.

Engine house No. 17, Mint avenue, San Francisco, Ward & Blohme, architects.

Cooling tower for Shell Company, C. I. Braun, contractor.

Two apartment houses on Jackson

STEEL FRAME, ARMSBY BUILDING, CALIFORNIA AND DAVIS STREETS, SAN FRANCISCO
O'Brien Bros., Architects   *J. H. Hjul, Contractor and Construction Engineer*

STEEL FRAME, WINDELER APARTMENTS, SAN FRANCISCO
August Nordin, Architect

street for Meyer Wood and A. Peyser, C. A. Meussdorffer, architect.

Garage for California Bakery, P. Righetti, architect.

Royal theatre, California and Polk streets, B. J. Joseph, architect, San Francisco.

Windeler apartments, Ellis near Jones street, San Francisco, August Nordin, architect.

Armsby building, California and Davis streets, H. J. Hjul, contractor and consulting engineer.

New Packing Plant

Messrs. Glass & Butner, Republican building, Fresno, are preparing plans for a new packing house to be erected at Reedley at an estimated cost of $15,000. Construction will be of concrete and wood. The building is for the California Peach Growers, Inc., of which Samuel J. Samuelson, Fresno, is manager.

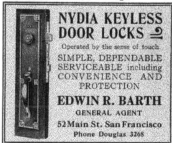

The Contractor

Plan to Avoid Forgotten Items in Estimating

ONE of the commonest causes of dispute between the retail lumber man and the customer that has just built a house is that the bill amounts to more than the estimated cost.

Very frequently this added cost is the result of some item being forgotten in the initial figuring of the house bill that, had it been incorporated in the beginning, would not have caused the slightest trouble. In almost all cases of this kind customers seem to think that the retailer is trying to "put something over," and raise so much objection that many a lumberman has suffered a considerable loss rather than run the risk of losing a good customer.

It is the duty of the architect to prepare a list of materials, but only too frequently there is no architect in the smaller towns and the local lumberman has to serve in his stead and do the estimating. With the progress of retailing lumber this is becoming increasingly necessary in the largest and smallest towns alike.

An estimate book that lists in detail all of the items that ordinarily go into the construction of a wooden house will be found to be of great help to retail lumbermen as a sort of a "mechanical memory," and may save time, money and friends if applied conscientiously.

It is a good plan to provide several types of books for buildings of different kinds; say one for houses of the two-story type, one for barns and one for buildings of small size. The initial cost will be small as compared to the saving to the lumberman, as their use will enable the estimate to be made with greater speed and allow him to rest assured that nothing has been forgotten in the estimate.

The following gives an idea of the form that is desirable for a two-story house, the list to be tabulated, giving number of pieces, their size and lengths:

Framing—Sills; cellar posts; first floor joists; first floor bottom plates; first floor outside wall studs; first floor partition studs; first floor top plates; first floor porch joists; first floor porch plates; first floor porch studs; first floor porch top studs; second floor joists; second floor bottom plates; second floor studs; second floor partition studs; second floor top plates; ceiling joists; ceiling rafters; second floor porch joists; second floor bottom porch plates; second floor studs; second floor top plates; ceiling joists; ceiling rafters; joist bracing for all floors; bracing for roof rafters.

Outside Sheeting—Sheeting; building paper; siding; roof sheeting; building paper (where used); shingles; sheeting under eaves (D & M or ceiling).

Floors—First floor subfloor; building paper; flooring; porch subfloor; flooring; second story subfloor; building paper; flooring; second story porch subfloor; second story porch floor.

Stairs—Porch stair horses; risers; stepping; molding; stair horses to second floor; risers; stepping; molding; railing; pickets.

Lath and Plaster—Lath; plaster (hair or wood fiber).

Interior Finish—Base molding; picture molding; floor molding; plate rail; mantel; shelving for closets; material for any special built-in features such as bookcases.

Exterior Finish—Water table; corner boards (or metal siding corners); ceiling for roof of porch first and second stories; molding to border ceiling; porch columns; cornice work; roof saddle boards (or metal ridge roll); material for outside beaming or brackets.

Mill Work—Inside doors; outside doors; transoms; outside door frames; inside door frames; door frame trim; thresholds; windows; window frames; transom frames; outside window trim; inside window trim; special items.

Hardware—Framing nails; sheeting nails; shingle nails; flooring nails; finishing nails; lathing nails; casing nails; door locks; window catches; pulleys; sash cord; sash weights; paint; hinges.—American Lumberman.

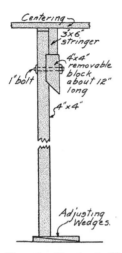

A Shore that Remains in Place

THE ordinary type of shore—that is, a plain 4 in. x 4 in. post—used for supporting floor or beam centering in reinforced concrete buildings has to be removed to strip the work after the concrete has set. This leaves nothing to carry the floor loads except the main column, and as the concrete has not usually reached its full strength when the forms are removed, this is undesirable. In the case of the usual 4 in. x 4 in. plain timbers, generally employed, it means resetting if the supplementary support is desired. To be able to keep the shores in place and yet strip the centering, the shore shown in the accompanying illustration was developed, and is finding wide application on account of its obvious advantages.

As shown in the sketch, this shore differs from the ordinary type, in that it has a removable block bolted to the side of the main strut. A mortice, about 1 in. deep, is cut in the main member to receive the block, which is about 4 in. x 4 in. in section and about 12 in. over all the length, one end being bevelled. This facilitates removal when the bolt is loosened. The stringers that carry the centering are carried on this block, instead of the strut proper.

When the concrete is sufficiently solid to warrant the removal of the form work, the block is removed by withdrawing the bolt, and the stringers and centers can be taken down. The shore remains in position, a board being inserted in the top to occupy the space previously taken by the centering

planks. Wedges in the bottom provide
for adjustment as usual.

The retaining of the shore in place
helps to support the dead floor load
and the live load caused by the equipment and men during the erection of
the next story. The advantage, of course,
lies in the fact that it is unnecessary to
reset the shores, as is the case with the
plain strut type. Time and labor are
saved, besides strengthening the structure during construction.—J. O. Smith
in Contract Record.

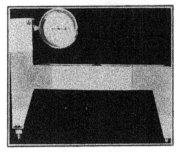

Special Strain Gage for Reinforced Concrete Building Tests

A SPECIALLY constructed strain gage
is used by the Building Department
of the city of Seattle, Wash., for measuring strains in reinforced concrete
buildings. This gage was supplied by
Prof. H. C. Berry of the University of
Pennsylvania, after a design prepared by
D. E. Hooker, Assistant Superintendent
of Buildings of Seattle. The unusual
features include a frame without rivets
or screws, the side plates being joined
to the spacing lugs by the electric
welding process; checkered side plates
to give better grip for the hands; a
clearance of 3 inches to enable readings
to be made on steel embedded deep in
the concrete; and a specially constructed
fulcrum joint for the movable leg.

The one-piece frame is so rigid that
side pressure, given unconsciously when
making observations, has comparatively
little effect on the readings, and there
are no rivets or screws to work loose
or throw unequal interior strains in the
frame. The 3-inch legs allow measurements on the deepest layer of steel in
four-way flat slabs and the checkered
plates reduce the strain of continued
reading by improving the grip of the
hands on the instrument.

The trunions of the movable leg are
held up into position in the notches of
the frame by a spring, guarded by a
cover plate. Both the spring and the
cover plate are square, with a square
hole in the center of each through which
the movable leg passes. The cover
plate is held in place by four countersunk screws, which are screwed "home"
in the frame and thus have no tendency
to work loose.

Typical Residence in which Armco Iron Spiral Lath is used as a Base for Stucco

Handsome and Lasting Stucco On a Pure Iron Base

The aesthetic values of perfect stucco work are appreciated by architects and owners alike. The slightly higher first cost as compared with shingles or weather-boarding is compensated by freedom from any necessity for painting and by greatly decreased fire risk.

The great question is the permanence of the metal base. Armco Iron has been developed to meet just such conditions. By reason of its remarkable purity and evenness and the painstaking care which marks every phase of its production

ARMCO IRON
Resists Rust

and in the forms of Metal Lath, Roofing, Pipes, Gutters, Cornices, Window Frames, Fire-Proof Doors and other exposed metal work is the material of Lasting Economy.

The trade mark ARMCO carries the assurance that iron-bearing that mark is manufactured by The American Rolling Mill Company with the skill, intelligence and fidelity associated with its products, and hence can be depended upon to possess in the highest degree the merit claimed for it.

THE AMERICAN ROLLING MILL COMPANY
MIDDLETOWN, OHIO

Licensed Manufacturers under Patents granted to the
International Metal Products Company

Armco Iron Sheets, Plates, Roofing, Pipe, Gutter and Metal Lath

Pacific Coast Sales Office—Monadnock Building, San Francisco; Other Branch Offices in New York, Washington, D. C,. Chicago, Pittsburgh, Cleveland, Detroit, St. Louis, Cincinnati and Atlanta.

An Ample Stock of Armco Iron Is Carried At San Francisco

Corrugated Iron Pipe as Well Curbing
By B. G. MARSHALL.

THE advantages of pure iron corrugated pipe as well curbing are just beginning to be appreciated. Everyone is familiar with the use of this material in the form of road culverts, but only here and there is it employed in the sinking and maintaining of wells, although for many situations it possesses advantages for this work practically equal to those of its more familiar applications.

The remarkable strength which pipe in this form has to resist external pressure is almost as important in well curbing as in highway and railroad drainage. Of course, the pressures are not nearly so severe since the thrust is entirely lateral, and this means that lighter gauges can be employed with safety than are advisable in road culverts of similar diameter.

Very deep wells are usually drilled or bored, but dug wells are often preferred for those of moderate depth, for two reasons: First, the assembling of the boring equipment involves a considerable expense and it often happens where the conditions are more or less favorable that comparatively shallow wells can be dug at a lower cost. Second, the diameter of a dug well is, of course, very much greater and when the amount of water needed is large, the supply is, of course, much more adequate than in a bored well. With the dug well the openings in the wall in strata where the water is found are so much greater in number and the storage in the well itself is so much greater as to furnish all the water that can be cared for by a pump of considerable capacity.

One use of corrugated pipe which is becoming more or less familiar in this way is that in which it simply serves as a curb to hold the sand or gravel of a more or less loose formation. In these installations it is customary to excavate for a certain distance, then let down a 10 or 12-foot section of corrugated pipe and continue to excavate, allowing the pipe to settle as the well is dug. When the first section is entirely below the surface of the ground, a second section is placed on end over it and coupled and the work goes on as before. Where the formation is very stable, it is sometimes possible to excavate the entire distance before installing the pipe.

It often happens that the surface water is objectionable for one reason or another and this condition sometimes obtains for a considerable depth; then the corrugated pipe is useful in excluding all the water that does not come from the desired depth, and some very interesting installations of this type have recently been made in various parts of California. The pipe is sometimes close riveted and soldered for water-tightness, but the most desirable installation is obtained where the well is lined with 1-inch lumber as excavated, the boards being held in place by iron rings of the proper diameter. Old wagon tires answer this purpose very well. Then the corrugated pipe of a somewhat smaller diameter is introduced and the space between the corrugated iron and the wooden casing poured full of concrete.

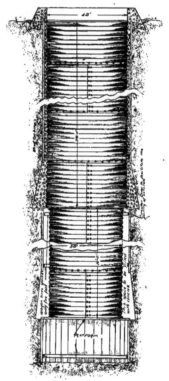

Diagram of practical corrugated iron and concrete well curbing.

The accompanying drawing shows the various stages in such an installation made by the Eldorado Oil Works of Berkeley, under the supervision of Mr. Edward Kalnin, a well boring contractor of that city. This well is very near the

Showing a simple but efficient derrick for handling curbing.

water of San Francisco bay. The surface water in that locality is bad, but that obtained from lower strata is exceptionally pure.

The well was dug four feet in diameter and forty-two feet deep. The entire circle was lined with 1-inch by 6-inch lumber, running up and down, with old wagon tires on the inside to keep it in place. The tires were about five feet apart. A platform had been built fourteen feet above the bottom to facilitate the installation of a piece of corrugated Armco iron pipe forty-two inches in diameter and twenty-eight feet long, which it was thought would serve to exclude all the impure water. For the last two feet above the platform the wooden curbing had been cut out and an excavation made in the walls that tapered outward from the bottom of the remaining board curbing and formed a shelf at the height of the platform, extending outward eight

inches around the entire circle. The corrugated curbing was lowered until it rested on the platform, then concrete was poured to fill between it and the wooden curbing as shown on the drawing. After the concrete had set the platform was broken and removed. It will be noted that the entire structure which went to make up the well curbing, including the corrugated and wooden curbs and the concrete, thus rested securely on the shelf formed by the excavation at the sides of the well at the twenty-eight foot depth.

It was found, however, that surface water continued to find its way into the well below the concrete. So another corrugated pipe thirty-eight inches in diameter and sixteen feet long was procured. A similar shelf was made near the bottom of the well. The thirty-eight inch pipe was lowered inside the first one and the operation repeated, the con-

"Armco" Iron Galvanized, Corrugated Well Curbing of 42" diameter being Installed on ranch of Geo. C. Russell near Enterprise, Oregon.

crete being poured through the two-inch space between the two pipes, twenty-eight feet from the surface. For convenience in pouring the concrete a round cover was made to set on the rodded end of the forty-two-inch pipe and this was afterward cut down so as to enable its use on the smaller pipe.

The installation is giving perfect service and the well affords an abundant supply of pure water.

Hoisting a length of corrugated well curbing into position for lowering.

Variations of this method are, of course, made necessary by circumstances in different localities. Sometimes quicksand is encountered, which makes it impossible to get the wooden shell tight enough to continue the excavation. Sand or silt runs so rapidly through the cracks as to form a very serious obstacle, or again there is a tendency for individual boards to sink before the next tier is in place. Under such circumstances well diggers lower a piece of corrugated pipe

A completed job.

to the point where the quicksand is encountered and this pipe sinks to some extent in the quicksand. They then dig inside the pipe, and as they dig, the pipe settles with them until they strike a more stable material. They leave the

pipe in the position to which it settles and continue their excavating in the regular way.

It is evident that where it is desirable to absolutely exclude water from certain levels, it is well to have a double-casing of some sort, either a combination of wood and corrugated iron or a combination of smooth and corrugated casing—in either case filling the intervening space with concrete.

Another effective and economical use for corrugated curbing is inside of existing wooden curbs that have become weakened by time and are going to pieces. These are usually square in shape and in a case of this kind the corrugated curbing would be of such diameter as would pass within the square.

Corrugated Well Curbing being placed in municipal well at Clovis, N. M. The installation of 240 feet of 36" diameter was accomplished in twelve hours. Material was No. 14 gauge galvanized "Armco" Iron.

When the corrugated curbing is lowered to place so that it rests at the bottom of the well and reaches to the top, earth or gravel can be thrown in the corners so as to fill between the pipe and the wood.

In cases of this kind where it is desirable to shut out surface water, the earth fill need only be brought up to the point above which it is desired to exclude the water, and the fill from that point up to the surface can be made with concrete.

In some localities there are many wells dug with an opening 6 feet by 8 feet and 100 feet deep. At the bottom two wells are drilled and a centrifugal pump is installed. The centrifugal pump will not draw up the water satisfactorily when it is located too far above it, but will readily lift water above the pump. In these wells the pumps are about 16 feet away from water and the water is lifted through the pumps and for 100 feet above to deliver it at the surface. There is no reason why corrugated pipe 7 feet in diameter and 100 feet long could not be used successfully to care for these situations.

Corrugated pipe may very readily be adapted to situations where it is desired to admit water from certain levels and to exclude it from others and to those in which water may be admitted from all levels. At comparatively slight additional expense the pipe can be perforated at the factory, the size and frequency of the holes being adjusted to the circumstances of each particular case. It is a simple matter also to perforate the pipe after it is in place, to care for unforeseen conditions, though this, of course, involves somewhat more labor. A very effective filter is secured by the use of perforated pipe with crushed rock and charcoal occupying the space intervening between the corrugated iron and the wall.

Corrugated Well Curbing—perforated.

The use of corrugated pipe by some of these methods serves to solve some very perplexing problems in well digging. It has the further advantage of maintaining a good clean interior surface which does not offer the opportunity for undesirable accumulations in the form of fungus. High purity in the base metal is, of course, of great importance in respect to durability. It makes a good appearance and stays clear and is the best possible means for shutting out surface water and quicksand.

"Keyhold Lath" Stands Remarkable Test

By an official test, under the auspices of the building committee of the Board of Supervisors, and by official invitation attended by Chief Murphy of the San Francisco Fire Department; Mr. Horgan, Chief Building Inspector; Mr. Robinson, Chief Engineer for the Board of Fire Underwriters, and by many prominent architects, engineers and contractors, held at the Civic Center lot, Friday, January 19th, "Keyhold Lath" gave a remarkable demonstration of its fire retardent qualities.

A house had been built on the site, three walls and the roof of which were composed of wood, and one wall being built of "Keyhold Lath" on wood studs, plastered with ordinary hardwall plaster. The interior of the house was filled with excelsior and fine dry wood, as well as the exterior against the "Keyhold Lath" wall. This entire mass was saturated with coal oil and then set afire.

The heat generated was so terrific that it was impossible to approach the fire closer than seventy-five feet, and in less than a few minutes the entire building had burst into flames. At the end of twenty minutes the house had almost entirely burned to the ground, and the side plastered with "Keyhold Lath," closest to the hottest fire, remained absolutely intact.

The Fire Department stood ready to test the effect of a stream of water on the standing wall and at this point the high-pressure system of the San Francisco Fire Department was brought into action, and a stream turned loose on the fire, the pressure at the hydrant registering 60 pounds to the square inch. It was then that the wonderful fire retardent qualities of "Keyhold Lath" became evident.

The superintendent of the Keyhold Lath company, who was assisting in directing the test, urged the firemen to bore a hole through "Keyhold Lath" with this tremendous water pressure, so as to lay bare before the officials the wood stud which had been used in

building the wall. The wood studs were found to be as bright and new as the day they left the mill, there being absolutely no evidence that a fire had been anywhere in their vicinity.

"The test," said a representative of the company, "demonstrated, aside from the wonderful fire retardent qualities of

'Keyhold Lath,' that the plaster became a permanent part of the lath or board by a perfect bond occasioned by the mechanical keys which held the plaster firmly to the 'Keyhold Lath' and prevented any separation, even though the plaster had become dead and almost ready to disintegrate from the tremendous heat.

"To the building world it is difficult to estimate the value of this monolithic construction, for had ordinary plasterboard been used that depends upon the affinity, bond or adhesiveness of one material for another, the same results could not possibly have been accomplished.

"Members of the Board of Supervisors present, as well as the building committee and other city officials, were more than pleased with the test, and, judging from their expressions, the future success of 'Keyhold Lath' would seem to be assured."

Engineers and Architects

The annual meeting of the Engineers' and Architects' Association of Los Angeles was held Saturday, January 28.

H. V. Mills, illuminating engineer of San Francisco, was present and addressed the association on the subject of "Interior and Exterior Illumination." His talk was illustrated with stereopticon views. Mr. Samuel Storrow, past president of the association, gave an interesting talk on grade crossings.

This being the time fixed for the annual election of officers, the following members who had previously been elected by letter ballot, were announced: A. H. Koebig, Sr., president; A. S. Bent, first vice-president; Ira J. Francis, second vice-president; J. J. Backus, Geo. P. Robinson, Albert C. Martin and H. L. Smith, directors.

Paraffine Paint Company Expands

The Paraffine Paint Company, one of the best known paint and roofing houses on the Pacific Coast, has had plans prepared by Leland S. Rosener, C. E., for a group of new factory buildings to be erected at Emeryville, just outside the Oakland city limits. The company intends to use a portion of this new plant for the manufacture or linoleum. The company also intends to build a $350,000 compo board plant at Port Angeles, Washington.

Old Friends Return

Foster Vogt & Co., who have not been active in the general contracting line for a year or more, owing to Mr. Vogt's private interests absorbing all his time and energy, are now back in the field again and ready to figure on good concrete jobs, especially the foundation work for buildings of heavy construction.

When writing to Advertisers please mention this magazine.

Will Improve Residence Tract

The most notable realty transaction the past month was the purchase of the John H. Spring holdings in Berkeley by a syndicate of Los Angeles capitalists, headed by A. C. Parsons, well known in connection with large country and suburban subdivisions in Northern and Southern California. When it comes to selling land it is conceded that no city can put anything over on a Los Angeles promoter. Mr. Parsons and his associates have invested $1,500,000 in the Berkeley deal and those familiar with his operations in the past say he will put Berkeley on the map in a more formidable manner than even the great University of California has been able to do.

Profit Sharing for Pioneer Employees

The Pioneer Paper Company, on its twenty-ninth birthday, announced the establishment of a profit-sharing plan by which every employee of the company will be benefited. This move was actuated not alone by the company's desire to treat its employees well, but by sound business reasons—an effort to promote the greatest possible harmony between employer and employee, to better the condition of the employees, and thus secure the maximum of loyalty and effort to further the company's interest, and to secure through greater efficiency a fuller measure of service to the company's patrons and customers.

The Pioneer Paper Company has been established as manufacturers and dealers in paper products and roofings and other building materials since 1888. It manufactures Pioneer roofings, building papers, etc., and is distributor for Buttonlath and the products of a new industry recently started by the Los Angeles Tissue Manufacturing Company.

Decorative Work Completed

I. R. Kissel, of 1747 Sacramento street, San Francisco, has just completed his contract for work on the Willys-Overland of California new building at Bush and Mason streets, San Francisco. This contract was for about $7000 and included the decoration of show rooms, canvassing of walls and finishing all the hard wood. Mr. Kissel has also recently done the painting of several fine residences, including those of Wm. Haas, Julius Newman and A. M. Shields.

Carnahan and Mulford Get Contract

Messrs. Carnahan and Mulford, San Francisco contractors with offices at 45 Kearny street, have the contract for building a two-story store and loft building at Twenty-first street and Broadway, Oakland, for H. S. Crane. Contract is close to $30,000. Wm. H. Weeks is the architect.

Illinois Thermo Vapor System

The Illinois Engineering Company, manufacturers of low pressure heating systems with graduated steam control, is now represented in San Francisco and vicinity by Mr. J. I. Krueger, with offices in the Pacific building. This company is experiencing a good demand for its Thermo vacuum return valves, which are installed on the discharge end of each radiator and are said to absolutely prevent the escape of steam from the radiator, resulting in an even and effective circulation of steam.

This system has many advantages. As compared with hot water, it is quicker in action, so that it is admirably adapted to take care of sudden drops or changes in outside temperature, and it can be readily handled in accordance with varying outside temperatures.

As compared with any one-pipe system, there is no opportunity for water to accumulate in the radiators, as occurs in any one-pipe system, unless the supply valve is either wide open or tightly closed off.

As compared with ordinary two-pipe heating systems, this system is controlled by a slight movement of a lever handle on one valve, instead of the necessity of working two ordinary valves at the bottom of each radiator. The Illinois System, it is claimed, prevents the noise which occurs in the radiators and piping of an ordinary two-pipe heating system, unless both the inlet and outlet valves are properly opened or closed.

Among the buildings on the Pacific Coast equipped with the Illinois automatic vacuum system are the Yeon building, Portland, Ore., Reid Bros., architects; Los Angeles Investment building, Los Angeles; Hotel Utah, Salt Lake City, and the Title Insurance building, Los Angeles, Parkinson & Bergstrom, architects.

Large Improvement to Suburban Tract

W. C. Duncan & Co., Sharon building, San Francisco, has secured the contract for extensive improvements to the 600-acre tract at Easton, San Mateo county, of R. B. Hale of Hale Bros., San Francisco. The betterments will include high-class buildings of every description suited to a gentleman's country residence, and a number of employees' cottages.

The first six months of W. C. Duncan & Co.'s business (since the old partnership was dissolved) makes a gratifying showing. Besides the American Beet Sugar Company's warehouse at Oxnard, and the Seamen's Institute, San Francisco, they have erected several fine residences, including Mrs. Janzt's at Montecito, Santa Barbara, and homes on the Peninsula for Mr. McCormick, Mr. Girvin, Dr. Lyman, Dr. Chidester and Mrs. Haynes.

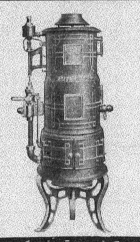

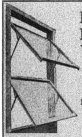

When writing to Advertisers please mention this magazine.

When writing to Advertisers please mention this magazine.

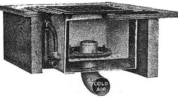

When writing to Advertisers please mention this magazine.

When writing to Advertisers please mention this magazine.

MONSON BROS.

Phone Market 2693

CONTRACTORS and BUILDERS

Office, 1907 Bryant Street   SAN FRANCISCO

Phone KEARNY 3021

GEORGE A. BOS

GENERAL CONTRACTOR   HEARST BUILDING
CONSULTING ENGINEER   SAN FRANCISCO

P. A. Palmer   Peter Petersen   W. L. Kelley   O. G. Hoaas

PALMER & PETERSEN

Contracting Engineers

774-776 Monadnock Building   SAN FRANCISCO, CAL.

AMERICAN CONCRETE CO.

JOSEPH PASQUALETTI, Manager

BUILDING CONSTRUCTION

1704 HUMBOLDT BANK BUILDING   785 Market Street, SAN FRANCISCO

CLINTON CONSTRUCTION COMPANY

Successors to CLINTON FIREPROOFING COMPANY

Concrete Construction

Phone Sutter 3440   140 TOWNSEND ST., near Third, SAN FRANCISCO

HOUGHTON CONSTRUCTION CO.

Successor to
VAN SANT, HOUGHTON & CO.

Engineering and Construction

Offices, Hooker & Lent Bldg., San Francisco   Century Bldg., Denver

---

J. D. HANNAH

Contractor and Builder

OFFICE: 725 Chronicle Building   Telephone Douglas 3895
San Francisco, Cal.   BUILDERS EXCHANGE, 180 JESSIE STREET

PHONE DOUGLAS 2370

McLERAN & PETERSON

GENERAL CONTRACTORS

SHARON BUILDING   SAN FRANCISCO, CAL.

ecifying
he stain
hat they

.   .

iancy are
IINGLE
orate and
oodwork

Co.

RODUCTS

Schaw=Batcher Co.
Pipe Works

SAN FRANCISCO
356 Market St.

Riveted Steel Pipe
Pressure Tanks
Storage Tanks
Well Casing

All Kinds Heavy Steel
Plate Work

Works, South San Francisco

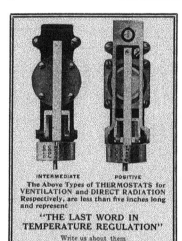

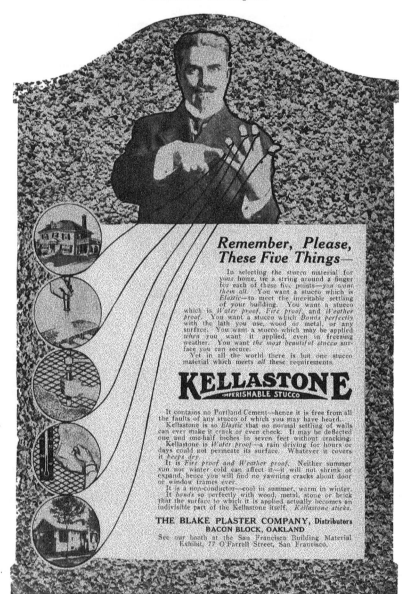

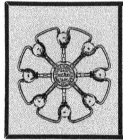

When writing to Advertisers please mention this magazine.

Architects' Specification Index

(For Index to Advertisements, see next page)

ACOUSTICAL CORRECTION
H. W. Johns-Manville Co., Second and Howard Sts., San Francisco.

ARBOR CULTURE
S. P. McClenahan, 738 Merchants Exchange Bldg., San Francisco.

ARCHITECTURAL SCULPTORS, MODELING, ETC.
G. Rognier & Co., 233 R. R. Ave., San Mateo.
Sculptors' Workshop. S. Miletin & Co., 1705 Harrison St., San Francisco.
A. F. Swoboda, modeler, 204 Second St., San Francisco.

ARCHITECTURAL TERRA COTTA
Gladding, McBean & Company, Crocker Bldg., San Francisco.
Steiger Terra Cotta and Pottery Works, Mills Bldg., San Francisco.

ASBESTOS ROOFING
H. W. Johns-Manville Company, San Francisco, Los Angeles, San Diego, Sacramento.

AUTOMATIC SPRINKLERS
Scott Company, 243 Minna St., San Francisco.
Pacific Fire Extinguisher Co., 507 Montgomery St., San Francisco.

BANK FIXTURES AND INTERIORS
Fink & Schindler, 218 13th St., San Francisco.
A. J. Forbes & Son, 1530 Filbert St., San Francisco.
C. F. Weber & Co., 365 Market St., San Francisco.
Home Mfg. Co., 543 Brannan St., San Francisco.
T. H. Meek Co., 1130 Mission St., San Francisco.
Mullen Manufacturing Co., 20th and Harrison Sts., San Francisco.

BLACKBOARDS
C. F. Weber & Co., 365 Market St., San Francisco.

BONDS FOR CONTRACTORS
Fidelity & Casualty Co. of New York, Merchants Exchange Bldg., San Francisco.
Robertson & Hall, First National Bank Bldg., San Francisco.
Fred H. Boggs, Foxcroft Bldg., San Francisco.
Casualty Company of America, Kohl Bldg., San Francisco.
J. T. Costello Co., 216 Pine St., San Francisco.
California Casualty Co., Merchants' Exchange Building, San Francisco.
Fidelity & Deposit Co. of Maryland, 701 Insurance Exchange, San Francisco.
Globe Indemnity Co., Insurance Exchange Bldg., San Francisco.
Edw. M. Jones, Merchants Exchange Bldg., San Francisco.

BOOK BINDERS AND PRINTERS
Hicks-Judd Company, 51-65 First St., San Francisco.

BRASS GOODS, CASTINGS, ETC.
H. Mueller Manufacturing Co., 589 Mission St., San Francisco.

BRICK—PRESSED, PAVING, ETC.
Gladding, McBean & Company, Crocker Bldg., San Francisco.
Los Angeles Pressed Brick Co., Frost Bldg., Los Angeles.
Livermore Brick Company, pressed, glazed and enameled, etc., Livermore, Cal.
Steiger Terra Cotta & Pottery Works, Mills Bldg., San Francisco.
United Materials Co., Crossley Bldg., San Francisco.

BRICK AND CEMENT COATING
Armorite and Concreta, manufactured by W. P. Fuller & Co., all principal Coast cities.
Wadsworth, Howland & Co., Inc. (See Adv. for Pacific Coast Agents.)
Glidden Products, sold by Whittier, Coburn Co., Howard and Beale Sts., San Francisco; California Glass & Paint Company, Los Angeles.
Paraffine Paint Co., 34 First St., San Francisco.
R. N. Nason & Co., 151 Potrero Ave., San Francisco.

BRICK STAINS
Samuel Cabot Mfg. Co., Boston, Mass., agencies in San Francisco, Oakland, Los Angeles, Portland, Tacoma and Spokane.
Armorite and Concreta, manufactured by W. P. Fuller & Co., all principal Coast cities.

BUILDERS' HARDWARE
Bennett Bros., agents for Sargent Hardware, 514 Market St., San Francisco.
Pacific Hardware & Steel Company, San Francisco, Oakland, Berkeley, and Los Angeles.

BUILDING MATERIAL, SUPPLIES, ETC.
Pacific Building Materials Co., 523 Market St., San Francisco.
C. Jorgensen, Crossley Bldg., San Francisco.
Richard Spencer, Hearst Bldg., San Francisco.

CEMENT
Mt. Diablo, sold by Henry Cowell Lime & Cement Co., 2 Market street, San Francisco.
Medusa White Portland Cement, sold by Building Material Co., Inc., Monadnock Bldg., San Francisco.

CEMENT EXTERIOR WATERPROOF PAINT
Bay State Brick and Cement Coating, made by Wadsworth, Howland & Co. (See distributing agents in advertisement.)
Glidden's Liquid Cement and Liquid Cement Enamel, sold on Pacific Coast by Whittier, Coburn Co., San Francisco.
Armorite, sold by W. P. Fuller & Co., all principal Coast cities.
Imperial Waterproofing, manufactured by Imperial Co., 183 Stevenson St., San Francisco.
Paraffine Paint Co., 34 First St., San Francisco.

CEMENT EXTERIOR FINISH
Bay State Brick and Cement Coating, made by Wadsworth, Howland & Co. (See list of Distributing Agents in adv.)
Concreta, sold by W. P. Fuller & Co., all principal Coast cities.

An Index to the Advertisements

ARCHITECTS' SPECIFICATION INDEX—*Continued*

CEMENT EXTERIOR FINISH—Continued
Glidden's Liquid Cement and Liquid Cement Enamel, sold on Pacific Coast by Whittier, Coburn Company, San Francisco.
Medusa White Portland Cement, California Agents, the Building Material Co., Inc., 587 Monadnock Bldg., San Francisco.
Samuel Cabot Mfg. Co., Boston, Mass., agencies in San Francisco, Oakland, Los Angeles, Portland, Tacoma and Spokane.

CEMENT FLOOR COATING
Bay State Brick and Cement Coating, made by Wadsworth, Howland & Co. (See list of Distributing Agents in adv.)
Fuller's Concrete Floor Enamel, made by W. P. Fuller & Co., San Francisco.
Glidden's Concrete Floor Dressing, sold on Pacific Coast by Whittier, Coburn Company, San Francisco.

CEMENT HARDENER
J. L. Goffette Corporation, 227 San Bruno Ave., San Francisco.

CEMENT TESTS—CHEMICAL ENGINEERS
Robert W. Hunt & Co., 251 Kearny St., San Francisco.

CHURCH INTERIORS
Fink & Schindler, 218 13th St., San Francisco.

CHUTES—SPIRAL
Haslett Warehouse Co., 310 California St., San Francisco.

CLOCKS—TOWER—STREET—PROGRAM
E. Howard Clock Co., Boston. Pacific Coast Agents, The Albert S. Samuels Co, 895 Market St., San Francisco. Joseph Mayer & Bro, Seattle, Wash.

COLD STORAGE PLANTS
T. P. Jarvis Crude Oil Burning Co., 275 Connecticut St., San Francisco.

COMPOSITION FLOORING
Germanwood Floor Co., 1621 Eddy St., San Francisco.
Malott & Peterson, Monadnock Bldg., San Francisco.
"Vitrolite," Vitrolite Construction Co., 34 Davis St, San Francisco.

COMPRESSED AIR MACHINERY
General Machinery & Supply Co., 39 Stevenson St, San Francisco.

COMPRESSED AIR CLEANERS
Spencer Turbine Cleaner. Sold by Hughson & Merton, 530 Golden Gate Ave., San Francisco.
Tuec, mfrd. by United Electric Company, 397 Sutter St, San Francisco, and 724 S. Broadway, Los Angeles.
Western Vacuum Supply Co., 1125 Market St., San Francisco.

CONCRETE CONSTRUCTION
American Concrete Co., Humboldt Bank Bldg., San Francisco.
Clinton Construction Co., 140 Townsend street, San Francisco.
Barrett & Hilp, Sharon Bldg., San Francisco.
Palmer & Peterson, Monadnock Bldg., San Francisco.
Pacific Coast Steel Company, Rialto Bldg., San Francisco.

CONCRETE HARDNER
Master Builders Method, represented in San Francisco by C. Roman, Sharon Bldg.

CONCRETE MIXERS
Austin Improved Cube Mixer. J. H. Hansen & Co., California agents, 508 Balboa Bldg., San Francisco.
Foote Mixers. Sold by Edw. R. Bacon, 40 Natoma St., San Francisco.

CONCRETE REINFORCEMENT
United States Steel Products Co., San Francisco, Los Angeles, Portland and Seattle.
Twisted Bars. Sold by Woods, Huddart & Gunn, 444 Market St., San Francisco.
Pacific Coast Steel Company, Rialto Bldg., San Francisco.
Southern California Iron and Steel Company, Fourth and Mateo Sts., Los Angeles.
Triangle Mesh Fabric. Sales agents. Pacific Building Materials Co., 523 Market St., San Francisco.

CONCRETE SURFACING
"Concreta." Sold by W. P. Fuller & Co., San Francisco.
Wadsworth, Howland & Co.'s Bay State Brick and Cement Coating. Sold by Jas. Hambly Co., Pacific Bldg., San Francisco, and Los Angeles.
Glidden Liquid Cement, manufactured by Glidden Varnish Co., Whittier, Coburn Co., San Francisco.

CONTRACTOR'S BONDS
Bonding Company of America, Kohl Bldg., San Francisco.
Globe Indemnity Co., 120 Leidesdorff St., San Francisco.
Fred H. Boggs, Foxcroft Bldg., San Francisco.
Fidelity & Casualty Co. of New York, Merchants Exchange Bldg., San Francisco.
Fidelity & Deposit Co. of Maryland, Insurance Exchange, San Francisco.
J. T. Costello Co., 216 Pine St., San Francisco.
Robertson & Hall, First National Bank Bldg., San Francisco.
Edwin M. Jones, 723 Merchants Exchange Bldg., San Francisco.

CONTRACTORS, GENERAL
Arthur Arlett, New Call Bldg., San Francisco.
Farrell & Reed, Gunst Bldg., San Francisco.
American Concrete Co., Humboldt Bank Bldg., San Francisco.
Barrett & Hilp, Sharon Bldg., San Francisco.
Carnahan & Mulford, 45 Kearny St., San Francisco.
Houghton Construction Co., Hooker & Lent Bldg., San Francisco.
W. T. & W. E. Commary, Crocker Bank Bldg., San Francisco.
Geo. H. Bos, Hearst Bldg., San Francisco.
Larsen, Sampson & Co., Crocker Bldg., San Francisco.
J. D. Hannah, 725 Chronicle Bldg., San Francisco.
Clinton Construction Company, 140 Townsend St., San Francisco.
Dioguardi & Terranova, Westbank Bldg., San Francisco.
Wm. A. Larkins, 1024 Hearst Bldg., San Francisco.
Teichert & Ambrose, Ochsner Bldg., Sacramento.
L. G. Bergren & Son, Call Bldg., San Francisco.
Grace & Bernieri, Claus Spreckels Bldg., San Francisco.
Geo. W. Boxton & Son, Hearst Bldg., San Francisco.
W. C. Duncan & Co., 526 Sharon Bldg., San Francisco.
A. P. Brady, Humboldt Bank Bldg., San Francisco.
Cameron & Disston, 831 Hearst Bldg., San Francisco.
Harvey A. Klyce, Sheldon Bldg., San Francisco.
Knowles & Mathewson, Call Bldg., San Francisco.

ARCHITECTS' SPECIFICATION INDEX—Continued

CONTRACTORS, GENERAL—Continued
Lange & Bergstrom, Sharon Bldg., San Francisco.
Foster Vogt Co., 411 Sharon Bldg., San Francisco.
Thos. Elam & Son, Builders Exchange, San Francisco.
Masow & Morrison, 518 Monadnock Bldg., San Francisco.
McLeran & Peterson, Sharon Bldg., San Francisco.
Monson Bros., 1907 Bryant St., San Francisco.
M. Dougan Co., Hearst Bldg., San Francisco.
Palmer & Peterson, Monadnock Bldg., San Francisco.
Robert Trost, Twenty-sixth and Howard Sts., San Francisco.
John Monk, Sheldon Bldg., San Francisco.
Ward & Goodwin, 110 Jessie St., San Francisco.
Williams Bros. & Henderson, 381 Tenth St., San Francisco.

CONVEYING MACHINERY
Meese & Gottfried, San Francisco, Los Angeles, Portland and Seattle.

CORK TILING, FLOORING, ETC.
David Kennedy, Inc., Sharon Bldg., San Francisco.
Be-ver Cork Tile. Sold by W. L. Eaton & Co., 812 Santa Marina Bldg., San Francisco.

CORNER BEAD
Capitol Sheet Metal Works, 1827 Market St., San Francisco.
United States Metal Products Co., 525 Market St., San Francisco; 750 Keller St., San Francisco.

CRUSHED ROCK
Grant Gravel Co., Flatiron Bldg., San Francisco.
California Building Material Company, new Call Bldg., San Francisco.
Niles Sand, Gravel & Rock Co., Mutual Bank Bldg., San Francisco.
Pratt Building Material Co., Hearst Bldg., San Francisco.

DAMP-PROOFING COMPOUND
Glidden's Liquid Rubber, sold on Pacific Coast by Whittier, Coburn Company, San Francisco.
Armorite Damp Resisting Paint, made by W. P. Fuller & Co., San Francisco.
Imperial Co., 183 Stevenson St., San Francisco.
"Pabco" Damp-Proofing Compound, sold by Paraffine Paint Co., 34 First St., San Francisco.
Wadsworth, Howland & Co., Inc., 84 Washington St., Boston. (See Adv. for Coast agencies.)

DOOR HANGERS
McCabe Hanger Mfg. Co., New York, N. Y.
Pitcher Hanger, sold by National Lumber Co., 326 Market St., San Francisco.
Reliance Hanger, sold by Sartorius Co., San Francisco; D. F. Fryer & Co., B. V. Collins, Los Angeles, and Columbia Wire & Iron Works, Portland, Ore.

DRAIN BOARDS, SINK BACKS, ETC.
Germanwood Floor Co., 1621 Eddy St., San Francisco.

DRINKING FOUNTAINS
Haws Sanitary Fountain, 1808 Harmon St., Berkeley, and C. F. Weber & Co., San Francisco and Los Angeles.
Crane Company, San Francisco, Oakland, and Los Angeles.
Pacific Porcelain Ware Co., 67 New Montgomery St., San Francisco.

DUMB WAITERS
Spencer Elevator Company, 173 Beale St., San Francisco.
M. E. Hammond, Humboldt Bank Bldg., San Francisco.

ELECTRICAL CONTRACTORS
Butte Engineering Co., 683 Howard St., San Francisco.
Goold & Johns, 113 S. California St., Stockton, Cal.
NePage, McKenny Co., 149 New Montgomery St., San Francisco.
Newbery Electrical Co., 413 Lick Bldg., San Francisco.
Pacific Fire Extinguisher Co., 507 Montgomery St., San Francisco.
H. S. Tittle, 245 Minna St., San Francisco.
Rex Electric and Construction Co., Inc., 1174 Sutter St., San Francisco.
Standard Electrical Construction Company, 60 Natoma St., San Francisco.

ELECTRICAL ENGINEERS
Chas. T. Phillips, Pacific Bldg., San Francisco.

ELECTRIC PLATE WARMER
The Prometheus Electric Plate Warmer for residences, clubs, hotels, etc. Sold by M. E. Hammond, Humboldt Bank Bldg., San Francisco.

ELEVATORS
Otis Elevator Company, Stockton and North Point, San Francisco.
Spencer Elevator Company, 126 Beale St., San Francisco.
Van Emon Elevator Co., 54 Natoma St., San Francisco.

ENGINEERS
Chas. T. Phillips, Pacific Bldg., San Francisco.
Hunter & Hudson, Rialto Bldg., San Francisco.

FIRE ESCAPES
Palm Iron & Bridge Works, Sacramento.
Western Iron Works, 141 Beale St., San Francisco.

FIRE EXTINGUISHERS
Scott Company, 243 Minna St., San Francisco
Pacific Fire Extinguisher Co., 507 Montgomery St., San Francisco.

FIREPROOFING AND PARTITIONS
Gladding, McBean & Co., Crocker Bldg., San Francisco.
Keyhold Lath Co., Monadnock Bldg., San Francisco.
Los Angeles Pressed Brick Co., Frost Bldg., Los Angeles.

ARCHITECTS' SPECIFICATION INDEX—*Continued*

FIXTURES—BANK, OFFICE. STORE. ETC.
T. H. Meek & Co., 1130 Mission St., San Francisco.
Mullen Manufacturing Co., 20th and Harrison Sts., San Francisco.
The Fink & Schindler Co., 218 13th St., San Francisco.
A. J. Forbes & Son, 1530 Filbert St., San Francisco.
C. F. Weber & Co,. 365 Market St,. San Francisco, and 210 N. Main St., Los Angeles, Cal.

FLAG POLE TOPS
Bolander & Son, 270 First St., San Francisco.

FLOOR TILE
New York Belting and Packing Company, 519 Mission St., San Francisco.
W. L. Eaton & Co., 112 Market St., San Francisco.

FLOOR VARNISH
Bass-Hueter and San Francisco Pioneer Varnish Works, 816 Mission St., San Francisco.
Fifteen for Floors, made by W. P. Fuller & Co., San Francisco.
Standard Varnish Works, Chicago, New York and San Francisco.
Glidden Products, sold by Whittier, Coburn Co., San Francisco.
R. N. Nason & Co., San Francisco and Los Angeles.

FLOORS—COMPOSITION
"Vitrolite," for any structure, room or bath. Vitrolite Construction Co., 1490 Mission St., San Francisco.
Malott & Peterson, Inc., Monadnock Bldg., San Francisco.
Germanwood Floor Co., 1621 Eddy St., San Francisco.

FLOORS—HARDWOOD
Gak Flooring Bureau, Conway Bldg., Chicago, Ill.
Strahle Mfg. Co., 511 First St., Oakland.

FLUMES
California Corrugated Culvert Co., West Berkeley, Cal.

GARAGE EQUIPMENT
Bowser Gasoline Tanks and Outfit, Bowser & Co., 612 Howard St., San Francisco.
Rix Compressed Air and Drill Company, First and Howard Sts., San Francisco.

GAS FURNACES
Cole Gas Furnace, Cole Heater Sales Co., Lick Bldg., San Francisco, 1764 Broadway, Oakland.

GAS GRATES
General Gas Light Co., 768 Mission St., San Francisco.

GAS RADIATORS
"The Paramount," sold by Modern Appliance Co., 128 Sutter St., San Francisco.

GLASS
W. P. Fuller & Company, all principal Coast cities.
Whittier, Coburn Co., Howard and Beale Sts., San Francisco.

GRANITE
California Granite Co., Sharon Bldg., San Francisco.
McGilvray-Raymond Granite Co., 634 Townsend St., San Francisco.
Raymond Granite Co., Potrero Ave. and Division St., San Francisco.

GRAVEL AND SAND
California Building Material Co., new Call Bldg., San Francisco.
Del Monte White Sand, sold by Pacific Improvement Co., Crocker Bldg., San Francisco.
Pratt Building Material Co., Hearst Bldg., San Francisco.
Grant Gravel Co., Flatiron Bldg., San Francisco.
Grant Rock & Gravel Co., Cory Bldg., Fresno.
Niles Sand, Gravel & Rock Co., Mutual Savings Bank Bldg., 704 Market St., San Francisco.

HARDWALL PLASTER
Henry Cowell Lime & Cement Co., San Francisco.

HARDWARE
Pacific Hardware & Steel Company, representing Lockwood Hardware Co., San Francisco.
Sargent's Hardware, sold by Bennett Bros., 514 Market St., San Francisco.

HARDWOOD LUMBER—FLOORING, ETC.
Dieckmann Hardwood Co., Beach and Taylor Sts., San Francisco.
Parrott & Co., 320 California St., San Francisco.
White Bros., cor. Fifth and Brannan Sts., San Francisco.
Strahle Mfg. Co., 511 First St., Oakland.

HEATERS—AUTOMATIC
Pittsburg Water Heater Co., 478 Sutter St., San Francisco.

HEATING AND VENTILATING
Gilley-Schmid Company, 198 Otis St., San Francisco.
Mangrum & Otter, Inc., 507 Mission St., San Francisco.
Charles T. Phillips, Pacific Bldg., San Francisco.
J. C. Hurley Co., 509 Sixth St., San Francisco.
Illinois Engineering Co., 563 Pacific Bldg., San Francisco.
William F. Wilson Co., 328 Mason St., San Francisco.
Pacific Fire Extinguisher Co., 507 Montgomery St., San Francisco.
Scott Company, 243 Minna St., San Francisco.
Thermic Engineering Company, Claus Spreckels Bldg., San Francisco.
C. A. Dunham Co., Wells Fargo Bldg., San Francisco.

HEAT REGULATION
Johnson Service Company, 149 Fifth St,. San Francisco.

HOLLOW BLOCKS
Denison Hollow Interlocking Blocks, Forum Bldg., Sacramento, and Chamber of Commerce Bldg., Portland.

ARCHITECTS' SPECIFICATION INDEX—Continued

HOLLOW BLOCKS—Continued
Gladding, McBean & Co., San Francisco, Los Angeles, Oakland and Sacramento.
Pratt Building Material Co., Hearst Bldg., San Francisco.

HOLLOW METAL DOORS AND TRIM
Edwin C. Dehn, 301 Hearst Bldg., San Francisco, representing Interior Metal Mfg. Co., Jamestown, N. Y.

HOSPITAL FIXTURES
J. L. Mott Iron Works, 135 Kearny St., San Francisco.

HOTELS
St. Francis Hotel, Union Square, San Francisco.

INGOT IRON
"Armco" brand, manufactured by American Rolling Mill Company, Middletown, Ohio, and Monadnock Bldg., San Francisco.

INSPECTIONS AND TESTS
Robert W. Hunt & Co., 251 Kearny St., San Francisco.

INTERIOR DECORATORS
Mrs. H. C. McAfee, 504 Sutter St., San Francisco.
Albert S. Bigley, 344 Geary St., San Francisco.
A. Falvy, 578 Sutter St., San Francisco.
The Tormey Co., 681 Geary St., San Francisco.
Fick Bros., 475 Haight St., San Francisco.
O'Hara & Livermore, Sutter St., San Francisco.

IRONING BOARDS
Western Equipment Co., Building Material Exhibit, 77 O'Farrell St., San Francisco.

KITCHEN CABINETS
Western Equipment Co., Building Material Exhibit, 77 O'Farrell St., San Francisco.
Hoosier Cabinets, branch 1067 Market St., San Francisco.

LIGHTING FIXTURES
"The Crystal Light," manufactured by Modern Appliance Co., 128 Sutter St., San Francisco.

LAMP POSTS, ELECTROLIERS, ETC.
J. L. Mott Iron Works, 135 Kearny St., San Francisco.
Ralston Iron Works, 20th and Indiana Sts., San Francisco.

LANDSCAPE GARDENERS
MacRorie-McLaren Co., 141 Powell St., San Francisco.

LATHING MATERIAL
"Buttonlath," manufactured and sold by Pioneer Paper Company, Los Angeles and San Francisco.
Keybold Lath Co., Monadnock Bldg., San Francisco.

LIGHT, HEAT AND POWER
Pacific Gas & Elec. Co., 445 Sutter St., San Francisco.
Union Gas Electric Company, Palace Hotel, San Francisco.

LIME
Henry Cowell Lime & Cement Co., 2 Market St., San Francisco.

LINOLEUM
D. N. & E. Walter & Co., O'Farrell and Stockton Sts., San Francisco.

LOCKS—KEYLESS
Nydia Bank Lock Co., 52 Main St., San Francisco.

LUMBER
Dudfield Lumber Co., Palo Alto, Cal.
Hooper Lumber Co., Seventeenth and Illinois Sts., San Francisco.
Sunset Lumber Co., Oakland, Cal.
Santa Fe Lumber Co., Seventeenth and De Haro Sts., San Francisco.
Pacific Manufacturing Company, San Francisco, Oakland and Santa Clara.
Pacific Mill and Timber Co., First National Bank Bldg., San Francisco.
Pope & Talbot, foot of Third St., San Francisco.
United Lumber Company, 687 Market St., San Francisco.

MASTIC FLOORING
Malott & Peterson, Monadnock Bldg., San Francisco.

MAIL CHUTES
Cutler Mail Chute Co., Rochester, N. Y. (See adv. on page 30 for Coast representatives.)
American Mailing Device Corp., represented on Pacific Coast by U. S. Metal Products Co., 525 Market St., San Francisco.

MANTELS
Mangrum & Otter, 561 Mission St., San Francisco.

MARBLE
Joseph Musto Sons, Keenan Co., 535 N. Point St., San Francisco.
Sculptors' Workshop. S. Miletin & Co., 1705 Harrison St., San Francisco.

METAL CEILINGS
San Francisco Metal Stamping & Corrugating Co., 2269 Folsom St., San Francisco.

METAL DOORS AND WINDOWS
U. S. Metal Products Co., 525 Market St., San Francisco.
Capitol Sheet Metal Works, 1927 Market St., San Francisco.

METAL FURNITURE
Capitol Sheet Metal Works, 1927 Market St., San Francisco.
Ralston Iron Works, Twentieth and Indiana Sts., San Francisco.
Edwin C. Dehn, Manufacturer's Agent, Hearst Bldg., San Francisco.

MILL WORK
Dudfield Lumber Co., Palo Alto, Cal.
Pacific Manufacturing Company, San Francisco, Oakland and Santa Clara.
National Mill and Lumber Co., San Francisco and Oakland.
The Fink & Schindler Co., 218 13th St., San Francisco.

OIL BURNERS
American Standard Oil Burner Company, Seventh and Cedar Sts., Oakland.
S. T. Johnson Co., 1337 Mission St., San Francisco.
T. P. Jarvis Crude Oil Burner Co., 275 Connecticut St., San Francisco.
Fess System, 220 Natoma St., San Francisco.
W. S. Ray Mfg. Co., 218 Market St., San Francisco.

ARCHITECTS' SPECIFICATION INDEX—*Continued*.

ORNAMENTAL IRON AND BRONZE
American Art Metal Works, 13 Grace St., San Francisco.
California Artistic Metal and Wire Co., 349 Seventh St., San Francisco.
Palm Iron & Bridge Works, Sacramento.
Ralston Iron Works, 20th and Indiana Sts., San Francisco.
J. L. Mott Iron Works, 135 Kearny St., San Francisco.
C. J. Hillard Company, Inc., 19th and Minnesota Sts., San Francisco.
Schreiber & Sons Co., represented by Western Builders Supply Co., San Francisco.
Sims, Gray & Sauter Iron Works, 156 Main St., San Francisco.
Schrader Iron Works, Inc., 1247 Harrison St., San Francisco.
West Coast Wire & Iron Works, 861-863 Howard St., San Francisco.

PAINT FOR CEMENT
Bay State Brick and Cement Coating, made by Wadsworth, Howland & Co. (Inc.) (See adv. in this issue for Pacific Coast agents.)
Fuller's Concreta Cement, made by W. P. Fuller & Co., San Francisco.
Samuel Cabot Mfg. Co., Boston, Mass., agencies in San Francisco, Oakland, Los Angeles, Portland, Tacoma and Spokane.

PAINT FOR STEEL STRUCTURES, BRIDGES, ETC.
Glidden's Acid Proof Coating, sold on Pacific Coast by Whittier, Coburn Company, San Francisco.
Paraffine Paint Co., 34 First St., San Francisco.
Premier Graphite Paint and Pioneer Brand Red Lead, made by W. P. Fuller & Co., San Francisco.

PAINTING, TINTING, ETC.
I. R. Kissel, 1747 Sacramento St., San Francisco.
D. Zelinsky & Sons, San Francisco and Los Angeles.
Fick Bros., 475 Haight St., San Francisco.

PAINTS, OILS, ETC.
The Brininstool Co., Los Angeles, the Haslett Warehouse, 310 California St., San Francisco.
Bass-Hueter Paint Co., Mission, near Fourth St., San Francisco.
Whittier, Coburn Co., Howard and Beale Sts., San Francisco.
Magner Bros., 419-421 Jackson St., San Francisco.
R. N. Nason & Company, San Francisco, Los Angeles, Portland and Seattle.
W. P. Fuller & Co., all principal Coast cities.
Standard Varnish Works, 55 Stevenson St., San Francisco.

PANELS AND VENEER
White Bros., Fifth and Brannan Sts., San Francisco.

PIPE—VITRIFIED SALT GLAZED TERRA COTTA
Gladding, McBean & Co., Crocker Bldg., San Francisco.
Pratt Building Material Co., Hearst Bldg., San Francisco.
Steiger Terra Cotta and Pottery Works, Mills Bldg., San Francisco.
G. Weissbaum & Co. Pipe Works, 127 Eleventh St., San Francisco.

PLASTER CONTRACTORS
C. C. Morehouse, Crocker Bldg., San Francisco.
MacGruer & Co., 180 Jessie St., San Francisco.

PLASTER EXTERIORS
"Kellastone," an imperishable stucco. Blake Plaster Co., Bacon Block, Oakland.
Keyhold Lath Co., Monadnock Bldg., San Francisco.
Buttonlath, for exterior and interior plastering, Pioneer Paper Co., San Francisco and Los Angeles.

PLUMBING CONTRACTORS
Alex Coleman, 706 Ellis St., San Francisco.
A. Lettich, 365 Fell St., San Francisco.
Gilley-Schmid Company, 198 Otis St., San Francisco.
Scott Co., Inc., 243 Minna St., San Francisco.
Wm. F. Wilson Co., 328 Mason St., San Francisco.

PLUMBING FIXTURES. MATERIALS. ETC.
Crane Co., San Francisco and Oakland.
California Steam Plumbing Supply Co., 671 Fifth St., San Francisco.
Gilley-Schmid Company, 198 Otis St., San Francisco.
Glauber Brass Manufacturing Company, 1107 Mission St., San Francisco.
Improved Sanitary Fixture Co., 632 Metropolitan Bldg., Los Angeles.
J. L. Mott Iron Works, D. H. Gulick, selling agent, 135 Kearny St., San Francisco.
Haines, Jones & Cadbury Co., 857 Folsom St., San Francisco.
H. Mueller Manufacturing Co., Pacific Coast branch, 589 Mission St., San Francisco.
Pacific Sanitary Manufacturing Co., 67 New Montgomery St., San Francisco.
Wm. F. Wilson Co., 328 Mason St., San Francisco.
C. A. Dunham Co., Wells Fargo Bldg., San Francisco.

POTTERY
Gladding, McBean & Co., San Francisco, Los Angeles, Oakland and Sacramento.
Steiger Terra Cotta and Pottery Works, Mills Bldg., San Francisco.

POWER TRANSMITTING MACHINERY
Meese & Gottfried, San Francisco, Los Angeles, Portland, Ore., and Seattle, Wash.

PUMPS
Simonds Machinery Co., 117 New Montgomery St., San Francisco.

RAILROADS
Southern Pacific Company, Flood Bldg., San Francisco.
Western Pacific Company, Mills Bldg., San Francisco.

REFRIGERATORS
McCray Refrigerators, sold by Nathan Dohrmann Co., Geary and Stockton Sts., San Francisco.

REVERSIBLE WINDOWS
Hauser Reversible Window Company, Balboa Bldg., San Francisco.
Whitney Windows, represented by Richard Spencer, 801-3 Hearst Bldg., San Francisco.

REVOLVING DOORS
Van Kennel Doors, sold by U. S. Metal Products Co., 525 Market St., San Francisco.

ROLLING DOORS, SHUTTERS, PARTITIONS, ETC.
Pacific Building Materials Co., 523 Market St., San Francisco.
C. F. Weber & Co., 365 Market St., S. F.
Kinnear Steel Rolling Doors, W. W. Thurston, agent, Rialto Bldg., San Francisco.
Wilson's Steel Rolling Doors, U. S. Metal Products Co., San Francisco and Los Angeles.

ARCHITECTS' SPECIFICATION INDEX—*Continued*

ROOFING AND ROOFING MATERIALS
Grant Gravel Co., Flatiron Bldg., San Francisco.
H. W. Johns-Manville Co., Second and Howard Sts., San Francisco.
Malott & Peterson, Inc., Monadnock Bldg., San Francisco.
Niles Sand, Gravel and Rock Co., Mutual Bank Bldg., San Francisco.
"Maltboid" and "Ruberoid," manufactured by Paraffine Paint Co., San Francisco.
Pioneer Roofing, manufactured by Pioneer Paper Co., 513 Hearst Bldg., San Francisco.
United Materials Co., Crossley Bldg., San Francisco.

RUBBER TILING
Goodyear Rubber Company, 587 Market St., San Francisco.
New York Belting & Rubber Company, 519 Mission St., San Francisco.

SAFETY TREADS
"Sanitread," sold by Richard Spencer, 801-3 Hearst Bldg., San Francisco.

SANITARY DRINKING FOUNTAINS
J. L. Mott Iron Works, 135 Kearny St., San Francisco.
Haws' Sanitary Drinking Faucet Co., 1808 Harmon St., Berkeley.

SCENIC PAINTING—DROP CURTAINS, ETC.
The Edwin H. Flagg Scenic Co., 1638 Long Beach Ave., Los Angeles.

SCHOOL FURNITURE AND SUPPLIES
C. F. Weber & Co., 365 Market St., San Francisco; 512 S. Broadway, Los Angeles.

SCREENS
Hipolito Flyout Screens, sold by Simpson & Stewart, Dalziel Bldg., Oakland.
Watson Metal Frame Screens, sold by Richard Spencer, 801-3 Hearst Bldg., San Francisco.

SEEDS
California Seed Company, 151 Market St., San Francisco.

SHEATHING AND SOUND DEADENING
Samuel Cabot Mfg. Co., Boston, Mass., agencies in San Francisco, Oakland, Los Angeles, Portland, Tacoma and Spokane.
Paraffine Paint Co., 34 First St., San Francisco.

SHEET METAL WORK, SKYLIGHTS, ETC.
Capitol Sheet Metal Works, 1927 Market St., San Francisco.
U. S. Metal Products Co., 525 Market St., San Francisco.

SHINGLE STAINS
Cabot's Creosote Stains, sold by Pacific Building Materials Co., Underwood Bldg., San Francisco
Fullen's Pioneer Shingle Stains, made by W. P. Fuller & Co., San Francisco.

SIDEWALK LIGHTS
P. H. Jackson & Co., 237-47 First St., San Francisco.

STEEL AND IRON—STRUCTURAL
Central Iron Works, 621 Florida St., San Francisco.
Dyer Bros., 17th and Kansas Sts., San Francisco.

STEEL AND IRON—STRUCTURAL—Con't.
Golden Gate Iron Works, 1541 Howard St., San Francisco.
Judson Manufacturing Co., 819 Folsom St., San Francisco.
Mortenson Construction Co., 19th and Indiana Sts., San Francisco.
Pacific Rolling Mills, 17th and Mississippi Sts., San Francisco.
Palm Iron & Bridge Works, Sacramento.
Ralston Iron Works, Twentieth and Indiana Sts., San Francisco.
U. S. Steel Products Co., Rialto Bldg., San Francisco.
Sims, Gray & Sauter, 156 Main St., San Francisco.
Schrader Iron Works, Inc., 1247 Harrison St., San Francisco.
Southern California Iron and Steel Co., Fourth and Mateo Sts., Los Angeles.
Western Iron Works, 141 Beale St., San Francisco.

STEEL PRESERVATIVES
Bay State Steel Protective Coating. (See adv. for coast agencies.)
Paraffine Paint Co., 34 First St., San Francisco.

STEEL FIREPROOF WINDOWS
United States Metal Products Co., San Francisco and Los Angeles.

STEEL REINFORCING
Pacific Coast Steel Company, Rialto Bldg., San Francisco.
Southern California Iron & Steel Company, Fourth and Mateo Sts., Los Angeles.
Woods, Huddart & Gunn, 444 Market St., San Francisco.

STEEL ROLLING DOORS
Kinnear Steel Rolling Door Co., W. W. Thurston, Rialto Bldg., San Francisco.

STEEL SASH
"Fenestra," solid steel sash, manufactured by Detroit Steel Products Company, Detroit, Mich.

STEEL WHEELBARROWS
Champion and California steel brands, made by Western Iron Works, 141 Beale St., San Francisco.

STONE
California Granite Co., 518 Sharon Bldg., San Francisco.
McGilvray Stone Company, 634 Townsend St., San Francisco.

STORAGE SYSTEMS—GASOLINE, OIL, ETC.
S. F. Bowser & Co., 612 Howard St., San Francisco.
Rix Compressed Air and Drill Co., First and Howard Sts., San Francisco.

TEMPERATURE REGULATION
Johnson Service Company, 149 Fifth St., San Francisco.

THEATER AND OPERA CHAIRS
C. F. Weber & Co., 365 Market St., San Francisco.

When writing to Advertisers please mention this magazine.

ARCHITECTS' SPECIFICATION INDEX—*Continued*

TILES, MOSAICS, MANTELS, ETC.
Rigney Tile Company, Sheldon Bldg., San Francisco.
Mangrum & Otter, 561 Mission St., San Francisco.
McElhinney Tile Co., 1097 Mission St,. San Francisco.

TILE FOR ROOFING
Gladding, McBean & Co., Crocker Bldg., San Francisco.
United Materials Co., Crossley Bldg., San Francisco.

TILE WALLS—INTERLOCKING
Denison Hollow Interlocking Blocks, Forum Bldg., Sacramento.
Gladding, McBean & Co., San Francisco, Los Angeles, Oakland and Sacramento.

TREES
California Seed Company, 151 Market St., San Francisco.

VACUUM CLEANERS
"Tuec" Air Cleaner, manufactured by United Electric Co. Coast agencies, 556 Sutter St., San Francisco, and 724 S. Broadway, Los Angeles.
Palm Vacuum Cleaners, sold by Western Vacuum Supply Co., 1125 Market St., San Francisco.
Spencer Turbine Cleaner, sold by Hughson & Merton, 530 Golden Gate Ave., San Francisco.

VALVES
Sloan Royal Flush Valves. T. R. Burke, Pacific Coast agent, Wells Fargo Bldg., San Francisco.
Crane Radiator Valves., manufactured by Crane Co., Second and Brannan Sts., San Francisco.

VALVE PACKING
N. H. Cook Belting Co., 317 Howard St., San Francisco.

VARNISHES
W. P. Fuller Co., all principal Coast cities.
Glidden Varnish Co., Cleveland, O., represented on the Pacific Coast by Whittier, Coburn Co., San Francisco.
R. N. Nason & Co., San Francisco, Los Angeles, Portland and Seattle.
Standard Varnish Works. San Francisco.
S. F. Pioneer Varnish Works, 816 Mission St, San Francisco.

VENETIAN BLINDS, AWNINGS, ETC.
Burlington Venetian Blinds, Burlington, Vt., and C. F. Weber & Co., 365 Market St., San Francisco.
Western Blind & Screen Co., 2702 Long Beach Ave., Los Angeles.

VITREOUS CHINAWARE
Pacific Porcelain Ware Company, 67 New Montgomery St., San Francisco.

WALL BEDS, SEATS, ETC.
Lachman Wall Bed Co., 2019 Mission St., San Francisco.
Marshall & Stearns Co., 1154 Phelan Bldg., San Francisco.
Peek's Wall Beds, sold by Western Equipment Co., 72 Fremont St., San Francisco.
Perfection Disappearing Bed Co., 737 Mission St., San Francisco.
Noack Disappearing Ironing Board Co., Sherman Kimball Co., selling agents, 199 First St., San Francisco.

WALL PAINT
Nason's Opaque Flat Finish, manufactured by R. N. Nason & Co., San Francisco, Portland and Los Angeles.
San-A-Cote and Vel--va-Cote, manufactured by the Brininstool Co., Los Angeles; Marion D. Cohn, Co., Hansford Bldg., San Francisco, distributor.

WALL BOARD
"Amiwud" Wall Board, manufactured by Paraffine Paint Co., 34 First St., San Francisco.

WALL PAPER
Uhl Bros., 38 O'Farrell St., San Francisco.

WATER HEATERS—AUTOMATIC
Pittsburg Water Heater Co. of California, 478 Sutter St., San Francisco, and Thirteenth and Clay Sts., Oakland.
Cole Heater Company, Lick Bldg., San Francisco.

WATERPROOFING FOR CONCRETE, BRICK, ETC.
Armorite Damp Resisting Paint, made by W. P. Fuller & Co., San Francisco.
J. L. Goffette Corporation, 227 San Bruno Ave., San Francisco.
Hill, Hubbell & Co., 1 Drumm St., San Francisco.
H. W. Johns-Manville Co., San Francisco and principal Coast cities.
Glidden's Concrete Floor Dressing and Liquid Cement Enamel, sold on Pacific Coast by Whittier, Coburn Company, San Francisco.
Imperial Co., 183 Stevenson St., San Francisco.
Samuel Cabot Mfg. Co., Boston, Mass., agencies in San Francisco, Oakland, Los Angeles, Portland, Tacoma and Spokane.
Wadsworth, Howland & Co., Inc. (See adv. for Coast agencies.)

WATER SUPPLY SYSTEMS
Kewanee Water Supply System—Simonds Machinery Co., agents, 117 New Montgomery St., San Francisco.

WHEELBARROWS—STEEL
Western Iron Works, Beale and Main Sts., San Francisco.

WHITE ENAMEL FINISH
"Gold Seal," manufactured and sold by Bass-Hueter Paint Company. All principal Coast cities.
"Silkenwhite," made by W. P. Fuller & Co., San Francisco.
"Satinette," Standard Varnish Works, 113 Front St, San Francisco.

WINDOWS—REVERSIBLE, CASEMENT, ETC.
Whitney Window, represented by Richard Spencer, Hearst Bldg., San Francisco.
Hauser Reversible Window Co., Balboa Bldg., San Francisco.
International Casement Co., represented by Edwin C. Dehn, Hearst Bldg., San Francisco.

WIRE FABRIC
U. S. Steel Products Co., Rialto Bldg., San Francisco.

WOOD MANTELS
Fink & Schindler, 218 13th St., San Francisco.
Mangrum & Otter, 561 Mission St., San Francisco.

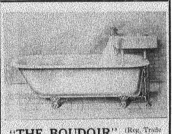

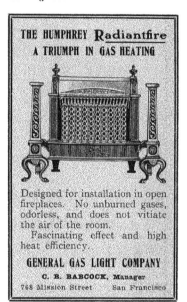

When writing to Advertisers please mention this magazine.

BUILDING FOR THE SIMMONS COMPANY, LOS ANGELES

Twelve-inch
RED RUFFLED BRICK
used with GOLDEN RUFFLED TRIM and TILE INSERTS.

MANUFACTURED BY

Los Angeles Pressed Brick Company
LOS ANGELES

UNITED MATERIALS COMPANY
CROSSLEY BUILDING, SAN FRANCISCO
Distributers for Northern California

When writing to Advertisers please mention this magazine.

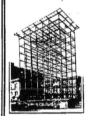

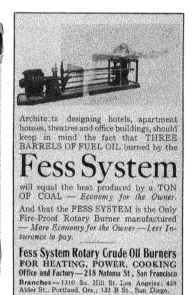

When writing to Advertisers please mention this magazine.

THE ARCHITECT & ENGINEER

25c Copy
$1.50 a Year.

OF CALIFORNIA

Volume XLVIII
Number 3

Issued monthly in the interest of Architects, Structural Engineers, Contractors and
the Allied Trades of the Pacific Coast.
Entered at San Francisco Post Office as Second Class Matter.

CONTENTS FOR MARCH, 1917

A LATIN-AMERICAN PATIO
ALBERT FARR, ARCHITECT

THE

Architect and Engineer
Of California
Pacific Coast States

VOL. XLVIII.　　　　　MARCH, 1917　　　　　No. 3.

Plans for the State Building on the San Francisco Civic Center

By B. J. S. CAHILL, Architect

COMPETITIONS, like matrimony, trial by jury and other institutions, are periodically railed against and found quite impossible. But they survive all opposition, for the good reason that no one has provided any satisfactory substitute.

And since we are going to discuss briefly the fourth building to be erected on the Civic Center, we might note in passing that the designs of three out of four of these were secured by competition; and they are generally conceded to be superior architecturally to the one that was secured without competition. And if Mr. Woollett has "criticised" the City Hall and Mr. Matthews has contested the library decision, and others in turn are now dissatisfied with Mr. Matthews' juryship on the State building, the profession has at least been well served in all these competitions. And if anyone thinks that heat and wrangling can be avoided by cutting out the competition, I would remind him that the heat and wrangling provoked over the Auditorium was even more bitter than the discontent engendered by all three of the competitions combined.

The main thing to be considered is the end achieved architecturally. With competitions we get at least quite worthy buildings and of course much personal dissatisfaction. It seems inevitable.

Without competition we got a distinctly less worthy design plus decidedly more personal dissatisfaction. The Psalmist declares that "a dinner of herbs and peace is better than a stalled ox and hatred therewith." But if more hatred is to be served up with the beans than with the beef, why then by all means let us have the beef.

※　　※　　※　　※　　※

The June, 1909, issue of The Architect and Engineer shows the original Civic Center plan made by the writer in 1904. It shows the two-block plaza west of the then City Hall with a library site and an art museum site on the two blocks opposite the City Hall. It also showed an auditorium where the Auditorium now stands and "a state building" on the exact block designated in this competition (McAllister and Redwood, Polk and Larkin).

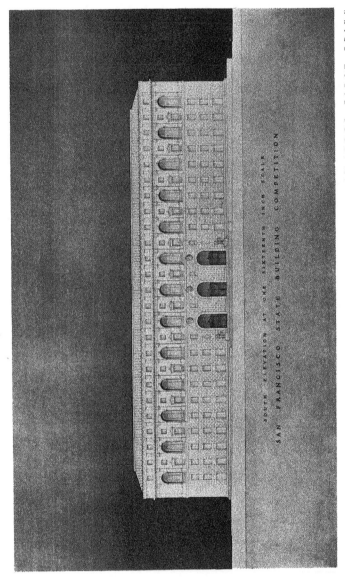

SOUTH ELEVATION AT ONE SIXTEENTH INCH SCALE
SAN FRANCISCO STATE BUILDING COMPETITION

AWARDED FIRST PRIZE
BLISS & FAVILLE, ARCHITECTS

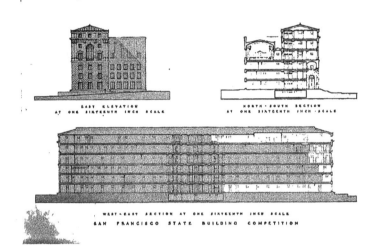

EAST ELEVATION
AT ONE SIXTEENTH INCH SCALE

NORTH-SOUTH SECTION
AT ONE SIXTEENTH INCH-SCALE

WEST-EAST SECTION AT ONE SIXTEENTH INCH SCALE
SAN FRANCISCO STATE BUILDING COMPETITION

Bliss & Faville, Architects

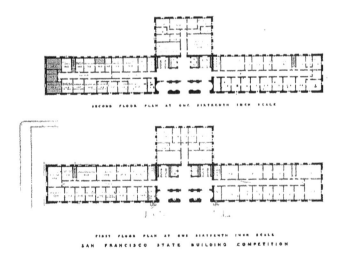

SECOND FLOOR PLAN AT ONE SIXTEENTH INCH SCALE

FIRST FLOOR PLAN AT ONE SIXTEENTH INCH SCALE
SAN FRANCISCO STATE BUILDING COMPETITION

Bliss & Faville, Architects

FOURTH FLOOR PLAN AT ONE SIXTEENTH INCH SCALE

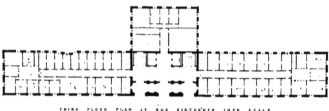

THIRD FLOOR PLAN AT ONE SIXTEENTH INCH SCALE
SAN FRANCISCO STATE BUILDING COMPETITION

Bliss & Faville, Architects

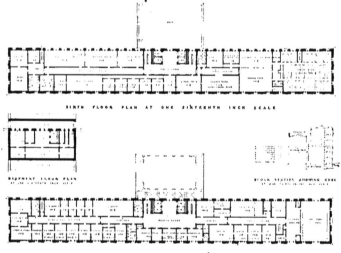

SIXTH FLOOR PLAN AT ONE SIXTEENTH INCH SCALE

BASEMENT FLOOR PLAN   BIOLA SECTION SHOWING CUBE

FIFTH FLOOR PLAN AT ONE SIXTEENTH INCH SCALE
SAN FRANCISCO STATE BUILDING COMPETITION

Bliss & Faville, Architects

The plan also showed Grove street extended into Marshall square and Hyde street also extended into Marshall square, exactly as now carried out. The Fulton street widening to Ash avenue and the extension of this boulevard to the Panhandle was not carried out. In consequence of the destruction of the City Hall, Fulton street was driven through into Market street instead.

To show that The Architect and Engineer can give sound prophetic advice, let us quote from the same issue, where, on page 72, it "submits the proposition that the library site recently acquired (the block southwest of Van Ness avenue and Hayes) be sold or exchanged for any one of the three available blocks around the proposed plaza," the place where I had originally placed the library in 1904.

This was literally carried out. At the time I made these carefully considered plans, begun in 1899, I was accused of "limited vision" and publicly described as a "nuisance"!

In view, then, of having conceived the Civic Center (and named it, too), I feel I may offer some suggestions, not merely as one who writes sympathetically of other men's work from time to time, but as one who worked single-handed through many years for this idea, without reward from the city or even credit from my fellow craftsmen, many of whom have reaped where I have sown!

*   *   *   *   *

No city plan should be too sophisticated. By this I mean that a too strict and formal programme for arranging a group of monumental buildings about a void will of itself come to grief. Personally I do not particularly favor the even cornice idea—the constant module, the uniform style, the monotone tint, the same material scale or texture. I distrust anyone with too positive convictions on these points. It may be a matter of blood and temperament, or of race, whether you are Celt, Latin or Teuton, or whether you are, as the French say, "particularist" or "communist."

There are as good arguments for a group of contrasted buildings as for wholly harmonious ones. A group of quite divergent structures can be immensely interesting. The greatest groups of the world are made up of contrasts rather than blends.

Any group of buildings around a space will show three fronts at once by the law of perspective, and a symphony with its three or four separate movements gives us an excellent analogy. Now, in music, incomparably the greatest of all the arts, the parts of a great composition in tempo, key and sentiment are invariably contrasted. Otherwise a symphony would be intolerably monotonous.

Much may be said for a reasonable resemblance of parts in a group of buildings, but assuming a group made at one time within the spirit of the prevailing mode, there should at least be contrast and variety. I feel that the demand for a uniform cornice line has been embarrassing from the beginning. It seems to me a very schooly and pedantic notion and it has already tended to make the Civic Center a little lame and tiresome.*

For this reason it seems important to secure a different architect for each of the six buildings of the Civic Center.

The chosen design by Bliss & Faville, therefore, should first be considered as the north end of the Civic Center, how it will link up or con-

*Editor's Note.—Mr. Cahill's point about a uniform cornice is well taken, but why did they put it in the programme?

SOUTH ELEVATION : SAN FRANCISCO STATE BUILDING COMPETITION

CHARLES PETER WEEKS, ARCHITECT

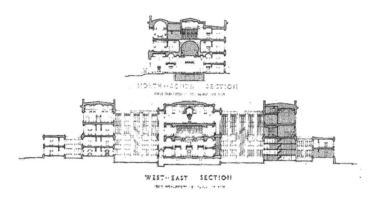

NORTH-SOUTH SECTION

WEST-EAST SECTION

SAN FRANCISCO STATE BUILDING COMPETITION

Charles Peter Weeks, Architect

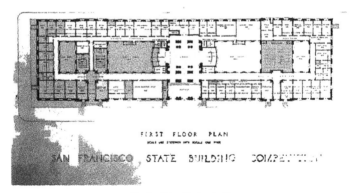

FIRST FLOOR PLAN

SAN FRANCISCO STATE BUILDING COMPETITION

Charles Peter Weeks, Architect

SOUTH ELEVATION. STATE BUILDING COMPETITION
WOOD & SIMPSON, ARCHITECTS

SECTION AND ELEVATION
Wood & Simpson, Architects

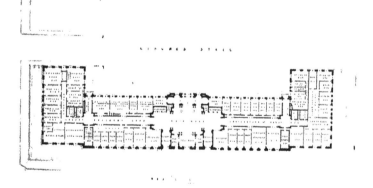

FIRST FLOOR PLAN
Wood & Simpson, Architects

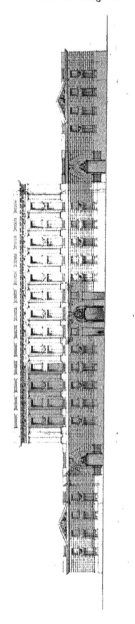

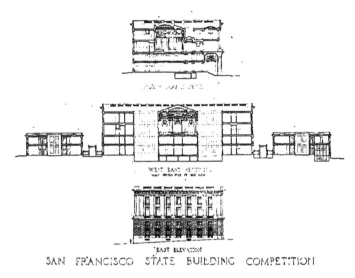

SAN FRANCISCO STATE BUILDING COMPETITION

Bakewell & Brown, Architects

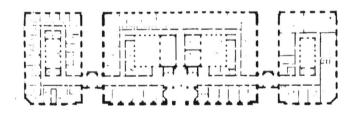

Bakewell & Brown, Architects

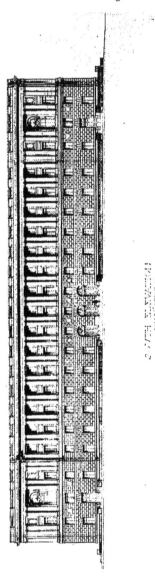

JOHN BAUR AND LORING P. RIXFORD, ARCHITECTS

EAST ELEVATION
SCALE 1/8"=1 FOOT

NORTH SOUTH SECTION
SCALE 1/8"=1 FOOT

John Baur and Loring P. Rixford, Architects

FIRST FLOOR PLAN
John Baur and Loring P. Rixford, Architects

SOUTH ELEVATION

SAN·FRANCISCO·STATE·BUILDING·COMPETITION·

LEWIS P. HOBART, ARCHITECT

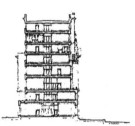

EAST ELEVATION   NORTH AND SOUTH SECTION

Lewis P. Hobart, Architect

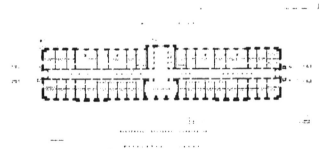

FIRST FLOOR PLAN

Lewis P. Hobart, Architect

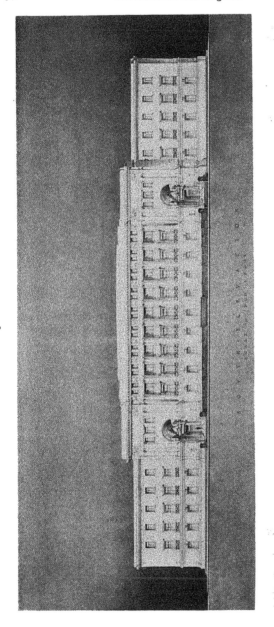

SAN FRANCISCO STATE BUILDING COMPETITION

WILLIAM C. HAYS, ARCHITECT

SAN FRANCISCO·STATE·BVILDING · COMPETITION

William C. Huys, Architect

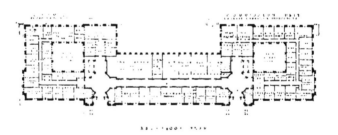

SAN FRANCISCO·STATE·BVLDING·COMPETITION

William C. Huys, Architect

SOUTH ELEVATION
ONE INCH EQUALS SIXTEEN FEET

SAN FRANCISCO STATE BUILDING COMPETITION

F. J. DE LONGCHAMPS, ARCHITECT

NORTH-SOUTH SECTION   EAST ELEVATION

WEST-EAST SECTION

ONE INCH EQUALS SIXTEEN FEET

SAN FRANCISCO STATE BUILDING COMPETITION

F. J. De Longchamps, Architect

·PLAN·OF·FIRST·FLOOR·

ONE INCH EQUALS SIXTEEN FEET

SAN FRANCISCO STATE BUILDING COMPETITION

F. J. De Longchamps, Architect

trast with the City Hall and the Library. Later will follow a brief analysis of the design in itself.

By a contrasting design, of course, we do not mean a conflicting design especially as regards bulk and scale.

I wish here to call attention to a very peculiar and embarrassing mistake made by the three gentlemen who laid out the delimiting lines of the various buildings bounding the Civic Center.

The basic principle of harmonics lies in an unequal ratio; the plan—rectangle, the very soul and essence of every beautiful room in the world. Now, two San Francisco blocks and three streets, north and south, yield $(2x275)+(3x68.9)$, or 756.3, and the short dimension is $412.6+(2x68.9)$, or 550, roughly as 15:11—a very pleasing ratio, giving a long side and a short end. In order that the City Hall on the original site should have its corner on the axis of Eighth street and Marshall square, the boundaries were squeezed in and the City Hall lot cramped to show almost the same broadside as the Auditorium at the end, thus absolutely destroying the beautiful rhythm of the original plaza. But there was, as we have pointed out, some excuse for this. When, however, the City Hall was changed over to the west side of the plaza, there was no longer any need to shorten the façade. But none the less it was shortened out of all reason. And now anyone with the least sense of proportion has only to glance at the City Hall to feel instantly the need of at least two bays on each side of the center. That the departments are crowded, it is already well known. How immensely the whole composition could have gained by being still more lengthened so as to do away with the courts and allow the dome to straddle a pavilion from the ground up instead of rising out of a void—how much better this would have been I leave those capable of visualizing the change to judge for themselves.

The result, then, of this shortening of the side that should be long—and the lengthening of the end which should be short—has brought about contradiction and confusion where there should have been rhythm and contrast. The pleasing 15:11 proportions of the Plaza have been deliberately and everlastingly spoiled. The State building suggests the side rather than the end of a rectangle—and the large gaps each side of the City Hall give a sense of something missing when we should have had a long and solid expression of a magnificent broadside adequately filling up and dominating the entire composition.

Regarding the Civic Center as a group composition and not a lot of separate units, it is important to find out how the end mass or State building will fit in with the flanks. Some of the competitors have evidently felt this need and have dropped the skyline of their buildings to a lower level at the ends so that at the two corners where City Hall and Library meet the State building at the end there shall be easy transition from each to its neighbor. Two wrongs do sometimes tend to right each other. The City Hall is too short for the long side of the Plaza and the high State building has too much length for the short end of the Plaza—relatively, if not absolutely. None the less, at the corner the distance of one cornice from the other remains about the same, and it does not appear that the bulk of the State building façade will really overpower or spoil the City Hall, whatever it may do to the library.

A plaster model of the City Hall has already been made. When one is made of the State building and library the three can be placed correctly to scale and it will be an easy matter to detect just how much, if at all, there is any need to modify the design for the State building. By reason of the short front on the City Hall and the wide gap at the end of it, I see no reason to make any change in the State building as it now stands. The similarity of the design helps, moreover, to harmonize it with the library.

And this brings us to consider the building itself.

The programme calls in the main for groups of small offices, with only a few requirements demanding monumental treatment. As all eight plans have already been selected from others, we can easily assume that within a reasonable margin they all provide well lighted, convenient and ample quarters for the public and private needs of the various State departments stipulated in the programme.

As the building is shallow, the ends are of minor importance. The rear backs on a small street and can be disregarded.

This reduces the whole field for competition to the one façade.

Which of the eight will best compose with the "Civic Center" and which of the eight develops the most architectural interest in itself?

It is remarkable that none of the designs develop articulation of the front in the plan. They all show a straight façade. In elevation, six designs show lower and subordinate wings, thus breaking the skyline. Half the designs make the main pavilion without any vertical subdivisions and half show rudimentary flanking wings. The diagram, which I have prepared to scale, shows exactly into how many parts each composition is divided and the proportions of each to the main mass. The winning design stands out unique and different from all the others in its absolute simplicity. The façade shows one plane of development only—all the rest show three, five and even eight.

It is all strictly in line with the present-day tendency towards simplicity, distinction and intensive rather than extensive development. With every opportunity to show strong features and articulation our architects instinctively make for plain façades and the plainer the better—the better chance of realization. And if the designs are graded by this process alone, as in the diagram, the result is of surprising interest.

The Bliss & Faville design develops rare distinction—a façade at once restrained, calm, broad and capable of diverse and charming subtleties of texture, form and color.

Like all real creations, it repels at first. It is not obvious, but on closer study one feels that there is something here expressed of real importance, of real value.

The high plain basement of three stories is something of a new note. One must not overlook the fact that by a device of draftsmanship this basement acquires a calm surface on paper which will disappear when this pale plane is peppered with window spots, as of course it will be when executed in granite.

Every designer is more or less mastered by his own moods and inclinations. He is obsessed with one idea on one occasion that makes no appeal on another. A certain perversity often takes possession of one's faculties, driving one on to defy all the conventions. It is hard to know how far to trust these fascinating infatuations. They lead quite often to brilliant results, but not always.

We cannot but feel that the basement fenestration would gain if the first row of windows had some slight variation at the heads. These win-

Diagrams of Design, State Building, Civic Center, Prepared by
B. J. S. Cahill, Architect

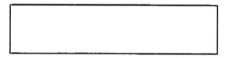

Bliss & Faville—One Plane

Baur & Rixford—One Plane in Effect, Three in Fact

Wood & Simpson—Three Planes

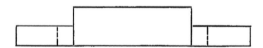

Bakewell & Brown—Three Planes in Effect, Five in Fact

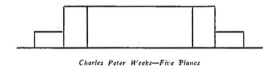

Charles Peter Weeks—Five Planes

F. J. De Longchamps—Five Planes

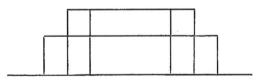

W. C. Hays—Five Planes

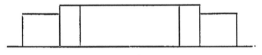

L. P. Hobart—Eight Planes

dows are larger than those above and seem to need additional differentiation. Some slight motive suggesting horizontality would give a touch of variety rather needed. The basement walls might be battered slightly and the upper stories should recede somewhat to soften the gaunt rigidity of the corners.

We think the three central arches in the upper part or the two extreme flanking ones might be deepened into belvederes and provided with projecting balconies, and the insides lined with colored marble. And of course the reveals should be deep throughout the arcade and perhaps of colored terra cotta. The front spandrils also call for color.

A slight widening of the arcades that are deepened—a few inches—would help kill a mechanical stiffness that might harden too much regularity in a design so abstemious of diversity.

But we have no doubt that these very matters will be successfully attended to by this firm of architects, who have abundantly proved their ability to accomplish something worth while in past undertakings.

*

The San Francisco State Building Competition

On account of the widespread interest in the outcome of the San Francisco State Building competition, the March issue of The Architect and Engineer of California is published two weeks in advance of the usual publication date. The designs, plans and sections of the eight architects who participated in the final stage of the competition are shown in this number and are the first to be published. After March 5th, the drawings will be hung in the rooms of the Building Material Exhibit, 77 O'Farrell street, San Francisco, where they may be viewed by the public and members of the profession.

In regard to the judgment of the jury in awarding first prize to Messrs. Bliss & Faville, Willis Polk states that had he been the judge he would have placed the design of Charles Peter Weeks first, with that of Messrs. Wood & Simpson second, and that of Bakewell & Brown third. Polk says that Mr. Hobart submitted a very intelligent piece of technique, but the imposition of an attic over the order he considered most unfortunate, and to his mind it was fatal to the success of the design. Referring to the Bliss & Faville award, Polk said:

"If the winning design disregards the cornice and does not in its main order reflect the scale of the buildings already constructed in the San Francisco Civic Center, it would, if built, be a disturbing note in the uniformity and harmony necessary for the successful completion of the Civic Center as a whole."

Charles Peter Weeks, whose design is reported to have been the second choice of the jury, suggests that if there is to be another competition for a second state building to be erected in Sacramento, the State officials should see to it that no local architects are invited to serve on the jury. He believes that better results would be accomplished by going outside the State for such professional talent.

Robert Farquahar Favored the Bakewell & Brown Design

THE, San Francisco Society of Architects on March 1 forwarded the following to Mr. Robert .Farquahar, who served on the jury, being the appointee of the Los Angeles 'Chapter, A. I. A.:

"Robert Farquahar, .architect, Los Angeles, California: The accepted design for the State building in the Civic Center of San Francisco does not in our opinion conform in any way to. the scale or scheme of buildings already forming three-fourths of the final group. We accept the result of the competition insofar as the appointment of Bliss & Faville as the architects is concerned, but strongly urge that they be requested to change their design so that it will add to, rather than detract from, the successful completion of the scheme as a whole.

"Did you fully concur in the final decision of the jury of which you were a member? A reply, if you feel·at·liberty to make one, would be appreciated.

"Frederick H. Meyer, John Reid, Jr., Clarence R. Ward, John Bauer, L. P. Rixford, Lewis P. Hobart, Charles Peter Weeks, William C. Hayes, John Bakewell, Jr., Arthur Brown, Jr., Charles Warren Perry, Ernest A. Coxhead, J. Harry Blohme, Willis Polk."

Mr. Farquahar's reply follows:

"I was not in favor of the Bliss & Faville drawings. I considered that plans No. 5 [Bakewell & Brown's] were better. Two of the three other architects, however, differed with me, and when the decision was announced two of the lay members who had sided with me ·accepted the opinion of a majority of architects.

"I considered that plans known as No. 5 were more beautiful and original and were evidence of higher architectural ability. I so stated to the jury. When the final vote was taken I asked permission to voice my objections if they were asked for. I did not put in a minority report because a majority ruled, and I was the only one finally who opposed the Bliss & Faville plans.

"The discussion and difference over the designs did not involve the matter of cost. I simply thought that San Francisco would have a more beautiful building, a creation of its own, under plans No. 5. What I am saying now I told Governor Johnson I would say if I were asked."

The San Francisco Chapter, at a meeting held on March 1, passed resolutions, of which the following is the principal paragraph:

"The San Francisco Chapter of the American Institute of Architects hereby denies these certain statements ·as emanating from this Chapter, and furthermore endorses the conduct of this competition and expresses the utmost confidence in the integrity of the award."

RESIDENCE OF BENJ. G. McDOUGALL, CLAREMONT COURT

Frederick H. Meyer Has Much New Work

Architect Frederick H. Meyer, Bankers Investment building, San Francisco, is preparing plans for a four-story steel and reinforced concrete warehouse to be erected at Twentieth and Illinois streets, San Francisco, for the Union Iron Works. The building will be 50x200 feet and will cost approximately $100,000. Mr. Meyer is also preparing plans for a three-story and basement frame and stucco store and apartment house to be erected at Post and Octavia streets, San Francisco, for B. W. Hartman. The estimated cost is $26,000. Mr. Meyer expects to let contracts this month for the construction of a six-story, steel frame, Class C office building, on Montgomery street near California, San Francisco, for the Pope Estate, which building will be the home of the San Francisco Stock and Bond Exchange and will cost approximately $100,000.

*ANTIQUE ITALIAN DOORWAYS IN POLYCHROME FROM OLD
VILLAS OF ITALY*

Some Interesting Fragments of Renaissance Architecture*

By WILLIAM L. WOOLLETT, Architect

"GIOVANNI PISANO, the lad whose uncle had just finished the great leaning tower, lingered at his work in the little workshop where he did his carving. The shop was in the alley just east of the Bishop's garden. * * * Giovanni lingered because of a certain panel. It was of wood, about two spans square and richly carved with a shield bearing the arms of a noble family. About the shield was a heavy ornamental scroll, deeply undercut and with long sweeping lines. The boy turned the panel this way and that—to the right and to the left. Walking across the room, he turned it upside down and set it upon the top of a shelf. Then, going to the bench, selected a large pair of wood

---

*Extract of an article in the Architectural Record for January, 1917. Illustrations loaned by the City of Paris, San Francisco, where the originals may be seen.

A BEAUTIFUL SPANISH FRAME

compasses, which were tipped with ivory points, and proceeded to measure and compare the various dimensions of the panel. 'Yes! It is not
square,' he muttered, 'but it looks quite so.' By skillful manipulation of
the lines in the carving on the edge of the panel and by means of the
proportions of the shield itself, which formed the central motif, he had
succeeded in obscuring the fact that the extreme boundary of the panel
was not a true square. 'I will test it,' he said, and, taking the panel
under his arm, he left the shop and alley and wound a devious way to
his chum, 'Rienzi, the armorer. A strong shoulder pressed against the
iron laden door of his friend sent it creaking open. The interior of the
smith's shop was disclosed, reeking of the soot of many forge fires, hung
with armor, some rusty, some glossy and fresh from the hammer. In
the midst of the litter, his finger on the point of the glistening blade of a
newly tempered dagger, stood Rienzi. 'What hast thou done now, Giovanni? Thine eyes like two suns look into my dusty cell. Why the fresh
beaming of so much joy?' 'I finished the panel for the Bishop's door and
I have brought it for you to see.' He stood the panel on the shelf, back

of the vise, where the light from a small window fell full upon the carving. 'It is well, Giovanni, but why so free in thy way with the forms—should not more of absolute symmetry prevail in the ornament?' 'Nay, I think not,' replied. Giovanni. 'It is just my play, anyway. The panel is square and true at least, think you, staid armorer?' 'Square? What meanest thou? Why jokest thou? Surely is the panel square, else hadst a hard time to fit it in the door. Ave Maria!' 'But, Rienzi, should I tell

AN ITALIAN PORTAL.

you that the panel was not square, how much wouldst wager me that it is not out more than the width of a finger either way?'

"Reaching under his leathern apron, Rienzi drew forth a long moleskin bag, which bulged a little with coin, and laid it on the open table near. 'Now, a pest on thy foolishness, I will wager the price of the Cardinal's dagger that my compass will prove thy panel to be square within the

GROUP OF RARE ANTIQUES

GROUP OF FINE REPRO-DUCTIONS

breadth of my little finger.' Giovanni leaped for the compass for which his friend had reached. Gauging the height of the panel accurately was the work of a moment; then swinging the tool deftly to the right, so that its span covered the width of the panel, he laid his two fingers into the space intervening between the edge of the panel and the ivory point of the compass. The stolid Rienzi looked askance. Then the ruddy hue of his countenance grayed a little. 'The evil eye,' he muttered. But Giovanni laughed a silvery laugh and took the purse. Then they were friends again, for these Machiavellian tricks came thick and fast from Giovanni, and Rienzi had really learned to like them."

* * *

In the accompanying photographs we have shown two Italian doorways and an old Spanish picture frame. These were done at a time when the craftsmanship of architecture was deemed to be an essential part of the lost art. The eternal egg-and-dart, the ogee molding and all the other paraphernalia of architectural details were fashioned by artisans who had learned, like Giovanni Pisano, the value of a line in architectural composition.

These examples of ancient architecture (sixteenth century) are now on sale in San Francisco, having been recently brought thither by collectors. They are richly carved, colored and gilded, toned by time to the subtle grays. It is stimulating to be reminded through them of other days when these gray whites were white, these reds like the red on a cardinal's coat, and the blue as cobalt of the sea—and to know that in the color drama of which they were part these fragments were but brilliant counterpart and complement to the rich trappings of rooms filled betime with the silks and satins and jewels of a people so discriminating as to note with pleasure minute fragments of form.

A lively appreciation of the value of subtle coloring in the rendering of architectural forms is stimulated by such examples. These trivial ornaments cast adrift on the shores of the Pacific in the midst of an alien civilization, poignantly point the finger of criticism at our modern methods in architecture. These simple egg-and-dart moldings, carved so carefully, so gracefully graded to suit some fine eye! How can we look with complacency upon the wagonload of egg-and-dart moldings just arrived from the factory to be placed in the drawing room of our favorite client?

Surely the love of simple things, made beautiful with care, is here made manifest, stimulating us with the thought that in the wide range of architecture there is a wealth of opportunity in a similar direction. And the architecture of the Renaissance, to many merely a derivative style, without claim to dignity or virility, as compared to the classic types, through such examples as these claims our larger human interest. These sermons in wood and gilt and color point away from a too formal, too symmetrical handling of our problems in architecture, even point away from a too great insistence on what may be termed "the ideals of the Beaux Arts." The sane but sometimes puerile insistence on mere mass and composition and function leaves little room for a kindly look at meaningful detail, subtlety of line and wealth of color.

The rendering of architectural details with finesse and imagination is so altogether worth while that the question naturally arises, Why do we not do our work more often in this way?

The answer to the above question can be found partly, perhaps, in the fact that our great schools of architecture, which no doubt have dominated to a great extent the aims of our well-trained architects, are not equipped, either through sympathy or knowledge, to teach these intimate and subtle tricks of the craftsman's art.

The schools naturally aim to give the formula for correct architecture, and if the term "correctness" may be deemed to omit the idea of inspiration and a consideration of the abstract values, the schools have accomplished their task. Too much cannot be said in appreciation of the rock-bottom value of technical education, as purveyed. We have been saved from the perdition of being illogical and illiterate in architecture, but we have not been instructed in many interesting phases of architecture, as practiced by the ancients. We have been amply fed on the A, B, C's of architecture, and when I say A, B, C's it is to be remembered that, whereas many great architects have passed through successfully the influence of the Beaux Arts training, there have been few buildings built in strict harmony with the precedents of that training that may be called great in the sense that we call some of the Gothic cathedrals great.

There is something beyond the T-square and triangle and compass and Vignola for the architect. The poet does not always linger with his sonnet, the traveler with his handbook, or the cabinet maker with his glue pot. There are other things in architecture and in architectural composition than mass and general proportions and function. In the subtleties of the Greek and Renaissance architecture we learn that curves as delicate as those of a butterfly's wing, or as suave as the swing of a glacier, may find a fitting place in the façade of a building or in the bedmolds of some otherwise insignificant doorway.

*

* *

Sure. a Concrete Spasm!

A Western cement man extracted this from his system: "I was sitting back this morning with my concrete pipe alit, and I fell into a pipe dream of when concrete would be it. I was lazy and the hazy curls of smoke around me whirled, and I dreamed about the time when this would be a concrete world. I could see the ardent lover woo a maid with concrete heart, and her father with his concrete foot suggests that they must part; see him sticking through the kicking, though he pleads in accents low, till at length he proudly leads her to a concrete bungalow. Then the dream gets slightly dimmer for a moment and gets clear, and I see a concrete cradle with the parents hovering near; I've a feeling that the squealing seems too real to be a dream, and my ears are rudely shattered by the semblance of a scream. Then the good wife comes a-running with a bucket in her hand, and she hurls a stream of water that benumbs to beat the band. She is yelling, too, and telling me that I sure do take a chance if I fall asleep while smoking, 'less I'm wearing concrete pants.'"

*

* *

Bohemians to Have Jinks Club House

The Bohemian Club of San Francisco has commissioned Louis C. Mullgardt, architect, to prepare plans for a club house to be built at Bohemian Grove, the club's summer rendezvous on the Russian River. A building in keeping with the surroundings is planned, construction to be largely of redwood and mountain stone. Preliminary sketches have been made and approved.

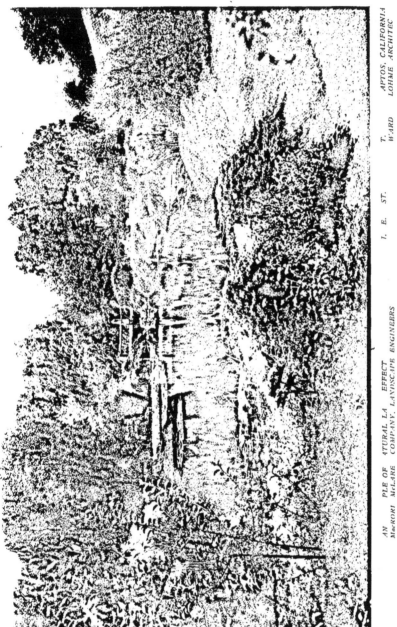

AN   PLE OF   ATURAL LA   EFFECT   I. E.   ST.   T.   APTOS, CALIFORNIA
MacRORI McLARE   COMPANY, LANDSCAPE ENGINEERS   WARD   LOHNE ARCHITEC

Beautifying the Country Estate and Importance of Expert Planning

By DONALD McLAREN

The Famous Belgian Bay.

MUCH has been written of late in regard to Landscape Gardening and Landscape Architecture in California, due to the interest which has been created in this subject within the last few years. There is no doubt but what there is a great movement throughout the entire State towards life in the country, and people generally are beginning to recognize the value and benefits of the outdoor country life.

Naturally, one loves spacious grounds and beautiful effects around the home. Values of land in the country are naturally far below those of city lots, and people are enabled to acquire considerable acreage for the price of one city lot.

This movement is noticed not only in large cities like San Francisco, but we find throughout the entire State that business men in towns the size of Sacramento, Fresno and Oakland are moving further out into the country, there to develop and beautify with nature's bounteous gifts picturesque suburban places.

Another factor which has had a large effect in developing landscape gardening in California is the fact that many Eastern people who have retired from business have migrated to California on account of our wonderful climate and have established permanent homes here.

Landscape gardening in our Eastern States, they being far older than California, has naturally been more highly developed, and the Eastern man coming to California recognizes this fact and upon establishing himself here looks first of all towards his home grounds. He appreciates the value of our wonderful climatic conditions, contrasting them in his mind to the harsh conditions prevailing in the State from which he came, and develops his estate accordingly.

As a matter of fact, one of the most encouraging signs that landscape gardening is becoming an important factor in this State is the fact that within the last few years a separate department has been established in the University of California for the expert training of landscape gardeners and architects. This undoubtedly will have a very material effect upon the future development of this profession, and its results cannot be anything but beneficial to all concerned.

Another element which has given impetus to landscape gardening in this State is the fact that the landscape work at both the Panama-Pacific International Exposition at San Francisco and the Panama-California Exposition at San Diego were such great successes; in fact, in each case these were revelations to many of our own people and are sure to have a lasting effect.

We are able to use in our planting work in this State a class of plants which cannot be grown anywhere else in the United States, with the ex-

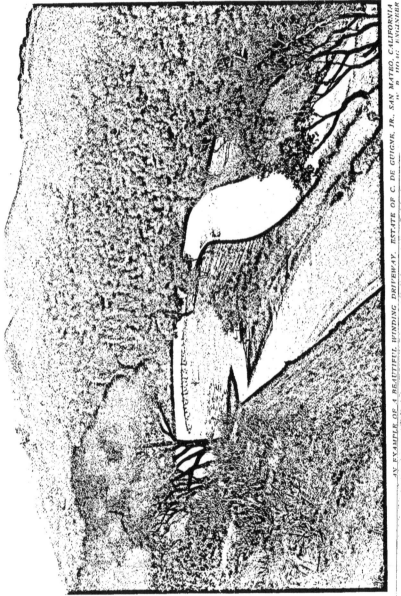

AN EXAMPLE OF A BEAUTIFUL WINDING DRIVEWAY. ESTATE OF C. DE GUIGNE, JR., SAN MATEO, CALIFORNIA
H. B. HOAG, ENGINEER

Specimen Plant of Raphis Flabelliformis.

ception of Florida and some of the most Southern States. We may use evergreen trees and shrubs throughout our plantings, so that a good effect is possible throughout the year.

The importance of having a definite plan worked out in every detail on paper, prior to starting any gardening operations, cannot at this time be too strongly emphasized. This plan should not be prepared in haste, but should be a matter of much study and consideration, not only by the owner but by the architect and landscape gardener working in conjunction. These three should work in unison and should give careful thought and care to every detail, as we all know that it is a matter of common occurrence to meet with people who have started to lay out their own gardens without the assistance of a competent adviser, and have become discouraged and given up hope of ever attaining their end, which is, of course, very deeply to be regretted, as beautiful gardens are obtainable here in California so easily and with comparatively little expense. Too much stress cannot be laid upon the importance of a complete and full understanding between the owner, architect and landscape gardener; in fact, the house site itself should not be selected without a decision having been reached by them all, as there are a great many angles and points of view to be considered and the matter must be threshed out from every standpoint.

Very Unusual Specimen of Sanda Sanderiana from the Island of Mindanao.

Another important element in connection with the garden and one which is often overlooked or not given sufficient attention is the class of help employed to direct the laying out of the work. It should always be borne in mind that a competent man in this line of labor is entitled to as much consideration as in any other occupation. It will be found

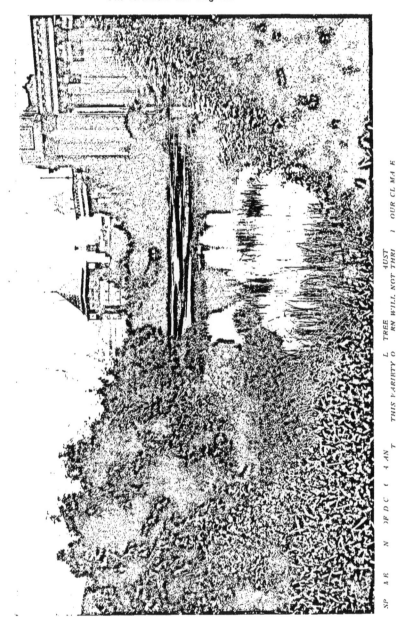

SP AE   N OF D C (4 AN   T   THIS VARIETY O   RN WILL NOT THRI   AUST
L TREE   1   OUR CL M A E

HYDRANGEAS, ESPECIALLY THE COMMON VARIETY (HYDRANGEA HORTENSIS), ESTATE OF F. H. AMES, SAN MATEO
GEORGE H. HOWARD, ARCHITECT *MacRORIE-McLAREN COMPANY, LANDSCAPE ENGINEERS*

HOUSE IN SAN MATEO COUNTY, SHOWING EFFECTIVE USE OF BELGIAN BAY
AND HEDGE

Specimen Plant of Cyclamen.

that any competent man will have served his apprenticeship for at least four years either before coming to America or on some of our large estates or public parks' in the East or abroad. Yet we frequently find the entire management of the garden left in the hands of some incompetent person who has had absolutely no training whatsoever. The results, of course, are unsatisfactory to the owner.

The importance of keeping up a garden after it has once been set out is not always realized and is often the source of much dissatisfaction and disappointment. Many owners install first-class gardens, but, failing to realize how important it is to give the plants good care at least for the first few years, they place in charge an inexperienced caretaker, with the result that their gardens prove absolute failures.

At this time it might be well to speak of a matter which is receiving deep consideration from many land owners, particularly owners of large barren tracts of land upon which few if any trees exist. People generally are coming to recognize the value of tree plantings, especially mass plantings on large naked acreage tracts. These plantings serve the double purpose of providing beauty in the landscape and needed protection from winds and storms. A good example of what has been accomplished in this direction is found on the hills back of San Mateo and Burlingame, which originally were barren of trees, with the exception of a sprinkling of natural oaks in the canyons. Due to the planting which was done approximately forty years ago, this section of the peninsula is today splendidly protected with an abundance of greenery almost as plentiful as in the highly cultivated foothills and flats lying between Millbrae and San Francisco.

In fact, the tree planting has been the making of that territory. Such plantings should consist only of very hardy varieties of eucalyptus and our native pines and cypress, they being self-sustaining after the first year and making very rapid growth.

Architects, Builders and the Law

Abstract of Court Decisions on Rights and Liabilities Created by Building Contracts

By A. L. H. STREET in Building Age

FROM the numerous Appellate Court decisions which have been handed down within the last few months in cases in which architects and builders have been parties, I have prepared the following abstract as covering those which should hold the largest general interest for members of the building trades.

The importance of definiteness in contract provisions is illustrated by a holding of the Washington Supreme Court to the effect that a contract whereby an architect was to be given the privilege of drawing plans and superintending the construction of a building for the defendants, if at any time in the future the defendants should desire to erect a building, was too uncertain in its terms to sustain an action for damages on the theory of a breach of the agreement. Claiming that he had been damaged in the sum of $600 through defendants' breach of the contract in the employment of another architect in connection with the construction of a building at a cost of at least $12,000, plaintiff sued defendants. In affirming a judgment which had the effect of dismissing the suit, the Supreme Court said:

"This contract has too many uncertainties, which neither time nor any other contingency can supply, save the making of a new contract between the parties. It fails to state on what terms the employment is to be entered upon, whether appellant or respondent is to name the terms and conditions, or whether they are to be determined mutually. * * * The courts can supply some elements in a contract, but they cannot make one; and when the language in a contract is too uncertain to gather from it what the parties intend, the courts cannot enforce it."

Because plans and specifications for a municipal building to be constructed in Brooklyn involved an estimated cost largely in excess of funds appropriated for the structure, a firm of New York architects were denied right to recover for the services, in a decision handed down by the Appellate Division of the New York Supreme Court. The contract contained a clause to the effect that the total estimated cost should be "well within the total appropriation." The only appropriation in existence was one for $500,000. The plans prepared under the contract involved a cost exceeding $3,000,000. .

It was urged on the part of plaintiffs, in their suit to recover compensation for their services, that a public building for the purpose that the one in question was to be used could not have been built for the sum appropriated, and that therefore the parties were justified in believing that further sums would be appropriated, but the Appellate Division declares that "the difficulty with this argument is that we are required to prophesy the future action of the board of estimate, or to exclude entirely the words referring to the appropriation. The contract may have been a foolish one for the parties to have made. We, however, are not required to make another for them, but to interpret the contract they have made according to the language used by them."

In adjudging liability of a firm of architects for damages resulting from collapse of the roof of a school building, they having furnished the plans therefor and superintended the construction, it was decided by the Supreme Court of Washington that the architects should have anticipated that a depth of nine inches of snow might rest upon the roof at times;

and that if the roof was not sufficiently strong to carry the weight of snow which reasonably might have beeh foreseen, the measure of damages recoverable by the school district was the amount of loss actually sustained. It was said to be the architect's duty to furnish plans for and secure construction of a building which would meet the conditions expected of it.

The fact that a building contractor has failed to complete a construction contract is held by the Appellate Division of the Supreme Court not to affect his right to recover for extra work performed and materials furnished at the request of the owner as a transaction independent of the principal contract. In the same opinion the court declares that the measure of damages recoverable against a contractor for failure to complete his contract is the difference between the contract price and the actual cost to the owner of completing the work agreed to be performed.

In litigation between a builder and an owner wherein the latter claimed that certain concrete construction work had not been performed according to agreement, it was held by the Pennsylvania Supreme Court that the trial judge properly excluded from evidence plans and specifications offered by the owner, it appearing that the specifications were not referred to in the contract. As to the plans, the Supreme Court said:

"Nor is there any merit in the suggestion that the trial court erred in rejecting defendant's offer to prove the meaning of the word 'plans' as used in this connection. The distinction between the use of plans, and of specifications, was pointed out in Knelly vs. Howarth, 208 Pa. 487, 57 Atl. 957. It was there suggested that plans are not, in the same sense, nor to the same extent, to be considered an integral part of the contract as are the specifications. Their office is rather to illustrate and explain what is to be done. In the present case the offer to show that the word 'plans' included the specifications was without any sufficient basis, and was not justified, and it was properly excluded."

The question as to when a general contractor is liable for injury sustained to a workman on a building through negligence of a sub-contractor was before the Appellate Term of the New York Supreme Court in the case of Brennan vs. George L. Walker Company, where a plasterer employed by a sub-contractor was injured through fall of a ceiling constructed by another sub-contractor. The court laid down this general rule:

"Ordinarily a general contractor, who sublets part of the work of construction on a building, relinquishing the right of control and direction over the work so sublet, and exercising only such general superintendence as is necessary to see that the subcontractor duly performs his contract, is not liable for any merely negligent acts of the sub-contractor, and mere knowledge that the work is being done in a negligent manner by the sub-contractor is not sufficient to charge the general contractor therewith, unless he actually participates in and exercises control and direction over the manner in which the work is done. If, however, the work is done not merely in a negligent manner, but in violation of law, and the general contractor has knowledge of the violation of the law during the progress of the work, makes no objection, and does nothing to endeavor to cause the work to be performed in a lawful manner, he is liable, with the subcontractor, for injuries resulting from such violation of law."

Striped Paint

A paint manufacturer recently received the following letter: "Gentlemen: Will you please send us some of your striped paint? We want just enough for one barber pole."—Southern Textile Bulletin.

Closer Co-operation Between Architects and Contractors

By EMERY STANFORD HALL, A. I. A.

THE relations between the architect and the material men and contractors have often been discussed, but it is generally by the latter two classes. An architect may be trained or untrained; may know or may not know. A material manufacturer or dealer may truthfully present the qualities of his wares or he can surround them with an atmosphere of mystery. A contractor may build with infinite care or shiftless neglect. The architect, material man and contractor may work together to the best interest of the owner or they may quibble and quarrel and get nowhere.

The architect must be qualified to diagnose his client's needs. His judgment must be predicated on established facts. He must know contract law, local trade terms and customs. In the taking of competitive bids he must use discretion in the choice of responsible bidders. He must take pains to see that all bidders are treated fairly and justly. He must recognize that his client is under obligation alike to all worthy contractors; that having received carefully prepared, legitimate bids, that the lowest capable bidder has justly earned the award of the contract. He must realize that a mistake on the part of a bidder is an injustice to the contractors who have submitted bids in good faith and should bar that bid from further consideration and justly entitle the bid of the next lowest contractor to first consideration. He should realize that all bidders should be required to stand by their bids or withdraw from consideration and should not tolerate changes in bids.

Having determined that the choice of materials is properly the function of the architect, we are now prepared to inquire how materials may be best presented to architects for their consideration. The successful entering wedge would seem to be descriptive advertising in architectural publications, followed by short personal letters drawing attention to the nature and availability of a product and suggesting the possibility of an early interview with the representative. Following this correspondence, a technically expert missionary should call upon the architect. The qualifications of this representative are of the utmost importance. There is nothing more annoying to an architect than to waste his time in an interview with a representative of a material manufacturer who lacks both information and tact. A special representative of a material manufacturer should carry with him a very carefully prepared catalogue or illustrated page substantially gotten up on architect standard size pages. This should give complete detailed information and illustrations of the product which he is presenting. This material should be especially trustworthy and exactly to the point. There must be no doubt as to the nature and proper application of the product.

During this interview, the material missionary should tell the architect where he may see full-sized working models of his product. There is no method so convincing to clinch an argument as to see the actual material in ample scale, and next to seeing the material actually in place, convenient exhibits of full-sized models are most effective. If the architect specifies the material, then he is in fact, if not in name, the purchasing agent. The wise material man will recognize his status as such and give him all of the data necessary for intelligent purchase. There can be no intelligence in purchase if there is not an accurate knowledge of actual price as well as comparative prices. The material man should remember that no architect of character will specify any material where he does not know the actual price which the reputable contractor will have to pay.

Why should not the material man be perfectly frank and give the architect the trade discounts at once, thus saving him the trouble of getting them in some other way? I have never been able to see the reason for the mystery with which so many material men surround their products—a mystery preserved both as to chemical composition and to price. To me it is an insult to the intelligence of the architect. Of course, the sensible architect knows that both the material man and contractor are making a profit. It is his duty, however, to see to it that this profit is no more, quality and efficiency considered, than is asked by responsible, legitimate competitors in fair competition on an equal article. Is there, then, a single worthy plea that can be entered against the spirit of frankest co-operation existing between the material man and the architect alike in reference to information as to cost, as to quality and as to manner of installation?

Now that we understand the limitations and function of both architect and material man, let us discuss the proper relation of the contractor to the remaining members of the triangle. Primarily, the contractor is one skilled in the cost and organization of construction. To command respect in his chosen calling, he must know cost, he must be able to estimate with accuracy the amount of labor required in any trade. To execute any piece of work which is presented for his consideration, he must at all times be an authority on building material and market conditions. He must know where, when and how much material can be obtained; he must know the possibilities of the labor market; he must be able to secure the right sort of men at the right time to execute any work on which he has assumed contracts. To meet these conditions, he must be able to look both into the past and the future; he must have an accurate system of cost accounting and an accurate index of men, giving full information as to their special qualifications and availability. With this information before him, he can speak with comparative certainty as to probable cost and the time required for execution of the work.

It is to be hoped that the time will soon come when the contractor will not be required to take off quantities from plans and specifications. The system in vogue at present which requires each contractor to make his own quantity survey is a duplication of the same service, which is not only wasteful but puts upon the contractor a duty for which he is not qualified by his training. This system has always been most productive of misunderstanding between owner, contractor and architect. All should co-operate to secure the early adoption of a system of independent quantity surveys, a system which would submit a duplicate and intelligently presented list of material to all contractors estimating on any given branch of work, making certain in this manner a uniform basis of estimating.

Another item which demands particularly close co-operation between the architect and contractor is the manner and method of inviting, preparing and handling of bids on proposed work. There is just as much reason for guaranteeing the secret system of bidding to the sub and original contractor and to the owner as there is for guaranteeing the secret ballot to the elector. There is the same argument against submitting more than one bid on the same subject-matter as there is against "repeating" at the ballot box. These conditions apply with equal force to bids submitted by the major contractor to the owner through the architect, and to bids submitted by minor contractors and material men to the major contractors.

If each contractor who submits a bid on any item to any person would exercise the necessary care in the preparation of such bid to insure himself that this bid represents the definite minimum for which he would be willing to accept the work, then the old bluff, "I have a lower bid," would not appeal to him. The submitting of bids to contractors' associations in advance of submitting them to the parties for whom they are intended constitutes a dangerous practice, which is ultimately certain to lead to scandal. Reputable architects do not peddle bids. The reputable contractor should refuse to submit bids through any other sort of architect. The real general contractor does not peddle bids. Sub-contractors and material men's associations should advise their members not to submit bids to so-called contractors who are known to peddle bids. They should go further than this. They should clearly state in their code of ethics that they consider it dishonorable practice for any competing contractor to secure information as to the bids submitted by other contractors, either through the architect's office, general contractor's office or from each other.

Within a few days after the contract is signed, all persons having to do with the award of the contract should make an announcement of the amounts of the bids submitted in order to satisfy the competing contractors as to the fairness of the award. Frank methods of this sort will do much to sustain the confidence which is essential to co-operation between architect, material man and contractor. Once the contract has been assumed, the contractor should immediately make out a programme of construction to insure the completion of his work, after making due allowance for unforeseen delays, at the time fixed by the contract. He should purchase his materials immediately, making contract for delivery according to his schedule.

The contractor's monthly requisitions for payment should be accompanied by an accurate statement of the entire amount of work essential for the completion of the work and the proportionate part of that work already completed. With such a statement before him, the architect may issue the proper certificates without undue delay. One of the chief causes of delay in the issuance of an architect's certificate is the vague and indefinite statements accompanying contractors' requisitions for payment. In a large majority of cases, through carelessness rather than evil intent, the statements submitted are misleading and are so worded as to make them impractical both to use as a basis for checking up the work already executed, as well as the work still to be completed.

It should be borne in mind that the architect's interest is not so much in the work already completed as it is the probable cost of executing the remaining work under contract. The architect is charged with the duty of reserving sufficient funds at all times to complete the contract and to secure all guarantees. With reference to the relation between the contractor and material man, it should be borne in mind that no warrantee on the part of the material man can be enforced unless the contractor is careful to comply strictly with the instructions of the material man as to the manner of use or installation of the material covered by the warrantee.

Having thus frankly discussed the controlling factors essential to co-operation between contractor, material man and architect, what is to hinder immediate procedure along these lines?

Floors and Floor Construction in Office Buildings*

THE types of floor construction most commonly found in the modern buildings are as shown in the accompanying designs. These sketches are by no means intended to cover the entire range or even include all of the common types. They show, however, in the opinion of the writer, the more common.

The essential features to be considered in any floor construction are strength, stiffness, durability, fireproofing qualities, light weight, small depth, and the cost. The construction of high buildings demands that the dead weight and the depth of the floor be reduced to a minimum consistent with good construction and the cost. In recent years various new types of floor construction have been placed before the designer and improvements have been made in the older types with the object of accomplishing these results. The forms used for concrete floors are also an important factor and have been subjected to much study and some reduction in the new types.

The partitions of office buildings are subject to continual rearrangement to suit different tenants, and the floor, therefore, should be designed to permit a partition to be placed in any position. This requirement is usually satisfied by assuming a certain weight (10 to 25 pounds per square foot) for partitions and adding this to the dead load of the floor.

Flat ceilings are also desirable and this requires the use of suspended ceilings for some of the types of floor construction. Ample fire protection should be given the beam on both flanges.

This paper does not attempt to discuss the relative advantages and disadvantages of various types of floor construction. The firms most interested have been quite successful in presenting the respective merits of their particular type and the designer must investigate these claims and make his choice accordingly.

The arrangement and the spacing of the floor beams are influenced by so many conditions, such as location of openings, the locations where comparatively deep beams are permitted, etc., etc., that it is impossible to suggest a particular set of rules to be followed.

The columns having been located and as it is desirable in all cases to transmit the floor loads as directly as possible to the columns, the main panels will be determined from this consideration. The economical span of the type of the floor construction will limit the size of the sub-panels. Thus, for terra cotta arches the usual span is from 5 feet to 6 feet, for reinforced concrete slabs the span will probably be larger, but not to exceed 8 feet to 9 feet, while for the concrete joist construction no intermediate panels will be required, as this construction may safely be used for spans up to 26 feet or 28 feet.

For large stretches of floor surface the arrangement of the beams may be influenced by the desire to give continuity to the floor construction. Also, usually there will be a number of floor beams in the panel and only one girder, and as the clearance may limit the depth of the girder it may be desirable to run the beams in the long direction and the girder in the short direction in order that the latter may not become too deep. Another factor which may determine the direction of the girder is the wind bracing, which may require that the deep girders run in the small direction of the building in order to obtain the advantage of the stiffness of the deep girder connections.

*From a paper, "Comparative Designs of Office Buildings," presented before the Western Society of Engineers by Fred Ruchts and printed in the October Journal of the Society.

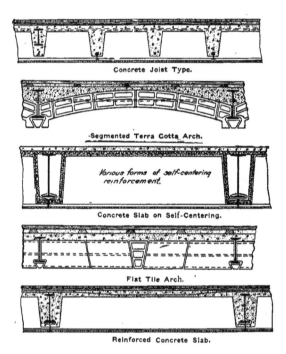

Concrete Joist Type.

-Segmented Terra Cotta Arch.

Various forms of self-centering reinforcement.

Concrete Slab on Self-Centering.

Flat Tile Arch.

Reinforced Concrete Slab.

In all cases, however, it should be the aim of the designer to make as many panels equal and rectangular as the general plan will permit. This will give duplication in the structural steel, concrete forms, and terra cotta blocks.

Beam to beam connections are made, in most cases, by simple web connections. These may consist of one or two angles, or in skew connections of bent angles or plates. It will be necessary at times to make a connection by resting one beam on top of another, in which case it may be necessary to investigate the webs of these beams for buckling resistance. Beams framing into shallower ones should be avoided, as this requires large cuts in order to clear the flanges of the shallow beam.

Unnecessary coping and blocking at the ends of the beams should be avoided and this may be done in many cases without injuring the construction in any way. For instance, very often the floor beams are not as deep as the girders into which they frame. By placing the beams at a slightly different elevation than the girder (1 in. to 1½ in.) connection may be made without any cutting. Holes in both the flanges and the web should be avoided where possible and only one size of hole should be used in any one beam. The cutting of beams and the punching of two sizes of holes in a beam, while of small importance in the design of the building, increases the cost of fabrication considerably, and may many times be avoided by a little thoughtfulness in designing.

Beam to column connections are probably most satisfactorily made by using top and seat angles, with stiffener angles if required by the load. This type of connection for the usual sizes of rolled beams is capable of transmitting a larger moment than the web connection and is, therefore, more desirable for wind bracing.

In many cases the clearance lines will not permit the use of stiffener angles. In such cases simple web connections must be used. A satisfactory wind bracing connection may very often be made by the use of web connection angles with top and bottom seat angles.

*

* *

Popularity of the Enclosed Porch

THE carpenter has finished his task and the long porch, veranda, piazza or stoop has been enclosed for the winter. The radiators, exposed to the weather five months in the year, have been regilded. Father has started a fire in the furnace. A comfortable warmth pervades the house. The French windows stand open. No one will consent to stay in the apartment known thirty years ago as the sitting room, twenty years ago as the parlor, ten years ago as the drawing room, and commonly designated as the living room today, says the New York Times. Everybody has moved into the enclosed porch; the whole family wants to live in the glass house.

The popularity of enclosed verandas is recent but striking. There are certain difficulties in the way of their universal installation. They call for large or long radiators. The plumber, with a serious air, tells you that one square foot of glass requires ten times as much radiating surface as a square foot of plastered wall. He shakes his head as he says you will have to have a boiler two sizes larger. He specifies that the lattice work beneath the porch shall be bricked up. You agree to all his conditions because you have tasted the pleasures of dwelling outdoors the year round.

There is a pleasanter style of country life. It really matters little whether the enclosed porch is an integral part of the house, a room with a hardwood floor, ivory trim and a fireplace, or just a pine floored stoop with rough shingles on one side. The point is that the other three sides are in glass. The glass may be beveled plate or may consist of mere latticed panes set in a hothouse frame and screwed in place. Either floods your outdoor room with sunlight; either lets you look out on the leafless trees and barren lanes, while, warm as toast, you lounge in a deep wicker chair, gay with flowered cretonne cushions, reading the morning paper. On a card table at your elbow rests the breakfast tray loaded with crisp toast and steaming coffee.

*

* *

Nearing the Roof

"I started to work on my twentieth story yesterday," said a busy looking man, "and I tell you I'm making it pay." "You are an author?" suggests his neighbor. "Certainly not! I'm an architect."—*Exchange*.

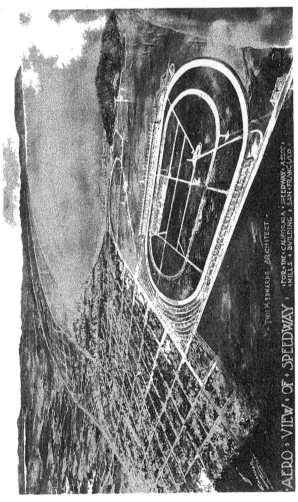

AERO · VIEW · OF · SPEEDWAY

THOS. A. EDWARDS · ARCHITECT ·

· FOR · THE · CALIFORNIA · SPEEDWAY · ASSO ·
· MILLS · BVILDING · SAN · FRANCISCO ·

MOTOR SPEEDWAY, SAN MATEO
THOS. M. EDWARDS, ARCHITECT

Proposed Motor Speedway at San Mateo

THE proposed motor speedway, drawings of which were a feature of the recent Salon de Luxe auto display at the Palace Hotel, San Francisco, will be the only track of the kind west of Chicago and will be patterned in many respects after the famous two-mile track at Sheepshead Bay. The San Mateo course will be one and one-quarter miles and with its buildings will represent an estimated expenditure of $400,000.

On account of the high cost of steel, the speedway will be constructed of wood and will have paraboloid turns 70 feet wide and 60 feet on the straightaway. There will also be the usual accessories pertaining to a racing plant. The grand stand will accommodate 20,000 chairs, with the box seats included, and the bleachers will seat 25,000 or more if necessary.

The club house on the infield will be a low-setting structure and large enough to accommodate club parties and others assembled on the parking spaces inside the track proper.

There will be four concrete-lined subways to afford an exit for the motorists who will fill up the infield.

The score boards, extensive wire fences to protect the public, racing car pits and all necessary conveniences for the public are also included in the general scheme of the architect, Thomas M. Edwards. The project is being promoted by the California Speedway Association, of which Ivan W. Gates is manager.

* * *

American Adaptation of the French Chateau Type

"OUR ablest architects," writes Mr. Dewitt H. Fessenden in a paper on "American Adaptation of the French Chateau Type" in a recent number of Arts and Decoration, "have won their art spurs by ability to tack on modern ideas to accepted types. No more pleasing example for this practice can be found than in the old chateaus that dot the banks of the Loire. So numerous and important are these that the region much traveled by artists and tourists is geographically known as the chateau district. Already many handsome erections in rural America owe their development to these French prototypes. It is the power to invest a new building suitable to modern requirements with an old worldly charm that proclaims the artist-architect. A very rare and precious product.

"The alliance between art, history and architecture is so subtle but at the same time so pronounced that they cannot be studied apart, each being a complement of the other. The styles and periods of architecture are merely the reflections of the men and women then living, just as today the houses we see to be effective must express the character and occupation to some extent of the people inhabiting them. Architecture has always played a very important part in France, which is easily intelligible when we bear in mind that the French, being artists, must perforce express themselves artistically, and where can they do that to better effect than in their homes?

"Mansard, who died in 1666, was one of the great French architects whom we know well. Montesquieu, another, who said: 'Love is an architect who builds palaces or ruins, if he pleases.' Architects ruined the reign of Louis XIV. The life of France and its people is well expressed in its architecture."

Architect vs. Liability Insurance

By F. E. DAVIDSON*

THE passage of the workmen's compensation laws in most of the commonwealths of the United States during the past five years has created a situation demanding the utmost vigilance on the part of architects if they are to protect the interests of their clients under the provisions of these laws.

No building contract can be so carefully prepared as to protect a client's interests under any and all circumstances; for the reason that most of the workmen's compensation laws now in effect provide that an injured workman of a contractor or a sub-contractor may claim compensation directly from the owner of the building in case injury is received, even though he may not be in any way employed by the owner; thus, if for any reason the employer of the injured workman, either the sub-contractor or the contractor, is not insured or is inadequately insured, or if for any reason the contractor or sub-contractor should become solvent, the whole burden goes directly upon the owner. It is, therefore, of the utmost importance to all owners that architects, in the interests of their clients, be thoroughly posted on the various compensation acts in the several States in which their work is done.

The architect's relation to the owner is such that there is the greatest moral obligation on him to see to it that the owner is thoroughly protected. The mere fact alone that the contractor or sub-contractor carries insurance should not be sufficient to satisfy the architect. He must be sure that the insurance is good insurance, that it is written in such manner as to describe all of the work covered, and that the insurance is not allowed to lapse or be cancelled and not replaced by other satisfactory coverage or insurance during the progress of the work.

Workmen's compensation insurance policies are often written for contractors by agents who are not familiar with all the provisions of the compensation laws and regulations, and the agent who writes insurance is naturally not as interested in his assured as the architect should be. Consequently, policies have oftentimes been found to have been written covering only a part of the work, and not on broad enough lines to cover any possible operations which may be undertaken by the contractor during the policy period.

In some States, notably Illinois, the Industrial Board has the power to require, and does require, that all insurance policies cover all operations and all employees of the assured, and while under this practice it is likely that the insurance companies could be forced to cover a loss, even though the specific kind of work from which the accident arose was not enumerated in the policy. Such matters require time and occasion vexatious delays and difficulties, and it is far better if the architect knows that the contractors and sub-contractors are thoroughly covered before the work is done, rather than rely upon straightening out the trouble should it arise.

Instances have been found where contractors of other States have come into Illinois to engage in work where their policy contract, written primarily to cover working conditions in other States, does not adequately take care of the situation in Illinois. This, too, is a matter which the architect should determine before the contractor undertakes the work on a building.

*President of the Illinois Society of Architects.

It is therefore quite evident, all facts considered, that the situation is far different under the Workmen's Compensation system than it was under the days of common law liability; where the owner was not liable to the injured employee of his contractor or sub-contractor unless he himself had been guilty of negligence. The new system which makes an accident a direct charge upon the owner, in the absence of adequate insurance carried by the immediate employer of the injured, creates a necessity for incessant vigilance on the part of the architect if he is to properly conserve the interests of his client. No matter how thoroughly satisfied he may be that the insurance carried by all the contractors or sub-contractors is adequate, he should also insist that the owner is adequately protected by contingent liability insurance.

A number of architects in Chicago have solved this problem to their satisfaction by having written an "Owners and Architects" contingent liability policy covering all of the work handled through their offices. It is only necessary where this system is followed to have a rider issued to the "blanket" policy, naming each new owner, as owner, as such new work is started. The cost of this kind of insurance is nominal, and in the writer's opinion gives to the architect and his client all the protection which can be afforded by law.

* * *

New York is Hotel Mad

MANHATTAN ISLAND seems to be in danger of going hotel crazy. Twelve giant structures, intended for hotel purposes, are either in course of planning or under way in the big metropolis. These will represent, when completed, an outlay of approximately $36,000,000, and will add something like 10,000 rooms to the city's hotel accommodations.

Experienced hotel men doubt the wisdom of so much hotel construction, while admitting that times are better than they have ever been. Fear that present conditions are only for a short period has caused them to urge caution. Times were when a hotel was not more than 75 per cent full during most of the year. Occasionally the average has been as low as 50 per cent. But those were other years. The year just ended and the present one tell a different story, a story of a country-wide prosperity; an era which is not to die for a long time. Some hotel men are of the opinion that, though caution is a good thing for a business man, it is out of place today. There is a scarcity of hotel accommodations in the city now.

The statement has been made that a few weeks ago 30,000 visitors found it impossible to get sleeping accommodations there and had to seek them in nearby cities and in the suburbs. The night before the Army and Navy football game, New York's hotels were crowded as they never were before. Folks slept two and three in a room, and space which had never before been used for sleeping quarters was used on that night. Fear of failure to get hotel rooms kept many out of the city until the day of the game. This state of affairs would not have been had the hotel capacity of the city been less taxed by transient business.—The Builder's Guide.

*

When a man says he is not influenced by advertising, make him prove it with an inventory of his possessions.

Some Notes on Tile

By W. B. WEBSTER*

TILES are an interesting study from an historical point of view because they are as old as history itself.   As far back as 747 years
before Christ the history of Babylon was written on sun-baked tables
or tiles which defied the ravages of time and the elements.

The manufacture of Encaustic or burnt clay tiles dates from a very
early period of the world's history. It is known that the Romans manufactured tiles of Encaustic colors 300 years before the Christian era.

During my visit to Pompeii I saw burned clay tile floors of exquisite
design and workmanship that had laid buried for nearly 2,000 years yet
were still in a perfect state of preservation. In Persia there are a great
many examples of the tile maker's art that are most beautiful, and in all
parts of Europe one sees a large number of pavements and floors that
were laid with tiles in the middle ages.

Spain is especially rich in exquisite tiles of antiquity, and the works
at Valencia in that country have been in active operation for 900 years.
In the old Alhambra at Granada are tile floors and walls made by the
early Moors which retain their brightness and colors to this day.

While in Holland I visited a tile factory which had been running
continuously for over 400 years, and the tile are still being made there in
the same crude way as when they first commenced. The primitive manner in which they purified their clays was indeed amusing. In one factory at The Hague I saw them filling a long sack with raw clay, which,
being saturated with water in a long wooden box, was tramped on by
barefooted Dutch girls who seemed to enjoy the sport. The kneading in
this way pressed the finer qualities· of the clay through the sack and
from this was made the bisque for the better class of tile, while the
residue left in the bag was used to make the coarser qualities. Other
parts of the process of manufacture were of the same crude character.

It was not until 1871 that the use of tile became at all general in California. At that time none whatever was manufactured in America. We
imported from Valencia, Spain, Stoke on Trent in England and Breslau
in Germany. The first piece of tile floor laid in San Francisco was in the
entrance to the old Baldwin Theater, the tile coming from England, and
from England we had to bring our first workman.

Tile manufacture in America had a very small beginning, starting
about the year 1873 with one kiln at Pittsburg. Since then it has expanded so rapidly that today there are over twenty manufacturers of over
two hundred kilns and it may surprise you to learn that today America
leads the world in tile making. In San Francisco some notable contracts
in tile have been carried out. In the Fairmont Hotel alone there is $120,-
000 worth of tile work, and nearly as much in the St. Francis. The Phelan building has over $30,000 worth of tile in it. Tiles are now being
used largely in veneering buildings in all parts of the world. In San
Francisco we have several buildings where the whole outside finish is
done in tile, notably the new California Market, fronting on Pine and
California streets. This building is universally admired and I'm sure it is
justly entitled to be called the finest market in the world. You all know
the delights of a tiled bathroom, with its glistening white cleanliness and
its sanitary effect, and there is hardly a residence of any pretentions but
what has one or more of the bathrooms tiled.

---

*Formerly manager of the tile and mantel department of W. W. Montague & Co., San Francisco.

The process of making tiles in this country is unique, as everything is done on a mammoth scale and by patented machinery not found in European factories, and most of this machinery is the result of the genius of American workmen. In the manufacture of tile several different kinds of clays are employed, some coming from Connecticut, some from New Jersey and some from Ohio, the Jersey ball clay and Connecticut spar being peculiarly fine classes of clay for tile work. The clays, after being sorted in the proper proportion, are put into the blunging mills to have all the foreign substances removed and reduce them to a liquid state. After being thoroughly mixed in Erastos, the liquid substance is passed through extremely fine filters, which are under a heavy pressure, thus removing the impurities and separating the water. The clays are then taken from the filter presses in a plastic state, cut into cakes of about two feet square and two inches thick and are then taken to the drying kilns. After all moisture has been evaporated by this process, the clays are taken to the grinding mills, where they are reduced to a superfine powder, finer than flour. The material is now ready for the hydraulic presses. These are electrically operated and are of great power. The fine clay powder is carried in conduits to the hoppers above the presses, and is there delivered to the die, to produce a tile one-half inch in thickness. The dies are about three inches in depth and upon being filled are pressed from a three-inch bulk to a bisque of one-half inch in thickness. Each bisque is then carefully placed on its edge in seggars. The latter are made of burnt clay and are about the size of a half bushel basket. After the seggar is full, say about ten square feet, the cover is placed on and the seam is covered with wet clay to keep out the air. The tile are now ready for the kiln for their first burning. The seggars are placed in the kilns so as to allow the heat of the fires free play around and through them. Each kiln holds from 5,000 to 10,000 feet of tile. The firing process is very important, for carelessness or inattention may lose the whole kiln, and the men that attend to the firing are the highest salaried workmen in the works. Before the fires are started four small cubes of the clay are placed in each of four openings in different parts of the kiln, so as to be reached from the outside, making sixteen pieces in all. This is to test the baking process to see when it has been sufficiently fired. The moment these test pieces show that the kiln is cooked, the fires are drawn. After the tile are burned, which occupies from thirty to forty hours, and are cooled gradually, they are taken from the seggars and carefully sorted for soundness, size and shape. The perfect ones are ready for the glazing process.

In most of the foreign factories the tile are dipped in the glazing solution by hand, but here they are coated by a marvelously constructed machine, which equally distributes the glazing solution, and they are now ready for the glazing kiln. After coming from the glazing kiln they are carried to the assorting rooms, where the imperfect tiles are again thrown out and broken up for the dump. They are then ready for the decorating room, if they are to be decorated, or for the packing room, if to remain plain. After one follows the clay from the clay bins to the finished product, the greatest wonder is how they can be sold so cheaply. The manufacture of tiles in America has been brought by the use of improved machinery to such an economical production, and such strides have been made in the artistic and ornamental effects produced, that they are now exported to countries where tile have been manufactured for ages, even to England, Egypt and India.

When the Prince of Wales visited Australia some four years ago, he used a bathroom lined with American tiles. When he visited India for the great Durbar, the railroad train in which he traveled had all its coaches paved with American tile. American tile were used for the decoration of the Khedive's Palace at Cairo, and large quantities of American tile were used in the royal palaces in London. This is bearding the lion in his den, as the British are very jealous of their clay products.

* * *

Salt Water Causes Cracking Concrete in Philippines

THE cracking of reinforced concrete structures is markedly prevalent in the Philippine Islands, according to a report by J. L. Harrison, District Engineer, Iloilo (in the "Bulletin" of the Bureau of Public Works, October, 1916). The accumulation of evidence of this trouble became so serious about two years ago that it was decided by the authorities to make some studies into the cause. They proceeded first on the assumption that the rusting was wholly chemical—stimulated by appreciable quantities of some determinable material; and a number of samples of concrete taken from structures in trouble were subjected to chemical analysis.

The samples submitted showed one foreign substance—chlorine—and that indicated the presence of salt. At first not much attention was paid to this, as it was known that it was largely used in the United States to prevent freezing of concrete during setting; but it was soon realized that the climatic conditions in the Philippine Islands are so different from those in the United States that the effect of the salt could not be neglected. The collection of analyzed samples has gone on for something over two years and not a single structure showing rusted steel has been found free from salt. The percentage of this salt has varied considerably—from that high enough to show that beach sand and sea water must have been used in making the concrete to a figure low enough to indicate that either brackish water was used or that salt water was used to wet down fresh-water concrete after the forms had been taken off. A typical sample (from the Constabulary Headquarters Building, Iloilo) showed 0.07 per cent chlorine. This was computed to be equivalent to 1.44 per cent salt in the water, assuming 12.5 lb. of water used per cubic foot of concrete. This is considered fairly salt water.

The presence of 0.10 per cent chlorine in the iron rust indicated too small a percentage of ferric chloride to explain all the indications of rusting to be observed; but it was realized that ferric chloride is not stable and that it readily oxidizes to ferric oxide, releasing the chlorine for further attack. High temperature and moisture are the only conditions necessary for the indefinite continuation of the process, and both of these conditions prevail throughout the Philippine Islands.

Not every structure in which salt water has been used, or in which salt is found, goes to pieces in this way. There are several such buildings in good condition. However, the concrete in them is unusually dense, and it is thought that their success in withstanding the influence of the salt is due to the density of the concrete.

Engineers in the Philippines have been accordingly advised that all use of salt water in concrete structures is dangerous and that the use of beach sand and beach gravel should be permitted only after thorough washing with fresh water.—*Engineering News.*

Effect of Plaster on Quiet Conditions in School Buildings

ONE of the important factors in producing quiet conditions in school buildings has been determined by prominent architects to be the kind of plaster that is applied to the walls. When a sound wave strikes a wall, the following occurs: Part of the sound is absorbed, part is transmitted and part is reverberated, the volume reverberated and transmitted being dependent entirely upon the volume absorbed and the volume absorbed is in turn dependent upon the character of the plaster. A dense, smooth surface will reflect sound waves much more readily than a material that is porous, as a dense surface absorbs very little of the sound wave at each impact and many reflections are necessary before it dies out, and in many auditoriums it has developed that an overlapping of syllables has persisted for several seconds after the source of sound has ceased. On the other hand, a surface porous in nature will absorb a greater quantity of energy at each impact and the sound quickly dies away. It will, therefore, be seen that the ideal material for plastering the interior of school buildings, from the viewpoint of acoustics and quiet conditions, would be that which reduces reverberation of sound waves to a minimum.

There are two kinds of plaster in general use today, viz: gypsum hard wall plaster and hydrated lime plaster. There is, however, one great advantage in favor of hydrated lime plaster—its ability to absorb and deaden sound—and it is this advantage which is now recognized by the school architect and impelling him to accept hydrated lime plaster as the standard plaster for school buildings or other buildings where good acoustics or quiet conditions are desirable.

Gypsum plaster, when passing through the process of hardening on the wall, takes up in chemical combination approximately 25 per cent water. This chemical addition causes the plaster to "set" or crystalize, each particle becoming firmly united to its nearest particle. When this action is completed, there results a panel of plaster which is dense, hard and brittle. Hydrated lime plaster hardens in an entirely different manner, this process being dependent upon the carbon dioxide in the atmosphere combining with the lime in the plaster, and this combination drives off all the water that was used in mixing the plaster. The mixing water originally required space, and this water, being driven off, leaves the hardened plaster with millions of tiny, dead air cells. These air cells are absorbers of sound and when a sound wave strikes the wall a large majority of it is absorbed, thus reducing to a minimum the reverberation which provides defective acoustics in a room or auditorium.

The durability of hydrated lime plaster cannot be questioned when one considers that for years it was the only plastering material on the market. Many readers probably well remember the days of construction when no other material was used for plaster except lump lime, sand and hair, and these jobs are still standing today in an excellent state of preservation. Hydrated lime plaster accomplishes the same fine results that were formerly gained by the use of lump lime. The old disadvantages of lump lime, such as pitting and popping, and the expense and inconvenience of slaking are eliminated with the use of hydrated lime. The material is delivered on the job all ready for the immediate addition of sand and water, and in some cities it is mixed with the sand at a mixing plant and delivered ready for mixing with water. The covering capacity of hydrated lime plaster is the same as that of gypsum plaster.—*School Board Journal.*

RESIDENCE OF DR. GILBERT GRAHAM, PIEDMONT
Albert Farr, Architect

RESIDENCE OF MR. J. H. TODD, BERKELEY
Walter D. Reed, Architect

Better· Buildings

By A. F. MORATZ, in the Ohio Architect.

IT is the intent of the writer to give in this article a few words of practical advice to those contemplating building. We have often observed structures which appeared substantial and enduring when first erected to have shown in a few years signs of decay, and we stop to determine the reason. Cracks in the walls have appeared caused by unequal settlement of the foundations. defective mortar has crumbled and fallen out of the joints. Then again we find the so-called galvanized iron which has been used for turrets, wall coping, buttress caps and what ·not, going to pieces. We find a piece of a substantial brick wall omitted to give space for a tin name plate. Would it not have been preferable to have omitted much of this tin ornamentation, often badly· designed, and applied this expense to making the essential portions, such as wall coping and buttress caps of an enduring material?

The tendency of the times is toward the construction of buildings for today only, and unfortunately this seems to apply more to churches than any other building, which on the contrary. should be the most enduring of structures. The most regrettable feature of this matter is that the same amount of money that is expended on these buildings would build good, permanent and enduring structures.

The first and the most vital step in any building operation is the selection of an architect, upon it depending much of the ultimate success or failure of the project. The architect should be selected on the merits of his completed work, and upon his honesty and integrity. The works and the character of the man who is commissioned to plan and supervise the construction of a building should be thoroughly investigated before he is employed.

Competitions as they are usually conducted are not conducive to the best results. The distinction must here be made between a draftsman and an architect. A good draftsman would be able to produce a very fine drawing, whereas the executed work is very apt to be unsatisfactory.

Another point to be considered where open competition is resorted to, even when only good architects are competing, is that men under these conditions will not thoroughly study and investigate the problem, consequently schemes will be presented that have been prepared in a hurried manner, the first that comes to mind. In order to be certain to obtain the best results, viewed from every phase, a problem in building must have the most careful study and investigation. This requires much thought, labor and expense, which men in competition cannot afford on account of the uncertainty of the result, and is also the principal reason for the difference in fees charged by different men, as this same thought and labor applies not only to the general scheme, but to every detail of the building. Any good architect is able to present a scheme in a very short time, usually, in the opinion of the layman, a good enough solution. If the result, however, is to be correct and certain, every possibility must be considered and good judgment exercised in the selection of what is best.

After an architect has been selected it is important, if the best results are to be obtained, that his advice be heeded and his drawings and directions faithfully adhered to. Absolute confidence must exist on the part of the owner toward the architect. both as to his honesty and ability, as many matters may arise during the progress of the work that will test this confidence to the limit.

It often occurs that an architect is commissioned to prepare only the drawings and specifications of a building, leaving the supervision to someone else. I have not in my experience found this satisfactory. Architects are held to blame for defective work on these buildings by the public who do not know the conditions, and even sometimes by the owners themselves.

Where several sites are under consideration it will be found advisable to consult with an architect on the selection, as an experienced man will often be able to offer some valuable advice in this connection. When locating a new building on a site, future buildings and additions to the present building should be most carefully considered. This is especially true in the case of institutions and in large or rapidly growing parishes.

Where a maximum amount that a building is to cost must be named, as is usually the case, this amount should be given the architect; the conscientious man will endeavor to remain within this limit. Owing to the variation in the proposals from contractors and in local conditions which are often difficult to foresee, the estimate on the cost of a proposed building often resolves itself more into a matter of judgment than of figures. The cost of a building cannot be definitely known until complete drawings and specifications are prepared and proposals received. However, by a careful calculation of the labor and material and the exercising of experienced judgment and by comparison with completed buildings an estimate can be given sufficiently accurate for practical purposes.

The style of architecture should be left largely to the architect. Permanent existing buildings belonging to the same group or prominent buildings in the near vicinity will affect the decision. The cost of the building and the personal preference of the owner will frequently have much bearing on this matter. With the many good styles of architecture in existence, it is to be regretted that there is so much sameness in church building. What a beautiful interior could be produced in the Roman Basilica style like St. Paul's, Rome, or exterior in the Romanesque like St. Theresa's, Rome, in the Renaissance like St. Peter's, Rome, the English Gothic, or the Byzantine, any of which are good if executed faithfully. In any case it is best by far to build a substantial permanent structure of good material, adhering strictly to the proportions and details in a style that can be built for the appropriated amount in preference to the reverse in another style of architecture.   ·

It would be preferable if more time were allotted than is customary to the preliminary sketches and also to working drawings and specifications of the building. Ample time should also be allowed for the preparation and receiving of proposals. Before awarding the various contracts the work and character of the men under consideration should be carefully investigated and only reliable and conscientious men employed. All contracts should be written on blanks known as the "uniform contract," and all contractors should give bond for the amount of the contract. All bonds should remain in effect for two months after the final completion and acceptance of the work. Drawings and specifications should have the most thorough study and inspection before letting the contract, but in case any additions or alterations, even of the most minor nature are found necessary, such alteration or addition should be made upon written order of the architect, strictly according to contract before work on such addition or alteration is commenced. Many lawsuits in connection with building operations would be avoided if all matters pertaining thereto were placed in writing in proper form.

Cost will largely determine the selection of materials; after that permanency should be the determining factor. The color and kinds of material, their size and disposition should be left to the discretion of the architect, and should conform to the style of architecture. It is far preferable to omit ornamentation, unless it can be executed in permanent material in good taste and correct style. In the selection of material only those having had a thorough test in the location in which they are to be used should be considered. Medium hard burned brick of regular form and concrete reinforced where required are good materials for structural parts of footings and walls. Close grained stone, terra cotta, marble or granite may be used for exterior walls wholly or in part where funds permit. Hollow tile is a good material for the structural part of floors, and for walls where the lateral strain is not too severe. Stucco for exterior walls on hollow tile makes a good construction where properly handled. Where competent and thorough inspection is not possible, stucco should be avoided as much as possible, as should also extensive operations in concrete construction. Mortar being under the most favorable conditions the weakest part of the wall, should be of the best quality and most carefully inspected. Avoid slow setting ingredients in mortar; Portland cement, one part to sand two parts, makes good mortar. It would be impossible for me to lay too much stress on the importance of good mortar; if the mortar is defective, the walls and the building are most seriously defective. Wall copings where required should be carefully inspected and made of the most permanent material. If water is permitted to penetrate a wall through wall coping or otherwise, it will soon disintegrate. It would often be possible to construct much of the structural parts of a building of masonry instead of wood without any very material increase in cost; this is certainly to be preferred, as it is practically impossible when wood is used for studding and joist to avoid future cracked plaster and other troubles caused by the shrinkage. Where wood trusses are used for roofs and other portions of the building they should be designed so that excessive shrinkage will not occur at the joining of the various members. Where plaster surfaces come in direct contact with the trusses, steel is much to be preferred.

* * *

The Architecture of the Small House

ARCHITECTS like to boast of the steady improvement in the design of expensive American houses and in the laying out of big estates, but when asked about our smaller domestic work they tell you it is still far below the standard. The reasons for this are obvious enough. No well trained architect whose education has been a matter of six or seven years and a great sum of money can afford to design small houses at the established rate. A small house looks like an insignificant problem— so easy of solution every untrained woman in the land is ready to solve it; but the truth is that a house at $4,000 requires twice as much time and study to design successfully as a house at $8,000, for the reason that there never lived a $4,000 client who did not want every convenience and comfort crowded into his little house that an $8,000 man demands in his. Moreover, he is usually a tyro in home-building; his little sum represents the first money he has been able to amass for the purpose; and it takes much patience to persuade him how really little he can expect for it— that he must not expect the number of closets and baths and dens and back staircases and piazzas that can be put into a costlier house.

If a small dwelling is to have any distinction whatever, its prime expression must be simplicity. It takes more art to leave out useless ornament and detail than to put it in. A small house is nothing more than the simplest form of shelter for a very few people. To make it an expression of refinement and good taste, and at the same time thoroughly modern as to comfort and convenience, requires more of the architect's time than he would put on a larger house where his commission would be both actually and relatively much higher.

"If the present minimum fee of six per cent were raised to eight per cent for work of $5,000 and under," says House Beautiful, "really good architects might be induced to design small houses; but in such a case clients of this order would, even more than now, seek the services of the 'builder architect,' forgetting that the quality which small houses lack most and yet need most is that subtle something called charm, and that the man least likely to impart this abiding quality is the builder. Charm is worth paying for. It is to a dwelling what it is to a woman—the imperishable attraction which outlives the pink of her cheek or the raven black of her hair. As Maggie sighs in 'What Every Woman Knows': ' If you have char-r-m, the bad things you do count nothing against you; and if you are without char-r-m, the good things you do count nothing for you.'".

* * *

The Cost of an Architect's Design Compared with that of a Structural Engineer

IT IS not often that a building designed by an architect is re-designed by a structural engineer. Recently, however, Mr. Louis Mulhausen, structural engineer, of Philadelphia, re-designed the structural part of a two-story commercial building in Wilmington, Del., with a resultant decrease in cost of nearly 8 per cent. The following table of costs is based on the actual sub-bids received on the two designs as given in Engineering News:

	Architect's design	Engineer's design
Permit, bonds, insurance, shoring, pumping foreman and watchman, miscellaneous expenses, etc.	$ 2,996	$ 2,985
Lumber	1,507	987
Millwork	2,500	2,500
Carpenter labor	3,095	2,595
Demolition, excavation and stone masonry	2,854	2,854
Brickwork	5,337	4,337
Cut stone	331	331
Ornamental terra cotta work	1,858	1,858
Structural steel	4,759	......
Reinforced concrete and cement	2,600	6,569
Ornamental iron	874	874
Dahlstrom door	288	288
Ash hoist	165	165
Stair work (wood)	185	185
Tile	192	192
Weather stripping	63	63
Roofing and sheet metal	317	317
Plastering	2,998	3,100
Hardware	618	618
Painting and glazing	984	984
	$34,521	$31,802

It will be noted that the engineer did not alter the architectural effect. What he did do was to substitute reinforced concrete columns and floors for steel columns and girders with wood floor and joists. He also substituted metal lath for wood lath. Thus he produced a thoroughly fireproof building at less cost than one that was not fireproof. The walls were 12x8-inch hollow tile with stucco finish outside.

The building was 45x65 feet for two floors and roof, with a 16x60-foot wing for one floor and roof, making a total of 10,695 square feet of floors and roof. The cost was $3.23 per square foot for the architect's design, and $2.97 for the engineer's design.

Forms for Concrete Work*

WE DO not often hear of failures occurring in reinforced concrete buildings after their completion, but generally during their erection, and although all failures cannot be attributed to defective forms, yet the forms are to blame in a sufficient number of cases as to render the forms for concrete work an important element in securing efficiency in construction, and not merely in the utilitarian aspect. Although it is not the practice, in England at any rate, for engineers to design their forms, that being generally left to the contractor, it is the author's belief that an engineer, for his own protection, should at least set out some typical portion of the forms for the contractor's guidance, thus doing all he can to circumvent failure in this direction at any rate. Of course good forms alone will not ensure safety, and we have to use vigilance likewise in detecting bad work, bad design and bad material. For, as Lieutenant-Colonel Winn has pithily put it, "A fool with a shovel may absolutely defeat the most elaborate calculation involving the calculus."

Formwork is a term embracing all kinds of moulds or centering set up to give shape to the concrete or similar plastic material. It is so employed in America. There is a consensus of opinion in favor of the definition "formwork" as an inclusive term, owing to the real meaning of the term "centering" having a more limited application than usually attributed to it. As the word "form" is the same, and has the same meaning in French, German, Italian and Spanish, the author believes it will be agreed we are on safe ground if we accept it for our purpose. The term has great merit, being superior to such terms as falsework or shuttering.

The contention that the engineer should prepare the design of formwork has much to recommend it. An engineer will generally have no hesitation in setting out the design of centering for a bridge or other equally important work, but for some reason or other the design of ordinary formwork which plays such an important part in the cost of reinforced concrete is never considered. There is no doubt that a thorough understanding of the principles underlying the every-day practice of concrete form design is one worthy of the best engineering talent. With this understood, the problem can be analyzed, the requirements realized and the design decided upon that will be the most economical and efficient, giving due consideration to the salvage of materials.

It is not merely that a design is required for a specific case which will safely support a certain volume of concrete; it is rather the problem of designing a set of forms which can be erected, taken down and many times re-used during the progress of work. The factors involved are many such as the type of centering, the kind of timber, how much to center at one time, and what clamps, bolts, nails, wire or strap steel should be used. These things properly considered will repay the trouble taken and result in better and more economical work.

Various authorities place the cost of formwork at anything from 20 per cent to 60 per cent of the total cost. The possibility of reducing this hindrance to the more general use of concrete ought to be sufficient inducement for us to give the matter close consideration. The great American constructional firms have struck out in many directions to reduce this cost to a minimum, and to this end the forms in most instances are designed in the drawing office, and this we are told at a cost of 2 per cent and a saving of 10 per cent.

*Summary of a paper read by Allan Graham at the 46th ordinary general meeting of the Concrete Institute, London.

The author then dealt with the kinds of timber that are used for formwork, the desirability of giving a camber to the bottom of beam boxes, the desirability of carefully checking the measurements, to see that the concrete members are actually carried out as designed, the necessity of having joints close to prevent the mixture escaping, the remedying of cracks, the removal of forms, clamps and nails to hold the forms together, the repair and re-use of formwork, the number of sets required in order to get on fast enough with the work of building, the importance of carefully clearing forms of all sawdust, dirt and chips before filling with concrete, the wetting of timber to prevent sticking, the use of sheet metal, the time for striking forms and methods of determining the strength.

He then dealt in detail with forms for various parts of construction, as, for example, floors, beams and pillars, culverts, conduits, tall chimneys, silos, tanks, gas holder tanks, domes and bridges.

The paper was illustrated by lantern slides and a considerable number of working drawings.

Keeping Reinforcement in Position

THE holding of reinforcing bars in proper position while concrete is being placed is a matter which merits the utmost attention. The labors of the best designer and detailer can be set at naught by the carelessness of those in charge of the construction of reinforced concrete structures, while placing steel and concrete, says The Improvement Bulletin.

A designer spends many days designing and detailing a complicated structure, the strength of which can be greatly impaired by comparatively slight displacement of the reinforcement at critical sections. Much time is spent in designing and detailing the reinforcement for a structure and the all-important matter of getting and keeping the bars in correct position is disposed of by a single note such as the following: "All reinforcement to be bent and placed as shown on plans and to be securely fastened or tied to prevent displacement during pouring of concrete and to insure proper position of reinforcement in the finished structure." It is left to the discretion of the construction foreman to devise a means of keeping the bars in position and as a result the strength of the structure may depend on whether the foreman thoroughly understands his business or not.

This is neither good practice nor economy. The method and means of supporting reinforced bars should be clearly indicated on the plans, since they are as important details as the location of bends of bars and stirrups. Where bars are bent up into the tops of slabs and beams they are best supported by cross bars resting on concrete blocks of a height to insure the exact location of bars. Bars in the bottoms of slabs can be kept at the proper height by small Z-shaped clips and spacing bars to which the main bars are wired.

It is just as important to show the supporting bars, supporting blocks and clips, and the spacing bars as it is to show the main reinforcement in detail. Before the structure can be built it is necessary for some one to devise a means for keeping bars in position during construction, and as a general rule, a good designer is more capable of handling these details to good advantage than anyone else. If it is left to the contractor, the owners pay dearly for this "designing service" rendered by the contractor if he is wide awake; and if he is not, he pays the bill. It can be seen at once that this is neither fair nor economical, and is very likely to lead to "wild" and "unbalanced" bids.

If a contractor is to bid intelligently and if all contractors are to enter their bids on the same basis, it is imperative that these details be shown on the plans when the work is at all complicated or important. The double purpose of keeping the bars in place and having more balanced and uniform bids is fulfilled at once by including these supporting details in the detail plans and the practice should be encouraged and should be more in evidence than in the past.

*

* *

The Importance of Town Planning

Mr. Thomas Adams, town planning advisor to the Conservation Commission, addressed the members of the Montreal Builders' Exchange at a luncheon held recently. One of the main points emphasized was the necessity for arteries in any town planning scheme. It would, said Mr. Adams, be futile to lay out a scheme for, say, Montreal, without taking into consideration the question of arteries leading off the main highways or boulevards. More attention to light and air is necessary, while it is also desirable to consider the possibility of cheapening building, in order that the artisan class may the more readily build or purchase their own houses. One advantage of a town planning scheme is that it conduces to beautiful surroundings, thus attracting population and inducing men with artistic tastes and with an appreciation of healthful and comfortable environments to settle in a town. For these reasons Mr. Adams urged the Builders' Exchange to support the proposed town planning bill for the Province of Quebec. Mr. James Ballantyne of Montreal West, Alderman Shephard of Westmount, Mr. A. Chausse, building inspector of Montreal; Mr. Ewing of the C. P. R., and Mr. J. P. Anglin spoke in support of this measure. Mr. Chausse pointed out the necessity for a comprehensive building code for Montreal. At present, owing to the annexation of outlying municipalities, different codes were in force, naturally making for confusion in the building by-laws. Mr. Ewing advocated the allocation of a given district for the concentration of all factories, which in Montreal, as in other places, would mean economy in the matter of transportation.

* *

Skyscraper Built in Forty-one Days

The great war is accountable for many records, none of which is more remarkable than the building of an eight-story (100x400 feet) reinforced concrete frame for a factory, having 360,000 square feet floor area, in forty-one days, sixteen of which it was impossible to work on account of rain and Sundays. In the twenty-five days of actual work, 20,000 cubic yards of concrete were placed, 5,000 being in the footings and 15,000 in the columns and Akme girderless floors. The carpenters, of whom there were 300, worked three eight-hour shifts daily. Forms were ⅞-inch tongue-and-groove, and 4x4's, of which 1,000,000 feet B. M. were used. Forms for four floors and one set of columns were provided. The laborers worked two shifts daily, one ten-hour, one twelve-hour. About 1,000 men of all classes were engaged on the work. The contractors were the F. W. Mark Construction Co. The building is owned by the Baldwin Locomotive Works and was designed by the Condron Co. of Chicago.

THE

Architect and Engineer
OF CALIFORNIA

Founded in 1905 by E. M. C. WHITNEY

A. I. WHITNEY	- -	*Manager*
T. C. KIERULFF	- -	*Legal Points*
FREDERICK W. JONES	- -	*Editor*

Published Monthly in the interests of the Architects, Structural Engineers, Contractors and the Allied Trades of the Pacific Coast by the Architect and Engineer.

BUSINESS OFFICE AND EDITORIAL ROOMS
627-629 Foxcroft Building, San Francisco
Telephone Douglas 1828

The publishers disclaim any responsibility for statements made in the advertisements of this magazine.

TERMS OF SUBSCRIPTION

(Including postage) to all parts of the United States $1.50 per annum; to Canada 50c additional; to all Foreign points $1 additional.

VOL. XLVIII.   MARCH, 1917   No. 3

INTELLIGENT NEED OF MORE SPECIFICATIONS

The question of specifications is not a new one. The first architect, whoever he was, upon completing his first set of plans, discovered that a set of specifications would be necessary to guide the builder. So he sat down to his desk and prepared the first set of specifications. If all this happened in the stone age, that first architect must have been something of a stone-cutter, for hacking out a set of specifications—as we know them to-day—on a stone tablet, or what is more likely, a series of stone tablets, must have been a job in itself.

Be that as it may, the first architect undoubtedly faced early in his career the task of preparing the first bill of specifications. We know local builders who are willing to swear that this same set, prepared back in the dawn of the ages, is still in use, but, then, builders are a prejudiced lot when it comes to specifications and we feel sure won't take it amiss if we decline to O. K. that particular theory.

It is a fact, however, that specifications are still a prolific bone of contention between the builder and the man behind the plans. The objection most frequently heard to the average specification is that it is not specific. For some reason or other, and despite the fact that architects have been writing specifications now for several thousand years, the objection is urged that the specification does not make the points it assumes to cover as clear and as readily grasped as builders think would be possible. The object of a specification is to specify with more or less clearness exactly what is in the mind of the specifier—i. e., the architect.

Some architects are very specific in their specifications. Others are not. Some believe in specifying an article without an alternative. Others specify the same article "or equal." Some use simply a general specification, without mentioning any particular brand or make.

Just how much attention some architects give to their specifications was emphasized rather forcibly the other day when a San Francisco contractor inquired of the editor of this magazine the address of the firm that was handling a certain waterproofing material. Investigation developed the fact that the article in question had not been on the market for several years. Yet that architect, having used the product at one time with satisfactory results, continued to specify it, ignorant of the fact that it was no longer manufactured. All of which leads one to wonder what substitute the contractors have been using on the jobs that have been carried out in this office since the waterproofing concern ceased business.

The above illustration would seem to bear out the oft-repeated assertion that some architects do not give enough of their personal time to the preparation of specifications. They leave it to their assistants or to so-called "experts" on the outside.

Architects, too, show a lamentable ignorance of trade terms. This lack of knowledge usually results in the contractor taking a big chance, guided by the little knowledge he is able to glean from the verbose description of the article in question.

It should be remembered that the specifications are for the contractor, and should be written in terms which he understands, and should not be a voluminous treatise which can only be interpreted by the writer. Every effort is put forth by the manufacturers of building materials to standardize their goods in such a way as to make specification writing easy for the architects. If the architect would only stop, look and listen for a minute, he would easily get acquainted with these trade terms, and, in addition to getting better bids, he would materially cut the size of his specifi-cations by the elimination of unnecessary descriptive matter.

While it is eminently proper that the architect should, insofar as he may, protect himself against the habit, common to a certain element of bidders, of running in for extra-elucidation, it ought to be easy to distinguish between **pests** of this class and the **reputable element** who come honestly seeking to clear up points in the specifications that are at once vague, ambiguous and misleading.

One reason for the present high cost of building material is ascribed by some to the op-
SUPPLYING EUROPE tions being taken
WITH BUILDING on supplies in gi-
MATERIALS gantic quantities by
companies which plan to ship building material by the millions of dollars' worth into Europe as soon as the war ends. Inquiries have been sent here from England, Russia and France in the last month to ascertain the per cubic foot cost of American standard shaped industrial buildings and quickly assembled houses for the employees. According to the specifications received from France within the last week, "prices must include complete mill construction ready for setting machinery on floors within thirty days from arrival of material on site, quotations to be f. o. b. New York and cover purchaser into the summer of 1918." One New York company has already made shipments of houses of this sort into South America, and is taking on capacity to meet the requirements of an export business in all kinds of basic building materials which seems sure to develop upon the closing of hostilities.

Not since the early part of the eighteenth century have basic building materials crossed the Atlantic. During and immediately following the American Revolution common brick was imported from Holland for use in New York and Philadelphia buildings. Since then there has been some German and Belgian cement imported, a little marble and some quarry and fine tile, but the exportation of basic building materials has always been considered impractical. Manufacturers now believe that basic building materials like steel, cement, brick, lime, glass and lumber will soon be exported in large quantities, and for that reason are making themselves prepared when the demand develops.

Expert Opinion

A man who kept a road house in Rhode Island, says the Public Health Journal, was called upon to testify in a suit as to the number of cubic yards that were handled in some filling work near his place. He showed very little knowledge of the matter and his idea of a cubic yard was so indefinite that it seemed doubtful whether he knew what the term meant. To make its meaning clear the judge said, "Listen, witness! Assume this inkstand to be three feet across the top this way and three feet that way and three feet in height; what would you call it?" "Well, your honor," replied the witness without hesitation, "I should say it was some inkstand."

S. P. Car Shops at Visitation

There is a possibility that the proposed car shops at Visitation Valley, planned by the Southern Pacific Company seven or eight years ago, will be built this year. The matter is now under advisement and a decision will probably be reached shortly. There will be a number of buildings constructed, including machine shops, car repair shops, painting shops, etc. They will be constructed of steel, concrete and corrugated iron. The plans were prepared by the engineering department of the railroad company.

New Court House

The Grand Jury has recommended the immediate construction of a new court house at Red Bluff, the cost to be met by a special bond issue.

American Institute of Architects

(ORGANIZED 1857)

OFFICERS FOR 1916-17

PRESIDENT.....JOHN LAWRENCE MAURAN, St. Louis
FIRST VICE-PRESIDENT......C. GRANT LA FARGE, New York
SECOND VICE-PRESIDENT....W. R. B. WILLCOX, Seattle, Wash.
SECRETARY....W. STANLEY PARKER, Boston, Mass.
TREASURER..........D. EVERETT WAID, New York

San Francisco Chapter

PRESIDENT...................EDGAR A. MATHEWS
VICE-PRESIDENT...........SYLVAIN SCHNAITTACHER
SECRETARY AND TREASURER........MORRIS BRUCE
TRUSTEES..................... { W. B. FAVILLE
                               { G. A. WRIGHT

Southern California Chapter

PRESIDENT......................J. E. ALLISON
VICE-PRESIDENT..................J. J. BACKUS
SECRETARY......................A. R. WALKER
TREASURER.............AUGUST WACKERBARTH
Board of Directors
ROBT. D. FARQUHAR   PERCY A. EISEN
            S. B. MARSTON

Portland, Ore., Chapter

PRESIDENT..................JOSEPH JACOBBERGER
VICE-PRESIDENT.............J. A. FOUILHOUX
SECRETARY.................W. C. KNIGHTON
TREASURER.................FOLGER JOHNSON
TRUSTEES................. { ION LEWIS
                          { M. H. WHITEHOUSE

Washington State Chapter

PRESIDENT............CHARLES H. BEBB, Seattle
1ST VICE-PRES...DANIEL R. HUNTINGTON, Seattle
2D VICE-PRESIDENT.........GEORGE GOVE, Tacoma
3D VICE-PRESIDENT.........L. L. RAND, Spokane
SECRETARY.............JOSEPH S. COTE, Seattle
TREASURER..........ELLSWORTH STOREY, Seattle
COUNCIL............. { JAMES STEPHEN, Seattle
                     { JAMES H. SCHACK, Seattle
                     { CHARLES H. ALDEN, Seattle

California State Board of Architecture

NORTHERN DISTRICT.

PRESIDENT..................EDGAR A. MATHEWS
SECRETARY-TREASURER.....SYLVAIN SCHNAITTACHER
Members
JOHN BAKEWELL, JR.   J. CATHER NEWSOM

SOUTHERN DISTRICT.

PRESIDENT..................JOHN P. KREMPEL
SECRETARY-TREASURER..........FRED H. ROEHRIG
MEMBERS.................. { OCTAVIUS MORGAN
                          { SUMNER P. HUNT
                          { WM. S. HEBBARD

San Francisco Architectural Club

OFFICERS FOR 1917

PRESIDENT ....CHAS. PETER WEEKS
VICE-PRESIDENT ....A. WILLIAMS
SECRETARY ....JOHN F. BEUTTLER
TREASURER ....WILLIAM HELM

San Francisco Society of Architects

PRESIDENT................CHARLES PETER WEEKS
VICE-PRESIDENT............GEORGE W. KELHAM
SECRETARY AND TREASURER.....WARREN C. PERRY
DIRECTORS................. { ERNEST COXHEAD
                           { FREDERICK H. MEYER

Engineers and Architects Association of Los Angeles

PRESIDENT.....................A. H. KOEBIG. SR.
FIRST VICE-PRESIDENT...............A. S. BENT
SECOND VICE-PRESIDENT...........IRA J. FRANCIS
Directors
J. J. BACKUS, GEO. P. ROBINSON, ALBERT C. MARTIN, H. L. SMITH

San Diego Architectural Association

PRESIDENT....................CHARLES CRESSEY
VICE-PRESIDENT.........W. TEMPLETON JOHNSON
SECRETARY....................ROBT. HALLEY, JR.
TREASURER....................G. A. HAUSSEN

San Joaquin Valley Ass'n of Architects

PRESIDENT....................W. J. WRIGHT
VICE-PRESIDENT..................E. B. BROWN
SECRETARY-TREASURER...........FRANK V. MAYO

With the Architects

Building Reports and Personal Mention of Interest to the Profession

One Thousand Houses Planned

The San Francisco Peninsula Company, capitalized for $2,000,000, is making progress with its plans to build one thousand modern workingmen's homes in the vicinity of South San Francisco and the Visitation Valley. Each house will contain from four to six rooms, and will be built in a substantial manner, yet sold for a reasonable price on the easy payment plan. The idea is to make these homes within the reach of the ordinary wage earner. The houses will be laid out with concrete streets and walks, gardens and lawns. The scheme is now being worked out by Chas. H. Cheney, Crocker building, San Francisco, specialist in house and city planning.

Personal

W. C. Pennell, formerly in the Baker-Detwiler building, Los Angeles, is now located at 1121-24 Hollingsworth building, Los Angeles.

Homer W. Glidden has moved his offices from 805 to 703-4 Wright & Callender building, Los Angeles.

I. J. Knapp, formerly of Los Angeles, is now practicing architecture in Fresno with offices at 402 Griffith-McKenzie building.

Romaine W. Myers, a consulting engineer on electrical and illuminating problems, with headquarters in Oakland, has been appointed California representative of the Illuminating Engineering Society.

H. C. Vensano has resigned his position as civil and hydraulic engineer of the Pacific Gas and Electric Company, and in connection with John R. and Edward G. Cahill has organized the Cahill-Vensano Company, contracting engineers. Vensano is a member of the American Society of Civil Engineers.

The firm of Henningsen & Co., 311 Security Bank building, Oakland, has been enlarged by the addition to its force of F. A. Sansome, a New York engineer. This firm is the consulting engineer for the Albers Brothers Milling Company, who are erecting an extensive plant near the Oakland mole.

Jas. C. Simms announces the opening of architectural offices at 14 Commercial Bank building, San Luis Obispo, where he will be glad to receive catalogues and trade literature. Mr. Simms has been associated with the engineering department of the Pacific Electric Railway Co., and was formerly with Walter Webber of Los Angeles.

New Architect Opens Offices

Earl Baldwin Bertz, for a number of years associated with Albert Farr, architect of many beautiful homes designed in the English-Tudor style of architecture, has taken up the practice of his profession independently with offices at 506 Foxcroft building, San Francisco. Mr. Bertz has a number of excellent prospects, among them a large apartment house, residence and some alteration work. He would be pleased to have trade literature, catalogues, etc.

Addition to Chevrolet Plant

The P. J. Walker Co., Monadnock building, San Francisco, are preparing the plans and will build on percentage, an addition 60x100 feet to the Chevrolet Automobile plant on the Oakland boulevard. The new building will be constructed of brick, and will be one story in height and used for the storage of new machines as soon as they have been assembled in the factory. About 5000 feet of Fenestra metal window sash will be used.

Richmond Building Reports

Jas. T. Narbett, architect, 906 Macdonald avenue, Richmond, has prepared plans for the following:

Store and flat building, 2-story brick. Approximate cost, $7500. Owner, W. A. Jones. Plans completed.

Seven-room bungalow to be built at Hercules, for the Hercules Powder Company. Estimated cost, $4500.

Four-story hotel, to be built on the northeast corner of Macdonald avenue and Tenth street, Richmond, of steel, reinforced concrete and brick, for Herbert F. Brown. Estimated cost, $40,000.

The City Council of the City of Richmond has authorized Mr. Narbett to prepare sketches for fire station No. 4, similar to fire station No. 3, which was also designed by Mr. Narbett.

St. Mary's College to Build

St. Mary's College, now located at Broadway and Hawthorne streets, Oakland, is to have a new home probably on the Foothill boulevard at San Leandro. Negotiations for the purchase of a large acreage are in progress. It is proposed to sell the present site in Oakland to an automobile concern, presumably the Studebaker Corporation, upon which will be built an assembling plant to care for the company's transbay business. According to the president of the college, Brother Zellesian, the new college buildings will represent an outlay of close to $250,000.

Oakland Architect Selected for Santa Barbara Schools

John J. Donovan, Perry building, Oakland, has been selected as the architect to prepare plans and specifications for a new group of high school buildings to be erected at Santa Barbara. Preliminary sketches and an estimate of cost will be prepared at once upon which to base the amount of the bond issue to be voted upon. The cost of an adequate group of buildings will probably be about $250,000.

Plans Being Prepared for Bridge

County Surveyor Chas. Richardson of Marin county, and County Surveyor Malcom Younker of Sonoma county, have been instructed to design a reinforced concrete bridge over the San Antone creek at the county line. The bridge will have 250-foot spans and will be of structural steel and concrete. It is estimated to cost $15,000.

$400,000 for Fort McArthur Barracks

The United States government will shortly commence work on the construction of barracks building and administration buildings to house the garrison which will be stationed at Fort McArthur, San Pedro. Major H. W. Newton, Coast Artillery, U. S. A., will have charge of construction work.

$20,000 Oakland Apartments

Plans have been prepared by E. W. Cannon, Central Bank building, Oakland, for a three-story frame apartment house for Robert McKilligan. It will be built on Twenty-fifth street, near Grove, and will cost approximately $20,000.

Louis C. Mullgardt Goes to Honolulu

Louis C. Mullgardt, Chronicle building, San Francisco, has sailed for Honolulu on a part business and part pleasure trip. Mr. Mullgardt will be away about six weeks. He may return with a commission to prepare plans for a new tourist hotel and a large residence.

On Market Street, San Francisco.

Supervisor—"Here's a fine-looking street."

Second Supervisor—"You're right. What's the best thing to do with it?"

"Let's have it dug up for a sewer."

"But wouldn't it be proper to pave it first?"

"Of course; I thought you would understand that. Then, after it is paved and a drain put in we'll have it repaved."

"All in readiness to be dug up again for the gas pipe? I see you understand the principles of municipal economy. And after we have had it repaired for the second time, then what?"

"Well, then it will be ready for widening. There's nothing I admire so much as system in the care and improvement of our roadways."

Harbor Improvements for Oakland

The Terminal Co-operative Shipbuilding & Dry Docks Company, through R. T. Stone, Greystone hotel, San Francisco, has applied to the Oakland city council for a twenty-five year lease on the waterfront property adjoining the site of the Albers Bros. Milling Company. They propose to build dry docks, marine ways and machine shops to cost $1,500,000. The petition has been referred to Commissioner of Public Works Harry S. Anderson.

Merced School Plans Ready

Complete drawings for the Merced High school group have been approved and are ready for figures. There will be four buildings—administration, domestic arts, manual arts and gymnasium. Construction will be either brick, concrete or hollow tile, alternate figures being taken on all three items. Exterior will be stucco, with clay tile roof. There will be vacuum cleaning, low pressure steam heat, showers, lockers, etc. Estimated cost, $150,000.

Theatre to Be Made Into Assembly Hall

The old Fillmore street theatre in San Francisco is to be renovated and converted into an assembly hall for lodge and public meeting purposes. A new floor will be put down and a gallery constructed. A new moving picture theatre, to cost $100,000, is to be built on the north side of Eddy, near Fillmore street. Reid Bros. have the plans for both jobs.

Another Factory for Emeryville

Plans are being prepared in the office of P. J. Walker, Monadnock building, San Francisco, for a two-story brick factory building to be erected at Emeryville for the Air Reduction Company of Detroit. Building will be about 100 feet square. Exterior will be of pressed brick.

A "Model" Roofing Specification

A Sacramento architect sends us the following copy of a "model" Roofing Specification, that was turned in by a local contractor. The architect suggests we print it in our humorous column, so here goes: (Note spelling.)

First lay one thickness of sheathing paper or unsaturated felt, Sheathing paper waying not les than five pounds to 100 square feat or one pound Dedning felt.

Second lay Four layers of Saturated felt waying Fourteen pounds to 100 square feat, shingle fashion, laping each sheat Twenty Four and one half inchs (24½) inches over the preceding one, and nailing as often as necessary to hold in place, moping solid with hot asfeltom betwean each sheat

then flud the same with a uniforme coating of asfeltum and when hot imbed a uniforme coat of washed crick gravel or crushed Brick gravel or brick one quater to Five Eights

The roof may be inspected before gravel or brick is spred By cutting a slit not less than three feat long at rite angles to the way the felt is laid. asfeltum shall be the best grade of Roofing asfeltum from 20 to 30 pentration

sed roof to be garentead by roofing contractor for a perid of five years from date of laying aginst ordnary ware and usage

Swimming Pool for Del Monte

Lewis P. Hobart, Crocker building, San Francisco, is completing plans for the Y. W. C. A. building to be erected on Sutter street at an estimated cost of $125,000. Mr. Hobart has made plans for a large concrete swimming pool at Del Monte. Plans have just been started for extensive alterations to the Ansel Easton home at Burlingame, which was recently bought by J. Cheever Cowdin, the famous polo player.

Office Buildings

Frederick H. Meyer of San Francisco has completed plans for a six-story office building on Montgomery street for the Pope estate. The ground floor will be especially arranged for the San Francisco Stock and Bond Exchange. Mr. Meyer is preparing plans for an office building to be erected in Palo Alto for the Pacific Gas & Electric Company. It will be similar to the building recently completed for the gas company in San Rafael.

Eight-Story Bank Building

The directors of the Fresno branch of the Bank of Italy of San Francisco, have voted to erect an eight-story Class "A" bank and office building at the corner of Tulare and "J" streets, Fresno. Structure will cost in the neighborhood of $100,000. L. Scatena is chairman of the board of directors and P. C. Hale of Fresno is vice-president.

Fresno Architect Busy

Recent work in the office of Ernest J. Kump of Fresno includes a $40,000 high school at Chowchilla, auditorium for the Edison school, Fresno; Odd Fellows building and stores and apartments for a client in Turlock.

To Build in Richmond

The Standard Oil Company is planning to build an office building on its property in Richmond. Construction will probably be of concrete and brick and the building will be either two or three stories. It is understood that it will be put up on percentage basis by the P. J. Walker Company, which concern built the Standard Oil Company's San Francisco office building. Washington J. Miller is the architect.

Architects for Santa Rosa Schools

Messrs. Herbert & Turton, the latter, L. M. Turton of Napa, have been selected by the Santa Rosa Board of Education to prepare plans for two new school buildings to be erected in that city. They will be Class "C" construction and will probably cost from $60,000 to $70,000 each. Messrs. Sexton & Ellery, Merchants National Bank building, San Francisco, will be consulting architect and engineer on the work.

Palo Alto Residence

Chas. S. Kaiser, Mechanics Institute building, San Francisco, has plans completed for a two-story and basement frame and plaster residence and garage at Palo Alto for R. S. Faxon of 1651 Waverly street, Palo Alto. The house, which will cost approximately $12,000, will have stucco exterior, slate roof, oak floors, mahogany and pine finish, furnace, automatic water heater, and four bathrooms.

Bakery to Erect Big Plant

The California Baking Company, with offices at Eddy and Fillmore streets, San Francisco, has announced through its manager, Chas. Loesch, that plans are being prepared and construction work will start shortly on a new plant for the company at 40th street and San Pablo avenue, Oakland. It will be one of the largest bakeries on the Pacific Coast.

Addition to Class A Building

John Reid, Jr., First National Bank building, San Francisco, has been commissioned to prepare plans for a Class A addition to the Balfour-Guthrie building on California street, San Francisco. It is estimated the work will cost $40,000. The present structure was designed by L. B. Dutton, who retired from active practice three years ago.

Four-Story Loft Building

C. H. Skidmore, 608 New Call building, San Francisco, is preparing plans for a four-story reinforced concrete loft building to be erected in San Francisco at a cost of $30,000. The building will be occupied by a manufacturing concern. It will have a 70 foot frontage. A sprinkler system will be installed.

TEN AND ONE-HALF MILES OF STEEL PIPING WELDED
TOGETHER FOR THE FORMATION OF AN ARTIFICIAL ICE POND

An Ice Palace Made Possible by Electricity

By ROBERT SIBLEY in the Journal of Electricity

ARTIFICIAL ice-skating on the Pacific Coast is not only creating a new health-giving, invigorating pastime for its people, hitherto unacquainted with the joys of winter sports, due to the temperate climate in which they live, but the net result to the electrical industry is an ever-increasing profitable power load of almost ideal demands.

The possibility of artificial ice-skating in the West was first heralded and put to a practical test in Portland, Ore., some two years ago. The new pastime proved so fascinating that it rapidly spread to other Coast cities. In San Francisco the sport has been especially cordially received by its frolicking, play-loving people.

On October 10, 1916, the new Winter Garden, a huge ice rink with exterior building dimensions of 275 by 144 feet was thrown open to the public. This building is situated at the corner of Pierce and Sutter streets. On the occasion of its dedication the ice palace was crowded to its limit and it is estimated that, in addition, some fifteen hundred people were refused admission.

The space devoted to ice skating is of the regulation hocky proportions and measures 210 by 90 feet.

The building has box seats, reserved seats and general admission seats that will accommodate two thousand spectators. Surrounding the rink are also to be found dressing rooms, hot and cold showers, a dance floor 100 by 90 feet, and confectionery stand.

An inter-connecting telephone system, a carefully appointed system of attendants and ice-skating instructors also add to the comfort and pleasure of the guests.

The principle of refrigeration employed in preparing the ice pond is that known as the indirect system. In this system liquid ammonia under high pressure is caused to expand into a gas at low pressure in the coils from A to B, as shown in the diagram. As in the formation of steam from water, an enormous amount of heat is necessary to be absorbed from the furnace gases, so in the formation of ammonia gas from its liquid, an enormous quantity of heat is necessary to be absorbed from the surrounding medium. Since brine is made the

surrounding medium, as shown at C in the diagram, this extraction of heat from the brine causes the temperature of the brine to be lowered considerably below the freezing point of water. If, now, this brine be pumped through pipes DCEF beneath the skating rink, where a thin layer of water—say 1½ to 2 inches in depth—is sprayed over the pipe, this water at once becomes frozen and thus furnishes the artificial ice pond GHIJ for the pleasure-seekers.

Reverting to the ammonia that has now been expanded into a gas at lower pressure, let us follow to a conclusion its cycle of operation. The low pressure ammonia gas at B is next drawn into a compressor K and subjected to such a pressure as will cause the ammonia gas to be sent forth at L ready for early condensation back again into a liquid. This compression of course causes the temperature of the ammonia gas to be raised to such a height that it must next be passed through a cooling condenser M. This condenser consists of a series of cool water tubes NOP, which absorb the excess heat from the heated high pressure ammonia gas in M and thus cause the conversion of the ammonia gas into a liquid at S, ready again to be expanded at A, in order to abstract the heat from the brine in the tank C so that ice may be maintained in the rink.

The water cooling tubes NOP, just mentioned, draw their supply of cool water from the tank R, which is fed from the spray nozzles Q on the roof of the building. The heated water, coming from the condenser M at P, is thus exposed to the atmosphere by means of sprays and returns to the coils NOP in the condenser, sufficiently lowered in temperature to permanently effect the

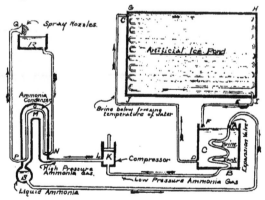

Diagramatic Sketch Showing How the Artificial Ice Pond is Maintained

necessary absorption of
heat from the high pressure ammonia gas in order to convert this gas
again to its liquid.

The construction of the
ice pond proved an interesting piece of work. The
building in which the Winter Garden is located was
formerly used as a roller
skating rink. Upon the
former skating rink floor
was laid eight inches of
heat insulating material
such as sawdust and
waterproof roofing. Upon
this was laid a sprinkling
of sand, and upon the sand
55,000 feet of two-inch
steel piping. This piping,

Artificial Ice Pond Supporting the Throng of Enthusiasts on the Opening Night

though remarkable for length, is also remarkable for the fact that it has but 134
joints. These were left to serve as expansion joints. The remaining 4,867 connections were done away with by welding the
ends together by the oxy-acetylene process.

In the various parts that make up the
refrigeration details for this ice rink, practically all units are installed in duplicate to
insure continuity of service. The ice plant
itself consists of two 50-ton units, each operated by electric motors of 100 horsepower
capacity. Twenty-five hundred gallons of
brine, composed of a 75 per cent solution, are used in the circulating system for
creating the artificial ice pond. The average quantity of brine circulated per minute
is about fifteen gallons. This is, however,

carefully regulated, so that the temperature
of the ice in the rink is kept as nearly 32
degrees F. as possible, since this temperature of freezing water has proven best for
maintaining a smooth surface of the ice.

It is found necessary to trim the ice three
times daily in order to maintain the surface
absolutely smooth. This is efficiently accomplished by means of an electrically
drawn ice planer, as shown in the diagram.
The ice pond is well lighted by means
of some 1200 lamps of 150 candlepower capacity, which are evenly distributed over
the skating area. Throughout the building
there are in all over 2,000 lighting outlets.

Mr. J. T. Ludlow, a consulting engineer
of San Francisco, acted as architect and
engineer for the complete installation.

*The Electrically Drawn Ice Planer Preparing the
Ice Surface for Skating*

Beauty and Utility in Lighting
By M. LUCKIESH

STRICTLY these two terms when applied to lighting and perhaps to all other activities, overlap considerably. Beauty cannot be considered to be completely separated from utility as is readily seen on perusing the extensive literature on the philosophy of the beautiful. Usefulness is a part of beauty and therefore a lighting fixture cannot be beautiful if it does not fulfill its purely utilitarian purpose regardless of the gracefulness of its lines or of its expressiveness as a work of art. Beauty is the result of harmony—the accord of all the elements; therefore, when a lighting fixture is extended to fulfill the double purpose of an object of art and of an utilitarian distributor of light, the fulfillment of the latter aim is essential to harmony and, hence, to beauty.

On surveying the past in lighting it is easy to imagine the designing artist so engrossed with such elements as form, grace, color, and expression that he neglected the other principal object of the fixture—its usefulness as a lighting fixture. Similarly it is equally easy to imagine the lighting engineer so occupied with the utilitarian aspect of lighting that he neglected the artistic aspect. It is no easy task for an individual to cultivate both viewpoints to a high degree of perfection. Dual experts of this character are rare, but the harmonizing of pure utility and art in lighting fixtures can be accomplished by a closer co-operation of the designing artist and the designing engineer. The past bears witness in many cases of the absence of such combined efforts. Fixture catalogues of today, although showing a gradual mingling of these two viewpoints, present a variety of examples which pictorially represent the progress of the two extreme viewpoints toward each other. Fixture design has largely evolved from the purely artistic viewpoint, and in this field lies the opportunity for perfecting the harmony of usefulness and beauty in lighting.

It is not a simple task to combine utility and art; that is, to design the skeleton of a lighting fixture and then to provide it with an artistic exterior. It is satisfying to note that such attempts are more frequent now than in the past and it is easy to discern by their output

MARYSVILLE SAND PLANT

The Pratt Building Material Co.'s sand plant at Marysville produces the best sand in California, so architects and contractors say. Phone Pratt Building Material Co. in the Hearst Building for prices.

those fixture manufacturers who are
working toward this ideal. An idea of
the amount of progress still to be made
can be gained by visiting fixture display-
rooms with the thought of this brief note
dominating the mind. If a sacrifice must
be made in harmonizing the artistic and
the purely utilitarian let it, in many cases,
be that of efficiency in its narrow sense.
The accomplishment of the purely utilitarian and artistic aims simultaneously,
even at the sacrifice of some light, results in an efficient unit in the broader
sense.

As stated in the beginning, usefulness
is a part of beauty; that is, beauty is useful and necessary. In lighting, the useful is often measured against the beautiful as if they were antagonistic; the
esthetic aspect is even ridiculed at times.
Those who ridicule the esthetic aspect
can readily ascertain the usefulness of
beauty if they will in their imagination
strike out all the beautiful from the world
and leave only the manifestly useful.
What a different world this would be!—
Lighting Journal.

Radiant Gas Heat
By C. B. BABCOCK.

FOR the first time in the United States
the principle of radiant gas heat is
being successfully applied in the form of
a fireplace heater.

Gas for heating purposes, if properly
applied, possesses superior advantages as
a fuel—instantaneous heat when wanted,
and with the Humphrey Radiantfire
heater, even after the gas is shut off, the
heat still continues to radiate from the
objects in the room which have been
brought to a higher temperature than the
air, a condition which eliminates the
sensation of chilliness in a room heated
by any other type of gas heater.

In this whole matter of superiority of
gas heating, the subject was very well
summarized a number of years ago by
the London Lancet in a report upon
"Smoke Prevention and Perfect Combustion." This report covered the advantages of gas over coal fires, and is as follows:

> None will deny the convenience of such a sys-
> tem. With gas, a bright fire can be obtained at
> any moment, night or day. The heat can be
> regulated to a degree, the fire can be stopped at
> will, the conveyance of coal is dispensed with, and
> the oftentimes troublesome process of lighting
> with wood and paper is avoided; while cleanliness
> is an inevitable result of a gas installation.

Radiant heat is derived from energy
waves projected through the atmosphere
from an incandescent mass. It carries its
warmth directly to that body upon which
the radiating heat waves fall, and it is
therefore very different from so-called
"convected heat," which merely warms
the air surrounding it.

The heat from the sun is radiant heat.
It is radiant heat you feel when seated

Radiant Gas Heater in Office of Mr. Holberton

close to an open fire, and now radiant heat with gas as a fuel, is available.

The advantage of this principle of gas heating is that it warms the body yet leaves the air in the room cool and fresh for breathing. In fact, it helps to create a circulation of air. A room thus heated will never feel close and stuffy.

A room heated by radiation is more comfortable to sit in and when we consider that the raising of the temperature of the air increases its capacity for absorbing moisture, we realize another very important aspect of the difference between heating by radiation and heating by convection.

It has been frequently noted that in a room heated by convection methods, one often gets cold feet, a hot head, a thirst, a headache, and a general feeling of lassitude.

There is very small heat loss up the flue or chimney. In fact, about 75 to 80 per cent of the heat thrown off is directed immediately into the room. A very simple method of proving this statement is to hold the hand directly above the heater and then directly in front of it.

Previous to the advent of the Radiant-fire gas heater, the architect and builder has been limited to the gas log and asbestos grate, which were at best, simply makeshifts, consuming a large amount of gas without efficient heating and hygienic results.

There are many homes where a central heating plant is now in use where the Radiantfire could be installed to advantage in rooms where there are fireplaces.

The Radiantfire heater is designed for installation in fireplaces, and is not intended as a portable heater.

Practically perfect combustion takes place in the Radiantfire. That is, there are no unburned gases, therefore no disagreeable or unhealthy products of combustion.

The heater is clean, odorless, and the elements which become incandescent are beautiful to behold, and have the same fascination as the flames from a coal or wood grate without the latter's dirt and ashes. The gas flame from this heater does not strike any part such as the fire clay elements, that are not hotter than the degree of combustion.

As an illustration of the strength of the radiant heat waves, you can place the Radiantfire facing a cake of ice, and feel the heat on your hand clear through the ice.

The heat is projected like light rays— it does not simply heat a column of air to rise to the ceiling.

It is particularly suitable for living rooms, halls, dining-rooms, sleeping chambers, libraries, or offices.

At the maximum heat the gas consumption will not exceed about 3 cents per hour.

A Useful Book for Motor Truck Owners

What wears a motor truck out? Wear and tear. But what wears a truck out in three or four years which is built to last ten or fifteen years? Overloading, over-speeding, reckless driving and lack of proper care by the driver. The abuse of trucks is admittedly one of the greatest problems facing the motor truck industry today.

The B. F. Goodrich Company recently asked the truck manufacturers of this country what subject they would like to see treated as an introduction to the 1917 issue of "Motor Trucks of America." A large majority of the replies indicated that the most urgent problem facing the industry was that of truck abuse.

In response to this demand, Mr. S. V. Norton has treated this subject under the title, "Lengthening the Life of the Motor Truck." The effect of overloading on the axles, springs, wheels, tires, frame, transmission, motor, etc., is clearly shown.

This article, however, is merely the introduction to the 164-page issue of the 1917 "Motor Trucks of America." This hand-book originated in 1913, and is awaited more and more eagerly at the beginning of each year by the motor truck industry. This year's edition contains the complete specifications of 118 makes of American motor trucks, with a photograph of each truck.

Mr. S. V. Norton, truck tire sales manager of The B. F. Goodrich Company, states that while the increased size of the book and the cost of paper and ink have made each copy cost 30 cents to produce, the company will adhere to its original policy of distributing it without charge to responsible persons interested. Requests, however, must be sent in on business letterhead and should be addressed to the Truck Tire Department of The B. F. Goodrich Company, Akron, Ohio.

House at Carmel

Edwin G. Garden, Phelan building, San Francisco, is preparing plans for a one-story frame rustic country residence and garage to be erected at Carmel for Louis Lyons.

The Contractor

General Contractors Association
OF SAN FRANCISCO
Officers
PRESIDENT....................HARVEY A. KLYCE
VICE-PRESIDENT.....................JOHN MONK
TREASURER........................CHAS. WRIGHT
SECRETARY.....................P. M. WUILLEMIN

Directors
A. H. Bergstrom	Harvey A. Klyce
John Biller	A. F. Lindgren
Harold Braunton	T. W. McClenahan
Percy J. Cole	John Monk
Thos. B. Goodwin	Clarence M. Moore
Chas. Wright	

New Form of Bidding

The Builders' Exchange of Rock Island, Ill., whose membership is made up of contractors, subcontractors and materialmen of Rock Island and Moline, Ill., and Davenport, Iowa, have formally adopted the Nelson system for choosing bidders upon work and awarding contracts. The form is by H. W. Nelson of Moline, and the Exchange adopting it reserves the right to change or modify the form as it may be necessary to cover certain conditions.

The contractors claim the Nelson form is a long step in the right direction towards solving the problem of unfair competition and provides that a buyer pay each contractor who bids on his job a certain sum for his time and labor. The sum to be paid is determined by the size of the job, the buyer limiting the number of contractors bidding to suit himself, and in this manner securing as much competition as he wishes to pay for, as alone derives the benefit.

"After all bids have been received and opened, the buyer shall, within ten days, pay to each bidder, who has bid in strict accordance and has complied with all the demands contained in the plans and specifications, and whose bids do not exceed by 50 per cent the amount of the bid upon which the contract is awarded, a sum equal to the square root of the average of all bids received, multiplied by .7. For example, if the average of all bids received shall be $90,000, the square root of which is $300, multiply $300 by .7, which equals $21, the amount which shall be paid to each competing bidder in payment for the labor and expense involved in estimating and as a complete waiver of all obligations."

The buyer may be the architect acting for the owner or any person requiring the services of a builder. As they have chosen their contractors in a fair manner and having paid a just and reasonable price for the competition they are under no obligations to the bidders and reserve a perfect right to reject any and all bids.

It would seem that with the adoption of this or a similar plan and operating on the plan of contract and general conditions contained in the standard documents advocated by the American Institute of Architects and Associated Builders' Exchanges that the happy day for the contractor is approaching.

Safety Nets for Falling Workmen

The Safety Department of the California Industrial Accident Commission has been responsible for the introduction of safety nets in San Francisco for buildings in course of construction. These nets are used in some of the large Eastern cities and there are European countries that require a similar safety precaution. It is intended to secure the co-operation of California's building contractors in order that the safety nets may come into general use.

It has been found that the law is impracticable that calls for the temporary flooring of all buildings under construction. High balconies, galleries, arch-trusses of theatres, auditoriums, churches, armory buildings, railroad train-sheds, towers, viaducts, bridges, domes and cupolas on which men are engaged are not safe in case men fall. The distance to the floor is too far. The safety net supplies the need. A man falling many feet into a net is uninjured. The cost of the net is nominal and it is easily adjusted and removed. It can be readily transported from one job to another.

. The safety nets are similar in character to those employed by fire departments in some of our large cities to catch persons jumping from blazing windows. Circus performers are protected in like manner.

Safety nets were used for the protection of structural steel workers employed on the erection of the California theatre at Market and Fourth streets, San Francisco. The four nets cost $60 each. They were the first used west of Chicago.

The need of these safety nets is best illustrated by California's experience in 1915. In the building industry 15 men lost their lives—10 of these men fell to death and 5 were struck by fal'ing objects. There were 91 permanent injuries. The temporary injuries numbered 1447. The installation of safety nets would have affected the seriousness of these 1553 deaths and injuries.

Millions for California Highways

The development in road bond issues during the year 1916 brings California into the foremost ranks as a progressive state in highway development. Besides the fifteen-million-dollar bond issue voted for new state roads last fall, the counties of Sacramento and Stanislaus have both voted more than a million dollars to be used on county highway work. Many counties have proposed bond issues which will be put to the vote of the people this year, and aggregate a proposed expenditure of $6,750,000 during the present year. Tulare leads with new road plans calling for a bond issue of two million dollars, while in Imperial, Santa Clara, Santa Cruz and Yolo counties similar plans are under way calling for less amounts.

A. T. de Forest in Eastern Wreck

Mr. A. T. de Forest recently returned to San Francisco from an extended business and pleasure trip in the East. Mr. and Mrs. de Forest were in one of three coaches which turned over at Green River, Wyo., and crawled out of the car windows, escaping without injury. Mr. de Forest is at the head of the San Francisco office of the United States Steel Corporation. He attended a convention at Pittsburgh as delegate of the Foreign Trades Council of San Francisco and was also a representative of the San Francisco Chamber of Commerce at a convention in Washington.

General Contractors Association Elects Officers

The following directors have been elected by the stockholders of the General Contractors Association of San Francisco for the year 1917-1918:

A. H. Bergstrom, John Biller, Harold Braunton, Percy J. Cole, Thos. B. Goodwin, Harvey A. Klyce, A. F. Lindgren, T. W. McClenahan, John Monk, Clarence M. Moore, Charles Wright.

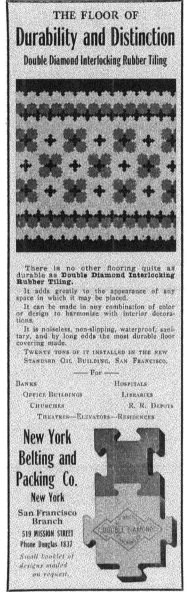

Cement Prices to Advance

Buyers of Portland cement are advised of a further advance in the price of this commodity within the near future, says the New York Sun. The immediate prospective jump will probably be ten cents a barrel, although conditions warrant an advance of fifteen cents. There is talk among manufacturers of putting the price up twenty-five cents a barrel. The new $1.77 price does not make up for the increased price of coal. There is no present doubt but that the price of Portland cement next spring will be $1.40 to $1.50, mill, making an approximate quotation for this market of $2 a barrel. This mill price of $1.40 to $1.50 a barrel is not record breaking, the highest previous quotation being $2 and $2.25, mill, or about $2.40 to $2.50 a barrel in New York.

"The sudden stiffening of the price of Portland cement was caused by a further advance in the price of coal.

"The price of wired, rough, ribbed and figured rolled glass has advanced ten to twenty cents on current lists. Window glass and plate glass are remaining firm and without change in discounts. Stocks are still ragged because the factories have just started up and have made no shipments."

New Oakland Bridge

An agreement for the joint construction, ownership and operation of a modern bascule bridge across Oakland's inner harbor, supplanting the two obsolete spans at Webster and Harrison streets, has been reached between members of the Alameda County Board of Supervisors and engineers of the Southern Pacific Company. It is proposed to place the matter before the people for a bond issue, the estimated cost of the bridge with its approaches being $1,000,000. The new type of bridge will eliminate, it is claimed, 90 per cent of the present delay to traffic in operating the two old bridges at Webster and Harrison streets, and will do away with the grade crossing at First and Webster streets. The plans as prepared by the Scherzer Rolling Lift Bridge Company of Chicago, call for a span 3450 feet in length with a maximum grade of 4 per cent, and 80 feet in width, subdivided into two 8-foot sidewalks, a 36-foot roadway for double street car tracks, and 28-foot right-of-way for S. P. R. R. trains.

To Have New High School

A special bond election has been set for March 15th to vote $80,000 bonds for a new high school building at Oroville. It is understood the plans of several architects for the proposed building are now under consideration.

When writing to Advertisers please mention this magazine.

Fish Gas-Electric Plant Ready for Operation

A New Fuel Produced
By GUIDO BLENIO.*

THE following is an extract of an article which appeared in the San Francisco Chronicle February 16, 1917, and relates to the development of the new Fish Gas-Electric System. The fact that a municipality has decided to install the system so early in the stage of manufacture, would seem to indicate unusual confidence in its practicability:

SAUSALITO IS TO OPERATE ITS OWN GAS PLANT

Contract Closed by Which Private Enterprise Is to Revert to City in Due Time

SAUSALITO, February 15.—Acting under authority given him by the Board of Town Trustees, Mayor E. G. Coughlin today signed a contract with the George L. Fish Company whereby this city is to have a municipally owned and operated gas plant built by outside capital, and transferred to the city as soon as the investment is repaid out of the earnings of the company. Work on the plant will be commenced within sixty days.

The contract with the Fish Company provides that the plant will be owned and operated by the city of Sausalito after it is built. Fish will provide all of the capital for building and operating the plant and will take all revenues until he has been repaid. Fish is also to receive a royalty of ten cents per thousand cubic feet for the use of his patent.

The writer has had ample opportunity of examining the Fish Gas System, as demonstrated at 72 Tehama street, San Francisco, during the past fortnight. He has not only his own opinion as a guide to his conclusions, but also the written testimony of many able engineers and the expressed sentiments of the throngs

which assembled every afternoon at this demonstration plant. Here is installed an ordinary equipment suitable for the furnishing of heat, light and power required for a good-sized apartment house, or other large buildings, and both gas produced for heating, cooking and lighting, also electricity generated for any and all similar uses. Thus the manifold possibilities of this system can be watched in actual operation and the results accurately tested. The result of my own observation and experiments have been to absolutely confirm the claims made for this system, and to prove that it is perfectly well adapted to furnish a cheap and efficient fuel, for all uses and capacities ranging from that required for a small camp or house to that required by any sized municipality.

The gas is produced from the use of distillates or oils (of quality from four cents per gallon upwards), and can be carried through standard pipes to any point at any distance for cooking, heating, lighting and power purposes. The operation of this system can be attended to by any ordinary person, without previous experience, and will take but very little of the operator's time. A system suitable for 100 families will comprise the following equipment, the whole outfit weighing less than a ton, and measuring three feet in width by eight feet in length.

1 two and a half horsepower gas engine.
1 fuel pump.
1 high pressure receiving and feeding tank.
1 breaker chamber.

*Professor Guido Blenio is a well-known chemical engineer, whose fireproofing processes were so successfully used at the P. P. I. E., when the fire loss was only $250 as against $478,000 at Chicago and $100,000 at St. Louis.

1 set belting and pulleys.
1 air blower.
1 set air and gas mixing apparatus.
3 pressure registers.
1 idling apparatus.
I governing apparatus.
1 fuel storage tank.

The claim is made by the Union Gas Electric Company, with offices in the Palace Hotel, San Francisco, who control and manufacture the Fish patents, that such an equipment can produce gas at a cost of 12 cents per 1,000 cubic feet and electricity at 1¼ cents per kilowatt or less. No change is necessary in the ordinary piping or wiring. The plant can be installed under a guarantee of efficiency in any apartment house or other large buildings or municipalities, under a royalty system.

Without going into the details leading up to same, I can epitomize and summarize my conclusions as to its results and benefits as follows:

1. The Fish Gas System produces a positive and fixed gas of a quality bordering on if not identical with the atmospheric gas known as nitrogen and oxygen, and will condense only as does air.

2. In its manufacture there is no application of heat or flame, or any exposure, which could produce a flame. It will not ignite at a distance of three inches from the burner and does not explode when coming into contact with the atmosphere. It may be called, therefore, a "safety first" gas generator.

3. Its combustion is complete and perfect, leaving no residue or fumes, and is odorless and non-poisonous. When burning, it is not injurious to animal life or to plants and flowers—and there is no discoloration of hangings, furniture, etc. The effect upon the occupants of a house will not be found to be depressing and no resultant headaches can follow its use.

4. The consumption of fuel will be in relation to its output, as 1 to 30 or less.

5. The simplicity of this machinery makes it almost "fool proof," and for engine use there can be no "fuel miss," no "foul spark plug," no "carbon deposit." Temperatures, altitudes and changes of atmospheric conditions have no effect upon the operation of the system or engine. The engine can be left alone for weeks and will operate idle or on a load as responsively as does steam in full response to the will of the operator.

6. The machine makes a cheap hot pure gas, the light being perfect and steady. It gave under actual test a greater heating power when using an ordinary open cooking burner than did other gas with a Bunsen burner.

7. My final conclusion is that architects and others interested in buildings, either in contemplation or construction, or in structures already completed, cannot profitably neglect to examine into the merits of a system so well calculated to give them satisfactory service, with a very substantial saving of money.

Pioneer Roofing Gives Satisfaction

Pioneer Flaxine Roofing was recently used in laying a new roof on the Emporium, San Francisco. Specifications called for two layers of Flaxine mopped solid and graveled in, which was similar to the specifications for State Piers Nos. 18, 24 and 37, upon which between 9,000 and 10,000 rolls or squares of Pioneer Flaxine Roofing were used.

Thousands of buildings all over the West are being roofed with Pioneer, according to Mr. H. H. Linton, San Francisco manager. Some prefer a sanded surface to the smooth or Flaxine brand—price, however, is the same and guaranteed for the same length of time.

"The history of the Pioneer Paper Company, manufacturers of Pioneer Rubber Flaxine Roofing and Pioneer Rubber Sanded Roofing," said Mr. Linton, "is interesting reading. Starting in a small building in 1888, their manufacturing plant has grown until today it covers nine acres of ground—a modern, up-to-the-minute factory, turning out Pioneer products of supreme quality.

"It is but reasonable to suppose that in that length of time we have acquired valuable experience—that means a great deal to the purchasers of roofing materials. In other words, we 'know how' to make roofing of durability at a reasonable price.

"Good roofing cannot be made from poor materials, and, with this in mind, emphasis upon the fact that everything that enters into the manufacture of Pioneer products is of the best quality obtainable.

"Not only are the finest ingredients used, but the best experts in the country are employed in the manufacture of Pioneer roofing—men who have studied the business in its every detail, and who know the why and wherefore of every part of the roofing business.

"It is presumed that partly this is the reason why Pioneer roofing has attained such an enormous sale all over the West and several foreign countries.

"Thousands of dealers are selling Pioneer products to at least a million consumers, who insist upon having Pioneer roofing materials."

New Distributors for Wall Board

The Key-Hold Lath Company, 251-57 Monadnock building, San Francisco, is now the general distributor and factory representative of the Schumacher Wall Board Company.

This wall board needs no introduction, as it has been sold on the Pacific Coast for some time. Its composition is a gypsum base with a magnesite and fibre filler, making it highly fire resistent, as has been shown in many successful official fire tests. This board may therefore be properly designated as a plaster wall board, differing from the wood and paper pulp boards, which are liable to warp and buckle by climatic changes.

According to Mr. J. A. Levensaler, general manager of the Key-Hold Lath Company, the Schumacher wall board is, as far as known, the only board of its type made in sheets up to twelve feet in length, thereby reaching from floor to ceiling, in ordinary buildings, and thus eliminating all horizontal joints. The boards are made in widths 32 inches and 48 inches, and as noted above, in lengths up to twelve feet. It is easy to cut and fit, thereby creating no waste and may be applied in any building, in any location, at all seasons, without plastering. The joints may be pointed and the board painted, tinted, papered or left in the natural finish. It is valuable particularly as a non-conductor of sound, heat and electricity.

Ample stock of all sizes will be carried in San Francisco, for the convenience of users in this territory, and particulars and samples may be had at the office of the Key-Hold Lath Company, 255 Monadnock building, San Francisco.

Plumbing in Public Buildings

The advantage of having shower baths in addition to the usual sanitary conveniences in buildings used by public officials has been demonstrated in many instances. Such provision has been made in old buildings by the office holder, and during hot weather the refreshment attending a shower bath better qualifies him for the exacting services required. Recognition of their value is being shown in the plans of new buildings in various centers. The new county-city building of Pittsburg, Pa., provides a private bath of the shower type in the lavatories for the heads of all departments and similar equipment in the lavatories used by the employees. This is in harmony with the equipment now provided in first-class hotels where the traveling man has had his demands satisfied in the provision of a shower bath in his room, even in some cases to the exclusion of the bathtub.

Wybro Veneered Panels Advance in Price

Wybro Veneered Panels have become such an important factor in modern architecture and are growing so rapidly in public favor that a brief discussion here will prove interesting to those who are not familiar with their true merits and beauty. Mr. C. H. White, of White Bros., manufacturers of Wybro veneered panels, says: "Our panels are suitable for wainscots, partitions, doors, etc. They are manufactured in three- and five-ply, the different layers running crosswise, in order to give stiffness and strength. The outside veneer is selected for its beauty, and the built-up structure gives a wider surface than could be obtained in the solid wood. Some people are inclined to regard veneering as a cheap substitute for solid wood. This is not the case. The veneered product is more expensive than the solid wood and is immeasurably superior. A wide solid board $\frac{1}{4}$ or $\frac{1}{8}$ of an inch thick would surely split when exposed to varying weather conditions, and it would also warp out of shape. This is entirely obviated when a veneered panel is used. The specific points of excellence of the veneered panel over the solid wood are found in the fact that a larger surface is obtainable, in their freedom from warping and checking, their wide range of grain and figure, and their superior beauty."

A new Wybro price list has just been published showing an advance in the cost of panels due to the advance in price of glue and veneers, and the higher wages paid for labor.

Pratt Building Material Company Expands

The Pratt Building Material Company of San Francisco has recently been reorganized and with its new directorate, composed of substantial business men, the company should be able to develop its properties and extend its range of operation very materially. Mr. Clarence F. Pratt continues as president and general manager, and his many years' experience, together with the wide acquaintanceship which he enjoys, will, of course, be an added factor toward future business expansion.

The other officers of the company are as follows: Andrew Mahony, of Olsen-Mahony Lumber Co., vice-president; James Brown, secretary; John D. McGilvray of McGilvray Stone Co., treasurer; directors, the officers and I. B. Clark. The Pratt Building Material Co. recently bought from the E. B. & A. L. Stone Co. their sand loading plant on the American river at Sacramento.

Metal Stamping Company Changes Ownership

The San Francisco Metal Stamping and Corrugating Company is no longer a corporation. Its stockholders have transferred their entire holdings to Mr. Theophile Lahaye, who, for the past ten years, has been manager and director of the business. The enterprise will hereafter be known as the S. F. Metal Stamping Works.

The many customers and friends of Mr. Lahaye will undoubtedly join in wishing him the same success with his labors as sole owner of the concern as marked his efforts when associated with the company as an incorporator and stockholder. The business has developed from very modest proportions to one of the foremost industries of its kind in San Francisco. Its customers are the leading sheet metal contractors in Northern and Central California. The factory and offices are at 2269 Folsom street, and the buildings extend through to Treat avenue. They are all substantial structures, being built of corrugated iron and heavy beam supports. The machinery is modern and complete. A large stock is carried for quick delivery, the stock comprising stamped and spun goods of varied patterns and sizes, metal tile roofing, drain pipe, fine copper and bronze work, and drawn metal ornaments.

New Face Brick Attracts Attention

The new style face brick used on the Santa Fe building at Second and Market streets, San Francisco, was supplied by the Richmond Pressed Brick Company through the agency of the United Materials Company. This brick is different from any other face brick thereabouts, not being as smooth as the regular pressed brick, nor as rough as rough-textured brick. It is of a texture somewhere between these two and the brick are variegated in color from light red to blue black. The general effect is a soft reddish hue which makes a splendid appearance. The brick are small, measuring 1⅞ by 7 inches. They were made to order after an idea furnished by the architects of the building. Seventy-five thousand were used on the building.

Plan Immense Warehouse

After many weeks of negotiations with owners of Oakland water front property, the Libby, McNeil & Libby Packing Company are reported to have obtained an option on a tract of land owned by Frank J. Woodward. The company is understood to be planning to build a $250,000 warehouse and packing plant.

TUEC STATIONARY CLEANERS FOR AMERICAN SCHOOLS

MANY SCHOOLS in Nearly Every State of the Union

have now installed the TUEC Stationary Cleaner.

WHY?

Simply because they know that the TUEC is the only vacuum cleaner that really cleans, and cleans thoroughly.

Tests have been made of the various cleaners in the New York schools, with the result that the

TUEC Stationary Cleaner

is the only machine that was purchased by the New York Board of Education. THE TUEC STATIONARY CLEANER does the work of cleaning your school, and does it right.

We *guarantee* every machine, and *stand* by our guarantee.

The United Electric Company
CANTON, OHIO

CALIFORNIA DISTRIBUTORS

S. F. COMPRESSED AIR CLEANING CO.
397 Sutter Street, San Francisco

BARKER BROS.
724-38 South Broadway, Los Angeles

When writing to Advertisers please mention this magazine.

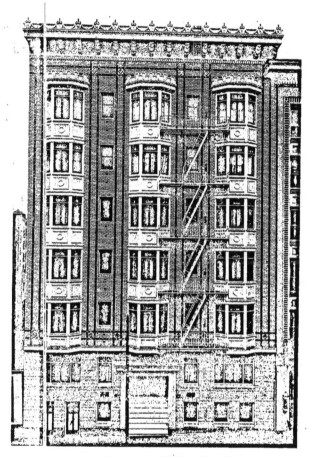

GEORGE BENNETT APARTMENT HOUSE, SAN FRANCISCO
C. O. CLAUSEN, Architect

Built by

Cameron & Disston, General Contractors

831 Hearst Building, San Francisco

Telephone Sutter 4120

When writing to Advertisers please mention this magazine.

GEORGE BENNETT APARTMENT HOUSE, SAN FRANCISCO
C. O. CLAUSEN, Architect

Built by

Cameron & Disston, General Contractors

831 Hearst Building, San Francisco

Telephone Sutter 4120

Automatic Sprinklers for Hotel Fire Protection

C. M. Thompson, city building inspector of Knoxville, Tenn., in his annual report has the following to say about the necessity for sprinkler protection in hotels:

I believe that when men offer their property for hire to the public for sleeping purposes they should be compelled to spare no reasonable known means for appliances for safeguarding the health and happiness and especially the lives of the public, who accept their implied guarantee of safety. Ever since I have had charge of this department this matter has confronted me more and more ominously. Knowing how jealously men guard their property rights I have hesitated to bring the matter to public attention, but it has been shown to me so conclusively that the sprinkler system in this class of buildings is the greatest known means for rendering them safe and in a sense fireproof, that I ask you for specific authority to compel the installation of the automatic sprinkler system in a number of buildings.

As an example of what sprinkler protection has done for one Knoxville hotel the following letter, dated October 19, 1916, from Col. C. B. Atkin, of the Hotel Atkin and Colonial hotel of Knoxville, is interesting:

In regard to the fire at the Atkin hotel about ten days ago, will report that the first we knew that there was any fire was from water running into the room below. Upon investigation we found that for some mysterious reason fire had broken out in the mattress which was on a bed immediately under one of the sprinkler heads. The mattress and box springs were completely destroyed, besides the brass bed being tarnished a little, this being the only fire damage excepting a little smoking of the wood work. The total loss of every description will probably be about $100. At the time of the fire there were over two hundred guests in the hotel and no excitement whatever was caused.

Mending Rubber Hose.

Rubber hose, on construction work, invariably develops leaks through rough handling. Leaks are a nuisance and often the hose is thrown away that, with a little trouble, could be easily repaired. The usual method of repairing leaks is by wrapping them with a piece of cloth, usually a cement bag, worth 10 cents, and the result is never satisfactory. A good and lasting repair job is very simply made. At an electrician's supply store buy a roll of ordinary tar insulating tape and a roll of rubber insulating tape. To mend the leak stop the water and wipe off the outside of the hose. Wrap the rubber tape around the hose over the leak and about one inch each way, letting the edges of the tape overlap. One thickness is enough. The rubber tape is soft and sticks to the hose. Then wrap rubber tape with the tar tape to protect it from wear.

Santa Cruz Has Woman Builder

Edwin J. Symmes, Pacific building, San Francisco, states that a contract on a percentage basis has been awarded to Mrs. Leila Sweet Martin, of Santa Cruz, for the erection of a two-story frame country residence for C. C. Moore at Santa Cruz. Building will be covered with resawed rustic and a shingle roof. A steam heating system is to be installed. Several small buildings have already been completed.

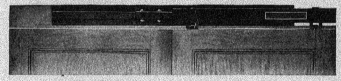

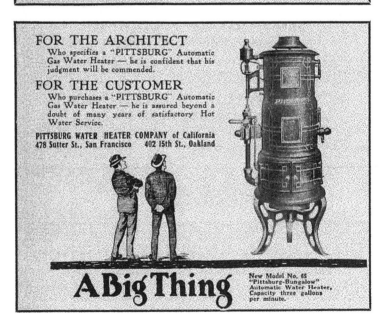

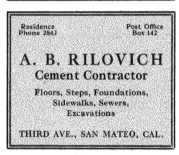
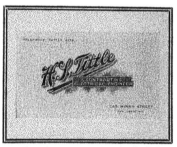

When writing to Advertisers please mention this magazine.

When writing to Advertisers please mention this magazine.

When writing to Advertisers please mention this magazine.

When writing to Advertisers please mention this magazine.

When writing to Advertisers please mention this magazine.

UNITED STATES STEEL PRODUCTS CO.

Rialto Building, San Francisco

SELLERS of the products of the American Bridge Co., American Sheet and Tin Plate Co., American Steel and Wire Co., Carnegie Steel Co., Illinois Steel Co., National Tube Co., Lorain Steel Co., Shelby Steel Tube Co., Tennessee Coal, Iron and Railroad Co., Trenton Iron Co.

MANUFACTURERS OF

Structural Steel for Every Purpose — Bridges, Railway and Highway — "Triangle Mesh" Wire Concrete Reinforcement — Plain and Twisted Reinforcing Bars — Plates, Shapes and Sheets of Every Description — Rails, Splice Bars, Bolts, Nuts, etc. — Wrought Pipe, Valves, Fittings, Trolley Poles — Frogs, Switches and Crossings for Steam Railway and Street Railway — "Shelby" Seamless Boiler Tubes and Mechanical Tubing—"Americore" and "Globe" Rubber Covered Wire and Cables — "Reliance" Weatherproof Copper and Iron Line Wire—"American" Wire Rope, Rail Bonds, Springs, Woven Wire Fencing and Poultry Netting — Tramways, etc.

United States Steel Products Co.
OFFICES AND WAREHOUSES AT
San Francisco - Los Angeles - Portland - Seattle

APRIL 1917

E A
D ENG
OF CALIFORNIA
BLISHED IN SAN FRANCISCO

of rushing and gurgling water can be heard from the *Kwy-eta* closet.

Kwy-eta suppresses those sounds your clients do not want to hear — yet has an extraordinarily strong flush.

Kwy-eta is an unusually attractive closet, made of pure white vitreous china.

Like all the "Pacific" line it is guaranteed forever against any defects in workmanship or material.

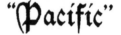

Plumbing Fixtures

For Sale by all Jobbers

Main Offices and Showroom, Factories,
67 New Montgomery St., Richmond,
San Francisco, Cal. California

Important to Architects

However excellent the plans you have drawn may be, the home or apartment building or hotel which you have designed will not do you proper credit, if inferior plumbing ware goes into it.

This makes it important that you specify

KOHLER WARE

always of one quality—the highest

"It's in the Kohler Enamel"

One-piece construction, hygienic designs and the beauty of the enamel are some of the features that contribute to the excellence of KOHLER WARE.

Our trade-mark, permanent in the enamel of every KOHLER product is a guarantee of *first quality*.

Where built-in tubs are called for specify the "Viceroy." Manufacturing economies enable us to maintain a low price on this remarkable *one-piece*, all-over enameled tub.

We make KOHLER Bath Tubs, Lavatories and Sinks— always of the highest quality — to suit homes of all types.

KOHLER CO., Founded 1873 Kohler, Wis.

Boston New York Philadelphia Atlanta Pittsburgh Detroit Chicago Indianapolis
St. Paul St. Louis Houston San Francisco Los Angeles Seattle London

★ The star indicates the location of the KOHLER permanent trade-mark in faint blue

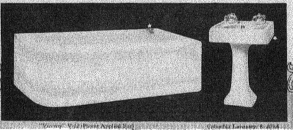

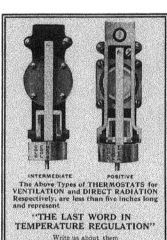

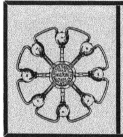

Architects' Specification Index

(For Index to Advertisements, see next page)

ACOUSTICAL CORRECTION
  H. W. Johns-Manville Co., Second and Howard
  Sts., San Francisco.
ARCHITECTURAL SCULPTORS, MODELING,
  ETC.
  G. Rognier & Co., 233 R. R. Ave., San Mateo.
  Sculptors' Workshop. S. Miletin & Co., 1705
  Harrison St., San Francisco.
  A. F. Swoboda, modeler, 204 Second St., San
  Francisco.
ARCHITECTURAL TERRA COTTA
  Gladding, McBean & Company, Crocker Bldg.,
  San Francisco.
  Steiger Terra Cotta and Pottery Works, Mills
  Bldg., San Francisco.
ASBESTOS ROOFING
  H. W. Johns-Manville Company, San Francisco,
  Los Angeles, San Diego, Sacramento.
AUTOMATIC SPRINKLERS
  Scott Company, 243 Minna St., San Francisco.
  Pacific Fire Extinguisher Co., 507 Montgomery
  St., San Francisco.
BANK FIXTURES AND INTERIORS
  Fink & Schindler, 218 13th St., San Francisco.
  A. J. Forbes & Son, 1530 Filbert St., San
  Francisco.
  C. F. Weber & Co., 365 Market St., San Fran-
  cisco.
  Home Mfg. Co, 543 Brannan St., San Fran-
  cisco.
  Rucker-Fuller Desk Co, 677 Mission St., San
  Francisco.
  T. H. Meek Co., 1130 Mission St., San Fran-
  cisco.
  Mullen Manufacturing Co, 20th and Harrison
  Sts., San Francisco.
BLACKBOARDS
  C. F. Weber & Co, 365 Market St, San Fran-
  cisco.
  Beaver Blackboards and Greenboards, Rucker-
  Fuller Desk Company, Coast agents, 677 Mis-
  sion St., San Francisco, Oakland and Los
  Angeles
BONDS FOR CONTRACTORS
  Fidelity & Casualty Co. of New York, Merchants
  Exchange Bldg., San Francisco.
  Robertson & Hall, First National Bank Bldg.,
  San Francisco.
  Fred H. Boggs, Foxcroft Bldg., San Francisco.
  J. T. Costello Co., 216 Pine St., San Francisco.
  Fidelity & Deposit Co. of Maryland, 701 Insur-
  ance Exchange, San Francisco.
  Globe Indemnity Co., Insurance Exchange Bldg.,
  San Francisco.
BOOK BINDERS AND PRINTERS
  Hicks-Judd Company, 51-65 First St., San Fran-
  cisco.
BOILERS
  "Franklin" water tube boiler, sold by General
  Machinery and Supply Co., 37 Stevenson St.,
  San Francisco.
BRASS GOODS, CASTINGS, ETC.
  H. Mueller Manufacturing Co., 589 Mission St.,
  San Francisco.

BRICK—PRESSED, PAVING, ETC.
  Gladding, McBean & Company, Crocker Bldg.,
  San Francisco.
  Los Angeles Pressed Brick Co., Frost Bldg., Los
  Angeles.
  Livermore Brick Company, pressed, glazed and
  enameled, etc., Livermore, Cal.
  Steiger Terra Cotta & Pottery Works, Mills
  Bldg., San Francisco.
  United Materials Co., Crossley Bldg., San Fran-
  cisco.
  California Brick Company, Niles, Cal.
BRICK AND CEMENT COATING
  Armorite and Concreta, manufactured by W. P.
  Fuller & Co., all principal Coast cities.
  Wadsworth, Howland & Co., Inc. (See Adv.
  for Pacific Coast Agents.)
  Paraffine Paint Co., 34 First St., San Francisco.
  R. N. Nason & Co., 151 Potrero Ave., San
  Francisco.
BRICK STAINS
  Samuel Cabot Mfg. Co., Boston, Mass., agencies
  in San Francisco, Oakland, Los Angeles, Port-
  land, Tacoma and Spokane.
  Armorite and Concreta, manufactured by W. P.
  Fuller & Co., all principal Coast cities.
BUILDERS' HARDWARE
  Bennett Bros., agents for Sargent Hardware,
  514 Market St., San Francisco.
  Pacific Hardware & Steel Company, San Fran-
  cisco, Oakland, Berkeley, and Los Angeles.
BUILDING MATERIAL SUPPLIES, ETC.
  Pacific Building Materials Co., 523 Market St.,
  San Francisco.
  C. Jorgensen, Crossley Bldg., San Francisco.
  Richard Spencer, Hearst Bldg., San Francisco.
  The Howard Company, First and Market Sts.,
  Oakland.
CEMENT
  Mt. Diablo, sold by Henry Cowell Lime & Ce-
  ment Co., 2 Market street, San Francisco.
  "Golden Gate" Brand, manufactured by Pacific
  Portland Cement Co., Pacific building, San
  Francisco.
CEMENT EXTERIOR WATERPROOF PAINT
  Bay State Brick and Cement Coating, made by
  Wadsworth, Howland & Co. (See distributing
  agents in advertisement.)
  Glidden's Liquid Cement and Liquid Cement
  Enamel, sold on Pacific Coast by Whittier, Co-
  burn Co., San Francisco.
  Armorite, sold by W. P. Fuller & Co., all prin-
  cipal Coast cities.
  Imperial Waterproofing, manufactured by Im-
  perial Co., 183 Stevenson St., San Francisco.
  Paraffine Paint Co., 34 First St., San Francisco.
CEMENT EXTERIOR FINISH
  Bay State Brick and Cement Coating, made by
  Wadsworth, Howland & Co. (See list of Dis-
  tributing Agents in adv.)
  Concreta, sold by W. P. Fuller & Co., all prin-
  cipal Coast cities.

An Index to the Advertisements

ARCHITECTS' SPECIFICATION INDEX—*Continued*

CEMENT EXTERIOR FINISH—Continued

Glidden's Liquid Cement and Liquid Cement Enamel, sold on Pacific Coast by Whittier, Coburn Company, San Francisco.
Pacific Building Materials Co., 523 Market St.
Samuel Cabot Mfg. Co., Boston, Mass., agencies in San Francisco, Oakland, Los Angeles, Portland, Tacoma and Spokane.

CEMENT FLOOR COATING

Bay State Brick and Cement Coating, made by Wadsworth, Howland & Co. (See list of Distributing Agents in adv.)
Fuller's Concrete Floor Enamel, made by W. P. Fuller & Co., San Francisco.

CEMENT HARDENER

J. L. Goffette Corporation, 227 San Bruno Ave., San Francisco.

CEMENT TESTS—CHEMICAL ENGINEERS

Robert W. Hunt & Co., 251 Kearny St., San Francisco.

CHURCH INTERIORS

Fink & Schindler, 218 13th St., San Francisco.

CHUTES—SPIRAL

Haslett warehouse Co., 310 California St., San Francisco.

CLOCKS—TOWER—STREET—PROGRAM

E. Howard Clock Co., Boston. Pacific Coast Agents, The Albert S. Samuels Co., 895 Market St., San Francisco. Joseph Mayer & Bro., Seattle, Wash.

COLD STORAGE PLANTS

T. P. Jarvis Crude Oil Burning Co., 275 Connecticut St., San Francisco.

COMPOSITION FLOORING

Germanwood Floor Co., 1621 Eddy St., San Francisco.
Malott & Peterson, Monadnock Bldg., San Francisco.
"Vitrolite," Vitrolite Construction Co., 34 Davis St., San Francisco.

COMPRESSED AIR MACHINERY

General Machinery & Supply Co., 39 Stevenson St., San Francisco.

COMPRESSED AIR CLEANERS

Spencer Turbine Cleaner. Sold by Hughson & Merton, 530 Golden Gate Ave., San Francisco.
Tuec, mfrd. by United Electric Company, 397 Sutter St., San Francisco, and 724 S. Broadway, Los Angeles.
Western Vacuum Supply Co., 1125 Market St., San Francisco.

CONCRETE CONSTRUCTION

American Concrete Co., Humboldt Bank Bldg., San Francisco.
Clinton Construction Co., 140 Townsend street, San Francisco.
Barrett & Hilp, Sharon Bldg., San Francisco.
Palmer & Peterson, Monadnock Bldg., San Francisco.

CONCRETE HARDNER

Master Builders Method, represented in San Francisco by C. Roman, Sharon Bldg.

CONCRETE MIXERS

Austin Improved Cube Mixer. J. H. Hansen & Co., California agents, 508 Balboa Bldg., San Francisco.
Foote Mixers. Sold by Edw. R. Bacon, 40 Natoma St., San Francisco.

CONCRETE REINFORCEMENT

United States Steel Products Co., San Francisco, Los Angeles, Portland and Seattle.
Twisted Bars. Sold by Woods, Huddart & Gunn, 444 Market St., San Francisco.

CONCRETE REINFORCEMENT—Continued

Pacific Coast Steel Company, Rialto Bldg., San Francisco.
Southern California Iron and Steel Company, Fourth and Mateo Sts., Los Angeles.
Triangle Mesh Fabric. Sales agents, Pacific Building Materials Co., 523 Market St., San Francisco.

CONCRETE SURFACING

"Concreta." Sold by W. P. Fuller & Co., San Francisco.
Wadsworth, Howland & Co.'s Bay State Brick and Cement Coating. Sold by Jas. Hambly Co., Pacific Bldg., San Francisco, and Los Angeles.
Glidden Liquid Cement, manufactured by Glidden Varnish Co., Whittier, Coburn Co., San Francisco.

CONTRACTOR'S BONDS

Bonding Company of America, Kohl Bldg., San Francisco.
Globe Indemnity Co., 120 Leidesdorff St., San Francisco.
Fred H. Boggs, Foxcroft Bldg., San Francisco.
Fidelity & Casualty Co. of New York, Merchants Exchange Bldg., San Francisco.
Fidelity & Deposit Co. of Maryland, Insurance Exchange, San Francisco.
J. T. Costello Co., 216 Pine St., San Francisco.
Robertson & Hall, First National Bank Bldg., San Francisco.

CONTRACTORS, GENERAL

Arthur Arlett, New Call Bldg., San Francisco.
Farrell & Reed, Gunst Bldg., San Francisco.
American Concrete Co., Humboldt Bank Bldg., San Francisco.
Barrett & Hilp, Sharon Bldg., San Francisco.
Carnahan & Mulford, 45 Kearny St., San Francisco.
Houghton Construction Co., Hooker & Lent Bldg., San Francisco.
Geo. H. Bos, Hearst Bldg., San Francisco.
Larsen, Sampson & Co., Crocker Bldg., San Francisco.
J. D. Hannah, 725 Chronicle Bldg., San Francisco.
Clinton Construction Company, 140 Townsend St., San Francisco.
Dioguardi & Terranova, Westbank Bldg., San Francisco.
Teichert & Ambrose, Ochsner Bldg., Sacramento.
L. G. Bergren & Son, Call Bldg., San Francisco.
Grace & Bernieri, Claus Spreckels Bldg., San Francisco.
Geo. W. Boxton & Son, Hearst Bldg., San Francisco.
W. C. Duncan & Co., 526 Sharon Bldg., San Francisco.
A. P. Brady, Humboldt Bank Bldg., San Francisco.
Cameron & Disston, 831 Hearst Bldg., San Francisco.
Harvey A. Klyce, Sheldon Bldg., San Francisco.
Knowles & Mathewson, Call Bldg., San Francisco.
C. L. Wold Co., 75 Sutter St., San Francisco.
P. R. Ward, 981 Guerrero St., San Francisco.
Lange & Bergstrom, Sharon Bldg., San Francisco.
Foster Vogt Co., 411 Sharon Bldg., San Francisco.

ARCHITECTS' SPECIFICATION INDEX—*Continued*

CONTRACTORS, GENERAL—Continued
T. B. Goodwin, 110 Jessie St., San Francisco.
Thos. Elam & Son, Builders Exchange, San Francisco.
Masow & Morrison, 518 Monadnock Bldg., San Francisco.
Monson Bros., 502 Clunie Bldg., San Francisco.
J. M. Dougan Co., Hearst Bldg., San Francisco.
Palmer & Peterson, Monadnock Bldg., San Francisco.
Robert Trost, Twenty-sixth and Howard Sts., San Francisco.
John Monk, Sheldon Bldg., San Francisco.
Williams Bros. & Henderson, 381 Tenth St., San Francisco.

CONVEYING MACHINERY
Meese & Gottfried, San Francisco, Los Angeles, Portland and Seattle.

CORK TILING. FLOORING, ETC.
David Kennedy, Inc., Sharon Bldg., San Francisco.
Be-ver Cork Tile. Sold by W. L. Eaton & Co., 812 Santa Marina Bldg., San Francisco.

CORNER BEAD
Capitol Sheet Metal Works, 1827 Market St., San Francisco.
United States Metal Products Co., 555 Tenth St., San Francisco; 750 Keller St., San Francisco.

CRUSHED ROCK
Grant Gravel Co., Flatiron Bldg., San Francisco.
California Building Material Company, new Call Bldg., San Francisco.
Niles Sand, Gravel & Rock Co., Mutual Bank Bldg., San Francisco.
Pratt Building Material Co., Hearst Bldg., San Francisco.
Saratoga Rock Company, Baker-MacDonald Co. representatives, First National Bank Bldg., San Jose.

DAMP-PROOFING COMPOUND
Armorite Damp Resisting Paint, made by W. P. Fuller & Co., San Francisco.
Imperial Co., 183 Stevenson St., San Francisco.
"Pabco" Damp-Proofing Compound, sold by Paraffine Paint Co., 34 First St., San Francisco.
Wadsworth, Howland & Co., Inc., 84 Washington St., Boston. (See Adv. for Coast agencies.)

DOOR HANGERS
McCabe Hanger Mfg. Co., New York, N. Y.
Pitcher Hanger, sold by National Lumber Co., 326 Market St., San Francisco.
Reliance Hanger, sold by Sartorius Co., San Francisco; D. F. Fryer & Co., B. V. Collins, Los Angeles, and Columbia Wire & Iron Works, Portland. Ore.

DRAIN BOARDS, SINK BACKS, ETC.
Germanwood Floor Co., 1621 Eddy St., San Francisco.

DRINKING FOUNTAINS
Haws Sanitary Fountain, 1808 Harmon St., Berkeley, and C. F. Weber & Co., San Francisco and Los Angeles.
Crane Company, San Francisco, Oakland, and Los Angeles.
Pacific Porcelain Ware Co., 67 New Montgomery St., San Francisco.

DUMB WAITERS
Spencer Elevator Company, 173 Beale St., San Francisco.
M. E. Hammond, Humboldt Bank Bldg., San Francisco.

ELECTRICAL CONTRACTORS
Butte Engineering Co., 683 Howard St., San Francisco.
Goold & Johns, 113 S. California St., Stockton, Cal.
NePage, McKenny Co., 149 New Montgomery St., San Francisco.
Newbery Electrical Co., 413 Lick Bldg., San Francisco.
Pacific Fire Extinguisher Co., 507 Montgomery St., San Francisco.
H. S. Tittle, 245 Minna St., San Francisco.
Rex Electric and Construction Co., Inc., 1174 Sutter St., San Francisco.
Standard Electrical Construction Company, 60 Natoma St., San Francisco.

ELECTRICAL ENGINEERS
Chas. T. Phillips, Pacific Bldg., San Francisco.

ELECTRIC PLATE WARMER
The Prometheus Electric Plate Warmer for residences, clubs, hotels, etc. Sold by M. E. Hammond, Humboldt Bank Bldg., San Francisco.

ELEVATORS
Otis Elevator Company, Stockton and North Point, San Francisco.
Spencer Elevator Company, 126 Beale St., San Francisco.
Van Emon Elevator Co., 54 Natoma St., San Francisco.

ENGINEERS
Chas. T. Phillips, Pacific Bldg., San Francisco.
Hunter & Hudson, Rialto Bldg., San Francisco.

FIRE ESCAPES
Palm Iron & Bridge Works, Sacramento.
Western Iron Works, 141 Beale St., San Francisco.

FIRE EXTINGUISHERS
Scott Company, 243 Minna St., San Francisco
Pacific Fire Extinguisher Co., 507 Montgomery St., San Francisco.

FIREPROOFING AND PARTITIONS
Gladding, McBean & Co., Crocker Bldg., San Francisco.
Keybold Lath Co., Monadnock Bldg., San Francisco.
Los Angeles Pressed Brick Co., Frost Bldg., Los Angeles.

ARCHITECTS' SPECIFICATION INDEX—Continued

FIXTURES—BANK, OFFICE, STORE, ETC.
T. H. Meek & Co., 1130 Mission St., San Francisco.
Mullen Manufacturing Co., 20th and Harrison Sts., San Francisco.
The Fink & Schindler Co., 218 13th St., San Francisco.
A. J. Forbes & Son, 1530 Filbert St., San Francisco.
C. F. Weber & Co., 365 Market St., San Francisco, and 210 N. Main St., Los Angeles, Cal.

FLAG POLE TOPS
Bolander & Son, 270 First St., San Francisco.

FLOOR TILE
New York Belting and Packing Company, 519 Mission St., San Francisco.
W. L. Eaton & Co., 112 Market St., San Francisco.

FLOOR VARNISH
Bass-Hueter and San Francisco Pioneer Varnish Works, 816 Mission St., San Francisco.
Fifteen for Floors, made by W. P. Fuller & Co., San Francisco.
Standard Varnish Works, Chicago, New York and San Francisco.
Glidden Products, sold by Whittier, Coburn Co., San Francisco.
R. N. Nason & Co., San Francisco and Los Angeles.

FLOORS—COMPOSITION
"Vitrolite," for any structure, room or bath. Vitrolite Construction Co., 1490 Mission St., San Francisco.
Malott & Peterson, Inc., Monadnock Bldg., San Francisco.
Germanwood Floor Co., 1621 Eddy St., San Francisco.

FLOORS—HARDWOOD
Oak Flooring Bureau, Conway Bldg., Chicago, Ill.
Strahle Mfg. Co., 511 First St., Oakland.

PLUMES
California Corrugated Culvert Co., West Berkeley, Cal.

GARAGE EQUIPMENT
Bowser Gasoline Tanks and Outfit, Bowser & Co., 612 Howard St., San Francisco.
Rix Compressed Air and Drill Company, First and Howard Sts., San Francisco.

GAS GRATES
General Gas Light Co., 768 Mission St., San Francisco.

GAS RADIATORS
"The Paramount," sold by Modern Appliance Co., 128 Sutter St., San Francisco.

GLASS
W. P. Fuller & Company, all principal Coast cities.
Whittier, Coburn Co., Howard and Beale Sts., San Francisco.

GRANITE
California Granite Co., Sharon Bldg., San Francisco.

GRANITE—Continued
McGilvray-Raymond Granite Co., 634 Townsend St., San Francisco.
Raymond Granite Co., Potrero Ave. and Division St., San Francisco.

GRAVEL AND SAND
California Building Material Co., new Call Bldg., San Francisco.
Del Monte White Sand, sold by Pacific Improvement Co., Crocker Bldg., San Francisco.
Pratt Building Material Co., Hearst Bldg., San Francisco.
Grant Gravel Co., Flatiron Bldg., San Francisco.
Grant Rock & Gravel Co., Cory Bldg., Fresno.
Niles Sand, Gravel & Rock Co., Mutual Savings Bank Bldg., 704 Market St., San Francisco.
Saratoga Rock Company, 703 First National Bank Bldg., San Jose.

HARDWALL PLASTER
Henry Cowell Lime & Cement Co., San Francisco.

HARDWARE
Pacific Hardware & Steel Company, representing Lockwood Hardware Co., San Francisco.
Sargent's Hardware, sold by Bennett Bros., 514 Market St., San Francisco.

HARDWOOD LUMBER—FLOORING, ETC.
Dieckmann Hardwood Co., Beach and Taylor Sts., San Francisco.
Parrott & Co., 320 California St., San Francisco.
White Bros., cor. Fifth and Brannan Sts., San Francisco.
Strahle Mfg. Co., 511 First St., Oakland.

HEATERS—AUTOMATIC
Pittsburg Water Heater Co., 478 Sutter St., San Francisco.

HEATING AND VENTILATING
Gilley-Schmid Company, 198 Otis St., San Francisco.
Mangrum & Otter, Inc., 507 Mission St., San Francisco.
Charles T. Phillips, Pacific Bldg., San Francisco.
James & Drucker, 450 Hayes St., San Francisco.
J. C. Hurley Co., 509 Sixth St., San Francisco.
Illinois Engineering Co., 563 Pacific Bldg., San Francisco.
William F. Wilson Co., 328 Mason St., San Francisco.
Pacific Fire Extinguisher Co., 507 Montgomery St., San Francisco.
Scott Company, 243 Minna St., San Francisco.
Thermic Engineering Company, Claus Spreckels Bldg., San Francisco.
C. A. Dunham Co., Wells Fargo Bldg., San Francisco.

HEAT REGULATION
Johnson Service Company, 149 Fifth St., San Francisco.

When writing to Advertisers please mention this magazine.

ARCHITECTS' SPECIFICATION INDEX—*Continued*

HOLLOW BLOCKS
Denison Hollow Interlocking Blocks. Forum Bldg., Sacramento, and the Howard Company, Oakland.
Gladding, McBean & Co., San Francisco, Los Angeles, Oakland and Sacramento.
Pratt Building Material Co., Hearst Bldg., San Francisco.

HOLLOW METAL DOORS AND TRIM
Edwin C. Dehn, 301 Hearst Bldg., San Francisco, representing Interior Metal Mfg. Co., Jamestown, N. Y.

HOSPITAL FIXTURES
J. L. Mott Iron Works, 135 Kearny St., San Francisco.

HOTELS
St. Francis Hotel, Union Square, San Francisco.

INGOT IRON
"Armco" brand, manufactured by American Rolling Mill Company, Middletown, Ohio, and Monadnock Bldg., San Francisco.

INSPECTIONS AND TESTS
Robert W. Hunt & Co., 251 Kearny St., San Francisco.

INTERIOR DECORATORS
Mrs. H. C. McAfee, 504 Sutter St., San Francisco.
Albert S. Bigley, 344 Geary St., San Francisco.
City of Paris, Geary and Stockton Sts., San Francisco.
A. Falvy, 578 Sutter St., San Francisco.
The Tormey Co., 681 Geary St., San Francisco.
Fick Bros., 475 Haight St., San Francisco.
O'Hara & Livermore, Sutter St., San Francisco.

KITCHEN CABINETS
Western Equipment Co., Building Material Exbibit, 77 O'Farrell St., San Francisco.
Hoosier Cabinets, branch 1067 Market St., San Francisco.

LIGHTING FIXTURES
"The Crystal Light," manufactured by Modern Appliance Co., 128 Sutter St., San Francisco.

LAMP POSTS, ELECTROLIERS, ETC.
J. L. Mott Iron Works, 135 Kearny St., San Francisco.
Ralston Iron Works, 20th and Indiana Sts., San Francisco.

LANDSCAPE GARDENERS
MacRorie-McLaren Co., 141 Powell St., San Francisco.

LATHING MATERIAL
"Buttonlath," manufactured by Buttonlath Mfg. Co., Pacific Bldg., San Francisco.
Keybold Lath Co., Monadnock Bldg., San Francisco.
Pacific Building Materials Co., 523 Market St., San Francisco.

LIGHT, HEAT AND POWER
Pacific Gas & Elec. Co., 445 Sutter St., San Francisco.
The Fish Fuel System, Palace Hotel, San Francisco.

LIME
Henry Cowell Lime & Cement Co., 2 Market St., San Francisco.

LINOLEUM
D. N. & E. Walter & Co., O'Farrell and Stockton Sts., San Francisco.

LOCKS—KEYLESS
Nydia Bank Lock Co., 52 Main St., San Francisco.

LUMBER
Dudfield Lumber Co., Palo Alto, Cal.
Hooper Lumber Co., Seventeenth and Illinois Sts., San Francisco.
Portland Lumber Co., 16 California St., San Francisco.
Pacific Manufacturing Company, San Francisco, Oakland and Santa Clara.
Pacific Mill and Timber Co., First National Bank Bldg., San Francisco.
Pope & Talbot, foot of Third St., San Francisco.
Sunset Lumber Co., Oakland. Cal.
United Lumber Company, 687 Market St., San Francisco.

MASTIC FLOORING
Malott & Peterson, Monadnock Bldg., San Francisco.

MAIL CHUTES
Cutler Mail Chute Co., Rochester, N. Y. (See adv. on page 30 for Coast representatives.)
American Mailing Device Corp., represented on Pacific Coast by U. S. Metal Products Co., 555 Tenth St., San Francisco.

MANTELS
Mangrum & Otter, 561 Mission St., San Francisco.

MARBLE
American Marble and Mosaic Co., 25 Columbus Square, San Francisco.
Joseph Musto Sons, Keenan Co., 535 N. Point St., San Francisco.
Sculptors' Workshop. S. Miletin & Co., 1705 Harrison St., San Francisco.

METAL CEILINGS
San Francisco Metal Stamping & Corrugating Co., 2269 Folsom St., San Francisco.

METAL DOORS AND WINDOWS
U. S. Metal Products Co., 555 Tenth St., San Francisco.
Capitol Sheet Metal Works, 1927 Market St., San Francisco.

METAL FURNITURE
Capitol Sheet Metal Works, 1927 Market St., San Francisco.
Ralston Iron Works, Twentieth and Indiana Sts., San Francisco.
Edwin C. Dehn, Manufacturer's Agent, Hearst Bldg., San Francisco.

MILL WORK
Dudfield Lumber Co., Palo Alto, Cal.
Pacific Manufacturing Company, San Francisco. Oakland and Santa Clara.
National Mill and Lumber Co., San Francisco and Oakland.
The Fink & Schindler Co., 218 13th St., San Francisco.

OIL BURNERS
American Standard Oil Burner Company, Seventh and Cedar Sts., Oakland.
S. T. Johnson Co., 1337 Mission St., San Francisco.

ARCHITECTS' SPECIFICATION INDEX—*Continued*

OIL BURNERS—Continued
F. P. Jarvis Crude Oil Burner Co., 275 Connecticut St., San Francisco.
Fess System, 220 Natoma St., San Francisco.
W. S. Ray Mfg. Co., 218 Market St., San Francisco.

ORNAMENTAL IRON AND BRONZE
American Art Metal Works, 13 Grace St., San Francisco.
California Artistic Metal and Wire Co., 349 Seventh St., San Francisco.
Palm Iron & Bridge Works, Sacramento.
Ralston Iron Works, 20th and Indiana Sts., San Francisco.
C. J. Hillard Company, Inc., 19th and Minnesota Sts., San Francisco.
Schreiber & Sons Co., represented by Western Builders Supply Co., San Francisco.
Sims, Gray & Sauter Iron Works, 156 Main St., San Francisco.
Schrader Iron Works, Inc., 1247 Harrison St., San Francisco.
West Coast Wire & Iron Works, 861-863 Howard St., San Francisco.

PAINT FOR CEMENT
Bay State Brick and Cement Coating, made by Wadsworth, Howland & Co. (Inc.) (See adv. in this issue for Pacific Coast agents.)
Fuller's Concreta for Cement, made by W. P. Fuller & Co., San Francisco.
Samuel Cabot Mfg. Co., Boston, Mass., agencies in San Francisco, Oakland, Los Angeles, Portland, Tacoma and Spokane.

PAINT FOR STEEL STRUCTURES, BRIDGES. ETC.
Glidden's Acid Proof Coating, sold on Pacific Coast by Whittier, Coburn Company, San Francisco.
Paraffine Paint Co., 34 First St., San Francisco.
Premier Graphite Paint and Pioneer Brand Red Lead, made by W. P. Fuller & Co., San Francisco.

PAINTING, TINTING, ETC.
I. R. Kissel, 1747 Sacramento St., San Francisco.
D. Zelinsky & Sons, San Francisco and Los Angeles.
Fick Bros., 475 Haight St., San Francisco.

PAINTS, OILS, ETC.
The Brininstool Co., Los Angeles, the Haslett Warehouse, 310 California St., San Francisco.
Bass-Hueter Paint Co., Mission, near Fourth St., San Francisco.
Whittier, Coburn Co., Howard and Beale Sts., San Francisco.
Magner Bros., 419-421 Jackson St., San Francisco.
R. N. Nason & Company, San Francisco, Los Angeles, Portland and Seattle.
W. P. Fuller & Co., all principal Coast cities.
Standard Varnish Works, 55 Stevenson St., San Francisco.

PANELS AND VENEER
White Bros., Fifth and Brannan Sts., San Francisco.

PIPE—VITRIFIED SALT GLAZED TERRA COTTA
Gladding, McBean & Co., Crocker Bldg., San Francisco.
Steiger Terra Cotta and Pottery Works, Mills Bldg., San Francisco.
G. Weissbaum & Co. Pipe Works, 127 Eleventh St., San Francisco.

PLASTER CONTRACTORS
C. C. Morehouse, Crocker Bldg., San Francisco.
MacGruer & Co., 180 Jessie St., San Francisco.
M. J. Terranova, Westbank Bldg., San Francisco.

PLASTER EXTERIORS
"Kellastone," an imperishable stucco. Blake Plaster Co., Bacon Block, Oakland.
Keyhold Lath Co., Monadnock Bldg., San Francisco.
Buttonlath, for exterior and interior plastering, Hearst Bldg., San Francisco.

PLUMBING. CONTRACTORS
Alex Coleman, 706 Ellis St., San Francisco.
A. Lettich, 365 Fell St., San Francisco.
Gilley-Schmid Company, 198 Otis St., San Francisco.
Scott Co., Inc., 243 Minna St., San Francisco.
Wm. F. Wilson Co., 328 Mason St., San Francisco.

PLUMBING FIXTURES. MATERIALS, ETC.
Crane Co., San Francisco and Oakland.
California Steam Plumbing Supply Co., 671 Fifth St., San Francisco.
Gilley-Schmid Company, 198 Otis St., San Francisco.
Glauber Brass Manufacturing Company, 1107 Mission St., San Francisco.
Improved Sanitary Fixture Co., 632 Metropolitan Bldg., Los Angeles.
J. L. Mott Iron Works, D. H. Gulick, selling agent, 135 Kearny St., San Francisco.
Haines, Jones & Cadbury Co., 857 Folsom St., San Francisco.
H. Mueller Manufacturing Co., Pacific Coast branch 589 Mission St., San Francisco.
Mark-Lally Co., 235 Second St., San Francisco, also Oakland, Fresno, San Jose and Stockton.
Pacific Sanitary Manufacturing Co., 67 New Montgomery St., San Francisco.
Wm. F. Wilson Co., 328 Mason St., San Francisco.
C. A. Dunham Co., Wells Fargo Bldg., San Francisco.

POTTERY
Gladding, McBean & Co., San Francisco, Los Angeles, Oakland and Sacramento.
Steiger Terra Cotta and Pottery Works, Mills Bldg., San Francisco.

POWER TRANSMITTING MACHINERY
Meese & Gottfried, San Francisco, Los Angeles, Portland, Ore., and Seattle, Wash.

PUMPS
Simonds Machinery Co., 117 New Montgomery St., San Francisco.

RADIATORS
American Radiator Co., Second and Townsend Sts., San Francisco.

RAILROADS
Southern Pacific Company, Flood Bldg., San Francisco.
Western Pacific Company, Mills Bldg., San Francisco.

REFRIGERATORS
McCray Refrigerators, sold by Nathan Dobrmann Co., Geary and Stockton Sts., San Francisco.

REVERSIBLE WINDOWS
Hauser Reversible Window Company, Balboa Bldg., San Francisco.
Whitney Windows, represented by Richard Spencer, 801-3 Hearst Bldg., San Francisco.

REVOLVING DOORS
Van Kennel Doors, sold by U. S. Metal Products Co., 525 Market St., San Francisco.

ROLLING DOORS, SHUTTERS. PARTITIONS, ETC.
C. F. Weber & Co., 365 Market St., S. F.
Kinnear Steel Rolling Doors, W. W. Thurston, agent, Rialto Bldg., San Francisco.
Wilson's Steel Rolling Doors, U. S. Metal Products Co., San Francisco and Los Angeles.

ARCHITECTS' SPECIFICATION INDEX—Continued

ROOFING AND ROOFING MATERIALS
Grant Gravel Co., Flatiron Bldg., San Francisco.
H. W. Johns-Manville Co., Second and Howard Sts., San Francisco.
Malott & Peterson, Inc., Monadnock Bldg., San Francisco.
Niles Sand, Gravel and Rock Co., Mutual Bank Bldg., San Francisco.
"Malthoid" and "Ruberoid," manufactured by Paraffine Paint Co., San Francisco.
Pioneer Roofing, manufactured by Pioneer Paper Co., 513 Hearst Bldg., San Francisco.
United Materials Co., Crossley Bldg., San Francisco.

RUBBER TILING
Goodyear Rubber Company, 587 Market St., San Francisco.
New York Belting & Rubber Company, 519 Mission St., San Francisco.

SAFETY TREADS
"Sanitread," sold by Richard Spencer, 801-3 Hearst Bldg., San Francisco.
Pacific Building Materials Co., 523 Market St., San Francisco.
C. Jorgensen, Crossley Bldg., San Francisco.

SCENIC PAINTING—DROP CURTAINS, ETC.
The Edwin H. Flagg Scenic Co., 1638 Long Beach Ave., Los Angeles.

SCHOOL FURNITURE AND SUPPLIES
C. F. Weber & Co., 365 Market St., San Francisco; 512 S. Broadway, Los Angeles.
Rucker-Fuller Desk Company, 677 Mission St., San Francisco.

SCREENS
Hipolito Flyout Screens, sold by Simpson & Stewart, Dalziel Bldg., Oakland.
Watson Metal Frame Screens, sold by Richard Spencer, 801-3 Hearst Bldg., San Francisco.

SEEDS
California Seed Company, 151 Market St., San Francisco.

SHEATHING AND SOUND DEADENING
Samuel Cabot Mfg. Co., Boston, Mass., agencies in San Francisco, Oakland, Los Angeles, Portland, Tacoma and Spokane.
Paraffine Paint Co., 34 First St., San Francisco.

SHEET METAL WORK, SKYLIGHTS, ETC.
Capitol Sheet Metal Works, 1927 Market St., San Francisco.
U. S. Metal Products Co., 555 Tenth St., San Francisco.

SHINGLE STAINS
Cabot's Creosote Stains, sold by Pacific Building Materials Co., Underwood Bldg., San Francisco.
Fuller's Pioneer Shingle Stains, made by W. P. Fuller & Co., San Francisco.

SIDEWALK LIGHTS
P. H. Jackson & Co., 237-47 First St., San Francisco.

STEEL TANKS, PIPE, ETC.
Schaw-Batcher Co., Pipe Works, 356 Market St., San Francisco.

STEEL AND IRON—STRUCTURAL
Central Iron Works, 621 Florida St., San Francisco.

STEEL AND IRON—STRUCTURAL—Con't.
Dyer Bros., 17th and Kansas Sts., San Francisco.
Golden Gate Iron Works, 1541 Howard St., San Francisco.
Judson Manufacturing Co., 819 Folsom St., San Francisco.
Mortenson Construction Co., 19th and Indiana Sts., San Francisco.
Pacific Rolling Mills, 17th and Mississippi Sts., San Francisco.
Palm Iron & Bridge Works, Sacramento.
Ralston Iron Works, Twentieth and Indiana Sts., San Francisco.
U. S. Steel Products Co., Rialto Bldg., San Francisco.
Sims, Gray & Sauter, 156 Main St., San Francisco.
Schrader Iron Works, Inc., 1247 Harrison St., San Francisco.
Southern California Iron and Steel Co., Fourth and Mateo Sts., Los Angeles.
Western Iron Works, 141 Beale St., San Francisco.

STEEL PRESERVATIVES
Bay State Steel Protective Coating. (See adv. for coast agencies.)
Paraffine Paint Co., 34 First St., San Francisco.

STEEL REINFORCING
Pacific Coast Steel Company, Rialto Bldg., San Francisco.
Southern California Iron & Steel Company, Fourth and Mateo Sts., Los Angeles.
Woods, Huddart & Gunn, 444 Market St., San Francisco.

STEEL ROLLING DOORS
Kinnear Steel Rolling Door Co., W. W. Thurston, Rialto Bldg., San Francisco.

STEEL SASH
"Fenestra," solid steel sash, manufactured by Detroit Steel Products Company, Detroit, Mich. Pacific Building Materials Co., 523 Market St., San Francisco, distributors.

STEEL WHEELBARROWS
Champion and California steel brands, made by Western Iron Works, 141 Beale St., San Francisco.

STONE
California Granite Co., 518 Sharon Bldg., San Francisco.
McGilvray Stone Company, 634 Townsend St., San Francisco.

STORAGE SYSTEMS—GASOLINE, OIL, ETC.
S. F. Bowser & Co., 612 Howard St., San Francisco.
Rix Compressed Air and Drill Co., First and Howard Sts., San Francisco.

TEMPERATURE REGULATION
Johnson Service Company, 149 Fifth St., San Francisco.

THEATER AND OPERA CHAIRS
C. F. Weber & Co., 365 Market St., San Francisco.

The Most Up=to=Date WALL BEDS

Perfect Concealment	Simple Installation
Economy of Space	Most Inexpensive
Only 16″ in depth required	Strong and Durable

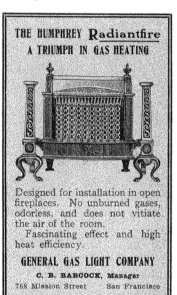

HARMON & FOGAL BUILDING, PHŒNIX, ARIZONA
MR. BURT McDONALD, Architect

EXTERIOR OF

CREAM PRESSED BRICK

MANUFACTURED BY

Los Angeles Pressed Brick Co.

FURNISHED THROUGH

VERNON L. CLARK, Phœnix, Arizona

AGENT FOR LOS ANGELES PRESSED BRICK
COMPANY'S MATERIALS

UNITED MATERIALS COMPANY

CROSSLEY BUILDING, SAN FRANCISCO

Agents for Northern California

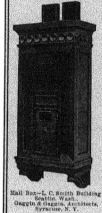

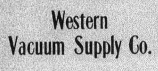

When writing to Advertisers please mention this magazine.

THE ARCHITECT & ENGINEER

25c Copy
$1.50 a Year.
OF CALIFORNIA
Volume XLIX
Number 1
Issued monthly in the interest of Architects, Structural Engineers, Contractors and the Allied Trades of the Pacific Coast.
Entered at San Francisco Post Office as Second Class Matter.

CONTENTS FOR APRIL, 1917

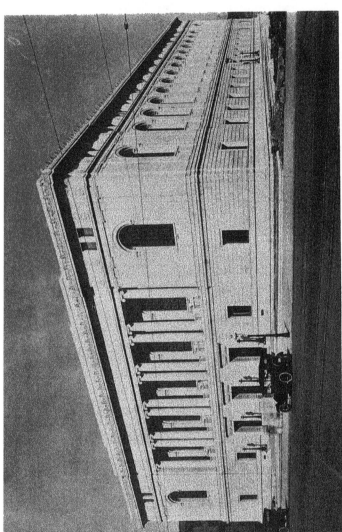

Frontispiece
The Architect and Engineer
of California
for April, 1917.

PUBLIC LIBRARY BUILDING, SAN FRANCISCO CIVIC CENTER
GEORGE W. KELHAM, ARCHITECT

THE
ARCHITECT
AND
ENGINEER
OF CALIFORNIA
APRIL · 1917.

VOL. XLIX. NUMBER 1.

The New San Francisco Public Library

By ARTHUR BROWN, Jr.*

THE salient characteristic of the new San Francisco Public Library seems to me to be its well distributed and organic plan. Mr. Kelham has molded the exacting requirements of a modern library building into a whole which adapts itself admirably to the difficulties of the shape of the lot, and at the same time harmonizes with the general conception of the Civic Center.

The expression of such a complicated group of requirements in beautiful and noble architectural forms has been accomplished in the simple and direct manner which characterizes all the best work in architecture, and great feeling and skill have been shown in the grasping of opportunities for monumental effects which make a universal appeal.

The new Library is free from puerile attempts at the picturesque and the slavish copying which mars so much of modern work. It is a nicely balanced arrangement of the elements necessary to a modern library, expressed without affectation or self-consciousness; and, to the very great credit of the architect, the exterior and interior have that close relation which good taste requires.

The exterior of the building consists of a delicately rusticated basement crowned by a belt course and surmounted by a high story pierced by ranges of graceful arches, which light the larger and more important units of the plan. This is the "piano nobile" of the building, and is admirably set off by the high basement. The arches facing the Civic Center are framed by free standing Ionic columns and form a feature strongly marked by the play of light and shade, and giving accent to the entrance façade. The side façade on Fulton street is very properly expressed by an unbroken arcade flanked at either end by flat pavilions.

*Member of the firm of Bakewell & Brown.

WEST FACADE, PUBLIC LIBRARY BUILDING, SAN FRANCISCO CIVIC CENTER
GEORGE W. KELHAM,   ARCHITECT

Over the principal story is a high entablature, which forms the wall of the top story in which are placed smaller units of the plan.

The north façade is a frank expression of the stacks, and the aspect of the high bays separated by simple piers is extremely decorative.

The architectural details of the exterior, inspired by the work of the Renaissance in Italy, are delicate and well adjusted, and are used with intention and comprehension of function, and in no place savor of blind imitation or affectation. Good proportion and directness seem to have been the guiding principles.

The composition of the façades is extremely simple, consisting of discreetly projecting corner pavilions joined by unbroken ranges of bays without central feature. This disposition shows a very sympathetic comprehension of the Civic Center scheme, and is very wisely chosen. The main cornice is at the same height as that of the neighboring Auditorium and City Hall.

Mr. Kelham had the happy idea of disposing his plan so that one is led to the main delivery and catalogue room, the heart of the mechanism of his plan, through a most pleasing and monumental succession of vaulted vestibule and noble stairway. The delivery room itself is of airy and ample proportion and forms a fitting climax to the monumental effects. Grouped around the delivery room are the reading and reference rooms, and the delivery desk of the stack room placed adjacent to its geometrical center. The important elements of the working plan are thus placed with the most limpid simplicity. The complicated service portions of the structure are combined with the main dispositions with rigid logic and common sense.

The circulations both horizontal and vertical are clear, direct and adequately lighted.

The main reading rooms are high, airy, of accentuated proportion, and of a gray tonality quite proper to their destination.

The harmonious result attained in this building is due in part to the sagacity shown in the combination of material. The cost of the building was limited, the demands of the Library great, and skill and judgment were necessary to reconcile these conditions.

The exterior is of the beautiful Raymond granite from the McGilvray quarry, treated with ornament generally in low relief, which is well adapted to this sort of stone.

The vestibule, main stairway and delivery room are in Travertine stone, part real and part in plaster imitation, skillfully executed by Mr. Paul Denivelle. The two materials are cleverly combined and the impression of color is extremely satisfactory. The decoration is in relief without introduction of applied color, allowing the full effect of the light and shade, and producing a result of great unity. The stairway is lighted from the ceiling of the side galleries, allowing the barrel vault of the stair-well its full value, entirely free of skylights. The effect of the broad stairway, rising between two rusticated walls crowned by noble colonnade and caissoned vault, is truly monumental, even if it is not gigantesque.

The use of Travertine for the pavement in the vestibules and stairs is a pleasing detail.

The reading rooms are simple in the extreme, with painted plaster walls and a high wainscot of stained oak. The ceilings, likewise in plaster, are stenciled in color, after the manner of the beamed ceilings of the early Renaissance, with a varied but subdued palette.

The metal work in bronze is simply wrought and sparingly used. The restriction of the kinds of materials used, and the simple color scheme through-

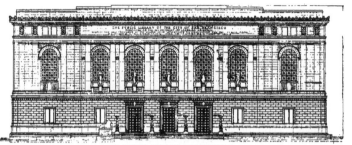

LARKIN STREET ELEVATION

ELEVATION, WEST FACADE AND DETAIL, SAN FRANCISCO PUBLIC LIBRARY
GEORGE W. KELHAM,   ARCHITECT

McALLISTER STREET FACADE, SAN FRANCISCO PUBLIC LIBRARY
GEORGE W. KELHAM,   ARCHITECT

ENTRANCE DOOR, SAN FRANCISCO PUBLIC LIBRARY
GEORGE W. KELHAM,   ARCHITECT

DELIVERY ROOM, LOOKING TOWARDS ENTRANCE, SAN FRANCISCO PUBLIC LIBRARY
GEORGE. W. KELHAM, *ARCHITECT*

BRONZE SCREEN, DELIVERY ROOM, SAN FRANCISCO PUBLIC LIBRARY
GEORGE W. KELHAM,   *ARCHITECT*

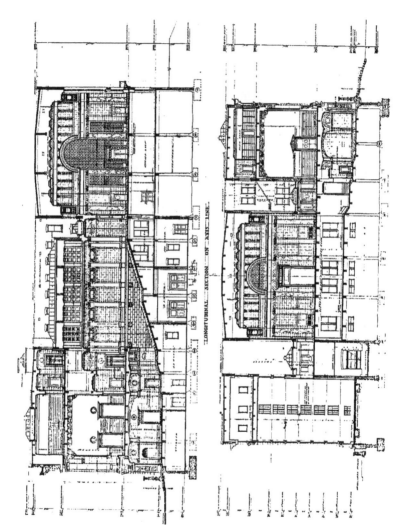

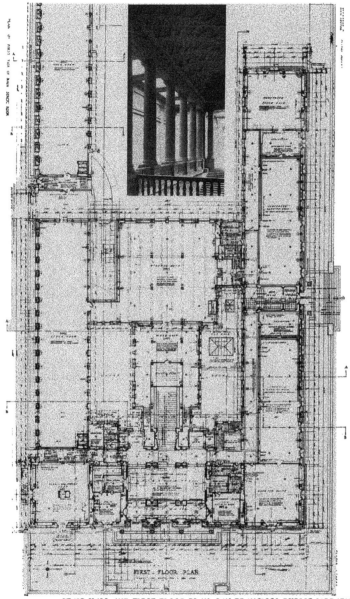

STAIR HALL AND FIRST FLOOR PLAN, SAN FRANCISCO PUBLIC LIBRARY
GEORGE W. KELHAM,   ARCHITECT

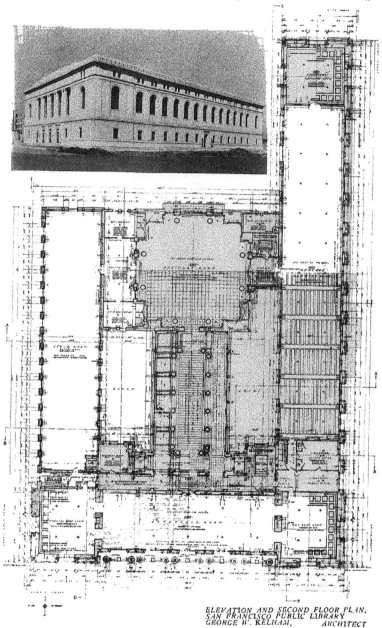

ELEVATION AND SECOND FLOOR PLAN,
SAN FRANCISCO PUBLIC LIBRARY
GEORGE W. KELHAM, ARCHITECT

ENTRANCE HALL, SAN FRANCISCO PUBLIC LIBRARY
GEORGE W. KELHAM,   ARCHITECT

STAIR HALL FROM DELIVERY ROOM, SAN FRANCISCO PUBLIC LIBRARY
GEORGE W. KELHAM   *ARCHITECT*

REFERENCE ROOM, SAN FRANCISCO PUBLIC LIBRARY

GENERAL READING ROOM, SAN FRANCISCO PUBLIC LIBRARY
George W. Kelham, Architect

COLONNADE, STAIR HALL, SAN FRANCISCO PUBLIC LIBRARY
GEORGE W. KELHAM, ARCHITECT

DELIVERY ROOM, SAN FRANCISCO PUBLIC LIBRARY

HYDE STREET ELEVATION, SAN FRANCISCO PUBLIC LIBRARY
George W. Kelham, Architect

*ENTRANCE
HALL,
SAN FRANCISCO
PUBLIC
LIBRARY*

*ENTRANCE
HALL,
SAN FRANCISCO
PUBLIC
LIBRARY*

*George W. Kelham
Architect*

STACK ROOM, SAN FRANCISCO PUBLIC LIBRARY
George W. Kelham, Architect

out has resulted in a degree of unity which is difficult to attain. The accessories throughout are designed with the same regard to the general harmony and fitness, and nothing jars or seems out of place. In fact, everything is thoroughly orderly and possessed of its reason for being.

The Library is a living organism, boldly conceived, and truly a reflection of its environment.

* ÷ *

Buy-a-Home Campaign Stimulates Building

Oakland's real estate dealers are conducting a "Buy-a-Home First" campaign that is having results beyond all expectations. The movement has been endorsed by leading organizations, including the Merchants' Association and Chamber of Commerce. The school children and even the churches have become interested. According to Mr. Fred E. Reed, chairman of the campaign committee and secretary-treasurer of the California State Federation, the idea originated in Birmingham, where the campaign was carried on for one week. In Oakland it will continue all summer. Efforts will be made to have every young man possessing a comfortable income deny himself certain luxuries so he may invest his money in a home of his own. "Everybody own a home" is the slogan. The movement already has stimulated the building industry. Architects and contractors are designing and building more homes across the bay than ever before. These houses range in cost from $2,500 to $6,000 and are sold on the easy payment plan.

Architectural Sketch Models

By BERTHOLD V. GEROW*

THOUGH scale models are by no means an innovation to the architectural profession, and many well-known architects use them, they have never taken the place in architectural practice that their usefulness unquestionably dictates. This is largely due, no doubt, to the fact that such models have had no place in architectural education. Practically speaking, the entire thought in teaching architectural design has been lavished upon flat surfaces and conventional shadows. Further than this, the impression prevails that an architectural model is justified only when the proposed structure is to be of considerable importance and cost. That this is true of plaster models cannot, of course, be denied. The making of such models by virtue of the highly technical processes involved requires the services of skilled artisans and for all usual purposes makes their cost quite prohibitive. Their very limitations, both as to manufacture and as to material, make them anything but "sketch" models.

These same limitations, even that of cost, apply to cardboard models. While apparently cheap, a well made cardboard building will cost as much as one of plaster, and, as with plaster models, their use is confined almost wholly to portraying designs for which every detail has been established. Once made, nothing can be changed.

Sketch models are a great time saver to both the architect and client, as they save a great deal of laborious mental translation from the technical drawings into solid forms. They portray the subject more accurately and faithfully than can be expected of any sketch elevation or perspective.

The material used by the writer is very similar to the plastic clay or plasteline used in the kindergartens and schools.

If it is desired merely to get form and shadow, a model in one color only is sufficient—preferably a grey green or sepia shade. But if it is desired to introduce color as well as form, this material can be secured in different shades. Modeling in the natural material leaves all the detail crisp and clear, obviating the clumsy and deadening effects of applying pigments to the surface of the model.

*509 Twenty-third avenue, San Francisco.

Unlike a perspective, the model will be expressive and correspondingly valuable in almost every stage of progress. One purpose may be served by the crudest blocking out, while for another purpose this same model might be carried to the limit of reality in color, texture and refinement of surface and detail. The possibilities of skilful technique in this direction are apparently endless.

Comparatively few architects, so far, have availed themselves consistently of this plastic method of study, or have taken the trouble to acquire the technique best suited to their individual needs.

Mr. Henry Rutgers Marshall of New York, the distinguished author, critic and architect, used this method in his office and advocated it strongly to the profession at large more than fifteen years ago. The writer's own introduction to sketch modeling was obtained in the office of Mr. Charles Sumner Kaiser of San Francisco, who himself has been very careful to acknowledge his indebtedness to Mr. Marshall.

MODELS OF CLUB HOUSE FOR SAN FRANCISCO GOLF AND COUNTRY CLUB
George W. Kelham, Architect

HOUSE IN ST. FRANCIS WOOD, SAN FRANCISCO
Henry H. Gutterson, Architect

The pictures on this page show a very good example of models made in plasteline. They were made for a house designed by Mr. Henry H. Gutterson and to be built in St. Francis Wood.

On page 58 are pictures of two excellent models made for Mr. George W. Kelham, architect of the San Francisco Golf and Country Club.

BIRDSEYE VIEW OF HOUSE IN ST. FRANCIS WOOD
Henry H. Gutterson, Architect

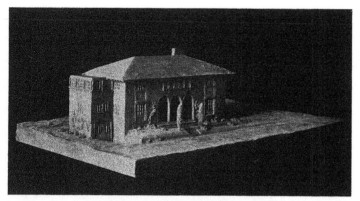

HOUSE IN ST. FRANCIS WOOD, SAN FRANCISCO
Henry H. Gutterson, Architect

All of the models illustrated were made entirely of plasteline, and at a scale of ⅛ inch to 1 foot.

*   *

The Dangers of "Skinning" Cement

A N Eastern newspaper recently published a short description of a building which collapsed, killing several workmen. In the story given it was stated that the building failed, due to the contractor "skinning cement." One workman, the paper alleges, overheard a foreman say to the contractor: "For God's sake have a heart; put some cement in, for if you keep on skinning the building will fail."

This story again brings forward the question, "Do contractors countenance the practice of skinning on cement?"

Unfortunately, we believe that this practice does obtain among some contractors. Just how prevalent it is cannot be stated. The custom dates back to the days when imported Portland cement sold from two and a half to five dollars a barrel and the contractor had to stand the loss of cooperage. Every pound of cement held out meant about a cent saved.

Then, too, contractors found that tables showing the amount of cement needed for certain proportions of mixed concrete do not hold out in actual practice, i. e., more cement is used than the theoretical figures call for, due to many reasons. Thus a contractor may order a thousand barrels of cement for a job, based upon the number of yards of concrete to be placed and the data given in the tables, yet when the job is finished, without the yardage on the concrete increasing, it is found that ten per cent more cement has been used. The increase at times may even exceed this.

(We know of a job in the heart of San Francisco where the architect's specifications called for a 1 to 6 mix. A disinterested inspector watched this job on several different occasions and took a record of the mix. His figures show that a 1 to 10½ mix was the rule.)

If the contractor uses more cement than called for, it is a dead loss to him. Thus it may become necessary for him to husband his cement. Even if the contractor means to be honest in this direction, and he tells his cement man to watch carefully that the cement does not overrun, there is the chance that the man; to save money for the contractor, may skin on cement.

We know of no valid excuse for a contractor to offer for skinning cement. He contracts to make mortar or concrete of certain proportions and there can be no doubt that he should do all he agrees to do. Nevertheless, some contractors may think it to their interest to save a little extra on cement.

Thus it becomes necessary to make it the interest of the contractor to use all the cement that the engineer specifies. Fortunatly, this incentive is not difficult to obtain, for in actual practice one prominent engineer has made the contractor as anxious to use the requisite amount of cement as the engineer is to have the proper amount in his concrete.

Thus on all the work under the Board of Water Supply of New York City, in charge of building the Catskill water system at a cost of about two hundred million dollars, the proposals on concrete masonry are made on a yard of concrete, including all work of mixing and placing and of all materials, except cement. In addition to this price, the contractor is asked to submit a price per barrel for furnishing cement. Thus the price submitted per barrel includes the cost of the cement, the handling, insurance, hauling and all work incidental to purchasing, caring for the cement and using it.

The inspector on the job orders into each batch of concrete the number of bags or barrels desired, keeps a record of the cement used, and upon this record, which the contractor can easily have checked, the payment for cement is made.

In submitting bids, the engineer furnishes the proportional mixtures to be used, the estimated yardage of concrete and the estimated number of yards of cement desired. This gives a ready means of comparing bids. It is a fair basis of payment for both the contractor and the owner and saves the engineer much worry. It is the only method that this journal knows of that is fair for all concerned.

Some cities and other corporations have tried the method of purchasing the cement direct from the manufacturer, and furnishing it to the contractor for use, making the latter responsible for the cement. This method has given but indifferent results. The expense of handling and storing the cement is thrown upon the contractor without paying him for it. The cement is more than likely to be wasted. The men, knowing it is not the contractor's, are indifferent as to the care they give it, and especially the empty cement bags, which represent money. There is a likelihood that some of the cement will be stolen. An incentive is not offered the contractor to care for the cement and use just what the specifications call for.

For these reasons we suggest, to both engineers and contractors, the New York method, to stop the practice of skinning on cement. It is also to the interest of cement manufacturing companies to advocate this method. —(The Contractor.)

* *

The Cover Design in this Issue

The unusual cover design for this month's Architect and Engineer was awarded second prize by the jury in a recent competition. The drawing is by Ernest E. Weihe, a draftsman in the office of Messrs. Bakewell & Brown, San Francisco. The author has produced a very realistic interpretation of the desert architecture, with the spirit of the West strongly in evidence.

COGSWELL POLYTECHNICAL COLLEGE, SAN FRANCISCO
FREDERICK H. MEYER, ARCHITECT

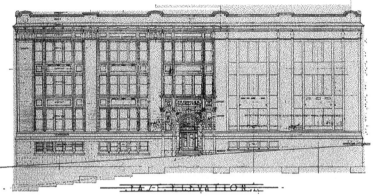

ELEVATION, COGSWELL POLYTECHNICAL COLLEGE, SAN FRANCISCO

Cogswell Polytechnical College, San Francisco

By FREDERICK H. MEYER, Architect.

THE question of vocational training has been discussed pro and con for many years and many interesting experiments are being made at various educational centers. The value of a mechanical training to a boy, who eventually may become an architect, engineer, or should follow another profession, is generally conceded to be doubtful but, judging from the many expressions of opinions one receives from men who employ boys as apprentices either in the drafting room or in the field, who have graduated from schools such as Cogswell or Lick-Wilmerding, in San Francisco, they are united in conceding that the student is filled with ambition and a keen desire to work and, what is infinitely more important, has some knowledge of how to work and make the best of his time and opportunity. If the Cogswell Polytechnical College can accomplish a result of this kind it certainly has the right to exist and can claim the support of our good citizens.

The average boy graduating from a grammar school has arrived at the stage where he has not the remotest idea of what he would like to do in after life and has shown no pronounced qualifications for any particular profession or trade. Of course, there are always exceptions to this rule. Facing a condition of this kind the parent is certainly in a quandary.

"The aim of the Cogswell Polytechnical College," says President Miller, "is to assist boys in finding themselves. We do not aim to make blacksmiths, carpenters, electricians, bricklayers or architects out of the boys who come to our schools, but we do claim that when the student graduates from our school he usually has fully made up his mind whether he wishes to take up a trade or profession."

Contrary to the general belief, Cogswell Polytechnical College is a free school and can be attended by any student with the necessary qualifications. The school was originally founded by Dr. H. D. Cogswell in the year 1887 and for some time occupied the present old building on the site at Twenty-sixth and Folsom streets.

FOLSOM STREET ENTRANCE, COGSWELL POLYTECHNICAL COLLEGE, SAN FRANCISCO
FREDERICK H. MEYER,   ARCHITECT

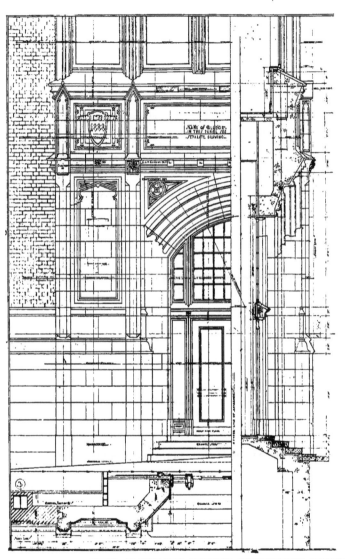

DETAIL OF ENTRANCE, COGSWELL POLYTECHNICAL COLLEGE
FREDERICK H. MEYER,   ARCHITECT

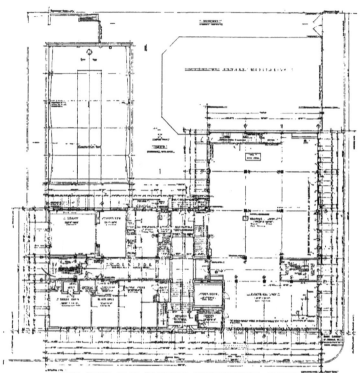

FIRST FLOOR PLAN, COGSWELL POLYTECHNICAL COLLEGE
Frederick H. Meyer, Architect

In the early part of 1915 it was finally decided to erect a new building and the accompanying photographs of the exterior and some of the various shops in the interior give an idea as to its general character. The construction is absolutely Class A throughout, steel frame, Meyer's form of floor construction, hollow tile partitions, white cedar trim, exterior walls of Port Costa red brick and dark headers, all trimmings of cast cement.

In plan, the main corridor running north and south terminates at each end with an enclosed fireproof stairway. The plan indicates the general arrangement of the class rooms, shops, etc. Special attention might be called to the arrangement of the forge shop and foundry which is one story. extremely well lighted from all sides through metal sash and a monitor roof with gear transom operated sash, with the control handle brought down near the floor. The operating fan for the forges is located in the boiler room. All the smoke and dust from the foundry is carried up to the roof, so that little dust is carried into the class rooms. The smelting cupola is located at the extreme west line as far as possible away from the main

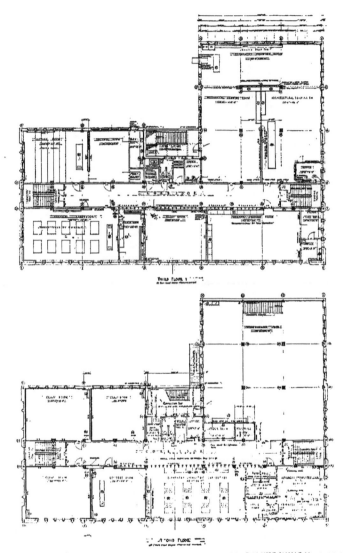

SECOND AND THIRD FLOOR PLANS, COGSWELL POLYTECHNICAL COLLEGE
FREDERICK H. MEYER, ARCHITECT

CHEMICAL LABORATORY, MACHINE AND AUTO ENGINEERING SHOP, FORGE SHOP AND
FOUNDRY, COGSWELL POLYTECHNICAL COLLEGE

CORNER OF CABINET AND JOINER SHOP, COGSWELL POLYTECHNICAL COLLEGE

FREE HAND ROOM, COGSWELL POLYTECHNICAL COLLEGE, SAN FRANCISCO
Frederick H. Meyer, Architect

building. The driveway on the south line of the building makes the foundry of easy access for the heavy materials which of necessity are used in this portion of the school.

The chemical laboratory is extremely well equipped. All the drains under the counters are of extra heavy lead and sloped in an even grade to the pot trap, the top of which can be seen in the photograph. At the extreme end of the table there is a door which can be opened and in case of a stoppage the pipe easily cleared. The sinks are all of soapstone and the sewer line leading from the laboratory of vitrious ironstone pipe. The tops of all tables, shelves, etc., are ebonized, which prevents the destruction of the wood by the acids used by the students.

* * *

Decay in Buildings

Much discussion during the year of interest to men of the electrical industry occurred in the technical lumber press over the decay of wood in buildings. Several cases of bad failure were reported. Research was started by the Forest Service to determine the "killing points" in temperature and humidity of common fungi found in American buildings. These studies have already yielded data of considerable importance. It was found, for example, that with a temperature approximately 100 degrees F., and a high humidity, the mycelia of certain fungi can be killed.

Field and laboratory studies indicate that much more care should be exercised in the selection of timber and in the construction of buildings to avoid conditions favorable to decay. A number of inspections of buildings which have given trouble on account of decay have shown that any one of the following causes may result in rapid deterioration of the building:

1. The use of green timber.
2. Allowing timber to get wet during construction.
3. Allowing the timber to absorb moisture after the building is finished, because of leaks or lack of ventilation.
4. The use of timbers containing too much sapwood.
5. The use of timbers which have already started to decay

The avoidance of these conditions will, as a rule, prevent decay. In special cases, however, decay can only be prevented by preservative treatment. For this purpose, salts such as zinc chloride and sodium fluorine are better than creosote for buildings.

CONCRETE
SWIMMING TANK,
ESTATE OF
MR. J. F. CARLSTON,
REDWOOD CANYON,
CALIFORNIA

G. E. McCrea, Architect

Why the New Law Regulating the Practice of Architecture?

By A. R. WALKER*

THE architectural profession within the State of California, seeking to maintain a high measure and standard of proficiency on the part of its members and all others entrusted with the designing and superintending of building operations and responsible to the public for the safety, sanitation and general character of its buildings as a safeguard to life and to the important financial, technical and aesthetic interests entrusted to them, are offering Assembly Bill No. 1126, as amended, as a substitute for the present statute, entitled "An Act to Regulate the Practice of Architecture," approved March 23, 1901.

.The two leading questions encountered in presenting this public safety measure may be summed up as follows:

What is the necessity?

Will the measure, if enacted into law, provide the best means and assure the attainment of its aims?

Under the first question, the following very relevant facts may be stated.

The architectural profession are initiating this measure because it is their duty so to do; because of their vocation, the one alone of those making up the building industry engaged exclusively in designing, specifying and superintending buildings, because of their intimate knowledge of existing conditions, and because they alone have an existing statute on the books about which such a measure may be built.

The present statute, above referred to, however, absolutely fails to serve the purpose of a public safety measure, in fact, serves no very definite end other than patenting the name "Architect," a feature which the proponents would still demand under a second form of certificate, by an additional educational examinatiin on clearly aesthetic subjects, and only as a protection to the public from misrepresentation.

The two reasonable methods of bettering the building conditions and accomplishing all the purposes sought which invited the attention of those who have been deeply studying this subject were, first, a state-wide building code, and, second, the determination of competency by examination.

The framing of a state-wide building code and the practical methods of enforcing it appeared to be a giant undertaking, cumbersome of enforcement, expensive to initiate and maintain, requiring as it would state appropriation for its formulating and administrating, and withal a solution illogical in that it sought to catch the trouble instead of preventing it.

The former method was more generally advocated by the civil and structural engineers, who through commendable loyalty to their society's ethics fundamentally oppose any form of licensing on the part of their members, but they are far from unanimous, and their contention is one similar in all respects to that of the architectural profession, which was by them subordinated in the interest of the public's best welfare.

The proposers of the law have taken the stand that a public safety measure to be effective must be sufficiently broad to compass all classifications of buildings wherein the public safety might be involved, and should bring within its jurisdiction all those engaged in the designing, specifying and superintending of such building operations.

They have, therefore, gone at the source of the trouble, choosing as a

*Secretary Southern California Chapter, American Institute of Architects.

more practicable, workable plan the second method, or that of state examination, whereby qualifications of practitioners shall be predetermined.

The two professions should demand of their members assurance of qualification in measure certainly no less than that required by the public whom they serve. They, the public, do require and we should make certain that ability and qualifications shall be **determined**, and shall in no case be **presumed**, whenever and wherever the public safety is involved. This is the answer to the only opposition thus far developed.

In brief summary, the law provides for a board appointed by the governor, consisting of four architects, two from the south and two from the north; two structural engineers, one from the south and one from the north; and one engineer from the state at large.

Matters of detail are covered in the act relative to the qualifications of board members, their terms of office, vacation of office, their compensation, which shall be expenses only; outlining the organization of the board; the number of meetings to be held; provisions outlined for special meetings, and the ordinary duties of the board; the various fees for examination payable to the board and to the state.

Two forms of certificate shall be issued, and under either certificate the qualified applicant may be permitted to design and superintend the construction of buildings of any character throughout the state.

The first form of certificate shall be issued to one who has passed the form of examination prescribed, which covers all subjects leading to a broad and comprehensive knowledge of building construction. They may use any title in handling their work which they may choose, "Engineer," "Designer," or what not. For the applicant, however, who elects to use the term "Architect" an additional examination is required, covering six subjects as set forth. Certain qualifications as to age and years of experience are outlined to establish eligibility for either examination.

Under the statute it shall be unlawful for any owner to erect a building used by human beings, for any purpose other than a one-family dwelling, and excepting buildings of temporary nature, unless such structures shall be designed by a holder of either form of certificate. The latter mentioned exception is sufficiently broad to exempt all forms of construction work in the oil fields and mines, in construction camps and elsewhere, where the structures are not of a permanent nature.

It shall be unlawful for anyone to use the word "Architect" unless he shall have passed, in addition to the first examination, the further examination prescribed entitling him to use the word "Architect."

Provision is also made for the securing of the proper certificate without examination by those demonstrating to the satisfaction of the board that they are actively engaged at the time of the passage of this act in the practice of structural engineering.

Proper provisions are made for cancellation and revocation of licenses.

The bill has received the hearty endorsement and active support of the state-wide architectural profession through its two chapters, the Southern California Chapter of the American Institute of Architects and the San Francisco Chapter of the American Institute of Architects, and the unanimous endorsement of the Los Angeles Builders Exchange and the Master Builders Association renders its approval full and complete by the recognized building fraternity. Individual endorsement has been received in letter and verbal form from many of the most prominent and influential civil and structural engineers.

Resolutions of endorsement have also been received by several other associations and societies of business and professional men.

Proposed Law Regulating Practice of Architecture in California

THE following is the text of the proposed amended law replacing the existing state law regulating the practice of architecture in California. The bill, known as Assembly Bill No. 1126, was introduced into the lower house by Assemblyman Wishard and is in the hands of the judiciary committee. The new provisions it contains define a policy designed to secure a larger degree of safety for the public in the design of buildings. The bill as introduced is in full:

An Act providing for public safety in buildings within the State of California by regulating the construction, alteration and repair of same, and to provide penalties for the violation thereof.

The People of the State of California do enact as follows:

Section 1. There is hereby created a board to be known as the State Board of Architecture. Said board shall consist of seven members, to be appointed by the Governor of the State; and for the period of sixty days from and after the date upon which this act becomes effective, unless a majority of said members are sooner appointed and qualify as herein provided, the members of the State Board of Architecture as organized under the provisions of an act entitled "An Act to regulate the practice of Architecture," approved March 23, 1901, and the acts supplemental thereto and amendatory thereof, shall constitute said board.

The membership of this board shall be composed as follows: All members shall be residents of the State of California; one member shall be a graduate of a recognized school of engineering, college or university, and shall have been engaged in continuous practice or teaching of structural engineering or both for a period of iot less than ten years; after the term of office of the original engineering member of the board shall have become vacant, each such member, in addition to the other qualifications herein named, shall hold a certificate to design and superintend the construction of buildings under this act. Each of the other members shall be an architect and shall hold a certificate to that effect under this act.

Three of the members holding certificates as architects shall be residents of that portion of the state north of the northerly line of the county of San Luis Obispo, the county of Kern and the county of San Bernardino, hereinafter known as the northern district; three members holding certificates as architects shall be residents of that portion of the state south of the northerly line of the county of San Luis Obispo, county of Kern and county of San Bernardino, hereinafter known as the southern district.

In making the original appointments to the board, the term of office of the member not holding a certificate as "architect" shall be three years. The term of office of one architect from the northern district and one from the southern district shall be two years each. The term of office of one architect from the northern district and one from the southern district shall be three years each. The term of office of one architect from the northern district and one from the southern district shall be four years each. After the original appointments the term of office of each member of the board shall be four years, or until a successor shall have been duly appointed and shall have qualified. Should any member of said board change residence from the district from which he was appointed during his term of office, said office shall become vacant. The governor shall have power to remove from office any member of the board for neglect of duty in the enforcement of this act, or for any cause which in his judgment renders such member incompetent to serve on said board. In the event of any vacancy occurring in the membership of the board, in any manner other than by expiration of the term herein set forth, the governor shall fill said vacancy by an appointment for the unexpired term. All members of the board, before entering upon the discharge of the duties of their offices as herein set forth, shall subscribe to and file with the secretary of state the constitutional oath of office.

It shall be the duty of the board to enforce all provisions of this act.

Sec. 2. The board, within thirty days from and after the appointment and qualification of a majority of the members thereof, shall meet and elect from its membership a president and a vice-president, one of whom shall be from the northern district and one from the southern district; and a secretary, and an assistant secretary, one of whom shall be from the northern district and one from the southern district, who shall act as treasurer and assistant treasurer, respectively. The term of office of such officers shall be two years each; the president shall be selected alternately from the northern and the southern districts every two years.

The board shall adopt all necessary rules, regulations and by-laws, not inconsistent with this act and the constitution and laws of this state or of the United States, requisite to the exercise of its powers and duties as in this act provided. The board shall adopt a seal, of which the secretary shall have the care and custody. The secretary shall keep a correct record of the proceedings of the board, of fees received and moneys disbursed, which record shall be open to the public at all times. Four members of the board shall constitute a quorum for the transaction of business.

Regular meetings of the board shall be held on the last Tuesday in April of each year in San Francisco, and on the last Tuesday in October of each year in Los Angeles, at each of which meetings examinations of applicants for certificates granted under this act shall be held. Special meetings to transact any business that may come before the board shall be called by the president within thirty days after the written request so to do from not less than three members of said board, and as prescribed in the by-laws adopted by said board.

An annual report of the work and proceedings of the board, embodying the report of the secretary and treasurer, together with a complete directory giving the names and addresses of all persons who hold unrevoked certificates granted under this act, shall be made by said board to the governor of the state and a copy of said report shall be mailed to each person who holds such certificate.

Sec. 3. Each member of the board shall serve without compensation for his services, but the board may incur such expenses as it shall deem to be necessary to carry out the provisions of this act, and the members of the board shall be reimbursed for the expenses incurred by them in the performance of their duties under this act. Expenses of the board shall be paid out of the fees collected and retained by the board, as in this act provided. At the end of each fiscal year any excess of fees received over moneys disbursed, after a working cash balance of one thousand five hundred dollars has been retained, shall be paid by the board to the state treasurer, to be retained by the state. All moneys and assets of the district and state boards of architecture existing at the time of the passage of this act shall become the property of the state board of architecture as organized under this act, and the secretary of each existing board shall turn such assets over to the secretary of the new board, together with a complete report and accounting of all such moneys and other assets.

Sec. 4. For the purpose of this act, unless it should be apparent from their context that they have a different meaning, words used in the singular include the plural, and the plural, the singular; words used in the present tense include the future; words used in the masculine gender include the feminine, and the feminine, the masculine; and "shall" as used shall be deemed to be mandatory. "The board" shall be deemed to be the state board of architecture as organized under this act. A "structural engineer" shall be deemed to be a person who has been engaged in the study of mathematics, strength of materials and allied subjects as applied to the computation of the stresses and strains in the structural features of a building and who is qualified thereby and by practical experience to design, specify, and superintend such structural work of buildings, and who is engaged in such operations as a vocation.

Sec. 5. It shall be unlawful for any person, firm or corporation to construct, erect, alter, add to, repair or reconstruct any building, or portion thereof, whenever such construction, erection, alteration, addition to, repair or reconstruction involves or affects the stability, strength or safety of such building or portion thereof, and whenever such building or portion thereof is occupied or used or is designed or intended to be occupied or used in whole or in part by human beings for the purpose of assemblage or the pursuit of vocation, or for living and sleeping purposes or either thereof, whenever the building or portion thereof is occupied or used, or is designed or intended to be occupied or used as a home by more than one family, unless such construction, alteration, erection, addition to, repair or reconstruction shall have been designed and specified and supervised or superintended by a person who has complied with all the requirements of this act and who holds an unrevoked certificate as "architect" or "to design and superintend the construction of buildings" in accordance therewith, and who has identified each and all of the drawings and specifications or reproductions thereof used in connection with such work by his signature thereon; provided, however, that nothing herein shall be construed to make it unlawful for a person qualified by this act to design, specify, supervise, or superintend the construction of buildings to assume the responsibility under this act for any of such operations when the drawings and specifications were made by a person not a resident of the State of California, if such responsibility shall (for the purpose of this act) be evidenced by the signature of such person on all the drawings, and specifications, or reproductions thereof, and by his direct supervision or direct control over the superintendence or supervision of the building work.

It shall be unlawful for any person who does not possess an unrevoked certificate as in this act provided, to in any manner, either directly or indirectly, use or attempt to use any certificate, license, registration or similar paper or document, for the purposes set forth in this act.

It shall be unlawful for any person who does not possess an unrevoked certificate as "architect" as in this act provided, to use, maintain or attempt to use or maintain in any sign or advertisement, or to stamp, sign, or label any drawing, specification, contract, correspondence, or to advertise or use the words "architect" or "architects," or any abbreviation or derivation of same, or any combination or words, or device of which such word or words form a part, with the object or result, either intentional or unintentional, of designating such person as "architect."

It shall be unlawful for any person who does not possess an unrevoked certificate to design and superintend the construction of buildings as in this act provided, to use or maintain or attempt to use or maintain in any sign or advertisement, or to stamp, sign, or label any drawing, specification, contract, correspondence, or to advertise or use the words "structural engineer" or "structural engineers," or any abbreviation of same, or any combination of words or device of which such words form a part, with the object or result, either intentional or unintentional, of designating such person as structural engineer.

Any person violating any of the provisions of this section shall be deemed guilty of a misdemeanor, and upon conviction thereof shall be punishable by a fine not exceeding five hundred dollars, or by imprisonment in a county jail not exceeding six months, or by both such fine and imprisonment; and in addition to the penalty therefor shall be liable for all costs, expense and disbursements by this act provided, which costs, expense and disbursements shall be fixed by the court having jurisdiction of the matter.

Sec. 6. Any person who has given to the board satisfactory proof that he is not less than twenty-one years of age, that he is of good moral character, and that for a period of not less than five years he has been continuously engaged in designing, making drawings and specifications and supervising or superintending the erection of buildings (not to exceed one of the five years may have been spent in travel for the purpose of study of such subjects), shall be entitled to an examination for a certificate "to design and superintend the erection of buildings" and for a certificate as "architect," or either of these, before and by said board. Upon payment by such person to the board of the fees as herein provided, the board shall examine such person at its next following regular examination of applicants for certificates.

The fee for examination for the certificate to design and superintend the construction of buildings shall be fifty dollars; for examination for the certificate as "architect," the applicant shall pay an additional fee of twenty-five dollars; which fees shall be retained by the board.

A person granted examination to either certificate by the board who shall fail to pass such examination to the satisfaction of the board, shall not be eligible for re-examination for a period of at least six months after such failure; and if such person has failed to pass the examination leading to either certificate in more than one-half of the subjects required therefor in such examination, upon re-examination such person shall pay the full fees as required for an original examination, which fees shall be retained by the board. If such person has failed to pass the examination leading to either certificate in less than one-half of the subjects required in such examination, upon re-examination such person shall pay a fee equal to one-half the full fees required for the original examination, which fees shall be retained by the board.

A person examined for the certificate as "architect," who shall pass to the satisfaction of the board the examination for a certificate to design and superintend the construction of buildings, but who shall fail to pass the remainder of the examination for the certificate as "architect," shall be granted a certificate to design and superintend the construction of buildings by the board and such person, or any person holding unrevoked a certificate to design and superintend the construction of buildings shall be granted an examination by the board, in the architectural subjects leading to the certificate as "architect" upon payment to the board of the fee of twenty-five dollars, which fee shall be retained by the board.

Whenever any person examined by the board shall have passed such examination to the satisfaction of the board, or whenever any person, whose place of residence and principal place of business are not within the state of California, shall have had issued to him and holds unrevoked in such state in which he resides a license or certificate of qualification wherein, in the judgment of the board, the qualifications of the person and the standard of examination for such license or certification are not less in any of their requirements than those prescribed by this act for certificates thereunder, and whenever such person shall have paid to the secretary of the board the annual current license fee, the secretary of the board shall issue to such person a certificate of the board signed by its president and secretary, sealed with the seal of the board and directed to the secretary of state, certifying that the person therein named has passed an examination satisfactory to the board, and that such person is entitled to a certificate "to design and superintend the construction of buildings" or to a certificate as "architect," as the case may be, in accordance with the provisions of this act.

Any structural engineer resident in the state of California who shall show to the satisfaction of the board that he is in good standing and has been engaged in the practice of structural engineering for a period of not less than eight years in said state, or who is engaged in the independent practice of his profession, and is so actively engaged at the time of passage of this act, shall upon application therefor by such person, be granted a certificate "to design and superintend the construction of buildings'' by the board without examination in the subjects herein set forth for examination leading to such certificate, upon the payment by him to said board of the regular fees for examination and certification as provided in this act; provided that such application shall be made within six months after this act shall go into effect.

To any person holding, at the time this act goes into effect, an unrevoked "certificate to practice architecture" issued by the state board of architecture under the provisions of the act entitled, "An act to regulate the practice of architecture," chapter 212, approved March 23, 1901, and amended March 26, 1903, the board shall, upon application to the board and without examination by the board, issue their certificate to the secretary of state, who, upon the payment of the fee by the applicant, as provided by this act, shall issue to such person a certificate as "architect"; provided, however, that if such application be not filed before the board on or before six months after this act shall be in effect, the holder of such "certificate to practice architecture" shall be liable to the penalties prescribed by this act for the unlawful use of the word "architect" or "architects" or any of its forms as provided by Section 5 of this act.

Upon presentation to him of a certificate from the board, and upon payment by said person to him of a fee of ten dollars, the secretary of state shall at once issue to the person named in such certificate from the board a certificate "to design and superintend the construction of buildings" or a certificate as "architect," as the certificate from the board shall show, in accordance with the provisions of this act, which certificate shall contain the full name of the person, the date of the issuance, and character of the certificate, and shall further certify that such person has passed an examination satisfactory to the state board of architecture, and the date of such examination. The secretary of the board shall transmit directly to the secretary of state the full report of the examination, and the secretary of state shall keep same on file in his office as public records, together with a proper index and file thereof.

All certificates heretofore issued by the state board of architecture under the provisions of the act entitled, "An act to regulate the practice of architecture, chapter 212, approved March 23, 1901, and amended March 26, 1903," shall have the same virtue, force and effect and shall be henceforth subject to the provisions of this act.

Sec. 7. The requirements of the examination, as in this section provided to be given by the board to determine the qualifications of the person for the certificate "to design and superintend the construction of buildings," or for the certificate as "architect," are hereby fixed to be the minimum requirements for examination by the board, and such requirements may be increased by the action of the board, but shall never be waived by the board, except when the person applying for examination, whose place of residence and principal place of business are not within the state of California, and where in such place of business a license or certificate of qualification is not required by law, is and has, for a period of not less than ten years previous to said time of application, been engaged in the active practice of architecture or of structural engineering, the board, upon satisfactory proof of ability and qualification of said applicant, may waive the written examination prescribed by this act.

The applicant for a certificate "to design and superintend the construction of buildings" shall be examined by the board in at least the following subjects, and the examination therein shall be in writing supplemented orally:

(a) His practical experience, its extent and responsibility; his technical knowledge of materials, their strength and use in practical construction; and his ability to compute mathematically the strength and stresses in materials and structures, and to design a building or structure, or any portion thereof, so as to insure inherent stability and strength in all its parts, and to meet the contingencies and problems of construction and public safety that arise in the erection of buildings or structures, or portions thereof. This portion of the examination shall be comprehensive, in order to insure that the applicant has a solid theoretical understanding and a working knowledge of the principles and mathematics involved in the computing of all stresses and strains in the mechanics of building operations.

(b) His theoretical and practical knowledge of sanitation as applied to buildings, and his ability to design plumbing systems therein.

(c) His knowledge of the theory and design of heating and ventilating of buildings, and his practical understanding of the various systems in use.

(d) His knowledge of stereotomy.

(e) His knowledge of specification work.

(f) His general education and knowledge of architectural terms, together with his character and fitness for a certificate.

The applicant for a certificate as "architect" shall be examined in all subjects leading to the certificate "to design and superintend the construction of building" and in addition thereto shall be examined in the following subjects:

(g) Elements of architecture.

(h) Architectural design.

(i) History of architecture.

(j) Freehand drawing.

(k) History of ornament.

(l) Shades and shadows, and the use of color.

Sec. 8. Every person to whom a certificate "to design and superintend the construction of buildings" or a certificate as "architect" has been issued, in accordance with this act, shall have his certificate recorded in the office of the county recorder in the county in this state in which the holder thereof resides, and shall pay to the recorder the same fee therefor as is charged for the recording of deeds.

Every person to whom a certificate "to design and superintend the construction of buildings" or a certificate as "architect" has been issued, in accordance with this act, shall pay an annual license fee of five dollars to the state board of architecture, such fee to be retained by the board. Such fee shall be payable in advance on the first Monday in January of each year. When paid the secretary of the board shall issue to each such person a receipt signed by the president and secretary under the seal of the board. If any such person shall fail, neglect or refuse to pay such annual license fee on or before the first Monday in April of each year, said fee shall be delinquent, and the certificate of such person shall thereupon become subject to revocation and cancellation.

Each certificate "to design and superintend the construction of buildings" or certificate as "architect" issued in accordance with the provisions of this act shall remain in full force until revoked and canceled for cause, as provided for in this section.

A certificate "to design and superintend the construction of buildings" or certificate as "architect" may be revoked and canceled for stamping or signing drawings, or specifications or reproductions thereof in any manner to certify to, or to appear to certify to, any such drawings, or specifications, or reproductions thereof, when any of these were not made directly by or for him as provided in Section 5 of this act; for failure to pay annual license fees; for conviction of fraud, misdemeanor under this act, felony, incompetency, gross carelessness or dishonest practice.

It shall be the duty of the State Board of Architecture, whenever charges in writing have been filed with the board and signed with the name of the person bringing such charges against any person holding a certificate "to design and superintend the construction of buildings" or as "architect," in the State of California, charging such person with any of the causes of revocation and cancellation of the certificate "to design and superintend the construction of buildings" or as "architect," as in this act provided, to notify such person in writing of the nature of the charges, and to cite him to appear before said board to show cause why such certificate should not be revoked and cancelled. Such notification and citation shall be given not less than thirty days before the time set for the hearing, and the delivery of such notice and citation to the place of buisness or last knows address of such person shall be deemed sufficient for the purpose of this notification and citation. Should such person so cited fail, neglect or refuse to appear at the time set by the board for the hearing, this shall be deemed evidence of guilt, and the board shall thereupon revoke and cancel the certificate of such person. The board shall investigate fully the charges against such person at the time set for the hearing, and the person charged shall be given opportunity to be heard in his own. defense or to be represented by counsel.

After such hearing, if, in the judgment of not less than four members of the board, the charges against such person have been proven, the secretary of the board shall issue to the Secretary of State a Board certificate revoking the certificate of such person, and the Secretary of State shall then cancel the certificate "to dsign and superintend the construction of buildings," or the certificate as "architect," as the case may be.

Upon the cancellation of such certificate, it shall be the duty of the secretary of the board to give notice of such cancellation to the county recorder of that county in the state in which said certificate has been recorded, whereupon the recorder shall mark the certificate recorded in his office "canceled." At the expiration of not less than six months after said cancellation, the person whose certificate "to design and superintend the construction of buildings," or as "architect" has been canceled may apply to the board for a new certificate, and the board may grant same upon the payment of every fee required in this act for any applicant for examination; but shall never grant any such certificate when the same has been revoked for incompetency or gross carelessness, without requiring such person to pass the examination therefor prescribed by this act.

Sec. 9. If any section, subsection, sentence, clause or phrase of this act is for any reason held to be unconstitutional, such decision shall not affect the validity of the remaining portions of this act. The legislature hereby declares that it would have passed this act, and each section, subsection, sentence, clause and phrase thereof, irrespective of the fact that any one or more sections, subsections, sentences, clauses or phrases be declared unconstitutional.

Sec. 10. An act entitled "An act to regulate the practice of architecture," approved March 23, 1901, and all acts amendatory thereof or supplementary thereto are hereby repealed.

Growing the Dahlia

By A. J. NEVRAUMONT*

Dahlia Roots

THESE are busy times for the landscape architect and gardener. Country and city homes are being made more attractive with the planting of trees, shrubs and blooms. One of the most satisfactory of the latter and among the easiest of all flowers to grow is the dahlia.

They can be grown in any good garden soil, but, if possible, plant in an open, sunny situation. Prepare the soil thoroughly by digging 12 to 18 inches deep, in the fall, if possible, and again in the spring. Plant any time between April 20 and June 1, digging holes 6 inches deep and from 3 to 4 feet apart. Then lay in the tuber flat on its side, the size of which makes no difference as long as it has one strong eye or sprout. Cover 3 inches deep, thus leaving the hole one-half full, to be filled after plant comes up 6 to 8 inches above ground. As soon as plant is large enough, cut out the top of it just above the second or third set of leaves, which causes the plant to grow a stout branch at the base of each of the four or six leaves left. Just as soon as the plants are up, the most important thing to do is to keep the soil loose and mellow by hoeing or cultivating once or twice a week and just as soon after each rain as the soil will permit. As soon as the buds appear, stop all cultivation and give the beds a mulch of rotted manure, leaves, grass clippings, etc., and around the base of each plant place a shovelful of well-rotted manure, if possible. Water the beds and plants thoroughly once or twice a week and specially during the dry weather. To have the greatest success is to keep them growing, but as strong and sturdy as possible. Never allow the faded flowers to remain on the plant, but cut them off with as much stem or stalk as you can. Dahlias will con-

*Manager California Seed Company, San Francisco.

Decorative Dahlia, Papa Charmet

tinue to bloom until a heavy frost kills the tops in late fall, after which the tops are cut off and the roots are dug and stored in a frost-proof cellar or basement, covering with dry soil, sand or anything that will keep them from shrivelling.

The following brief history of the dahlia will be found interesting:

The dahlia is a native of Mexico, and before the invasion of Mexico by Cortez was grown by the Aztecs under the name acoctli.

It was named dahlia in honor of Prof. Andrew Dahl, a Swedish botanist, and was first cultivated in Europe about 130 years ago.

Staghorn Cactus Dahlia, Wodan

Cactus Dahlia, California

Dahlia Variabilis, the forerunner of the common or show dahlias, was single in its wild state. The first perfectly double flowers were obtained by M. Dankelaar of the Botanical Gardens of Belgium in 1814, and from this source came the well known double varieties so common in the gardens of the East a half century ago.

Dahlia Juarezi, the original Cactus dahlia, was named after a former President of Mexico and was discovered in Juxphaor, Mexico, in 1872, by J. T. Vanderberg, and sent by

Decorative Dahlia, Champion

him to an English florist, who exhibited it in England in 1882. The graceful form and brilliant color of the flower ?t once captured the fancy of flower lovers, and today there is no flower more popular.

The progeny of Dahlia Juarezi not only "broke" into various colors, but into different shapes as well. It was by selecting the most desirable of these and reselecting the finest from each succeeding generation of plants, that the Cactus dahlia has been worked up to its present state of perfection. The contrast between Juarezi and some of its gorgeous descendants is so great that it almost staggers belief.

The Pompon form appeared about 1858-1860. Next came the decorative type, which is about forty years old, and most recently the Hybrid Cactus and the peony class, which dates back but a few years and are becoming very popular.

Indeed, the marvelous transformation wrought in the wonderful flower in the past thirty-four years must seem to those unacquainted with the possibilities of plant life more like a tale from Arabian Nights than actual reality.

Decorative Dahlia, Minna Bergle

San Francisco's Experience with Concrete Wharf Supports

THE present practice of the Board of State Harbor Commissioners, San Francisco, calls for the use of concrete for wharf foundations wherever the conditions permit. The methods and experience of the commissioners in this work were set forth by Mr. Thomas S. Williams in a paper presented at the fifth annual convention of the American Association of Port Authorities. The notes that follow are taken from Mr. Williams' paper:

Concrete supports, used in the piers, wharves or seawall, have been of two main types, called cylinders and pre-moulded piles. Pre-moulded concrete piles were first driven in the San Francisco harbor in 1911, for work close in shore, but emboldened by apparent success their use was extended until a new pier just completed, 200 feet wide and 900 feet long, is entirely supported by concrete driven piles.

The first piles used were 66 feet long, 16 inches square, and were employed to sustain concrete masses under ferry aprons. In a pier just completed the length of piles varies from about 40 to 106 feet, and they were placed with centers 11x12 feet apart.

The pile is reinforced with longitudinal steel rods, four of them, each ⅝ inch square, being set in piles 16 inches square and from 35 to 40 feet long, and eight rods each 1 inch square in piles 20 inches square and from 90 to 100 feet long. In order to facilitate driving, the piles are given a taper, beginning about 10 feet from the point, tapering to 10 inches square. In setting the reinforcement, soft steel wire, ¼ inch in diameter, is wound spirally around the rods, with spacing for the wire of about 6 inches. One of these piles, 20 inches square and 100 feet long, weighs about 20 tons.

In designing such a pier it is necessary to drive test piles of wood in advance, so as to determine bottom conditions. Borings are also made. In the plans, the length of each pile is specified. If it turns out to be too long when actually driven to refusal, the top of the pile is blasted off with dynamite, and if it turns out to be too short, it is built up by concrete to the proper level.

The top of the pile, during the driving, is protected by a rope cushion, and a wooden block about 6 inches thick, and usually the point is not protected at all. In seawall construction, however, where a loose rock fill is first put in at the base and then piles are driven through the rock as supports for the deck or bulkhead wharf, a hole is made for the pile by driving a wooden "bulldozer" ahead of it, and the point of the pile is often protected by a steel shoe.

Thus far piles have been driven only into good, firm holding-ground, securing usually a penetration of about 30 to 40 feet. Much of the water-front is very soft mud, running frequently to a depth of 100 feet or more, before stiffness is found, and in such regions the concrete pile has not yet been used.

Results already obtained in handling piles up to 106 feet long and 20 inches square are encouraging the commission to try even larger piles in some contemplated work, and very likely before long piles 115 and 125 feet long and 2 feet square may be tried. Of course, such piles will necessitate specially built drivers.

The cylinder form of concrete supports may be divided into two main types as used in the harbor of San Francisco. The first type was introduced about fifteen years ago and has been entirely abandoned because of its deficiencies manifested by the lapse of time in many piers.

The composition of this type was as follows: Wooden piles, sometimes one, sometimes three close together, were driven to refusal, the tops coming up to near the wharf deck, then a wooden stave form of cylindrical shape was placed around them and driven into the bottom, no steel reinforcement being used, and then the concrete was poured in and allowed to set as best it might. Generally speaking, the mud was too deep to permit one to say that there was any bedrock or hard bottom at all under this construction. Such cylinders were about 3 feet in diameter.

The design of such cylinders, which almost uniformly proved failures, contemplated that the bottom of the concrete would extend about 2 feet below the mud line. The calculation was that this was sufficiently deep to guard against shifting or other removal of the mud, that might in consequence expose the wooden piles to the attacks of the voracious teredo. This calculation proved futile. Modern vessels with their swift and powerful propellers raised such a disturbance of the waters that the mud was whipped or sucked away from the supporting wooden piles, the teredos thereupon honeycombed them in short order, and the concrete columns above them necessarily fell into the water. This was a common occurrence in piers so designed.

Such cylinders were all built without steel reinforcement, but the absence of the reinforcement was manifestly not the particular cause of failure in this instance, as the whole cylinder fell when the wooden supports were eaten off by the teredo.

Another serious mistake, with costly consequences, was made by pouring the wet concrete mixture into the cylinders without removing the water from the bottom of the form. The result invariably was that such wet mixture deposited in water never did set into true concrete at all, since the cement was practically washed out of it. Disintegration of the bottoms of such cylinders followed rapidly.

Profiting by the experience of their predecessors, the engineers in the past four years have improved on the old type of concrete cylinder and in the actual work of installing them in several noticeable respects. This type is really founded on an entirely different principle.

If wooden piles are used to support the cylinder, as they must be in mud bottoms where there is no bedrock, the piles are driven to about 8 feet below the permanent dredge line and come up into the concrete cylinder only about 5 feet, the theory being that the wood supports the cylinder and then the cylinder supports the wharf. This arrangement, it is believed, guards sufficiently against the possibility that the wood will by shifting of the mud become exposed to teredo attacks.

The method is first to drive a steel shell, or caisson, in cylindrical shape into the bottom, so that it can be sealed. The mud is dredged out of it and the water pumped out, and the wooden form with the steel reinforcement already set in it is lowered into the steel shell. Great care is taken to clean and dry the bottom of the form as thoroughly as possible, and then the concrete mixture is poured in and tamped down by hand. After the concrete is set, the steel shell is pulled off by the pile-driving apparatus and again used elsewhere. Steel reinforcing rods are always used, usually ¾ inch square, and from 8 to 12 rods in each cylinder. The concrete columns when finished are from 3 to 4 feet in diameter. Spiral wire hooping is also used around the reinforcement, as already described with respect to the concrete piles.

The mixing of the concrete is carefully inspected by competent inspectors; the cement, steel and concrete are tested by the testing engineer; and the cement is bought by the commission and furnished to the contractor for the work. The concrete mixture now used in the harbor of San Francisco, the proportion of cement to the aggregate is 1 to 5 in the pile, and 1 to 6 in the wharf deck and cylinders.

The experience with cylinders has warranted the deduction that where at all practicable the cylinders should rest on any bottom hard enough to carry the load, thus avoiding the use of wooden supports below them.

In San Francisco harbor, as far as it has been improved, such bedrock has been found in only one limited district, and in that stretch seven piers have been built, supported by concrete columns or cylinders of the type last described, and going down to hardpan and without any wooden supports under them at all. These piers range from 130 to 200 feet wide, and from 650 to 800 feet long.

*   *

Proposed Legislation Affects Building

THREE bills are pending in the California legislature which will materially affect the building interests of the state. These are the new State Tenement House Act, the Hotel and Lodging House Act and the Dwelling House Act. A brief outline of the bills with their proposed changes follows:

The size of courts are regulated by the size of the building and are not all one size as the law now provides. The height of frame tenement houses is limited to thirty-six feet or three stories. Where the basement is occupied it will class as a story. Side yards are provided for instead of back yards but the space at the rear of tenements must never be less than seven feet from the ground. Fire escapes must open directly from hallways, and there must be two means of egress from every floor. Hallways must be semi-fireproof, and in places where automobiles are stored the compartment must be fireproof.

Mosquito screening of sixteen mesh to the inch must be placed on each door and window or other opening. In tenements of more than eight families there must be a housekeeper, janitor or someone living on the premises to be responsible for sanitation, heat and light. Bedding must be stored in dry, vermin free rooms. Dark rooms must be painted or papered in light colors. Building inspectors or any city officials charged with enforcing the bill will appeal directly to the Superior Court. The present provision requiring the filing of plans in duplicate before construction can be commenced is not amended nor changed in the proposed law.

The hotel bill (S. B. 433) is practically a new measure. The present act is regarded as only an entering wedge, but the proposed new law will cover all subjects and prescribe regulations similar to the Tenement House Act but applicable to hotels.

One of its important provisions is that all rooms shall be outside, opening upon streets or courts. Height of frame hotels and plumbing are regulated. The bill applies to dormitories as well as to hotels. Courts will vary with the size of the structure, and combination buildings will be made to conform to the regulations. Safety and sanitation is given especial attention.

The Dwelling House Bill (S. B. 457) regulates the construction, reconstruction, moving, altering, maintenance, use and occupancy of dwellings erected in any part of the state. A few of the regulations which must be followed in building dwellings if this bill becomes a law are:

Substantial construction so as to exclude dampness. Cellar living prohibited. No basement living quarters shall be used where the ceiling is not seven feet or more above the ground. All walls, floors or ceilings of such dwelling places shall be damp-proof and water-proof. Air space under the lower floor of six inches or more. No room of less than ninety square feet shall be built.

Rooms must be at least seven feet and eight feet in height. Every water-closet compartment shall not be less than thirty-six inches in width, and bathrooms shall not be less than seven feet six inches in width. Every room must have a window opening directly upon a street or unoccupied area containing at least thirty-six square feet. There are numerous regulations affecting plumbing, sanitation and ventilation.

Senate Bill 440 provides that where buildings are required to have fire-escapes they shall also be equipped with counterbalance stairways.

The examination and certification of plumbers is provided for in Senate Bill 100. The bill also would restrict the employment upon any public work to plumbers so licensed.

Senate Bill No. 6 provides that seperate bids be asked on public buildings. One to cover the structure itself and other the plumbing.

Senate Bill 963 provides that all State brick, stone, terra cotta or concrete work done in the future shall be inspected by a State Masonry Inspector before accepted by the State.

* * *

To Build Workingmen's Homes of Brick

The problem of housing workingmen and persons of moderate means in and around Reading, Pa., has resulted in an ambitious attempt at its solution by the borough of Wyomissing, the town that is located within a park and just across the Schuylkill river from Reading. Plans are about to be carried out, and work has been begun upon one of the largest operations of its kind ever undertaken in Berks county, Pennsylvania. It is believed that the sequel to the same will be the erection of several hundred model homes, upon a tract of one hundred and fifty acres, which will involve an expenditure of $1,000,000.

Each house will consist of six or seven rooms, varying from single and twin construction up to blocks of five or six, but with a diversity of architecture.

In the construction of these dwellings brick will be the chief commodity used. The plans include the elimination of the back yard, and all the houses will have practically two fronts, with front and rear lawns and with no fences or divisions, except ornamental hedges. The whole area will be interspersed with malls, open circles and parking places, planted with shrubbery and flowers. The grouping will be around a pretty park, which contains a lake of spring water.

In their disposition and location with regard to each other, in exterior form and interior finish, the homes will be planned for convenience and comfortable living. Provisions will be made for space, light, air, outlook, and in attractive, cleanly, agreeable surroundings, which will compare favorably with the most expensive homes, and to be more free than the average of such homes from disagreeable, sordid and unsightly environment.— Brick and Clay Record.

* *

Officers of Oakland Realty Board

The Oakland Real Estate Board has elected the following officers: President, Mr. Pearson W. Morehouse; vice-president, Mr. Frank K. Mott; secretary, Mr. S. H. Masters; treasurer, Mr. Wickham Havens; directors, Mr. Geo. W. Austin, Mr. F. Bruce Maiden, Mr. C. P. Murdock, Mr. Fred E. Reed, Mr. Willard W. White, Mr. Chas. M. Wood, Mr. Fred T. Wood.

Advantages in Using Architectural Terra Cotta†

By HERMAN A. PLUSCH, M. S., Cr. E.*

WITH a predetermined lot size and a definite amount of money available for the erection of a building, be it church, school, office building, skyscraper or what not, one of the very important questions to be decided is the kind of material to use.

Terra cotta offers the solution to this and many other of the problems which arise. It is probably the lightest building material, meeting all requirements, that can be obtained. Thus, at once, there is a saving in foundation work. Being of a lighter weight than most materials, less transportation charges are incurred than on other more solid and heavy building materials.

Another advantage of the light weight terra cotta (this material weighs about 65 lbs. to the cubic foot) as against stone (about 125 lbs. to the cubic foot) was noticeable in the San Francisco earthquake, where it was decidedly illustrated that, due to its lightness and method of anchorage to steel frames, terra cotta was better able to withstand the shock than any other building material.

The time element is always a most important factor in construction work and here terra cotta comes to the front. Most manufacturers, after the receipt of complete information, can make deliveries in from six to eight weeks, and can continue deliveries as fast as the material is needed.

Terra cotta, being made only four inches thick—on the average—makes thinner walls possible and consequently permits greater room space.

Color, texture and style must be considered in the erection of any important building. It is in the settlement of these three considerations that terra cotta stands pre-eminent.

Terra cotta gives the widest range and most liberal choice in the selection of color, texture and style, more so than any other building material obtainable.

Smooth or textured surfaces to match or to harmonize with plain cut stone, tooled surfaces to harmonize with or to have the apperance of stone, granite surfaces and color applications may be combined to produce granite effects, which are so like the original material that the casual observer, and often more careful critic, cannot distinguish the imitation from the natural stone.

Granite terra cotta, like many of the natural stones which bear this name, will not crumble away or be attacked by the weather or by acid-laden air, and in case of a conflagration, will be much less injured, as it has already been proved by fire, as well as being fireproof.

Matt and lustrous glazed terra cotta is serviceable where the building is of such a nature that surface cleanliness is desirable. Buildings of this type, when washed constantly, present a fresh and clean appearance.

An example of this, as well as the startling difference between the appearance of the terra cotta wall before and after cleaning, may be found in the Bulletin building, Philadelphia. Erected only eight years ago, its lines have been gradually hidden under a coat of dust and soot, which has settled on it. Thanks, however, to the forethought of its designers, it is an easy matter to restore the whole structure to its original spotless appearance by washing its glazed sides with soap and water, mixed with a little lye, in much the same manner that a housewife washes and rinses her dishes.

---

†From a series of articles written for Brick and Clay Record.
*Research Engineer, Abrasive Company of Philadelphia, and Consulting Ceramic Chemist and Engineer.

The dome on this building is done in white ornament with a light green background and has now been cleaned. It looks as bright and is as capable of presenting contrast as the day it was erected. The Bulletin building is very prominently located in the City Hall Square in Philadelphia. The terra cotta on this structure was furnished by the Conkling-Armstrong Terra Cotta Company of that city.

The introduction of polychrome or colors as desired may be resorted to where the style of architecture permits or demands it, or where the purpose for which the building is erected may be consistently displayed. In no other building material is there offered such latitude for choice of ornament as in terra cotta, especially when cost and results obtainable are compared.

The economy in reproduction enters in here and places ornamental terra cotta in a cost class of its own.

Besides the many advantages in the use of terra cotta enumerated thus far, is the ease with which contractor and architect can secure the material. All of the manufacturers of terra cotta employ trained draftsmen and they will carry out the architect's plan in detail, and often from rough sketches only work up the architect's drawings. In fact, some terra cotta manufacturers will not only design but will even erect buildings, thereby assuming nearly all of the responsibility with the added assurance to the owner that the manufacturer will place his material in the best possible manner and to the best advantage, resulting in their mutual benefit.

So much for the advantages of terra cotta as applied to exteriors.

Next comes light wells, and here large ashlar blocks of white glazed terra cotta make an ideal light-reflecting and sanitary building material. Elevator shafts with floor numbers in color are effective as well as satisfactory.

The swimming pool, scum gutters, balustrades, and such rooms as cafes and grills, may be executed in faience or polychrome terra cotta in permanent colors—colors that never have to be done over and which are easily cleaned and kept clean.

The patio of a residence may be executed in cream and matt terra cotta at one-tenth the cost of marble and if properly done, will be more beautiful than marble and present a softer and more pleasing appearance. Less formal entrance halls in apartments will lend themselves to permanent color treatment, and hard wear and hard usage will not affect a well-burned material.

We know of no other manufacturers of building materials so willing, so anxious and so well equipped to co-operate with architects, builders and owners in giving them what they want as are the manufacturers of terra cotta as a whole.

The New York Times of May 14, 1911, states that "terra cotta is the only building material that combines practical economy with architectural beauty," and further, in part, that "altogether it is apparent that the influence of terra cotta on architecture has been of considerable moment, and judging by the past few years, it seems that terra cotta will loom even larger actually and figuratively, on the architectural horizon of the future. Certainly, the architect can find no material more flexible, more easily modeled to his design. Nothing could be more durable. Its economy insures its use for a commercial building, and its dignity when properly employed, for the monumental. The fact that it is thoroughly tested by time and that improvement and development are steadily advancing, insure an ever-growing demand."

The above prediction, made six years ago, has proved true and terra cotta is now more largely and widely used than ever before. We venture to predict that the industry as such in this country is still in its infancy.

No Mysteries Left in Reinforced Concrete Construction

By D. E. A. CAMERON, Architectural Engineer

THE article entitled "Advantages and Disadvantages of Reinforced Concrete" by Percy J. Waldram, which appeared in your publication of February, 1917, is without doubt very unjust and far-fetched in its adverse criticism of reinforced concrete. Inasmuch as no reference was made to the status of the author, it is difficult to believe that it is such that his statements are to be given much weight. However, the lay reader is liable to give too much credulance to an article of this nature appearing in a well established publication, and as a result, reinforced concrete construction will suffer—at least from the natural skepticism resulting from the susceptibility of the lay mind to sarcastically clothed statements as made in the article referred to. I trust you may find space to publish the following excerpts from standard works on the subject of reinforced concrete with a few remarks whose authority is our eastern practice, and will at least tend to eradicate a part of the misconception of such a splendid structural material, caused by the article in question.

The reference to reinforced concrete—the combination of a metal to resist tensile stresses and concrete to resist compressive stresses—as an "ill-matched team" is most ridiculous to an engineering mind. A combination of conditions or materials in which each acts in its capacity of highest efficiency and produces an advantageous, economical and satisfactory result, is certainly to be lauded and appreciated. This is accomplished in reinforced concrete. To substantiate this, I shall present the following quotation from "Reinforced Concrete Construction," by G. A. Hool, Vol. 1, pages 26 and 27:

"The highest success in the use of concrete and steel in combination is attained only when maximum strength is secured at minimum cost. This is accomplished when the steel and concrete are placed in such a manner as to derive their greatest strength, and when economical proportions of these materials are employed.

"Steel can be put in a form to resist a given tensile stress much more cheaply than it can be put in form to resist a corresponding compressive stress. * * * Concrete, on the other hand, cannot be used in tension, except to a very limited extent, but its compressive strength is fairly high. It is also a good fireproof material and has great durability. * * *

"From the above considerations, it follows that reinforced concrete construction is advantageous to varying degrees in different types of structures. In structural forms subjected to both tension and compression, such as beams, the proper combination of the two materials meets with the best success. Steel rods embedded in the lower side of the beam carry the tensile stress, while the compressive stresses are carried by the concrete. Here, then, the steel is used in its chapest form and the whole structure may be made strong, economical and very durable. For columns, also, a combination of the two materials is quite advantageous, although to a varying degree, and in any case, not to such a large extent as beams."

Thus we find that the proper practice in the design of reinforced concrete gives us a willing, efficient, and economical team—a combination to be greatly desired.

But again, we read of the "intricate nature of the mathematics and formulas" involved, or supposed to be involved, and how it suffers from the incubus of tedious and intricate calculations. This criticism, while perfectly true, is decidedly unfair. All adjectives as indefinite in sense as those used are understood only when that which they are compared with is known. "Intricate" and "tedious" calculations in comparison with what? It is assumed that the author refers to those of wood and steel, since he has mentioned their superiority over reinforced concrete elsewhere in his article. To be sure, computations for the determination and design of structural timbers are more simple than for reinforced concrete, but how about steel? Has the author ever gone into the mathematics involved in the computation of the strength of an I beam, a channel, a Z bar or any other structural steel shape from the fundamentals of mechanics? Has he figured out the moment of inertia, radius of gyration or section modulus of a structural steel shape in order that he may know the strength and capacity of a member for which this shape was to be used? It is doubtful, for were it necessary to go through these computations, the computations and mathematics involved in reinforced concrete beams would be found comparatively simple. Structural steel shapes can, thanks to the steel companies, who, through their Pocket Companions, hand books, etc., have performed all these computations for us, be picked out quite readily from tables, which operation, even after investigating for web shear, etc., reduces to a very simple procedure in comparison with the complete computation otherwise necessary. Reinforced concrete computations reduce to a similarly simple procedure by the use of curves. This important feature of commercial design was brought out by Mr. Waldram, but he does not properly credit it with being the relief from the "intricate" and "tedious" computations. Curves of this nature have been employed in this vicinity as early as 1905 that I know of, and every office possesses a set which are as necessary as "Carnegie" or "Cambria" to its designers. However, there is a remedy superior to Mr. Waldram's suggestion of curves for the solution of reinforced concrete members. Hand-books which cover this branch of design as thoroughly as the steel hand-books are now available. Reference to the excellent work of Thomas and Nichols (McGraw-Hill), which is fresh from the press, will show that reinforced concrete design may be handled quite as simply as steel design.

But why should Mr. Waldram leave the estimating of advantages and disadvantages of reinforced concrete to surveyors? (I suppose the quantity surveyor of the type employed under the English system is referred to.) Does it not seem more logical that the statements of our foremost engineers in theory, design and construction should be accepted as the conditions upon which we should base our condemnation or approval? The "physical properties" and "conditions" essential to its proper production are known to us only through the results of laboratory and field tests. These tests and investigations are carried on by our foremost engineers, whose intimate knowledge of the materials in question undeniably fit them to be judges of the results. The surveyor could do no better than to repeat the decision of these men. Let us have our knowledge first hand. It would be a useless repetition to quote from these many authorities as to the relative advantages and disadvantages of reinforced concrete. I would refer the doubting Thomases to I. O. Baker's "Treatise on Masonry Construction," chapter 7; Turneaure and Maurer's "Principles of Reinforced Concrete Construction," chapter 1; F. E. Kidder's "Building Construction," Vol. 1, chapter 10. All declare that the disadvantages are greatly outweighed by the advantages and that the capabilities and capacities of reinforced concrete are definitely known and that it is admirably suited to its purpose in withstanding the imposed strains in foundations, columns, walls, etc. Taylor and Thompson in their work, "Concrete—Plain and Reinforced," which is fresh from the press and is without doubt the last word on the subject, say, "The theory of the design of reinforced concrete is definitely established. The action of combinations of steel and concrete in tension and compression and shear has been analyzed so that a thoroughly rational treatment is possible."

There are no mysteries left. All conditions have been met with convincing analysis and reinforced concrete becomes the obedient servant, of a knowing master.

* * *

Seattle Architect Wrongly Criticised

SOME time ago an article was published in the Seattle Municipal News criticising the new Court House in that city and the architect of the structure, Mr. A. Warren Gould. The Mayor of Seattle was quoted as condemning the absence of mail chutes and letter slots in the doors, blaming the architect for the alleged oversight. According to Mr. Gould, the criticism was just but wrongly placed. It appears that Mr. Gould was in no way to blame for the absence of these two essential features in the building, as the following letter would seem to indicate. We are very glad, indeed, to put Mr. Gould right in this matter before the architectural profession of the Coast:

Seattle, Wash.

Mr. Geo. B. Littlefield,
    Editor Seattle Municipal News,
        Seattle, Washington.
Dear Sir:

In the current issue of the News, I notice an article referring to the new Court House, which essays to criticise me as architect for some of the omissions in that building.

The Mayor is quoted as condemning the lack of mail chutes and letter slots in the doors. His criticism is just, but wrongly placed.

I endeavored to have these modern appliances, together with others, installed in the building, but they were ruled out by the Citizens' Committee, whose praises have been sounded for saving sixty-three thousand dollars ($63,000), at the expense of real necessities required, on the ground of economy.

As to the offices and arrangement of same, occupied by the various departments, they were decided upon at variance with my plans, and in most instances by the officials themselves; and the city office divisions were made by the City Architect, Huntington. Veritably, it is a case of "too many cooks spoil the broth."

But the public in general will find, if they desire the information, that I am on record in favor of the equipment, the lack of which is complained of, and that other things equally essential to a well-appointed building were eliminated from my plans and specifications on the advice of the Citizens' Committee, and, in my opinion, will have to be installed sooner or later, at much greater cost than would have been the case had they been provided as recommended.

I also wanted ventilation of all large offices, but was overruled by the Citizens' Committee.

Yours respectfully,

(Signed) A. WARREN GOULD.

* * *

$1,500,000 for New Construction Work in Honolulu

Mr. Louis C. Mullgardt, Chronicle building, San Francisco, recently returned from Honolulu, where he was commissioned to prepare plans by a group of capitalists and bankers for a new business center to comprise seven different buildings, all of fireproof construction, and ranging in size from two to five stories. All will be designed along monumental lines. There will be two banks, a store and office building and two other structures of a business character and probably a hotel. By June 1 all preliminary sketches will have been worked out. While in Honolulu Mr. Mullgardt was also commissioned to prepare plans for a splendid fireproof residence. The total cost of the work involved is in the neighborhood of $1,500,000.

CHURCH AND MONASTERY, SANTA CLARA, CALIFORNIA
MESSRS. MAGINNIS & WALSH, ARCHITECTS
ALBERT CAULDWELL, ASSOCIATE

Carmelite Monastery a Good Example of Spanish Renaissance with 16th Century Architecture

THE accompanying plate shows the architect's perspective of the new church and monastery of the Discalced Carmelite Nuns at Santa Clara. The edifice is now under construction from plans by Messrs. Maginnis & Walsh and Albert Cauldwell. The work is being supervised by the latter, he having come to San Francisco from New York, where for many years he was attached to the office of Mr. Bertram G. Goodhue, formerly of the firm of Cram, Goodhue & Ferguson.

In plan the church and monastery conform to the monastic traditions of the Carmelite Order. Roughly speaking the building is shaped like a hollow square with one side prolonged. This elongation is the nave of the public chapel, the sanctuary being within the quadrangle proper. Immediately behind the high altar is the nuns' choir, beyond this the chapter room. To the left of the high altar is the lady chapel and near the chapel entrance in the facade is the semi-detached octagonal chapel in memory of Alice Phelan Sullivan, the foundress of this monastery.

Around the courtyard at the ground level is a brick-paved and vaulted cloister; in the second floor there is an upper cloister with wooden posts and carved consoles of the Spanish type supporting the heavy overhanging roof. On the east side of the court are the nuns' choir and the chapter room, while in the south side is the convent proper. In the basement are the laundries, drying rooms and storerooms; on the first floor the kitchen, refectory, offices and the recreation room. Being an eremetical order the Carmelites have no community room. The second floor contains the novitiate and cells for the sisters.

From an architectural point of view the structure will be a perfect example of the Spanish Renaissance of the sixteenth century, the type in use during the lifetime of St. Teresa, the reformatrice of the Order. As it is well known the Gothic architecture of Spain was for the most part designed by foreigners, especially brought in for the purpose, mostly from France and the Low Countries, and as a whole Gothic was never thoroughly understood or practiced by the native Spanish. In consequence the traditions of Romanesque work, the precursor of Gothic, persisted not only up to the epoch of the Renaissance but many of them were preserved and incorporated in the work of the sixteenth and seventeenth centuries; in fact the Romanesque coloring is a distinctive feature of the later Spanish work. Thus in this chapel at Santa Clara many details absolutely medieval, such as the columns and arches of the nave and sanctuary, are found in juxtaposition with the ornament and forms characteristic of later periods.

The building is constructed of brick plastered on the outside with cement in a faint greyish rose color; the chapel and tower alone have a steel frame. The ornamental work of the chapel and convent entrance wing will be matt enameled terra cotta in the soft Tennesse shade of greyish pink such as enhances the new hospital of the University of California in San Francisco. There is no reinforced concrete work save in the tower and cloister floors, the architects and owners believing in utilizing the natural products of a clay-producing country. Even the firm erecting the building were chosen in virtue of their being experts in brick work and terra cotta.

It may not be amiss to indicate at this juncture that the monastery is not designed in this hackneyed and vulgar modern mission style, which seems to be associated so intimately with concrete in the minds of some architects.

Among the ornamental features of the building are the main entrance and belfry of the chapel, both inspired by prototypes at Avila, Spain, where lived Teresa de Jesus first as a religious in the Monastery of the Incarnation, a community following the mitigated rule, and later as the first prioress of St. Joseph's, the foundation house of the reform which she inaugurated, the discalced Order following the primitive observance. The belfry follows a type peculiar to the Order for many centuries.

The interior of the entire structure, as well as the exterior, is noteworthy for its extreme simplicity, in keeping with the austerity and asceticism of the community whose home it is.

The lighting fixtures of the chapel will be of hammered Spanish iron work touched with red, black and gold, a combination found in so many rejas in the Iberian cathedrals. The pavement, like that of the cloisters and outquarters, will be of brick laid in herringbone pattern; the sanctuary, Lady Chapel and Memorial having floors of foreign marbles. The seats will be rush bottomed chairs which will be stacked up at the sides of the chapel when not in actual requirement.

The whole structure represents a studied effort to avoid the commercialism and materialism of the present day, as exemplified in many of our churches, and to return to that phase of Christian idealism in architecture so well observed in the honest and frank work of the times of the early Renaissance. As of old bishops and clergy built for ages to come, so those responsible for this splendid structure have had the principles of honesty, durability and permanence constantly before them, and it will stand, a monument to their piety and foresight, for many years to come.

The Archdiocese is most fortunate in having in this building the services of the premier Catholic architects of America, men who, having broken away from the sordid and uninspired types unfortunately so prevalent in our midst, have finally made Catholic architecture recognized in this country and comparable with that done abroad. The total cost of the building, enclosure walls and improvement of grounds, is estimated at $250,000.

The general contractors for the monastery are the Larsen-Sampson Company of San Francisco, under whose efficient management the building has made rapid progress since the breaking of ground on the 15th of last November.

The terra cotta and roofing tiles are being fabricated by the Gladding, McBean Company; the plumbing is in the hands of J. E. O'Mara of San Francisco. The millwork is being supplied by the Pacific Manufacturing Company.

*   *   *

Novel Apartment House Planned by Woman Architect

A new apartment house, demonstrating the feminine idea of correct planning, has just been designed by Miss Josephine W. Chapman, architect. The sixteen-story structure is to be located on Park avenue, New York City, and many innovations are to be introduced.

The kitchens are to be in white porcelain and no flame of any kind is to be permitted, as it would tend to eventually soil the porcelain. Instead, electricity is to be used for cooking, for the running of a new type of refrigerator, for a dish washer, ironing, clothes washing machine, clothes wringer, vacuum cleaner, etc. The odors arising from cooking are to be disposed of by an electric ozonator. Electric conveniences are also to be provided for in the bathrooms and other rooms. Each apartment is to contain an open fireplace.

The center court is to be fixed up as a flower garden, with tea tables in summer and a glass enclosed cloister for all year round use. Apartments facing on inner courts are to have balconies. Individual vestibules from the elevator shaft are to replace the usual long hall.

BUILDING FOR THE NATIONAL CARBON CO., SAN FRANCISCO
Maurice C. Couchot, Constructing Engineer

Advanced Factory Building in the West

By MAURICE C. COUCHOT, C. E.

THE National Carbon Company of Cleveland, Ohio, with a branch in San Francisco at 755 Folsom street, is erecting a $400,000 building on its new location at the corner of Eighth and Brannan streets in San Francisco. This building is to be the most advanced factory in the West. The main building dimensions are 295 feet long by a depth of 120 feet. The building is a four-story and basement reinforced concrete structure, with a high tower enclosing the gravity tanks for the sprinkler system. There is also an annex of one story, 80 by 120 feet, to be used as a garage and mill. The plant will be equipped with the most modern conveniences for both men and women. There are four sets of stairs and four elevators, hot water and heating and ventilating system, the latter supplying an entire change of air throughout the building every thirty minutes. The roof will be used for the drill of autopeds, which this company is manufacturing at present.

The main offices will be situated on the fourth floor, and will have a complete system of intercommunicating telephones, pneumatic tubes, spiral chutes for handling material, dumb waiters, etc. All windows will be metal with wired glass.

The Acme system of flat slab reinforcing will be used throughout and all of the panels will be exactly equal, being 19 feet 6 inches square. A spur track at the back of the building will give quick freight connections to the factory.

This company intends to employ about 500 people in this new building which was designed by and is being built under the supervision of the writer.

Some Observations on Paint*

By A. J. CAPRON

PAINT! Thy name is legion! There was a beginning but there seems to be no end. What with honest and dishonest makers and painters, the row of the "Tribe of Paint" has been a hard one, both for the manufacturer and the "innocent bystander." The whole realm of the paint world has been exploited seemingly for mere gain, and the factory product has been sent to the four winds on its journey of war and peace—mostly war.

It is not improbable that less is known about real paint chemistry than any of the sciences with which the average engineer has to deal. It is marvelous why so important a subject has been allowed to roll along by itself all these years without legislation and with so little study given to its requirements. Costly buildings have been erected and then painted with any old thing, so long as it had a name, and ruined completely.

Paint chemistry is less understood than paint mechanics, and this brings me to the point of differentiating between the two kinds. By chemically prepared paint we mean where the ingredients have been brought together by chemical process. This operation requires some six months to complete, that is, effecting the changes which the ingredients undergo, when assembled, including the "curing"; while on the other hand, where the composition is simply dumped into a receptacle, stirred and is "ready" for the brush—this latter is known as a "mechanically prepared" product.

Chemists will inform you that ingredients entering into the composition of paint undergo changes, known as "chemical changes." They will also say that some of them have an affinity for each other, while some may act as "reagents." A druggist compounds his prescription by the rotating process, otherwise he might get a poisonous compound instead of a medicine, and the same argument will apply in making a true paint. The process, in most instances, is slow, as the ingredients of paint are not any too "active," and to thoroughly unite them requires time and considerable expense.

These "chemical changes" must take place either in the process of manufacture, or afterward, when the product is in service, as when applied to an exposed surface. If outside exposure, then fatal results will follow, and one has only to note the many failures—some so bad that it would be as much as the life of the manufacturer is worth for him to meet the owner.

The whole paint world seems to be judged by the failures and not by the successes which some, the best of the paints, have attained. Lead, oil and other pigments simply mixed together do not make paint any more than iron ore, reduced to billets and rolled into steel rails, make good rails. The best chemists obtainable are employed to see that the chemical composition of steel rails is such as will give the maximum of service required by the roads, and we may also say that cost does not enter entirely into the bargain either. If, then, so much care is necessary in the manufacture of rails, why not employ the same discrimination in the making of paint?

Mechanical mixtures of so-called paint do not unite the ingredients entering therein; witness field results where the vehicle has washed out, leaving the pigments without a "binder," and failure follows. Costly steel structures have been ruined by improper paint—the hidden rusting process is covered with a "coating," but not a preservative, and before the fault has been discovered the ruin is wrought. The vehicle is the weak link in the

*Written from the standpoint of a manufacturer's agent.

paint family; while the pigment is presumed to "protect" the vehicle, that which lasts the longest is the ingredient which commands our best attention. It follows, therefore, that the closer the vehicle and pigments are united the better the results. Any combination that drys hard, that is, hard to inelasticity, will not give permanent results.

Any paint may be a failure wherein the ingredients entering into their composition are not chemically united. It requires a perfect chemical union to make a "paint film"—one that will hold together on a section of steel, for instance.

This is not all; there is something aside from a mere "film," and that one thing is—a paint must unite with the metal if it is to religiously preserve and protect the steel. This will not be accomplished by mechanically mixed paints—the union must be a "chemical combination."

Again, if all the chemical changes have taken place in the factory, then there will be none in the field. A chemically prepared product will have the same co-efficient of expansion as the metal, and no cracking, scaling or peeling off will occur. True, time and weather will wear it off, but there will be no breaks or pin holes on the surface, and the preservation of the steel will be assured.

When paints have been properly prepared by the true process of manufacturing, the ingredients will be held in "suspension," and the last drop will be of the same consistency as the first, doing away with frequent stirring when being used, and assuring an even coat throughout the work. Such paints will cost somewhat more, but this is more than overcome in the wear. Two coats will last under average conditions from twelve to fifteen years, as against four to six of the poorer product. Moreover, one may get a covering capacity of approximately 1000 square feet to the gallon, as against four to four fifty of the other.

In addition to this, it has another valuable feature, one commending itself to the owner, viz.: chemically prepared paints are not easily adulterated by unscrupulous painters, who desire to "get over the work." Being chemically prepared, any "dope" that may be stirred in will easily be detected by natural difficulties, reasonably assuring the owner that the paint must be applied as taken from the package.

I might cover the subject of concrete paints, but will leave that for possibly another article.

* * *

Largest Movie Theatre on the Pacific Coast

PLANS are being completed by Messrs. Cunningham & Politeo, architects, with offices in the First National Bank building, San Francisco, for the largest moving picture theatre yet to be constructed on the Pacific Coast. The owner is the McCreery Estate Company, and the location the site of the old Central Theatre on the southeast corner of Eighth and Market streets. The theatre is to be unique in many ways. Its exterior has been designed in the style of modern art, the composition being on the principle of a triumphal arch. The execution is in multi-colored terra cotta. More than double the number of exit ways demanded by the building laws have been provided. The theatre is to be located in the center of the lot, which is 275 feet on Market street and 550 feet on Eighth street. The play house will have an entrance lobby 55 feet in width leading from Market street to a promenade foyer, 50 feet wide by 250 feet long.

The auditorium will have a seating capacity of 6000 persons on one floor only, there being no balconies. The proscenium arch will be 80 feet wide by 40 feet high, the exact size of the arch of the largest theatre in New York city. The seats have been arranged in the form of a fan, which makes the sight line and acoustics perfect. The interior of the theatre is to be highly ornamental in plaster decorations and fresco painting. The investment will represent an outlay close to $500,000.

* * *

Genezero or Jenisero

By C. H. WHITE*

THIS well known high-class cabinet wood comes principally from the west coast of Central America. In that section of the continent genezero forests are very plentiful and thrifty and the lumbering operations there produce extremely large-sized logs. The size of the timber admits of the manufacture of wide boards, which is a very great advantage in cutting the stock up into house trim.

The figure in genezero is very beautiful. The grain is a little larger and more pronounced than in mahogany, but on account of the texture of the wood it lends itself to a greater variety of stains and finishes. The wood itself is hard and durable and when finished natural has the neutral brown tones so much desired at the present time. When finished in one of the light gray shades now so popular it shows itself to be the most suitable of all hardwoods for this purpose. In price genezero is lower than quartered oak and, in addition to being less costly, it works up more economically on account of the great widths obtainable. Genezero stock panels are carried by the hardwood houses and are priced very economically.

At the present time the San Francisco hardwood yards are very well stocked with fine old dry genezero in all dimensions, and plenty of the thicker door veneers are also available.

Two famous examples of genezero interiors, put up soon after the fire, are the Fairmont hotel and the Monadnock building. These are finished with a very slight stain and are good examples of the durability and beauty of the wood. One of the newer examples of genezero interiors is J. R. Hanify's residence at Lombard and Vallejo streets, San Francisco. Reid Brothers are the architects of this handsome domicile, the millwork is by the California Mill Company, and the finish is in brown. The Whitcomb hotel on Market street, between Eighth and Ninth streets, San Francisco, is another of the latest examples of genezero trim for a large building. This building was used as the San Francisco City hall until the present magnificent structure was completed. Since the city vacated, the owners have reconstructed the interior, making the large edifice into a hotel, and they have used genezero throughout, even the furniture being made of this wood.

One of the most beautiful examples of genezero trim is the interior of the new Webster street branch of the Alameda National Bank in Alameda. In these fixtures the wood was finished a French gray and the strongly defined grain of the genezero softened by the gray stain makes a most pleasing and effective interior.

Mahogany, a much higher priced wood, has been plagued with imitations galore. Mahoganized birch, mahoganized gum, mahoganized laurel, Philippine mahogany, Polynesian mahogany, and many other woods have been substituted for mahogany; in fact, red stain applied to almost any wood causes it to pass with most people as mahogany. Genezero, however, has never been imitated. It is in a class by itself. Its distinctive grain and its smooth and durable surface are so entirely original that genezero remains inimitable and unapproachable.

*Manager of White Brothers, hardwood dealers, San Francisco.

Choosing an Architect

By ALFRED BUSSELLE

ASSUMING that the prospective builder has bought or decided upon his land, that he has taken into consideration the general questions of location, accessibility and social conditions which make the neighborhood desirable, and that the particular site chosen has favorable exposure, outlook, good water supply and drainage, he is now ready for the architect.

It may sometimes happen that the architect should be called in to help decide between two or more possible sites, when their suitability would depend on some study of the completed scheme—in such a case the client should go to the architect somewhat in this frame of mind:

"I want a house of such and such requirements and cost, and I want your best advice in regard to the general feasibility on this site, or these sites. As far as I know your work, and from what I hear, I think I should like you to design my house, but however this may be, I want this preliminary service now. I am willing to pay for it, but I do not want your work carried needlessly far so as to entail great expense, in case nothing comes of it. I am not shopping around to various architects, 'but giving you my whole confidence at the present time, and want you to treat me in the same spirit."

This attitude is by no means so common in architecture, although universal in medicine and law. Architects should not permit their profession to be less respected than these others; they should on the one hand understand the position of the sincere would-be client, and on the other they should positively refuse to furnish free sketches on the chance of getting a job. A moment's thought will show you that the man who is making this mad scramble for your work must, if he gets it, neglect it for the next mad scramble for other jobs.

One of the main objections to this practice is that the architect is necessarily in the wrong relation to his clients, he is spending time and money to "cinch the job," and must be, to say the least, as optimistic as possible in regard to the possibility of getting all that the client wants for what he is willing to pay. He is obviously not in a good position to delay that happy moment when the client will order him to proceed with the working drawings by offering much advice contrary to his patrons' preconceived ideas. A young architect may properly point to such work as he has had a real part in designing or carrying out, and must trust to his own personality for the rest.

I have a great deal of sympathy for the person who starts out to choose an architect, without any clue whatever. He sometimes feels that he must have his little free competition, which I have said is so improper, or else that he must stake his all on a more-or-less haphazard choice. He feels that he must not speak to any architect until he is ready to commit himself, so he sleuths through the magazines hoping to find some house he likes, and gives his work to the author of the best one he finds. That is not a bad way, but he need not fear to go into an architect's office, talk briefly with him, see what other work he has done, and if convenient see the work itself. Most previous clients, if thoroughly pleased, feel that they still owe a good word, and a glimpse of their houses, to others in the same position they once were themselves. Of course, a man should be chosen who has done the same general sort of work as that contemplated, but not necessarily any particular house which exactly or even approximately suits the new client. In fact, every architect knows that he has never done a house for one set of conditions which he would want to reproduce for another set, even if it were fair to do so. Occasionally a client recognizes this and chooses an architect from some piece of work which seems a good solution of some other fellow's problem, even though there is nothing about it which he wants himself. Both should bear in mind that the successful house is made by the architect and owner working sympathetically together. The man who boasts that he planned and designed his house and "simply had an architect draw it out for the builder," has a house that looks the part; likewise the architect should not belittle the help of his client who has enabled him to express his ideas in a creditable way.

There is still to be mentioned the choice of the architect by direct recommendation of a friend, and this is perhaps the safest way if the friend's problem has been in a general way similar to yours, as it takes in other matters than those of design, such as general efficiency, care in handling the work, and good business judgment on the financial side. This may be reinforced by the examination of other work. It is by this method that the architect is most proud to extend his practice.

The architect having been chosen by some one of these means, the requirements should be carefully stated to him as to number and uses of rooms and any special matters which have been thought of, also as clear an idea of the family life as possible.

Preference as to outside materials can generally be observed, the house being thought of from the start in terms of a material—brick, wood, stone, stucco, etc.—and take its shape accordingly.

Cost is almost always an important condition, and this should be frankly stated, neither less nor more, and with this in mind, a sharp difference should be made between the things that are essential and those merely desirable. The architect should advise his client, as nearly as he can, as to how much house he can expect, perhaps showing him drawings of other houses and telling their cost. He should be willing to make necessary changes at their net cost to him if the estimates require it, but should avoid making his employment conditional upon producing so many rooms of such a size for a given amount. The real protection the client has is the architect's experience and his willingness to use it truly.

Some people feel it necessary to prepare a rough sketch of their plan showing the general arrangement of the rooms. This practice I have found to be more of a hindrance than a help because one cannot tell where the real emphasis of the idea lies. Several times after puzzling over some important looking arrangement which, however, conflicted with other things more important, I have abandoned it in my sketch-plans, armed with reasons and apologies, only to be met with: "Oh, I didn't mean anything by that; it just seemed to work out that way."

In settling down to the design and plan (or rather, plan and design, for the plan comes first), the first important consideration is an accurate idea of the site. This should be gained by a visit if possible. If not, by a map, photographs, accurate description, any and all means which will give a correct mental picture. In the case of a suburban lot, the plan of the lot itself, approach, points of compass, and the immediate surroundings on adjoining lots may be sufficient, but designing for a rugged and picturesque site should be done on the ground itself in its main features, and the inspiration of the spot carried back to the office.

A guest-book at a certain country house bears a little piece of yellow paper about five inches square, with a plan of the house done on a rock in a broiling summer noon. The owner has enjoyed pointing out that the exact plan of that house appears on that sketch. That is the best way to plan.

As the sketch-plans are being prepared the architect will at the same time be thinking of the exterior, how his plan will take shape in the material, how it will compose as a whole in the style he has in mind, or perhaps what style will best compose with his plan, and other considerations of the site. It is impossible to separate the plan and the design in thought, but it should be unnecessary to sacrifice any important arrangement of plan in order to force some preconceived exterior.

The sketches are finally made and the working drawings are started. At this stage, as the specification is now imminent, the client will be asked to consider not only the suggested interior treatment of the rooms, but all practical matters which he will or will not think it worth while to pay for, such as vacuum cleaner, metal weather strips, ice machine, kind of heating plant, insulation of roof and walls, garbage receptacle, as well as the fittings in closets, kind of range, plumbing fixtures, etc. The architect should be able to advise on all such matters. Although the architect is not a builder, and cannot guarantee more than faithful supervision on a properly prepared specification, it is reasonable to expect him to know such things as how the building should be framed, how the fire-places should be built to draw, how big the flues should be, how the plumbing pipes should be arranged, how the activities of mice and rats should be frustrated, and many other things of a strictly practical nature.

The list of bidders who are to estimate on the work will probably be discussed, and this subject is of more importance than most people imagine. The idea has been prevalent (happily it is less so now) that it is only necessary to secure a bid which is very low by comparison with others, sign a contract binding the builder to complete the work by a certain date, and let the architect worry about the rest, convincing one's self that "that's what he's paid for." Now this matter is subject to the same human nature and needs the same business judgment as any other transaction of similar importance. Many owners would not spend a hundred dollars with anything like the reckless abandon with which they will agree to spend thousands on a contract with some inferior builder. It is not always possible to limit the bidding to the highest class of men; in fact, not always desirable. Neither is it necessary to place all bidders on the same footing, but it is necessary and fair to confine the bidding to those who will be considered on some basis or other. It is utterly unfair to allow any one to bid just to please him, with no intention of letting him do the work.

The architect may say something like this: "A. and B. are of the highest class; it costs them a little more to do their work and it would be worth while to pay a thousand dollars more for the lowest of those two over the others. C. has such and such faults which you must allow for because of his lower price, and do not imagine that I can get A.'s class of work out of C., for he is not equipped to furnish it. D. is slow, and if you can wait you will get a good job, but if you are in a hurry do not take him, for you would be fretting all the time at delays, in spite of all I can do. E. and F. I cannot recommend, and they should not bid." I have had many cases where a low-priced man has done a job very acceptable, because he did it the best he could, and other cases where the money saved was but poor economy. The fact is that by the time this stage is reached the architect should be on such terms with his client that he can advise him freely.

The decorations and furnishings of the interior, and the treatment of the grounds are also really inseparable from the architect's work. It is his province to create a home, not merely to put a house on a piece of land. Fortunately his place in that creation is being better understood and appreciated as time goes on.—Realty.

MR. ARTHUR BROWN, SR.

Death of Arthur Brown, Sr.

THE architectural and engineering professions will be grieved to learn of the death early in March of Mr. Arthur Brown, father of Arthur Brown, Jr., of the firm of Bakewell & Brown, architects of the new San Francisco city hall.

Arthur Brown, civil engineer, was born in Kentore, Scotland, in 1830. He gained his early experience in railroad work in New York, Pennsylvania and Missouri, coming to California in the early sixties. He entered the employ of the Central Pacific railroad as Superintendent of Bridge and Buildings Department, and remained in that capacity for thirty-five years. During his term with the Central and Southern Pacific companies he designed and executed a vast number of structures, including the snow-sheds and bridges of the Central Pacific railroad as far as Ogden, and later the bridges and structures of the Northern and Southern branches of Southern Pacific Company. Included in the work executed under his direction was the ferry-boat Solano, the Oakland Terminal station, the Sacramento and Los Angeles stations, and numerous other depots throughout the state; also a number of shops and roundhouses, the Hotel del Monte, and waterworks system for the Pacific Improvement Company, and power houses, etc., for the Market street cable system.

OAKLAND MOLE TERMINAL DEPOT

Mr. Brown took a very keen interest in his profession for its own sake, and gave his greatest care and thought to the theory and rational design of wooden bridges and roof trusses and other framed structures. While he was not primarily an architect, the beauty and good proportions of his engineering designs were a constant preoccupation.

*   *   *

Tribute to Ernest L. Ransome

ERNEST L. RANSOME, a pioneer of reinforced concrete construction, is dead. Mr. Ransome was well known as an inventor of concrete machinery, the Ransome mixer being familiar to builders all over the United States. The editor of Engineering and Contracting pays Mr. Ransome the following tribute:

Mr. Ransome's mind was always active upon some improvement or some new device, yet, unlike many inventors, he did not cease his labors on an invention before it was fully developed. He was exceedingly practical and painstaking. But the necessity of carrying on his business often left him with but few hours to devote to inventive work.

Mr. Ransome was a man who took the kindliest and most gracious interest in those about him. No person could see him often without feeling both a profound respect for his ability and a great liking for his character. He was modesty personified as to his achievements, and told how each invention had "evolved" in such a simple, matter-of-fact way that it seemed as if almost anyone might have "evolved" it. But, as some one remarked, the ease with which a powerful and skilled intellect works is the most deceptive ease in the world, as speedily becomes apparent when a weak and untrained mind attacks the same sort of a problem.

Mr. Ransome's father, Frederick Ransome, had also been an inventor, and had patented an artificial stone in 1844. The early training under his father, coupled with his inherited originality, made Mr. Ransome eager to follow a career as an inventor.

It is related of Mr. Ransome that many years ago, when an architect in San Francisco wished to find a cheaper sidewalk "roof" for a basement than one made of steel I-beams and brick arches, Mr. Ransome's advice was asked. Within a few hours Mr. Ransome had solved the problem, and in a characteristically novel fashion. For brick arches he substituted a concrete slab, and for steel I-beams he substituted steel rods bedded in the concrete. But, as he said, he feared that under the tension of a load the rods would slip in the concrete; so his first idea was to thread the ends of the rods and put nuts on the ends. Then it flashed upon him that he could make the entire rod into a "threaded rod" and the entire concrete into a huge "nut" threaded thereon. Forthwith he took a rod of rectangular section and twisted it in a lathe, making what afterward became famous as the "Ransome twisted bar reinforcement."

The first reinforced concrete slab was made, and a new era of building construction was initiated. Nor was Mr. Ransome slow in perceiving the economic possibilities that now presented themselves. He began to design and erect reinforced concrete bridges and buildings, improving steadily in his designs of details, and coincidentally in his methods of manufacturnig and placing concrete. His "non-tilting batch mixer"—a device of extreme simplicity—was first designed for his own contract work, and later put upon the market. His tower and hoisting bucket for building work was a still later step, and then came his system of chuting concrete from the tower into the forms.

* * *

Hardwall Plaster Noted for Its Strength and Durability

By R. B. KNOX

THE best hardwall plasters are made by calcining gypsum rock, during which process about 75 per cent of the moisture content is driven off.

This basic product, generally termed "Plaster of Paris," forms a plastic mass by the addition of water, and upon setting, or crystallizing, unites chemically with the same amount of water driven off during calcination, and upon application to the wall reverts back to its original rock state.

Gypsum or hardwall plaster has almost entirely supplanted lime for plastering purposes. A lime mortar wall requires months and often years to attain its full strength and to harden throughout, and unless properly hydrated and applied never develops the strength necessary for durability. During this period of hardening, lime mortar gives off water in exchange for the carbon gases absorbed from the air, and until it is entirely hardened throughout the building is damp and unsanitary.

This condition is entirely impossible with gypsum hardwall plaster. It sets up uniformly hard and homogeneously within about two to three hours after application, and inside of thirty-six hours the walls are dry, with no further possibility of dampness or sweating, so common with lime mortars, and the building is immediately habitable from a hygienic standpoint.

The outstanding features of hardwall plaster, in addition to the foregoing, are its fire resistant qualities, the strength and durability of the finished wall, which effectively withstands the wear and tear of occupancy, and its hardness and density, which resist the inroads of vermin and prevent leakage from defective pipes and roofs.

One of the chief arguments advanced by the opponents of hardwall plaster is the claim that it tends to rust and corrode metal lath. Aside from the fact that actual use in numberless buildings has amply proved the contrary, the Underwriters' Laboratories, Inc., of Chicago, have conducted tests along these lines with very interesting results. About four years ago a panel of metal studs was made up with an uncoated special iron lath. This was plastered in the usual manner with a scratch, brown and finish coat all of hardwall gypsum plaster. The back was exposed, and the panel kept in a damp sub-basement. After two years the panel was broken up and critically examined under a magnifying glass, with the following result of the observation: The metal, where not covered with plaster, was considerably corroded and the corrosion was evidently progressive. There was less corrosion on the metal whère thinly covered with plaster, and only slight initial corrosioh, which had not progressed, was found on the metal wherever it was completely imbedded in the plaster. The plaster in which the metal lath was completely imbedded fully protected the metal against the access of damp air, which is the principal corroding agency.

* * *

War Will Not Cause Building Slump on Pacific Coast

Bankers say there will be no tightening of the loan market on account of war with Germany, at least not on the Pacific Coast. This part of the country is too far away from the seat of conflict to interfere seriously with business conditions, the financial men say. Architects and others dependent upon the building industry will find encouragement in these words, especially those of the pessimistic class who could see only doom ahead when the war clouds thickened. San Francisco, Los Angeles and all the large cities in California and on the Coast will go right on building. Money will be loaned at a better rate of interest than two years ago, on all legitimate building projects. The only thing that may lessen the volume of new construction work will be the advances in cost of materials. But the increase here has been no greater than for wearing apparel and foodstuff.

There are many big projects to be carried out in San Francisco and vicinity this year and for which money already is available. One of the largest will be the construction of immense wharfs and docks at Dumbarton Point, plans for which have been prepared by Architect H. M. Banfield, 36 Essex street, San Francisco. The promoters of this $3,000,000 project have incorporated as the Pacific Terminal Company. Besides this enterprise, the new California State building will be erected in the San Francisco Civic Center at a cost of $1,000,000. Other big projects include the expenditure of several million dollars by the Union Iron Works for a new ship building plant, the erection of an immense warehouse in Oakland by Libby, McNeil & Libby, and the building of a municipal water works in Marin county at an outlay of $1,500,000.

* * *

State Realty Federation Elects Officers

The California State Realty Federation has elected the following officers for 1917:

President, W. L. Atkinson, San Jose; vice-president, Benjamin F. Wright, Monterey; second vice-president, W. W. Mines, Los Angeles; third vice-president, S. G. Buckbee, San Francisco; secretary-treasurer, Fred E. Reed, Oakland.

Directors—W. H. Akin, Los Angeles; W. L. Atkinson, San Jose; C. P. Austin, Santa Barbara; Geo. W. Austin, Oakland; S. G. Buckbee, San Francisco; D. W. Carmichael, Sacramento; W. G. Cockrane, Fresno; Francis Cutting, Stockton; C. C. Juster, Berkeley; A. F. Kern, Tulare; Mabry McMahan, San Francisco; W. W. Mines, Los Angeles; J. P. Pryor, Pacific Grove; Fred E. Reed, Oakland; C. C. C. Tatum, Los Angeles; W. C. Thompson, Napa; H. S. Wanzer, Sacramento; J. R. Wilson, Vallejo; Geo. J. Wren, Modesto; Benjamin F. Wright, Monterey; Alexander Young, Tulare.

THE

Architect and Engineer

OF CALIFORNIA

Founded in 1905 by E. M. C. WHITNEY

A. I. WHITNEY	Manager
T. C. KIERULFF	Legal Points
FREDERICK W. JONES	Editor

Published Monthly in the Interests of the Architects, Structural Engineers, Contractors and the Allied Trades of the Pacific Coast by the Architect and Engineer.

BUSINESS OFFICE AND EDITORIAL ROOMS
627-629 Foxcroft Building, San Francisco
Telephone Douglas 1828

The publishers disclaim any responsibility for statements made in the advertisements of this magazine.

TERMS OF SUBSCRIPTION
(Including postage) to all parts of the United States $1.50 per annum ; to Canada 50c additional ; to all Foreign points $1 additional.

VOL. XLIX.   APRIL, 1917   No. 1

Architects and builders are coming to realize that misplaced taxes **MISPLACED TAXES** stand in the way **HURT BUILDING** of normal building **INDUSTRY** development. It will be worthwhile to sum up briefly the reasons which make this fact of prime importance to all who are engaged in the building professions and trades.

First let us consider the demand for buildings and sites. It may be taken for granted that the average man desires a home of his own— usually also at least a little ground for the children to play on. Every home creates a demand for household necessities—food, clothing and the comforts of life. Thus arises a demand for farms and factories to supply these things, and stores through which to market them.

With the growth of towns and cities comes an increased demand for office buildings, churches, schools, power stations and every other kind of structure which gives employment to architects, builders and mechanics.

It goes without saying that all buildings must have sites. The cost of building is high enough, and when the cost of a site is too high the chances are that building plans will be postponed or abandoned.

The more heavily buildings are taxed, the more difficult it becomes to secure sites at a reasonable price, because owners often expect more profit from holding them. As a matter of fact, interest and taxes usually eat up the expected increase; otherwise everyone would be tempted to engage in holding land unimproved to the exclusion of other business, and disaster would speedily result. But, strange to say, enough people are ignorant of this truth to keep building development at a low level.

The natural course would be to use for public revenue the values which grow up with the growth of every community. This always suffices to meet any public expense short of extravagance, and entirely relieves buildings, household furniture and other personal property from needing to be taxed.

The transition from old methods to this modern plan of assessment has to be moderately rapid, in order to offset inflation of land prices, as the demand for buildings is greatly stimulated by relieving them of taxation. Houston, Texas, increased its building operations fifty per cent in two years by this plan, which has been followed in numerous other cities and is especially popular in Canada.

Equally effective would be the same principle applied ·to iron mines, stone quarries, brick clay deposits and other sources of structural materials.

Another factor not to be overlooked is labor cost. Any measure tending to make the home environment of laborers more pleasant, as the house-and-garden plan does; to reduce living costs by productive use of farm land now idle; and to increase opportunities for young blood by encouraging the development of our vast ·natural resources, would go far toward solving the labor problem and easing the builder's mind of many worries.

It must appear obvious to everyone who seeks capital for building purposes that the transfer of taxes suggested would make such funds more readily available. It will be easy, to persuade oneself that the idea deserves wider attention and should be encouraged by individual and organized influence. Our public councils would do well to adopt it as the foundation of their finances, with a view to the most favorable growth of the communities entrusted to their care.

"Despite the vast volume of war orders, it is my belief, based upon **AFTER WAR** a two months' inti- **ORDERS CEASE,** mate and first-hand **—THEN WHAT?** study of the industrial and agricultural areas of France, that the reconstruction period after the war will make a call upon American industries that will tax all of our resources and lead to a reciprocal trade that will be markedly larger and infinitely more enduring than the mushroom trade of the 'past two years," declares Noble Foster Hoggson, president of Hoggson Brothers, the New York builders.

Mr. Hoggson bases his conclusions on information he obtained while a member of the American Industrial Commission, which last Fall made a survey of the devastated region of France.

According to Mr. Hoggson, some of the materials and equipment which France will need when the war comes to an end are ·rolled steel for quick construction; sanitary and plumbing fixtures; concrete-mixing and concrete-block machinery; stock factory sashes and doors; wire glass; factory lighting fixtures; cranes, carrying belts and conveyors; elevators and lifts; pneumatic riveters; metal furniture and lockers; standard factory hardware, automatic sprinklers; farm equipment; labor-saving machinery of practically every kind; modern factory structures; and hotel equipment.

In discussing the opportunity for American farm machinery, buildings and equipment, Mr. Hoggson said:

"Contrary to the usual belief, France has not been an industrial nation. It is distinctly a land of farms. Yet because of peculiar local conditions, it has not heretofore furnished a market for farm machinery.

"Now, however, out of the 5,500,-000 farms in the country, 85,000 are at present the market for American implements and machinery. Factories throughout France are engaged in making ammunition and other war material, so the manufacture of even such farm implements as were previously produced has ceased. The demand for American made machinery will therefore, at the close of the war, be of permanent importance both to this country and the people of France.

"But it is in its industrial reorganization that France needs American co-operation more urgently, and it is here that the greatest chance for the American manufacturer lies. Under normal conditions, the demand for modern American machinery would be slight. As a result of its lack of modern machinery, its business in different centers has been dropping off during the past few decades. With modern methods and modern labor-saving machinery, it is probable that France might have held a large part of this lost trade. The war has awakened France to this need which has become so strikingly manifest.

"The war has made France conscious of her industrial needs, and has created an infinitely greater demand for labor-saving machinery than would have prevailed under normal conditions of peace.

"With the need of labor-saving machines comes the even more immediate want of modern structures in which to house them. This need it not merely a need of the future; it is felt poignantly right now. Temporary houses are wanted immediately while the more permanent ones are being erected.

"Lumber is needed right now and needed in great quantities. There is a demand for plumbing and sanitary fixtures. After the war there will be a vast amount of construction to be done both in France and Belgium."

American Institute of Architects

(ORGANIZED 1857)

OFFICERS FOR 1916-17

PRESIDENT.....JOHN LAWRENCE MAURAN, St. Louis
FIRST VICE-PRESIDENT......C. GRANT LA FARGE, New York
SECOND VICE-PRESIDENT....W. R. B. WILLCOX, Seattle, Wash.
SECRETARY:...W. STANLEY PARKER, Boston, Mass.
TREASURER.........D. EVERETT WAID, New York

San Francisco Chapter

PRESIDENT...................EDGAR A. MATHEWS
VICE-PRESIDENT..........SYLVAIN SCHNAITTACHER
SECRETARY AND TREASURER........MORRIS BRUCE
TRUSTEES.......................{ W. B. FAVILLE
                                { G. A. WRIGHT

Southern California Chapter

PRESIDENT..................J. E. ALLISON
VICE-PRESIDENT.................J. J. BACKUS
SECRETARY ....A. R. WALKER

TREASURER...............AUGUST WACKERBARTH
Board of Directors
ROBT. D. FARQUHAR   PERCY A. EISEN
S. B. MARSTON

Portland, Ore., Chapter

PRESIDENT...............JOSEPH JACOBBERGER
VICE-PRESIDENT.................J. A. FOUILHOUX
SECRETARY....................W. C. KNIGHTON
TREASURER.....................FOLGER JOHNSON
TRUSTEES.................{ ION LEWIS
                         { M. H. WHITEHOUSE

Washington State Chapter

PRESIDENT.............CHARLES H. BEBB, Seattle
1ST VICE-PRES....DANIEL R. HUNTINGTON, Seattle
2D VICE-PRESIDENT....GEORGE GOVE, Tacoma
3D VICE-PRESIDENT.........L. L. RAND, Spokane
SECRETARY..............JOSEPH S. COTE, Seattle
TREASURER.............ELLSWORTH STOREY, Seattle
                      { JAMES STEPHEN, Seattle
COUNCIL............... { JAMES H. SCHACK, Seattle
                      { CHARLES H. ALDEN, Seattle

California State Board of Architecture

NORTHERN DISTRICT.

PRESIDENT.................EDGAR A. MATHEWS
SECRETARY-TREASURER.....SYLVAIN SCHNAITTACHER
Members
JOHN BAKEWELL, JR.   J. CATHER NEWSOM

SOUTHERN DISTRICT.

PRESIDENT...................JOHN P. KREMPEL
SECRETARY-TREASURER........FRED H. ROEHRIG
                          { OCTAVIUS MORGAN
MEMBERS................... { SUMNER P. HUNT
                          { WM. S. HEBBARD

San Francisco Architectural Club

OFFICERS FOR 1917

PRESIDENT ....CHAS. PETER WEEKS
VICE-PRESIDENT ....A. WILLIAMS
SECRETARY ....JOHN F. BEUTTLER
TREASURER ....WILLIAM HELM

San Francisco Society of Architects

PRESIDENT...............CHARLES PETER WEEKS
VICE-PRESIDENT..........GEORGE W. KELHAM
SECRETARY AND TREASURER.....WARREN C. PERRY
                        { ERNEST COXHEAD
DIRECTORS.............. { FREDERICK H. MEYER

Engineers and Architects Association of Los Angeles

PRESIDENT................A. H. KOEBIG, SR.
FIRST VICE-PRESIDENT..............A. S. BENT
SECOND VICE-PRESIDENT..........IRA J. FRANCIS
Directors
J. J. BACKUS, GEO. P. ROBINSON, ALBERT C. MARTIN, H. L. SMITH

Washington State Society of Architects

PRESIDENT..................A. WARREN GOULD
SECRETARY......................WM. J. JONES
TREASURER..................J. L. MCCAULEY
                        { HARRY H. JAMES
                        { WM. J. JONES
TRUSTEES................ { ALFRED BREITUNG
                        { J. L. MCCAULEY
                        { G. F. ROWE

San Diego Architectural Association

PRESIDENT..................CHARLES CRESSEY
VICE-PRESIDENT.........W. TEMPLETON JOHNSON
SECRETARY..................ROBT. HALLEY, JR.
TREASURER..................G. A. HAUSSEN

San Joaquin Valley Ass'n of Architects

PRESIDENT....................W. I. WRIGHT
VICE-PRESIDENT.................E. B. BROWN
SECRETARY-TREASURER..........FRANK V. MAYO

With the Architects

Building Reports and Personal Mention of Interest to the Profession

ANNUAL HOUSE NUMBER

The annual House Number of The Architect and Engineer is in course of preparation and will be an issue of exceptional interest and merit. Leading architects of the Coast will contribute, the range of illustrations covering the country house, city home and suburban bungalow. Special articles on city planning, landscape gardening and interior decoration will also appear in this number.

High Recognition for Mr. Kaiser

Mr. Charles S. Kaiser, architect, with offices in the Mechanics Institute building, San Francisco, has been advised that a dissertation on "School Building Finance," relating chiefly to school bonds, recently prepared by him, has been accepted for publication by the Houghton Manufacturing Co. of Boston to form part of a forthcoming textbook on school buildings. Professor Elwood P. Cubberley, head of the Department of Education at Stanford University, is the editor of the volume.

Alameda Bank Building

Plans are being prepared by Messrs. Edward T. Foulkes and E. H. Hildebrand, Crocker building, San Francisco, for a two-story Class C bank building, to be erected in Alameda. The name of the bank is withheld until such time as the site is definitely determined upon. There have been rumors that the Alameda National Bank and Alameda Savings Bank would build a branch institution in the West End.

Y. W. C. A. Building

Working plans for a six-story Class A building for the San Francisco Y. W. C. A, to be erected on Sutter street adjoining the Woman's Athletic Club, are being completed by Mr. Lewis P. Hobart, Crocker building.

Will Build Two Residences

Messrs. Austin & Sanford, Hearst building, San Francisco, have completed plans for two large residences.

A Couple of Good Polk Stories

Mr. Willis Polk tells this one on himself, so it must be true. Willis has in his office a right-hand man, a secretary-manager, or, as Willis calls him, "a trained soldier," called Kinne. Kinne is the only man who chides Willis in the way Willis likes to be chided for his shortcomings. "He plucks the pin feathers out of me, and I respect him for it," says Willis. Willis leans heavily on Kinne, so heavily that when anything of importance comes up in the course of business, Willis' first remark is, "Ask Kinne." This formula has become second nature with Willis. The architect was at the recent subscription ball, and when a lady said to him: "How is Mrs. Polk?" Willis replied without thinking: "Ask Kinne." The lady's look of surprise brought Willis to, and he explained elaborately.—Town Talk.

* * *

The other Sunday the San Francisco Examiner published a forecast of building news in various architects' offices. "Willis Polk Leads," read the heading.

"Who's second?" asked Clarence Ward in calling Polk's attention to the article Monday morning.

"Why, Willis Polk's staff, of course," replied Polk dryly.

Bank Buildings

Mr. R. F. Felchin, Rowell building, Fresno, has been commissioned to prepare plans for an eight-story Class A bank and office building for the Bank of Italy, Fresno branch. Mr. Will T. Shea of San Francisco, who attends to the architectural work of the Bank of Italy in San Francisco, will act as consulting architect. The building will probably cost $250,000.

At Eureka two bank buildings are planned. One will be erected by Lindgren company of San Francisco and the other is being designed by Mr. G. A. Applegarth of San Francisco and Mr. Fay Spangler of Eureka. The last named will be a five-story building for the Bank of Eureka.

Sketches for Apartment House

Miss Grace Jewett, Holbrook building, San Francisco, is preparing preliminary sketches for a frame apartment house.

Architects' Registration Law

The proposed architects' registration law is still pending before the Washington Legislature. Considerable discussion of the measure has taken place since its introduction and a number of amendments have been offered. The bill does not presume to legislate anyone out of business and would not preclude anyone from practicing who can and will show that he is qualified by passing such examination as the state board of examiners may deem necessary to prove such qualifications. In other words, only those who are entitled through experience and training to call themselves architects shall be permitted use of the title on plans, stationery or other mediums. If such a law can be passed without leaving it open to the curse of political manipulation, the public will be protected and benefited, while the professional title will no longer be subject to abuse

Many Houses Planned

Many new houses are being planned for the Thousand Oaks district, near Berkeley. Mr. Noble Newsom has prepared plans for several $3,000 bungalows which the George Friend Co. will build on Solano avenue in Thousand Oaks. Frank Spring will build fifteen bungalows, costing $3,000 each, in the same section, and E. B. Spitler will erect four residences on Solano avenue Terrace and ten houses in Thousand Oaks. Chas. Mason will build ten houses on Colusa street, Thousand Oaks, ranging in cost from $5,000 to $8,000. E. I. Krosca will build seven houses in Thousand Oaks, all with cement exteriors and costing about $4,000 each.

Falch & Knoll Busy

Messrs. Falch & Knoll, Hearst building, San Francisco, report much work on hand. Besides designing a number of new residences for St. Francis Wood and Forest Hill, they have prepared plans for an apartment house of five stories and basement to be erected on Geary street, west of Leavenworth, for Mr. 'A. Rulfs, at an estimated cost of $80,000. They also have prepared plans for a one-story and mezzanine floor automobile sales and store building to be erected at the gore of Broadway and Piedmont avenue, Oakland, for Mr. C. A. Iceberger. The latter building will cost approximately $75,000.

Fresno Auditorium

Plans by Mr. Ernest J. Kump, Rowell building, Fresno, for a new auditorium to cost about $12,000 for the Edison school, have been completed and approved by the Board of Education.

Ten-Story Building

Plans have been completed by Messrs. Reid Bros., California-Pacific building, San Francisco, for a ten-story Class A office building, to be erected at Market and Main streets, San Francisco, for the Matson Navigation Company. This will be in close proximity to the new Southern Pacific building and will help to make lower Market street a very lively district. The new structure will represent an outlay of close to $500,000.

Market Building for Richmond District

Messrs. Fabre & Bearwald, Merchants National Bank building, San Francisco, have completed plans for a one-story reinforced concrete market building at Sixth avenue and B street, Richmond District, San Francisco, for the Lackmann Grocery Company. The same firm has let contracts for altering a frame flat building at 1850-4 Sacramento street, property of B. Siersty, into modern apartments.

Mr. George Sperry to Build

The country place of Mr. and Mrs. George Sperry at Redwood City will be rebuilt from plans by Mr. Charles Peter Weeks of Weeks & Day, Phelan building, San Francisco. The house will have a stucco exterior with a superstructure of either hollow tile or wood. There will be a patio and numerous sun porches.

Addition to Piedmont Town Hall

Mr. Albert Farr has prepared plans for a $7,000 addition to the Piedmont Town Hall. Mr. Farr also has made plans for a $5,000 home for Mr. Henry Hansen at San Rafael. In the same city Frank Anderson of the Bank of California, San Francisco, will erect a $7,500 house from Mr. Farr's plans.

Apartment House for Stanford

Julius Krafft & Sons, Phelan building, San Francisco, have prepared plans and taken figures for the construction of a three-story frame apartment house on the Stanford University campus, Palo Alto. The building will contain twenty-six apartments and will be owned and managed by Mrs. Burt Estes Howard. The estimated cost is $30,000.

Two Oakland Buildings

Mr. F. D. Voorhees, Central Bank building, Oakland, is preparing plans for a one-story Class C garage to be erected on Broadway, near Twenty-sixth street, for Mr. Jules Abrahamson. Mr. Voorhees is also designing a one-story building to front on Broadway, Oakland.

A Striking Face Brick

Many favorable comments are heard concerning the beautiful face brick being used on the new Southern Pacific office building under construction in San Francisco. The bricks are a soft salmon pink and were turned out by Gladding, McBean & Co. As the architectural lines of the big structure are developed the treatment reminds one not a little of the Gorham building in New York City, by McKim, Mead & White.

The new Southern Pacific building, when completed, will be the largest office structure of its kind west of Chicago.

It will house the San Francisco general offices of the railroad. It will require 20,000 cubic yards of concrete, equal to eighty cars of cement. The building will weigh, when completed, 55,000 tons, the steel averaging 3,500 tons and the piling 6,600 tons.

A Hotel with 2600 Baths

The largest and most costly hotel building in the world is being erected in New York City by the Pennsylvania Railroad interests. It is located in the block on Seventh avenue, just opposite the Pennsylvania depot, and on completion will comprise rooms and suites priced to suit the millionaire or the guest whose tastes demand only a modest service and furnishing. Some idea of the magnitude of this building may be gained from the fact that 2800 Royal flush valves, manufactured by the Sloan Valve Company, are being installed. There will be about 2600 private baths in the house.

New Hotel for Colorado Springs

Plans for a unique yet utilitarian structure in pink and gray, designed after some of the famous hotels of Europe, have been accepted by the Broadmoor Hotel Company for its new hotel in Colorado Springs, Colo. That city is one of the famous summer resorts and industrial centers on the Santa Fe Railway. The new hotel will be completed for the 1918 season.

Class A Theater for Lodi

Messrs. Stark & Hodges of the Tokay Theater at Lodi have purchased a lot on South Lodi street, 50x160 feet, next to the Hotel Lodi. The owners will erect a Class A theater.

Fire House for Fresno

The Fresno City Council will receive competitive plans from architects for a two-story fire station building to replace station No. 2 on Van Ness avenue. It will cost about $15,000.

Stockton Society of Architects

Several important committees were appointed by President Wright at the last meeting of the San Joaquin Valley Architects' Association.

Mr. Joseph Losekann reported to the architects that so much interest had been shown in the proposed building ordinance for the city that the council had ordered sixty copies made for the use of those caring to study them. G. McM. Ross addressed the association and congratulated the members upon their work for the public welfare.

Messrs. Frank Mayo, Louis Stone and W. B. Thomas were appointed a committee to make a programme and arrange for a competition for plans for a civic center in Stockton.

Messrs. J. Losekann, E. B. Brown and Peter Sala were appointed to make arrangements for an architectural exhibition there some time during the year.

A public welfare committee was created by the president. He named Messrs. J. Losekann, W. B. Thomas and Charles Young. This committee will have as its duty the inspection of all buildings constructed in the city to see that they do not conflict with the building ordinance.

Messrs. Peter Sala, C. Ryland and Louis Stone will compose the committee to draw up rules and regulations to guide the local architects in their competitions for work.

A publicity committee, whose duty it will be to keep the public informed of what the architects are doing and of matters pertaining to public welfare along building lines, was named in the persons of Messrs. Frank Warner, J. Losekann and Peter Sala.

Palo Alto Residence

Mr. John K. Branner has completed plans and specifications for a one-story frame and plaster residence and garage to be erected by Dewar & Son for Mr. Payson J. Treat at Palo Alto. The interior is to be finished in white cedar and hardwood floors and white enamel. A feature will be a 40-foot living-room and large open fireplace. A hot air heating system will be installed. The building will cost about $10,000.

Death of Mr. Jules Godart

Mr. Jules Godart, one of the old-time architects of San Francisco, died March 18th, aged 75 years. Mr. Godart was one of the most distinguished of the ante-earthquake architects—was the architect of the Metropolitan Temple on Fifth street, the Windsor hotel at Fifth and Market streets, the Alameda County Hall of Records in Oakland, and many other buildings in San Francisco and Portland.

Personal

Mr. George B. Sturgeon, for ten years construction engineer at the University of California, is now in southern California in charge of the construction of an irrigation system in recently opened tracts of farming land.

* * *

Mrs. Vera I. Felt of Salt Lake City, Utah, has been appointed chief draftsman in the United States Surveyor General's office. She is the first woman to hold the position.

* * *

The Associated Engineers, heretofore united only for the purpose of designing a San Francisco-Oakland bridge, announce that they have organized as the Watson Davis Miller Company and will hereafter jointly conduct a general consulting, designing and inspecting engineering business with offices in Cleveland, Ohio; Albany, N. Y., and Merchants Exchange building, San Francisco. The personnel of the firm comprises Messrs. Wilbur J. Watson, William R. Davis and Harlan Miller.

* * *

Mr. Alfred F. Rosenheim has moved his offices from the Herman W. Hellman building to 1121 Van Nuys building, Los Angeles. Mr. Rosenheim was the architect for the Hellman building and had maintained his office there since the structure was completed.

* * *

Among the distinguished visitors to the office of The Architect and Engineer the past month was Mr. Tachu Naitoun, professor of architecture in the University of Waseda, Tokyo, Japan. Mr. Naitoun complimented the publishers and asked that his name be entered as a regular subscriber to this magazine.

Another State Building Competition

A programme has been prepared and architects of the State shortly will be invited to submit plans in a competition for two new Capitol extension buildings to be erected in Sacramento. The competition will be conducted in two stages, in accordance with a programme approved by the American Institute of Architects. There will be two stages—the first stage to be open to all qualified architects in California; the second stage to be participated in by eight architects selected in the first stage. Bonds amounting to $3,000,000 have been voted for the buildings.

Washington State Society of Architects

President, A. Warren Gould; secretary, Wm. J. Jones; treasurer, J. L. McCauley; trustees, Harry H. James, Wm. J. Jones, Alfred Breitung, J. L. McCauley and G. F. Rowe.

Rousseau & Rousseau Busy

Messrs. Rousseau & Rousseau, 110 Sutter street, San Francisco, report that they have completed plans for two four-story brick apartment buildings to be erected on Hyde street, between Post and Geary streets.

The same architects report that they are preparing plans for a three-story and basement frame apartment building to be erected on the southwest corner of Washington and Leavenworth streets. This building will contain eighteen apartments of three rooms each.

The same firm also announce that they are preparing plans for three beautiful flats to be erected on Union street near Taylor street. They have completed plans for twelve one and one-half story bungalows to be erected on Forty-seventh avenue near Cabrillo street.

Church and Business Buildings

Mr. Smith O'Brien, architect, in the Humboldt Bank building, San Francisco, is preparing plans for a $50,000 church for St. Edwards parish. It will be Gothic in design and constructed of reinforced concrete. The parish owns a splendid site on California street, between Walnut and Laurel streets. Mr. O'Brien has completed plans for two store and loft buildings to be erected at Sutter and Stockton streets, San Francisco, at a total outlay of $20,000. Both structures will have brick and terra cotta exteriors.

$100,000 Portland Club Building

Messrs. W. W. Lucious and Chas. B. Martin, associate architects, 316-17 Lewis building, Portland, Ore., are preparing preliminary plans for a $100,000 building for the Laurelhurst Club, same to be 85x140 feet, brick, concrete and wood construction.

Piedmont Residence

Dr. Roscoe A. Day of Oakland will spend $12,000 in the construction of an English brick and half timber house in Piedmont from plans by Mr. Washington J. Miller, Lachman building, San Francisco.

Baptist Church for San Jose

Mr. Warren F. Skilling of San Jose has prepared plans for an attractive frame and stucco church for the Second Baptist Society. It will be built at Seventh and Santa Clara streets.

$80,000 Farming College Proposed

The Assembly at Carson City passed the bill providing for a bond issue of $80,000 to be used in the erection of an agricultural building at the University.

ELECTRICAL DEPARTMENT

Electricity in the Hospital

By F. C. MYERS in the Modern Hospital

NOT all physicians realize the important part electricity plays in alleviating suffering, facilitating the care of the sick, and making life in confinement more bearable.

First impressions are always important and lasting. First impressions on patients many times come a long time after they have entered, but usually the first impression is made immediately on entering the building. Therefore, the entrances, whether reception hall or ambulance receiving room, should be well lighted and ventilated and equipped with the conveniences necessary to create a feeling of security and good treatment. With the hall and reception rooms well lighted and ventilated, visitors are favorably impressed and in a mood to view with favor the work being done and all arrangements for comfort and convenience.

The lighting, of course, will be by electricity, which can always be available under even the most adverse conditions. The safety, convenience and effectiveness of electric light is too well understood by the medical profession to need any defense here. It must be pointed out, however, that quantity of light is not a measure of quality of illumination.

Certain rules and conditions must be observed if satisfactory results are to be obtained. There must be sufficient light to eliminate eye strain. There must be no glare, which means that the source of light must be out of the line of vision and no direct rays from the lamp should strike the eye. These requirements are easily complied with and no complications appear when the conditions are considered in connection with the large variety of fixtures available.

Ventilation is another important consideration for hospitals. The extent to which the air in a hospital is controlled will depend on the authorities themselves. Fans, of course, are well known and understood, and apparatus is now available not only for positively controlling the amount of air that enters the halls, wards and rooms, but also for washing and controlling the temperature and humidity of all the air entering the building.

In certain industries buildings have been erected with the windows sealed and the doors air tight when closed. Air is pumped through air washers, tempering equipment and humidifiers, so that the temperature and moisture content is constant throughout the year regardless of outdoor conditions. At the same time there are no drafts, and sufficient air is provided for every person inside. This can be done for hospitals as easily as for any other institution. Most air-controlling apparatus is driven by electric motors on account of their safety, quietness and reliability.

The next part of the hospital with which the public and patients come in contact may be the elevator. Electric elevators in many styles and sizes are available. Their safety is proverbial and if maintained in good condition are noiseless. Quietness is an essential if the best interests of patients are to be conserved. Electric elevators can be operated by an attendant or automatically by push buttons without an attendant.

Comparison of the cost of attendance and the interest on the increased investment necessary to install the automatic elevator, if the amount of service required is limited, will determine whether or not the investment should be made. Whenever the wage of an attendant will be more than the interest on the investment, the hospital management will find the automatic elevator advantageous. If the elevator will be in constant service or if there is an employee who can operate an elevator in connection with his other duties, the hand-controlled equipment will be satisfactory.

All designers of hospitals strive to locate all rooms and wards so as to have ample natural light and good, fresh air. As has been pointed out, artificial ventilation can be provided to meet every requirement and insure a constant circulation of clean, pure air at any desired temperature. Daylight, especially sunlight, cannot be surpassed, but frequently light is required on dark days and during the night, and electricity is the most practicable method of illumination.

Electrical installations can be made to meet any condition and light of any intensity can be provided. Lighting fixtures that give a restful, steady light, not trying to the most sensitive nerves, can be had and the new "daylight" lamps permit almost exact duplication of natural light. Electric light throws very little heat into the room and does not vitiate the air.

The diet kitchens are especially susceptible of electric treatment. Electric hot-plates can be used to advantage because they are heated by turning a switch instead of using a match or keeping a fire constantly burning. Fuel —in this case electric current—is consumed only when cooking is actually being done and the air is not fouled or vitiated. There is absolutely no fire danger. Electric water-heaters that will hold the temperature automatically at any predetermined point are available. These devices use current only in accordance with the amount of water used and can be operated constantly.

Coffee percolators, egg-boilers and other equipment can be operated electrically to excellent advantage and under absolute control at all times. This is a material advantage and eliminates much of the danger of spoiling the food being prepared for patients. Electric stoves with or without ovens and provided with time switches are available to meet any requirement.

In considering electricity for the diet kitchens, the requirements of the main kitchen are faced in miniature. Electric ranges with all the features of gas or coal ranges are being manufactured and used with marked success. Electric cooking has several marked advantages: The heat is under absolute control always. The heat is constant and regular under all conditions, not being affected by varying drafts, temperatures or the conditions of flues. There is no oxidation to vitiate the air and no smoke or obnoxious gases. Practically all of the heat is used, very little escaping into the room to raise the temperature abnormally. Cool, comfortable kitchens enable chefs not only to do their work easier, but to do it better.

In the main kitchen, electrically operated dish-washing machines can be used with the assurance of absolute sanitation by thoroughly cleansing the dishes and eliminating the use of the insanitary dish towel. There is other electrically operated equipment suitable for kitchens, such as bread-mixers, food-choppers, coffee-grinders and roasters, and vegetable-peelers.

If the hospital is more than one story high, some means must be provided for elevating food, drugs, etc., from the lower floors or basement. The elevators may be used for handling large quantities, but for individual service dumb waiters will be most convenient. They must be noiseless and easily operated and nothing can be quieter than an electric motor located in the basement some distance from the sick-rooms and operated by pressing a button to lift or lower the dumb waiter. Several kinds are available and their action is positive and reliable. They materially

facilitate and improve the service duties of the nurses.

The operating room and operating service rooms will require plenty of light and ventilation. Special lighting arrangements will be necessary for the operating room, in order that there shall be no shadows to interfere with the surgeon and his work. A special adjustable light that can be set to throw its light directly into the wound will be of material assistance. Electric sterilizers can be installed so that there need be no fire near the operating room. Ventilators can be installed to remove foul odors, to maintain the correct temperatures and to insure clean, fresh air for the patient, the surgeon and his assistants.

All these have a powerful influence that will help to lighten the operation for everyone. The equipment of the operating room is most important and should have the most careful study. The danger of infection is great and a slip of the knife due to fatigue or the mistaking of a part due to shadow may prove fatal.

Electric fans are an important part of every hospital equipment. Moving air under any circumstances is more beneficial than still air. Extensive experiments have demonstrated that moving air low in oxygen and high in carbon dioxide will have a less depressing effect than still air of the same or even better quality. Fans cost little to buy and little to operate. A 12-inch fan will consume about 55 watts and can be operated continuously for almost twenty hours for the cost of one kilowatt. This is at full speed. At lower speeds the current consumption will be proportionately less.

Fans can be used to insure proper distribution of heated air, cold air, or simply to keep the air in circulation. Fans have been used for drying clothes, for drying hair after washing the head. Set in transoms, they are used for expelling or impelling air. The same work can be done by placing them in open windows. They are especially welcome during the hot summer months, but their use is not limited to that season. If forced ventilation is installed for the entire institution, the need for fans may be limited to a certain extent.

Satisfactory signal systems must be electrically operated. No other method has been developed for doing this satisfactorily. Nothing is simpler or easier than pressing a button. Various methods of utilizing the energy thus set at work have been devised. Some hospitals depend on bells, buzzers or lights, others on combinations of these. Some arrangements start the operation of recording apparatus which registers the time the button was pressed and the

time elapsing before the call is answered.

Laundry machinery is especially well adapted to electric drive and operation. Washing and ironing can be done by electricity with less danger, quicker and easier than by any other means. Current is consumed only while the equipment is being used.

Mention should be made of refrigeration. Electrically driven refrigerating and ice-making plants can be had so arranged that temperatures can be regulated automatically within narrow limits. Electricity is used only for a short time daily. By installing refrigerating plants, low temperatures can be had where they are wanted and there will be no ice to be handled. A sanitary advantage in this arrangement is that the air will be dry in refrigerators, thus providing a dry cold instead of a moist germ-breeding atmosphere where food is to be stored. Lower temperatures are also obtainable and can be maintained indefinitely.

There are two sources of electric current: It can be purchased from a company making a specialization of its generation or a private plant can be installed. Which method is to be preferred can be determined only by a careful study of each individual case. In the past the service of central stations was not so reliable as it might have been, but now guarantees are made for constant service day and night. Private plants will be reliable in exact ratio with the quality of the equipment and the care taken in their operation.

Sanitary and safe hospitals are the objectives of all builders. Electricity plays an important part in producing these conditions. Even heating can be provided by electricity under the proper conditions, but usually it will be found cheaper to install a heating plant. By locating this in a building away from the hospital proper it will be possible to have the hospital entirely free from fire and without high-pressure steam.

Pratt Building Material Co.'s Plastering and Brick Mortar Sand Loading Plant at Sacramento.

The Pratt Building Material Co. (Clarence F. Pratt, President), main office Exanimer building, have a sand plant at Sacramento, where they screen and wash American River Sand and produce the best plastering and brick mortar sand in California. Pratt also has a sand plant on the Yuba river, at Marysville—the best Concrete Sand in California.

CONTRACTOR AND BUILDER

"The Golden Rule"*

By JOHN LAWRENCE MAURAN†

All mankind has one or another task or duty in common with his neighbor, but it is only of late years that our best citizens realized either the responsibilities of the service we owe our fellow men, or were willing to grant for a moment that we have a common heritage; and so, it is scarcely surprising that you, the master-builders of the country, and we the architects of the very buildings you were rearing in steel and masonry. should fail to see through the cloud of petty details—and some of them I must admit were "full sized"—but details none the less of divergent interests, into the heart of things where builder and architect are first of all men—men with the same God-given rights—the same common responsibilities and the same ambition and aim to serve the man who makes their common effort possible. I always like the theory which my predecessor and, I venture to say, our mutual friend, Mr. Sturgis, has spoken of to you, "that no matter how widely men may think they differ, personal contact in discussing those differences is bound to establish points in common which grow until those differences are dissolved in an atmosphere of understanding.

Just a year ago, when your convention passed those splendid resolutions to aid me in my fight against the erection of the power house in the park area of Washington, I had a striking instance of this truth. Perhaps you know the very general feeling which has always existed between architects and engineers, the engineer looking upon the architect's work with a certain amount of disdain because engineering is an exact science and architecture has so wide a latitude that the slide rule cannot well cover its possibilities. On the other hand, the architect has always felt that the engineering problems incident to building are handled by the engineering profession with a rigidity which evidences a lack of sympathy in what should be a mutual effort, and hence—when five of the most distinguished engineers hurried to Washington in re-

*Paper read at the Sixth Annual Convention, National Association of Builders' Exchanges, Atlanta, Ga.
†President American Institute of Architects.

sponse to our invitation we naturally felt that we could count on their interest in so far only as the power house might appeal to them as a poor engineering proposition. So you can imagine our surprise—our delightful surprise—when we found them individually and collectively opposed to the erection of this unsightly array of smoke stacks in the park area, not only from a strictly utilitarian viewpoint, but more particularly on account of their appreciation of the fact that it would be a blemish on the face of our beautiful Washington from an artistic standpoint. Here again, personal contact brought out a surprising number of viewpoints common to both professions, and when I suggested to some of these men that there ought to be an established means of co-operation on those new found interests, the idea was enthusiastically received.

As a result, I am engaged in forming a sort of "clearing house" or "forum"—a joint conference committee of architects and engineers to make permanent the cordial relations established at that time. Even if you have never stopped to think of it before, you must have noticed that while the bridges and viaducts designed and erected by engineers for many decades were scarcely "things of beauty," no matter how perfect the engineering solution of the problem might be, there have been built more recently structures for the same purpose just as perfect in combination of economy and strength, but through the association of an architect in the problem, embracing lines of beauty and accessories of interest which have made them real monuments to their joint designers. This is but one of the many fields of common interest to the two professions and the dawning of a new day of co-operation is typical of this area of "getting together" which all of us believe points to a rapid constructive progress impossible under the old regime.

Now all of you remember the old order of things, which our labors together have done so much to revolutionize—except in the offices of architects of the highest type, the master builder found himself on the one side and the owner and architect on the other. Wherever the fault lay, whether with the architect

in defending drawings insufficiently explicit, or with the builder in exacting the last extra the "traffic would stand," is now happily of no consequence, for in the last analysis the fundamental trouble was that neither architect nor builder realized that "understanding" and "co-operation" are essential to success within the grasp of both. Our disinterested labors together over the Standard Documents has proved the fact, and their usage has emphasized its application. The Standard Documents come nearer than anything else to stating in legal form the true instinctive relationship between men of the highest ethical standards—both in the field of construction and of creation.

I am sure every builder here present has seen that excessively clever cartoon of the "successful bidder"—the builder who has just read the letter informing him that he has been successful in landing a big job, depicted in a state of complete collapse, vainly cudgeling his brains as he stares wild-eyed into space—for the answer to the question escaping from his lips "what did I forget?" Now that truism, for it is a truism—is all wrong. No right-minded owner wants to profit by human fallibility—no decent architect wishes to see his co-worker the victim of an oversight, nor is it pleasant to enforce the proper applications of the terms of the contract under such conditions, and most of all it is hard for the builder to show a broad-minded interest in a contract which like the unbaptized Presbyterian infant is thus "damned at its birth." Some way will be found to overcome this common evil and the friends of the Quantity Survey claim that their system is the "cure all" that will prove efficacious. They may be right—very likely they are—you have evidenced your interest and have suggested co-operation between our organizations to determine its value.

The American Institute of Architects has been interested for a long time in this method which has been in vogue in other countries for a great many years but it has felt no compelling impulse to accept or reject the principles involved. It undoubtedly has its merits and it undoubtedly has its shortcomings, which must be as apparent to you as it is to us, and our board of directors had determined to take no definite action until we could observe the workings of this system on some typical job from the time the drawings were ready for the Quantity Surveyor to the moment of adjustment of the final certificate. I know it will be of interest to you to learn that such an opportunity has just come to our notice and I have appointed three conscientious, painstaking members of the Institute a special committee to make this observation for our mutual benefit and to report its findings to the Board of Directors.

As we meet here today our country stands upon the brink looking into that hell's cauldron of war which has convulsed a divided Europe. Whether national honor forces us over that fateful brink or happily we remain in honorable peace with our friends and brothers throughout the world—let us thank God we learned our eternal lesson in that baptism of blood and fire which settled forever in 1865 whether it should be "united we stand" or "divided we fall"—and made absolute the assurance that through the years to come there stands Republican and Democrat, bricklayer and banker, merchant and manufacturer, builder and architect, a vast army united as one man behind our constituted authority—the President of these, **our** United States.

Opportunities for American Contractors in Europe*

IT is a common remark among business men on the Continent that Europe will be made over after the war. Perhaps there will be a greater amount of new construction than reconstruction. It is almost the universal wish of the people involved that they may be able to incorporate in their new construction and reconstruction the latest and best ideas from America.

If American contractors are alive to their opportunities and go after this business not with the intention of dictating to the European people how they must do business, but with the idea of conforming to the regular methods followed in these various countries, American contractors will have little difficulty in securing the very cream of this business if they lose no time in going after it.

Plans are already evolved and are being put into operation for the reconstruction of the whole of France in the

*Detailed information may be obtained by writing the American Society of Engineering Contractors, 40 Whitehall street, New York.

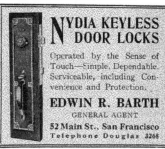

New Architectural Firm for Honolulu

Mr. William W. Harper and Mr. William C. Furer announce a partnership under the name of Harper & Furer, architecture and architectural engineering, with offices in the Kanikeolaui building, Honolulu. Mr. Harper was formerly in the employ of D. H. Burnham & Co., and Mr. Jarvis Hunt of Chicago; also he has held responsible positions with Mr. Frederick H. Meyer, Mr. Charles Peter Weeks and Mr. Lewis P. Hobart of San Francisco. Mr. Furer is a graduate of the Department of Architecture, Massachusetts Institute of Technology.

Building material houses are invited to send them trade catalogues and other data pertaining to building construction.

Architectural Competition

A competition for plans of almshouses, county infirmaries and county hospitals in the nature of photographic or perspective drawings of completed or prospective buildings, is announced by the National Conference of Charities and Correction. The work is to be exhibited at the forty-fourth annual meeting to be held in Pittsburg, June 6-13. For further particulars, architects should address Francis Bardwell, 315 Plymouth Court, Chicago.

New San Francisco Architects

Mr. Irving J. Gill, architect of Los Angeles and San Diego, has opened an office for the practice of his profession at 12 Geary street, San Francisco. Mrs. M. E. Strange of Los Angeles has also established an office in the same building for the practice of architecture.

Bridge Plans Ordered

The Sacramento and Solano County Supervisors have awarded the plan bids for the proposed bridge at Rio Vista to the Strauss Bascule Bridge Co. of Chicago. It will cost approximately $150,000. Bids for construction are now being taken.

war area. Spain has plenty of labor, money and materials for business now, and is anxious for Americans to do the work. Italy also has plenty of labor and material for contracts at the present time and is anxious to begin even now.

A large number of the contracts in Italy and in Spain that are ready at the present time are from first-class public service institutions whose bonds are endorsed by the government, making their securities strictly first-class, having not only special property that is bonded as security, but the guarantee of the government itself to make up any deficit.

In almost all European countries it is a rule not to give the contract directly to a foreign corporation or individual, because neither of them is subject to the laws of the foreign country. Most of the desirable propositions in Europe consist of concessions granted to individuals or corporations, temporarily, so as to enable them to arrange their finances, and when these are arranged the final concession is granted and work can begin at once.

For instance, suppose the matter under consideration is a railroad. The "concessionaire," at his own expense or at the expense of his firm or syndicate, must employ first-class engineers and lay out with the minutest detail his entire line. This is then presented to the government for consideration with a view to securing its endorsement on the company's bonds. Such changes as may be necessary are then made, and the plans are accepted by the government. Finally an agreement is entered into whereby that government undertakes to endorse the bonds and grant the concession when the "concessionaire" is prepared to show his financial ability to carry out the construction of the work and to take the company's bonds endorsed by the government for his pay.

When it comes to taking the contract for the construction of the road, the concessionaires generally seek the con-

tractor who has the banking facilities for handling their bonds. This contract is usually given to a contractor of their own country, who in turn sub-lets the contract to the American or other foreign contractor on a cost-plus-percentage basis. Thus the American contractor will run practically no risk at all in carrying out work of this kind.

The reconstruction contracts in France will be handled in two ways. First, to furnish money for the rebuilding of homes and private business buildings, the government intends to issue bonds to raise the money in order that the individual may borrow it from the government at a reasonable rate. On the other hand, the public work will be done in the usual French manner, which is as follows: If the work is reconstruction, a strong contractor, through his organization, prepares plans, drawings and complete estimates covering the whole or some special part of the work. At an appointed time the contractors who have so prepared themselves have an opportunity to submit bids on the contract, and only one who can prove his financial ability to carry out the contract, should he get it, meets with success.

Each country has its own peculiar customs, which we are not now prepared to go into, as to the giving out of these contracts, but only contractors who can prove large experience may hope to secure them. Furthermore, it is useless for an American contractor to bid for such work unless he has tentatively arranged with his banking connections or otherwise to take the bonds which he receives in payment. If preferred, these bonds can be issued direct to his financial backers. There will be little difficulty in agreeing upon the terms.

Back Numbers Wanted

The publishers will pay 35 cents apiece for copies of the May and June, 1905, Architect and Engineer. Also 25 cents each for one or more copies of the January, 1917, Architect and Engineer.

The Building Industries Association (Inc.)

This is the name of a new association which is now under process of formation. It will succeed to the assets and good will of the San Francisco General Contractors' Association, provided it is successfully organized. It is proposed to weld with it all other associations or societies representing building and allied interests. Every line of business represented shall have equal vote. Each trade organization shall have one representative in the Board of Governors, such representative to be selected by a ballot of members in his own craft.

A mass meeting of about 250 persons representing some thirty separate trades and interests was held on Thursday, March 29th, at the General Contractors' Association, Mr. Chas. W. Gompertz presiding. Addresses were made by H. P. Stow, president of the Thos. Day Company; A. H. Bergstrom, of Lange & Bergstrom, and D. Zelinsky. There seemed to be a general feeling of favor to the new association. The following expression of the purposes of the association states same in a terse and interesting manner:

The objects of this association shall be to promote the organization of the entire building business into one efficient institution for the various purposes as hereinafter set forth and to maintain suitable quarters for the use of its members; to adjudicate by arbitration or otherwise all differences among members, or between members and their employees; to foster the interests of those engaged in the building industry; to promote just and equitable principles in the conduct of their business; to discourage ruinous competition and to promote harmony and justice in their business relations; to advocate the public opening of bids; to discourage the peddling of bids; to bring about the adoption of a standard form of bid and contract; to encourage mutual trading among members of the different crafts belonging to the association; to discourage unfair and restrictive combinations, and finally to make a membership in this association a guarantee of honesty, fairness and reliability.

New Contractors' Society

Articles of incorporation of the Contractors' Pastime Society of San Francisco have been filed. The announced purpose of the corporation is to promote social intercourse and literary advancement among the contractors of San Francisco, to build, later on, a club house, equipped with a gymnasium, and to give entertainments of various kinds. The incorporators are George S. Hall, O. R. Hale, Howard S. Williams, A. Carlson and Tony Daniels.

In Union There Is Strength

The General Contractors' Association of San Francisco is working for a consolidation with the Builders' Exchange. Commenting on the recent merging of the two Oakland organizations, the Review, published by the General Contractors' Association, says:

Members of this Association have learned that the General Contractors' Association and the Builders' Exchange of Oakland have joined hands and are now meeting in common headquarters and by their united efforts will be able to accomplish more in the future than they have in the past.

Following along the lines laid out in other articles in this Review, we may say that it is a matter of congratulation that Oakland has taken this step and we only regret that they took the lead and set a pace which it is up to us to follow.

We extend our sincere congratulations to the Oakland contractors and builders and hope that their combined efforts will bring them the success to which they are justly entitled.

And with the example set us by our sister city across the Bay it is up to us to "go and do likewise."

The Marble Contract for the Public Library

This contract is only one of many similar ones satisfactorily handled by the American Marble and Mosaic Co. of San Francisco. This concern has offices at 25-29 Columbus square, San Francisco, with factory on Canal, South San Francisco. The officers of the company are as follows: President, A. F. Edwards; vice-president, J. M. Fabbris; secretary, J. A. Mackenzie; assistant managers, Chas. F. Eisele and J. Rubiolo.

Among the many prominent buildings of recent construction for which the marble was furnished, cut and set by this concern may be mentioned the following: U. S. Sub-Treasury, Hotel Whitcomb, Yolo County Court House, Standard Oil building, Chas. Holbrook building, Call-Post building, San Francisco Public Library, U. S. National Bank, Portland; Stockton Savings Bank building (exterior), Insurance Exchange building, Rialto building, Security National Bank, Los Angeles; Merchants National Bank, Los Angeles, and U. S. Grant Hotel, San Diego.

Women Make Good Concrete Mixers

The University of California has started a class in concrete work in which women are being taught concrete construction in connection with clay modeling. They make ornamental lawn posts, flower pots, garden sets and various other articles, besides learning to make sidewalks and curbs. Visitors stare in amazement at the women students who carry hods and get down on the ground and work with trowels and tamps. The work started last summer and the course was taken by a large-number of teachers, who are now trying to introduce it in their schools.

When writing to Advertisers please mention this magazine.

State Building News Culled Down

R. J. Tredor will build a two-story brick building on Yosemite avenue, Manteca.

The Christian Church, Visalia, will erect a $20,000 edifice.

Selma Presbyterians will spend $20,-000 for a new church.

A $60,000 high school at Sparks, Nev., is being planned by F. J. De Longchamps, Reno architect.

William Knowles, Hearst building, San Francisco, has made plans for a $30,000 Congregational Church at Pittsburg, Contra Costa county.

Messrs. Richardson & Burrell, Albany block, Oakland, are preparing plans for a five-story and basement Class C apartment house, to be erected by Sommarstrom Bros., on Grand avenue, Oakland. Estimated cost, $75,000.

A hotel costing $100,000 is planned for Woodland, Yolo county. Chas. S. Stern of the California State Highway Commission is interested in the project.

Announcement

The Capitol Sheet Metal Works announces that a larger company has been organized to be known as the Capitol Art Metal Company, which company has absorbed the Capitol Sheet Metal Works. The factory, which comprises 45,000 square feet, will be located at Richmond, Contra Costa county, Cal., with main offices in San Francisco.

In addition to the lines heretofore manufactured, the new company will make a specialty of the metal furniture line and of steel library stacks and other products.

Mr. G. A. Wieland and Mr. W. F. Aldrich will assume the active management of the new company and respectfully solicit a continuance of your valued patronage.

Appreciation

Dallas, Oregon, Apr. 2, 1917.

Architect and Engineer,
  San Francisco, Cal.

Gentlemen—Find enclosed check for $1.00 in payment for my subscription for the year 1917, for the best magazine in the world for the money.

Very truly yours,
  F. H. MORRISON,
   Architect.

The Hauser Window Decision

The decision of the U. S. District Court, after long delay, in sustaining the patents of the Hauser Reversible Window Co., calls attention anew to the weakness of U. S. patent laws. The government, for a consideration, awards a patent, but with this patent goes no guarantee. Any competitor can, with or without reason, attack the validity of the patent, enjoin and embarrass the patentee's business and involve him in large legal expenses in his efforts to sustain what he may have secured in good faith and after long delays and circumlocution. In foreign countries a patent means something. The foreign government having satisfied itself that the claim or application is a just one, backs up its opinion and protects the patentee. A decided reform in this respect should be inaugurated in the United States, and while we are endeavoring to secure justice for the world in general we should endeavor to protect the individual whose brains have accomplished improvements in our materials and manufactures.

J. M. Dougan Gets Contract

The J. M. Dougan Co., Hearst building, San Francisco, has been awarded a contract for erecting the Hoffman school, Portland, Ore., for approximately $50,-000. The plans were prepared by School Architect F. A. Noramore. There will be six class rooms, two playrooms, an assembly hall, quarters for teachers and a private room for the principal. The building will be of reinforced concrete.

FOXCROFT BUILDING, 68 Post Street, San Francisco. Offices Single and in Suite.

New 1917 Model Ray Rotary Crude Oil Burner

1 B' and S Gear Pump
2 Worm Reduction Gear
3 Oil Regulating Valve
4 Motor
5 Air-Inlet
6 Blower
7 Atomizer
8 Guide Vanes and Air Nozzle
9 Stationary Oil Supply Tube
10 Hollow Drive Shaft
11 Annular Ball Bearings
12 Furnace
13 Oil Jacketed Motor Casing
14 Strainer

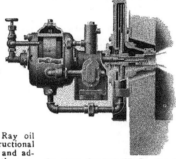

This improved type of the Ray oil burner has many new constructional features, both in improvements and advantages. Among these are the enclosed, oil-cooled and bearingless motor, the Split Field, the Hollow Shaft, the Single Lubricating Point and the Splash Lubrication to Bearings. These secure the following advantages: Less noise; oil, dust and water proof; 75 per cent less temperature and longer life; accessibility, preventing accumulation of excess oil in winding or switch; expediency in repairing; there is no danger of over or under lubrication and washes bearings free from grit; preheats the oil while passing through motor and necessitates larger bearings.

The Ray crude oil burner is less than two years old, and while only fifty-three burners were disposed of the first nine months, the second nine months showed sales of 503 burners.

Among the users, besides a long list of apartment houses, hotels and apartments too numerous to enumerate, may be mentioned the following:

Armsby, J. K., Bldg., San Francisco
Clinton Cafeteria, San Francisco
Calif. School of Mechanical Arts, San Francisco
Carmen Johnson Bldg., San Francisco
California Evergreen Co., San Francisco
Davis Schonwasser Bldg., San Francisco
Daniel Webster School, San Francisco
Detention Home, San Francisco
Ford Motor Co., San Francisco
Ford Apts., San Francisco
Ferrari Bros. Nursery, San Francisco
Grosjean Rice Milling Co., San Francisco
Hansford Block, San Francisco
Hewes Bldg., San Francisco
Hygienic Bakery Co., San Francisco
Independent Cracker Co., San Francisco
Lipman Bldg., San Francisco
McLaughlin Bldg., San Francisco
Mission Dolores Parochial Res., San Francisco
Methodist Book Concern, San Francisco
Noe Valley Library, San Francisco
New Mission Theater, San Francisco
Overland Bldg., San Francisco
Pacific States Hotel, San Francisco
Pac. Tel. & Tel. Co., Mkt. Ex. Bldg., S. F.
Pac. Tel. & Tel. Co., Operating Sch., S. F.
Pac. Tel. & Tel. Co. Exec. Of. Bldg., S. F.
Reading School, San Francisco
Second Church of Christ, Scientist, San Francisco
St. Francis Girls' Directory, San Francisco
St. Mary's Parish & Urselene Convent, S. F.
Union Iron Works, Office Bldg., San Francisco
Zellerbach, Bldg., San Francisco
Str. Astral, Standard Oil Co., San Francisco
Str. Acme, Standard Oil Co., San Francisco
Str. Col. Drake, Standard Oil Co., San Francisco
Str. H. C. Folger, Standard Oil Co., S. F.
Str. J. A. Moffit, Standard Oil Co., S. F.
Str. D. G. Schofield, Standard Oil Co., S. F.
Str. Paulsboro, Standard Oil Co., San Francisco
Str. Van Dyke, Standard Oil Co., San Francisco
Bishop Theater, Oakland
Fenton Creamery, Oakland
South Methodist Church, Oakland
Shuey Creamery, Oakland
University Laundry, Oakland
Varsity Creamery, Oakland
American Dairy Co., San Jose
Aero-Cushion Tire Co., San Jose
City Hall, San Jose
German Catholic Church, San Jose
Hawthorne School, San Jose
Muireson Label Co., San Jose
Pac. Tel & Tel. Co., San Jose
Rainier Bottling Works, San Jose
St. Joseph Church, San Jose
St. Joseph School, San Jose
Sisters of Charity, San Jose
Twohy Bldg., San Jose
Wilson Dairy, San Jose
Y. W. C. A. Bldg., San Jose
Masonic Bldg., Los Angeles
Father Maloney Church, Los Angeles
California Orange Jelly Co., Los Angeles
Neuner Bldg., Los Angeles
St. Agnes Church, Los Angeles
St. Cecilia School, Los Angeles
Kiatz Bldg., Los Angeles
Physicians Bldg., Los Angeles
Marine Ave. School, Albany, Cal.
State Hospital, Agnews, Cal.
Bath Shipbuilding Co., Bath, Me.
Dome Laundry, Berkeley, Cal.
First Natl. Bank, Berkeley, Cal.
Marshal Steel Co., Berkeley, Cal
Telegraph Ave. School, Berkeley
St. Patrick's Church, Bisbee, Ariz.
Str. Talabot, Christiania, Norway
Reichardt Duck Co., Colma, Cal.
Mt. Olivet Crematory, Colma, Cal.
Park Hotel, Chico, Cal.
Enloe Hospital, Chico, Cal.
Chico Steam Laundry, Chico, Cal.
N. Y. Motion Pic. Co., Culver City
Western Mercury Co., Cloverdale
Clovis High School, Clovis, Cal.
Culver City School, Culver City, Cal.
McGuire Bldg., Douglas, Ariz.
Downey School, Downey, Cal.
Theo. Roosevelt School, Exeter
Harts Bros. Restaurant, Fresno
Dohoto Bros. Nursery, Fruitvale
Nevada Co. Bank, Grass Valley
Public Library, Grass Valley, Cal.
O. K. Soda Water Co., Honolulu, Hawaii
Oahu Bakery, Honolulu, Hawaii
Mormon Church, Honolulu, Hawaii
Queen's Hospital, Honolulu, Hawaii
Oahu Insane Asylum, Honolulu, Hawaii
Leves Bakery, Honolulu, Hawaii

U. S. Government, Ft. Shafter, Honolulu
Hayward Grammar School, Hayward, Cal.
Grangers Union, Hollister, Cal.
Products Development Co., Ione, Cal.
Kauai Hospital, Kauai, Hawaii
Newcomer's Crematory, Kansas City, Mo.
Saunders Bros. Mill, Modesto, Cal.
La Salle Bros., Martinez, Cal.
California Nurseries, Niles, Cal.
Yacht Cyprus, New York, N. Y. ·
Butte Co. Infirmary, Oroville, Cal.
Rideout Bank, Oroville, Cal.
Herbert E. Law Nursery, Portola
Stanford Grammar School, Palo Alto
U. S. Government, Panama Canal
Petaluma Co.-op. Creamery, Petaluma
Redwood City Jail, Redwood City
Central California Canneries, Rio Vista
Wildwood Dairy, Santa Rosa, Cal.
Public Library, Santa Monica, Cal.
Public Library, Santa Barbara
Cal. Chemical Co., Summerland, Cal.
Kell's Dairy, Stockton, Cal.
Levee Bldg., Vallejo, Cal.
Visalia Court House, Visalia, Cal.
Van Nuys City Hall, Van Nuys, Cal.

New Firm of Plumbing and Heating Contractors

Mr. J. C. James, formerly of Peterson & James, and Mr. Clarence Drucker, until recently engaged in the manufacture of heating apparatus in Chicago, have formed a partnership and will engage in the plumbing and heating contracting business, with shops and offices at 450 Hayes street, San Francisco. Mr. James in his former connection handled more than $1,000,000 in plumbing and heating contracts for San Francisco buildings, and this experience, joined with Mr. Drucker's special training, should fit them to render efficient service on any work entrusted to them. The new firm intends to figure on both large and small work, and, according to Mr. James: "Our prices will be low, despite our slogan, 'Quality our motto.' "

Big Order for Master Builders Floor Hardner

In the construction of the cement floors of the new Terminal market buildings on East Seventh street, Los Angeles, over two hundred tons of Master Builder Floor Hardner will be used. This large order was awarded by the Wurster Construction Company, the contractors, to the Master Builder Company of Cleveland, Ohio, through their Los Angeles representative, A. E. Banks, 208 Wright & Callender building. C. Roman, Sharon building, is the San Francisco representative of the Master Builder company.

Dissolution of Partnership

The firm of Ward & Goodwin, general contractors, has dissolved partnership by mutual agreement. Both Mr. Ward and Mr. Goodwin will continue in the contracting business independently. They have been very successful in their building operations, which have covered a period of more than seven years. All outstanding bills contracted by Ward & Goodwin will be paid under the firm name.

Spencer Elevators

The Spencer Elevator Company of San Francisco reports business conditions much improved since the beginning of the year. The company has completed a number of good-sized installations, while new orders will keep the force busy for some time to come. The United States envelope factory being erected by Palmer & Petersen, will be equipped with both a passenger and a freight elevator. The new Goodyear Rubber Company building will have a Spencer freight elevator, as will the garage on Van Ness avenue designed by Clarence Tantau. A Spencer passenger lift has been installed in the Union Iron Works hospital, also two passenger cars in the store and office building designed by Henry H. Meyers at Palo Alto. The splendid Native Sons Hall at Sacramento, now being constructed from plans by Washington Miller, will have a Guerney type passenger elevator, the installation to be in charge of the Spencer company.

Flag Poles in Demand

In these days of patriotism, architects are specifying flag poles for both public and private buildings, and even some residences are using them. Bolander & Son's patent flag pole and tops are being quite generally specified. They are to be used on the new Colusa high school, Watsonville high school, South San Francisco and Tracy, all designed by William H. Weeks, architect of San Francisco.

Telephone Annex

The Pacific Telephone and Telegraph Company will build a six-story $100,000 annex to its present exchange building on Franklin, near Fifteenth street, Oakland. Mr. E. V. Cobby, Sheldon building, will prepare the plans.

To Build Brick Church

The Vallejo Methodist Church will shortly start the erection of a brick church building on Virginia street. Plans are now being prepared.

Special Furniture of the Library

One of the features of the new San Francisco Public Library which evokes much commendation is the furniture of the various rooms, such as reading desks and tables, book rests, special chairs, setees, etc. These were made by the Mullen Manufacturing Co. of 64 Rausch street, San Francisco, who have a considerable trade in similar work for public buildings, churches, etc. Their work is marked by skillful turning and a correct interpretation of the architect's ideas and plans.

Library Building's Lathing Contract

This was satisfactorily executed by the National Lathing and Furring Co., Monadnock building, San Francisco. This concern has carried out many big contracts in their line which have been awarded during the past ten years. Their recent orders include lathing and furring of the following buildings: The Civic Auditorium, Clift Hotel, Southern Pacific building, Casino Theatre, Native Sons Hall, and the Sacramento Court House.

American Radiator Company to Rebuild

The plant of the American Radiator Company at Second and Townsend streets, San Francisco, which was almost totally destroyed by fire, is being rebuilt from the original plans. The present brick walls will be retained, but an entire new interior will be necessary, also roof and windows. The building is owned by the Sharon Estate.

Automobile Machine Shop

Mr. August G. Headman, New Call building, San Francisco, has let a contract to V. Filippis for the construction of a one-story and basement reinforced concrete auto machine shop at Golden Gate avenue and Gough streets, San Francisco, for $17,000. Contract for the heating has been let to the Scott Co. for $1,325.

Insert Shows Magnitude of Paraffine Paint Company's Plant

Elsewhere in this issue is a striking folded insert of the Paraffine Paint Co. This insert is a miniature reproduction of a large broadside or folder which was recently sent out to the company's thousands of customers.

This insert graphically shows the company's five great plants—located at strategic positions along the Coast—and the extensive line of products manufactured.

The folder gives a brief history of the Paraffine Paint Company's wonderful growth during the last thirty-three years. From the small original plant built in 1884 for the manufacture of preservative paint and pile covering, the company now has mills and refineries for the manufacture of roofing, felts, building papers, asphaltums, wallboards and paint.

The field of operation has been steadily extended until today the Paraffine Paint Company's products are sold in every city, town and village in the West and in every country bordering on the Pacific and Indian Oceans.

California Exports Cement Now

It is a new thing in American foreign trade to read of California as an exporter of Portland cement. Still with the growth of the industry in the State, and with the ocean at her door, there is nothing surprising in the fact that San Francisco exported last year 50,438 barrels of cement. In this connection only recently the Japanese steamer Iko Masan took a cargo of 5,000 barrels of cement from California Portland Cement Co. at Colton for delivery to purchasers in Peru.

Mr. Hunt Visits Coast Architects

Mr. Clarence J. Hunt of Wadsworth, Howland and Co., Inc., Boston, recently paid his customary visit to the Pacific Coast and called upon a number of the architects in the interest of Bay State Brick and Cement Coating. Mr. Hunt has been with the Wadsworth, Howland company for nearly a quarter century. He is one of the best posted paint men in the country.

TRANSMISSION EQUIPMENT

FOR MILL OR FACTORY

Pulleys	Bearings
Hangers	Clutches
Sprockets	Gears
Floor Stands	Rope Sheaves
Belt Tighteners	Take Ups
Shafting	Chain Belt

Meese & Gottfried Company

ENGINEERS AND MANUFACTURERS

CONVEYING, ELEVATING, SCREENING AND MECHANICAL POWER TRANSMITTING MACHINERY

SAN FRANCISCO
660 Mission Street

SEATTLE
558 First Ave. So.

PORTLAND
67 Front Street

LOS ANGELES
400 East 3rd St.

HAVE YOU OUR CATALOG?

Carnegie Library Plans

Plans and specifications for three of the four branch library buildings to be built by funds of the Carnegie corporation in Oakland, totaling $140,000 in all, have been sent to James Bertram, secretary of the corporation at New York, by City Librarian Charles S. Green.

When writing to Advertisers please mention this magazine.

A Development in Belt Driving at Short Centers

The "Meeseco Belt Drive"
By J. A. BRIED

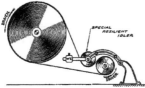

The Principle of the Short Center Drive

One particular source of loss in most industrial plants is in the slippage of belts, for even the best of regular belt drives involve some 2 per cent slip and some drives 5 per cent or more. This represents a direct power loss, and. going on day after day in any fair sized plant will total thousands of dollars at the end of each year.

The slipping of belts is greater in drives in which the pulleys are relatively near together and it has therefore been customary to use long belts or greater tension to get more traction, or belt tighteners were forced with great pressure against the belts in the attempt to prevent belts from slipping, and while slippage can be overcome to a certain extent by such means, it more frequently results in excessive bearing pressures, overheating, etc., and simply consumes power by friction at the bearings instead of by belt slippage.

This condition of affairs is the reason for the considerable use of silent chain drives, especially for short center drives, for by their use bearing pressures may be kept down and efficient drives secured with entire freedom from slip, but such drives are limited in their application on account of high first cost, expense of upkeep and the constant attention they require, together with the fact that the highest speed practicable with silent chains is only about a quarter of what is frequently used with good belts and pulleys.

Therefore, it was with great interest that the experiments carried on in Europe with short center belt drives controlled by yielding idlers were watched by the engineers of this country.

The new system involved the use of especially constructed pivoted idlers, mounted on ball or roller bearings, operating against slack belts somewhat in the nature of a belt tightener, though in principle quite different, and it permitted of very short centers, at the same time giving greatly increased horsepower, with practically no slip.

This system was studied by the engineers of the Meese & Gottfried Company of San Francisco, Seattle, Portland and Los Angeles, and developed to a high state of mechanical perfection; in fact, this firm is the only one that has gone thoroughly into the engineering of the subject in this part of the country, and though a new undertaking, has already furnished these drives to handle some 10,000 horsepower.

The principle on which it operates can be gathered from the diagram at the head of this article, and is totally different from a belt tightener in several important features:

First—It does not cause an increase in belt tension for a given horsepower.

Second—It operates just as satisfactorily on very short centers—where formerly a belt drive would have been impossible.

Third—It does not increase the bearing pressure with consequent overheating and rapid wear of the bearings.

MEESECO BELT DRIVE

150 horsepower from motor at 700 revolutions per minute to a duplex double acting air compressor at 140 revolutions per minute. Distance between centers of shafts, 6 feet 6 inches.

Fourth—It makes possible the transmission of much more horsepower than heretofore considered practicable with a leather belt.

Fifth—It is easy on the belt and with a good flexible grade of belting it causes no injury.

The average mechanical man first seeing one of these drives would class it as a swinging belt tightener drive, but would be in error, as can be seen from its distinctive features enumerated above, for it is not merely a "device," but is more properly a system, the successful installation of which depends on the proper position of the idler, its effective weight relative to the horsepower and speed of the drive, together with the pre-determined slack in the belt, as the belts are purposely made very loose.

The angle and direction at which the drive runs must also be considered, as the idler may be controled by weights on levers arranged at the proper angle or may be pulled upward or sidewise by ropes and counterweights. On heavily pulsating loads pneumatic shock absorbers are sometimes connected to the oscillating frame to steady it.

This new development in short center belt driving undoubtedly has a great future, as it accomplishes what can be done by no other means—transmitting from the smallest to the heaviest horsepowers smoothly and silently at high efficiency and at speeds which would be utterly impossible with silent chains. Practically all belt drives, from the heaviest main drives down, come easily within its scope, and it is particularly suitable for the higher speed belts running in saw mills and other woodworking plants.

The Golden Gate Decorating Co.

This is a new concern, located at 704 Polk street, San Francisco, which is out after good contracts for painting, paperhanging and interior decoration. It makes a specialty of apartment house and hotel work. Mr. R. E. McQuade, the manager, was formerly connected with the Tiffany Decorating Co. of New York City, and he offers his services to architects and owners in the way of furnishing sketches or color schemes for drapes, curtains, hangings or wall decoration. He refers to his work in the East, also the interior decoration of the Holt residence in Honolulu.

Paint Company to Enlarge Plant

The Bass-Heuter Paint Company will build a $15,000 addition to its San Francisco plant. The improvements will be in charge of P. A. Palmer, constructing engineer.

S. P. Car Shops

The Southern Pacific Company has taken bids for constructing three large frame and brick shop buildings at Visitacion, South San Francisco. Messrs. Lange & Bergstrom submitted the low bid for approximately $86,000.

When writing to Advertisers please mention this magazine.

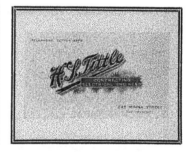
When writing to Advertisers please mention this magazine.

When writing to Advertisers please mention this magazine.

When writing to Advertisers please mention this magazine.

THE
ARCHITEC
AND
ENGINEER
CALIFORNIA

HOUSE NUMBER

MAY, 1917

UNITED STATES STEEL PRODUCTS CO.

Rialto Building, San Francisco

SELLERS of the products of the American Bridge Co., American Sheet and Tin Plate Co., American Steel and Wire Co., Carnegie Steel Co., Illinois Steel Co., National Tube Co., Lorain Steel Co., Shelby Steel Tube Co., Tennessee Coal, Iron and Railroad Co., Trenton Iron Co.

MANUFACTURERS OF

Structural Steel for Every Purpose — Bridges, Railway and Highway — "Triangle Mesh" Wire Concrete Reinforcement — Plain and Twisted Reinforcing Bars — Plates, Shapes and Sheets of Every Description — Rails, Splice Bars, Bolts, Nuts, etc. — Wrought Pipe, Valves, Fittings, Trolley Poles — Frogs, Switches and Crossings for Steam Railway and Street Railway — "Shelby" Seamless Boiler Tubes and Mechanical Tubing—"Americore" and "Globe" Rubber Covered Wire and Cables — "Reliance" Weatherproof Copper and Iron Line Wire—"American" Wire Rope, Rail Bonds, Springs, Woven Wire Fencing and Poultry Netting — Tramways, etc.

United States Steel Products Co.
OFFICES AND WAREHOUSES AT
San Francisco - Los Angeles - Portland - Seattle

THE

RCHITEC

AND

NGINEER

OF CALIFORNIA

HOUSE NUMBER

MAY, 1917

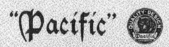

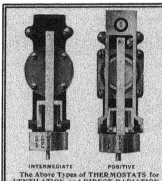

When writing to Advertisers please mention this magazine.

For Modern Store-Fronts

OUR DISAPPEARING

AWNINGS

are constructed with no outside attachments below recess, above windows. Gears entirely concealed.

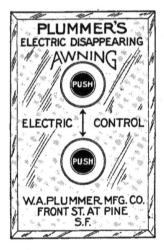

Absolutely Practicable when Extended

and when rolled up is contained in recess 8 inches by 8½ inches, with front board, which can be utilized as a sign board, covering front of recess. Operated either by crank or electric control, from any part of building.

Send for Architect's Sheet of Specifications

The new Southern Pacific Building, San Francisco, is being equipped with

Plummer's Disappearing Awnings

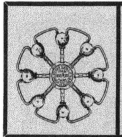

ACOUSTICAL CORRECTION
H. W. Johns-Manville Co., Second and Howard Sts., San Francisco.

ARCHITECTURAL SCULPTORS, MODELING, ETC.
G. Rognier & Co., 233 R. R. Ave., San Mateo.
Sculptors' Workshop. S. Miletin & Co., 1705 Harrison St., San Francisco.
A. F. Swoboda, modeler, 204 Second St., San Francisco.

ARCHITECTURAL TERRA COTTA
Gladding, McBean & Company, Crocker Bldg., San Francisco.
Steiger Terra Cotta and Pottery Works, Mills Bldg., San Francisco.

ASBESTOS ROOFING
H. W. Johns-Manville Company, San Francisco, Los Angeles, San Diego, Sacramento.

AUTOMATIC SPRINKLERS
Scott Company, 243 Minna St., San Francisco.
Pacific Fire Extinguisher Co., 507 Montgomery St., San Francisco.

AWNINGS
W. A. Plummer Mfg. Co., Pine and Front Sts., San Francisco.

BANK FIXTURES AND INTERIORS
Fink & Schindler, 218 13th St., San Francisco.
A. J. Forbes & Son, 1530 Filbert St., San Francisco.
C. F. Weber & Co., 365 Market St., San Francisco.
Home Mfg. Co., 543 Brannan St., San Francisco.
Rucker-Fuller Desk Co., 677 Mission St., San Francisco.
T. H. Meek Co., 1130 Mission St., San Francisco.
Mullen Manufacturing Co., 20th and Harrison Sts., San Francisco.

BLACKBOARDS
C. F. Weber & Co., 365 Market St., San Francisco.
Beaver Blackboards and Greenboards, Rucker-Fuller Desk Company, Coast agents, 677 Mission St., San Francisco, Oakland and Los Angeles.

BONDS FOR CONTRACTORS
Fidelity & Casualty Co. of New York, Merchants Exchange Bldg., San Francisco.
Robertson & Hall, First National Bank Bldg., San Francisco.
Fred H. Boggs, Foxcroft Bldg., San Francisco.
J. T. Costello Co., 216 Pine St., San Francisco.
Fidelity & Deposit Co. of Maryland, 701 Insurance Exchange, San Francisco.
Globe Indemnity Co., Insurance Exchange Bldg., San Francisco.

BOOK BINDERS AND PRINTERS
Hicks-Judd Company, 51-65 First St., San Francisco.

BOILERS
"Franklin" water tube boiler, sold by General Machinery and Supply Co., 37 Stevenson St., San Francisco.

BRASS GOODS, CASTINGS, ETC.
H. Mueller Manufacturing Co., 589 Mission St., San Francisco.

BRICK—PRESSED, PAVING, ETC.
Gladding, McBean & Company, Crocker Bldg., San Francisco.
Los Angeles Pressed Brick Co., Frost Bldg., Los Angeles.
Livermore Brick Company, pressed, glazed and enameled, etc., Livermore, Cal.
Steiger Terra Cotta & Pottery Works, Mills Bldg., San Francisco.
United Materials Co., Crossley Bldg., San Francisco.
California Brick Company, Niles, Cal.

BRICK AND CEMENT COATING
Armorite and Concreta, manufactured by W. P. Fuller & Co., all principal Coast cities.
Wadsworth, Howland & Co., Inc. (See Adv. for Pacific Coast Agents.)
Paraffine Paint Co., 34 First St., San Francisco.
R. N. Nason & Co., 151 Potrero Ave., San Francisco.

BRICK STAINS
Samuel Cabot Mfg. Co., Boston, Mass., agencies in San Francisco, Oakland, Los Angeles, Portland, Tacoma and Spokane.
Armorite and Concreta, manufactured by W. P. Fuller & Co., all principal Coast cities.

BUILDERS' HARDWARE
Bennett Bros., agents for Sargent Hardware, 514 Market St., San Francisco.
Pacific Hardware & Steel Company, San Francisco, Oakland, Berkeley, and Los Angeles.

BUILDING MATERIAL, SUPPLIES, ETC.
Pacific Building Materials Co., 523 Market St., San Francisco.
C. Jorgensen, Crossley Bldg., San Francisco.
Richard Spencer, Hearst Bldg., San Francisco.
The Howard Company, First and Market Sts., Oakland.
James P. Dwan, 1113 Hearst Bldg., San Francisco.

CEMENT
Mt. Diablo, sold by Henry Cowell Lime & Cement Co., 2 Market street, San Francisco.
"Golden Gate" Brand, manufactured by Pacific Portland Cement Co., Pacific building, San Francisco.

CEMENT EXTERIOR WATERPROOF PAINT
Bay State Brick and Cement Coating, made by Wadsworth, Howland & Co. (See distributing agents in advertisement.)
Glidden's Liquid Cement and Liquid Cement Enamel, sold on Pacific Coast by Whittier, Coburn Co., San Francisco.
Armorite, sold by W. P. Fuller & Co., all principal Coast cities.
Imperial Waterproofing, manufactured by Imperial Co., 183 Stevenson St., San Francisco.
Paraffine Paint Co., 34 First St., San Francisco.

CEMENT EXTERIOR FINISH
Bay State Brick and Cement Coating, made by Wadsworth, Howland & Co. (See list of Distributing Agents in adv.)
Concreta, sold by W. P. Fuller & Co., all principal Coast cities.

An Index to the Advertisements

ARCHITECTS' SPECIFICATION INDEX—*Continued*

CEMENT EXTERIOR FINISH—Continued
Glidden's Liquid Cement and Liquid Cement Enamel, sold on Pacific Coast by Whittier, Coburn Company, San Francisco.
Pacific Building Materials Co., 523 Market St.
Samuel Cabot Mfg. Co., Boston, Mass., agencies in San Francisco, Oakland, Los Angeles, Portland, Tacoma and Spokane.

CEMENT FLOOR COATING
Bay State Brick and Cement Coating, made by Wadsworth, Howland & Co. (See list of Distributing Agents in adv.)
Fuller's Concrete Floor Enamel, made by W. P. Fuller & Co., San Francisco.

CEMENT TESTS—CHEMICAL ENGINEERS
Robert W. Hunt & Co., 251 Kearny St., San Francisco.

CHURCH INTERIORS
Fink & Schindler, 218 13th St., San Francisco.

CHUTES—SPIRAL
Haslett Warehouse Co., 310 California St., San Francisco.

CLOCKS—TOWER—STREET—PROGRAM
E. Howard Clock Co., Boston. Pacific Coast Agents, The Albert S. Samuels Co., 895 Market St., San Francisco. Joseph Mayer & Bro., Seattle, Wash.

COLD STORAGE PLANTS
T. P. Jarvis Crude Oil Burning Co., 275 Connecticut St., San Francisco.

COMPOSITION FLOORING
Germanwood Floor Co., 1621 Eddy St., San Francisco.
Malott & Peterson, Monadnock Bldg., San Francisco.
"Vitrolite," Vitrolite Construction Co., 34 Davis St., San Francisco.

COMPRESSED AIR MACHINERY
General Machinery & Supply Co., 39 Stevenson St., San Francisco.

COMPRESSED AIR CLEANERS
Spencer Turbine Cleaner. Sold by Hughson & Merton, 530 Golden Gate Ave., San Francisco.
Tuec, mfrd. by United Electric Company, 397 Sutter St., San Francisco, and 724 S. Broadway, Los Angeles.
Western Vacuum Supply Co., 1125 Market St., San Francisco.

CONCRETE CONSTRUCTION
American Concrete Co., Humboldt Bank Bldg., San Francisco.
Clinton Construction Co., 140 Townsend street, San Francisco.
Barrett & Hilp, Sharon Bldg., San Francisco.
Palmer & Peterson, Monadnock Bldg., San Francisco.

CONCRETE HARDNER
Master Builders Method, represented in San Francisco by C. Roman, Sharon Bldg.

CONCRETE MIXERS
Austin Improved Cube Mixer. J. H. Hansen & Co., California agents, 508 Balboa Bldg., San Francisco.
Foote Mixers. Sold by Edw. R. Bacon, 40 Natoma St., San Francisco.

CONCRETE REINFORCEMENT
United States Steel Products Co., San Francisco, Los Angeles, Portland and Seattle.
Twisted Bars. Sold by Woods, Huddart & Gunn, 444 Market St., San Francisco.
Clinton Welded Wire Fabric, L. A. Norris Co., 140 Townsend St., San Francisco.

CONCRETE REINFORCEMENT—Continued
Pacific Coast Steel Company, Rialto Bldg., San Francisco.
Southern California Iron and Steel Company, Fourth and Mateo Sts., Los Angeles.
Triangle Mesh Fabric. Sales agents, Pacific Building Materials Co., 523 Market St., San Francisco.

CONCRETE SURFACING
"Concreta." Sold by W. P. Fuller & Co., San Francisco.
Wadsworth, Howland & Co.'s Bay State Brick and Cement Coating. Sold by Jas. Hambly Co., Pacific Bldg., San Francisco, and Los Angeles.
Glidden Liquid Cement, manufactured by Glidden Varnish Co., Whittier, Coburn Co., San Francisco.

CONTRACTOR'S BONDS
Bonding Company of America, Kohl Bldg., San Francisco.
Globe Indemnity Co., 120 Leidesdorff St., San Francisco.
Fred H. Boggs, Foxcroft Bldg., San Francisco.
Fidelity & Casualty Co. of New York, Merchants Exchange Bldg., San Francisco.
Fidelity & Deposit Co. of Maryland, Insurance Exchange, San Francisco.
J. T. Costello Co., 216 Pine St., San Francisco.
Robertson & Hall, First National Bank Bldg., San Francisco.

CONTRACTORS, GENERAL
Arthur Arlett, New Call Bldg., San Francisco.
Farrell & Reed, Gunst Bldg., San Francisco.
American Concrete Co., Humboldt Bank Bldg., San Francisco.
Barrett & Hilp, Sharon Bldg., San Francisco.
Carnahan & Mulford, 45 Kearny St., San Francisco.
Houghton Construction Co., Hooker & Lent Bldg., San Francisco.
Geo. H. Bos, Hearst Bldg., San Francisco.
Larsen, Sampson & Co., Crocker Bldg., San Francisco.
J. D. Hannah, 725 Chronicle Bldg., San Francisco.
Clinton Construction Company, 140 Townsend St., San Francisco.
Dioguardi & Terranova, Westbank Bldg., San Francisco.
Teichert & Ambrose, Ochsner Bldg., Sacramento.
L. G. Bergren & Son, Call Bldg., San Francisco.
Grace & Bernieri, Claus Spreckels Bldg., San Francisco.
Geo. W. Boxton & Son, Hearst Bldg., San Francisco.
W. C. Duncan & Co., 526 Sharon Bldg., San Francisco.
A. P. Brady, Humboldt Bank Bldg., San Francisco.
Cameron & Disston, 831 Hearst Bldg., San Francisco.
Harvey A. Klyce, New Call Bldg., San Francisco.
Knowles & Mathewson, Call Bldg., San Francisco.
C. L. Wold Co., 75 Sutter St., San Francisco.
P. R. Ward, 981 Guerrero St., San Francisco.
Lange & Bergstrom, Sharon Bldg., San Francisco.
Foster Vogt Co., 411 Sharon Bldg., San Francisco.

ARCHITECTS' SPECIFICATION INDEX—*Continued*

CONTRACTORS, GENERAL—Continued
T. B. Goodwin, 110 Jessie St., San Francisco.
Thos. Elam & Son, Builders Exchange, San Francisco.
Masow & Morrison, 518 Monadnock Bldg., San Francisco.
Monson Bros., 502 Clunie Bldg., San Francisco.
J. M. Dougan Co., Hearst Bldg., San Francisco.
Palmer & Peterson, Monadnock Bldg., San Francisco.
Robert Trost, Twenty-sixth and Howard Sts., San Francisco.
John Monk, Sheldon Bldg., San Francisco.
Williams Bros. & Henderson, 381 Tenth St., San Francisco.

CONVEYING MACHINERY
Meese & Gottfried, San Francisco, Los Angeles, Portland and Seattle.

CORK TILING, FLOORING, ETC.
David Kennedy, Inc., Sharon Bldg., San Francisco.
Be-ver Cork Tile. Sold by W. L. Eaton & Co., 812 Santa Marina Bldg., San Francisco.

CORNER BEAD
Capitol Art Metal Works, 1927 Market St., San Francisco.
United States Metal Products Co., 555 Tenth St., San Francisco; 750 Keller St., San Francisco.

CRUSHED ROCK
Grant Gravel Co., Flatiron Bldg., San Francisco.
California Building Material Company, new Call Bldg., San Francisco.
Niles Sand, Gravel & Rock Co., Mutual Bank Bldg., San Francisco.
Pratt Building Material Co., Hearst Bldg., San Francisco.
Saratoga Rock Company, Baker-MacDonald Co. representatives, First National Bank Bldg., San Jose.

DAMP-PROOFING COMPOUND
Armorite Damp Resisting Paint, made by W. P. Fuller & Co., San Francisco.
Biturine Co., 24 California St., San Francisco.
Imperial Co., 183 Stevenson St., San Francisco.
"Pabco" Damp-Proofing Compound, sold by Paraffine Paint Co., 34 First St., San Francisco.
Wadsworth, Howland & Co., Inc., 84 Washington St., Boston. (See Adv. for Coast agencies.)

DOOR HANGERS
McCabe Hanger Mfg. Co., New York, N. Y.
Pitcher Hanger, sold by National Lumber Co., 326 Market St., San Francisco.
Reliance Hanger, sold by Sartorius Co., San Francisco; D. F. Fryer & Co., 513 B. V. Collins, Los Angeles, and Columbia Wire & Iron Works, Portland, Ore.

DRAIN BOARDS, SINK BACKS, ETC.
Germanwood Floor Co., 1621 Eddy St., San Francisco.

DRINKING FOUNTAINS
Haws Sanitary Fountain, 1808 Harmon St., Berkeley, and C. F. Weber & Co., San Francisco and Los Angeles.

DRINKING FOUNTAINS—Continued
Crane Company, San Francisco, Oakland, and Los Angeles.
Pacific Porcelain Ware Co., 67 New Montgomery St., San Francisco.

DUMB WAITERS
Spencer Elevator Company, 173 Beale St., San Francisco.
M. E. Hammond, Humboldt Bank Bldg., San Francisco.

ELECTRICAL CONTRACTORS
Butte Engineering Co., 683 Howard St., San Francisco.
Goold & Johns, 113 S. California St., Stockton, Cal.
NePage, McKenny Co., 149 New Montgomery St., San Francisco.
Newbery Electrical Co., 413 Lick Bldg., San Francisco.
Pacific Fire Extinguisher Co., 507 Montgomery St., San Francisco.
H. S. Tittle, 245 Minna St., San Francisco.
Standard Electrical Construction Company, 60 Natoma St., San Francisco.

ELECTRICAL ENGINEERS
Chas. T. Phillips, Pacific Bldg., San Francisco.

ELECTRIC PLATE WARMER
The Prometheus Electric Plate Warmer for residences, clubs, hotels, etc. Sold by M. E. Hammond, Humboldt Bank Bldg., San Francisco.

ELEVATORS
Otis Elevator Company, Stockton and North Point, San Francisco.
Spencer Elevator Company, 126 Beale St., San Francisco.
Van Emon Elevator Co., 54 Natoma St., San Francisco.

ENGINEERS
Chas. T. Phillips, Pacific Bldg., San Francisco.
Hunter & Hudson, Rialto Bldg., San Francisco.

FIRE ESCAPES
Palm Iron & Bridge Works, Sacramento.
Western Iron Works, 141 Beale St., San Francisco.

FIRE EXTINGUISHERS
Scott Company, 243 Minna St., San Francisco
Pacific Fire Extinguisher Co., 507 Montgomery St., San Francisco.

FIREPROOFING AND PARTITIONS
Gladding, McBean & Co., Crocker Bldg., San Francisco.
Keyhold Lath Co., Monadnock Bldg., San Francisco.
Los Angeles Pressed Brick Co., Frost Bldg., Los Angeles.

FIXTURES—BANK, OFFICE, STORE, ETC.
T. H. Meek & Co., 1130 Mission St., San Francisco.
Mullen Manufacturing Co., 20th and Harrison Sts., San Francisco.
The Fink & Schindler Co., 218 13th St., San Francisco.
A. J. Forbes & Son, 1530 Filbert St., San Francisco.
C. F. Weber & Co., 365 Market St., San Francisco, and 210 N. Main St., Los Angeles, Cal.

ARCHITECTS' SPECIFICATION INDEX—*Continued*

FLAG POLE TOPS
  Bolander & Son, 270 First St., San Francisco.
FLOOR TILE
  New York Belting and Packing Company, 519 Mission St., San Francisco.
  W. L. Eaton & Co., 112 Market St., San Francisco.
FLOOR VARNISH
  Bass-Hueter and San Francisco Pioneer Varnish Works, 816 Mission St., San Francisco.
  Fifteen for Floors, made by W. P. Fuller & Co., San Francisco.
  Standard Varnish Works, Chicago, New York and San Francisco.
  Glidden Products, sold by Whittier, Coburn Co., San Francisco.
  R. N. Nason & Co., San Francisco and Los Angeles.
FLOORS—COMPOSITION
  "Vitrolite," for any structure, room or bath. Vitrolite Construction Co,. 1490 Mission St., San Francisco.
  Malott & Peterson, Inc., Monadnock Bldg., San Francisco.
  Germanwood , Floor Co., 1621 Eddy St., San Francisco.
FLOORS—HARDWOOD
  Oak Flooring Bureau, Conway Bldg., Chicago, Il
  Strable Mfg. Co., 511 First St., Oakland.
FLUMES
  California Corrugated Culvert Co., West Berkeley, Cal.
FURNACES—WARM AIR
  Miller-Enwright Co., 907 Front St., Sacramento.
  Pacific Blower & Heating Co., 224 Fifth St., San Francisco.
GARAGE EQUIPMENT
  Bowser Gasoline Tanks and Outfit, Bowser & Co., 612 Howard St., San Francisco.
  Rix Compressed Air and Drill Company, First and Howard Sts., San Francisco.
GAS GRATES
  General Gas Light Co., 768 Mission St., San Francisco.
GLASS
  W. P. Fuller & Company, all principal Coast cities.
  Whittier, Coburn Co., Howard and Beale Sts., San Francisco.
GRANITE
  California Granite Co., Sharon Bldg., San Francisco.
  McGilvray-Raymond Granite Co., 634 Townsend St., San Francisco.
  Raymond Granite Co., Potrero Ave. and Division St., San Francisco.
GRAVEL AND SAND
  California Building Material Co., new Call Bldg., San Francisco.
  Del Monte White Sand, sold by Pacific Improvement Co., Crocker Bldg., San Francisco.
  Pratt Building Material Co., Hearst Bldg., San Francisco.

GRAVEL AND SAND—Continued
  Grant Gravel Co., Flatiron Bldg., San Francisco.
  Grant Rock & Gravel Co., Cory Bldg., Fresno.
  Niles Sand, Gravel & Rock Co., Mutual Savings Bank Bldg., 704 Market St., San Francisco.
  Saratoga Rock Company, 703 First National Bank Bldg., San Jose.
HARDWALL PLASTER
  Henry Cowell Lime & Cement Co., San Francisco.
  Empire Plaster sold by Pacific Portland Cement Co., Pacific Bldg., San Francisco.
HARDWARE
  Pacific Hardware & Steel Company, representing Lockwood Hardware Co., San Francisco.
  Sargent's Hardware, sold by Bennett Bros., 514 Market St., San Francisco.
HARDWOOD LUMBER—FLOORING, ETC.
  Dieckmann Hardwood Co., Beach and Taylor Sts., San Francisco.
  Parrott & Co., 320 California St., San Francisco.
  White Bros., cor. Fifth and Brannan Sts., San Francisco.
  Strable Mfg. Co., 511 First St., Oakland.
HEATERS—AUTOMATIC
  Pittsburg Water Heater Co., 478 Sutter St., San Francisco.
HEATING AND VENTILATING
  Gilley-Schmid Company, 198 Otis St., San Francisco.
  Mangrum & Otter, Inc., 507 Mission St., San Francisco.
  Charles T. Phillips, Pacific Bldg., San Francisco.
  James & Drucker, 450 Hayes St., San Francisco.
  J. C. Hurley Co., 509 Sixth St., San Francisco.
  Illinois Engineering Co., 563 Pacific Bldg., San Francisco.
  William F. Wilson Co., 328 Mason St., San Francisco.
  Pacific Fire Extinguisher Co., 507 Montgomery St., San Francisco.
  Pacific Blower & Heating Co., 224 Fifth St., San Francisco.
  Scott Company, 243 Minna St., San Francisco.
  Thermic Engineering Company, Claus Spreckels Bldg., San Francisco.
  C. A. Dunham Co., Wells Fargo Bldg., San Francisco.
HEAT REGULATION
  Johnson Service Company, 149 Fifth St., San Francisco.
HOLLOW BLOCKS
  Denison Hollow Interlocking Blocks. Forum Bldg., Sacramento, and the Howard Company, Oakland.
  Gladding, McBean & Co., San Francisco, Los Angeles, Oakland and Sacramento.
  Pratt Building Material Co., Hearst Bldg., San Francisco.

When writing to Advertisers please mention this magazine.

ARCHITECTS' SPECIFICATION INDEX—*Continued*

HOLLOW METAL DOORS AND TRIM
Edwin C. Dehn, 301 Hearst Bldg., San Francisco, representing Interior Metal Mfg. Co., Jamestown, N. Y.

HOSPITAL FIXTURES
J. L. Mott Iron Works, 135 Kearny St., San Francisco.

HOTELS
St. Francis Hotel, Union Square, San Francisco.
Hotel Whitcomb, facing Civic Center, San Francisco.

INGOT IRON
"Armco" brand, manufactured by American Rolling Mill Company, Middletown, Ohio, and Monadnock Bldg., San Francisco.

INSPECTIONS AND TESTS
Robert W. Hunt & Co., 251 Kearny St., San Francisco.

INTERIOR DECORATORS
Mrs. H. C. McAfee, 504 Sutter St., San Francisco.
Albert S. Bigley, 344 Geary St., San Francisco.
City of Paris, Geary and Stockton Sts., San Francisco.
A. Falvy, 578 Sutter St., San Francisco.
The Tormey Co., 681 Geary St., San Francisco.
Fick Bros., 475 Haight St., San Francisco.
O'Hara & Livermore, Sutter St., San Francisco.

KITCHEN CABINETS
Western Equipment Co., Building Material Exhibit, 77 O'Farrell St., San Francisco.
Hoosier Cabinets, branch 1067 Market St., San Francisco.

LIGHTING FIXTURES
"The Crystal Light," manufactured by Modern Appliance Co., 128 Sutter St., San Francisco.

LAMP POSTS, ELECTROLIERS, ETC.
J. L. Mott Iron Works, 135 Kearny St., San Francisco.
Ralston Iron Works, 20th and Indiana Sts., San Francisco.

LANDSCAPE GARDENERS
MacRorie-McLaren Co., 141 Powell St., San Francisco.

LATHING MATERIAL
"Buttonlath," manufactured by Buttonlath Mfg. Co., office, Building Material Exhibit, San Francisco.
Keyhold Lath Co., Monadnock Bldg., San Francisco.
Pacific Building Materials Co., 523 Market St., San Francisco.

LIGHT, HEAT AND POWER
Pacific Gas & Elec. Co., 445 Sutter St., San Francisco.
The Fish Fuel System, Palace Hotel, San Francisco.

LIME
Henry Cowell Lime & Cement Co., 2 Market St., San Francisco.

LINOLEUM
D. N. & E. Walter & Co., O'Farrell and Stockton Sts., San Francisco.

LUMBER
Dudfield Lumber Co., Palo Alto, Cal.
Hooper Lumber Co., Seventeenth and Illinois Sts., San Francisco.
Portland Lumber Co., 16 California St., San Francisco.
Pacific Manufacturing Company, San Francisco, Oakland and Santa Clara.
Pacific Mill and Timber Co., First National Bank Bldg., San Francisco.
Pope & Talbot, foot of Third St., San Francisco.
Sunset Lumber Co., Oakland, Cal.
United Lumber Company, 687 Market St., San Francisco.

MASTIC FLOORING
Malott & Peterson, Monadnock Bldg., San Francisco.

MAIL CHUTES
Cutler Mail Chute Co., Rochester, N. Y. (See adv. on page 30 for Coast representatives.)
American Mailing Device Corp., represented on Pacific Coast by U. S. Metal Products Co., 555 Tenth St., San Francisco.

MANTELS
Mangrum & Otter, 561 Mission St., San Francisco.

MARBLE
American Marble and Mosaic Co., 25 Columbus Square, San Francisco.
Joseph Musto Sons, Keenan Co., 535 N. Point St., San Francisco.
Sculptors' Workshop, S. Miletin & Co., 1705 Harrison St., San Francisco.

METAL CEILINGS
San Francisco Metal Stamping & Corrugating Co., 2269 Folsom St., San Francisco.

METAL DOORS AND WINDOWS
U. S. Metal Products Co., 555 Tenth St., San Francisco.
Capitol Art Metal Works, 1927 Market St., San Francisco.

METAL FURNITURE
Capitol Art Metal Works, 1927 Market St., San Francisco.
Ralston Iron Works, Twentieth and Indiana Sts., San Francisco.
Edwin C. Dehn, Manufacturer's Agent, Hearst Bldg., San Francisco.

MILL WORK
Dudfield Lumber Co., Palo Alto, Cal.
Pacific Manufacturing Company, San Francisco, Oakland and Santa Clara.
National Mill and Lumber Co., San Francisco and Oakland.
The Fink & Schindler Co., 218 13th St., San Francisco.

OIL BURNERS
American Standard Oil Burner Company, Seventh and Cedar Sts., Oakland.
S. T. Johnson Co., 1337 Mission St., San Francisco.
T. P. Jarvis Crude Oil Burner Co., 275 Connecticut St., San Francisco.
Fess System, 220 Natoma St., San Francisco.
W. S. Ray Mfg. Co., 218 Market St., San Francisco.

ARCHITECTS' SPECIFICATION INDEX—*Continued*

ORNAMENTAL IRON AND BRONZE
American Art Metal Works, 13 Grace St., San Francisco.
California Artistic Metal and Wire. Co., 349 Seventh St., San Francisco.
Palm Iron & Bridge Works, Sacramento.
Ralston Iron Works, 20th and Indiana Sts., San Francisco.
C. J. Hillard Company, Inc., 19th and Minnesota Sts., San Francisco.
Schreiber & Sons Co., represented by Western Builders Supply Co., San Francisco.
Schrader Iron Works, Inc., 1247 Harrison St., San Francisco.
West Coast Wire & Iron Works, 861-863 Howard St., San Francisco.

PAINT FOR CEMENT
Bay State Brick and Cement Coating, made by Wadsworth, Howland & Co. (Inc.) (See adv. in this issue for Pacific Coast agents.)
Fuller's Concreta for Cement, made by W. P. Fuller & Co., San Francisco.
Samuel Cabot Mfg. Co., Boston, Mass., agencies in San Francisco, Oakland, Los Angeles, Portland, Tacoma and Spokane.

PAINT FOR STEEL STRUCTURES, BRIDGES. ETC.
Biturine Company, 24 California St., San Francisco.
Glidden's Acid Proof Coating, sold on Pacific Coast by Whittier, Coburn Company, San Francisco.
Paraffine Paint Co., 34 First St., San Francisco.
Premier Graphite Paint and Pioneer Brand Red Lead, made by W. P. Fuller & Co., San Francisco.

PAINTING. TINTING. ETC.
Art Wall Paper Co., 508 Ellis St., San Francisco
Golden Gate Decorating Co., 704 Polk St., San Francisco.
I. R. Kissel, 1747 Sacramento St., San Francisco.
D. Zelinsky & Sons, San Francisco and Los Angeles.
The Tormey Co., 681 Geary St., San Francisco.
Fick Bros., 475 Haight St., San Francisco.

PAINTS, OILS, ETC.
The Brininstool Co., Los Angeles, the Haslett Warehouse, 310 California St., San Francisco.
Bass-Hueter Paint Co., Mission, near Fourth St., San Francisco.
Biturine Company, 24 California St., San Francisco.
Whittier, Coburn Co., Howard and Beale Sts., San Francisco.
Magner Bros., 419-421 Jackson St., San Francisco.
R. N. Nason & Company, San Francisco, Los Angeles, Portland and Seattle.
W. P. Fuller & Co., all principal Coast cities.
Standard Varnish Works, 55 Stevenson St., San Francisco.

PANELS AND VENEER
White Bros., Fifth and Brannan Sts., San Francisco.

PIPE—VITRIFIED SALT GLAZED TERRA COTTA
Gladding. McBean & Co., Crocker Bldg., San Francisco.
Steiger Terra Cotta and Pottery Works, Mills Bldg., San Francisco.
G. Weissbaum & Co. Pipe Works, 127 Eleventh St., San Francisco.

PLASTER CONTRACTORS
C. C. Morehouse, Crocker Bldg., San Francisco.
MacGruer & Co., 180 Jessie St., San Francisco.
M. J. Terranova, Westbank Bldg., San Francisco.

PLASTER EXTERIORS
"Kellastone," an imperishable stucco. Blake Plaster Co., Bacon Block, Oakland.
Keyhold Lath Co., Monadnock Bldg., San Francisco.
Buttonlath, for exterior and interior plastering, Hearst Bldg., San Francisco.

PLUMBING CONTRACTORS
Alex Coleman, 706 Ellis St., San Francisco.
A. Lettich, 365 Fell St., San Francisco.
Gilley-Schmid Company, 198 Otis St., San Francisco.
Scott Co., Inc., 243 Minna St., San Francisco.
Wm. F. Wilson Co., 328 Mason St., San Francisco.

PLUMBING FIXTURES. MATERIALS. ETC.
Crane Co., San Francisco and Oakland.
California Steam Plumbing Supply Co., 671 Fifth St., San Francisco.
Gilley-Schmid Company, 198 Otis St., San Francisco.
Glauber Brass Manufacturing Company, 1107 Mission St., San Francisco.
Holbrook, Merrill & Stetson, 64 Sutter St., San Francisco.
Improved Sanitary Fixture Co., 632 Metropolitan Bldg., Los Angeles.
J. L. Mott Iron Works, D. H. Gulick, selling agent, 135 Kearny St., San Francisco.
Haines, Jones & Cadbury Co., 857 Folsom St., San Francisco.
H. Mueller Manufacturing Co., Pacific Coast branch, 589 Mission St., San Francisco.
Miller-Enwright Co., 907 Front St., Sacramento.
Mark-Lally Co., 235 Second St., San Francisco, also Oakland, Fresno, San Jose and Stockton.
Pacific Sanitary Manufacturing Co., 67 New Montgomery St., San Francisco.
Wm. F. Wilson Co., 328 Mason St., San Francisco.
C. A. Dunham Co., Wells Fargo Bldg., San Francisco.

POTTERY
Gladding. McBean & Co., San Francisco, Los Angeles, Oakland and Sacramento.
Steiger Terra Cotta and Pottery Works, Mills Bldg., San Francisco.

POWER TRANSMITTING MACHINERY
Meese & Gottfried, San Francisco, Los Angeles, Portland, Ore., and Seattle, Wash.

PUMPS
Simonds Machinery Co., 117 New Montgomery St., San Francisco.

RADIATORS
American Radiator Co., Second and Townsend Sts., San Francisco.

RAILROADS
Southern Pacific Company, Flood Bldg., San Francisco.
Western Pacific Company, Mills Bldg., San Francisco.

REFRIGERATORS
McCray Refrigerators, sold by Nathan Dohrmann Co., Geary and Stockton Sts., San Francisco.

REVERSIBLE WINDOWS
Hauser Reversible Window Company, Balboa Bldg., San Francisco.
Whitney Windows, represented by Richard Spencer, 801-3 Hearst Bldg., San Francisco.

REVOLVING DOORS
Van Kennel Doors, sold by U. S. Metal Products Co., 525 Market St., San Francisco.

ROLLING DOORS, SHUTTERS, PARTITIONS, ETC.
C. F. Weber & Co., 365 Market St., S. F.
Kinnear Steel Rolling Doors. W. W. Thurston, agent, Rialto Bldg., San Francisco.
Wilson's Steel Rolling Doors, U. S. Metal Products Co., San Francisco and Los Angeles.

ARCHITECTS' SPECIFICATION INDEX—*Continued*

ROOFING AND ROOFING MATERIALS
Grant Gravel Co., Flatiron Bldg., San Francisco.
H. W. Johns-Manville Co., Second and Howard Sts., San Francisco.
Malott & Peterson, Inc., Monadnock Bldg., San Francisco.
Niles Sand, Gravel and Rock Co., Mutual Bank Bldg., San Francisco.
"Malthoid" and "Ruberoid," manufactured by Paraffine Paint Co., San Francisco.
Pioneer Roofing, manufactured by Pioneer Paper Co., 513 Hearst Bldg., San Francisco.
United Materials Co., Crossley Bldg., San Francisco.

RUBBER TILING
Goodyear Rubber Company, 587 Market St., San Francisco.
New York Belting & Rubber Company, 519 Mission St., San Francisco.

SAFETY TREADS
"Sanitread," sold by Richard Spencer, 801-3 Hearst Bldg., San Francisco.
Pacific Building Materials Co., 523 Market St., San Francisco.
C. Jorgensen, Crossley Bldg., San Francisco.

SCENIC PAINTING—DROP CURTAINS, ETC.
The Edwin H. Flagg Scenic Co., 1638 Long Beach Ave., Los Angeles.

SCHOOL FURNITURE AND SUPPLIES
C. F. Weber & Co., 365 Market St., San Francisco; 512 S. Broadway, Los Angeles.
Rucker-Fuller Desk Company, 677 Mission St., San Francisco.

SCREENS
Hipolito Flyout Screens, sold by Simpson & Stewart, Dalziel Bldg., Oakland.
Watson Metal Frame Screens, sold by Richard Spencer, 801-3 Hearst Bldg., San Francisco.

SEEDS
California Seed Company, 151 Market St., San Francisco.

SHEATHING AND SOUND DEADENING
Samuel Cabot Mfg. Co., Boston, Mass., agencies in San Francisco, Oakland, Los Angeles, Portland, Tacoma and Spokane.
Paraffine Paint Co., 34 First St., San Francisco.

SHEET METAL WORK, SKYLIGHTS, ETC.
Capitol Sheet Metal Works, 1927 Market St., San Francisco.
U. S. Metal Products Co., 555 Tenth St., San Francisco.

SHINGLE STAINS
Cabot's Creosote Stains, sold by Pacific Building Materials Co., Underwood Bldg., San Francisco
Fuller's Pioneer Shingle Stains, made by W. P. Fuller & Co., San Francisco.

SIDEWALK LIGHTS
P. H. Jackson & Co., 237-47 First St., San Francisco.
Jas. P. Dwan, Hearst Bldg., San Francisco.

STEEL TANKS, PIPE, ETC.
Schaw-Batcher Co. Pipe Works, 356 Market St., San Francisco.

STEEL AND IRON—STRUCTURAL
Central Iron Works, 621 Florida St., San Francisco.
Dyer Bros., 17th and Kansas Sts., San Francisco.
Golden Gate Iron Works, 1541 Howard St., San Francisco.
Judson Manufacturing Co., 819 Folsom St., San Francisco.
Mortenson Construction Co., 19th and Indiana Sts., San Francisco.
Pacific Rolling Mills, 17th and Mississippi Sts., San Francisco.
Palm Iron & Bridge Works, Sacramento.
Ralston Iron Works, Twentieth and Indiana Sts., San Francisco.
U. S. Steel Products Co., Rialto Bldg., San Francisco.
Sims, Gray & Sauter, 156 Main St., San Francisco.
Schrader Iron Works, Inc., 1247 Harrison St., San Francisco.
Southern California Iron and Steel Co., Fourth and Mateo Sts., Los Angeles.
Western Iron Works, 141 Beale St., San Francisco.

STEEL PRESERVATIVES
Bay State Steel Protective Coating. (See adv. for coast agencies.)
Paraffine Paint Co., 34 First St., San Francisco.
Biturine Company, 24 California St., San Francisco.

STEEL REINFORCING
Pacific Coast Steel Company, Rialto Bldg., San Francisco.
Southern California Iron & Steel Company, Fourth and Mateo Sts., Los Angeles.
Woods, Huddart & Gunn, 444 Market St., San Francisco.

STEEL ROLLING DOORS
Kinnear Steel Rolling Door Co., W. W. Thurston, Rialto Bldg., San Francisco.

STEEL SASH
"Fenestra," solid steel sash, manufactured by Detroit Steel Products Company, Detroit, Mich.

STEEL WHEELBARROWS
Champion and California steel brands, made by Western Iron Works, 141 Beale St., San Francisco.

STONE
California Granite Co., 518 Sharon Bldg., San Francisco.
McGilvray Stone Company, 634 Townsend St., San Francisco.

STORAGE SYSTEMS—GASOLINE, OIL, ETC.
S. F. Bowser & Co., 612 Howard St., San Francisco.
Rix Compressed Air and Drill Co., First and Howard Sts., San Francisco.

When writing to Advertisers please mention this magazine.

ARCHITECTS' SPECIFICATION INDEX—*Continued*

TEMPERATURE REGULATION
Johnson Service Company, 149 Fifth St., San Francisco.

THEATER AND OPERA CHAIRS
C. F. Weber & Co., 365 Market St., San Francisco.

TILES, MOSAICS, MANTELS, ETC.
Rigney Tile Company, Sheldon Bldg., San Francisco.
Mangrum & Otter, 561 Mission St., San Francisco.
McElhinney Tile Co., 1097 Mission St., San Francisco.

TILE FOR ROOFING
Gladding, McBean & Co., Crocker Bldg., San Francisco.
United Materials Co., Crossley Bldg., San Francisco.

TILE WALLS—INTERLOCKING
Denison Hollow Interlocking Blocks, Forum Bldg., Sacramento.
Gladding, McBean & Co., San Francisco, Los Angeles, Oakland and Sacramento.

VACUUM CLEANERS
Arco Wand Cleaners, sold by American Radiator Company, Second and Townsend Sts., San Francisco.
"Tuec" Air Cleaner, manufactured by United Electric Co. Coast agencies, 556 Sutter St., San Francisco, and 724 S. Broadway, Los Angeles.
Palm Vacuum Cleaners, sold by Western Vacuum Supply Co., 1125 Market St., San Francisco.
Spencer Turbine Cleaner, sold by Hughson & Merton, 530 Golden Gate Ave., San Francisco.

VALVES
Sloan Royal Flush Valves. T. R. Burke, Pacific Coast agent, Wells Fargo Bldg., San Francisco.
Crane Radiator Valves., manufactured by Crane Co., Second and Brannan Sts., San Francisco.

VALVE PACKING
N. H. Cook Belting Co., 317 Howard St., San Francisco.

VARNISHES
W. P. Fuller Co., all principal Coast cities.
Glidden Varnish Co., Cleveland, O., represented on the Pacific Coast by Whittier, Coburn Co., San Francisco.
R. N. Nason & Co., San Francisco, Los Angeles, Portland and Seattle.
Standard Varnish Works, San Francisco.
S. F. Pioneer Varnish Works, 816 Mission St., San Francisco.

VENETIAN BLINDS, AWNINGS, ETC.
Burlington Venetian Blinds, Burlington, Vt., and C. F. Weber & Co., 365 Market St., San Francisco.
Western Blind & Screen Co., 2702 Long Beach Ave., Los Angeles.

VITREOUS CHINAWARE
Pacific Porcelain Ware Company, 67 New Montgomery St., San Francisco.

WALL BEDS, SEATS, ETC.
Lachman Wall Bed Co., 2019 Mission St., San Francisco.
Marshall & Stearns Co., 1154 Phelan Bldg., San Francisco.
Peek's Wall Beds, sold by Western Equipment Co., 72 Fremont St., San Francisco.
Perfection Disappearing Bed Co., 737 Mission St., San Francisco.

WALL PAINT
Nason's Opaque Flat Finish, manufactured by R. N. Nason & Co., San Francisco, Portland and Los Angeles.
San-A-Cote and Vel--va-Cote, manufactured by the Brininstool Co., Los Angeles; Marion D. Cohn Co., Hansford Bldg., San Francisco, distributor.

WALL BOARD
"Amiwud" Wall Board, manufactured by Paraffine Paint Co., 34 First St., San Francisco.

WALL PAPER
Uhl Bros., 38 O'Farrell St., San Francisco.
The Tormey Co., 681 Geary St., San Francisco.
Art Wall Paper Co., 500 Ellis St., San Francisco.

WATER HEATERS—AUTOMATIC
Pittsburg Water Heater Co. of California, 478 Sutter St., San Francisco, and Thirteenth and Clay Sts., Oakland.

WATERPROOFING FOR CONCRETE, BRICK, ETC.
Armorite Damp Resisting Paint, made by W. P. Fuller & Co., San Francisco.
Biturine Company, 24 California St., San Francisco.
J. L. Goffette Corporation, 227 San Bruno Ave., San Francisco.
Hill, Hubbell & Co., 1 Drumm St., San Francisco.
H. W. Johns-Manville Co., San Francisco and principal Coast cities.
Imperial Co., 183 Stevenson St., San Francisco.
Pacific Building Materials Co., 523 Market St., San Francisco.
Samuel Cabot Mfg. Co., Boston, Mass., agencies in San Francisco, Oakland, Los Angeles, Portland, Tacoma and Spokane.
Wadsworth, Howland & Co., Inc. (See adv. for Coast agencies.)

WATER SUPPLY SYSTEMS
Kewanee Water Supply System—Simonds Machinery Co., agents, 117 New Montgomery St., San Francisco.

WHEELBARROWS—STEEL
Western Iron Works, Beale and Main Sts., San Francisco.

WHITE ENAMEL FINISH
"Gold Seal," manufactured and sold by Bass-Hueter Paint Company. All principal Coast cities.
"Silkenwhite," made by W. P. Fuller & Co., San Francisco.
"Satinette," Standard Varnish Works, 113 Front St., San Francisco.

WINDOWS—REVERSIBLE, CASEMENT, ETC.
Whitney Window, represented by Richard Spencer, Hearst Bldg., San Francisco.
Hauser Reversible Window Co., Balboa Bldg., San Francisco.
International Casement Co., represented by Edwin C. Dehn, Hearst Bldg., San Francisco.

WIRE FABRIC
U. S. Steel Products Co., Rialto Bldg., San Francisco.

WOOD MANTELS
Fink & Schindler, 218 13th St., San Francisco.
Mangrum & Otter, 561 Mission St., San Francisco.

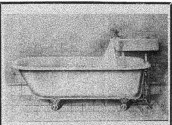

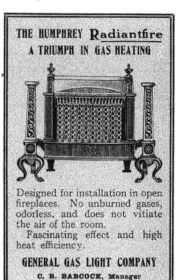

When writing to Advertisers please mention this magazine.

CRANE
CAST IRON
BRASS
CAST STEEL
FERROSTEEL

FLANGED FITTINGS

We have the largest line of patterns for flanged fittings for low pressure, standard, extra heavy, hydraulic, superheated and extreme hydraulic pressures, ranging in size from one-inch to sixty-inch, and for working pressures from fifty pounds to three thousand pounds.

The dimensions of the low pressure, standard and extra heavy fittings are in accordance with the 1915 *American Standard.*

Castings for special fittings also may be made at a minimum expense owing to our large equipment of special patterns which may be altered at very low cost.

CRANE CO.
PLUMBING SUPPLIES

2nd and Brannan Sts., SAN FRANCISCO.

348 9th Street
OAKLAND

Architects designing hotels, apartment houses, theatres and office buildings, should keep in mind the fact that THREE BARRELS OF FUEL OIL burned by the

Fess System

will equal the heat produced by a TON OF COAL — *Economy for the Owner.*

And that the FESS SYSTEM is the Only Fire-Proof Rotary Burner manufactured — *More Economy for the Owner — Less Insurance to pay.*

Fess System Rotary Crude Oil Burners
FOR HEATING, POWER, COOKING
Office and Factory—218 Natoma St., San Francisco
Branches—1310 So. Hill St. Los Angeles; 428 Alder St., Portland, Ore.; 131 B St., San Diego.

Hipolito

EVEN TENSION
Window Screens   Screen Doors

ROLLER SCREENS
For Casement Windows

METAL FRAME SCREENS

SEE DISPLAY AT
Building Material Exhibit
77 O'Farrell St.   San Francisco

Simpson & Stewart
FACTORY DISTRIBUTORS

565 16th St., Oakland, Cal.
TELEPHONE LAKESIDE 415

Better than Window Shades
BURLINGTON VENETIAN BLINDS
can be adjusted to *let in* light and air, yet *keep out* the sun and the gaze of outsiders. They make your sunny rooms cool and restful, your porch a shady, airy and secluded haven of comfort.

Also order Burlington Window Screens (inside or outside) and Screen Doors with Rust-proof wire cloth, they have the quality. Instead of old-fashioned *folding* blinds insist on BURLINGTON Patent Inside *Sliding* Blinds. Look for the name "Burlington": best for cottage or mansion.

Burlington Venetian Blind Co.
BURLINGTON, VT.   365 MARKET ST., SAN FRANCISCO

When writing to Advertisers please mention this magazine.

When writing to Advertisers please mention this magazine.

THE ARCHITECT & ENGINEER

25c Copy
$1.50 a Year.
OF CALIFORNIA
Volume XLIX
Number 2

Issued monthly in the interest of Architects, Structural Engineers, Contractors and the Allied Trades of the Pacific Coast.

Entered at San Francisco Post Office as Second Class Matter.

CONTENTS FOR MAY, 1917

DETAIL OF TERRACE, HOUSE OF MR. EDSON F. ADAMS, PIEDMONT
CHARLES PETER WEEKS,   ARCHITECT

THE
ARCHITECT
AND
ENGINEER
OF CALIFORNIA
MAY · 1917

VOL. XLIX.   NUMBER 2.

Domestic Architecture in California
By FREDERICK JENNINGS

MUCH has been written of domestic architecture, and, like the discussion of many other subjects, the authors have covered such a wide range of thought that some doubt penetrates the reader's mind as to just what constitutes really good house planning. It is not surprising that many of our architects are thoroughly disgusted with some of the dreadful abortions that disfigure the residence sections of our large cities.

There are two types of this class of houses — first, the misnamed bungalow or cottage—thrown together from stereotyped plans usually prepared by a contractor or copied from a twenty-five-cent catalog. The profession refers to these homes as "mushrooms," probably because they spring up over night. The second type is the two-story box-like house that is planned by the architectural draughtsman of limited professional standing who is satisfied to take a couple of hundred dollars from his client in payment for a very poor set of blue prints and specifications. The owner does his own supervising and uses his own judgment in hiring labor and buying materials. When his home is finished he finds it has cost

ENTRANCE DETAIL,
HOUSE OF
MR. J. O. GANTNER
SAN FRANCISCO
Louis M. Upton, Architect

GARDEN AND WEST ELEVATION, HOUSE OF MR. EDSON F. ADAMS, PIEDMONT
CHARLES PETER WEEKS,
ARCHITECT

ENTRANCE ELEVATION, HOUSE OF MR. EDSON F. ADAMS, PIEDMONT

POOL, HOUSE OF MR. EDSON F. ADAMS, PIEDMONT
Charles Peter Weeks, Architect

DETAIL, MAIN FACADE, HOUSE OF MR. EDSON F. ADAMS, PIEDMONT
CHARLES PETER WEEKS,   ARCHITECT

DETAIL OF ENTRANCE, HOUSE OF MR. EDSON F. ADAMS, PIEDMONT
CHARLES PETER WEEKS,   ARCHITECT

ENTRANCE HALL, HOUSE OF MR. EDSON F. ADAMS, PIEDMONT
Charles Peter Weeks, Architect

LOGGIA, HOUSE OF MR. EDSON F. ADAMS, PIEDMONT
Charles Peter Weeks, Architect

ENTRANCE DETAIL, HOUSE OF MR. GEORGE H. LENT, WOODSIDE
Bakewell & Brown, Architects

GARDEN VIEW, HOUSE OF MR. GEORGE H. LENT, WOODSIDE
Bakewell & Brown, Architects

HOUSE OF MR. GEORGE H. LENT, WOODSIDE
Bakewell & Brown, Architects

HALL AND STAIRWAY, HOUSE OF MR. GEORGE H. LENT, WOODSIDE
Bakewell & Brown, Architects

HOUSE OF PROF. A. U. POPE, CRAGMONT, BERKELEY
Wood & Simpson, Architects

him double what he anticipated and he has a shack on his hands, devoid of good lines on the outside and far from refined within.

The time is coming, and that not far distant, we hope, when home building of the sort described will be impossible. Our cities will have commissions, made up of reputable architects, engineers and landscape experts, and it will be their duty to pass upon plans before building is started. This will assure us residence blocks laid out in an attractive manner with houses designed on dignified lines and harmonious, one with the other. The monotonous repetition of style will be done away with and it will not be possible to thrust a huge two-story and attic house alongside a squatty, rambling bungalow. The bungalow, by the way, should have its own environment, if its full charm is to be realized. It should not be crowded between or alongside a two-story house, and the grounds about it should be large enough to give the bungalow a proper setting.

♪ ♪ ♪

The pictures of homes in this issue cover a wide range. The pretentious city mansion is seen in the house for Mr. Edson F. Adams at Piedmont,

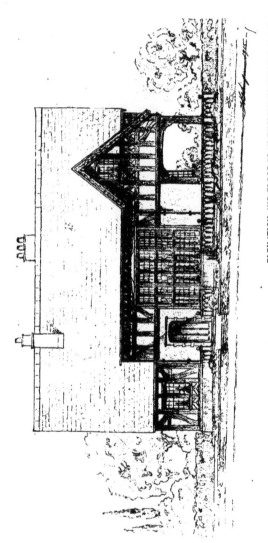

ELEVATION AND FLOOR PLAN ENGLISH COTTAGE, P. P. I. E.
NOW THE RESIDENCE OF PROF. A. U. POPE
BERKELEY, CALIFORNIA

ENGLISH COTTAGE, AS IT APPEARED AT THE EXPOSITION

THE SAME COTTAGE, REBUILT AND ENLARGED, NOW THE PROPERTY OF
PROF. A. U. POPE, CRAGMONT
Wood & Simpson, Architects

LIVING ROOM, HOUSE OF PROF. A. U. POPE, CRAGMONT
Wood & Simpson, Architects

DINING ROOM, HOUSE OF PROF. A. U. POPE, CRAGMONT
Wood & Simpson, Architects

LIVING ROOM, HOUSE OF PROF. A. U. POPE, CRAGMONT
Wood & Simpson, Architects

LIVING ROOM, HOUSE OF PROF. A. U. POPE, CRAGMONT
Wood & Simpson, Architects

DINING ROOM, HOÙSE OF PROF. A. U. POPE, CRAGMONT
Wood & Simpson, Architects

GUEST ROOM, HOUSE OF PROF. A. U. POPE, CRAGMONT
Wood & Simpson, Architects

ENTRANCE DETAIL, HOUSE OF MR. SIDNEY M. EHRMAN, SAN FRANCISCO
LEWIS P. HOBART,   ARCHITECT

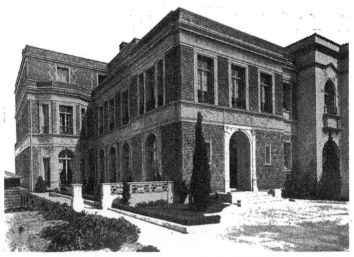

HOUSE OF MR. SIDNEY M. EHRMAN, SAN FRANCISCO
Lewis P. Hobart, Architect

COURT, HOUSE OF MR. CRIMMINS, LOS ANGELES
Morgan, Walls & Morgan, Architects

RESIDENCE OF MR. WALTER MOORE, PIEDMONT
Albert Farr, Architect

HOUSE OF MR. GEORGE W. KELHAM, SAN FRANCISCO
George W. Kelham, Architect

WEST ELEVATION,.HOUSE OF MR. GEORGE W. KELHAM
George W. Kelham, Architect

designed by Mr. Charles Peter Weeks. It is a splendid American adaptation of the French school.

In the series of pictures of the charming home of Professor Arthur U. Pope in the Berkeley hills. (Wood & Simpson, architects) one recognizes parts of the little English cottage, designed by Mr. Simpson, which attracted so much attention at the late Panama-Pacific Exposition. The building was transported across the bay on a flat boat, moved up over the hills on wheels by the aid of two powerful "Holt" tractors and set upon a new foundation which had been prepared for it. The task of the designer then began anew as cost limitations and the strong affection of the clients for the early New England colonial architecture made it necessary to depart somewhat from the style of the original part. Client and architect, co-operating in the most enthusiastic fashion, invented a sort of historical fiction, assuming a lapse of about two hundred years between the dates of the two parts of the house and the result has produced a building of much charm and distinction and that pleasant rambling effect usually obtained only by successive additions extending over a long period of years. A point which requires special notice is the manner in which the house has been adapted to the local climate. In this

RESIDENCE OF MR. NICKERSON, BERKELEY
WALTER H. RATCLIFF, JR., ARCHITECT

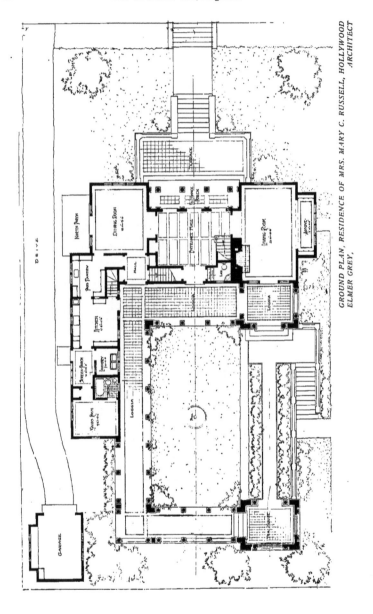

GROUND PLAN, RESIDENCE OF MRS. MARY C. RUSSELL, HOLLYWOOD
ELMER GREY, ARCHITECT

RESIDENCE OF MRS. MARY C. RUSSELL, HOLLYWOOD
Elmer Grey, Architect

PORCH AND PATIO, RESIDENCE OF MRS. MARY C. RUSSELL
Elmer Grey, Architect

HOUSE OF MR. EDWIN LEACH, PIEDMONT
Louis M. Upton, Architect

RESIDENCE AND STUDIO FOR MR. HAIG PATIGIAN, SAN FRANCISCO
Ward & Blohme, Architects

ENTRANCE HALL AND STAIRWAY, RESIDENCE AND
STUDIO OF MR. HAIG PATIGIAN,   SAN FRANCISCO
WARD & BLOHME,   ARCHITECTS

HOUSE OF MR. W. S. CRISMON, LOS ANGELES
Arthur R. Kelly, Architect

connection it is interesting to quote from an article by Mr. Simpson in the
Architect and Engineer of February, 1916.

"The question of windows requires a very special study to fit our
peculiar local climate, as we require an abundance of sunlight at certain
seasons, while at others the glare from this source is oppressive. This
requires a sort of adjustable glass area, best secured by very large
windows on the south side of the rooms, with shutters or heavy curtains
to temper the light in sultry weather. This large glass area requires
skilful treatment in order to obtain good scale and domestic character.
It must be suitably divided to harmonize with the other windows of the
house, as the large sheets of plate glass, which we often see, remind us
of shop windows, and are a certain indication of vulgar taste."

The reader may know how well this principle has been embodied by
noting the flood of sunshine in the various rooms.

Several interesting photographs are shown of Mr. J. O. Gantner's new
home at Vallejo and Baker streets, San Francisco. The architect, Mr. Louis

COUNTRY HOUSE FOR MR. ANSEL M. EASTON
LOUIS CHRISTIAN MULLGARDT, ARCHITECT

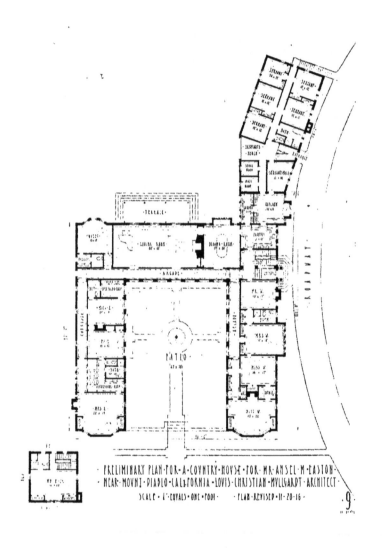

PRELIMINARY PLAN·FOR·A·COVNTRY·HOVSE·FOR·MR·ANSEL·M·EASTON·
NEAR·MOVNT·DIABLO·CALIFORNIA·LOVIS·CHRISTIAN·MVLLGARDT·ARCHITECT·
SCALE·⅛·EQVALS·ONE·FOOT·   ·PLAN·REVISED·11·20·16·

FRONT VIEW MANSUR RESIDENCE, NEAR LOS ANGELES
Morgan, Walls & Morgan, Architects

PATIO, COUNTRY HOME OF MR. W. L. GROWALL, ATHERTON
Albert Farr, Architect

RESIDENCE OF MR. R. A. ROWAN, PASADENA, CALIFORNIA
Robert D. Farquhar, Architect

HOUSE OF MR. DUNCAN McDUFFIE, BERKELEY, CALIFORNIA
John Galen Howard, Architect

M. Upton, has developed a rather pleasing style that is a mixture of Spanish and Italian Renaissance. The house is much larger than the pictures indicate, having twenty or more rooms, many halls and numerous baths, besides a spacious roof garden at the rear, with a glass inclosed pergola, and a garage with accommodations for two machines. Some very satisfactory results have been obtained by using fumed gum for the interior woodwork. The bedrooms are papered and all woodwork on the second floor is finished in ivory enamel. The Gantner house cost approximately $30,000.

❧ ❧ ❧

In an article on "Country House Architecture on the Pacific Coast" in the Architectural Record, Mr. John Galen Howard says:

"There has of late years been a great advance in planning the house. There is less appearance of torture of the program in order to get exact symmetry of outer form. There is also less ready acceptance of the perfunctory and stereotyped layout, though such planning will always be much in evidence, I suppose. The architect himself is not always to be blamed for this. But fresh thought and childlike acceptance of the special program, no matter where it may lead, go hand in hand. The delightful new solution of the house plan, with all that this implies as to the exterior aspect, comes about by reason of the easy and receptive relation of the architect's mind to the client's requirements. A charming and individual client has a right to a charming and individual house, and the architect can produce the result only by going along with his client, instead of imposing some arbitrarily conceived form upon him. In this way unexpected rhythms and appealing balances are struck, which seem to take a house out of the everyday world and make it a part of romance.

"It goes almost without saying that a house is never wholly successful, no matter how fine it may be in itself, if it does not fit its surroundings. Our architects are more and more being permitted to give, let me say, the most careful study to the development of the site. This has not always been the case, and it is only within comparatively recent years, in this part of the world, that owners have realized that the garden and landscape about a house are as much a part of the design as the walls and roof. The great artistic successes have been, I think, without exception, cases where the designer of the house has designed the setting as well. The principle involved here is fundamental and so obvious as not to seem to require argument. To separate the design of the landscape setting from the design of the house is to preclude vital success in the ensemble. An old Californian once told me of his experience of building his country house in the early days, and of his, and the architect's, surprise, after the drawings had been completed and the contracts let, to find on laying the house out on the site that one corner was twenty feet out of the ground. That may have been the old way of doing things, but it is so no longer. One finds many rarely beautiful examples of unity of house and setting among the newer works.

"The study of the garden as an architectural work in itself is coming more into recognition, too, aside from its relation to the house. Garden architecture is essentially domestic in its appeal. Even in the cases, few and far between on this coast at present, where they form part of public parks or the setting of public buildings, they introduce the needed note of amenity, and give the human, personal touch. How much more valuable are they, then, in rounding out and completing the country house. A jarring note here kills all the music.

"It is with great sense of satisfaction that one recognizes the fine qualities of so much of the country house work of today. But one cannot help

RESIDENCE OF DR. JNO. R. HAYNES. LOS ANGELES
Robert D. Farquhar, Architect

wondering what the next step is to be. Are we always going to be satisfied with the pike-staff plainness which is so grateful to us now? Are there not other worlds to conquer? I hope we shall never return—there is surely little danger of our returning—to cheap lugged-in elaboration, to tortured and whimsical forms, to stereotyped planning. But, after all, architecture is essentially an alliance in which painter and sculptor are partners, too, and the deepest and highest notes of architectural design cannot be struck without their co-operation. Think of the exquisite work to be found all about the Mediterranean (to whose climate and landscape, and perhaps also to whose people, this coast is most akin) ; work which, while possessing all the restraint and quietness which appeal to us so deeply now, yet finds place for painter and sculptor, too! We have found a common ground with fine tradition as to fundamentals. It is not difficult to see the direction in which we should turn to make still further progress. Let us give our fellows of the allied arts their chance."

Garden Gates and Entrances

By E. I. FARRINGTON, in The Craftsman

THERE is a strong national sentiment in America against the exclusiveness which walled gardens seem to imply. Yet some kind of garden enclosure is highly desirable, and, of course, an enclosed garden must have an entrance. This makes possible what is coming to be an interesting and delightful feature of many gardens in this country, even though the emphasis is being laid rather unduly, perhaps, on the pergola design. American houses and American gardens are being pergolized to an extent that is almost amusing; it is even bewildering to see pergolas attached to little farm cottages and old-fashioned houses, where they look about as appropriate as a bandmaster's coat on a clergyman.

When a garden is wholly informal and close by a house of the cottage type, the best kind of garden gate is designed with a simple arch, over which vines may be trained. If the house is somewhat more pretentious and the garden a trifle more formal, there is no good reason why a gateway with a pergola top should not be used, and on large estates or at entrances opening into a strictly formal or Italian garden the pergola type of gateway is ideal.

When the garden encloses a Colonial house, it is most appropriately surrounded with a white picket fence or with a low brick wall, possibly a combination of both. In either case, the gate should be simple and of wood painted white with posts at the side having molded caps. If the fence is made of wood or wood on a low brick wall, the gate posts will naturally be of the same materials, or if brick alone is used in the walls, the gate posts will naturally be brick, too, and square, with a ball on top, perhaps, or an urn for growing plants. The entrance gate to the grounds of a large estate may appropriately be made of iron when a brick wall is used, but a wooden gate painted white is also satisfactory for the garden of a Colonial house. Of course, the design and color of the dwelling must be considered, and a white gateway might not be at all suitable for a California bungalow or a stone house or one built of stucco. But, then, neither would a brick wall or a picket fence. Gardens adjoining houses of this type are best surrounded with hedges, and then the entrance gate may be painted the same color as the house. Sometimes a simple lattice-work fence with vines growing over it can be substituted for a hedge, especially if the owner desires considerable privacy. Lattice-work fences of this kind and gates to match can be purchased ready made and set up in a very short time.

Mediaeval gardens, we discover, when reading the quaint and charming descriptions of the old writers, were beset with "thick-set hedges of green," or "battlemented walls." Gardens were "circummured with brick," "enclosed with walles—strong, embanked with benches to sytt and take my rest." Though at first the walls were erected as strongholds of the home, their beauty was so apparent, so compelling, that after strict need of them had passed people built them because of their fitness and the sense of privacy they gave. The gateways piercing those old walls were as beautiful and impressive as the owner's rank and purse permitted. Upon the great posts of the nobleman's gateways were carved or emblazoned the family coat of arms, upon the gates of peaceful monastery walls were nailed crosses of wood or else Latin inscriptions were deeply graved, kings' palaces were protected by gates of iron wonderfully wrought, and on either side stood guards costumed magnificently. Whatever we do to our gateways at the present day keeps alive some faint memory of those old times. Walls are not so high nor so thick, are ornamental instead of defensive. In place of the gaily bedecked guards standing watchfully at the gate posts we plant stiff little trees, instead of the ominous cannon on the top of each post we place an urn filled with flowers and overflowing with vines.

But whatever the time, the gate invariably represents the station and the taste of the owner. A stranger idling along a village street or motoring swiftly along country roads past the estates of the wealthy may get a very fair idea of the people dwelling back of the entrances. Some humble cottages are ennobled by a rose-arched gateway, some by simple evergreens, others are disgraced by ignoble sagging gates or disfigured by unsuitable, showy ornamentation. Some of the entrances to the rich man's grounds are too large, too ostentatious, others badly proportioned, but on the whole American gateways both small and great are exceedingly interesting, for they are nearly always graced with vines. The plainest of walls with rudest of posts becomes beautiful when covered with creepers or vines, fortified with flowers instead of bayonets and cannon. Fences are now constructed so that the passerby may see the green stretch of lawn and noble trees through the pickets instead of having all knowledge of the dweller within shut from sight by towering walls.

The thought commonly associated with gates is that they are intended to be a barrier against the entrance of unwelcome guests. Doubtless the original purpose of gates was to offer protection and security to those inside, but in these days a garden entrance may seem to invite rather than to warn away. A walk or drive marked by posts at each side, perhaps entwined with vines or supporting growing plants, suggests that the visitor will do well to pass that way.

When one penetrates to the heart of a garden, he is likely to find gates of a different type, narrow often, and vine-covered, and altogether intimate in their nature. In the heart of the garden the rustic form is most satisfactory; but if a high wall is to be passed through, there may be only an arched opening with a little iron gate to suggest privacy. A vine-covered arch makes one of the prettiest of garden entrances, with or without a gate. In some gardens the old-time turnstile has been revived and is decidedly picturesque with rural surroundings.

ENTRANCE GATES, HOUSE OF MR. DUNCAN McDUFFIE
John Galen ·Howard, Architect

Some garden entrances may be beautified by the use of shrubs, plants and climbing vines. When ornamental posts are used, planting of some kind is especially desirable, and if the posts be made of stone or brick, it can be laid down as a rule that something green should be made to grow upon them or at the base. If the gate is set back from the lot line and joined to the wall by a reverse curve, there may be planting on the street side, but otherwise it is best limited to within the yard or garden. Low growing evergreen trees are very attractive when used in a situation of this sort, but rather expensive. Vines like Boston ivy, ·Hall's honeysuckle and climbing roses soften the general lines and give color and fragrance.

Next to the ivies in popularity is, perhaps, the Virginia creeper. Though it has not the fine evergreen trait of the ivies, it has the delightful habit of changing its quiet robes of green to harlequin garb of gayest reds and yellows in the fall. It spins its own trellis as it climbs, fastening the long runners to the walls with tenacious fingers. In the winter the fine lacy network of stems revealed after the leaves have fallen is extremely decorative, especially when cutting across a glaring red brick wall.

The wisteria lends itself with especial grace to large entrance pergolas or to archways. The stems of an old wisteria are very beautiful and if trained properly and preserved to good old age will make a living arch of themselves. The trellis which supported it when young could be removed and thus a really beautiful living arch crowned all summer with delicate leaves and adorned in the spring with fragrant lavender flower streamers could be. had.

Effective results are gained in the West with passion flowers, for they grow to gigantic size. They are valued for the rare blue shade of their flowers and for the ambition of their growth. They are often seen covering the tops of tall trees with a crown of blue. Another beautiful blue vine which can be depended upon to give beauty to an entrance is the plumbago.

LIBRARY, RESIDENCE OF MR. MANSUR, LOS ANGELES
Morgan, Walls & Morgan, Architects

The Library in the Home

EXCEPT it be the vast and simple stage of nature, nothing is more conducive to the inspirational mood than a room wherein great books dwell. Here is the torch-light of civilization; the heritage of intellect. "A library may be regarded as the solemn chamber in which a man may take counsel with all who have been wise, and great, and good, and glorious among the men that have gone before him."

In the real library—the one that is born, not made—how uplifting is the atmosphere! How exalting! It is intimate and inviting in its splendid spirit of companionship and comfort. There is an air of comradeship apparent about every book on the shelves. It is so thoroughly satisfying to the mind and to the physical being as well.

A real library is the Heaven to which all good books should find their way; where their reward shall be one of everlasting life and where each volume may be proud in the knowledge that it is of true and real service. It will matter not, how costly their binding, nor how "dog-eared" their leaves.

The hearth-stone is the heart of the home; the library is its soul. Like a sad and mournful place where the sweet voices of childhood are unknown, is the house that has no library.

Every home that is to be a home in the truest sense, should have a library, a place for thought and meditation, a haven of refuge and of solitude. "'We enter our studies, and enjoy a society which we alone can bring together. We raise no jealousy in conversing with one in preference to another; we give no offense to the most illustrious by questioning him as long as we will, and leaving him as abruptly. Diversity of opinion raises no tumult in our presence; each interlocutor stands before, speaks or is silent, and we adjourn or decide the business at our leisure."

A library is the room to fit any mood and the place to which we turn instinctively, sure in the knowledge that it will not fail us, either in comfort or in opening the wells of inspiration.

"Nothing conduces more to making our life happy than to know things as they really are; and this wisdom must be acquired by frequent reflections upon men and the affairs of the world, for otherwise books will contribute but little to it," is a sage maxim of Rochefoucauld. It was also this fashioner of epigrams who first shrewdly observed that: "A great many people are fond of books as they are furniture which serves to dress and set off their rooms rather than adorn and enrich their souls."

The foundation of spiritual satisfaction and repose is physical comfort and practical good taste. Comfort is essential in a library, and in the designing of a new home consideration of this important element begins, of course, with the architectural plans. In remodeling the old home, grown dear through years of occupancy and association, one has the whole house to choose from, for it does not matter greatly that the library be in conventional juxtaposition to the other rooms. What does matter seriously is that it be a room which will satisfy and fulfill its destiny; it must not be too large nor too small, and the furniture whether elaborate or simple must be comfortable; the decorations must be in perfect harmony. It must captivate. One must sense the whole with a feeling of pleasurable content, entirely oblivious of the attractive but unobtrusive details directed to that end, else there can be no real spiritual comfort and peace.

A real library is a room where you meet and enjoy the companionship of the greatest thinkers of the ages, past and present; no mere room full of books gathered as "first editions." It is a place where only your best known and most beloved books can enter; where you feel their companionship without even opening the cover of any. One touches books like these with a caress, and reads their titles with a heart full of memories, as one looks into the face of a dear friend. It is a place to settle down in and lose oneself in his "first" or "last" edition; a place so quiet and dreamy that the only sounds are those made by the soft crinkling of the fire, the settling of a log, or the rustling of leaves outside the windows; a place from which to set sail to far countries, to fairyland; or to join in great adventures across the sea.

* * *

Our Architects of the Future

Public aeroplane landings and private landings and hangars may furnish problems that will tax the skill and ingenuity of the architects and consulting engineers of the next decade, according to men who have watched the rapid development of the science of aeronautics.

Architects may spend many sleepless nights trying to devise a method of making a hangar harmonize with modern residence or landscape architecture. A three-machine hangar with living rooms for the aviator on the second floor will not add to the attractiveness of a Dutch Colonial residence and the spectacle of a hangar in the immediate vicinity of an Italian garden, would jar the aesthetic sensibilities of an Esquimo. Perhaps some architectural genius of the future will introduce the world to an aero era of architecture.

False Standards in Modern Apartment Building

A MODERN building which does not perform any useful function, and whose only claim for existence is the beauty of its facade, is not in a true sense a product of architecture and it cannot permanently live. Yet in what a large number of buildings today do we see this false standard asserting itself! What in many cases serves to make matters worse are the vain attempts at securing architectural effect through the lavish smearing of facades with atrociously ugly forms, representing a waste of money that should more properly be used to secure a better form of construction or more adequate equipment. To cite one type of building in which false standards are evident, let us consider the modern apartment house.

It would seem that in planning such a building to house from three to one hundred families, and in some cases even more under one roof, the practical considerations insuring quietness, comfort, privacy, and convenience to the occupants would take precedence over all others; but the percentage of the apartment buildings constructed every year in which these necessities for comfortable living are provided is very low. When this fact is considered, the reason for the rapid depreciation in the value of apartment property is not far to seek. Tenants are free to take advantage of greater value for the money they pay if they find it, and any building which it is hoped to maintain as a permanent earning power solely through its marble entrance foyer or the number of cartouches and swags that its street facade parades, is doomed to become a losing property.

Sound proof floors and walls between apartments so that one occupant will not disturb another, ample water heating apparatus, a properly designed heating plant, elevator shafts located so that the noise of operation will be confined to the smallest space, well fitted hardware, conveniently placed gas and electric outlets, well lighted and ventilated service staircases and lifts, reasonable closet area—these and as many more service-giving features as are practicable, depending upon the type of tenants it is proposed to attract, should surely be provided first in every apartment house. Clothe the structure thus planned with a facade of dignified materials, honestly treated, and expressing in form the purpose of the building, and the result, if influenced by a correct knowledge of proportion and a discriminating use of ornament, will be architecture in its true and complete sense.

Another important factor in modern practice is the duty of safeguarding human life against destruction by fire. The fire in the Lenox hotel in Boston is a case in point, showing the great value of such fireproofing as actually existed, even though it was not developed to the highest degree. All the conditions for a bad fire were present: a high wind, freezing temperature, an early morning hour. The fire started in an occupied room, a window was open, the guest discovering the fire ran to the corridor leaving the door open, and the flames rapidly spread. Despite the serious handicaps, the fire was confined to two stories. The walls and floors which were fireproofed with hollow tile remained intact, with no material damage except to furniture and interior finish. Such examples are conclusive evidence that fireproofing is an actual possibility and that it only remains to be generally applied to reduce greatly our annual fire loss.—The Architectural Forum.

LIVING PORCH, HOUSE OF MR. L. A. REDMAN
Louis M. Upton, Architect

Fundamental Principles of Interior Decoration

MR. FRANK ALVAH PARSONS, president of the New York School of Fine and Applied Art, and author of "Interior Decoration, Its Principles and Practice," has a splendid article in The New Country Life for February, dealing rather fully with the fundamental principles of interior decoration. The author says, among other things:

"History is recorded in the objects that man uses to express his normal life interests, and the house not only meets his physical requirements, but is a mental necessity for rest, reflection, and natural intercourse. This stamps the house as one of the fundamental expressions of a man's intelligence, his standards of taste, and his knowledge of the relation of surroundings to character development.

"This idea is strongly expressed in architecture. The best architects see historic architecture as the representation of needs and taste. They view it as the conception of the past readapted to various national periods, impressed by geographical conditions, local requirements and psychological phenomena. This viewpoint makes an epoch in our domestic architecture somewhat slow, owing to traditional architectural training, but no less distinctly seen.

"The interior of the house shows changes much more quickly, but no less certainly, and for these very reasons there is a greater danger here and greater care is necessary.

"There are two distinct ways to look at the question of interior decoration. First, a house is a place in which to rest the body, feed it, and pre-

RECEPTION HALL AND ART GALLERY, HOUSE OF MR. J. O. GANTNER

STAIRWAY AND HALL, HOUSE OF MR. J. O. GANTNER, SAN FRANCISCO
Louis M. Upton, Architect

pare it for vigorous action in life's melee. Second, it is the place for rest, recuperation and mental reorganization, where one's standards of taste are formed, stimulated and expressed. Both these views must be acknowledged, considered, and used in a discussion of this subject.

"On the other hand there are vicious points of view that should be avoided, so far as a sane conception of the problem of interior decoration is concerned. Traditions of antiquity, personal sentimentalities, individual antipathies, and a mind closed to argument are great stumbling blocks to clear thinking. They do not express general truths; but are one's own personal idols taking the place of truth.

"The relation of architecture to interior decoration is vital. Not seeing what this relation is and how the harmonies of relationship may be maintained is to invite the destruction of the architect's ideal and to make interior decoration a farce. In fact, there can be no interior decoration without a definite concept of something to decorate and what and where it is. Then there can be no decorative effect unless both the architect and the decorator have the same ideal and each understands the other's viewpoint.

"Architecture is structure, therefore it is fundamental. Its forms, lines, and scale are the real clues to where the decoration must go, to follow out the architect's plan or concept. Inasmuch, also, as there is any architectural decoration at all, its kind, its amount, its placement, and its treatment all relate directly to what the decorator must select and to how he will arrange it so that harmony or unity of expression may follow unity of idea. Architects and decorators should be one and the same, or they should work in the closest harmony to secure the best results. A client who has little knowledge of architecture and less of what is decorative may so hamper either the architect or the decorator that good results are impossible.

"In considering the composition of a room, all objects placed in it may be seen first as decorative materials with which to add beauty to the architectural framework; hence the importance of the principles of arrangement. On the other hand, every object is considered from the point of its use and its comfort. Two qualities, utility and artistic unity, form the basis for room composition. Every good picture has a centre of interest, a dominating idea to which prominence is given and around which other elements are grouped as accessories. Every good room also has one or more centres around which, and in connection with which, every other object is placed. In the bedroom, it is the bed, in the dining room, the table, in the living room a large table or chimney piece or other family possibility. This centre of interest answers the leading question of what the room is for.

"One of the most hopeful signs of the times is the more recent viewpoint as to using period furnishings. Useful and beautiful things have been created in every period as the expressions of conditions, any one of which has something definite to contribute to our modern life. The present problem is one of adaptation or selection and arrangement of elements in the expression of the individual man's conception of his house. Some of the most charming rooms in America contain not only French, English and Italian pieces, but objects selected from various periods in each of these national art expressions.

ENTRANCE HALL, HOUSE OF MR. E. B. KIMBALL, PIEDMONT
Albert Farr, Architect

"There is a danger, to be sure, in mixing period objects, lest one allow his personal fancy or appreciation for an article to blind him to its real value as a decorative element in a room design. Not only every object, like a chair, a table, commode, lighting fixture, mirror frame, or lamp, is to be considered as to its meaning or value as an element, but every line, form, scale, relation, ornament and color combination bears a definite relation to the room composition. The same discretion is essential in combining period objects as is necessary in selecting these things. The future charm of American homes lies largely, first, in knowing what idea is to be desired in each individual room; second, in understanding the value of period art objects in a room design; and third, in the knowledge and ability to arrange these objects so that each expresses its fullest measure of usefulness, and at the same time by its design, contributes all the beauty of which it is capable from the standpoint of a cultivated taste.

"The final test of every room is its unity. Of course there should be unity in the idea of use, but there should also be unity in the decorative idea, and in the way this idea is expressed. A very good test is to apply an eminent writer's statement as to what a unit is. 'A unit is that to which nothing can be added and from which nothing can be taken without destroying the idea for which the unit stands.' This test applied to any room will cause the removal of much that is non-essential and disturbing, and will prevent the storing of further senseless or sentimental objects after a room is already complete."

Some Unusual Fireplaces

By ERI. H. RICHARDSON*

THE editor proposed the caption as bait. It was alluring and offered possibilities of brevity.

Brevity is not only the soul of wit; it is of necessity the soul of joy to the busy architect who must draw plans, write specifications and familiarize himself with the thousand changing requirements of his own work and modern design and construction between incessant interruptions. Thus the architect sometimes condemns a lamb for a fox—or otherwise gets the vendor's goat.

It is not entirely clear to me just what the unusual fireplace is. I have never built nor recall seeing two alike, so all may be unusual in some respect. Some—in fact, many—are unusually bad; rarely we find an unusually fine one.

The illustrations are chosen from a limited number of photographed mantels, with regret that others have not or could not be obtained. They have been chosen with the idea of illustrating various types of work which would offer possibilities of variation and adaptation to meet given requirements. More helpful and specific suggestions could be offered in particular cases.

The Woodbridge mantel (Mr. Chas. S. Kaiser, architect) represents a type of work of superb possibilities, the adaptation of period design to a simple modern fireplace within reach of any modern house. In pieces of large size in dull, unglazed colors, which simulate the old Italian marbles or English stones, these mantels offer a permanent material of character and beauty.

The fireplace is often the one interior feature of distinct architectural possibilities. Lack of knowledge of materials, unsympathetic co-operation from the builder, poor workmanship and defective construction have all contributed in the past to the ill success of many fireplaces and its consequent loss of importance in the interior scheme. In many cases it is the one permanent piece of furniture installed by the architect, often observed more than any

*411 Bankers Investment building, San Francisco. The mantels shown in this article were built under Mr. Richardson's supervision.

MANTEL IN HOUSE OF MR. CHARLES BROCK, THOUSAND OAKS, BERKELEY.   HENRY GUTTERSON, ARCHITECT

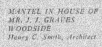

MANTEL IN HOUSE OF
MR. J. J. GRAVES
WOODSIDE
Henry C. Smith, Architect

MANTEL IN HOUSE OF
MR. J. E. WOODBRIDGE
Chas. S. Kaiser, Architect

MANTEL IN
BUILDING MATERIAL
EXHIBIT

MANTEL IN THE
BUILDING
MATERIAL
EXHIBIT,
A STUDY IN
BROWNS AND
DULL BLUES.

other single feature of the residence, and is therefore deserving of more study, intelligent co-operation and care in design, color and finish than it usually receives. If from three to five per cent of the total cost of the home were to be specifically appropriated for the fireplace, hearth, fireback and throat construction it would be ample allowance to secure the deserved results and often make possible the avoidance of much dissatisfaction due to a poor fireplace.

When we consider how little there has been in the way of working material for the architect to turn to and the difficulties encountered in obtaining co-operation, it is surprising that the fireplace is as generally used as it is today. Future years will

MANTEL IN HOUSE OF MR. CLARKSON BRADFORD
SAN MATEO PARK

see the development of the fireplace to the importance it deserves as the center of the home.

The fireplace which is designed to fulfill the owner's requirements, to meet fully and enhance the architectural scheme, to contrast pleasingly or blend well with the color scheme and to work properly and give real marrow-warming heat, is, after all, the unusual fireplace.

MANTEL IN HOUSE
OF MR. EMORY
SINGLETARY,
SAN JOSE
*Warren Skillings,
Architect*

War and the Architect*

By RICHARD F. BACH, Columbia University

SPECIALIZATION, in its ruthlessly logical advance, is entrenched before the realities of war itself. In the course of the European war to date a lack of specialization—that is, a lack of proper regard for specially developed capabilities on the part of individuals or of professional groups and bodies—has repeatedly appeared as an obstacle to complete success and as a hindrance to thoroughness and effective equipment; and this without mention of the loss of highly trained types of minds in the regular course of attack and advance, minds devoted to trench digging, though equipped by years of schooling, training and practice to a skillful use of pencil, rule and instruments; minds whose capabilities might have been diverted to a score of channels of greater service, with distinct advantage at the moment and with the even greater hope of resources to be available when reconstruction shall have superseded carnage. Those of us who have had access to the Journal of the Royal Institute of British Architects, to the gazettes of the various ateliers in Paris, or to the German architectural periodicals that still reached this country in the first months of the war, are aware of the long lists of architects killed in action or permanently disabled, having found death or mutilation as regulars on the firing line. With the example of European countries before us, now that our entry into the struggle has made it a world conflict, it is to be hoped that the architect's ability will be given its proper position in the service of the nation.

Far be it from us to discourage regular military service, and there are many architects who will feel themselves called upon to serve as regulars; nor need it here be repeated that all citizens of military age are subject to the call of arms as provided for in the Constitution of the United States. But it may also be said that service to the home land is of the greatest variety and that fighting is but one type of service, even at the front.

The architect's training has made him professionally useful in a special field in time of peace; why should that special usefulness be forgotten or ignored in time of war? While banks were depicted on his drafting board in 1916, there may be barracks in 1917, and in similar fashion museum buildings will cede place to munitions plants, hotels will be replaced by hospitals. The suggestion is too apparent to need further expatiation here.

Let the architect's training be the nation's resource. Let his specialized type of knowledge, duly organized, be an anchor of reliance. Above all, let us by this very service likewise conserve these trained minds for service after the war.

And we must emphasize the need for organization in such service. Specialized minds individually can render but a modicum of the assistance that they can easily give when once they are welded into a unit. The Federal Government must be assured that there are in New York or in Chicago or in San Francisco a stated number of architects ready to be used as draftsmen, as topographers, as surveyors, as superintendents of construction of bridges, landings, roads, as designers and builders of war

---

*Editor's Note.—This article is printed in response to the following letter from the author: "In the hope that the material may be of interest to you or to the person in charge of The Architect and Engineer of California, I beg leave to send you under separate cover a copy of the American Architect of April 18, 1917, which contains articles on possible war service by architects. Yours very truly, Richard F. Bach, Curator Columbia University, School of Architecture, New York."

buildings of fifty different kinds. And these but suggest the possible fields that would be fertile ground for the architect's specialized training.

Obviously, when such work must be done—and conditions demand an always increasing efficiency and effective accomplishment in these directions—shall we be considered unpatriotic if we regard the use of such minds for cannon targets as an economic waste? And again, what of the number of those physically unfit in the ranks of the architects? Shall the service of these capable men be lost to the nation because the ranks of the fighting men are closed to them? And, finally, when the war has run its length and men's minds again are set in the course of peace, what of the work of the architects then? In the labor of reconstruction, rebuilding the sinews of the land, the architect bears a great responsibility, and, even though destruction by invasion is the least of our fears, ordinary building will in the very nature of things be retarded during the war, so that the aftermath will make heavy demands upon the profession, and at a time when the greatest judgment will be required. Above all, then, let us remember that, though as a nation we may fight for ideals, the conservation of these ideals must be our chief recompense. Such conservation can and should begin at once, and that by an organization of all specially trained minds into available units, classified according to type and length of experience and according to particular field or parts of a given field in which they are best able to be of direct service to the country.

Even as we indite these lines there is brought to our desk a circular and questionnaire sent to its members by the American Institute of Architects. Specially important is the itemized list of branches of service in which training and specific qualifications can prove of assistance at once, under the Quartermaster's Corps and the Corps of Engineers in the Army. No doubt the Navy can avail itself, although only to a certain extent, of like services. It is our honest hope that success may come to the Institute's plan, that organization will result and the nation profit thereby. By using the local influence of its chapters and thus bringing individuals more nearly within reach, such organization may be made very closely effective and immediately available service units established.

Assuming, however, that the Institute's circular was sent to members only, we are prompted to ask how those not members shall be organized, especially the great number of younger draftsmen. One way, of course, immediately suggests itself—namely, a census within each office and a report to a local chapter of the Institute, whether the chief of the firm is a member or not. We venture to feel assured that the various chapters would be content to undertake such clerical work as might be attached to the gathering of these office reports, and, after due classification, of sending them to the Institute's headquarters in Washington.

It may be well to point out that the established architect can render still another kind of service. Several of the larger firms have offered their entire facilities—office space, drafting rooms and equipment—to the War Department to be used at any time and in any manner that may be deemed necessary. What a wealth of resource there is again in this type of contribution toward national defense. All honor to those who have blazed the way in this direction, for they have offered gladly a type of sacrifice that nations are usually driven to exact under military law.

Even the schools have fallen into line. Columbia has set the pace by offering its spacious and well-equipped drafting rooms to the Government for military purposes. No doubt other schools will soon follow.

The universities generally throughout the land have promptly put the facilities of their various departments at the nation's command.

And, finally, let all architects bear in mind that success can come to our arms only if they are adequately supported; that service is manifold; that the specialized training of the architect is an asset to the land in war as well as in peace, and that, with proper organization, professional services rendered will redound to the profit and glory of the United States.

* * *

Once Again—Who Invented the Modern Skyscraper?

THOMAS NOLAN, professor of architectural construction of the University of Pennsylvania, recently delivered a public lecture in which he said:

There has been some controversy in regard to priority of invention of first use of metal skeleton construction. It is generally agreed that it was first developed in Chicago in 1889 and recognized as a definite and new contribution to the science of construction in American architecture.

Professor Nolan said that the steel skeleton frame has been classified as the last of the four great developments of structural advances, which have given architecture really new resources, the first being the Roman vaults, the second the Gothic ribbed vault and flying arch and buttress and the third the metallic truss. Steel beams were first manufactured in 1895 by the Carnegie Steel Company at Pittsburgh, Pa.

Who invented the steel skeleton frame and made possible the modern skyscraper?

Prof. Nolan said:

The inception and growth of the high building has been made possible by the introduction and rapid development of structural steel, light fireproof materials, passenger and freight elevators, and by great advances in the mechanical equipment, isolated foundation supports and wind bracing.

Previous to 1885 "tall" buildings were not more than eight or ten stories high—this height was very nearly the practical limit—and their construction was then sometimes referred to as "elevator architecture." The next stage in the evolution of the tall building was the one in which the entire weight of the floors and roofs and the loads on them were carried by a system of metal columns, the exterior walls thus supporting no load but their own weight. Buildings were carried by this form of construction to the height of eighteen or nineteen stories.

With the introduction of cheap structural steel the steel "skeleton" or "cage" construction came rapidly into use. Formerly the "skeleton" type was carefully distinguished from the "cage" type of tall building construction, the former term being applied to buildings which might have the outside walls self-supporting and which depended somewhat for stiffness upon walls, partitions, floor filling, etc.; and the term "cage" being applied to buildings which consisted of a complete and well-connected framework of metal designed to carry not only the floors, but the walls, roof and all other parts of the structure, and furnished with wind-bracing members.

* * *

Integral Waterproofing

By a mail canvass of 10,000 architects and engineers, "Structural Conservation" secured more than 2600 replies to queries relative to integral waterproofing. More than 94 per cent favored integral waterproofing of concrete under hydrostatic pressure, and 92 per cent stated that their observation had shown that integral waterproofing is beneficial in filling the pores of concrete and preventing the absorption of moisture, whereas concrete not waterproofed is absorptive of moisture.

Artistic Stucco: Its History and Development and How It Should Be Done*

By JOHN B. ORR

ARTISTIC stucco! What great possibilities can be conjured up in these two words! Stucco which is among the oldest, in some form or other, of man's early attempts at the artistic. With all the possibilities and, despite the fact that there can be found to this day portions of stucco in a good state of preservation after standing the wear of many centuries, there is no other form of building material that has fallen more into disrepute than stucco. This is especially so in the United States.

The causes can be traced largely to the slip-shod methods that have gradually crept into our building industry. Today, the main point of view or the achievement that is looked for is that a contractor shall complete in 60 days what should take three or four times longer. They take short cuts wherever they can; essentials that appear small in the successful completion of the work are sacrificed for time. The boy learning the business does not learn how good to do it but how fast to do it. The view he gets as a successful craftsman is not to do better and try to improve on the specifications for the work, but just how much he can scamp and get away with. Some contractors govern their costs by these methods and we get the results so often noticeable in modern construction—competition in price instead of competition in value or good work. The good contractor who tries to figure at a price that will permit good work is in many cases forced out of business, leaving the field open to the cheaper man and his cheaper methods.

The old school craftsman had a different view; he tried to make his work a masterpiece just as much so as the artist did his on canvas. He wanted to look at it years afterward and be able to say, "I did that" or "I worked on that" and feel the pride that comes from viewing a masterpiece. I never will forget an early lesson I got during my apprenticeship, which I served under two master craftsmen, John Forbes, of Glasgow, Scotland, and his general manager, John Monroe, both of whom I look up to to this day as experts in their line of business. I was doing a piece of ornamental work in cement and was worried because an older apprentice was doing his faster. I commenced to scamp my work to gain speed; Mr. Monroe came on the scene and his sharp eye took in the situation. His cure was drastic; he took up a hammer and smashed my work, then proceeded to administer a lecture, namely, first to learn just how good I could do it and then speed in manipulation would follow. I took his advice to heart and found it to be good. I believe every form of encouragement and instruction should be given the craft to get good work.

We find that stucco was used in building almost as soon as buildings were found to be necessary. It grew from the crude mud huts to the most artistic treatment of exteriors to be found in the old world today. Stucco is an Italian term usually applied in Italy to an exterior plastering, although we can trace it further back under a different name. The old Egyptians and the classical Greeks used a form of exterior plastering extensively; however, I have always looked upon Italy as the mother of the plastic art and responsible to a great extent for the artistic effects of exterior plastering generally known in this country as stucco. In Great Britain stucco is a somewhat indefinite term for various plastic mixtures.

*Presented at 13th Annual Convention of the Am. Concrete Inst., Chicago, Feb. 8–10, 1917.

To great Robert Adam is due credit for the advancement of exterior stucco in Great Britain. He adopted it as a covering over houses built of brick and cobblestone and it was used extensively during his period.

I find that the Temple of Apollo at Delos and even the' first Parthenon under Aegis of Pallas was plastered with stucco. Vitruvius calls the exterior plastering Tectorum Opus. This was composed of three coats of lime and sand and three coats of lime and marble, the united thickness not being more than one inch. The first coat was of common but very old lime and sand (lime that had been "soured" three or more years) ; when it was nearly dry a second and third coat was applied and left fairly straight. The work was then laid over with another two coats of lime and marble and finished with a coat of fine marble powder, this finish of marble powder being troweled into it before it was dry. The marble mortar was beaten to render it tough and plastic. The successive coats of marble mortar were troweled into each other before they were dry. The tectorum was then painted in brilliant colors while it was still fresh. In certain conditions the surface was then rubbed with wax and pure oil for the purpose of adding to the brilliancy and endurance of the colors. Slabs of this tectorum have been found and preserved from the ruins of Pompeii and Herculaneum and are in the Museum of Portici; specimens also from the same place are in the South Kensington Museum, London. It was found that some of this work was colored integrally, while in others it was colored by the use of a wash, which was applied over the surface while it was still fresh.

The early workers in stucco had each his different formula for treating the stucco to make it weather-proof. Pliny mentions fig juice as being used in exterior plaster; elm bark and hot barley water was mixed with the stucco used on Justinian's church of the Baptist, Constantinople.

Bullocks' blood was employed for ' this purpose in the mortar for Rochester cathedral, England. Whites of eggs and strong malt were used in the lime for Queen Eleanor's Cross, Charing Cross, London, in the year 1300. It is an historic fact that during the building of the Duke of Devonshire's house at Chiswick, the exterior of which was plastered with stucco, the surrounding district was impoverished for eggs and buttermilk to mix with the stucco. My mention of these different methods and treatments is to show the care and wide range of methods and mixtures that were used in the endeavor to make the stucco weatherproof, and the difficulty that the old craftsmen had to contend with in getting these results. Modern manufacture has overcome this to a large extent and has made the path of the stucco workers easier.

It is a curious fact that the fountain of possibilities in modern stucco has hardly been tapped. I give for the reasons, first, fear of the permanency of the material; second, neglect by the architects in not studying the possibilities; third, the difficulties in getting the work executed owing to the ignorance of the craftsman in this branch of the plastic art. In reply to the first, anyone who has traveled or has gone into stucco historically can prove the permanency of the material before and after the introduction of Portland cement as the binding material. By the introduction of Portland cement and waterproofing compounds much has been done to simplify and make permanent the mixture. The danger in most cases to be overcome is in the manipulation. My greatest obstacle to overcome has been crazing or check cracking. This I have cured by what I believe to be the only sure method. The richer you get the mix, the more danger there is in check cracking; rapid drying, heat in cement, soft sand, these all help to cause check cracks. I have taken precautions against these dangers and have done what I could with the local materials that are obtainable in Miami. I had good results in some cases and in some others check cracks did appear despite the fact that I had made every effort to avoid them; I never yet had any stucco scale or fall off. My next attempt I made using an overwash of liquid stucco. This last method has proven very satisfactory and I have jobs that are two years old on which there has been no appearance of crazing.

A Few Suggestions to Architects

To the architect and designer, as a layman, I offer a few suggestions and criticisms. As a general rule they do not give enough study to the possibilities in color effect such as are to be seen in Europe, Cuba and other Latin countries. Then, in ornamentation they seem to forget that they are working in a very plastic material that lends itself to the fullest extent in obtaining lights and shadows. I believe that to get the full effects, relief work in stucco should have the appearance of being modeled in place with this material. It should not have hard lines and in no case should it have the appearance of carving as in stone. · The work should retain all the touches of the modeling, these touches that give the sketchy effect which is lost in the carving in stone. In preparing the models ·the modeler should accentuate the detail and not attempt to smooth up the model. These markings, when brought out, all serve to make the work plastic and alive. It also helps in obtaining light and shade when colors are used as the finish. Even when the work is colored integrally these markings of the tool all stand out and bring out the work better to the eye when the buildings weather; in other words, he should not attempt to get in the clay any smoother work than he could get if he were modeling with stucco right in place instead of modeling in clay.

By proper manipulation of colors and attention to these details, great beauty can be obtained from work in low relief. On several jobs which I have under way at present I am using this method and getting what I believe to be good results. I am not attempting to confine the relief work to panels but am using the walls as the background, getting an effect as if the work were actually modeled in stucco and keeping the relief work very low and plastic. These are the touches that give the sketchy effect that is lost in the carving of stone. As a general rule it seems to be the practice of designers in stucco to copy stone; this, in my opinion, is entirely wrong. Stucco is a distinctive material and should be used as such. In my ornamental molding and relief work I use a combination of several colors (which match with the general color scheme of the exterior of the house) to bring out the effect and give light and shade. I use the darker tints in the background and work out the lighter tints in the high-lights, blending all the tints by rubbing the one color into the other; by doing this you bring out all the plastic beauty of the modeling and give an artistic appearance to the whole scheme. My colors on stucco I bring out by the use of a wash of liquid stucco. I am quite enthusiastic about this color work and I think it wonderful the effects that can be obtained with its intelligent use.

A study in colors for the stucco of buildings is the work of an artist and should be given this care with due consideration to the surroundings in which the house is to be built. My idea in getting effect and tone in a residence is that a study of the whole scheme, including the landscape work, should be taken into consideration and let the residence become a part of the landscape in which it sets and not make it look like an obstacle that has been put in the way of the beauty of nature.

In public buildings there is a big field for the stucco worker in producing the effects that are obtained by the use of terra cotta. Stucco can be made a formidable competitor of this material. It can be made permanent and has as wide a range of colors as polochrome terra cotta. When this is the result that is required, I use this method. In such work I use manufactured cement paints as a background applied over a stucco surface for the color effect. I apply the stucco according to the accompanying specifications. When the stucco is thoroughly dry I then apply a priming coat of a good cement paint, using the material thin and working it into the stucco surface with a brush, being careful not to use the material so thick as to spoil the texture of the surface. This texture should be a smooth sand finish. If the effect wanted is in a blend of several colors my system is to cover the surface of the stucco with two coats of cement paint as mentioned above. I then mix up my blending materials in the form of a stain, using good mineral colors ground in oil. which I thin down with prepared oil. I apply this stain over my relief and ornamental work in the various tints desired. I then rub off the high lights and in general blend in the colors to give it the soft effects. On the plain surfaces I apply the stain in the color desired, then rub off as much as possible; this gives a very pleasing mottled effect that blends in with the under-coating of cement paint and takes away the hard appearance. I have just completed a building on which I used in my relief work blue, golden buff and cream and got a beautiful effect that resembles old bisque china. On some of my work I get these effects by coloring integrally. It is then rubbed over with an oil preparation.

On residence work my methods are entirely different. I apply the stucco as specified, getting the texture desired, preferably medium rough cast. In some cases, I color the work integrally, a liquid form of the stucco of the same colors with a binder and hardener and waterproofing added. This material, when properly applied over a fairly rough texture makes a fine finish and when one becomes familiar with its working fine color effects are obtained. This liquid stucco is applied with a brush, like paint. The stucco surface, when finished, does not look like paint but retains the softness of the stucco with an unlimited range of color effects. On the ornaments and trim I use color effects with this wash in very much the same way as I specify for my treatment on public buildings except that the material is a stucco composition. To get the shading great care and taste must be used. This liquid stucco coat should be applied before the stucco surface is dry, usually, wherever possible, a day after the stucco is finished. It then dries and sets along with the stucco and makes a good bond. Spraying with water helps to make the surface bind; use a very fine spray. It gets harder with age and, being of practically the same composition as stucco, it retains all the soft tints and makes a house very attractive, especially when the latter has good surroundings. It seems to catch all the shadows and to change with different positions of the sun, reflecting the color of the surrounding foliage. It is this soft color effect that has made the homes of Italy and the south of France the mecca of the students of art. To me, the difference between this treatment and a surface that has been treated with some technical cement paint is like the difference between a cheap colored lithographic print and a painting. It retains the stucco surface, it keeps out check cracks and avoids the use of artificial paint, which is manufactured for this purpose but which, while curing check cracking, gives an artificial appearance and adds considerable to the cost.

The specifications which I give are taken from an article I wrote some time ago and which cover practically all conditions and treatments except possibly the texture for obtaining the Italian effects. The stucco in this case should not be perfectly straight except in the molding and trim. The molding and trim should be treated as specified, but the plain surfaces should give the appearance of stucco applied over cobblestone. No straight-edges should be used. The surface should be worked up to a condition with easy modulations, after it is partially set, go over it with the edge of a trowel to roughen the surface slightly, being careful not to leave trowel marks. Apply over this the liquid stucco with the desired tints. I could give my method for mottling the color but I am afraid it might be dangerous; the same applies to the texture. I did a very large stucco job here on which I have been working for two years. This was the effect desired. I had a lot of trouble in getting the texture; the plasterers would either make it too rough or too smooth. I simply had to take a few of my men, train them into the method I wanted; then I chose the ones who seemed to get the idea of the effect desired. These few men I then used on the actual finishing of the work so as to insure the same texture throughout the entire work. I have another style of finish which gives a splendid effect and which is very popular. I bring up the work to the straightening coat as specified. For the finish I apply over this surface a very thin coat of cement and sand troweled with a good pressure; I then apply a dash with a whisk broom, being careful not to throw the whole contents of the broom in one place but to spread it and get it with the texture about the size of peas, uniformly over the surface. I then apply over this the liquid stucco coating. A visit to Miami would show the results I have obtained.

* * * * *

Mr. Orr's Stucco Specifications

Preparation of Surface—The entire surface is examined and all loose form scale removed from the surface, i. e., the scale is caused by cement adhering to forms from previous pours. (When the form is not entirely filled in one day's operations, a film of cement adheres to the form in places and sets when the pour is made. This film invariably forms a scale surface on the face of the concrete when the forms are removed.) The entire surface is gone over with a hand pick or an axe to roughen the surface; if brick, rake out joints. This is for the purpose of forming key for stucco. The surface to be brushed clean and thoroughly soaked, ready for application of stucco.

Proportions: Straightening Coat—The proportions of this coat shall consist of four parts of Portland cement of approved brand to 12 parts of sand and two parts of hydrated lime. The above material to be thoroughly mixed dry, then tempered with water, to which has been added three parts of concentrated waterproofing paste to every 25 parts of water.

Finish Coat—The proportions of this coat shall consist of five parts of Portland cement to 12 parts of sand and 15 per cent of hydrated lime. (If white color is desired, use Medusa white cement and local white sand.) The above materials to be well mixed dry, then tempered with water, to which has been added one part of the waterproofing paste to every 18 parts of water.

Application of Stucco: Straightening Coat—Care has to be taken that the surface is thoroughly saturated with water to insure perfect bond, then apply straightening coat. Bring the surface to a true and straight condition, using a traversing rod. (No darby float to be used on first coat.) Then scratch the surface with a wire or nail scratch. (This gives an under cut and insures good bond.)

Application of Finish Coat for Smooth Surface—If stipple, use same process, only stipple before set. If rough cast, dash the finish material with a broom. Thoroughly saturate the first coat surface with water until it presents a glaze appearance; when this glaze disappears, which will be in a few minutes, apply the finish mortar, which should not be too soft, and bring the surface to a true condition with darby float. When the mortar will permit, go over the surface with hand float, bringing to a true finish free of cat-faces or voids; the entire surface to be gone over with burlap or hand float and patted to take out float marks. No joints to be allowed in the work where they can be seen. The entire surface to present a uniform appearance in color and texture. Mortar should be applied as quickly as possible and at all times protected from the sun.

Protection—Special care should be taken to avoid too rapid drying; if in the direct rays of the sun, the mortar shall be protected with burlap or wet canvas, and when sufficiently resistive, should be sprinkled with water for at least six days.

Stucco on Metal Lath—If stucco on metal lath, specify three-coat work with good fiber in first and second coats, waterproof in second and third coats.

Forming Molding—Cores for molding shall be formed of concrete by concrete contractor, allowing about one inch for finish. All molding to be run and finished with hand float to give same texture as rest of surface and to help bind the surface. When a condition arises where a heavy coat of mortar is necessary, a key for the mortar shall be formed by driving galvanized nails into the core.

*

* *

Architect's Right to Compensation

WHEN a statute or ordinance requires an architect to obtain a license before pursuing his occupation, an unlicensed person is not entitled to recover compensation for services in preparing plans and specifications, although his employer may have known that no license had been obtained. This point was declared by the Michigan Supreme Court recently in the case of Wedgewood vs. Jorgens.

Plaintiff prepared plans and specifications for a building which defendant contemplated but later abandoned, and plaintiff sued to recover the agreed compensation. The defense interposed was based on plaintiff's non-compliance with a local ordinance requiring architects to obtain annual licenses, pay a $5 fee, and furnish a $1,000 bond. The ordinance defines an architect as being any one who plans or supervises the erection or alteration of buildings for others, the construction work being done by third parties. Plaintiff, a builder and contractor, did not do the work in question himself, having it done by an unlicensed architect, with the assent of the owner.

In determining that plaintiff was not entitled to recover, the Supreme Court holds that the employing owner's knowledge that no license had been obtained did not avoid invalidity of the contract of employment; and that the fact that the city authorities had not enforced the ordinance did not deprive the regulation of its binding effect.

An architect employed to superintend the construction of a building for lump sum compensation is entitled to extra pay for prolongation of the work by changes in the plans made at the owner's instance, holds the Texas Court of Civil Appeals in the case of Shear vs. Bruyere. The court cites an earlier decision in the same state wherein it was decided that notwithstanding a contract had been made to superintend the construction of a building for a lump sum, still, if the owner made changes during the progress of the work, requiring longer time to complete the building than originally contemplated, and the work was done with the owner's knowledge, the architect could recover extra compensation for such additional services.—Building Age.

Some Needed Inventions

AN article entitled "What to Invent" was printed by The Electrical Experimenter (New York). Ever since, we are told in the February issue, the editors have been besieged by would-be inventors for another list of the kind. Evidently there are hosts of inventive-minded persons who want to invent something, but feel the need of a shove in some particular direction. In other words, "there exists an unsatiated demand for practical ideas of this kind." The editor, therefore, makes the suggestions quoted below, prefacing them with what he calls "a few words of advice to fortune-hunters via the Patent Office."

"The practical-minded inventor, as well as the one who has but a modest income, should always ask himself these important questions, before spending his money on models or patent fees:

"First, Is the device useful? Secondly, Does it fill an actual want? Thirdly, If so, is the device practical and can it be readly manufactured and marketed? Fourthly, Is there a similar article on the market already?

"Only if these questions have been answered satisfactorily to the inventor should he begin spending money on the device. Too many inventors are prone to rush to the Patent Office without asking themselves these all-important questions, with the net result that out of one thousand patents issued by the United States Patent Office less than three are ever taken up by a manufacturer or are actually exploited by their inventors.

"Then, again, far too many inventors are anything but practical-minded. Most of them lack business sense, and for this reason every inventor should submit his idea to at least one trusted business friend, who is not intoxicated with enthusiasm, as is almost every inventor worthy of the name."

The suggestions below are believed by the writer to cover all requirements. There is, he says, a positive demand for all, and if the correct solution is found, each invention will undoubtedly prove a handsome money-maker. Here are the needed inventions:

"Electric Air Cooler.—At the present time we use fans in the summer to 'cool' our sweltering humanity. Fans really don't cool, but simply stir up the heated atmosphere, and by causing drafts evaporate the moisture on our skins. This gives a cooling sensation. Electric fans, however, do not reduce the room temperature to any great extent, and for that reason are makeshifts at best. We should produce cold (lowering of the temperature) by some other electrical means. Peltier showed us that cold can be produced by crossing a bar of bismuth with a bar of antimony and sending an electric current through it in a certain direction. This is Peltier's cross. Why can not this principle—or a similar one—be supplied on a commercial scale, and incidentally make a fortune for its inventor?

"Electric Insect-Destroyer.—Every summer we are exasperated by flies and mosquitoes. Why not keep them out of the house of kill them by some electrical means? Electrically charged wire-netting has been used already, but if has many inherent faults. As a rule such netting can not be used on windows, as water or moisture puts the device out of order. Something more practical is required. Insects as a rule keep away from highly charged conductors (high frequency or Tesla currents). Perhaps this hint will put somebody on the right track.

"Electric Toys.—There is an immense market for cheap, electric toys. Something is wanted to keep a boy amused with a good electric toy operated by a dry cell. Years ago we saw an electric motor that sold for ten cents and actually ran. It was badly designed and badly made, otherwise the five- and ten-cent stores would be selling a million or more of them, a year. Here is a rich field, and it matters little if the article can be marketed for ten cents or one dollar—if the toy is right.

"Electric Window Attractions.—A vast field for the clever inventor. Movable window attractions are in ever-growing demand. Everybody stops and looks at the least mystifying movable sign or what not. Electricity and magnetism supply unending combinations, and, providing the device is novel and cheap, thousands can be sold. Every retail store can use one. 'Can you supply it?

"Bell 'Softener.'—A poor title for want of a better one. The harassed modern business man is of late developing what is termed as the 'telephone heart.' Every time the phone rings he starts, and if he is very nervous he jumps involuntarily. At home his wife is developing the same disease. What is wanted—badly wanted—is a device that will do away with the harsh, abrupt sound. Something 'soft' and mellow that doesn't jar one's nerves, and at the same time is not too muffled, otherwise the calling signal can not be heard in the next room. Simply unscrew the gongs and replace with your device. Can you furnish half a million at, say, one dollar each?"

*   *   *

National Highway System Needed

THE present strained relations with Germany, growing out of what is popularly designated as the latter's "ruthless" submarine warfare, should forcibly bring the people of the United States to a serious realization of the crying need for a gigantic system of concrete roads of the kind that in crises would be available for military operations in defense of the country.

These highways should not be constructed for the exclusive use of pleasure vehicles, such as the Lincoln highway, but should be built of materials of the most durable and strongest character possible. They should, of course, by reason of the most important strategical viewpoint, skirt both the Atlantic and Pacific coasts and be so constructed of concrete and other material to be able to withstand the movement of coast defense batteries from one point to another along the two coasts without injury to the roadbed.

Not only the east and west coasts should be provided with such a system of highways, but there should be other roadways capable of sustaining the heaviest possible conveyance, penetrating the country east and west as well as north and south.

Chambers of Commerce throughout the United States when contemplating the construction of new roads should always bear in mind the possibility that some day the Federal Government may take over these highways for the transportation of not only troops but guns of the heaviest calibre as well. With this view in mind they should be so constructed that the roadways in each State would be a connecting link in one great system of continuous highways running from the Atlantic to the Pacific, as well as from the Great Lakes to the Gulf.

With such a gigantic chain of roads built to be able to sustain the heaviest possible load, the Federal Government in case of any emergency would be enabled to move its entire army and guns with the greatest expediency. In the event of trouble involving only one particular State—such as a strike—where it is unnecessary for the State to call upon the Federal Government for aid, the National Guard of the commonwealth could be hurriedly transported from one end of the State to another with the least possible delay.

In the event of war with a foreign nation the importance of such a continuous chain of highways would be utterly indescribable. They would permit the United States Government to transport its troops located at the various forts throughout the country to strategical points for mobilization and thence to the actual scenes of hostilities. Along the coast country the heaviest of coast defense guns could be transported from one point of vantage to another as the situation might require, with the greatest possible facility. With such a roadway it would be unnecessary to load these heavy guns upon railroad cars for transportation from one point to another. Their own carriage, so constructed, would complete an individual vehicle for the movement of its own particular gun to any point along or the entire distance of the concrete roadway. An electrical motor system would provide the necessary motive power.

In time of peace, which happily is almost all the while, these roads with their connecting State links, would provide one of the most splendid systems of highways to be found anywhere in the world, over which could be transported agricultural products from one end of the country to the other. In deploring the bad roads of the country Secretary of Agriculture Houston declared that bad roads are expensive possessions and that it costs twenty-three cents to haul a ton one mile on the average country road as against only thirteen cents on a properly improved road.

Good roads are also essential to the development of suburban and rural property. By all means give us good roads of the kind that will withstand all requirements.—Realty.

*   *   *

The New Pacific Coast Naval Station

At a recent meeting of the Downtown Association of San Francisco Congressman John I. Nolan made an address in which he dwelt at length on the proposed naval base on San Francisco bay. He stated that the Helms Commission, which had been sent to the Pacific Coast, reported at length on conditions along the Pacific Coast, and their findings were that no harbor and no site in Southern California were adequate for the establishment of such a plant, but their recommendations included submarine and aeroplane bases at certain Southern California points. On the other hand, they reported favorably on four sites on San Francisco bay, viz: at Hunter's Point, in Alameda County near Bay Farm Island, Goat Island, and the Albany-Richmond site. This Commission recommended that Congress appropriate $1,500,000 for the purchase of a site on San Francisco bay. In addition to this, they requested an appropriation of $2,500,000 for extension work at Mare Island, and also as a submarine and aeroplane base at this point. It was the consensus of opinion in this Commission that the Mare Island Navy Yard was capable of doing a great deal of minor shipbuilding, but that a larger naval site is necessary on San Francisco bay to build capital ships with deeper draught of water. There was no doubt in the Congressman's mind but that the Helms Commission had fully determined on the selection of Hunter's Point as the site which they would ultimately recommend.

*   *   *

Take all the advertising out of the best newspaper in the world and see how quickly its circulation will dwindle.

A Good Home for Every Wage-Earner

By JOHN NOLEN*

A GOOD home for every wage-earner is possible only by recognizing that housing is intimately and permanently related to a number of large and difficult problems. Some of these are planning problems, some questions of broad economic policy. For example, we have the close relation between city planning and housing,—how it is influenced by the location of factories; by the proper districting of the city and by other building regulations; by the street system, and especially by means of transportation; by the proper distribution and development of parks, playgrounds, and neighborhood facilities for recreation. Many housing schemes have been carried through as if they were isolated phenomena, and thus have often failed of their purpose.

Then, housing is, of course, closely related to the building interests, materials of construction, and the loss by depreciation and fire. It is affected directly by policies with regard to land and taxation, the prevailing practice as to public health and sanitation, and especially standards of living and their dependence upon the minimum wage.

From the point of view of economics, and I believe that the ultimate solution of this problem is to come mainly in that direction, housing is big business, and should be handled as big business is handled. Building operations in the United States amount annually, it is said, to $4,000,-000,000. More than half of this great total is spent in dwellings—much of it, in fact from an economic point of view most of it, is not either well constructed nor permanently invested. By far too large a percentage of the houses, especially the cheaper sorts, are poorly conceived for their purposes, and 80 per cent of all of them are built of wood. A frame house may be a satisfactory house, provided the space between and around houses makes it reasonably safe. Usually there is an excessive depreciation and a fearfully costly fire risk. This constitutes a huge economic loss, amounting, by the most conservative estimate, to hundreds of millions of dollars annually, which sum must be paid, as other carrying charges are paid, out of production, and finally must be taken care of in the wage-earner's pay-roll.

Closely related to housing is the question of wages and standards of living. Consider, for example, these four points and their relation to one another:

1. The minimum desirable house of four or five rooms cannot be provided in the United States, even under favorable conditions, for less than about $1,800 or $2,000; that is, for house and lot, with street improvements, essential public utilities, and neighborhood recreation.

2. A house costing that sum cannot be offered on the basis of an economic rent of, say, 5 per cent or 6 per cent net, for less than $15 per month.

3. Unless a wage-earner with a normal family of wife and three dependent children has an income of $15 a week, or $800 a year, he cannot afford to pay as much as $15 a month for the rent of his home.

4. More than one-half of all workingmen earn less than $15 a week.

Thus we see that under the present conditions no solution of the housing problem in its most acute form, affecting more than 50 per cent of all wage-workers, is possible until a better adjustment can be made in the relation of these four points. Here is our choice. Either the cost of the

*From an address at American Civic Association Conference, Washington, 1916.

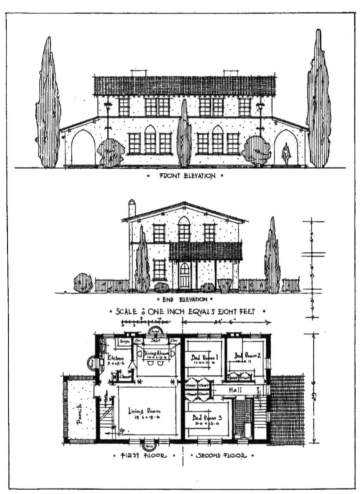

FOUR-ROOM SINGLE FAMILY DOUBLE HOUSE
J. THEODORE HANEMANN,   ARCHITECT

(National Americanization Committee Housing Competition)

house and lot must be very substantially reduced; or the actual standard of healthful living must be lowered; or—the wages of the poorest paid workmen must be raised. The other three possible alternatives, if they may be so considered, are to put the wife and children to work to add to the family income, to take in boarders or lodgers, or to count upon private philanthropy or the public treasury to provide not a few but great masses of wage-workers with a house at less than an economic rent. Are we content to accept any of these alternatives?

What, then, is the first step toward a solution of this large and important problem? I believe it is to recognize that the subject is primarily one for the right application of broad economic principles. We must in some thoroughgoing way convert the great forces, working through regular channels, which now produce bad housing, to produce good housing, and we must do it by bringing into control and co-operation with them the forces that believe in good housing and will gain from it, which are mainly the manufacturing and business interests that depend upon the efficient and happy workman. This great change in housing methods will come, if it does come, from the substitution for exploitation and excessive return, of the reasonable profits of business, from the transfer of housing from the field of speculation to that corresponding to legitimate manufacturing. We shall then proceed in very much the same way that the manufacturer proceeds. We shall want to know the facts as to the nature and extent of the demand. We shall have definite aims as to the produce we require. We shall use our best skill and experience and efficient factory methods. We shall back the enterprise with adequate capital, and then count upon obtaining a fair rate of interest.

The experiment of the Woodlawn Company, at Wilmington, Del., is an example of the financial basis on which permanent housing can be provided for the wage-earning class as a good business investment yielding full 5 per cent interest.

The houses are mostly built in rows, containing four six-room houses, four four-room houses, and six two-family houses. Some of the houses in the district differ from these, but most of them come within these four types. There are 270 houses in the twenty rows which have thus far been built, which provide accommodations for 390 families in all.

It has been difficult to determine the exact cost of each type because the contracts usually covered building at least two rows of houses, but the cost, without the cost of the ground, is estimated for the six-room house, which rents for $16, at about $1,775; the four-room, with rents at $13.50, $1,425; and the two-family house, of which the first floor rents for $11.50 and the second floor for $12, $2,475.

Houses are built of brick, with slate and slag roofs. All have sewer connections, city water and gas, and some have electric wiring. A range is installed in each kitchen, with water-boiler attached. Bath-tubs and kitchen sinks are porcelain enameled. Stationary laundry tubs are installed in the second-floor flats. There are both front and back yards, and parts of the tract have been set aside for park or playground purposes.

The first houses were built in 1903 and the last ones in 1913. They were not built for sale, but are to be kept in the ownership of the Woodlawn Company. The six-room house has been found to be as large, if not larger, than the majority of wage-earners want. It is of actual value to know that more applications have been made for four-room houses and flats than for any other kind. This development represents an investment of $583,000, and has yielded an average net profit of about 5 per cent.

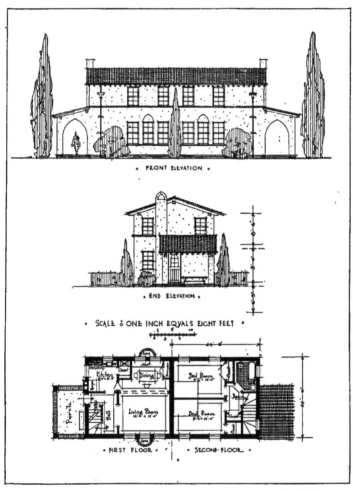

DOUBLE SINGLE-FAMILY HOUSE WITH FOUR LODGERS
J. THEODORE HANEMANN,   ARCHITECT

(National Americanization Committee Housing Competition)

The larger part of low-cost housing in the United States is not today satisfactory in character, but a peculiar opportunity for improvement is now presented. Employers of labor are having such great difficulty in getting and holding employees, that they are ready to consider any practicable proposition that will lessen their troubles. It is now easy to draw their attention to the poor character of much of the housing of wage-earners, and more especially to the utter inadequacy of the supply of small houses of suitable types available at rents which the working-man can afford.

From a recent study of conditions in four cities, Waterbury and Bridgeport, Conn., Kenosha, Wis., and Akron, O., I believe that there is today an opportunity for a substantial and permanent advance. In some respects the problems are similar to all these cities; in other respects, they are local and peculiar.

In all cases the local organization resolved that before plunging in and building something, they would find out by careful investigation the extent and character of the demand for houses, and also the experience of other places in meeting somewhat parallel conditions and requirements. The first step, it seemed to them, was a social and economic survey, a diagnosis that would give them confidence in the prescription for immediate needs, and at the same time enable them to adopt measures that would be preventive in character and apply to meeting the situation in more normal times.

The recommendations submitted to these four cities, of which those for Bridgeport are typical, have been framed to meet the actual housing needs of working-men, on terms which their wages make possible. The proposals are not essentially new; in fact, they follow conservative and well-tried-out schemes of other housing companies. Virtually everything recommended has been successfully executed elsewhere in this country for the same classes of working-men, with the same income or even less. No one house or method is endorsed as the only one, although the emphasis is put upon the single family, self-contained, detached house or cottage, as on the whole most desirable when possible. In addition to the single one-family house, detached, the recommendations include an endorsement of the use of one-family houses in groups; also of well-arranged, well-lighted apartments or flats. All of these types have some advantages of economy of land cost or of land improvement cost, or of house construction, and all take into account the fact that different people have different tastes and preferences, as well as different needs in housing, as in all other matters. What is best depends upon conditions and circumstances, and, finally, the cost.

In Waterbury, two large manufacturing concerns have begun operations, and a considerable number of new houses of desirable types will be completed and available this autumn. Furthermore, the attention of the manufacturers of the city has been effectively drawn to the subject, and through the publication of the report in the Waterbury Republican, as a Sunday supplement, public interest has been aroused and found favorable to the energetic prosecution of the subject. No joint action, however, on the part of manufacturers or of business interests generally, has yet been secured, and it will be interesting to observe how much can be accomplished without it.

In Kenosha, the movement was begun by the Manufacturers' Association, and had the approval and support from the start of all the business interests of the city. Although the investigation was not taken up until

May, the Kenosha House Building Company and the Kenosha Homes Company were successfully organized in July. Land was purchased and building begun early in August. Plans have been made for the construction of at least 400 single family houses. Some are already completed and occupied, and a new house is started every day. So far the operation is confined to the detached cottage type of five or six rooms. The price of the first houses, on 40-foot lots which had already been laid out when purchased, will be under $2,500. It is hoped that later operations will make possible houses at about $2,000 on a minimum of 50-foot lots.

Some forces are now being used in Kenosha for good housing that formerly built houses less good or were relatively inactive in adding to the supply of houses. These forces have been stimulated, directed and helped by the effective organization of the manufacturing, business, and financial interests of the city. The work is on a good business basis, yielding a good return. It places no dependence upon philanthropy and charity. It is being done by the entire community for the entire community. It is free from any taint of paternalism or embarrassing relation of employer and employee. It is permanent, and intends to occupy the field so long as there is any need for it. It is of inestimable benefit to the four parties most affected; namely, the employers of labor, the people of the city as a whole, the legitimate real-estate operators and builders, and above all, to the wage-earner himself. With slight modifications to meet local conditions, the method of Kenosha is, I believe, capable of wide application.

The Bridgeport story is just begun. After the presentation of the report entitled "More Houses for Bridgeport," and the careful consideration of the whole matter by the Chamber of Commerce, the Housing Company was incorporated, with a capital of $1,000,000. A capable manager has been engaged by the company to give all his time to the problem, offices have been opened and negotiations are now under way for the acquisition of land and the construction of buildings. Definite plans have been prepared by Schenck & Mead, architects, of New York city, for the Bridgeport Housing Company. They include provision for 86 houses and 138 families. The plan includes also a liberal playground, and arrangements for agreeable planting of the entire property.

If successful, I believe that the movement in Bridgeport will be particularly instructive and significant, because the demand is so great, and the conditions that the company has been organized to combat are typical of a modern industrial city in the throes of very rapid growth.

Advance in solving the problem of housing will come as men and women of vision recognize its controlling importance and discover ways of effectively promoting it. I believe we shall solve these problems on strictly economic lines, and so we shall make one of the greatest contributions to the welfare of the wage-earner and to the increase of our industrial efficiency.

* * *

Test of Strength of Hollow Tiles

At the request of several manufacturers of hollow tile, a series of investigations of the strength of this material as developed in walls of varying thicknesses has been started in the U. S. Bureau of Standards by the construction of a number of these walls 5 feet long by 12 feet high. The walls so far constructed are of three thicknesses—6, 8 and 12 inches. Those already laid up have been set with the tile placed on their sides. Other variables will enter into the work, and when the investigation is completed about 50 will have been built.

New Building Laws Passed by California Legislature

MR. CHARLES H. CHENEY, city planning expert, with offices in the Crocker building, San Francisco, attended the City Planning Conference recently held in Kansas City. Mr. Cheney is well pleased with the efforts of the State Housing Institute at Sacramento, in securing the passage of at least three important bills at the late session of the California Legislature. These bills amend the state tenement house and hotel laws and create an entirely new act regulating the construction of private dwellings. Despite strong opposition to some features all these bills were passed practically as they were drafted by the Housing Institute. The clause in the original tenement and hotel bills providing for combined tenement and rooming houses was eliminated and a compromise was made on the provisions prohibiting garbage chutes in tenement houses by permitting their installation when the chutes to be used are approved by the building department.

Three bills designed to aid city planning were also passed by the legislature and await the governor's signature. They provide for the establishment of zones, set-back lines and excess condemnation.

The following will serve to give a brief outline of some of the more important provisions prescribed by the three bills:

Tenement House Law

The Tenement House Act is not in any manner radically different from the present state law, though greatly improved upon in its entirety. Particular pains have been taken to write the law so that the sections and subjects are grouped in their logical sequence. This arrangement makes it very handy for use. The scope of the law has been extended to all parts of the state. This includes territory either in incorporated towns or cities, or outside in the suburban or country districts. The present law has applied only to territory within incorporated towns and cities, etc.

The enforcement of the law has been definitely centralized, thereby eliminating the possibility of officials shirking their duties and also eliminating much inconvenience to the general public. The present law is very ambiguous on this particular phase. This will also assist very materially as to the obtaining as well as the issuing of permits and certificates required by the law.

The definitions of words and phrases used in the law have been elaborated upon and made quite more extensive and specific. This will tend to eliminate much confusion which has been caused by the present law, due to its conflicting and ambiguous phrases and terms.

The definitions of "courts," "lots' and "yards," also of the three classes of buildings, to wit, "fireproof," "semi-fireproof," "wooden," might well be studied, as they are of particular significance throughout the act. The provisions for a yard on a lot extending from street to street have been cleared up and all reference to the 150-ft. depth limit eliminated. Rear tenements and rear hotels, i. e., a tenement house or hotel erected behind another building, carry certain restrictions, one of which is that a front yard not less in width than 50 per cent of the actual width of the rear building must be provided in front of such tenement house or hotel.

The maximum height of a fireproof tenement house or hotel is fixed at 150 ft. and for a semi-fireproof building is fixed not to exceed six stories at any point, nor more than 65 ft., and the limit for a wooden tenement house is three stories and not more than 36 ft. In the case of a semi-fireproof and a wooden tenement house, a variation of 10 ft. over the above figures is permitted for lots with sloping ground, this will permit of the stepping down or up of a building to follow the grade of the lot. No building can exceed one and a half times the width of the widest street to which the lot on which it is situated abuts, though the building may be set back from the street line to gain a greater height.

A basement is specifically defined in the new law and is considered a story for the purpose of computing the height of buildings. This will eliminate much confusion that has existed heretofore.

Percentages of lot to be left unoccupied and size of rear yards remain practically the same as in the present law.

The definition of "court" has eliminated the present so-called "street to yard court." This, however, is taken care of by a "side yard." The minimum width of a side yard is the same as an outer court, except that the provision of outer courts as to the maximum lengths does not apply. Further, the width of a side yard may be reduced 12 in. when the building is erected on the lot so that a side yard is provided on each side thereof, and that the side yards are connected across the rear by a rear yard. In other words, 12 in. more space may be covered by the building on each side in the event that it is kept away from the property lines so as to provide free circulation of air around the entire building.

"Outer" and "inner court" sizes remain the same as in the present law, except that "lot line courts" will, under the new law, come under the same provisions as an inner court and therefore will be a few inches wider than required by the present law. However, this is not a bad provision, as it simply encourages the construction of outer courts, and under the new law the heretofore known "outer lot line court" is an "outer court."

Ventilation in Tenements

The new law provides for ventilation under the first floor of all buildings, except where the lowest floor is of masonry; also requires rat-proofing of the lowest floor of buildings. There are several simple methods in which this can be done and which are permitted by the new law.

Every apartment must be provided with a separate watercloset in a compartment within the apartment. Windows from rooms will be permitted to open through open porches, except windows from kitchens. This will permit the construction of sleeping porches and also legalizes the use of front porches on bungalow design buildings. Technically this is a violation under the present act.

The fan exhaust system of ventilation for amusement, entertainment and reception rooms and rooms used for similar purposes, where it is not practicable to get windows to the outer air, has been recognized. Under the present law this cannot be done, and in many cases has worked a hardship to those desiring to construct rooms for these purposes.

A new section in both the tenement and hotel laws prescribes that every building must be so designed that every apartment in a tenement house and every room in a hotel be provided with at least two means of egress, and that the means of egress must be either by stairways or fire escapes.

The stairway and fire escape provisions have been gone into at quite length in the new laws. The present acts contain nothing of any consequence on these subjects. Fireproof tenement houses and hotels, under the new law, will require one stairway 3 ft. 6 in. wide for each 6000 sq. ft. or fractional part thereof of floor area in any one floor above the first floor; and in semi-fireproof buildings one for each 4000 sq. ft. or fractional part thereof, and one for every 3000 sq. ft. or fractional part thereof in wooden buildings. Stairways must be readily accessible and located to provide the best means of egress from the buildings. A stairway on more than one side of an elevator shaft will not be allowed, nor one located over a steam boiler, gas meter, gas heater or furnace, except that the boiler or other apparatus be located in a boiler room. Also prohibits a stairway from either terminating in or passing through a boiler room. Circular and winding stairways are prohibited and all stairways are required to be continuous, i. e., one flight above another, or so that each flight shall be in plain view of each succeeding flight. The fire escape provisions are all based on standard practice and as now used in this city and other cities in the state. One fire escape must be provided for each 3000 sq. ft. of floor area in any building above the second floor thereof, and one additional fire escape for each additional 4000 sq. ft. of floor area, or fractional part thereof. Construction of elevator shafts and similar shafts is well taken care of under the new law.

Maintenance, sanitation, cleanliness, and privacy are covered much more extensively than in the present law.

The cubical contents of a room for any number of occupants is arrived at in the new laws on the basis of floor area, i. e., not less than 60 sq. ft. must be afforded each occupant of more than 12 years of age, or two persons under 12 years of age. Additional floor area in the same ratio must be provided for additional persons.

The Hotel Law

The new hotel law, under its provisions, includes every building, or portion thereof, containing six or more guest rooms, i. e., any building which has six or more rooms to rent or hire out to the public for living and sleeping purposes, and in a general way requires all of the same standards as are fixed in the tenement house law for tenement houses; except that the provisions of percentages of lot unoccupied and rear yard requirements do not apply to hotels. Of course, those things that are required in a hotel and not in a tenement house have been added, and vice versa, things required in a tenement house and not in a hotel, eliminated.

The hotel law makes a marked change over the present state hotel law, inasmuch as the present law has served no purpose other than to cause confusion and difficulties to those who attempted to use it.

The new hotel law also will regulate the construction as well as the maintenance and occupancy of large dormitories similar to those that now exist in the east part of the city and which are rented out for cheap lodging houses. Its provisions will require that proper toilet and other conveniences are installed, and limits the occupants of any one dormitory to not more than twenty persons. It requires windows opening to the outer air and provides other sanitary features.

The third bill, which is the dwelling house law, will take in all single dwelling houses, double houses, and the 3 and 4-family flats; in fact, all buildings which may be designed so as not to come within either the provisions of the tenement house or hotel laws. Its provisions are not at all severe, though will supply a much felt want, especially in cities which do not have any kinds of building or sanitary laws.

Its provisions require that all buildings be constructed in a substantial manner and so as to provide shelter to the occupants against the elements, and to exclude dampness in inclement weather; that all sleeping rooms contain at least 90 sq. ft. of superficial floor area; that the room in no part be less than 7 feet in width; and that it have a ceiling height of not less than 8 ft.; that every such room have windows opening to the street or to some unoccupied area on the lot, which unoccupied area must not be less than 4 ft. in its least dimensions and contain an area of not less than 36 sq. ft.

It requires that a certain amount of floor area be afforded each occupant of a room which is used for sleeping purposes, in the same manner as fixed by the tenement and hotel laws.

* * *

$75,000,000 for Buildings for New U. S. Army

Plans are well advanced for the construction of the cantonments to shelter the emergency army of the United States of 43,000 officers and 1,034,000 enlisted men. The estimated cost of providing temporary construction, etc., is $75,650,000. The item for erection of temporary buildings amounts to $40,290,800. Temporary hospitals are to be built to cost $2,014,540; water and sewer systems will cost $2,490,000; electric lighting systems, $604,000; roads, $5,036,000. The location and size of these camps have not been determined, and it is still a question whether the War Department will purchase the material and engage general construction companies to erect the buildings or award contracts for the complete work. It is planned to erect at Fort Myer, Va., a series of sample buildings arranged in units of various types of construction, and the departmental designation of a type will be governed, not only by price and availability of material, but by considerations of climate. One of the types will be of metal, another of concrete (which includes the roof), and a third of frame (of the "knockdown" variety). The buildings will be of one story and of the simplest design. The "layouts" will be for brigade headquarters, a regiment, a battalion, and a company. The officers' quarters for a regiment, for example, will be 84 feet in length and contain at one end the kitchen and mess room with offices at the other; between will be separate sleeping rooms for six officers.

* * *

"Portland" with a Small "P"

The Portland Cement Association suggests that there is no good reason for writing "portland cement" with a capital "P," since the product is not made in Portland, Me., Portland, Ore., nor Portland, England. The association recommends this practice to members in the following paragraph:

The emphasis resulting from the capitalization of the letter "P" contributes to the erroneous impression so prevalent that Portland cement is all made by a single corporation—hence such frequent expressions as, "Oh, yes! you are with the Portland people," or "What is the address of the Portland Cement Company?" The word "Portland" is properly to be considered as a qualifying adjective used to distinguish a kind of cement, not a brand of cement or a trade-mark. The case is quite similar to that of "macadam roads," where the word "macadam" has become a common adjective, though derived from MacAdam, the name of the man who invented this type of road. It is believed that departing from the custom of capitalizing the word "portland" will do much to correct the present troublesome misconception.

THE
Architect and Engineer
OF CALIFORNIA

Founded in 1905 by E. M. C. WHITNEY

A. I. WHITNEY	- - -	*Manager*
T. C. KIERULFF	- - -	*Legal Points*
FREDERICK W. JONES	- -	*Editor*

Published Monthly in the interests of the Architects, Structural Engineers, Contractors and the Allied Trades of the Pacific Coast by the Architect and Engineer.

BUSINESS OFFICE AND EDITORIAL ROOMS
627-629 Foxcroft Building, San Francisco
Telephone Douglas 1828

The publishers disclaim any responsibility for statements made in the advertisements of this magazine.

TERMS OF SUBSCRIPTION

(Including postage) to all parts of the United States $1.50 per annum; to Canada 50c additional; to all Foreign points $1 additional.

VOL. XLIX.   MAY, 1917   No. 2

It is both amusing and annoying to pick up an Eastern publication every now and then **THE "REAL" CALIFORNIA BUNGALOW** and find in it a picture of a one and one-half story cottage, and not infrequently a two-story house with this caption beneath it: "A California Bungalow." To educate the East into an intelligent comprehension of the difference between a bungalow and an ordinary cottage seems a most difficult task, strange to say. We've been telling them about bungalows for at least eight years—telling them that a bungalow is a one-story house, first, last and always, yet they go right on talking about the two-story house that is "modeled after" or a "prototype of" the California bungalow.

Recently the Building Age published a photograph of a house—a frame cottage, the architecture of which, according to the text, is supposed to have been influenced our California bungalow. Here is what Mr. F. A. Schilling of Los Angeles wrote in .contradiction:

In the first place, the roof is too steep. A bungalow roof is about one-sixth or one-eighth pitch.

Again, a bungalow never has an upper story. We call such houses "cottages"—not bungalows.

The windows certainly show the Eastern Colonial influence both in design and size. Bungalow windows are not mullioned, and are wide. The pergola shows no bungalow influence—it is Colonial. The dormers surely are not "bungalonial," to coin a new word; neither are the boxed eaves.

As for the interior, it is just as Eastern as the exterior—no built-in buffets, beds, coolers, etc., even a broad, cased opening is lacking, which, of course, is natural in a cold climate. Even the porch has been made a part of the interior by inclosing it.

Mr. Francis Wilson, a Southern California architect, has the right idea about art com- **WHY AN ART COMMISSION?** missions and what they may do for a community. Mr. Wilson has long been an ardent advocate of an art commission for the city of Santa Barbara. Some of his thoughts along these lines were expressed by him recently in the public press. We quote a few paragraphs:

With a setting, a climate and an environment that is the envy of all the rest of the world, we owe it to ourselves, to our self-respect, as well as to the whole country to provide man-made improvements that will do full justice to the bountiful gifts or nature. So far we have fallen lamentably short of such a standard.

No one could go to Paestum and gaze on those three lovely temples and think the while of Santa Barbara without a shudder. There they stand in an open plain, backed by mountains, lonely and dignified and beautiful. They have been there for 2600 years, and they certainly represent honest and permanent construction.

Is there any reason why we should not do as well, nay better, than those Greeks of long ago?

I think it is hard for the American temperament to confine itself for any great length of time to one thing. We want things done quickly. If it is a question of a house we want to move in within six months when proper planning and careful building should require not less than a year.

I believe the most practical method of getting the public to realize the necessity for beauty, neatness and charm is to demonstrate its commercial value.

Biarritz, on the Bay of Biscay, owes its fortunes to its irresistible charm. Every one who goes there looks forward to a return, all faces are smiling, business is good, the people are happy, and the tourist is pleased. It pays; it certainly does pay to make your city, the place where you live and earn your daily bread, a place of beauty and attraction.

These arguments inevitably lead to a plea for a commission to regulate the artistic expression of our citizens. It is probably true that the less exact and definite a person's knowledge of a subject is the more confident and vociferous that person is in expressing his opinions.

An art commission would be a distinct benefit, both esthetically and commercially, and after it has been in service long enough to have its work fairly judged, we would all bless the day it was created.

Comparing the small house of 1916 with those of earlier date, it will be noticed that the lines are simpler, the useless addition of "features" is more subdued, colors are more harmonious and friendly.

The clinker brick is losing its popularity, and stucco of a roughness and harshness quite incredible is giving way to a plaster of gentler habit.

Exaggerated roofs are not quite so exaggerated, and rafter ends seem less riotous and exhuberant. Even the "picture window" is coming under control.

How Architects May Serve Country

The American Institute of Architects has sent out, through its Central Committee on Preparedness, a circular to members of the profession telling of the needs of the United States Army, and in what manner architects and draftsmen may serve their country.

The circular in part is as follows:

The United States Army is in greatest need of line officers, and it would be of the greatest service if the younger men of the profession, particularly those who have had military training, would enter this branch.

The branches of the service in which an architect's training and knowledge would render him particularly valuable are the Corps of Engineers and Quartermaster Corps. In both of these there is no age limit.

The Quartermaster Corps is primarily the business organization of the Army. It has charge of the equipment, supplies, commissary, pay, transportation and building.

The duties of the Corps of Engineers comprise reconnoitering and surveying for military purposes, including the laying out of camps; selection of sites and formation of plans and estimates for military defenses; construction and repair of fortifications and their accessories; the installation of electric power plants and electric power cable connected with sea-coast batteries; construction and repair of military roads, railroads and bridges; military demolitions. In time of war within the theater of operations it has charge of the location, design and construction of wharves, piers, landings, storehouses, hospitals, and other structures of general interest, and of the construction, maintenance and repair of roads, ferries, bridges, and incidental structures, and of the construction, maintenance and operation of railroads under military control, including the construction and operation of armored trains.

The buildings erected under the Q. M. C. comprise barracks, warehouses, hospitals, etc., of which many would be needed in time of trouble, and therefore the architect's services are particularly valuable.

The special qualifications for members of an engineer company comprise:

Engineers specializing in Bridges	Concrete
Construction	Wharves
Earth	Piers
Electrical	Buildings
Highway	Quarrymen
Mining	Miners
Railroad	Carpenters
Sanitary	Bridge Carpenters
Topographical	Blacksmiths
Construction Superintendents	Plumbers and Pipefitters
Topographical Surveyors and Sketchers	Electricians
Draftsmen	Enginemen, Steam
Photographers and Blueprint men	Engineers, Gas
Lithographers and Zincographers	Firemen
	Machinists
	Masons
	Caulkers
	Riggers
	Axemen

From the above it is evident that the architect can fit in somewhere in the Corps of Engineers, particularly in construction, topography, draughting, sanitary and electrical work. The architect would be in charge of much the same class of trades as he is in his professional superintendence, although military engineering technique is quite a different matter. In France many architects are engaged in translating photographs from aeroplanes into maps.

Mr. Evarts Tracy, the Octagon, Washington, is chairman of the Central Committee.

Concrete Industry Loses Pioneer Builder

Mr. Ernest L. Ransome, pioneer in reinforced concrete building construction in the United States, whose death was noted last month, is credited with having built the first reinforced concrete buildings in America. Bulletin No. 12 of the Association of American Portland Cement Manufacturers in 1906 says:

Ernest L. Ransome, then of San Francisco, from 1885 to 1890 was engaged in applying his discoveries to works of the most elaborate and extensive character—we can bestow the greater credit and honor upon him for the courage and splendid mechanical and engineering ability which he displayed in undertaking the construction of steel concrete buildings of such magnitude in a country subject to earthquakes; and the value of his discoveries has been further accentuated by the fact that during the recent great earthquake in California all of the above structures came through the ordeal unscathed, where buildings of brick and stone in their immediate vicinity were entirely wrecked.

It is said of Mr. Ransome that he was the inventor of more machinery for the purpose of mixing and placing concrete than all the other inventors combined.

Engineers Ready to Aid Cause

For the purpose of holding a survey of the engineering talent in the Bay region with the idea of offering it to the United States Government in case of necessity, a meeting of engineers was held recently at the Oakland Chamber of Commerce. The meeting included all branches of the profession, civil, electrical, mechanical and mining.

The following officers were elected: President, Harlan D. Miller; vice-president, R. S. Chew; secretary-treasurer, John A. Britton, Jr.; directors, A. Vander Naillen, Jr., Romaine W. Meyers and T. J. Allen. A committee was appointed to confer with the State Council of Defense. Seventy-five engineers attended the meeting.

American Institute of Architects
(ORGANIZED 1857)
OFFICERS FOR 1916-17

PRESIDENT.....JOHN LAWRENCE MAURAN, St. Louis
FIRST VICE-PRESIDENT......C. GRANT LA FARGE, New York
SECOND VICE-PRESIDENT...W. R. B. WILLCOX, Seattle, Wash.
SECRETARY....W. STANLEY PARKER, Boston, Mass.
TREASURER..........D. EVERETT WAID, New York

San Francisco Chapter

PRESIDENT..................EDGAR A. MATHEWS
VICE-PRESIDENT.........SYLVAIN SCHNAITTACHER
SECRETARY AND TREASURER........MORRIS BRUCE
TRUSTEES...................... { W. B. FAVILLE
{ G. A. WRIGHT

Southern California Chapter

PRESIDENT...................... ..J. E. ALLISON
VICE-PRESIDENT................. ...J. J. BACKUS
SECRETARY ....A. R. WALKER
TREASURER...............,...AUGUST WACKERBARTH

Board of Directors
ROBT. D. FARQUHAR   PERCY A. EISEN
S. B. MARSTON

Portland, Ore., Chapter

PRESIDENT...................JOSEPH JACOBBERGER
VICE-PRESIDENT.................J. A. FOUILHOUX
SECRETARY....................W. C. KNIGHTON
TREASURER....................FOLGER JOHNSON
TRUSTEES................. { ION LEWIS
{ M. H. WHITEHOUSE

Washington State Chapter

PRESIDENT..............CHARLES H. BEBB, Seattle
1ST VICE-PRES...DANIEL R. HUNTINGTON, Seattle
2D VICE-PRESIDENT.........GEORGE GOVE, Tacoma
3D VICE-PRESIDENT........L. L. RAND, Spokane
SECRETARY.............JOSEPH S. COTE, Seattle
TREASURER...........ELLSWORTH STOREY, Seattle
COUNCIL............... { JAMES STEPHEN, Seattle
{ JAMES H. SCHACK, Seattle
{ CHARLES H. ALDEN, Seattle

California State Board of Architecture
NORTHERN DISTRICT.

PRESIDENT..................EDGAR A. MATHEWS
SECRETARY-TREASURER...SYLVAIN SCHNAITTACHER
Members
JOHN BAKEWELL, JR.   J. CATHER NEWSOM
SOUTHERN DISTRICT.
PRESIDENT.....................JOHN P. KREMPEL
SECRETARY-TREASURER.........FRED H. ROEHRIG
MEMBERS..................... { OCTAVIUS MORGAN
{ SUMNER P. HUNT
{ WM. S. HEBBARD

San Francisco Architectural Club
OFFICERS FOR 1917

PRESIDENT ....CHAS. PETER WEEKS
VICE-PRESIDENT ....A. WILLIAMS
SECRETARY ....JOHN F. BEUTTLER
TREASURER ....WILLIAM HELM

San Francisco Society of Architects

PRESIDENT................CHARLES PETER WEEKS
VICE-PRESIDENT...........GEORGE W. KELHAM
SECRETARY AND TREASURER......WARREN C. PERRY
DIRECTORS............... { ERNEST COXHEAD
{ FREDERICK H. MEYER

Engineers and Architects Association of Los Angeles

PRESIDENT....................A. H. KOEBIG, SR.
FIRST VICE-PRESIDENT..............A. S. BENT
SECOND VICE-PRESIDENT...........IRA J. FRANCIS
Directors
J. J. BACKUS, GEO. P. ROBINSON, ALBERT C. MARTIN, H. L. SMITH

Washington State Society of Architects

PRESIDENT..............:.....A. WARREN GOULD
SECRETARY....................WM. J. JONES
TREASURER....................J. L. MCCAULEY
TRUSTEES.................. { HARRY H. JAMES
{ WM. J. JONES
{ ALFRED BREITUNG
{ J. L. MCCAULEY
{ G. F. ROWE

San Diego Architectural Association

PRESIDENT....................CHARLES CRESSEY
VICE-PRESIDENT........W. TEMPLETON JOHNSON
SECRETARY....................ROBT. HALLEY, JR.
TREASURER....................G. A. HAUSSEN

San Joaquin Valley Ass'n of Architects

PRESIDENT....................W. J. WRIGHT
VICE-PRESIDENT.:.................E. B. BROWN
SECRETARY-TREASURER..........FRANK V. MAYO

With the Architects

Building Reports and Personal Mention of Interest to the Profession

Portland Architects Getting Busy

Portland building operations seem to be taking new life, much to the satisfaction of the architects, many of whom have had little to do the past two or three years.

Messrs. Sutton & Whitney are especially busy. They report a fifty-thousand-dollar fruit drying plant in The Dalles, to be repeated in Salem for the same company; a 100x100 four-story reinforced concrete garage for Frazer & McLean, to cost $60,000, the building to be finished in white throughout; a 100x100 two-story store building for the Spaulding Estate, to cost $40,000, in addition to five residences costing from five to fifteen thousand dollars each.

The United States National Bank building, Mr. A. E. Doyle architect, is nearing completion. When finished it will be one of the most monumental banking structures in Oregon.

Messrs. Houtalling & Dougan have let the contract for the Moose building, the upper portion of which will be devoted to lodge purposes and the first floor rented for stores.

Mr. John V. Bennes having finished two fine business blocks in Portland, is working on plans for the O. A. C., which, together with other construction, is keeping his office busy.

Stockton Architect Has Much Work

Mr. Ralph P. Morrell, Odd Fellows building, Stockton, is preparing plans for a large country home to be erected at Jamestown, near Sonora, Tuolumne county, for Dr. Congdon. The estimated cost is $12,000.

Mr. Morrell is also making plans for a one-story frame and stucco house to be built at Newman for William J. Burris, cashier of the First National Bank of Newman. The Frank Lloyd Wright style will be followed. House will cost $7,500.

F. P. Roper, editor of the Lodi Sentinel, will build a $4,500 Swiss Chalet at Lodi from plans by Mr. Morrell.

University of California to Build

Messrs. Willis Polk & Company are preparing plans for a seven-story reinforced concrete store and office building, to be erected on Sutter street, between Montgomery and Kearny, San Francisco.

Idaho's New License Law

Architects throughout the Coast undoubtedly will take keen interest in the announcement that the state of Idaho now has an up-to-the-minute State License Law for architects. The Governor has appointed the following board of examiners to act under the provisions of this law:

Mr. L. J. Corbett, Professor of Engineering, State University, Moscow, Idaho.

Mr. Fritz C. Hummel, First Lieutenant Second Idaho Infantry, Boise, Idaho.

Mr. J. B. Boyer, Pocatello, Idaho.

Mr. George Williams, Coeur d'Alene, Idaho.

Mr. Burton E. Morse, Twin Falls, Idaho.

Bank Building for Palo Alto

The Bank of Palo Alto will spend $50,000 in constructing a handsome new home at University avenue and the Circle. Construction will be of reinforced concrete, with terra cotta front, clay tile roof and interior of marble and birch. The architects are Messrs. Tantau and Branner and the engineer is Mr. Clarkson Swain.

Country Estate

Mr. Charles Peter Weeks, architect, and Mr. W. P. Day, engineer, are preparing plans for a palatial country home to be built near Napa for Mr. D. P. Doak. The house and outbuildings, landscape architecture, swimming pool, etc., will entail an expenditure in excess of $100,000.

Ceres Bank

Mr. Hugh Y. Davis of Fresno is the architect of a new bank building to be erected by the Bank of Ceres. It will be one story with cement plaster exterior and cast cement and marble ornamentation.

Factory and Warehouse

Mr. Geo. W. Kelham is making the plans for the new factory and warehouse which the Hills Bros. Coffee Company plan to build in San Francisco.

Polo Player's New Home

Mr. Lewis P. Hobart is preparing plans for extensive alterations to the country house at Burlingame of Mr. H. Cheever Cowden, the polo player.

Personal

The recent death of Mr. Charles M. Enwright, son of Mr. T. L. Enwright of the Miller, Enwright Co. of Sacramento, left a void in the business of this pioneer company that cannot be readily filled. Young Enwright was devoted to his work as one of the managers of the Miller, Enwright Company, and although a comparatively young man he was a member of the Sacramento Civil Service Commission and a life member of Sacramento Lodge, No. 6, B. P. O. Elks.

Messrs. Howells & Stokes, architects, announce the dissolution of their New York partnership. Mr. I. N. Phelps Stokes will continue the office at 100 William street. Mr. John Mead Howells has opened a new office at 470 Fourth avenue. The Western practice of the firm will be maintained with offices in Seattle, Wash., and at 100 William street, New York.

Mr. Carl Nuese, whose work at the Panama-Pacific Exposition is still fresh in the minds of many architects, has opened an office at 728 Montgomery street, San Francisco, and will make perspectives for architects and others having prospective architectural work.

Mr. O. R. Thayer has moved his offices from San Francisco to 443 Dargia street, Vallejo, in which city he has a number of buildings under construction and in prospect. Mr. Thayer also has considerable work at Manteca.

Mr. James A. Magee has opened an office at 202 Lick building, San Francisco, for the practice of architecture.

Mr. Harvey A. Klyce has moved his office from the Sheldon building to the new Call building, San Francisco.

Office Building and Apartments

Mr. Benjamin G. McDougall, architect in the Sheldon building, San Francisco, has completed plans for a two-story class C office building to be erected on Sansome street, near California, San Francisco, for Mr. T. C. Kierulff, attorney, and one of the owners of The Architect and Engineer of California. The building will cost $30,000. Mr. McDougall is also preparing plans for the first unit of a $250,000 apartment house to be erected by the Nightingale Estate in Haight street, San Francisco.

Concrete Automobile Factory

Mr. Maurice C. Couchot, C. E., has prepared plans for a reinforced concrete factory building to be erected on the Foothill boulevard, Oakland, for the Fageol Motor Car Company. The structure will cover a ground area 50 by 250 feet.

Legislature Authorizes New State Work

The California State Legislature has approved appropriations amounting to several thousand dollars for new construction work and additions to present State buildings this year. The plans will be gotten out by the State Engineering Department under the direction of Mr. W. F. McClure, engineer, and Mr. Geo. B. McDougall, architect. Following is a partial list of appropriations:

New cottage at Agnew Hospital	$ 4,500
Water system for University School at Davis	15,000
Creamery building at Davis	15,000
Completion of Normal School grounds, Fresno	3,600
Equipment for Fresno Normal School	17,000
Convalescent cottage for females at Napa Hospital	15,000
Pathological hospital at Napa	20,000
Tubercular ward at Veteran's Home	10,000
Group of small buildings at Davis Farm	15,000
Cottages for females at Sonoma Home	15,000
Bakery building for Sonoma Home	15,000
Water plant at Mendocino Hospital	7,500
Repairs to flooring, Mendocino Hospital	9,500
New bathrooms, Stockton Hospital	1,000
Tubercular ward for Stockton Hospital	10,000
Riverside Citrus Experiment Station	40,000
Prison school building, Folsom	10,000
Blacksmith shop and other improvements, Folsom	30,000
Repairs to employees' cottage, Folsom	12,500
New sewer disposal system, Folsom	11,000
Water development, Home for Blind, Berkeley	4,250
New training schools for all the State Normals	191,580
Repairs to Relief Corps Home	5,000

Heiman-Schwartz Have Much Work

The firm of Heiman-Schwartz, 212 Stockton street, San Francisco, has considerable important work under way. They have taken bids for a seven-story concrete apartment house to be erected on the southwest corner of Sacramento and Gough streets, San Francisco, at an estimated outlay of $150,000. They have also completed drawings for a one-story and basement Class C office building for the south side of Pine street, east of Sansome, for Mr. L. A. Meyer.

Apartments for East Oakland

Plans have been completed by Mr. Earle B. Bertz, architect in the Foxcroft building, San Francisco, for a two-story frame and plaster apartment house at Thirteenth street and Third avenue, East Oakland, for Mr. W. E. Whalen. Mr. Bertz has also planned several attractive houses for construction by the Roeding Estate in Fresno.

Mr. Farr Has Residence Work

New work in the office of Mr. Albert Farr, architect, with offices in the Foxcroft building, San Francisco, includes a $30,000 residence at Piedmont for Mr. John Spohn, a $12,000 home at Twin Oaks Crossing, near Napa, for Mrs. Christopher Chinn, and a $3,000 bungalow at Mt. Diablo for Mr. Morrie Sims.

More Packing Houses Planned

Messrs. Glass & Butner, Republican building, Fresno, are preparing plans for several more packing houses to be built for the California Peach Grower's Association and to cost from $15,000 to $20,-000 each. One plant will be at Hanford, another at Selma, and a third at Parlier. These are in addition to a packing house to be built in Fresno and for which a contract was recently let.

Class A Theater

Mr. A. B. Rosenthal, 407-408 Lankershim building, Los Angeles, is preparing plans for a three-story class A reinforced concrete theater and store building to be erected on the east side of Main street, south of 8th street, for Col. J. B. Lankershim. The theater has been leased to Fred A. Miller, proprietor of Miller's theater, and associates.

Fairmont Hotel Changes

Some extensive alterations and additions are planned for the Fairmont Hotel on California street, San Francisco. The new management has in mind building an immense porch which will be glassed in and will be used for dinner dansants. A special hardwood floor will be laid. Other improvements are under advisement.

Clinton Company Gets Big Contract

The Clinton Construction Co., 140 Townsend street, San Francisco, has been awarded the contract for about $90,-000 to construct a group of brick and timber factory buildings at Emeryville for the Paraffine Paint Co. There will be four structures. The Clinton Co.'s contract does not include the machinery and equipment.

Will Rebuild Concord Bank

Fire destroyed the building of the Bank of Concord and also the Concord Inn on April 23. The bank building was designed by Mr. G. A. Applegarth, architect in Claus Spreckels building, San Francisco. It will be rebuilt in accordance with new plans by Mr. Applegarth.

$20,000 San Francisco Home

Plans have been drawn and figures taken for a two-story frame and stucco house and garage to be erected on Jackson, near Spruce street, San Francisco, for Mr. Abraham Rosenberg. The house and other improvements will cost $20,-000. Miss Julia Morgan is the architect.

Menlo Park Residence

Mr. Henry Shermund has completed plans for a $12,000 residence for Mrs. F. E. Foster. It will be built in Menlo Park.

Mr. Arthur G. Scholz Busy

Mr. Arthur G. Scholz, architect in the Phelan building, San Francisco, has recently awarded a contract for a $7,500 frame and stucco house at Burlingame for Mr. George Binning. Mr. Scholz has also let a contract for alterations to a three-story frame flat building on Fairmont street, San Francisco, for Mr. F. Weiss. Plans for a $10,000 house and garage in St. Francis Wood are being prepared.

New Factories

The Fleischhacker Paper Box Company will build a four-story reinforced concrete factory at Harrison and Second streets, San Francisco. The plans were prepared by Mr. George Wagner and the building will be put up on percentage by the Clinton Construction Company. The latter has also taken a contract to build extensive additions to the Paraffine Paint Company's plant at Emeryville.

$75,000 Alterations

Mr. W. H. Toepke is the architect of the alterations and additions planned for the seven-story building at 942 Market street, formerly occupied by Brittain & Co. The improvements will cost $75,-000. The original plans for this building were made by Messrs. Reid Bros.

New Lodi Theater

Messrs. Stone & Wright, San Joaquin Bank building, Stockton, are preparing working plans for a two-story theater and office building to be erected at Lodi for Mr. Bauer. The estimated cost is $20,000.

Theater Addition

Messrs. Reid Bros., architects in the California-Pacific building, San Francisco, have awarded a contract to Stockholm & Allyn for building a $40,000 addition to the Mission theater, owned by the Keil Estate.

Flagstaff, Arizona, Hotel

Preliminary plans have been made by Messrs. Coxhead & Coxhead, Hearst building, San Francisco, for a two-story class A store, hotel and office building for Babbitt Bros. of Flagstaff, Arizona. Between $100,000 and $200,000 will be expended on the work.

Presbyterian Church

Mr. John H. Thomas, architect of Berkeley, has prepared plans for a $15,-000 edifice for the Northbrae Presbyterian Church. It will contain a Sunday school and social rooms, bowling alleys, dining room, kitchen, etc. The main church will not be built until later.

City Plan for Turlock

Following the recent visit of Mr. C. H. Cheney of San Francisco, city planning expert, a classified arrangement of data in regard to the improvement of the civic center of Turlock will be presented to the local city planning commission within a few weeks and a permanent city plan will be adopted.

$50,000 Stockton Warehouse

Mr. E. B. Brown, architect, with offices in the Masonic Temple building, Stockton, is preparing plans for a five-story reinforced concrete warehouse to be built on North California street for H. S. Dawson of that city. The estimated cost is $50,000.

Church and Rectory

Mr. Smith O'Brien, Humboldt Bank building, San Francisco, is completing working drawings for a class C church and rectory for St. Edward's Parish. The site is on California street, between Walnut and Laurel streets, San Francisco.

Buys Apartment House Site

Mr. A. H. Bergstrom of Lange & Bergstrom, San Francisco, has purchased the southeast corner of California and Stockton streets, San Francisco, and in the near future will build on the site a modern apartment house.

$10,000 Colonial House

Messrs. Milwain Bros., architects of Oakland, have completed plans for an attractive Colonial house to be built in Crocker Terrace for Mr. Andrew Dalziel. The improvements will cost $10,000.

S. P. May Build at Stockton

The engineering department of the Southern Pacific Co. has prepared preliminary plans for a large reinforced concrete building at Stockton. It will cost in the neighborhood of $100,000.

Seacliff Residence

Mr. Charles Warren Perry, architect, has prepared plans and taken bids for a two-story frame residence to be erected at Seacliff, San Francisco, for Dr. Phillip King'Brown. House will cost $7,500.

Concrete Loft Building

A reinforced concrete loft building will be erected on the southwest corner of Pacific avenue and Trenton place, San Francisco, for the S. & G. Gump Co., from plans by Mr. Milton Lichtenstein.

San Jose Gets Orphan Home

The State Odd Fellows have decided to build a new home at San Jose instead of at Lodi as at first planned. The size and cost of the home has not been fully determined upon.

Agricultural Building, Nevada University

Mr. Walter O. Lewis of Reno, Nev., has been commissioned by the Regents of the University of Nevada to prepare the plans for the new Agricultural building, the work to begin at once. The building is to be of the Class C type, with brick walls laid up in Flemmish bond and Indiana limestone trimmings. The structure will be two stories and full basement and will cover an area 180x60 feet. The estimated cost is $80,000.

Mr. Lewis will have associated with him in this work Mr. N. B. Ellery, formerly California State Engineer, and Mr. N. W. Sexton, architect of San Francisco. Mr. Ellery will be in charge of the engineering and Mr. Sexton will act as the consulting architect, dealing with the aesthetic branches.

Watsonville Architect Busy

Mr. Ralph Wyckoff, Pajaro Valley Bank building, Watsonville, reports the following new work in his office:

Two-story brick and terra cotta store and apartment building in Monterey for Mr. L. D. Lacey. Concrete foundation, composition roof, tile vestibules, marble base, prism glass, etc. Cost, $8000.

Packing house for Hihn-Hammond Lumber Co., to be built in Watsonville for the Corralitos Fruit Growers Association, 173x200 feet, with dampproofed concrete basement. Cost, $20,000.

Alteration of Ford & Sanborn Co.'s store building in Salinas. New tile vestibules, galvanized iron cornice covered with terra cotta tile. Exterior to be painted with cement paint. Cost, $4000.

$200,000 Salinas Hotel

Mr. Theodore Lenzen, architect, Humboldt Bank building, San Francisco, is preparing plans for a $200,000 reinforced concrete Mission style hotel for the Salinas Hotel Company. There will be over 200 rooms, with connecting baths. W. W. Breite is the engineer.

Park Improvements

The Fresno city planning commission is making extensive preparations for the beautification of streets, parks and public places in Fresno. Chas. H. Cheney, Crocker building, San Francisco, will be recommended to take charge of the work for a six months term.

San Jose Apartments

A $40,000 apartment house will be erected for V. Luba at First and San Carlos streets, San Jose, from plans by Messrs. Binder & Curtis. There will be twenty-seven apartments.

Want City Pool

The Modesto Trustees plan to call an election to vote $80,000 in bonds, $10,000 of which will be used to build a municipal swimming pool.

ELECTRICAL DEPARTMENT

Further Experiments in Electrical Heating*

Data Gathered from Eight Installations in Seattle (Wash.) Residences.

FOR about four years the lighting department of the city of Seattle, Wash., has been investigating electric heating for the home to see just what could be done to make this form of heat cheap enough for general use.

In the recently-issued biennial report of the Seattle Lighting Department, of which J. D. Ross is superintendent, an account is given of progress of the investigation since 1913.

Since the electric heater, states the report, of whatever type, transforms all the energy supplied to it into heat, there is nothing to be gained by attempting to raise the efficiency of the heaters themselves. The problem is to generate and distribute current at a lower price than ever before, and then to utilize the heat so that the least amount will bring the desired result, which is the maintenance of a comfortable temperature with ample ventilation in the home.

The first side of the problem, that of reducing the cost of current, may be solved in Seattle, at least in part, by the development on a large scale of the water power which is so abundant in this section of the country, and by the distribution of this power for heating by special heating circuits of higher voltage than the lighting circuits and without the expensive voltage regulators used on the lighting circuits.

The other phase of the problem, the most economical use of the heat, has been very clearly defined by the experiments carried on by the department during the past four years. Data have been gathered from eight different homes equipped by the department for using electric heat in every way that appeared advantageous, both as an auxiliary and as the sole method of heating.

The first installation, at 1119 Grand avenue, was in a small five-room cottage, and consisted of open-air resistance heaters. No restriction was placed on the time or amount of current used, and the bills were paid by the owner so that the tenant was free to use as much current as he chose. Record of current was kept by recording meter, and temperature (average, maximum and minimum), were recorded every day for one year. These records are in the department files.

The consumption of current for the year was 12,360 kilowatt hours, and the maximum was 6,100 watts. Good ventilation was maintained, and the average inside temperature was kept at 68 degrees to 70 degrees Fahrenheit. The recording meter showed that the most current was used between 6:30 and 8:00 a. m. and 9:00 to 10:00 p. m., with a considerable amount between 5:00 and 9:00 p. m.

The heaviest demand, then, comes at almost the same time as the lighting peak. In order to make electric heating load an off-peak load, some heat storage is necessary. Electric heaters adapt themselves to hot water, steam, hot air or direct heating or to any combination of methods.

At 802 Thirty-third avenue an electric water heater was installed to work in conjunction with the boiler of the hot water heating system. In the coldest weather both electric and coal heaters were used; in mild weather the electric coil alone was used, and very often the coal heater alone was used. This arrangement gave excellent satisfaction in heating the house, and the two heaters worked together without trouble.

Another method of using electric heat as an auxiliary was tried at 516 Thirtieth avenue South. The house had a hot water heating system. The radiators in the rooms most used were equipped with individual electric heaters placed in the basement directly under them. Each heater was connected so as to permit the water in its radiator to circulate through it, and at the same time the circulation from the coal-fired boiler was not interfered with. No valves of any kind were used. The hot water system can be operated entirely by electric current or by coal as desired, or only enough coal may be used to keep the entire house at about 60 degrees Fahrenheit, and each electric heater may be used to bring its room to the temperature desired.

The first heaters used here were simply coils wound around a section of the pipe, using the pipe for a short-circuited secondary and getting the heating effect from the hysteresis and eddy currents in the iron pipe. These heaters were inferior to the resistance type used later on the same system in that their power-factor was low and it was next to

---

* A description of the original equipment, together with a report of the tests as made up to that time, were published two years ago in The Heating and Ventilating Magazine and reprinted in The Architect and Engineer of California.

impossible to eliminate the humming sound. An induction-type heater has lately been developed that has a better power factor, and is so solidly constructed that it is practically noiseless.

Experiments using electric heat as an auxiliary prove that it is most convenient, but give little information on the economy of using current alone. Data on this point were gathered from four houses using electricity alone for heating. The first of these, on Thirty-seventh avenue, was fully equipped with heaters, heat-storage tanks, circulation pump, automatic heat control, recording wattmeters and all the apparatus that was needed for a complete test. There were nine rooms, four on the first floor and five above. The downstairs rooms were kept at 70 degrees Fahrenheit during the day and allowed to run down to 60 degrees Fahrenheit during the night. The upstairs part was maintained at about 65 degrees Fahrenheit during the day. Heat control was entirely automatic; thermostats were used to keep the temperature within 2 degrees of the desired mark, and current was turned on in the morning by timeswitch so that the house would be warm before time to arise.

The installation was made in February, 1914, and the house has been maintained at a comfortable temperature at all hours since, with practically no attention. Characteristics of the house are as follows:

First floor—
Exposed wall area .... 2,492 sq. ft.
Window area .... 180 sq. ft.
Contents ....10,475 cu. ft.
Second floor—
Exposed wall area .... 2,357 sq. ft.
Window area .... 197 sq. ft.
Contents ....12,275 cu. ft.

Floor surface is included in the wall area of the first floor to care for the unheated basement. Three-fourths of the ceiling is included in the wall area of the second floor.

The house is of first-class frame construction. The hot water heating system is of liberal design, with a total

of 690 sq. ft. of radiation. Four 10½-kilowatt bayonet-type ' heaters were used, arranged in parallel with a storage tank of 500 gal. so that the water could circulate from the radiator through the heaters or through the storage tank. Time switch was used to disconnect the current entirely during the hours of lighting peak, amounting to 4½ hours in the winter months. Readings were taken daily for four months, beginning with September, 1914, of the average, maximum and minimum air temperatures, inside, upstairs and downstairs. Readings were also taken of the temperature of the circulating water, both outgoing and returning, to show the action of the storage tank. This tank has proved able to care for the hours when the current is cut off. The temperature at the end of the 4½ hours peak in December never dropped below 70 degrees F. On the coldest days the water in the tank dropped from 190 degrees to 104 degrees F. during the peak, and the usual range of temperature during cold weather was from 170 degrees to 180 degrees F. in the tank at the time the current was turned off to 110 degrees to 120 degrees at the time it was turned on again. Readings on temperatures have not been made regularly since the four months' test.

Three other houses were equipped with the same system of electric hot water heat, and data collected for periods covering approximately two years. Synopsis showing the current used per year are given below. Characteristics of each house are omitted; the square feet of radiation, which was figured on the same basis as that in the Thirty-seventh avenue house, is given in each case, and serves as a measure of the estimated heat requirements.

Experiments with Oil-Filled Radiators

During 1915 a number of heating installations were made with oil-filled, electric-heated radiators. These consist of an ordinary hot-water radiator filled with oil and having a cartridge-type heater inserted in the top. This scheme

Result of Experiments with Oil-Filled Radiators in Two Seattle Houses

Address	2541 11th Ave. W.	1238 E. Fir
Number of rooms	5	9
Kilowatt heaters	10½	31½
Square feet radiation	160	640
Duration of test—months	7	7
Consumption, kilowatt hours	9,777	50,960
Estimate for one year, K.W.H	16,000	85,000
Estimate per square foot radiation, K.W.H	100	134

Electric Heating Experiment in Four Houses

Address	225 37th N.	1505 36th	615 Terry	802 33d
Number of rooms	9	9	6	7
Kilowatt heaters	42	32	12	10
Square feet radiation	690	640	330	350
Consumption, first year, K.W.H	42,850	39,320	57,210	54,930
Consumption, second year, K.W.H	63,860	41,880	*18,100	*23,990
Average consumption, K.W.H	53,355	40,600	....	....
Consumption per square foot of radiation per year, K.W.H	77.3	63.4	....	....

*Used as auxiliary only during second year.

of heating has the advantage that each room has its own heater, and no piping is necessary. The radiator in each room may be turned off when not needed, although nothing is to be gained by turning off the heat where a comfortable temperature is to be maintained for most of the day, because more heat will be needed to warm the room again than was saved while it was cooling. Results obtained with the oil radiators are the same in current required and temperatures maintained as with the hot water system, with the exception that there is very little storage of heat in the oil radiators to tide over the time when current is turned off.

Sufficient data has been collected to enable the lighting department to make a definite statement as to what can be done in any given case. So many variable factors enter into the heating of a home that each house must be studied and estimated by itself. The problems presented are almost entirely the same that have been met with regularly in heating and ventilating, except that we have kilowatt hours to deal with instead of British thermal units. With electric heat the energy is, in general, several times as expensive as in the form of coal, so that every device for saving heat is valuable.

In the ordinary building with good ventilation the heat loss is about four-fifths through the walls, while one-fifth is used to heat the air. With improved heat insulation in buildings it is conceivable that half the heat now required may do the same work, without in any way impairing ventilation, which requires about 30 cu. ft. per minute for each person. Any improvement tending to reduce the amount of heat necessary gives an advantage to electricity as compared with lower priced sources of heat.

The hot water heating system, with ample storage tank, seems to present the most advantages for use with electric heaters. This is due to the fact that the heat storage keeps a uniform temperature, for less heat is required for comfort with steady than with intermittent heat.

The tank, fitted with a small centrifugal circulating pump, will keep the house at an even temperature during the lighting peak when the current is shut off. Heating, however, cannot be permanently classed as an off-peak load. This is evident from the fact that about ten times the capacity of installation is necessary for heating a house than is used for lighting it. When one house in ten is electrically-heated, then the load curve valleys will be filled up. After that the success of heating by electricity demands cheap current at all times, which is only to be had from water power, generated in large units and distributed at comparatively high voltages. It may be feasible to serve heating customers at 400 to 500 volts three wire, which would materially reduce distribution cost.

The comparative cost of this method of heating is fairly well established. It is from 25 to 50 per cent more expensive for electricity at one-half cent per kilowatt hour than for coal at $6 per ton. At one cent per kilowatt hour the electricity is two and one-half or three times as costly. These figures are borne out by theory, which says that the 10,-000 B.T.U. in a pound of coal cost 0.3 cents, while in the form of current the 3,413 B.T.U. in one kilowatt hour will cost one-half cent, making the current roughly five times as expensive. Then allowing for a furnace efficiency of 40 per cent, which is fair for the ordinary furnace, the current would prove twice as expensive. The showing of less than one and one-half times made in the experiments is probably due to more care in the use of the heat so that less was wasted.

It is very noticeable that once electric heat is installed in a home the occupants do not like to consider its removal. It delivers the home from the drudgery of building fires and handling coal and ashes, and banishes the disagreeable and injurious extremes of temperature so often tolerated now. It generates no poisonous gases and does not vitiate the air. It is, indeed, the ideal heat in everything save expense.

CONTRACTOR AND BUILDER

Builders' Will-o'-the-Wisps

"WILL-O'-THE-WISP" was what the inhabitants of the border lands between England and Scotland called the vain fire that was sometimes seen to flicker and gleam at night over bogs and swampy places. Whether there is any such thing, like a phosphorescent gleam or a bright spot made up, perhaps, of particularly dense patches of fog that arise at night from low, wet places, or whether they were the sheer product of the imagination of those who thought they saw them, I do not know. They were generally reported as having been seen by late revellers returning to their beds in a condition that is sometimes characterized as "lit-up." Many a man lost his way and many a one, too, his life led by their deceptive gleam, the victims thinking them to be the light in some window where, of course, there must be a house and as a consequence shelter.

You know the stories told by the folks who used to see them and mayhap escaped to tell the tale—for not all who followed them were destroyed. They kept receding—some weary Willie, burdened with too much drink, lost in the bog and struggling on toward the false light, would afterward tell how they kept moving further and further on.

Real will-o'-the-wisps no longer mislead anybody, but the imaginary ones remain and do more harm than the old kind ever possibly could have done.

There are many kinds, from the great ones, such as now, to my fond imagination, mislead the bewitched Kaiser and his Junkers, to the little ones that are at the bottom of so many of our own individual and personal errors of judgment.

Institutions follow them, too, and Systems, such as Thomas W. Lawson wrote about.

They are everywhere, deceiving ardent souls and causing endless trouble.

They particularly beset the beneficiaries of existing systems and cause them to fight and fight against things that were better for them than what they have.

For instance, a trade union is a will-o'-the-wisp. It promises so much and performs so little.

That is the pity of advanced unionism. Like a will-o'-the-wisp, it keeps luring the poor dupes on.

"Oh, if I can only get $1 an hour," says the mechanic, "then I can live." And when he gets it the dollar won't buy what the old fifty cents would.

Isn't this true, little mechanics? You know it is. But you can't believe the evidence of your own senses; you keep hoping and hoping that it is not true, for Will-o'-the-wisp is leading you on.

And what will-o'-the-wisps the poor little builders have in their experiences. Good fellows—fine fellows—the salt of the earth, yet they are dragged farther and farther into the mire and bog because there seems to be no one to guide them, to warn them. At least there's none that they will listen to.

I think I could tell a dozen different kinds of stories of builders' will-o'-the-wisps, from general contractors at the one end to materialmen at the other, and almost all of them point to one moral, one lesson, and that is, the amazing slowness with which the building industry recognizes modern conditions and the fact that we are living in an age of intense enlightenment. The little, average general contractor who used to get contracts on which he could make 25 per cent profit and not have to bestir himself very much at that finds when he is dealing with his customers nowadays that they know too much for him. The materialman in his way has the same experience, and yet they both seem to cling to the belief that some day, somehow, things will be as they used to. They seem to think it is only a matter of waiting for the turn of the tide.

These are the days of advertising, which is just another name for enlightenment. Advertising is busy revolutionizing all industry; it is making a terrible pother for all of us middlemen. We seem to have no friends; everywhere we turn the cry is against the middleman, which is just another way of saying that we are abusing one another. It is a case of the pot calling the kettle black.

The general contractors can shift themselves today while you listen to this story for materialmen.

They all advertise—at least all who make any pretensions. One of the best advertisers in the game is a concern which discovered new possibilities in a certain building material and advertised it most faithfully. The concern's name is known to every architect in the country and samples of their material are doubtless to be found in every office of any pretension.

Every time I pass a certain building on one of the prominent streets of New York I am reminded of this concern, because I see that the material used in the

front of this building is similar to that which our friends might almost be said to have originated. But "another received the honors"; one of the numerous imitations, that flooded the market as soon as this concern made itself well felt, is used in place of the genuine goods.

Part of this concern's trouble is due to the fact that it does not advertise to those who buy its goods. It follows a will-o'-the-wisp: the notion that if you can only get specified the job is yours and the profits thereof.

I could write a whole book about this interesting phase of the building game, but I won't.

Don't you know, little paint man and little lumber man, that architects don't specify you without some string or other that always lets you out? The architect who specifies may accept your hospitality and your attentions, but remember that as man proposes and somebody else disposes so it is with a good many other things; the architect specifies—somebody else buys.

The material man who pins his faith to the architect reckons without the host.

The difference in the case of the building that I speak of, as in most cases of this kind of substitution, is not large; it is just about the difference of a modest profit for the concern which did the advertising.

Of course everybody knows that substitution is said to be one of the evils of the age. General advertising in newspapers, for instance, is directed to the consumer, and even in this direct advertising substitution has been found to be one of the great drawbacks. It has been met by more advertising and by repetition and by warning and by appeal to those who read—that is, the consumers. But when you are reckoning without the host what good is an appeal? All your eloquence is wasted on a third party who has private reasons for turning a deaf ear when at a conference, at which you are not present—the owner or—somebody—who knows little and· cares less about you and your advertising, actually settles the matter.

One of the reasons why the architect consents to the substitution, if indeed he does not actually advise it, is because all the rising architects, all the comers, as I would call them, are out to save their clients every dollar that they can. They have found that that is the way to success. Another reason is that there is an atmosphere of suspicion about all businesses where the consumer has to deal through a third party and to pay large sums for things that he does not know anything about. A great many people who buy buildings—that is, owners— have this feeling. In my goings around

I have been surprised to see how much there is of it. The breed of the architects which caused this suspicion to be engendered is out of business, but the suspicion remains.

And the building business is being modernized, revolutionized, in spite of the infatuation of those who cling so tightly to the old ideas of secrecy. Everything you do is being dragged out to the light of day.

Little builder, I am not trying to teach you the whole thing at one lesson. If I did it would be forgotten as quickly as it was learned. I want to repeat over and over again examples that point the way to a certain conclusion; I want to wake you up so that you will solve your problem for yourself.—Theodore Starrett in Architecture and Building.

Plumbers' State Law Approved

The California State law requiring an examination for plumbers and a license to do business has been passed by the Legislature and signed by the Governor. The Board of Health is empowered to appoint a committee of three, consisting of a master plumber, a journeyman plumber and a physician as an examining board, in all towns having sewer systems. Applicants for a certificate must pay a fee of $2.50, the certificate to be renewable each year at a cost of $2.

Safety-Nets on Structural Work

THE State of California believes that
a laborer doing useful work at a
height of several hundred feet needs at
least as much protection as a trapeze
performer in a circus. The state law requires the use of temporary p ank flooring on each floor of a structure to protect workmen below from falling objects, and in case this cannot be provided, safety-nets are now to be prescribed. Writes J. J. Rosenthal, safety
engineer of the California Industrial Ac-

*Safety Net Used to Protect Structural Workers
on New California Theatre*

cident Commission, in the Engineering
Record (New York, March 3):

"The requirements are that there
should be a plank floor for each story
as the structural work progresses. But
the difficulty of adhering strictly to this
ruling in special cases, such as auditoriums, arch trusses in theaters, towers,
bridges, etc., is such that it has in many
cases been impracticable to comply with
the legal requirements.

"The Department of Safety of the Industrial Accident Commission of California, after devoting considerable attention to the subject, decided that the use
of rope safety-nets would afford a meas-

ure of protection for workmen who might
fail from above; at the same time they
can be used in many cases where plank
floors would be impracticable. Accordingly the department has now ordered
the use of such nets on all structural
work where the use of plank floors is
not feasible.

"The safety-nets are made of half-inch
manila rope with three-quarter-inch bor-
uer, and 4x4-inch mesh. The nets come
in 10x30 feet sections, borders being provided with loops at suitable intervals so
that they can be readily combined and
attached to convenient points on the
structural frame.

"The nets are patterned after the type
which has been used successfully for
about a year in Chicago. In this time
there have occurred at least two accidents, according to the Illinois records,
which would have resulted in fatalities
had it not been for the use of the nets.
In these instances workmen fell into the
nets without injury, instead of dropping
about 100 feet to a concrete floor.

"The illustration shows the safety-nets
in service. These nets, the first of the
kind to be used west of Chicago, were
made in San Francisco at a cost of $60
apiece and are shown in service in the
accompanying photograph of the California Theater, under construction at
Fourth and Market streets, San Francisco."

When Is a Day a Working Day?

A difference of opinion between the C.
J. Kubach Co., contractor for the foundation of a twelve-story and basement
theater and office building at Third and
Broadway, Los Angeles, and the Stability Building Co., owners, regarding the
"bonus" time gained by the contractor,
has resulted in suit being filed by the
contractor to enforce a claim for $5,400.
The contract was to be completed in
ninety working days from November 1,
1916, and the agreement provided a bonus
or penalty of $100 a day. The Kubach
Company claimed it had completed its
work in thirty-six days and was entitled
to bonus for fifty-four days' time gained.
The owners conceded sixteen days' bonus
to the contractor and tendered a check
for $1,600 in payment, which the con-
tractor refused to accept and filed suit.

What constitutes a working day under the terms of the contract and a working day so far as actual construction
work is concerned will be threshed out
in the court. Some interesting questions
are raised. For example: Are Sundays
and holidays working days or non-working days when work is performed on
those days; also is a rainy day a working day or a non-working day if construction work is performed on those
days?

How Hard Wall Plasters Are Manufactured*

By EDWARD DURYEE

HARD wall plasters are made principally from "Plaster of Paris," or calcined gypsum rock. They set in about two hours and dry out quickly, becoming very hard. These two characteristics have enabled the builder to complete his work rapidly, strong walls and rapid building being characteristic of modern methods that have superseded the old-fashioned lime and sand methods. Modern hard wall plasters save weeks in time in completing large buildings and give greatly better results than did lime mortars.

The manufacture of Plaster of Paris, Hard Wall plasters, Stucco and Casting plasters from gypsum involves some interesting physical and chemical conditions and reactions. Gypsum is a hydrated sulphate of lime having a formula $CaSO_4.2H_2O$ and containing in percentages:

Lime	32.6
Sulphur trioxide	46.5
Water	20.9
	100.0

When this gypsum is heated above 212 degrees F. and below 400 degrees F., the moisture and part of the water of crystallization is driven off and the product becomes Plaster of Paris with a formula $CaSO_4.\frac{1}{2}H_2O$ or in percentages as follows:

Lime sulphate ($CaSO_4$)	93.8
Water (H_2O)	6.2
	100.0

Three-fourths of the original combined water is driven off in the calcining process.

This calcining process is carried on in steel kettles usually from 8 to 14 feet in diameter by similar heights. The kettles are surrounded by flues for heating and enclosed in brick settings.

The crushed and ground gypsum in quantities of ten to twenty tons is fed into the kettles and gradually heated and agitated by means of rotating arms or sweeps, during the boiling process. As the water is driven off the material becomes violently agitated and resembles a kettle of boiling mush. The calciners judge the correct stage of completion of the boiling by settling down and quieting of the mass and the registrations of a thermometer. As the temperature rises the gypsum boils with escapement of steam until at 269 F. the mass settles slightly, marking the hydrite stage, then as the temperature continues to rise the mass boils again till another settling stage indicative of the anhydrite form is reached at 350, F.

*From Southwest Contractor, Los Angeles.

to 380, F. The boiling process usually takes about two and a half hours and after its completion the product is discharged into a cooling pit. From the pit it is elevated and discharged into regrinding mills; after final grinding it is stored in bins till required for shipment. In this condition the material is known as stucco and hardens when water is added, in five minutes.

When fibred hard wall plaster is ordered the quick setting stucco is drawn into a mixer in which the proper proportions of fibre (either hemp or hair), and a catalizer (usually a preparation made from tannery scraps and soda) are added, the retarder regulates the setting time, usually making it for wall plaster about two hours. After thorough mixing the finished plaster is discharged into sacks for shipment. The fibred plaster is used for the brown or scratch coat in plastering walls, the fibre facilitates the clinching of the plaster between the laths and makes a better bonding surface preparatory to the finish coat. The fibre is not added to the finish plaster. The quantities of fibre and retarder added are exceeding small, usually about five pounds of retarder to a ton of plaster will slow the setting time from five minutes to two hours and six pounds of fibre to a ton of plaster is all that is required.

The manufacturer can make plasters of any required setting time, but to do so he should have samples of the sand that is to be used for mixing with the plaster in order to determine correctly the proportions needed, as different sands affect the setting times and spreading quality of plasters variously, the same plaster that gives satisfactory sand carrying qualities with some sands and with some treatment may prove quite unsatisfactory with others. Usually the setting times required for plasters are about as follows:

Ordinary fibred hard wall plaster, 2 hours 30 minutes.

Unfibred hard wall plaster, 2 hours.

Finishing plaster, 45 minutes.

Casting plaster, 15 minutes.

* * *

A correspondent supplements the foregoing with the following additional data:

The factory should be equipped with regrinding mill and separators for promoting fineness and uniformity in products. The plant is best located close to the deposit of raw materials, which must be of uniform whiteness, and of the highest degree of purity, producing a plaster which, when used with good sand, results in superior surfaces.

In buildings, an air of distinction and superior finish can be secured at small outlay by panelling and moulding walls and ceilings with finish plaster and casting plaster. White, hard-finished, sanitary walls may be obtained by specifying trowelled hard-finished surfaces.

In conclusion it will be useful to draw attention to the very common misuse of the term "Plaster of Paris." This is applied by the unthinking public to each and all of the various grades of plaster mentioned above and thereby leads to considerable confusion in the minds both of the manufacturer and retailer, when trying their best to serve their clients. It has been well suggested, therefore, that the term "Plaster of Paris" be entirely discarded, as not being sufficiently definitive of the material which is meant by the user, and that the expressions "Fibered Hardwall," "Unfibered Hardwall," "Finishing Plaster," "Casting Plaster," and "Dental Plaster" be used instead.

The New Building Industries' Organization

The San Francisco Building Industries' Association, which already has 331 members, held a largely attended meeting on May 9 at the rooms of the General Contractors' Association, for the election of a temporary board of governors, who will complete the organization. Following this, a permanent board will be elected and installed composed of one representative for each industry which has five or more members enrolled. The following comprise the temporary board of governors:

Chas. W. Gompertz, general contractors.
William Williams, plastering contractors.
J. A. Korell, sheet metal contractors.
M. A. DeSolla, building materials dealers.

A. H. Vogt, concrete contractors.
P. Montague, grading and teaming contractors.
Roy Geary, hardwood floor contractors.
R. G. Guyett, insurance men.
M. A. Harris, lumber dealers.
H. P. Stow, lighting fixture contractors.
H. J. Ralston, iron works.
D. Zelinsky, painting contractors
M. S. Neugass, Sr., planing mills.
Herman Lawson, plumbing contractors.
Steven Hurst, plumbers' supplies dealers.
J. W. Asher, electrical contractors.
Habenicht & Howlett, glass and glazing.
Malott & Peterson, roofing contractors.
Jos. Musto Sons-Keenan Co., marble, mosaic and terrazzo dealers.

Examination for Architectural Draftsman

The California State Civil Service Commission announces an examination for architectural draftsman to be held in Sacramento, San Francisco and Los Angeles, on June 2, 1917, to provide a register of eligibles from which to fill positions in the State service. The salary range is from $1200 to $1800. Applications must be filed before May 26th. Application blanks may be obtained from the State Civil Service Commission, Forum building, Sacramento, or from the Los Angeles County Civil Service Commission, 1007 Hall of Records, Los Angeles.

Packing House

Messrs. Allison & Allison have made a decided departure from their usual line of architectural work and are preparing plans for a large packing house to be built at Santa Paula for the Santa Paula Citrus Fruit Association. The building will be two stories and basement, 350x125 feet. It will have reinforced concrete frame, hollow tile filler walls and mill interior construction.

Engineers' Reserve Corps, U. S. A.

Among the architects and engineers who have enlisted in the United States Reserve Corps is Mr. Ernest L. Norberg, of the former architectural firm of Edwards & Norberg, with offices in the Phelan building, San Francisco, and the Bank building, Burlingame. Mr. Norberg has been made a first lieutenant and the Government has commissioned him to assist in recruiting. The headquarters of the Western Department, U. S. Army, are at 204 Pine street, San Francisco. The various district engineer officers are located at the following points and applications will be received either by mail or in person from men skilled in civil and electrical engineering, draftsmanship and various other engineering and mechanical lines:

204 Pine street, San Francisco.
Third District, 405 Custom House, San Francisco.
723 Central building, Los Angeles.
602 Burke building, Seattle, Wash.
First District, 806 Couch building, Portland, Ore.
Second District, 321 Custom House, Portland, Ore.
U. S. Engineer Office, Yellowstone Park, Wyo.
U. S. Engineer Sub-Office, Eureka.

Applications may also be made to any of the following engineers, all of whom have been commissioned or recommended for commissions as officers of the engineers' section of the Reserve Corps:

Major S. H. Hedges, 432 Central building, Seattle, Wash.
Major Seeley W. Mudd, 2232 Harvard boulevard, Los Angeles, Cal.
Major Geo. S. Binckley, Central building, Los Angeles, Cal.
Major Wm. A. Cattell, Foxcroft building, San Francisco, Cal.
Major H. H. Wadsworth, 405 Custom House, San Francisco, Cal.
Major Wm. F. Allison, 5264 Nineteenth avenue, N. E., Seattle, Wash.
Capt. W. D. Peaslee, 125 East Eleventh street, Portland, Ore.
Capt. Clarence B. Lamont, Hoge building, Seattle, Wash.
Capt. Alfred B Lewis, 310 Burke building, Seattle, Wash.
Capt. Carl A. Heinze, 1415 W. Forty-ninth street, Los Angeles, Cal.
Capt. John A. Griffin, 428 E. Fifty-second street, Los Angeles, Cal.
Capt. John Harisberger, 4015 Fourth avenue, N. E., Seattle, Wash.
Capt. F. J. Fitzpatrick, Fort Rosecrans, Cal.

Capt. Henry M. Parks, Corvallis, Ore.
Capt. Walter H. Adams, 1661 Rose Villa street, Pasadena, Cal.
Capt. J. T. Kelly, Jr., 711 Pittock block, Portland, Ore.
Capt. K. D. Schwendener, 2158 W. Twenty-ninth street, Los Angeles, Cal.
Capt. J. L. Bacon, 1101 American National Bank building, San Diego, Cal.
Capt. Delmar S. Clinton, Mill Valley, Cal.
Capt. C. R. Adams, 912 Griffith-McKenzie building, Fresno, Cal.
Capt. Carl E. Grunsky, Jr., 57 Post street, San Francisco, Cal.
First Lt. William Hague, Grass Valley, Cal.
First Lt. K. J. Zinck, box 929, Portland, Ore.
First Lt. John G. Kelly, Jr., 711 Pittock block, Portland, Ore.
First Lt. C. A. Meyer, 633 W. Eighteenth street, Los Angeles, Cal.
First Lt. Ross Henry Rook, 1443 W. Thirty-seventh drive, Los Angeles, Cal.
First Lt. C. C. Bartlett, P. O. box 308, Corona, Cal.
First Lt. Kirby B. Sleppy, 1019 Florida street, Los Angeles, Cal.
First Lt. Earl W. Fassett, 723 Central building, Los Angeles, Cal.
First Lt. C. M. Hurlburt, Hood River, Ore.
First Lt. E. E. Schliewen, 927 Grattan street, Los Angeles, Cal.
First Lt. J. P. Growden, Pittock block, Portland, Ore.
First Lt. C. I. Signer, 1702 Yew street, Olympia, Wash.
First Lt. D. J. Young, 935 Sixth street, San Diego, Cal.
First Lt. Wm. P. Belcher, 405 Custom House, San Francisco, Cal.
First Lt. Charles H. Lee, 1103 Central building, Los Angeles, Cal.
First Lt. Blaine Noice, 5436 Carlton way, Los Angeles, Cal.
First Lt. L. A. Henderson, Hood River, Ore.
First Lt. F. L. Weisenheimer, 405 City Hall Annex, Los Angeles, Cal.
First Lt. R. E. Whitaker, City Engineer's Office, Los Angeles, Cal.
First Lt. Guy B. Donald, 3942 Walton avenue, Los Angeles, Cal.
First Lt. Leslie W. Nims, care Utah Power and Light, Salt Lake City, Utah.
Second Lt. Paul S. Jones, Hermiston, Ore.
Second Lt. Happer K. Phelps, 731 Wells Fargo building, San Francisco, Cal.
Second Lt. Edgar R. Perry, P. S. T. L. & P. Co., Seattle, Wash.
Second Lt. E. D. Clabaugh, 115 So. Olive street, Anaheim, Cal.
Second Lt. Wm. E. Dickinson, 416 Couch building, Portland, Ore.
Second Lt. Wales MacPerdue, 2734 W. avenue 31, Los Angeles, Cal.
Second Lt. C. F. Toklas, Union League Club, San Francisco, Cal.
Second Lt. V. H. Bell, Calexico, Cal.
Second Lt. R. F. Dean, Pacific Power & Light, Pomeroy, Wash.
Second Lt. S. J. Benedict, 2651 Forty-ninth street, S. E., Portland, Ore.
Second Lt. Clarence C. Jacob, 421 Federal building, Salt Lake City, Utah.

No Change in Cement Delivery Points

Oregon Portland cement manufacturers, being fearful that they would be shut out from competition in bidding upon 67,000 barrels of cement to be delivered at Seattle or San Francisco for Government shipment to Hawaii, endeavored to have the delivery point changed to embrace Portland as well as the two cities first named, at both of which the Government has its own shipping facilities. The matter went down to Washington, where Senator Chamberlain brought it up before the War Department, but the Quartermaster-General sustained the form of specification and delivery points, basing his decision upon the fact that each of the shipments of cement would go in a vessel, including lumber and other miscellaneous articles, and the Government would not be warranted in view of the fact that no entire cargo of cement was to be shipped at one time, in sending a transport to Portland for partial ship loads.—Cement.

Book Acknowledgments

"The Nelson Form of Choosing Bidders and Awarding Contracts," is the title of a booklet whose author evidently has given long study to a modern problem and has made copious personal investigations. Architects and builders individually and collectively have endorsed Mr. Nelson's plan of submitting bids, the basic idea of his plan being to eliminate the losses incurred by the builders themselves in preparing estimates and making bids.

This plan was unanimously approved at the sixth annual convention of the National Association of Builders Exchanges at Atlanta on February 12th.

The treatise cannot be charged with having "advertising earmarks," for it really appears to be securing the favor of architects and builders because it offers a solution of a more or less vexatious problem.

Greater Whittier College

Messrs. Allison & Allison of Los Angeles have been commissioned to prepare plans for the proposed Greater Whittier College at Whittier, an institution conducted under the patronage of the Friends' Church. Plans for the new institution to be reared on the present college site provide for a group of fourteen or more buildings, estimated to cost half a million dollars. A campaign to raise half this amount immediately has been inaugurated. The new buildings will be of masonry construction, with tile roofs. In architecture they will be reminiscent of Italian Renaissance with a suggestion of English Georgian. The president's residence will be a replica of the birthplace of John Greenleaf Whittier, the poet.

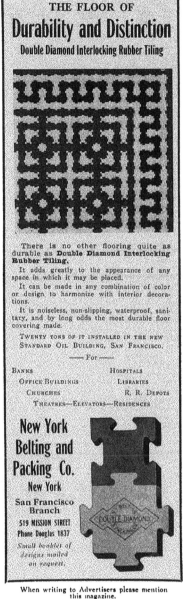

Tell Them Where You Saw It

Every reader can render a service, greater than he may realize, if he will mention the publication in which he has seen the advertisement, when he writes to a manufacturer for a catalogue or information. The service is three-fold: (1) To the advertiser, (2) to the paper, and (3) to the reader. The first two services are obvious, and it takes but little thought to appreciate that in proportion as a periodical thrives financially it gives a better service to its readers. Note the contrast between English and Continental engineering periodicals and those in America. Americans have learned the educational efficacy of advertising, while Europeans scarcely know, as yet, what can thus be accomplished. Consequently the American technical and trade press leads the world as pronouncedly in its articles and news as it leads in its advertising.—Contracting and Engineering.

Shredded Wheat Building Work

G. W. Courtney, 160 Eddy street, San Francisco, who has just completed his contracts for masonry, carpentry and fireproofing in the new shredded wheat factory in Oakland, reports that he has recently secured a big job on the Peninsula. Mr. Courtney is not a newcomer here, having satisfactorily executed contracts for Lewis P. Hobart, Henry H.

Meyer, J. J. Donovan, L. P. Dutton, Osier Bros. and other well-known architects.

Sand Prices Soaring

The prices on sand are likely to go considerably higher-this summer. Everything that goes into the sand business, except the sand itself, has gone away up in price. Engineers at the plants and on the river boats are getting much larger wages than ever before. Common labor is paid fully 40 per cent more than 18 months ago. Added to these troubles the sand companies are having great difficulty in getting shipments in many places.

Mr. Roy H. Baker in Business

Mr. Roy H. Baker, well known in San Francisco as a painter and decorator, has opened a studio at 508 Ellis street, where he will keep an extensive stock of wall papers for selection. His concern is called the Art Wall Paper Co. and is in the field for any contracts in its line from architects and contractors. Besides a splendid reputation Mr. Baker is prepared to give any size bond required for satisfactory execution of work entrusted to him.

Many a new house looks as if it had been designed by the man who put the bungle in bungalow—Youth's Companion.

When writing to Advertisers please mention this magazine.

Glauber Brass Mfg. Co.'s Pacific Coast Branch in New Quarters

The Glauber Brass Manufacturing Company, makers of high class brass goods for plumbing, gas and water works, has moved to larger and more convenient quarters at 567 Mission street, near Second, San Francisco. The new offices and show rooms will enable the company to better take care of its increasing Pacific Coast business. The showrooms are now very accessible to architects and their clients. The newest fixtures are shown under actual water pressure.

The Glauber concealed bath and basin fixtures are claimed to be the most up-to-date in the plumbing brass goods line. Buildings like the University Hospital, the Lane Hospital of San Francisco, and the new Statler Hotel, St. Louis, are a few of the more recent buildings equipped with Glauber concealed bath and basin fixtures.

This firm is also furnishing the Gary steel mills, as well as the Bethlehem steel works with mixing valves and showers to be used on high pressure steam and water supply, and even under such severe conditions, the valves are guaranteed to mix perfectly.

Glauber self-closing work stood a test at the Panama-Pacific International Exposition, equal to eighty to ninety years actual use in a hotel or public washroom, being opened and closed 370,000 times without once requiring the least repair.

"The quick opening or Nu Rapid style of bibbs, basin cocks and bath cocks manufactured by Glauber are among the simplest and most efficient in use today," said Mr. M. W. Wuesthoff, Pacific Coast manager. "The only part that could ever need replacing," he continued, "is the washer, and that being countersunk will last for years. Plumbing brass goods that will require the least repair is a matter receiving closer attention today than ever before and so it is no wonder that the extreme simplicity of all Glauber products appeals to architects and building owners when selecting this important part of the plumbing fixtures.

"Drinking fountains of the Glauber patent are made in accordance with the United States health report and are the most sanitary fountains in use today, it being impossible for the lips to touch the water jet."

At the P. P. I. Exposition, Glauber brass goods were awarded three medals of honor and three gold medals, the highest honors ever awarded any manufacturer of plumbing brass goods at an American or European exposition. Glauber catalog "H," showing the most complete line of mixing valves, self-closing work, concealed bath room fixtures and other plumbing brass goods, may be obtained upon request.

Mr. M. W. Wuesthoff, Pacific Coast manager, who has been in charge of the company's interests on the Pacific Coast for 15 years, is fully conversant with requirements in this territory and is ready at any time to give further information.

Have Done Much Painting

The Terminal station in Los Angeles, said to comprise the largest group of railway buildings west of New York, will be painted by D. Zelinsky & Sons of San Francisco, a firm that has the reputation of having painted more large buildings in San Francisco and the bay region than any other concern in the same line. Thirty years of continued service is a record which the Zelinskys—father and two sons—may well be proud of. Besides general painting they have done much high-class interior decorating. The following is a partial list of buildings recently painted or contracted for by Zelinsky & Sons:

University of California hospital, De Luxe Apartments for Meyer Wood and A. L. Peyser, Piers 28 and 29, Waterfront of San Francisco; Officers' quarters, Presidio; Northeast wing, San Francisco Hospital, Emporium Service building, Hotel Johnson, Visalia; Home Economics and Gymnasium at San Jose High, Union Iron Works office building, Los Angeles Union Terminal Co.'s group of buildings, Pacific Envelope Co.'s new factory building, Santa Fe building, Regents building, First and Market streets; Stock Exchange building for Pope Estate, Tynan residence, California Theater, San Francisco City Hall, Merchants Bank, Los Angeles; El Paso High School, and Davenport hotel, Spokane.

Silent Button for Lights Patented

Dr. Graham Biddle, an Oakland physician, has made arrangements with a large concern for the manufacture of his "silent push button" invention. The patent for Dr. Biddle's invention has been recently granted. The silent push button is to replace the wall electric light switch. It was designed by Dr. Biddle for hospitals, but is applicable for homes and buildings. It consists of a single button, which flashes on the lights silently and shuts them off when pressed again. Inside the button is a small electric bulb, which makes it possible for the button to be found in the darkness.

Something New—Wybro Board, Not Wybro Panels

White Bros., pioneer San Francisco hardwood dealers, have recently published a circular describing an Oregon pine board which is different from other Oregon pine boards on the market, in that it will not split. It is called Wybro Board. It may be used for a multiplicity of purposes, including cigar and cigarette boxes and cases, mounting boards for blue prints, drawing boards, shirt boards and trays, art frames, photograph frames, type trays, flower boxes, fruit cases, sample cases, etc. Wybro Board cannot split, because it is cross plied.

Modesto Factory and Garage

The Milk Products Corporation of Delaware has leased property 100x150 feet in the Southern Pacific reservation near "L" and 9th streets, Modesto, as a site for a factory and garage. The company manufactures caseine. H. R. Hewelecke, of San Francisco, is secretary of the company, and will be resident manager.

May Get Naval Base

In a letter from J. M. Helm, Rear Admiral, U. S. N., and senior member of commission inspecting various naval base sites, to the Alameda Chamber of Commerce and the 'Mayor, a request is made to have the city cede to the government certain waterfront lands that the state had previously granted to Alameda.

Richmond May Have Big Docks

According to Mr. John H. Nicholl of Richmond and Oakland, plans are being formulated to build a $5,000,000 deep water railroad and manufacturing terminal on the Inner harbor at Richmond. Bonds for the project are to be placed in the East.

When writing to Advertisers please mention this magazine.

The Palm System of Vacuum Cleaning

Palm vacuum cleaners are intended for standard high, medium and low duty and are handled in California by the Western Vacuum Supply Company, 1125 Market street, San Francisco.

The Palm System is capable of maintaining a maximum vacuum at the producer of 10 to 12 inches mercury, which with the properly proportioned air piping and hose furnished by the Palm System makes it possible to maintain the requisite amount of vacuum in the cleaning tool for efficient work on heavy fabrics.

The amount of air moved at the cleaning tool in the standard types of the Palm System varies from 65 cubic feet per minute per sweeper, for carpet cleaning, to 90 cubic feet per minute per sweeper for bare surface sweeping. An ample amount of air for thorough and efficient cleaning is thus moved under all conditions.

The sanitary feature of the Palm System confines the dust and other objects —depositing by gravity the heavier articles in the settling tank, and discharging the finer dust directly to the sewer.

The substantial construction of the vacuum producer used in the Palm System, the extremely slow speed of its moving parts and their entirely automatic lubrication, makes it very simple in operation, renders it nearly independent of any attention or care and reduces the expense of maintenance to the minimum.

Pioneer Roofing

"A Book on Pioneer Roofing" has been issued by the Pioneer Paper Company. It is not a book on roofing, but a booklet on Pioneer Roofing, and gives in detail the manufacture and adaptability of the various brands of-composition roofing turned out by this concern. For the past 28 years Pioneer Roofing in its various, forms has been before the public, and the fact that a business that has increased from the confines of a small city lot to one covering nine acres illustrates progress with a big "P."

Score One for the Plumber

During the course of a lecture in Southern California, John E. D. Trask of the Panama-Pacific Exposition's art department declared that "There is no subject more worthy of human consideration than art."

In answer to this assertion, an enthusiastic but anonymous plumber comments in the Los Angeles Contractor and Builder as follows:

I beg to disagree. If I have to choose between a picture and plumbing, plumbing wins. The plumber is the pioneer of civilization. An esthetic life in the mountain solitudes is utterly ruined for want of a plumber. Try it. Minus good plumbing, there is no dignity for humanity.

There are precious few homes which would not trade their wall pictures for a little good plumbing, if they could not have both. Artists would have us believe that until we can make the common people yearn for pictures, our civilization is a failure. I maintain that because the vast majority of us have a marked respect for good plumbing, our civilization is a success. By our plumbing ye shall judge us. From the fact that we are slow to buy pictures and quick to install plumbing, I should say that we have sagaciously decided which subject is the more worthy of human consideration.

New Building Laws for Oakland

The Oakland City Council has accepted a new ordinance framed by the building laws committee of the Chamber of Commerce. The measure makes drastic revisions in the present building laws. It was prepared by a committee comprising lawyers, bankers, real estate operators, architects and engineers.

Some of the changes will be the abolition of the Class A and B fire zones and Class C buildings will be permitted within fire limits, but subdivided into two classes, Class C-1, with a height limit of eighty-five feet, and Class C-2, with a height limit of sixty feet for metal lathes and forty-five feet if wood.

The height of all buildings is limited to 150 feet or one and one-half times the width of the street, with additional allowance for towers. Brick and tile wall specifications are altered to permit their use for home construction. At a later date an additional ordinance covering special buildings will be framed.

How to Take Care of Oak Floors
By W. L. Claffey, Chicago.

ALL floors require a certain amount of care. No housewife expects to keep her floors looking beautiful without some attention. Naturally every housewife wants to find the simplest way of giving her floors the attention they need. In searching for this simplest way many housewives have adopted methods that experts on floor finishes know are very ruinous to the finish, and very often to the wood itself.

If one only knows how, nothing is easier than the care of a well-finished oak floor. Usually the care of floors is entrusted to the discretion of servants whose intentions may be good but whose methods are more often bad.

There are several preparations put up by varnish and wax manufacturers that give excellent results for cleaning and the care of oak floors which can be bought at any department or paint store.

Never use water, oil, kerosene, turpentine, soap, Gold Dust, Dutch Cleanser, or any other cleansing agents, except as follows:

Shellac finish: If water has been spilled upon the floor and it has turned white in places, moisten a soft cloth with a little alcohol and lightly rub the spots, which should immediately disappear. Do not repeat this operation too often, however, or the finish will be entirely removed. Shellacked floors some-

When writing to Advertisers please mention this magazine.

times take on a clouded or grayish appearance due to dampness in the air. This condition can usually be greatly improved by the same treatment as above. If the finish has become so dirty that it is necessary to remove same entirely, first scrub the floor with wood alcohol and then bleach it with oxalic acid—never use lye as it turns the wood black and ruins the surface permanently. After all moisture has evaporated, the original finish may be applied.

Varnish finish: If the finish has become badly worn, thoroughly scrub it with a brush and Sapolio and water (never flood the floor). After it has dried out, apply a thin coat of varnish, or in case time cannot be allowed for the varnish to dry, wax may be substituted. Do not use shellac on top of old varnish or varnish on top of old shellac.

Wax finish: Waxed floors should be dusted daily with a broom covered with canton flannel. Keep a can of wax on hand, and should the finish become worn in the doorways or elsewhere, apply a thin coat, rubbing well into the wood. Allow the wax to dry for one hour and then polish thoroughly. Before rewaxing the floor, scrub it thoroughly with turpentine and a piece of cheese cloth.

Record Sales of Pressed Brick

The Livermore Fire Brick Works of Livermore, Cal., report a great rush of business for their pressed, enameled and glazed brick, and find that they must now take orders for not earlier than July delivery. This despite the fact that their kilns are running full blast and up to greatest capacity.

The California Brick Co. is also enjoying a rush of new business and; like their allied concern, the Livermore Brick Works, sees no indications of dull times in construction work.

Pioneer Paper Co. Working Three Shifts

The Pioneer Paper Co. of Los Angeles and San Francisco reports unequaled business, requiring its factory to run day and night. Orders for Pioneer roofings aggregated for one day the past month ten carloads, which is said to be a fair example of what every other day brings forth for this growing concern.

STATEMENT OF THE OWNERSHIP,
MANAGEMENT, CIRCULATION, ETC.
(Required by the Act of Congress,
August 24, 1912),
Of The Architect and Engineer of California, published monthly at San Francisco, California, for April 1st, 1917.

State of California, }
County of San Francisco, } ss.

Before me, a Notary Public in and for the State and County aforesaid, personally appeared A. I. Whitney, who, having been duly sworn according to law, deposes and says that she is the sole owner of The Architect and Engineer of California, and that the following is, to the best of her knowledge and belief, a true statement of the ownership, management, etc., of the aforesaid publication for the date shown in the above caption, required by the Act of August 24, 1912, embodied in section 443, Postal Laws and Regulations, printed on the reverse of this form, to wit:

1. That the names and addresses of the publisher, editor, managing editor and business managers are:
Publisher..................A. I. WHITNEY
        627 Foxcroft Bldg., San Francisco
Editor.............FREDERICK W. JONES
        627 Foxcroft Bldg., San Francisco
Business Manager............A. I. WHITNEY
        627 Foxcroft Bldg., San Francisco

2. That the owner is A. I. WHITNEY, Sole Owner, 627 Foxcroft Bldg., San Francisco.

3. That the known bondholders, mortgagees, and other security holders owning or holding 1 per cent or more of total amount of bonds, mortgages, or other securities are: None.

4. That the two paragraphs next above, giving the names of the owners, stockholders, and security holders, if any, contain not only the list of stockholders and security holders as they appear upon the books of the company but also, in cases where the stockholder or security holder appears upon the books of the company as trustee or in any other fiduciary relation, the name of the person or corporation for whom such trustee is acting, is given; also that the said two paragraphs contain statements embracing affiant's full knowledge and belief as to the circumstances and conditions under which stockholders and security holders who do not appear upon the books of the company as trustees, hold stock and securities in a capacity other than that of a bona fide owner; and this affiant has no reason to believe that any other person, association, or corporation has any interest direct or indirect in the said stock, bonds, or other securities than as so stated by him.

5. That the average number of copies of each issue of this publication sold or distributed, through the mails or otherwise, to paid subscribers during the six months preceding the date shown above is .... (This information is required from daily publications only.)
                        A. I. WHITNEY,
Signature of Editor, Publisher, Business Mgr. or Owner
Sworn to and subscribed before me this 20th day of March, 1917.
                        SID S. PALMER,
Notary Public in and for the City and County
(SEAL)   of San Francisco, State of California.
(My commission expires Dec. 31st, 1918.)

Railway Shops

The Pacific Electric Railway Company has decided to proceed at once with the erection of new shops at Torrance. An appropriation of $1,000,000 has been authorized for the construction and equipment of the buildings. The work will be handled by the construction office of the Pacific Electric, M. C. Halsey, 695 Pacific Electric building, Los Angeles, superintendent.

$10,000 Residence

Chas. Haber, Monadnock building, San Francisco, has completed plans for a $10,000 addition to a two-story frame and plaster residence and a two-story frame and plaster servants' quarters and garage building for Carl Raiss at Atherton.

When writing to Advertisers please mention this magazine.

When writing to Advertisers please mention this magazine.

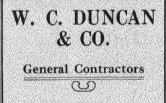

When writing to Advertisers please mention this magazine.

THE ARCHITECT & ENGINEER OF CALIFORNIA

JVNE
1917

This label appears on every "ℙacific" Plumbing Fixture. It denotes that this fixture is of superior quality and design — that it has attained the standard set for all "ℙacific" Plumbing Fixtures, and it is guaranteed forever against any defects in workmanship or materials.

To make sure that your clients get the highest quality specify

"ℙacific"

PLUMBING FIXTURES
FOR SALE BY ALL JOBBERS

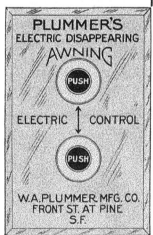

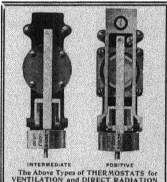

When writing to Advertisers please mention this magazine.

When writing to Advertisers please mention this magazine.

Architects' Specification Index

(For Index to Advertisements, see next page)

ACOUSTICAL CORRECTION
H. W. Johns-Manville Co., Second and Howard Sts., San Francisco.

ARCHITECTURAL SCULPTORS, MODELING, ETC.
G. Rognier & Co., 233 R. R. Ave., San Mateo.
Sculptors' Workshop. S. Miletin & Co., 1705 Harrison St., San Francisco.
A. F. Swoboda, modeler, 204 Second St., San Francisco.

ARCHITECTURAL TERRA COTTA
Gladding, McBean & Company, Crocker Bldg., San Francisco.

ASBESTOS ROOFING
H. W. Johns-Manville Company, San Francisco, Los Angeles, San Diego, Sacramento.

AUTOMATIC SPRINKLERS
Scott Company, 243 Minna St., San Francisco.
Pacific Fire Extinguisher Co., 507 Montgomery St., San Francisco.

AWNINGS
W. A. Plummer Mfg. Co., Pine and Front Sts., San Francisco.

BANK FIXTURES AND INTERIORS
Fink & Schindler, 218 13th St., San Francisco.
A. J. Forbes & Son, 1530 Filbert St., San Francisco.
C. F. Weber & Co., 365 Market St., San Francisco.
Home Mfg. Co., 543 Brannan St., San Francisco.
Rucker-Fuller Desk Co., 677 Mission St., San Francisco.
T. H. Meek Co., 1130 Mission St., San Francisco.
Mullen Manufacturing Co., 20th and Harrison Sts., San Francisco.

BLACKBOARDS
C. F. Weber & Co., 365 Market St., San Francisco.
Beaver Blackboards and Greenboards, Rucker-Fuller Desk Company, Coast agents, 677 Mission St., San Francisco, Oakland and Los Angeles

BOOK BINDERS AND PRINTERS
Hicks-Judd Company, 51-65 First St., San Francisco.

BOILERS
"Franklin" water tube boiler, sold by General Machinery and Supply Co., 37 Stevenson St., San Francisco.

BRASS GOODS, CASTINGS, ETC.
H. Mueller Manufacturing Co., 589 Mission St., San Francisco.

BRICK—PRESSED, PAVING, ETC.
Gladding, McBean & Company, Crocker Bldg., San Francisco.
Los Angeles Pressed Brick Co., Frost Bldg., Los Angeles.
Livermore Brick Company, pressed, glazed and enameled, etc,, Livermore, Cal.
United Materials Co., Crossley Bldg., San Francisco.
California Brick Company, Niles, Cal.

BRICK AND CEMENT COATING
Armorite and Concreta, manufactured by W. P. Fuller & Co., all principal Coast cities.
Wadsworth, Howland & Co., Inc. (See Adv. for Pacific Coast Agents.)
Paraffine Paint Co., 34 First St., San Francisco.
R. N. Nason & Co., 151 Potrero Ave., San Francisco.

BRICK STAINS
Samuel Cabot Mfg. Co., Boston, Mass., agencies in San Francisco, Oakland, Los Angeles, Portland, Tacoma and Spokane.
Armorite and Concreta, manufactured by W. P. Fuller & Co., all principal Coast cities.

BUILDERS' HARDWARE
Bennett Bros., agents for Sargent Hardware, 514 Market St., San Francisco.
Pacific Hardware & Steel Company, San Francisco, Oakland, Berkeley, and Los Angeles.

BUILDING MATERIAL, SUPPLIES, ETC.
Pacific Building Materials Co., 523 Market St., San Francisco.
C. Jorgensen, Crossley Bldg., San Francisco.
Richard Spencer, Hearst Bldg., San Francisco.
The Howard Company, First and Market Sts., Oakland.
James P. Dwan, 1113 Hearst Bldg., San Francisco.

CEMENT
Mt. Diablo, sold by Henry Cowell Lime & Cement Co., 2 Market street, San Francisco.
"Golden Gate" Brand, manufactured by Pacific Portland Cement Co., Pacific building, San Francisco.

CEMENT EXTERIOR WATERPROOF PAINT
Bay State Brick and Cement Coating, made by Wadsworth, Howland & Co. (See distributing agents in advertisement.)
Glidden's Liquid Cement and Liquid Cement Enamel, sold on Pacific Coast by Whittier, Coburn Co., San Francisco.
Armorite, sold by W. P. Fuller & Co., all principal Coast cities.
Imperial Waterproofing, manufactured by Imperial Co., 183 Stevenson St., San Francisco.
Paraffine Paint Co., 34 First St., San Francisco.

CEMENT EXTERIOR FINISH
Bay State Brick and Cement Coating, made by Wadsworth, Howland & Co. (See list of Distributing Agents in adv.)
Concreta, sold by W. P. Fuller & Co., all principal Coast cities.

An Index to the Advertisements

ARCHITECTS' SPECIFICATION INDEX—*Continued*

CEMENT EXTERIOR FINISH—Continued

Glidden's Liquid Cement and Liquid Cement Enamel, sold on Pacific Coast by Whittier, Coburn Company, San Francisco.

Pacific Building Materials Co., 523 Market St.

Samuel Cabot Mfg. Co., Boston, Mass., agencies in San Francisco, Oakland, Los Angeles, Portland, Tacoma and Spokane.

CEMENT FLOOR COATING

Bay State Brick and Cement Coating, made by Wadsworth, Howland & Co. (See list of Distributing Agents in adv.)

Fuller's Concrete Floor Enamel, made by W. P. Fuller & Co., San Francisco.

CEMENT TESTS—CHEMICAL ENGINEERS

Robert W. Hunt & Co., 251 Kearny St., San Francisco.

CHURCH INTERIORS

Fink & Schindler, 218 13th St., San Francisco.

CHUTES—SPIRAL

Haslett Warehouse Co., 310 California St., San Francisco.

COLD STORAGE PLANTS

T. P. Jarvis Crude Oil Burning Co., 275 Connecticut St., San Francisco.

COMPOSITION FLOORING

Germanwood Floor Co., 1621 Eddy St., San Francisco.

Malott & Peterson, Monadnock Bldg., San Francisco.

"Vitrolite," Vitrolite Construction Co., 34 Davis St., San Francisco.

COMPRESSED AIR MACHINERY

General Machinery & Supply Co., 39 Stevenson St., San Francisco.

COMPRESSED AIR CLEANERS

Spencer Turbine Cleaner. Sold by Hughson & Merton, 530 Golden Gate Ave., San Francisco.

Western Vacuum Supply Co., 1125 Market St., San Francisco.

CONCRETE CONSTRUCTION

American Concrete Co., Humboldt Bank Bldg., San Francisco.

Clinton Construction Co., 140 Townsend street, San Francisco.

Barrett & Hilp, Sharon Bldg., San Francisco.

Palmer & Peterson, Monadnock Bldg., San Francisco.

CONCRETE HARDNER

Master Builders Method, represented in San Francisco by C. Roman, Sharon Bldg.

CONCRETE MIXERS

Austin Improved Cube Mixer. J. H. Hansen & Co., California agents, 508 Balboa Bldg., San Francisco.

Foote Mixers. Sold by Edw. R. Bacon, 40 Natoma St., San Francisco.

CONCRETE REINFORCEMENT

United States Steel Products Co., San Francisco, Los Angeles, Portland and Seattle.

Twisted Bars. Sold by Woods, Huddart & Gunn, 444 Market St., San Francisco.

Clinton Welded Wire Fabric, L. A. Norris Co., 140 Townsend St., San Francisco.

Pacific Coast Steel Company, Rialto Bldg., San Francisco.

Southern California Iron and Steel Company, Fourth and Mateo Sts., Los Angeles.

Triangle Mesh Fabric. Sales agents, Pacific Building Materials Co., 523 Market St., San Francisco.

CONCRETE SURFACING

"Concreta." Sold by W. P. Fuller & Co., San Francisco.

Wadsworth, Howland & Co.'s Bay State Brick and Cement Coating. Sold by Jas. Hambly Co., Pacific Bldg., San Francisco, and Los Angeles.

Glidden Liquid Cement, manufactured by Glidden Varnish Co., Whittier, Coburn Co., San Francisco.

CONTRACTOR'S BONDS

Bonding Company of America, Kohl Bldg., San Francisco.

Globe Indemnity Co., 120 Leidesdorff St., San Francisco.

Fred H. Boggs, Foxcroft Bldg., San Francisco.

National Surety Co. of N. Y., 105 Montgomery St., San Francisco.

Fidelity & Casualty Co. of New York, Merchants Exchange Bldg., San Francisco.

Fidelity & Deposit Co. of Maryland, Insurance Exchange, San Francisco.

J. T. Costello Co., 216 Pine St., San Francisco.

Robertson & Hall, First National Bank Bldg., San Francisco.

CONTRACTORS, GENERAL

Arthur Arlett, New Call Bldg., San Francisco.

Farrell & Reed, Gunst Bldg., San Francisco.

American Concrete Co., Humboldt Bank Bldg., San Francisco.

Barrett & Hilp, Sharon Bldg., San Francisco.

Carnahan & Mulford, 45 Kearny St., San Francisco.

Houghton Construction Co., Hooker & Lent Bldg., San Francisco.

Geo. H. Bos, Hearst Bldg., San Francisco.

Larsen, Sampson & Co., Crocker Bldg., San Francisco.

J. D. Hannah, 725 Chronicle Bldg., San Francisco.

Clinton Construction Company, 140 Townsend St., San Francisco.

Dioguardi & Terranova, Westbank Bldg., San Francisco.

Teichert & Ambrose, Ochsner Bldg., Sacramento.

L. G. Bergren & Son, Call Bldg., San Francisco.

Grace & Bernieri, Claus Spreckels Bldg., San Francisco.

Geo. W. Boxton & Son, Hearst Bldg., San Francisco.

W. C. Duncan & Co., 526 Sharon Bldg., San Francisco.

A. P. Brady, Humboldt Bank Bldg., San Francisco.

Harvey A. Klyce, New Call Bldg., San Francisco.

Knowles & Mathewson, Call Bldg., San Francisco.

C. L. Wold Co., 75 Sutter St., San Francisco.

P. R. Ward, 981 Guerrero St., San Francisco.

Lange & Bergstrom, Sharon Bldg., San Francisco.

Foster Vogt Co., 411 Sharon Bldg., San Francisco.

T. B. Goodwin, 110 Jessie St., San Francisco.

Thos. Elam & Son, Builders Exchange, San Francisco.

Masow & Morrison, 518 Monadnock Bldg., San Francisco.

ARCHITECTS' SPECIFICATION INDEX—*Continued*

CONTRACTORS, GENERAL—Continued
Monson Bros., 502 Clunie Bldg., San Francisco.
J. M. Dougan Co., Hearst Bldg., San Francisco.
Palmer & Peterson, Monadnock Bldg., San Francisco.
Robert Trost, Twenty-sixth and Howard Sts., San Francisco.
John Monk, Sheldon Bldg., San Francisco.
Williams Bros. & Henderson, 381 Tenth St,. San Francisco.

CONVEYING MACHINERY
Meese & Gottfried, San Francisco, Los Angeles, Portland and Seattle.

CORK TILING, FLOORING, ETC.
David Kennedy, Inc., Sharon Bldg., San Francisco.
Be-ver Cork Tile. Sold by W. L.-Eaton & Co., 812 Santa Marina Bldg., San Francisco.

CORNER BEAD
Capitol Art Metal Works, 1927 Market St., San Francisco.
United States Metal Products Co., 555 Tenth St., San Francisco; 750 Keller St., San Francisco.

CORK TILE AND INSULATION
Van Fleet-Freear Co., 120 Jessie St., San Francisco.

CRUSHED ROCK
Grant Gravel Co., Flatiron Bldg., San Francisco.
California Building Material Company, new Call Bldg., San Francisco.
Niles Sand, Gravel & Rock Co., Mutual Bank Bldg., San Francisco.
Pratt Building Material Co., Hearst Bldg., San Francisco.
Saratoga Rock Company, Baker-MacDonald Co. representatives, First National Bank Bldg., San Jose.

DAMP-PROOFING COMPOUND
Armorite Damp Resisting Paint, made by W. P. Fuller & Co., San Francisco.
Biturine Co., 24 California St., San Francisco.
Imperial Co., 183 Stevenson St., San Francisco.
"Pabco" Damp-Proofing Compound, sold by Paraffine Paint Co., 34 First St., San Francisco.
Wadsworth, Howland & Co., Inc., 84 Washington St., Boston. (See Adv. for Coast agencies.)

DOOR HANGERS
McCabe Hanger Mfg. Co., New York, N. Y.
Pitcher Hanger, sold by National Lumber Co., 326 Market St., San Francisco.
Reliance Hanger, sold by Sartorius Co., San Francisco; D. F. Fryer & Co., B. V. Collins, Los Angeles, and Columbia Wire & Iron Works, Portland, Ore.

DRAIN BOARDS, SINK BACKS, ETC.
Germanwood Floor Co., 1621 Eddy St., San Francisco.

DRINKING FOUNTAINS
Haws Sanitary Fountain, 1808 Harmon St., Berkeley, and C. F. Weber & Co., San Francisco and Los Angeles.

DRINKING FOUNTAINS—Continued
Crane Company, San Francisco, Oakland, and Los Angeles.
Pacific Porcelain Ware Co., 67 New Montgomery St., San Francisco.

DUMB WAITERS
Spencer Elevator Company, 173 Beale St., San Francisco.
M. E. Hammond, Humboldt Bank Bldg., San Francisco.

ELECTRICAL CONTRACTORS
Butte Engineering Co., 683 Howard St., San Francisco.
Goold & Johns, 113 S. California St,. Stockton, Cal.
NePage, McKenny Co., 149 New Montgomery St,. San Francisco.
Newbery Electrical Co., 413 Lick Bldg., San Francisco.
Pacific Fire Extinguisher Co., 507 Montgomery St., San Francisco.
H. S. Tittle, 245 Minna St., San Francisco.
Standard Electrical Construction Company, 60 Natoma St., San Francisco.

ELECTRICAL ENGINEERS
Chas. T. Phillips, Pacific Bldg., San Francisco.

ELECTRIC PLATE WARMER
The Prometheus Electric Plate Warmer for residences, clubs, hotels, etc. Sold by M. E. Hammond, Humboldt Bank Bldg., San Francisco.

ELEVATORS
Otis Elevator Company, Stockton and North Point, San Francisco.
Spencer Elevator Company, 126 Beale St., San Francisco.
Van Emon Elevator Co., 54 Natoma St., San Francisco.

ENGINEERS
Chas. T. Phillips, Pacific Bldg., San Francisco.
Hunter & Hudson, Rialto Bldg., San Francisco.

FIRE ESCAPES
Palm Iron & Bridge Works, Sacramento.
Western Iron Works, 141 Beale St., San Francisco.

FIRE EXTINGUISHERS
Scott Company, 243 Minna St., San Francisco
Pacific Fire Extinguisher Co., 507 Montgomery St., San Francisco.

FIREPROOFING & PARTITIONS
Gladding, McBean & Co., Crocker Bldg., San Francisco.
Los Angeles Pressed Brick Co., Frost Bldg., Los Angeles.

FIXTURES—BANK, OFFICE, STORE. ETC.
T. H. Meek & Co., 1130 Mission St., San Francisco.
Mullen Manufacturing Co., 20th and Harrison Sts., San Francisco.
The Fink & Schindler Co., 218 13th St, San Francisco.
A. J. Forbes & Son, 1530 Filbert St., San Francisco.
C. F. Weber & Co., 365 Market St., San Francisco, and 210 N. Main St., Los Angeles, Cal.

ARCHITECTS' SPECIFICATION INDEX—*Continued*

FLOOR TILE
New York Belting and Packing Company, 519 Mission St., San Francisco.
W. L. Eaton & Co., 112 Market St., San Francisco.

FLOOR VARNISH
Bass-Hueter and San Francisco Pioneer Varnish Works, 816 Mission St., San Francisco.
Fifteen for Floors, made by W. P. Fuller & Co., San Francisco.
Standard Varnish Works, Chicago, New York and San Francisco.
Glidden Products, sold by Whittier; Coburn Co., San Francisco.
R. N. Nason & Co., San Francisco and Los Angeles.

FLOORS—COMPOSITION
"Vitrolite," for any structure, room or bath. Vitrolite Construction Co., 1490 Mission St., San Francisco.
Malott & Peterson, Inc., Monadnock Bldg., San Francisco.
Germanwood Floor Co., 1621 Eddy St., San Francisco.

FLOORS—HARDWOOD
Oak Flooring Bureau, Conway Bldg., Chicago, Ill.
Strable Mfg. Co., 541 First St., Oakland.

FLUMES
California Corrugated Culvert Co., West Berkeley, Cal.

FURNACES—WARM AIR
Miller-Enwright Co., 907 Front St., Sacramento.
Pacific Blower & Heating Co., 224 Fifth St., San Francisco.

GARAGE EQUIPMENT
Bowser Gasoline Tanks and Outfit, Bowser & Co., 612 Howard St., San Francisco.
Rix Compressed Air and Drill Company, First and Howard Sts., San Francisco.

GAS GRATES
General Gas Light Co., 768 Mission St., San Francisco.

GLASS
W. P. Fuller & Company, all principal Coast cities.
Whittier, Coburn & Co., Howard and Beale Sts., San Francisco.

GRADING
P. Montague Co., 110 Jessie St., San Francisco.

GRANITE
California Granite Co., Sharon Bldg., San Francisco.
McGilvray-Raymond Granite Co., 634 Townsend St., San Francisco.
Raymond Granite Co., Potrero Ave. and Division St., San Francisco.

GRAVEL AND SAND
California Building Material Co., new Call Bldg., San Francisco.
Del Monte White Sand, sold by Pacific Improvement Co., Crocker Bldg., San Francisco.

GRAVEL AND SAND—Continued
Pratt Building Material Co., Hearst Bldg., San Francisco.
Grant Gravel Co., Flatiron Bldg., San Francisco.
Grant Rock & Gravel Co., Cory Bldg., Fresno.
Niles Sand, Gravel & Rock Co., Mutual Savings Bank Bldg., 704 Market St., San Francisco.
Saratoga Rock Company, 703 First National Bank Bldg., San Jose.

HARDWALL PLASTER
Henry Cowell Lime & Cement Co., San Francisco.
Empire Plaster sold by Pacific Portland Cement Co., Pacific Bldg., San Francisco.

HARDWARE
Pacific Hardware & Steel Company, representing Lockwood Hardware Co., San Francisco.
Sargent's Hardware, sold by Bennett Bros., 514 Market St., San Francisco.

HARDWOOD LUMBER—FLOORING, ETC.
Dieckmann Hardwood Co., Beach and Taylor Sts., San Francisco.
Parrott & Co., 320 California St., San Francisco.
White Bros., cor. Fifth and Brannan Sts., San Francisco.
Strable Mfg. Co., 511 First St., Oakland.

HEATERS—AUTOMATIC
Pittsburg Water Heater Co., 478 Sutter St., San Francisco.

HEATING AND VENTILATING
Gilley-Schmid Company, 198 Otis St., San Francisco.
Mangrum & Otter, Inc., 507 Mission St., San Francisco.
Charles T. Phillips, Pacific Bldg., San Francisco.
James & Drucker, 450 Hayes St., San Francisco.
J. C. Hurley Co., 509 Sixth St., San Francisco.
Illinois Engineering Co., 563 Pacific Bldg., San Francisco.
Neil H. Dunn, 786 Ellis St., San Francisco.
William F. Wilson Co., 328 Mason St., San Francisco.
Pacific Fire Extinguisher Co., 507 Montgomery St., San Francisco.
Pacific Blower & Heating Co., 224 Fifth St., San Francisco.
Scott Company, 243 Minna St., San Francisco.
C. A. Dunham Co., Wells Fargo Bldg., San Francisco.

HEAT REGULATION
Johnson Service Company, 149 Fifth St., San Francisco.

HOLLOW BLOCKS
Denison Hollow Interlocking Blocks. Forum Bldg., Sacramento, and the Howard Company, Oakland.
Gladding, McBean & Co., San Francisco, Los Angeles, Oakland and Sacramento.
Pratt Building Material Co., Hearst Bldg., San Francisco.

ARCHITECTS' SPECIFICATION INDEX—*Continued*

HOLLOW METAL DOORS AND TRIM
Edwin C. Dehn, 525 Hearst Bldg., San Francisco, representing Interior Metal Mfg. Co., and Dahlstrom Metallic Door Company, Jamestown, N. Y.

HOSPITAL FIXTURES
J. L. Mott Iron Works, 135 Kearny St., San Francisco.

HOTELS
St. Francis Hotel, Union Square, San Francisco
Hotel Whitcomb, facing Civic Center, San Francisco.

INGOT IRON
"Armco" brand, manufactured by American Rolling Mill Company, Middletown, Ohio, and Monadnock Bldg., San Francisco.

INSPECTIONS AND TESTS
Robert W. Hunt & Co., 251 Kearny St., San Francisco.

INTERIOR DECORATORS
Mrs. H. C. McAfee, 504 Sutter St., San Francisco.
Albert S. Bigley, 344 Geary St., San Francisco.
City of Paris, Geary and Stockton Sts., San Francisco.
A. Falvy, 578 Sutter St., San Francisco.
The Tormey Co., 681 Geary St., San Francisco.
Fick Bros., 475 Haight St., San Francisco.
O'Hara & Livermore, Sutter St., San Francisco.

KITCHEN CABINETS
Western Equipment Co., Building Material Exbibit, 77 O'Farrell St., San Francisco
Hoosier Cabinets, branch 1067 Market St., San Francisco.

LAMP POSTS, ELECTROLIERS, ETC.
J. L. Mott Iron Works, 135 Kearny St., San Francisco.
Ralston Iron Works, 20th and Indiana Sts., San Francisco.

LANDSCAPE GARDENERS
MacRorie-McLaren Co., 141 Powell St., San Francisco.

LATHING MATERIAL
"Buttonlath," manufactured by Buttonlath Mfg. Co., office, Building Material Exhibit, San Francisco.
Pacific Building Materials Co., 523 Market St., San Francisco.

LIGHT, HEAT AND POWER
Pacific Gas & Elec. Co., 445 Sutter St., San Francisco.
The Fish Fuel System, 50 Eighth St., San Francisco.

LIME
Henry Cowell Lime & Cement Co., 2 Market St., San Francisco.

LINOLEUM
D. N. & E. Walter & Co., O'Farrell and Stockton Sts., San Francisco.

LUMBER
Dudfield Lumber Co., Palo Alto, Cal.
Hooper Lumber Co., Seventeenth and Illinois Sts., San Francisco.

LUMBER—Continued
Portland Lumber Co., 16 California St., San Francisco.
Pacific Manufacturing Company, San Francisco, Oakland and Santa Clara.
Pacific Mill and Timber Co., First National Bank Bldg., San Francisco.
Pope & Talbot, foot of Third St., San Francisco.
Sunset Lumber Co., Oakland, Cal.
United Lumber Company, 687 Market St., San Francisco.

MASTIC FLOORING
Malott & Peterson, Monadnock Bldg., San Francisco.

MAIL CHUTES
Cutler Mail Chute Co., Rochester, N. Y. (See adv. on page 30 for Coast representatives.)
American Mailing Device Corp., represented on Pacific Coast by U. S. Metal Products Co., 555 Tenth St., San Francisco.

MANTELS
Mangrum & Otter, 561 Mission St., San Francisco.

MARBLE
American Marble and Mosaic Co., 25 Columbus Square, San Francisco.
Joseph Musto Sons, Keenan Co., 535 N. Point St., San Francisco.
Sculptors' Workshop, S. Miletin & Co., 1705 Harrison St., San Francisco.
Vermont Marble Co., Coast branches, San Francisco, Portland and Tacoma.

METAL CEILINGS
San Francisco Metal Stamping & Corrugating Co., 2269 Folsom St., San Francisco.

METAL DOORS AND WINDOWS
U. S. Metal Products Co., 555 Tenth St., San Francisco.
Capitol Art Metal Works, 1937 Market St., San Francisco.

METAL FURNITURE
Capitol Art Metal Works, 1937 Market St., San Francisco.
Ralston Iron Works, Twentieth and Indiana Sts., San Francisco.
Edwin C. Dehn, Manufacturer's Agent, Hearst Bldg., San Francisco.

MILL WORK
Dudfield Lumber Co., Palo Alto, Cal.
Pacific Manufacturing Company, San Francisco, Oakland and Santa Clara.
National Mill and Lumber Co., San Francisco and Oakland.
The Fink & Schindler Co., 218 13th St., San Francisco.

OIL BURNERS
American Standard Oil Burner Company, Seventh and Cedar Sts., Oakland.
S. T. Johnson Co., 1337 Mission St., San Francisco.
T. P. Jarvis Crude Oil Burner Co., 275 Connecticut St., San Francisco.
Fess System, 220 Natoma St., San Francisco.
W. S. Ray Mfg. Co., 218 Market St., San Francisco.

ARCHITECTS' SPECIFICATION INDEX—*Continued*

ORNAMENTAL IRON AND BRONZE
American Art Metal Works, 13 Grace St., San Francisco.
California Artistic Metal and Wire Co., 349 Seventh St., San Francisco.
Palm Iron & Bridge Works, Sacramento.
Ralston Iron Works, 20th and Indiana Sts., San Francisco.
C. J. Hillard Company, Inc., 19th and Minnesota Sts., San Francisco.
Schreiber & Sons Co., represented by Western Builders Supply Co., San Francisco.
Schrader Iron Works, Inc., 1247 Harrison St., San Francisco.
West Coast Wire & Iron Works, 861-863 Howard St., San Francisco.

PAINT FOR CEMENT
Bay State Brick and Cement Coating, made by Wadsworth, Howland & Co. (Inc.) (See adv. in this issue for Pacific Coast agents.)
Fuller's Concreta for Cement, made by W. P. Fuller & Co., San Francisco.
Samuel Cabot Mfg. Co., Boston, Mass., agencies in San Francisco, Oakland, Los Angeles, Portland, Tacoma and Spokane.

PAINT FOR STEEL STRUCTURES, BRIDGES, ETC.
Berry Bros., 250-256 First St., San Francisco.
Biturine Company, 24 California St., San Francisco.
Glidden's Acid Proof Coating, sold on Pacific Coast by Whittier, Coburn Company, San Francisco.
Pacific Coast Paint Corp'n, Security Bank Bldg., Oakland.
Paraffine Paint Co., 34 First St., San Francisco.
Premier Graphite Paint and Pioneer Brand Red Lead, made by W. P. Fuller & Co., San Francisco.

PAINTING, TINTING, ETC.
Art Wall Paper Co., 508 Ellis St., San Francisco
Golden Gate Decorating Co., 704 Polk St., San Francisco.
I. R. Kissel, 1747 Sacramento St., San Francisco.
D. Zelinsky & Sons, San Francisco and Los Angeles.
The Tormey Co., 681 Geary St., San Francisco.
Fick Bros., 475 Haight St., San Francisco.

PAINTS, OILS, ETC.
The Brininstool Co., Los Angeles, the Haslett Warehouse, 310 California St., San Francisco.
Bass-Hueter Paint Co., Mission, near Fourth St., San Francisco.
Berry Bros., 250-256 First St., San Francisco.
Biturine Co., 24 California St., San Francisco
Pacific Coast Paint Corp'n, Security Bank Bldg., Oakland.
Whittier, Coburn Co., Howard and Beale Sts., San Francisco.
Magner Bros., 419-421 Jackson St., San Francisco.
R. N. Nason & Company, San Francisco, Los Angeles, Portland and Seattle.
W. P. Fuller & Co., all principal Coast cities.
Standard Varnish Works, 55 Stevenson St., San Francisco.

PANELS AND VENEER
White Bros., Fifth and Brannan Sts., San Francisco.

PIPE—VITRIFIED SALT GLAZED TERRA COTTA
Gladding, McBean & Co., Crocker Bldg., San Francisco.

PLASTER CONTRACTORS
C. C. Morehouse, Crocker Bldg., San Francisco.
MacGruer & Co., 180 Jessie St., San Francisco.
M. J. Terranova, Westbank Bldg., San Francisco.

PLASTER EXTERIORS
Buttonlath, for exterior and interior plastering, Hearst Bldg., San Francisco.

PLUMBING CONTRACTORS
Alex Coleman, 706 Ellis St., San Francisco.
A. Lettich, 365 Fell St., San Francisco.
Gilley-Schmid Company, 198 Otis St., San Francisco.
Scott Co., Inc., 243 Minna St., San Francisco.
Wm. F. Wilson Co., 328 Mason St., San Francisco.

PLUMBING FIXTURES, MATERIALS, ETC.
Crane Co., San Francisco and Oakland.
California Steam Plumbing Supply Co., 671 Fifth St., San Francisco.
Gilley-Schmid Company, 198 Otis St., San Francisco.
Glauber Brass Manufacturing Company, 1107 Mission St., San Francisco.
Holbrook, Merrill & Stetson, 64 Sutter St., San Francisco.
Improved Sanitary Fixture Co., 632 Metropolitan Bldg., Los Angeles.
J. L. Mott Iron Works, D. H. Gulick, selling agent, 135 Kearny St., San Francisco.
Haines, Jones & Cadbury Co., 857 Folsom St., San Francisco.
H. Mueller Manufacturing Co., Pacific Coast branch, 589 Mission St., San Francisco.
Miller-Enwright Co., 907 Front St., Sacramento.
Mark-Lally Co., 235 Second St., San Francisco, also Oakland, Fresno, San Jose and Stockton.
Pacific Sanitary Manufacturing Co., 67 New Montgomery St., San Francisco.
Wm. F. Wilson Co., 328 Mason St., San Francisco.
C. A. Dunham Co., Wells Fargo Bldg., San Francisco.
Neil H. Dunn, 786 Ellis St., San Francisco.

POTTERY
Gladding, McBean & Co., San Francisco, Los Angeles, Oakland and Sacramento.

POWER TRANSMITTING MACHINERY
Meese & Gottfried, San Francisco, Los Angeles, Portland, Ore., and Seattle, Wash.

PUMPS
Simonds Machinery Co., 117 New Montgomery St., San Francisco.

RADIATORS
American Radiator Co., Second and Townsend Sts., San Francisco.

RAILROADS
Southern Pacific Company, Flood Bldg., San Francisco.
Western Pacific Company, Mills Bldg., San Francisco.

REFRIGERATORS
McCray Refrigerators, sold by Nathan Dohrmann Co., Geary and Stockton Sts., San Francisco.

REVERSIBLE WINDOWS
Hauser Reversible Window Company, Balboa Bldg., San Francisco.
Whitney Windows, represented by Richard Spencer, 801.3 Hearst Bldg., San Francisco.

REVOLVING DOORS
Van Kennel Doors, sold by U. S. Metal Products Co., 525 Market St., San Francisco.

ROLLING DOORS, SHUTTERS, PARTITIONS, ETC.
C. F. Weber & Co., 365 Market St., S. F.
Kinnear Steel Rolling Door Co., Rialto Bldg., San Francisco.
Wilson's Steel Rolling Doors, U. S. Metal Products Co., San Francisco and Los Angeles.

ARCHITECTS' SPECIFICATION INDEX—Continued

ROOFING AND ROOFING MATERIALS
Grant Gravel Co., Flatiron Bldg., San Francisco.
H. W. Johns-Manville Co., Second and Howard Sts., San Francisco
Malott & Peterson, Inc, Monadnock Bldg., San Francisco.
Niles Sand, Gravel and Rock Co, Mutual Bank Bldg., San Francisco.
"Malthoid" and "Ruberoid," manufactured by Paraffine Paint Co., San Francisco.
Pioneer Roofing, manufactured by Pioneer Paper Co., 513 Hearst Bldg., San Francisco.
United Materials Co., Crossley Bldg., San Francisco.

RUBBER TILING
Goodyear Rubber Company, 587 Market St., San Francisco.
New York Belting & Rubber Company, 519 Mission St., San Francisco.

SAFETY TREADS
"Sanitread," sold by Richard Spencer, 801-3 Hearst Bldg., San Francisco.
Pacific Building Materials Co., 523 Market St., San Francisco.
C. Jorgensen, Crossley Bldg., San Francisco.

SCENIC PAINTING—DROP CURTAINS, ETC.
The Edwin H. Flagg Scenic Co., 1638 Long Beach Ave., Los Angeles.

SCHOOL FURNITURE AND SUPPLIES
C. F. Weber & Co., 365 Market St., San Francisco; 512 S. Broadway, Los Angeles.
Rucker-Fuller Desk Company, 677 Mission St., San Francisco.

SCREENS
Hipolito Flyout Screens, sold by Simpson & Stewart, Dalziel Bldg., Oakland.
Watson Metal Frame Screens, sold by Richard Spencer, 801-3 Hearst Bldg., San Francisco.

SEEDS
California Seed Company, 151 Market St., San Francisco.

SHEATHING AND SOUND DEADENING
Samuel Cabot Mfg. Co., Boston, Mass., agencies in San Francisco, Oakland, Los Angeles, Portland, Tacoma and Spokane.
Paraffine Paint Co., 34 First St., San Francisco.

SHEET METAL WORK, SKYLIGHTS, ETC.
Capitol Sheet Metal Works, 1927 Market St., San Francisco.
U. S. Metal Products Co., 555 Tenth St., San Francisco.

SHINGLE STAINS
Cabot's Creosote Stains, sold by Pacific Building Materials Co., Underwood Bldg., San Francisco
Fuller's Pioneer Shingle Stains, made by W. P. Fuller & Co., San Francisco.

SIDEWALK LIGHTS
P. H. Jackson & Co., 237-47 First St., San Francisco.
Jas. P. Dwan, Hearst Bldg., San Francisco.

STEEL TANKS, PIPE, ETC.
Schaw-Batcher Co. Pipe Works, 356 Market St., San Francisco.

STEEL AND IRON—STRUCTURAL
Central Iron Works, 621 Florida St., San Francisco.
Dyer Bros., 17th and Kansas Sts., San Francisco.
Golden Gate Iron Works, 1541 Howard St., San Francisco.
Judson Manufacturing Co., 819 Folsom St., San Francisco.
Mortenson Construction Co., 19th and Indiana Sts., San Francisco.
Pacific Rolling Mills, 17th and Mississippi Sts., San Francisco.
Palm Iron & Bridge Works, Sacramento.
Ralston Iron Works, Twentieth and Indiana Sts., San Francisco.
U. S. Steel Products Co., Rialto Bldg., San Francisco.
Schrader Iron Works, Inc., 1247 Harrison St., San Francisco.
Southern California Iron and Steel Co., Fourth and Mateo Sts., Los Angeles.
Western Iron Works, 141 Beale St., San Francisco.

STEEL PRESERVATIVES
Bay State Steel Protective Coating. (See adv. for coast agencies.)
Paraffine Paint Co., 34 First St., San Francisco.
Biturine Company, 24 California St., San Francisco.

STEEL REINFORCING
Pacific Coast Steel Company, Rialto Bldg., San Francisco.
Southern California Iron & Steel Company, Fourth and Mateo Sts., Los Angeles.
Woods, Huddart & Gunn, 444 Market St., San Francisco.

STEEL ROLLING DOORS
Kinnear Steel Rolling Door Co., Rialto Bldg., San Francisco.

STEEL SASH
"Fenestra," solid steel sash, manufactured by Detroit Steel Products Company, Detroit, Mich.

STEEL WHEELBARROWS
Champion and California steel brands, made by Western Iron Works, 141 Beale St., San Francisco.

STONE
California Granite Co., 518 Sharon Bldg., San Francisco.
McGilvray Stone Company, 634 Townsend St., San Francisco.

STORAGE SYSTEMS—GASOLINE, OIL, ETC.
S. F. Bowser & Co., 612 Howard St., San Francisco.
Rix Compressed Air and Drill Co., First and Howard Sts., San Francisco.

ARCHITECTS' SPECIFICATION INDEX—Continued

TEMPERATURE REGULATION
Johnson Service Company, 149 Fifth St., San Francisco.

THEATER AND OPERA CHAIRS
C. F. Weber & Co., 365 Market St., San Francisco.

TILES, MOSAICS, MANTELS, ETC.
Rigney Tile Company, Sheldon Bldg., San Francisco.
Mangrum & Otter, 561 Mission St., San Francisco.
McElhinney Tile Co., 1097 Mission St., San Francisco.

TILE FOR ROOFING
Gladding, McBean & Co., Crocker Bldg., San Francisco.
United Materials Co., Crossley Bldg., San Francisco.

TILE WALLS—INTERLOCKING
Denison Hollow Interlocking Blocks, Forum Bldg., Sacramento.
Gladding, McBean & Co., San Francisco, Los Angeles, Oakland and Sacramento.

VACUUM CLEANERS
Arco Wand Cleaners, sold by American Radiator Company, Second and Townsend Sts., San Francisco.
Palm Vacuum Cleaners, sold by Western Vacuum Supply Co., 1125 Market St., San Francisco.
Spencer Turbine Cleaner, sold by Hughson & Merton, 530 Golden Gate Ave., San Francisco.

VALVES
Sloan Royal Flush Valves. T. R. Burke, Pacific Coast agent, Wells Fargo Bldg., San Francisco.
Crane Radiator Valves., manufactured by Crane Co., Second and Brannan Sts., San Francisco.

VALVE PACKING
N. H. Cook Belting Co., 317 Howard St., San Francisco.

VARNISHES
Berry Bros., 250-256 First St., San Francisco.
W. P. Fuller Co, all principal Coast cities.
Glidden Varnish Co, Cleveland, O., represented on the Pacific Coast by Whittier, Coburn Co., San Francisco.
Pacific Coast Paint Corp'n, 112 Market St., San Francisco; Security Bank Bldg., Oakland.
R. N. Nason & Co, San Francisco, Los Angeles, Portland and Seattle.
Standard Varnish Works. San Francisco.
S. F. Pioneer Varnish Works, 816 Mission St., San Francisco.

VENETIAN BLINDS, AWNINGS, ETC.
Burlington Venetian Blinds, Burlington, Vt., and C. F. Weber & Co., 365 Market St., San Francisco.
Western Blind & Screen Co., 2702 Long Beach Ave., Los Angeles.

VITREOUS CHINAWARE
Pacific Porcelain Ware Company, 67 New Montgomery St., San Francisco.

WALL BEDS, SEATS, ETC.
Lachman Wall Bed Co., 2019 Mission St., San Francisco.
Marshall & Stearns Co., 1154 Phelan Bldg., San Francisco.
Peek's Wall Beds, sold by Western Equipment Co., 72 Fremont St., San Francisco.
Perfection Disappearing Bed Co., 737 Mission St., San Francisco.

WALL PAINT
Nason's Opaque Flat Finish, manufactured by R. N. Nason & Co., San Francisco, Portland and Los Angeles.
San-A-Cote and Vel-va-Cote, manufactured by the Brininstool Co., Los Angeles; Marion D. Cohn Co., Hansford Bldg., San Francisco, distributor.

WALL BOARD
"Amiwud" Wall Board, manufactured by Paraffine Paint Co., 34 First St., San Francisco.

WALL PAPER
Uhl Bros., 38 O'Farrell St., San Francisco.
The Tormey Co., 681 Geary St., San Francisco.
Art Wall Paper Co., 500 Ellis St., San Francisco.

WATER HEATERS—AUTOMATIC
Pittsburg Water Heater Co. of California, 478 Sutter St., San Francisco, and Thirteenth and Clay Sts., Oakland.

WATERPROOFING FOR CONCRETE, BRICK, ETC.
Armorite Damp Resisting Paint, made by W. P. Fuller & Co., San Francisco.
Biturine Company, 24 California St., San Francisco.
Hill, Hubbell & Co., 1 Drumm St., San Francisco.
H. W. Johns-Manville Co., San Francisco and principal Coast cities.
Imperial Co., 183 Stevenson St., San Francisco.
Pacific Building Materials Co., 523 Market St., San Francisco.
Samuel Cabot Mfg. Co., Boston, Mass., agencies in San Francisco, Oakland, Los Angeles, Portland, Tacoma and Spokane.
Wadsworth, Howland & Co., Inc. (See adv. for Coast agencies.)

WATER SUPPLY SYSTEMS
Kewanee Water Supply System—Simonds Machinery Co., agents, 117 New Montgomery St., San Francisco.

WHEELBARROWS—STEEL
Western Iron Works, Beale and Main Sts., San Francisco.

WHITE ENAMEL FINISH
"Gold Seal," manufactured and sold by Bass-Hueter Paint Company. All principal Coast cities.
"Silkenwhite," made by W. P. Fuller & Co., San Francisco.
"Satinette," Standard Varnish Works, 113 Front St., San Francisco.

WINDOWS—REVERSIBLE, CASEMENT, ETC.
Whitney Window, represented by Richard Spencer, Hearst Bldg., San Francisco.
Hauser Reversible Window Co., Balboa Bldg., San Francisco.
International Casement Co., represented by Edwin C. Dehn, Hearst Bldg., San Francisco.

WIRE FABRIC
U. S. Steel Products Co., Rialto Bldg., San Francisco.

WOOD MANTELS
Fink & Schindler, 218 13th St., San Francisco.
Mangrum & Otter, 561 Mission St., San Francisco.

When writing to Advertisers please mention this magazine.

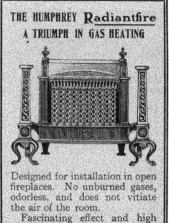

THE HUMPHREY Radiantfire
A TRIUMPH IN GAS HEATING

Designed for installation in open fireplaces. No unburned gases, odorless, and does not vitiate the air of the room.

Fascinating effect and high heat efficiency.

GENERAL GAS LIGHT COMPANY
C. B. BABCOCK, Manager
768 Mission Street   San Francisco

House of Mrs. D. T. Murphy, Hillsborough, Cal.

LAWN AND GARDEN ORNAMENTS

Garden Furniture, Flower Pots, Vases

Made by

G. Rognier & Co.
233 Railroad Ave., San Mateo, Cal.

PEEK'S WALL BEDS

Many beautiful designs in woods or metals. Mechanical parts all of steel—no castings.

SELF SUPPORTING NARROW DOOR

concealment and other practical methods. We inspect semi-annually (without charge) all installations of our beds.

SHOWN AT

The Building Material Exhibit
77 O'Farrell St., San Francisco
Phone Sutter 5712

Western Equipment Co.

When writing to Advertisers please mention this magazine.

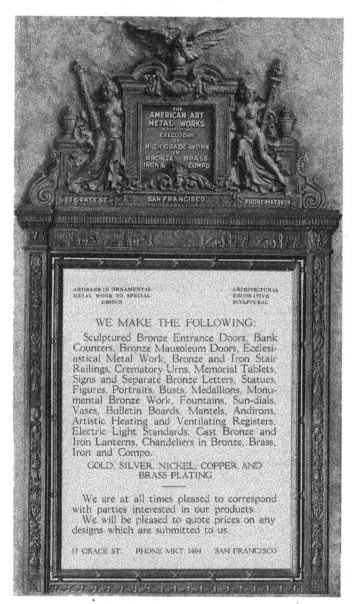

THE AMERICAN ART METAL WORKS

EXECUTORS OF HIGH GRADE WORK IN BRONZE BRASS IRON & COMPO

13 GRACE ST.   SAN FRANCISCO   PHONE MKT. 1404

ARTISANS IN ORNAMENTAL
METAL WORK TO SPECIAL
DESIGN

ARCHITECTURAL
DECORATIVE
SCULPTURAL

WE MAKE THE FOLLOWING:

Sculptured Bronze Entrance Doors, Bank Counters, Bronze Mausoleum Doors, Ecclesiastical Metal Work, Bronze and Iron Stair Railings, Crematory Urns, Memorial Tablets, Signs and Separate Bronze Letters, Statues, Figures, Portraits, Busts, Medallions, Monumental Bronze Work, Fountains, Sun-dials, Vases, Bulletin Boards, Mantels, Andirons, Artistic Heating and Ventilating Registers, Electric Light Standards, Cast Bronze and Iron Lanterns, Chandeliers in Bronze, Brass, Iron and Compo.

GOLD, SILVER, NICKEL, COPPER AND
BRASS PLATING

We are at all times pleased to correspond with parties interested in our products.
We will be pleased to quote prices on any designs which are submitted to us.

13 GRACE ST.   PHONE MKT. 1404   SAN FRANCISCO

CHESTER HALL APARTMENTS, 955 BUSH STREET, SAN FRANCISCO
Dr. Clyde Payne, Owner   W. G. HIND, Architect

Exterior Faced with

Richmond Red Pressed Brick

MANUFACTURED BY

Los Angeles Pressed Brick Company

LOS ANGELES, CALIFORNIA

SOLD THROUGH

UNITED MATERIALS COMPANY

Distributors for Northern California

CROSSLEY BUILDING, SAN FRANCISCO

The GOLD MEDAL MAIL CHUTE

INSTALLED IN
THE NEW
SAN FRANCISCO
CITY HALL
AND THE
WHITE MARBLE
MERRITT
BUILDING,
LOS ANGELES

Given highest
award at Panama-
Pacific Interna-
tional Exposition,
1915.

Represented on the
Pacific Coast by

United States Metal Products Co.

525 Market Street
SAN FRANCISCO
Agents for California
and Oregon

F. T. CROWE & CO.
Seattle

Agents for Washington,

American Mailing
Device
Corporation

The Cutler Mail Chute

*Pacific
Coast
Represen-
tatives:*

San Francisco,
Cal.,
THOMAS DAY
COMPANY.

Portland,
Ore.

C. W. BOOST.

Seattle and
Tacoma,
Wash.,
D. E. FRYER
& Co.

Spokane,
Wash.

E. C.
TOUSLEY.

Mail Box—L. C. Smith Building
Seattle, Wash.
Gaggin & Gaggin, Architects,
Syracuse, N. Y.

Cutler Mail Chute Co.,

ROCHESTER, N. Y.
Cutler Building.

BIGLEY'S

*Curtains
Decorated Lamps
and Pottery
Fine Upholstered
and Period
Furniture*

498 GEARY STREET
San Francisco, Cal.

Telephone: Franklin 5919

THE·L· SCHREIBER & SONS CO

ORNAMENTAL IRON&BRONZE STRVCTVRAL STEEL

CINCINNATI

SAN FRANCISCO
WESTERN BVILDERS SVPPLY CO
155 NEW MONTGOMERY ST.
LOS ANGELES
SWEETSER & BALDWIN SAFE CO
200 EAST 9TH ST

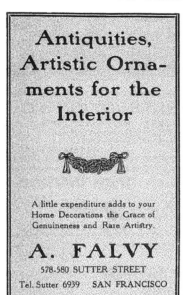

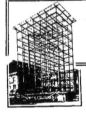

THE ARCHITECT & ENGINEER

OF CALIFORNIA

25c Copy
$1.50 a Year.

Volume XLIX
Number 3

Issued monthly in the interest of Architects, Structural Engineers, Contractors and the Allied Trades of the Pacific Coast. Copyright 1917–By Annie I. Whitney, all rights reserved

Entered at San Francisco Post Office as Second Class Matter

CONTENTS FOR JUNE, 1917

*OUR LADY'S CHAPEL OF THE PARISH
PRIEST, LANZI CHURCH, ITALY*

Frontispiece
The Architect and Engineer
of California
for June, 1917.

THE
ARCHITECT
AND
ENGINEER
OF CALIFORNIA
JUNE · 1917

VOL. XLIX.　　　　　　NUMBER 3.

Highbourne Gardens—A Southern California Bungalow Court

By WILBUR DAVID COOK, JR., Landscape Architect*

ENTRANCE TO HOUSES 7 AND 8

IN THE Highbourne Gardens and bunga-low court at Los Angeles, California again takes precedence in accomplishing the unusual. The aim of the owners was to build a court that should be distinctly different.

In this they have been most successful.

The problem was how to build twenty-two bungalows and ten garages on less than 1.5 acres of land without unduly crowding them, or shutting out the sunshine, and still have enough land left to provide an adequate landscape setting for the buildings. How this was finally accomplished is best shown by the accompanying photographs.

At the time the work was started there was a one-story bungalow at the northerly end of the property. This had to be remodeled to conform architecturally to the rest of the group.

By referring to the section on the general plan, some idea of the lay of the ground can be gained. That portion of the property below the brook was comparatively level, sloping only four feet in a frontage of 320 feet from north to south. It will be noted that Highbourne Gardens is a series of units, each unit possessing features of interest peculiar to itself. For instance, Unit 1 was developed along informal lines, with curvilinear paths and

*915 Marsh-Strong building, Los Angeles.

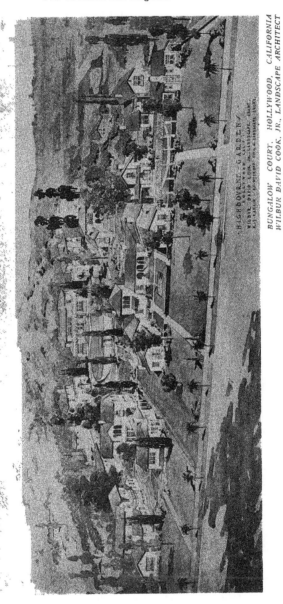

BUNGALOW COURT, HOLLYWOOD, CALIFORNIA
WILBUR DAVID COOK, JR., LANDSCAPE ARCHITECT

LOOKING INTO COURT 1 FROM THE PERGOLA, TOWARDS HOUSES 1, 2, 3 AND 4

an informal lily pool with rustic stone borders. Its approach from the street, however, is direct. Houses 1 to 5 are tied together with a pergola treatment with a central raised feature. A low privet hedge across the front of this pergola insures privacy to the occupants of the surrounding houses and makes this unit in reality a large outdoor living room.

LOOKING NORTH FROM THE PERGOLA NEAR HOUSE 1, TOWARDS HOUSES 4, 6 AND

VISTA TO ENTRANCE OF HOUSE 7, COURT 2

Another interesting feature of this unit is the treatment of the entrances to houses 1 and 2. Note the little terrace between with its pergola treatment and latticed background, screening out the yard between the two houses.

Unit 2 was developed along formal lines, with straight paths and a rectangular lily pool in a central panel of turf. Its approach is direct from the street, but it may also be reached by making use of the entrance to Unit 1 and the stone steps.

The method of tying houses 6 and 7 together is interesting, and the entrances to these two houses is unusual. The living rooms of all of the houses facing the various units were so arranged as to command views of at least two of them, showing the variation in the landscape development of each.

The bowling green might really be termed Unit 3 for purposes of identification. From the major axis of this unit the longest sweep of the property is obtained, some 300 feet deep. One looks across a sunken panel of turf to a bridge, across a driveway to a pergola tea house, over this to a two-story house which will crown the vista. The absence of walks in the immediate foreground of this unit should be noted. The bowling green pergola closes this unit back of house 10 and is a feature of interest.

ENTRANCE TO HOUSE·3—NOTE HOMELIKE FEELING OF COZINESS

Unit 4 is a combination of formal and informal development. Its approach is direct; passing house 10 it branches as shown on the plan. This unit vista will be closed by house 13 when built. An informal oval pool is shown on the axis line.

Units 1 and 2 have a service walk for the delivery of household supplies to the back doors. Unit 4's service arrangements are by means of the north driveway, which is also the approach to the garage courtyard. This driveway passes through an archway between the garages, climbs the hill on an easy grade and finds a point of exit at the southeast corner of the property at Emmett Terrace. The driveway is designed to carry heavy supplies to the houses.

ENTRANCE TO HOUSES 5 AND 6—NOTE ARRANGEMENT OF BACK YARDS

A GLIMPSE OF COURT 2, SHOWING HOUSES 5, 6, 7 AND 9

HOUSE 10, "HONEYMOON" COTTAGE, BOWLING GREEN AND PERGOLA

LOOKING NORTH TOWARDS HOUSES 5, 9, 10 AND 11

Unit 5, surrounded by houses 17 to 25, occupies the higher ground, enjoys a splendid outlook over the units below and an unrestricted distant view to the mountains beyond. Two fine sycamores growing by the brookside add picturesqueness to the site. The brook itself has been given a boulder treatment and the adjoining banks have been covered with periwinkle.

Complete planting plans were made for the gardens and the plants set into place, but they are not yet sufficiently advanced to make much of a showing. In another year the trellises will be covered with flowering vines, softening the architecture of the court.

Highbourne Gardens may be said to be an adaptation of the architecture of Italy modified to meet Southern California conditions—the houses are of gray stucco with moss green roofs. The houses run from three to six rooms; many have balconies and outdoor sleeping porches; all have hardwood floors, tiled bathrooms, tiled fireplaces, white enameled kitchens, and built-in features. Many of the rooms are finished in mahogany and fumed oak.

There is a growing demand for individual houses in park-like surroundings, where one can step from the house into a garden of evergreen beauty, with the feeling that it is yours to enjoy without the responsibility of its upkeep. The courts have been planted so that an abundance of cut flowers can be obtained for house decoration the year round. Tubbed plants will be found on the terraces, hanging baskets in the pergolas, and many window boxes for flowers.

The houses have been rented as fast as completed and the owners have a waiting list months in advance, showing the appreciation of the public of this type of court. The investment is yielding the owners something more than 16 per cent.

MARY BAKER EDDY MEMORIAL
EGERTON SWARTWOUT, ARCHITECT

DETAIL OF COLUMNS AND CORNICE, MARY BAKER EDDY MEMORIAL
Egerton Swartwout, Architect

The Mary Baker Eddy Memorial

By EGERTON SWARTWOUT, Architect

THE design of the memorial for Mary Baker Eddy was not a spontaneous product. It was a gradual development from the original scheme, and was influenced by the character of the memorial, by the site, and by the material that was finally adopted. It was essential that the memorial be simple and dignified in character; not overornamented, and yet worthy of its high purpose; strong, and yet expressing in its detail feminine rather than masculine strength; and above all, it should not be in any sense a copy of any existing structure.

The original scheme was essentially a marble design, as it seemed that in no other material could the requisite fineness of detail be obtained, but after

STEPS LEADING TO COLONNADE, MARY BAKER EDDY MEMORIAL
Egerton Swartwout, Architect

much investigation it was decided to abandon marble as not sufficiently durable and lasting, and white granite from the Bethel quarries was finally selected. It then occurred to me that it might be advisable to use bronze for the more delicate ornament that could not be carved in granite, and that this bronze might be white bronze, instead of the more customary color, so that there would not be too much contrast with the granite, and a sample was made which was extremely interesting and beautiful. After great deliberation this idea was given up, because the ornament looked a little spotty, due to the fact that practically all the work was curved, and the bronze was constantly seen in different lights.

Mr. Menconi, the modeler and carver, then made a series of experiments with the granite under the direction of the Christian Science Board of Directors and myself, to determine just to what extent the carving could be carried, and much to our satisfaction, we found that with the aid of modern methods this hard granite could be carved with the delicacy of marble, and that marvelous results could be obtained. It took a long time, it is true, to carve the granite in this manner, on account of the hardness of the material and its brittleness, and the greatest care had to be exercised, but the result has, in our opinion, justified the time and expense spent upon it. I think it can be said without fear of contradiction that, leaving aside entirely any artistic excellence, such perfection and delicacy have never been attained before in this unyielding and enduring material. There is certainly nothing in modern times that can approach it nor, as far as I know, in any of the monuments of antiquity. The Greeks and Romans employed granite but little, and while the Egyptians have left some wonderful carving in that material, they did not carry their work to such an elaborate or delicate extent. The detail is novel; it is not a copy of any highly conventionalized type, but is living and vibrant and at the same time it still retains its classic feeling; and in that connection it is interesting to note that in the best period of Greek and Roman art the detail was not the stiff formal thing that is usually imagined by modern restorers; it was highly conventionalized, but yet it was free, and the greatest individuality was displayed by the carver; no one piece of ornament was exactly a replica of another piece, and this same feeling has been obtained in the memorial, perhaps even to a greater extent than in any classical monument.

The memorial itself consists of a circular colonnade of eight columns, 15 feet in height, surmounted by a cornice and a cheneau course or cresting. There is no roof or covering; the colonnade is open, and similarly there is no pavement in the circle inclosed by the columns, nor is there any stone structure of any kind over the grave itself, but the space between the columns will be filled entirely with growing flowers, rhododendrons possibly, or plants whose flowers will be large enough to be in scale with the memorial. This colonnade rests upon a stylobate of three steps, which stylobate is surrounded on the road side by a broad platform of Pompton pink granite, which contrasts admirably with the white granite of the memorial itself, while on the lake side there are, as before mentioned, the double flight of circular steps, flanked on each side by large pylons, on the top of which are inscriptions of white bronze, let into the surface of the granite. There is also an inscription on the top step of the stylobate, and a dedicatory inscription in the frieze of the entablature.

I have been often asked in what style the memorial was designed; was it Greek or Roman, or was it Ionic of Corinthian; and I have been forced to answer that it was none of these. It was classic, I hoped, but yet it was modern. The columns and the caps have a certain resemblance to an order which was transitional between the Doric and the Corinthian and is best known from its use in the little Clypsedra of Andronicus Cyrrhestes, in Athens, sometimes called the Tower of the Winds. I do not mean to infer that the columns of the memorial are copies of, nor are they similar to, the order of the Tower of the Winds. They are merely of the same type, infinitely more refined in detail and better in proportion. The entablature is not similar to any entablature that I know of; it is extremely simple, relying for its ornamentation on the exterior chiefly upon the carved cresting and the bronze inscription in the frieze, and on the interior upon the elaborate and effective frieze, which is carved in high relief.

* * *

Making Tunnel Plans

Plans for the construction of a combination bridge and tunnel between the foot of Folsom street and Oakland mole are being prepared by the Watson-Davis-Miller Company, Merchants Exchange building, San Francisco.

This type of construction has been resorted to because of objections of the army engineers to a bridge. The plans provide for a bore accommodating three tubes, two for fast electric trains and one for vehicular traffic. The points at which the roadways dip from the bridge into the tunnel under the bay would be marked by lighthouses, with a clear waterway of 3000 feet between. The estimated cost is $26,000,000. The promoters of the project believe the traffic would pay a good return on a considerably larger investment.

PLAN AND FRONT ELEVATIONS FOR THREE HOUSES IN FOREST HILL, SAN FRANCISCO
FABRE & BEARWALD.   *ARCHITECTS*

HOTEL WHITCOMB, SAN FRANCISCO
Wright & Rushforth, Architects

The New Hotel Whitcomb
By EDWARD F. O'DAY

IN THE matter of hospitality, public or private, San Francisco has never been "serene, indifferent," but always enthusiastic and alert. As public hospitality is dispensed to a great extent in hotels, there is here, it may be, an explanation of the fact that no city of its approximate size has so many distinctive hotels as San Francisco.

The individuality which invests the great hotels of San Francisco is sensed readily by the experienced traveler; the elements which combine to make that individuality do not escape him if he has an aptitude for drawing comparisons. The great San Francisco hotels "stick in the mind." Though visited in the course of a long journey with many stopping places, they imprint an image which is not blurred when a succession of other hotel pictures supervenes.

It would seem, therefore, that the person who undertook to add another to the list of San Francisco's outstanding hostelries would be hard put to achieve a new kind of distinction—to satisfy the conventions of hotel building and still strike the note of originality. Difficult as this is, it appears to have been done in the construction of the new Hotel Whitcomb. The San Francisco family which built the Whitcomb gave the hotel three individual characteristics; the Whitcomb is unique in location and has one unique feature of architecture and one of management.

LOBBY, LOOKING TOWARDS DINING ROOM, HOTEL WHITCOMB, SAN FRANCISCO
Wright & Rushforth, Architects

LOBBY, NEAR ENTRANCE, HOTEL WHITCOMB, SAN FRANCISCO
Wright & Rushforth, Architects

Market street is usually referred to as the main artery of San Francisco, but the metaphor is inexact, for the blood has never flown freely the entire length of this artery. There has always been congestion on Market street. For years lower Market street and upper Market street have been neglected while central Market street was enjoying intensive development. This condition is passing rather rapidly. Had there been no catastrophe of 1906 it would have passed long since. In the years of rehabilitation immediately following 1906, however, it looked like a condition which would continue for an indefinitely long period. But there are always a few who have a keener vision than the generality in sighting the trend of municipal development. When these far-seeing ones have the pioneering impulse and the means to indulge it, a city profits. Usually they profit, too, reaping the just reward of their prescience.

Plans for the Hotel Whitcomb were started by Messrs. Wright & Rushforth, architects, in 1910; work was commenced the following year and consumed about twelve months. The architects had an unusual problem to solve. While a hotel structure was contemplated, a temporary City Hall was the immediate need; they had, therefore, to prepare a duplicate set of drawings, superimposing, as it were, the plans for a municipal building upon the plans for the hotel. With a hotel always in mind, they built a city hall, using all the ingenuity at their command in effecting a compromise. Architectural compromises are never wholly satisfactory. It is not surprising, therefore, that while the building as prepared for temporary municipal tenancy cost $700,000, it required the additional expenditure of $450,000 to make the structural changes which obliterated the city hall and gave the building the hotel character originally intended. Today the visitor, ignorant of this bit of local history, does not dream that the big building was ever anything but a hotel.

The point to be emphasized, however, is that as early as 1910—within four years of San Francisco's overwhelming disaster—the Whitcomb Estate anticipated the development of upper Market street by planning a hotel for that thoroughfare between Eighth and Ninth. Since then has occurred that awakening of civic consciousness testified by the development of a Civic Center which, when completed, will compare in beauty of architecture and landscape treatment with any civic center in the world; and which already boasts a City Hall, a Public Library and an Auditorium of true metropolitan distinction. The Hotel Whitcomb faces this Civic Center. This is one condition which makes its location unique—using that much-abused word in its literal sense. Another condition is that, unlike the other big hotels, it stands on the main thoroughfare, easily accessible to depots, the business and residence sections, and yet avoids the hurly burly of centermost San Francisco. However, with the rapid growth of upper Market street it cannot long retain this latter distinction.

What the unique features of architecture and management are will appear in the course of a more detailed description of the Whitcomb. The hotel has a frontage of 200 feet on Market street and extends south for a depth of 375 feet. The building is a fireproof one, consisting of steel columns encased in concrete and reinforced concrete walls, floors and roof. An idea of its massiveness may be obtained from the architects' statement that the walls have a minimum thickness of twelve inches. The partition walls are either concrete, brick or metal, with hard wall plaster surfaces on both sides. The entire inside finish is Jenisero hardwood, a very beautiful and highly prized inside finish. The building is seven stories high, not counting the sunroom.

DINING ROOM, HOTEL WHITCOMB, SAN FRANCISCO
Wright & Rushforth, Architects

SUN PORCH, HOTEL WHITCOMB, SAN FRANCISCO
Wright & Rushforth, Architects

TYPICAL GUEST ROOM, HOTEL WHITCOMB, SAN FRANCISCO
Wright & Rushforth, Architects

which crowns the roof. The six upper stories contain 400 large rooms, all with outside exposure. While most of these rooms have private baths, there are 24 public baths and the same number of lavatories. All baths are of the "built-in" variety.

Entering the hotel, the visitor finds himself in a lobby 50 feet wide and 120 feet deep. To his left is the flower stand, beyond that a barber shop and lavatory. To his right is the news and cigar stand, with the wine room beyond. As he approaches the desk, which is on the left, he passes four elevators, two on either hand. Beyond the desk are the private offices of the hotel. Opposite the desk on the right are the telephone exchange, telephone booths, check room and ladies' dressing room.

On this right side, too, is a large banquet room and a smaller room for private luncheon parties. Opening off the lobby at the rear is the main dining room, a spacious room splendidly lighted and ventilated. Immediately adjoining this to the right is the kitchen. Commanding the lobby is a mezzanine floor, with manicuring parlors to the right.

The lobby, the dining rooms and the mezzanine floor have great decorative distinction, having received special attention from Albert Herter, whose establishment devised the entire scheme of Whitcomb decoration. The lobby, in addition, has remarkable architectural dignity. It is in the truest sense what most hotel lobbies are only by courtesy—a marble lobby. Several varieties of marble have been used in its adornment. The columns and pilasters are of Verd d'Estee, while the wainscot is of Pavonazzo. Other marbles used in treating this part of the hotel are Grey Siena, Campan Vert, Tinos, Skyros and Numidian.

Mention has been made of one unique architectural feature possessed by the Whitcomb. This is the sunroom on the roof, named for its daytime attractiveness, though it is achieving an even greater popularity by night. An enclosed glass observation room and promenade was at that time contemplated for the hotel purposes, an idea which finally developed into the roof lounge scheme as it is today. The lounge, which is nearly 200 feet long, is provided with a dancing floor and furnished with tables, chairs, cushions, etc., in gay colors. It thus becomes a very important feature of the hotel, for it is used during the morning as a lounge, during the afternoon for tea and cards, and during the evening for music and dancing. Of course, its prime attraction is the magnificent view it commands of the city, the bay and the hills. There is no room in San Francisco open to the general public which affords anything like the panorama to be enjoyed by the traveler in this sunroom.

When the big building was in use as a temporary ·city hall, two small buildings immediately back of it on Stevenson street were also used by the city. These small structures have been joined, and are now part of the hotel plant. One is used as a laundry, the other as a garage. This garage is the unique feature of management which distinguishes the Whitcomb. For this garage is placed free of charge at the disposal of·all Whitcomb patrons. As the sunroom is the only room of its kind in the West, so this free garage stands alone in Western hoteldom. It has 5,000 square feet of floor space.

The basement of the Whitcomb is exceptionally well lighted and ventilated. It contains the servants' dining room, as well as a cafeteria for their use; ice plant; cold storage; bakery, etc. The boiler room equipment includes two 50-horsepower boilers, pumps, vacuum cleaning machinery, etc. A sterilizing and filtering plant purifies all the water used throughout the building.

In their work on the Whitcomb Messrs. Wright & Rushforth were assisted by the consulting engineers, W. T. Hanscom and Thomas Morrin, in the electrical and mechanical equipment respectively. Mr. P. J. Cole was superintendent of construction.

*   *

"The Girl He Left Behind Him"

"The Girl He Left Behind Him" is the heroine of an anecdote by Frances Pritchard, fair dancer in the "Passing Show of 1915."

A negro died without medical attendance, and the coroner went to investigate.

"Did Samuel Williams live here?" he asked the weeping woman who answered the door.

"Yussah," she replied between sobs.

"May I see the remains?" asked the coroner.

"I is de remains," she answered proudly.

*   *

$400,000 Shop for Union Iron Works

Plans are being prepared by Mr. John Reid, Jr., for an immense machine shop to be erected in Alameda for the Union Iron Works. It will cover an area 200 x 600 feet and will probably cost close to $400,000. Mr. C. H. Snyder is the engineer.

Structural Steel Prices, 1898 to 1917

THE accompanying diagram, reproduced from the December, 1916, Bridge Manual of the Oregon State Highway Commission, shows price fluctuations in steel from year to year at various stages in its progress from furnace to the erected bridge. The lowest line in the diagram represents pig iron (Pittsburgh District), the next two lines steel bars and structural steel in the Pittsburgh District, the second line from the top fabricated steel at site (average for Oregon), and the top line steel in bridge erected in Oregon.

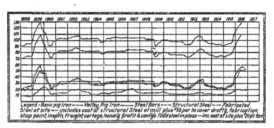

PRICE PER TON OF STRUCTURAL STEEL
FROM FURNACE TO BRIDGE

The curves representing the costs of pig iron, steel bars and structural shapes are drawn up from data from The Iron Age and are based on prices at Pittsburgh.

The line representing fabricated steel at the bridge site is obtained by adding $50 to these Eastern prices on structural shapes to provide for: Steel inspection, fabrication, shop inspection, waste in fabrication, draughting, shop painting, freight to Portland district, road haul and handling.

While this assumed figure of $50 is not a maximum, it is stated to be considerably higher than the mean or average cost of the sum of the items it is intended to cover, within the present zone of steel bridge construction in Oregon.

The line representing steel erected in place is obtained by adding $20 to the cost of the fabricated material at the site, to cover all costs of falsework, handling, erection and painting, and is a little better than a fair average price for steel bridge erection in Oregon. This line suggests in a graphical way, for the term of years which it covers, a base line about which, in comparative proximity to it, the prices paid for this work should have ranged themselves. The costs from mill to site and for erection and painting are based on the cost of a large number of structures built in Oregon. The Manual states that actual costs should run under, rather than over, the figures given.

Teaming rates vary considerably according to the topography of the country and condition of the roads. They also are subject to conditions of supply and demand, but, according to the Manual, a fair average price for teaming throughout the state is 30 cents per ton mile.

PLENTY OF SUNL'GHT ADDS A CHEERY WARMTH TO THE COUNTRY HOME

"EVEN THE SHADOWS HAVE A NEW SOFTNESS"

The Country Home of Today

By NOBLE FOSTER HOGGSON*

IF man's habitation gauges the status of humanity in the civilization of any period, an earnest of flowering into finer times is vouchsafed in the growing popularityof the country home. The country home manifests a mellowing and maturing of civilization. More and more are Americans, in all sections, inspired to build homes in the country and this indicates our happy departure from the crude youthfulness typical of new peoples, the arrival of public consciousness at the age of discretion. The Italian villa, the English landed estate, the French chateau, the Russian datcha are varying expressions of the same maturity. The process of transformation. is in accord with a natural law. In the earliest years in the life of a people men dwelt perforce in the wilderness, pioneers battling with the elements for food, for shelter, and for raiment; the youth of a people's commerce forces them to crowd together so they flock to the cities; entering into their manhood as a people or nation they seek again the country, finding, on their return, the pleasures of the pioneer but none of his hardships, the conveniences of the city but none of its distractions. The modern country home thus adjusts a balance for sane living; it is the combining of the best of yesterday's romance with the best of today's comfort.

When the feeling of the spring is in the air, and the grass in the parks puts forth furtively its first tiny blades of greenness, and the trees show that they are really alive again, and the sun gets up earlier in the morning and goes to bed later, when the joyous twitter of the birds and even the shadows have a new softness, and there's a new glow and warmth in all things, it is then that the heart of the city man turns, with tenderness and longing, to his real home in the country.

*Illustrations courtesy of Hoggson's Magazine.

"IN THE COUNTRY MAN REALLY LIVES"

He 'realizes, then, that it is in the country he really lives and that his town house has become to him, more and more, a place where he and his family stay during the winter, a place of convenience and of necessities associated with business, education, social engagements and duties. As the years go by, he notices a tendency to go to the country earlier and to stay later, for June is such a delightful month, with its perfume and roses, and the crisp, cool days of late October have a freshness and sparkle that give a glad, free boldness to his step as he walks briskly through the woods.

The country home means relaxing from the tension of life as we know it in the city, where, for the most part, carried on by the pressure of insistent

"TO STEP INTO ONE'S OWN GARDEN OF SWEETNESS"

duties we must do, there seems little time for the things one most ardently wishes to accomplish. In the country home, with fewer artificial distractions, there seems leisure for simpler hospitality, and a general freer spirit of living, for the reading of books one really tries to read in town, for one's own music which has been put aside because one has had to listen to the music of others at the opera and at concert.

The country home means an outdoor life, for many hours of every day, of direct communion with nature instead of speaking with her through an interpreter in even the best of the nature books. There is the glory of sunset behind the hills, where the royal coloring of the western sky is seen with proper distance, and the expanse of view is one rarely to be had in

"BY THE FIRESIDE AND——

the city for lack of proper vantage ground for observation. There is a new sense of reverence for the Infinite in the majesty and wonder of revelation of a summer sky at night with its millions of stars, as a tremendous sweep of uninterrupted vision.

——LIBRARY TABLE HE LINGERS"

There is a suggestion of the joy of creation in saying, "There will I plant a tree where one has never grown before, or that patch of barren land will blossom into a garden of beauty and perfume under my inspiration, or a lake will fill that hollow in the hills, because it will mean my realization of a dream of years." All this means much to the man or woman who sees the bigness and broadness of life in its true spirit.

To step into one's own garden of sweetness when the day is gently dusking into night, to know the flowers and the birds and to be calmed by the quiet plash of the fountain, to feel that special kinship with nature, that peculiar closeness that comes from feeling that one is walking on one's own land, that the earth itself there is one's own—is all part of a country home.

In the building or the remodeling of a house, to make a home in the country, so little may make it a lasting charm in the general scheme, so little may lose this charm. Every detail should be considered to make the house harmonize with its special needs, to take advantage of every possibility of situation and environment. Graciousness and generous hospitality should find expression in all of the many outer aspects and on the inside the sweet cheer and comfort of happy realization. It is not a mere matter of cost, but the sympathy, skill, spirit, and unity inspiring the building of a house that will make it the finest setting for a real home, a country home.

One may have, as Mr. Kipling says, "a little place at Tooting" or "a country house and shooting." For some, the large estate elaborately laid out with mansion ornately furnished is a necessary condition of their position.

No longer are we content to have our country homes mere storage places of pictures, books and furniture discarded from city houses. Those who live thus are still in the pioneer stage. We have come to see that the country home worthy its name must combine with the joy and the privilege of the glad, free, outdoor life the comfort and the convenience of the city dwelling. Herein the remodeller brings to his work the best in all the past modified by the best in our current civilization; he feels the olden spirit and expresses it in modern terms; he establishes a harmony between the life outside and the life within, and from original bareness evolves a country home of comfort, charm, and individuality.

In the problem of remodelling a country house three elements are vital in determining the plans: the site, the surroundings and the amount of money to be expended. The extent of the plot of ground, if restricted to a small area with little likelihood of future increase by accession, will be an important factor in deciding the general changes of the house, as some types of building require more space, further distance from the road and other essentials to bring out their best lines.

A country house should harmonize with its surroundings in design, color and materials. A house standing out boldly on the top of a hill and visible for miles should differ essentially in appearance from one nestling in among the trees at the edge of the woods, from a house on the banks of a lake or from a villa set back from the village street. Every natural advantage from the standpoint of health, view, light, and convenience should be utilized, every disadvantage neutralized. The amount of money to be expended is a factor determining the extent and manner in which the other two vital element may be best met and mastered.

A TYPICAL COUNTRY HOME IN SAN MATEO COUNTY

VIEW FROM THE TEA HOUSE

An Artistic California Garden

A S EVERY picture requires its frame, so every well-designed home should have its garden surrounding. Many times the perfect work of a clever architect has been marred by the failure of the owner to permit him to develop a harmonious garden scheme. The beauty of design is always augmented by a well-planned garden. No home plan is really complete without its outdoor living room. In California this is made easy because of the soil and favorable climatic conditions.

The Panama-Pacific International Exposition has had a large influence in the development of gardens in this community. The Exposition was the inspiration and Milton Roller the designer who made the grounds of Mr. Charles M. Whitney at Palo Alto, Cal., a veritable fairyland of charm and beauty.

"It is said that the garden should always be considered simply and wholly as a work of art and should not be made to look like nature. That is true enough. Nothing, indeed, can be poorer taste than the landscape gardener's imitations of nature, but there is another plan. Nature should have her own way in certain parts of your garden."

This seems to have been one of the principal thoughts in working out the scheme shown in the accompanying illustrations. From the entrance trellis, covered with purple wistaria over the stepping stones, past the sundial to the tea house, there is a constantly varying picture. The iris garden, with the rice bowl placed upon a juniper-covered rock, the Japanese corner surrounded by dwarf maples, magnolia and flowering crab-apple trees, the water splashing over the rocks to the lily pond skirting the wild flower covered hillock

LOOKING INTO A RIOT OF BLOOMS

SUMMER HOUSE AND SUNDIAL

appear on one side, while the rose garden, flower beds, grape arbor, Japanese stone lantern and dove cote attract the attention on the other.

One of the greatest ornaments to the garden is a fountain, but many are fatally ineffective. At the side of the house in front of the dining room windows a bird bath has been placed on a slender Pompeian standard. This is surrounded by tall grasses, Japanese iris and white-stemmed cut-leaf birches affording one of the most attractive features.

> "A garden is a lovesome thing, God wot!
>   Rose garden,
>   Fringed pool,
>   Fern'd grot—
> The veriest school of peace."

Here is an ideal spot for the family to have tea, to loiter and to dream.

* * *

Complete Cities to be Erected for U. S. Government

PLANS have been made and locations are now being selected for the 32 towns to be erected by the U. S. Government for mobilization camps for the new army of 1,000,000 men. Each camp will be of sufficient size to provide for about 22,000 soldiers and will be a complete city in itself. As soon as the camp sites are chosen the surveys will be made and contracts will be let. The construction work will be done by contract, under the supervision of Army officers.

To direct this undertaking Col. I. W. Littell of the Quartermaster General's Division, Washington, D. C., has been placed, by order of the Secretary of War, in general charge of cantonment construction. Col. Littell has already begun organizing his forces for the work.

It is estimated that 600,000 M feet of lumber will be required, and arrangements are being made to secure this in all parts of the country, preferably in the section where the camps will be located. Each of the 32 cantonments contain about 2,000 houses. These will include quarters for the men, officers' quarters, kitchens, mess halls, bathhouses, storehouses, and all the various buildings needed for housing the troops and providing for the varied activities of a big camp. Most of the buildings will be long, one-story structures, with some two-story houses. They will be of plain construction but will be of modern type, and the plans and sanitary arrangements will carry out the most approved methods. They are expected to be the best arranged, cleanest, and most up-to-date barracks yet erected.

Each town will cover about 720 acres, a little over a square mile, and this does not include the large area required for drill grounds at each camp.

The contractors who are to do the construction work will organize their own forces of carpenters, laborers, etc., but the building will be done under the direction of Army officers. Several officers from the Quartermaster's Department, Government inspectors, timekeepers, foremen, engineers, plumbers, etc., will be stationed at each camp town, and Col. Littell has already begun to arrange for the men required for this work.

In addition to the 32 camp towns, the Quartermaster's Department will erect groups of warehouses at points where Army stores are to be concentrated. The exact number and location of these has not yet been determined, as they are to be erected to meet the needs of the Army as they arise.

MR. CLARENCE R. WARD, ARCHITECT

Mr. Clarence R. Ward Discusses Architects and Architecture*

"WHY do the architects of San Francisco get along so badly?"

"Because there are so many clever men of so many schools. Though really there is only one school of architecture, the school of harmony, of harmonious relations of individuals and styles."

The answer is characteristic of Clarence Ward. In our architectural controversies his voice is rarely silent, and his words are always listened to with respect because he speaks with authority and avoids jarring, unnecessary personalities. Clarence Ward helps to resolve differences, not to embitter them....

"Would it be a good thing if all San Francisco architects lived in amity?"

"No. Because a great many stick to what they call 'the schools.' They spend six years in Paris, and the knowledge thus acquired they bring to America and apply to conditions based upon a life that is entirely different commercially, socially and so forth. To apply the ideas of 'the schools' to such conditions as well as to our totally different conditions of construction is very difficult. The problem is a fight to start with. So we must have fighting among the architects if there is to be anything accomplished.

"The architects lived in perfect amity, there was no fighting, when San Francisco was in the grip of the 'jigsaw' and the 'Queen Anne in front and Mary Ann in back' school of architecture. Yes, we must have fighting. The Willis Polks are more or less a necessity."

I think Clarence Ward is the only architect who can differ from Willis Polk without exciting Willis unduly. In essentials, however, they usually agree. The "stormy petrel" profoundly respects the attainments of Clarence Ward and covets his good opinion. Perhaps Willis sees in Clarence Ward what I see in him—the poet and the philosopher as well as the architect. Ward has not written a poem as Galen Howard has, but he has built several in stone and wood. Because he had the poet's vision he, before all others, picked the site of our World's Fair. As one of the great aggregation of architects who designed that Fair he wrought the poetry of his personality into the huge mass of Machinery Hall, making that tremendous building sing. He is also a philosopher, as were many great architects before him. On this account he'd rather build a home than any other structure.

"Do architectural controversies result in good?"

"In the long run they must," replied Ward. "The whole history of architecture is a controversy as to the right and the wrong. Angelo and Bramante's adherents had their controversy, not to mention others. Sometimes the most powerful had to give way before the consensus of opinion of those who knew what they were talking about, technically speaking."

This brought us directly to that delicate subject of controversy, William Faville's design for the State Building in the Civic Center. In that controversy Faville stands against "the consensus of opinion of those who know what they are talking about, technically speaking." These—and Ward is one of them—hold that Faville's design is out of harmony with the rest of the Civic Center. Faville appears to take the position of the Irish recruit who was reprimanded by the drill sergeant for being out of step and replied indignantly that he was keeping step, while the rest of the company was not.

I asked Ward to express himself concerning the current controversy.

"Speaking of the Civic Center generally," he said, "the first effort was to place it right. Many hold that it is a back door Civic Center. I maintain

*An interview by Edward F. O'Day in Town Talk.

that traffic should not pass through a Civic Center. The governmental portion of a city should be a quiet spot so that the buildings may be given the necessary dignity.

"Once the Civic Center has been placed, it would seem that the clever men who manage to win the competitions should at least endeavor to preserve harmony of proportion.

"The school boy knows that French and Italian Renaissance have their orders based on the same proportions, and as to the matter of scale, it is certain that it is impossible to place three stories in the basement of one building and one story in the basement of another, and still produce what is known as scale.

"Willis Polk, approaching one of the judges in the State Building competition, put the case very nicely by saying that the Place de la Concorde and the Piazza of St. Peter's enjoyed harmony of scale. He was answered by the judge calling attention to the fact that the Court of the Louvre was out of scale. Polk replied by asking if it wasn't a fact that all the French architects had been endeavoring to correct this.

"These matters of harmony are in no way intricate either technically or personally. I don't think they depend on the point of view so much as on the personality of those who attempt the work. Every man needs a safety valve. He can only find it by associating with his colleagues and discussing pure reason in the preparation of design. This was done with considerable success in the Exposition work."

"What do you think of our architects as a whole?"

"There are more clever architects here per capita than in any other place I know of. This is due to the fact that the younger men got their chance after the fire. Competition was very keen, and they had to prove their worth. They did.

"The local group is entitled to great credit for the upbuilding of the city, and for the selection of the site, the architecture, sculpture and artists of the Fair. They have not been given proper credit for this Fair work. The Fair gave us the opportunity to make comparisons: the local men compare favorably with their Eastern brethren. Personally I found those Easterners prepared to work with us in the greatest harmony, and I found them nearly all satisfied with the general result. This is very unusual with the big men in our profession."

"What do you think of the effort to preserve the California Building?"

"I don't think it possible to preserve any portion of the Fair. I think it is structurally impossible. But I should like to see the design of the California Building preserved in some concrete form. Much as I admired the Palace of Fine Arts in its former setting, I do not feel that it can be either in scale or in harmony with anything so far projected in its neighborhood."

"What is the original note in American architecture?"

"The application of architecture and decoration to the steel structure. The skyscraper was called into being in America by the necessity of congregating large numbers of people in restricted areas. It was made possible by the fast running elevator."

"Was San Francisco among the first to sound this new note?"

"San Francisco was not particularly alert in the matter. The Chronicle Building was the first attempt to clothe a tall skeleton with some sort of decent investiture. It was followed by the Crocker-Building, and closely thereafter by the Mills.

"But in architectural detail and decoration there is nothing new under the sun. The old forms may be beautifully applied, provided there be true knowledge of the problem to be solved. The Woolworth Building is a notable instance of success in this line."

"Has San Francisco done anything distinctive in the architecture of the home?"

"Not in the city proper. We have nothing very distinctive here, due to the fact that the fire stopped at Van Ness, on, the boundary of the principal residence district. If that district had burned, we might have developed something, slowly but along the right line. We have the talent here. But our suburban architecture compares favorably with any in the United States. I refer particularly to the peninsula and the surrounding bay country."

"Is the apartment house well regarded by architects?"

"It is a necessary evil. In San Francisco we have many fine apartment houses, and very livable for those who have moderate incomes. Personally I'd rather build one home than two apartment houses, though the intrinsic emoluments are vastly out of proportion. My biggest joy is to build a home—I don't mean a house. The architect is the one artist who is able to express the personality of the dweller—and he may even develop that personality. The housing of a family is most important. So, for that matter, is the housing of a commercial project. I know of many cases where buildings made for success or failure in business. Who knows but that may be true of families too?"

This was the philosopher talking—the architectural philosopher with ideals—the Clarence Ward who not only builds but dreams.

* * *

Factors Affecting the Cost of Structural Steel

THE factors affecting the cost of producing and the cost of purchasing structural steel work were discussed in two papers presented recently before the Engineers' Society of Western Pennsylvania. Abstracts of the paper read by Mr. George H. Danforth, structural engineer, Jones & Laughlin Company, follow:

"An item of design in which a high cost is frequently incurred to save a small amount of material is in the use of riveted trusses for roofs and similar places, when a simple beam will answer all purposes, and there are a great many cases where roof trusses are used on spans of 30 to 40, or even 45, feet, where a simple beam would answer all the purposes, weigh possibly a trifle more, but cost in dollars and cents considerably less. This feature is. of course, subject to modifications, due to the variation in the price of material and the price of labor. At the present time it would probably be economical in material, but even at the present time the saving, under these conditions, would not be as great as might be imagined, and the greater stability and ease of cleaning and painting that attaches to the use of a simple beam over that of a roof truss, which has a considerable portion of its surface inaccessible, is plainly evident.

"This idea of getting economy by the use of simple sections in place of complex riveted sections is nothing new. In the days when channels were held at prices of 3c and over, with angles and plates about half this price, it was a common practice to make bridge chords, even of small highway bridges. of four angles, two web plates and a cover plate, in place of two channels, and a cover plate, the conditions in the prevailing prices for material more than offsetting the additional shop work of using the plate and angle section.

"Another item that will occasionally affect costs and also affect delivery is the number of sizes that a designer will put into a structure. For instance, there is not sufficient difference between the dimensions of a 6x4-inch and a 6x3½-inch angle to prevent the use of either size throughout a job, rather than use both sizes. This is also true of 5x3½-inch and 5x3-inch angles, 3½x2½-inch and 3x3-inch angles; also 2½x2½-inch and 2x2½-inch angles. Each size that can be thus eliminated from a job means one less size to be realized before the fabrication of the job can be taken up, and so expedites delivery and reduces the work and troubles in putting through a piece of work.

"In this connection it might be well to mention that even nowadays we occasionally run across work wherein tees have been specified by the designer, in happy ignorance of the fact that there is probably not a more difficult section to get, even under normal mill conditions, than such tees.

"The same is similarly true, although in a lesser degree, of small beams and channels. Many designers use these sections for lintels, when two or three angles could just as well be used, and which would eliminate any necessity for punching or for separators or separator bolts, and with no appreciable increase in weight.

"Going further into detail, you will find the matter of detail design, which of course involves the question of shop drawings. It seems impossible to some people to make details without getting rivets into pockets, where they are very difficult, if not impossible, to drive! or of building up a section which has to be partially assembled and partially riveted before the balance of the section can be put together and the piece finished. There is also a tendency to use an excessive number of rivets. A few excess shop rivets are not serious and do not appreciably increase costs unless the excess is great.

"The contrary, however, is true in regard to field rivets, as we frequently find field rivets put in with a free hand, utterly regardless of what it will cost the erector to drive them. In one instance which occurs to me the designer insisted upon using 24 rivets to hold up one end of a 24-inch beam, which was not subject to any excessive load, and very carefully arranged the details so that 18 of these 24 rivets would be down in a pocket where it was impossible to properly back up the rivet in driving.

"Another detail item that seems to receive little attention, outside of drawing rooms that are directly in charge of a shop superintendent, are changes in sizes of holes and in sizes of rivets. This is a frequent item of expense and a constant source of trouble, as, unless everyone connected with a job is constantly on guard, the condition will arise where a member that has been built using ¾-inch rivets will connect with a member that has been built using ⅞-inch rivets, and the holes for the field connections, instead of being the same size, will be of different sizes. In other words, of sizes suitable for the use of rivets used in the individual member.

"Column splices constitute another item wherein much money is often uselessly spent. With the ordinary plate and angle columns there is not much need of any splices other than plates on the flanges. An attempt to splice the web also frequently results in bad holes and other difficulties, while a web splice arranged with angles generally serves no useful purpose other than covering up, possibly, a case of a poorly milled end.

"Due attention is rarely given to the economies of duplication. To build one truss is expensive, but to build a large number of duplicate trusses is a relatively cheap operation, and it would frequently be an economy to make a large number of parts of a structure exact duplicates, even though it involved more material than it would to make each separate and individual truss or part specifically designed for its work."

The Ninth National City Planning Conference

By CHARLES HENRY CHENEY, Architect

TO the San Francisco Chapter, American Institute of Architects.
Gentlemen:

I have the honor to submit herewith my report on the proceedings of the Ninth National Conference on City Planning, held in Kansas City on May 7, 8 and 9, 1917, which I attended as your delegate. About 140 delegates were present at the Conference, and most of the important cities in the United States were represented. This convention was declared by its president, Frederick L. Olmsted, to have been the most important and useful one ever held by the Conference. The local newspapers gave much publicity to the work of the convention and it is interesting to quote from an editorial in the Kansas City Times (May 10th):

"A few years ago nobody knew what city planning meant. We all understood that a well-managed business is planned for the future. But we had a notion that a city could grow in a haphazard way and there was no occasion to attempt to direct its growth along rational lines. A city plan was supposed to be merely a civic center about a city hall or court house.

"Now we have learned that we were mistaken. We have discovered that we can plan for traffic ways, for industrial additions, for correct housing. Experience has taught us that too wide streets in the residence districts are wasteful. We have found that convenience and beauty and healthfulness are important city assets, and now we are discovering that there are trained men who can help us get these things—not visionaries, but men who have based their work on experience."

Large Cities Now Have Permanent Commissions.

It was reported that practically all the large cities of the country with the exception of San Francisco—in fact, something over two hundred cities in all—have appointed permanent city planning commissions to advise and recommend to the mayor, city council or board of supervisors, as the case may be, well-thought-out plans and ordinances for zoning the city and for initiating and guiding city development in a business-like way, which politically elected boards find it difficult to do. By making it definitely somebody's business officially to plan and advise, these cities as a result are doing most constructive work, often effecting definite economies on a large scale. They seem to have overcome the continual bickering in each little local district which fights the improvements of other sections of the city, a matter from which San Francisco has long suffered, as our Mayor and Board of Supervisors can testify.

City planning involves consideration of zoning or districting so as to limit the height and bulk and use of all buildings, the study of railway terminals, traffic ways, street widenings, parks and playgrounds and housing. Mr. Olmsted says that city planning is to show the divergent interests in the city's growth how to pull together for the best use of the natural opportunities of the community.

Zoning or Districting of Cities

The great importance of zoning or districting of cities was emphasized at practically every session of the Conference. It was evident that the experts present without question regarded it as the first fundamental step. California's progress came in for a great deal of favorable comment, particularly as the decisions of the United States Supreme Court upholding the Los Angeles Zone Ordinance seemed to be the basis for districting in New York and most of the other cities of the country.

At the special session on zoning, papers on different phases of the subject were read and discussed by Lawson Purdy of New York City, Charles H. Cheney of San Francisco, Edward M. Bassett of New York City, Frank D. Stringham of Berkeley, and a number of others. Mr. Purdy during his address said:

"Every city contains horrible examples of homes ruined by the intrusion of garages, stores or factories. Every large city in this country has buildings so high that they steal their neighbors' light and air and monopolize the streets. Every one of these buildings is an extra hazardous investment. When its light and air has gone its tenants go, and the rent goes and the mortgagee can have the deed.

"Some of the dearest things of life may not be reasoned in money, but all the advantages of city life and city ownership may be measured by money. Surely the general welfare demands that we shall zone our cities to protect our homes, protect life and protect values."

Mr. Purdy stated that one building which was assessed at $3,900,000, and which was mortgaged for $3,500,000, actually sold for $3,000,000 after its light had been taken away by surrounding high buildings. One 22-story building which rented its floor space at $1 per square foot per year so long as it had light and air borrowed from its neighbors, now rents its space for 45 cents per square foot per year, its original tenants having vacated on account of the want of light and air resulting from the construction of new buildings on three sides. The reduction of values below Twenty-fourth street in New York has been enormous on account of the construction of too high buildings. When the Equitable Insurance Company contemplated the erection of its new building on Broadway the neighboring buildings got together and offered the company two and a quarter million dollars if the company would not build above the ninth story; that is to say, they would pay that amount for the light and air above that height. The company asked two and a half million dollars for that privilege and the project fell through. The company then built its present 40-story building. Economic waste results from such haphazard construction, and there is no doubt but that New York should have long ago adopted an ordinance limiting the height of the buildings to be constructed in any part of the city. In July of last year New York passed an ordinance covering the entire city, in which it has limited the height and bulk of buildings and divided the city into three classifications of uses.

The Berkeley districting plan is much more complete than that of New York in segregating the different uses of buildings most carefully to protect residence districts. As probably more than 90 per cent of the buildings in Berkeley, as in Los Angeles and most other Western cities, are used for single family residences only, the problem out here is to protect that type of building. In New York City, where a very large proportion of the buildings are high, congested apartment buildings, the problem is different. The Berkeley plan makes the formation of districts optional, which evidently would leave open a large area of the city undistricted for many years to come unless the city takes steps to classify the remainder of the city without waiting for the petition of the local residents in each neighborhood. It seemed to be the general opinion of this Conference that it was advisable to district the whole city at once and that Berkeley had best do this immediately to protect its standing in court. The Berkeley and Los Angeles ordinances do not, of course, establish heights of building districts or area districts as in New York, although the new California State Zoning Law now directs all California cities to do so.

Railway Terminals

George A. Damon of Pasadena presented an interesting paper on "Interurban Passenger Terminals." He showed how important it was that Los

Angeles secure better terminals for its suburban trains; that the latter could only successfully compete with the jitney bus when the street cars were not hampered by other traffic in going through the densely populated districts of the city and could operate trains with sufficient speed. Los Angeles should have all of its suburban terminals connected underground so that passengers could pass through the city without their being transferred over the crowded surface thoroughfares.

The chief engineer of the Public Service Railway Corporation of New Jersey showed by lantern slides how Newark, New Jersey, had partially solved its transportation problem by constructing a modern central street car terminal and arranging for the taking on and discharge of passengers upon different levels.

Lawson Purdy told how the electrification of the New York Central Railroad removed the smoke nuisance and added millions of dollars to the value of the property upon the street which lies over the underground portion of the road. The trains are 26 feet underground in an open cut and no vibrations can be felt in the buildings.

Kansas City has an excellent Union Railroad Station, where trains of all roads pass through the city with the greatest economy of operation. Station and adjuncts cost approximately $40,000,000, the cost being borne by twelve railroads.

Denver has a modern end-on union station, but trains have to back out, which of course is not the best kind of an arrangement.

A. Pearson Hoover of New York read a paper on the subject of "The Industrial Terminal and Its Relation to the City Plan." This paper discussed the economic advantage of an industrial terminal, such as the famous Bush Terminal of New York.

Parks and Playgrounds.

Mr. Jay Downer, engineer of the Bronx Parkway Commission, in an illustrated lecture, demonstrated how the Bronx river for the entire distance from Bronx Park to Croton Dam had been reclaimed from an unsanitary, unsightly water course and converted into a beautiful stream bordered by parks and playgrounds, with a driveway along its course, all of which is destined to become the recreation ground of millions of people.

Chicago has found in recent years that many of the smaller children in the city could not use the larger parks, for the reason that they were generally located too far apart and too far from the homes of these children. The city, therefore, recently created a special park commission to study this question. As a partial result of the labors of this commission, Chicago purchased during the year 1915 forty-eight small parks scattered throughout the city.

During the last twenty years Kansas City (population approximately 250,000) has spent $16,000,000 upon its park and boulevard system, paid for on the district assessment plan. This system is a source of health and much pleasurable enjoyment to that city, and one of which they are justly proud. One of the Park Commissioners of Kansas City suggested that cities hereafter in their park development provide landing spaces for aeroplanes. City planners generally are recommending that playgrounds be required in close vicinity to school buildings. In certain parts of New York traffic is excluded from some of the streets during a portion of the day, in order that children may have a place to play.

Traffic Ways

The increased traffic resulting from the introduction of motor cars presents a most serious problem. In some instances the only remedy is to cut through new streets or to widen existing streets. Mr. Nelson P. Lewis pointed out that there are four ways of meeting this necessity:

1. The setting back of the curb.
2. The actual widening of a street by purchase of land.
3. Requiring new buildings to be set back from the property line, the city acquiring an easement until such time as it may wish to acquire the fee.
4. Putting the sidewalks under arcades, the city acquiring an easement for that purpose through the ground floor of existing buildings which are remodeled to include the arcade.

The second method, which is the most efficient, is, of course, the most expensive. When the right to excess condemnation is once clearly established, the expense to cities' of widening streets would be reduced. We shall have an opportunity to vote on a constitutional amendment granting cities this power in California at our next general election.

In the last ten years Chicago widened Michigan avenue at an expense of about $8,000,000 and widened Twelfth street at an expense of $4,000,000.

New York has recently widened, or is now widening, two streets at a total expense of about $5,000,000 each. Mr. Lewis gave one illustration where an owner received in damages for the taking of land for the widening of the street a sum equal to what he had paid for the property, and the owner then sold the remaining portion of his lot for a sum equal to the damages paid, and this same owner had protested against the amount of damages which he had been allowed.

Mr. Hill, City Engineer of Kansas City, urged the separation of the light fast-moving vehicular traffic from the slower and heavier vehicles. Traffic ways must form a complete system, and if they are not in the direct flow of business upon easy grades they fail of their functions. Traffic is sure to follow the line of least resistance. It will go out of its way to avoid a bad road or a grade. There is no doubt but that a great deal has been accomplished by merely making traffic rules and regulations. A tremendous amount of traffic can be taken care of when well handled. This is well illustrated by the intensive use made of the Great White Road to Verdun during the time of the German assault in February. All refugees and all of the munition supplies and ambulances to take care of the force of 800,000 men had to pass over this road. Over 30,000 passed one point of this road in one day, counting the vehicles going in both directions. If any one vehicle became disabled, it had to be immediately thrown out of line.

City Planning

Most of our cities have not been scientifically planned and there is a common misconception that city planning and the city beautiful are synonymous terms. I quote Mr. J. Horace McFarland, president of the American Civic Association:

"There are people who imagine that city planning consists of covering lamp posts with wriggling dolphins and ornamenting buildings with bunches of grapes and flowers tied with impossible stone ribbons. Some cities have been built with this idea. Most of them look like a man in evening dress to his waist and with overalls the rest of the way down. A city plan has to be either right or wrong. Pompeii, Babylon and the most ancient of cities had their city plans.

"There is one city planning crown of which we can always boast; it is the National Capital. It was designed for a national capital by the man for whom it was named. At a time when the colonists were hanging onto a strip of the Atlantic coast by their eyebrows, George Washington planned a city for future years. All cities should be planned in this way, for a purpose and for the future."

Mr. Charles E. Merriam, former Alderman of Chicago, well expressed the purpose of city planning:

"City planning is city conservation. It is the same work on a small scale as national conservation is on a larger. We may measure our gains in square feet of land. We may appraise them in dollars and cents. We may chronicle them by the clock in terms of transportation time. We may gauge them by the reduction in the grim reaper's toll of death and the sweeping ravages of disease. But we cannot measure by rule, scale, compass or computer the precious human values, the warmth and brightness of more abundant life, the happiness and joy of larger living, those personal values which transcend all others, and whose protection and promotion is the supreme end of government."

I have the honor to report my election to the Board of Governors of the American City Planning Institute, newly organized at this Conference to increase the efficiency and service of the country's trained city planners for the benefit of the cities which employ them.

* * *

Let Engineering Students Finish Their Courses

There is a steadily growing feeling that engineering classes should not be broken up because of war. We are glad to note that at least two engineering periodicals voice that sentiment.

Chancellor Brown of New York University has advised engineering and medical students to finish their courses, the engineers to take military tactics as part of their curriculum.

There are about 10,000,000 men between the ages of 21 and 30, of whom less than 17,000 are taking courses in engineering colleges, or one in 600. About an equal number of engineering students are below the age of 21. As operators of machine guns or users of rifles, these partly trained engineers would be no more effective than men entirely without engineering training. As graduate engineers, however, they will be vastly more useful to the nation.

If the war is to be short, these undergraduate engineers will be of little or no use as engineers in the war. If it is to be long, their usefulness after graduation will be great, particularly if during the remainder of their course at college they are required to study the principles of military engineering.

Already many engineering students have enlisted in the officers' reserve corps, and are not only continuing their regular engineering studies, but are studying military engineering. In addition they are spending their recreation hours is physical training under military instructors. Engineering students at Yale were among the first to volunteer for this strenuous double duty.— Engineering-Contracting.

* * *

A Scheme to Produce Artistic Buildings

One method of accelerating the artistic impulse, and one that would seem to offer great possibilities, has, says the American Architect, been adopted in the South American city of Buenos Ayres. That municipality exempts from taxation each year the most beautiful building erected during the preceding twelve months, and in addition awards a medal to the architect. A more direct form of encouragement, or one that would possess a greater appeal for the average owner, it would be difficult to devise. It is possible that the decoration of the architect may be unnecessary to the success of the plan, but doubtless it is with the idea of taking cognizance rather than paying a reward that the medal is bestowed. The plan might well receive consideration by municipalities in this country. Then, possibly, the average citizen would learn to appreciate the inherent as well as the commercial value of good architecture to an extent that might render unnecessary the offer of any special prize or distinction to induce him to co-operate in the production of architecturally meritorious buildings.

"Doing Our Bit"*

By CHARLES H. BEBB, Architect

A YEAR ago at our last annual meeting it was my privilege to speak to you on the relations of the architect to the contractor, pointing out, among other things, that the best results were always produced by co-operation, and that, looking back into history, the great epochs in the evolution of the human family found permanent and concrete expression only when the nations producing them became unified and thought and acted as a single intelligence. I dwelt on the rampant commercialism of this, our passing era, the desire of wealth for wealth's sake and for what it could bring in the way of ease, luxury and idle gratification, for the most part, and its entire lack of national spirit. But I also said, if you will remember, that the dawn of a new era was with us. In the midst of our feverish endeavors a pause had come. While a year ago we were ourselves at peace with the world, a mighty cry had reached us, had penetrated our self-assumed national isolation, and we listened. The din of strife was in our ears. Nations far removed from us were in battle and as a great nation ourselves we paused to listen, to inquire, to think. Perhaps because of our wonderful geographical isolation from other powers we failed to understand at first the underlying reason for the awful conflict. Now we know and fully realize the issue at stake. The liberty of the nations of the world is at issue, liberty from the dominating influence of an arrogant power that has taken as its motto that force and force only is the supreme reason, has proclaimed it to the world and for forty years has prepared to bring the peoples of the world under its yoke.

Not, therefore, for territorial acquisition, or for vain glory, or for the possible greed of huge indemnities, not primarily because some American lives have been lost and some of our ships sunk, but because liberty, liberty the ethical basis and reason of our national existence, is at stake. Two years and ten months ago today war was declared in Europe, and thirty-two days ago, the 2d of April, we as a nation entered the conflict. Ever during that period the struggle has grown fiercer and more awful, and on one side more brutal and more barbarous. Why the hesitation on our part for so long a time? It was because the vital forces of national unification were in process. To my mind the proof that we are a great nation is this very hesitation. Press and platform could not stampede us into war. The strident voice of unjust criticism did not avail. We were accused of "slothful cowardice bred of mammon serving peace, that we hesitated from inner division and distraction, that we were not a nation but a huge boarding house for the accommodation of alien peoples, that we had become corrupted by over-much prosperity and a sentimentally humanitarian pacifism." But it was not so. The masses, the American people, were being fused into a single being, the national mind was made up, and on the 2d day of April the hour struck and our great President spoke for the nation and Congress re-echoed his voice. On that day the national standard, the stars and stripes, the emblem of life, liberty and happiness, took its rightful place in the fight for the freedom of nations against the aggressive militarism of a great power.

You have seen and heard and read the nation's response to the government's call. From every city, town and village, from every corner of our vast country, the will to serve has been expressed in no uncertain tones. Let me quote a few out of the thousands of incidents. "Producers of copper are now supplying the government's war needs at less than half the market price. Producers and manufacturers of steel are doing likewise. The free use of the largest plants suitable to the manufacture of war supplies and munitions has been offered to the government. The leaders in every industry, trade and

*Address delivered at Second Annual Banquet, Washington State Chapter, American Institute of Architects and Master Builders Association of Seattle, May 4, 1917.

profession have offered the facilities at their disposal for the use of the government without thought of remuneration. More patriotic action, and action speaks louder than words, can scarcely be imagined." (American Architect.)

Every American man, woman and child wants to do his or her bit. What are we doing, we architects, we builders, and, represented with us tonight, what can organized labor do? The American Institute of Architects, of which the Washington State Chapter is a branch, through its president has offered the President of the United States the services of its members. A committee, going beyond their own membership, has sent out applications for any qualified service they can render to 8,241 architects in the country. I do not know what the Master Builders' Association of Seattle has done, but the National Association has tendered the services of its members to the President. I do not know what organized labor in Seattle has done, but the national representatives are in line with the government. David Lloyd George, in a speech before the British Parliament last December, said: "We realized that it is impossible to conduct war without getting the complete and unqualified support of labor, and we were anxious to obtain their assistance and their counsel for the purpose of the conduct of the war." The new ministry of labor was formed not only for the purposes of settling disputes about labor conditions or wages, but having also the well-being of labor in its charge. Labor is the great branch and sinew of the American people and I am certain allows no peer in its feelings of national patriotism. *It will do its bit, and its bit will be a large one.

Effective national organization of our entire citizenship is the essential factor for victoriously and expeditiously terminating this awful struggle.

And what of the future, when this fight for international right, international honor, international good faith, has been won and strife has ceased? Borne in upon our minds is a vision of triumphant democracy for the peoples of the world, government of the people, by the people, for the people. This is the message that the standard of our country bears with it as it is carried on the battlefields of Europe. Already one great autocratic dynasty has fallen, the Romanoffs and their traditions are now inscribed in the archives of past history, and Russia, the newest republic, seeks guidance in the formative stage of its government from the United States; a commission is going to that country, if it has not already started. The voices of other people of other nations lacking self-government are distinctly heard above the din of battle, crying for the inalienable right of mankind, crying for freedom from the dictation of any king or caste or oligarchy. If in the throes of all the pain, all the torture, all the suffering of the nations now fighting, a new child is brought forth, freedom for the race, then perhaps the price paid in blood and anguish will not have been too great. And when Time's gentle hand has effaced the evidence in Europe's battlefields of this great war, and the plow and the furrow bear testimony to man's peaceful industry, and wounds are seared, and a new generation of little children pluck flowers in the sunlit fields, a new religion will come to the world, the religion of tolerance and complete consideration of your neighbor, and peace, universal peace, will be the most militant sentiment in the human heart.

*   *   *

Miss Julia Morgan Plans Private School

Miss Julia Morgan, Merchants Exchange building, San Francisco, has let a contract to D. B. Farquharson to build a $60,000 girls' school on Jackson street, east of Lyon, San Francisco, for Miss Katherine Burk. Miss Morgan has also prepared plans for a private garage and play garden for Mr. E. W. Newhall on Pacific avenue. A garage to accommodate forty machines is being built for the State Y. W. C. A. at Asilomar from plans by Miss Morgan.

Steam Heating—Reminiscent and Otherwise

By JAMES I. KRUEGER*

THE first instance of where steam heating for buildings was applied in this country was in the building known as the Eastern Exchange Hotel in Boston, Mass. This steam job was installed about the year 1847. Heating in those days was done entirely by pipe coils. Some years afterward different forms of cast iron radiators were made use of. A very popular radiator in those days, and used all through New England, was the Mattress Radiator. It was made of sheet iron in such a way that the steam passed up and down as in the case of hot water radiators of today. In the early sixties the Nason Radiator was gotten out. This is the old pipe radiator where each length of pipe contained just one foot of radiation and was screwed into a cast iron base. This radiator had to be made exactly right, as it could not be enlarged, as is possible today with cast iron radiators. This is the same Nason who went into partnership with Mr. J. J. Walworth, from which sprung the great manufacturing firm known as the Walworth Manufacturing Company.

Among the other individuals who helped to perfect the first steps in steam heating may be mentioned Mr. Miles Greenwood of Cincinnati, who originated the nest or coil of upright pipes connected by bends. The first closed system whereby the water of condensation is returned to the boiler was perfected by Mr. Thomas Tasker of Philadelphia. Several have laid claim to having invented the first steam trap. Professor Mapes of New York is, however, given credit for this by the best authorities. One of the best treatises on steam heating was written by Baldwin and for years this was recognized as the standard book on heating. This was in the days when every steam fitter in the country made his own plans, and, as they were more commonly called, lay-outs of heating system. Such a confusion arose from this fact because each fitter had his own notions as to the size of mains, boilers, radiators, etc., that some very queer installations resulted. This was in the days of two-pipe jobs, which eventually merged into one pipe and from which it graduated into vacuum and is now getting into vapor system of heating. The confusion was so marked when fitters were making their own plans that it was reported by a trade paper, which made inquiry as to pipe sizes from thirty different steam fitters, that the answers did not agree in all respects from any of them. This resulted in the laying out and making of plans for heating systems going into the hands of technical engineers, where it properly belongs.

This is by the way of preface to the comparative merits in the trade as it exists between this country and Europe. In the writer's humble opinion, America is so much farther advanced than Europe in the way of heating buildings and in the proper installation of sanitary appliances that there is no comparison.

While traveling in Europe, nearly twenty years ago, the writer had letters of introduction to firms in the heating line both in France and Germany. He also had letters of introduction from the old American Boiler Company, which concern old-timers no doubt will remember.

We first visited the firm of Nahrun & Pertsch in Berlin. We found at that time that they were procuring the material for heating from this country. While some sort of a boiler was made in Germany, it did not compare at all with the American make. The installations over there were of the very primitive kind. When speaking to the firm of the superior quality of our

*California representative of the Illinois Engineering Company, Pacific building, San Francisco. Mr. Krueger has spent thirty years in the heating line and enjoys the confidence of the trade throughout the coast.

material, they would fly into a rage, but when we asked them why they found it necessary to order the material from this country they could not answer. In France we visited Mr. Henry Hammill. Mr. Hammill is a very fine gentleman, who was still alive and hearty upon our last visit, five years ago. Mr. Hammill is a wealthy bronze manufacturer residing in Paris. He visited our Chicago Fair in 1893. He was so favorably impressed with the exhibits of heating houses by steam that he took up this study in Philadelphia. Being an educated civil engineer, it took him a comparatively short time to master the scientific end of the business. Mr. Hammill was one of the commissioners of the Paris World's Fair in 1899. We found Mr. Hammill a very liberal-minded gentleman and more than willing to give the United States all credit due for excelling in steam and hot water heating. Up to Mr. Hammill's introduction of our system of heating there was not a steam heating plant in the city of Paris, although there were a great many hot-air heating plants. Mr. Hammill, like his German contemporaries, was procuring his heating material from this country.

Since 1897 the American Radiator Company has established factories both in France and in Germany for the manufacture of heating appliances and both countries are trying to keep up with us at the present time. Germany has something like a dozen factories making heating appliances. Mr. Monahan had charge of the American Radiator Company in Paris. He joined the French Red Cross Society and died in France about two or three months ago. The American Radiator Company's manager in Berlin is Mr. Kluckeman, and he, too, was very glad to see anyone engaged in the heating business from the United States.

Of course, heating is not installed over there nearly as universal as here. Only the more pretentious homes and the larger important buildings have heating plants. Back in '97 Paris was full of cesspools. To these all the plumbing in the buildings was attached and they were cleaned out by scavengers periodically. Venting is hardly known over there. They simply run a 4-inch stack through the roof and install a combination sewer and tide trap just inside of the foundation. Many of the joints to the fixtures are made with putty.

It appears to American visitors that there is a lack of sanitation existing abroad which fortunately does not exist in the United States. The fixtures are not nearly as neat in appearance and in some of the houses the toilets are constructed to within a few inches of the floor. It is not an uncommon thing in Paris that when one wants a bath a hot water vender is called from the street, who brings a sort of rubber bath tub and furnishes hot water from his cart in the street by the bucket until the necessary amount has been supplied. The only thing attractive about this is the cheapness, which, of course, does not appeal to the average American.

In the last ten or fifteen years cesspools are gradually being done away with and connections made to the very fine sewer system in Paris. It is hard to understand why this sewer was used only for rain water in the past years. Of course, conditions are improving right along and getting better each year. The same thing related of Paris as to their plumbing holds good in Berlin, except that in the latter city the system of connecting all houses to the sewer has been made use of. The Berlin sewer system is considered a very fine one and it is claimed it was introduced by an American. All the soil coming from the Berlin sewer is, through an elaborate system of pumping, used as a fertilizer for the surrounding country. One thing the writer thinks they can teach us over there is the universal use of public comfort stations. A city the size of San Francisco should have at least a dozen comfort stations in place of the single one existing in Union Square.

SPERRY FLOUR COMPANY'S NEW PLANT, VALLEJO
Maurice C. Couchot, C. E.

BUNGALOW IN MADERA, CALIFORNIA
Ralph P. Morrell, Architect

SLATE ROOF ON TUDOR RESIDENCE, NEAR LOS ANGELES
Morgan, Walls & Morgan, Architects

Roofing the Home*
I—Slate Roofs

T IS only recently that Pacific Coast architects have taken to using or rather specifying slate roofs. The high cost of this material has doubtless been a considerable factor in discouraging its general use. The average owner is satisfied with a shingle or tile roof, although for some types of houses these materials are not altogether suitable. The slate roof is most popular in sections of the country where it is produced. The fact that it is not more widely used in other parts of the country is due first to the high cost of transportation and second to a lack of progressiveness on the part of the manufacturers and vendors of slate in the matter of popular education (advertising) as to the merits of this material.

Within the past two years, however, some efforts have been made on the part of manufacturing concerns to bring before the building public general knowledge of the subject in hand through the medium of attractive literature and advertising which is not made up principally of a careful description of the weaknesses of other roofing materials and methods; but rather devoted to a description of the aesthetic and physical qualities of slate and its logical appeal to the home builder and home owner.

Slate shingles are, of course, natural rock products. The solid rock formations from which slate is quarried were the result of terrific heat and pressure applied simultaneously, resulting in a hard, non-porous rock varying considerably in color and grade.

*A series of articles intended to give the reader some assistance in the selection and construction of roofs. Acknowledgment is made to the publishers of Realty for much valuable data and to the Merrill Roofing Company of San Francisco. Succeeding articles will be published on terra cotta tile, redwood and cedar shingles, tar and gravel and ready prepared roofs. There will be no reference made in these articles to any particular brand or make of roof, the purpose of the series being merely to acquaint the reader with the merits of each material, leaving a final selection to his own judgment.

SLATE ROOF FOR OFFICE BUILDING, OAKLAND
BENJ. G. McDOUGALL,   ARCHITECT

By the careful use of explosives the slate is taken from deep quarries in blocks weighing several tons. These blocks are conveyed to buildings where skilled workmen split them into sheets of required thickness. The sheets are then trimmed to size on a machine and the slate piled in yards for shipment. Slate shingles run about three-sixteenths of an inch in thickness and may be had in stock sizes varying from 12x6 inches to 24x14 inches. For residence use, and on small buildings, the sizes varying in width from 6 to 10 inches and in length from 12 to 20 inches are recommended.

Slate may be had in a wide variety of soft and attractive colorings. Some of the popular shades offered by quarries are: Unfading green, blue black; unfading mottled purple; variegated green and purple; unfading crimson red; black weathering green; variegated purple; rustic grey and sea-green. It will be noted that slate comes in unfading colors and in colors which fade or change through weathering. In the purchasing of slate the color question should be given careful consideration and purchases made from quarries or dealers of known standing, whose guarantee has value.

In common with other types of roofing, there are many reported instances of the failure of slate roofing and careful investigation almost invariably results in the discovery that the human equation is at fault through the various mediums of carelessness, stupidity or plain dishonesty. The writer knows of instances where steel nails were used and rust ensued, allowing loosening of the slates; where slates were loosened by failure of the substructure; where snow was driven up under slates, melted and frozen lifting the units; where flashings and valleys were improperly constructed.

In applying slate shingles steel nails should never be used because of their tendency to rapid deterioration due to rust. Bronze composition or galvanized nails only should be used. Nails with lead washers are invariably the most satisfactory. The slate should be drilled and countersunk, as it will be found that in the ordinary "punched" slate the countersunk surface is always rough and almost invariably the nail-heads will be found holding at one point only. Sharp shouldered nails should never be used.

To the matter of carelessness on the part of those having to do with the construction and maintenance of the roof may be ascribed many of the complaints which are offered in regard to various types of roofing. For instance, painters may work about the house some time after the roof is laid, or the chimney may need repairing. The work is done and some time later there is trouble about leaks in the roof. Naturally one does not think to blame the painter or mason for roof trouble. Complaint is made and in many cases it is found that shingles have been cracked or broken off by accidental contact of ladders, scaffolding supports, walking on the roof or other natural causes which did not arise from any defect in the roofing itself.

In the construction of the roof the builder should insist that great care be taken in laying the shingles, that the right nails are used and used properly, that flashings are properly laid, that slating at hips is done in the standard manner. It is well in this connection to see that the roofer selected to do the work has a good reputation to stand on and that he understands thoroughly how to lay slate shingles. Too often the owner leaves this matter in the hands of others and later regrets that he has done so.

Slate shingles constitute a fairly heavy deadload, ordinary commercial slate running in weight from 650 to 750 pounds per square. (A "square" is the standard of roof measure and means the amount of roofing material necessary to cover 100 square feet. A "square" of slate, then, would mean a sufficient number of any size of slate to lay 100 square feet of roof, allowing for the standard 3-inch lap.) This fact must be given some consideration in the

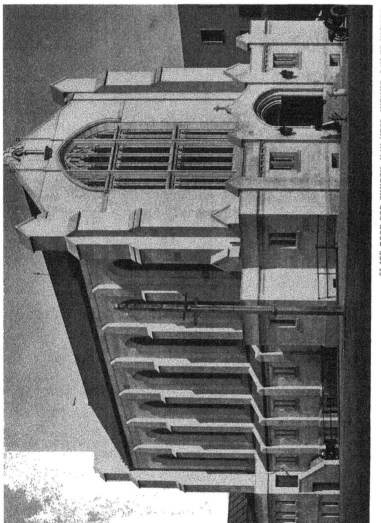

SLATE ROOF FOR CHURCH, VAN NESS AVENUE, SAN FRANCISCO
BENJ. G. McDOUGALL, ARCHITECT

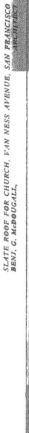

design of the roof substructure, although the necessity for having this structure particularly heavier than that of the ordinary shingle roof is somewhat over-emphasized.

· Slate roofs are usually laid either on the ordinary wood frame with sheathing boards or on a steel frame with angle purlins where fireproof steel construction is used in the building.· On the wooden frame the sheathing boards are laid in the usual manner, after which a layer of felt paper is placed over the sheathing, the roof marked off with chalk lines for guidance in placing the rows of slate and the slate carefully laid, care being taken to leave the roof without crack or loose unit.

In fireproof steel construction the slate shingles are placed on metal angle purlins instead of sheathing. These purlins are spaced so that each slate unit is supported at the middle and both ends. The nailing is through the center of the shingle, soft metal clinch nails being driven down beside, and clinched around, the purlin. This results in a rigid and indestructible roof construction, providing the work has been carefully done.

Another interesting type of roof construction in which slate is employed is that of the reproduction of old Tudor stone roofing so often seen in the picturesque sections of England. In this type of roofing, for the purpose of obtaining a great degree of strength and durability the slate shingles are laid in a weak lime-cement mortar. Incidentally this type of roof construction is considerably more expensive than ordinary slate roofing, running in cost approximately $17.50 per square laid.

Several other methods of breaking away from the regularity of appearance created by the use of equal sized units in slate roof construction are known generally under the title of Old English Method of slate roofing. This consists of using slates decreasing in thickness from the eaves to ridge of the roof; using slates decreasing in size from eaves to ridge for the purpose of relieving monotony of equal rectangles and adding to perspective; or using slates of random widths which tend to break up vertical and diagonal line effects.

Where the dwelling has a flat roof there is available a type of slate roofing which gives excellent service and may be walked upon without damage or danger of causing leakage. This is what is known as slate paving for flat roofs.

It consists of a built up roofing on concrete deck or wooden sheathing. Sheathing paper, and alternate layers of pitch and tarred felt are built up to the required thickness. .The slate units are then embedded in asphalt to cover the entire surface and the result is a leakproof and practically indestructible roof.

The cost of slate roofing is figured by the square. Cost of slate sufficient for one square constitutes the cost unit of quotations from quarriers. This varies from $10 to $12, depending entirely on color, quality and size of slate. Prices are usually quoted f. o. b. at shipping point or water connection.

The total cost of slate roofing of the ordinary type is from $12 to $16 a square. From this price the cost varies upward. depending on nature of construction and quality of slate selected.

The matter of space forbids entering into the technical details of each of the problems in the construction of slate roofs and in the selection of color and design.

It will be readily realized that slate in its various forms offers many possibilities of architectural beauty and that by the use of care in color selection this material can be made to harmonize remarkably with any type of dwelling

The Architect and Engineer

SLATE ROOF FOR HOSPITAL, SAN MATEO, CALIFORNIA
LEWIS P. HOBART, ARCHITECT

exterior. The various colors and fading and unfading slates can easily be worked in together to form a pattern at once distinctive and of high aesthetic value.

Slate roofing, properly selected and applied, makes a long-wearing fire and element-resisting roof, possessing the inherent good qualities of a nature-made mineral material.

*

*

Why Cement Costs More

THIS comment on the higher price of cement comes from the Portland Cement Association: In connection with the advance in the prices of building materials in the last two years, information reaches the public occasionally which indicates that the manufacturer, in dealing with labor and raw materials, has the vexing problem of high prices before him quite as well as the consumer.

One manufacturer of cement, in discussing his difficulties, said:

"As compared with 1915, cost results for January, 1917, show that coal for power and burning was 25 cents higher per barrel for finished cement. In other words, the amount we are obliged to pay for fuel now has increased the cost of manufacturing a barrel of cement 25 cents, as compared with the early part of 1915. We are paying 35 per cent higher wages, which has increased the cost of manufacturing cement several cents per barrel. All repair and renewal material has increased in cost by percentages varying from 30 per cent to 250 per cent. The increase in the cost of insurance, due to the general adoption of the compensation insurance, and the increase in taxes, have also added to our cost of doing business 1 cent per barrel. We have been compelled to pay higher salaries. Our operating costs are considerably higher than formerly by reason of frequent interruptions due to shortage of cars and delays in transportation. All of these factors and the general increase in the cost of all items entering into the problem of manufacturing cement have vexed the cement makers and have compelled them to charge more for their product, a situation which is not at all relished by them because of the fact that one of their most prominent arguments for the use of concrete is not only its economy and permanence, but its relative low cost as compared with other materials which for many purposes are rivals of concrete."

*

*　*

Should Hats Come Off in Office Building Elevators?

Whether or not a gentleman should take off his hat in an elevator when a lady is a passenger is a question of manners which all large cities ought to settle at once and for all time. An elevator being a public conveyance, many argue it ought to be governed by the same rules of politeness as a street car, in which no gentleman is ever expected to go bareheaded.

New Orleans apparently is perplexed as to just what is the right thing to do, for some of her gentlemen take their hats off and others keep them on, and the same thing happens quite often in San Francisco. Most of those who uncover do so reluctantly, we are sure, lacking the courage to keep them on when someone else takes his off.

"It is a foolish custom," says an exchange. "The men would abolish the custom if they had the courage. Every last one of them hates it for its silliness, and the annoyance it causes to men when in a crowded car. Some day some lady is going to win applause by remarking 'As you were!' or 'Be covered!' or 'Resume your hats, gentlemen!' and all the men will take their hats off to her."

Inclined Walk for Theatre Balconies

By HORACE BARNES, Patent Attorney

THE new Liberty Theatre in Seattle includes several unique features in theatre construction and design of interest to the architectural and engineering professions. The seal of approval of the patent office has been placed on the novelty of one of such features, and a patent will soon be issued to Mr. Henderson Ryan of Seattle, the architect and inventor, covering the arrangement of the ramp, or inclined walk by which the balcony is reached.

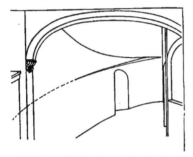 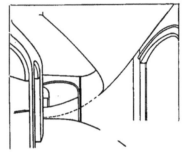

Foyer of Liberty Theatre, Seattle, Looking Inward From Lobby   *Foyer of Liberty Theatre, Looking Outward Toward Lobby, with Ramp Crossing Over*

Ramps are a very desirable factor in theatre design, as they make easy access to the balcony and are inviting to the theatre patrons, but they are installed at a sacrifice of space and not many building sites are sufficiently large to permit of their use.

Heretofore where ramps have been employed they have been located between the foyer at the rear of the auditorium and the building wall, which required that the available depth of the auditorium be contracted to admit the foyer and the ramp between the rear of the auditorium and the building wall.

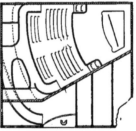

Plan of Liberty Theatre

By Mr. Ryan's arrangement, as exemplified in the Liberty Theatre, the ramp springs from the entrance lobby and ascends by an easy curvature and incline between the entrance to the foyer and the wall of the building toward the center axis of the auditorium. When the center line of the auditorium and the foyer has been reached the ramp has attained a sufficient height so that it can cross the foyer without subtracting from the head room in the foyer, or being noticeable except as a pleasing element of the foyer design. After the foyer has been crossed, the ramp is continued in the same easy inclination in two branches, one to either side of the balcony, or as is provided in Mr. Ryan's patent claims, a ramp may continue in the axial line of the auditorium by a tunnel coming out into the middle of the balcony.

By either arrangement the ramp lands the theatre patrons at a point equidistant to all parts of the balcony, whether upon the two sides or in the middle. By the old style of ramp, to attain the necessary elevation, the ramp extended the entire length of the theatre and landed the patrons upon the further side of the balcony, which tended to cause a congestion upon that side and an unequal distribution of the patrons about the balcony.

A further advantage in Mr. Ryan's design resides in the increased space available in the auditorium on the main floor. By extending the foyer under the ramp and against the side wall of the building, the auditorium is enlarged to occupy space formerly utilized by the foyer, and four or five more rows of seats may be added—thus increasing the seating capacity of the auditorium by several hundred.

The People's Theatre of Butte, Montana, is being built with the improved ramp, and Mr. Ryan is now preparing plans for a moving picture theatre in Helena, Montana with the same equipment.

The patent on Mr. Ryan's ideas presented peculiar difficulties, as the practice of the patent office is adverse to the granting of patent protection on a mere architectural design or plan of a building, these being held to be non-patentable subject matter.

* * *

"The High Cost of Building"

MR. THEODORE STARRETT, who came to San Francisco immediately after the big fire in 1906 and whose construction company took a prominent part in rebuilding the city, has written reminiscently of those strenuous days in Architecture and Building, relating how one of San Francisco's big architects sought to persuade him to put up a building at a loss for the "advertising" it would bring him (Query—Who is the architect?) Mr. Starrett writes:

There's food for thought in a bulletin of an architectural society that appeared lately. It is not a New York publication; I do not know whether New York has such a thing, and it does not make a particle of difference anyway.

Two interesting references are to be noted in this bulletin; one, to the high cost of building, and the other to the building report nuisance.

Now, the high cost of building is a condition and not a theory, as the late President Cleveland might have said. I have spoken of it myself on several occasions. Whether it is due, as the architects imply and in fact baldly state, to combinations of builders and material men—"gentlemen's agreements"—is another question that does not make such a great deal of difference.

Building is a costly thing. How much of the heaped up expense is due to architects who insist on designing everything so that it is special and not standard, and how much to the difficulties of building management, per se, I do not pretend to state, either. Combinations are pretty hard things to keep up in these giddy-paced times. There are too many candidates, too many mouths to feed, for me to believe that combinations in the building business are much of a burden on the body politic.

I am reminded of a story of an architect out in San Francisco. It was just after the great fire. The town was full of builders from all over the United States. They got a glad hand and a cold shoulder—if you can imagine such a combination—from all the local builders. The town was also full of architects from all over the United States. The clubs were bulging with them. Highbrows met who hadn't seen one another since the days of dear old Paris and the Ecole des Beaux Arts. I suppose there was a lot of glad-handing and cold-shouldering among them, too.

Well, in spite of the competition of numbers, there was no competition in price. It was too risky. The California law was too strenuous for the outsiders to take any chances with, and it resulted in what our friends of the bulletin above referred to call a gentleman's agreement. No gentleman would take a contract except on percentage.

The architect, whom I propose to tell you about, was one of the local contingent; he had a number of clients and when he talked it was business that was not exactly up in the air. He wanted to induce some deep-chested general contractor to take a straight old-fashioned contract, and he sounded a number of them to see if they could not be persuaded to break the gentleman's agreement.

Now I will pause here to impress on your mind, little builder, that there was no gentleman's agreement this time. There was no combination. It was simply a case where once in their lives the builders who were gathered in the city were all impressed with the seriousness of their work and all stood fast in their resolve to let the profiteers of building, namely, the owners, take the chances.

But my architectural friend persisted in his efforts. One builder that he attempted to exploit was made the object of a great many attentions, entertainments, dinners and all that sort of thing.

The builder listened to his plea.

"Now, what I want you to do," said the architect, "is to take a contract for this work. Show these percentage fellows that you have some nerve."

Then, to the suggestion from the builder that if such a thing was done it would, of course, be at a prohibitive price, the architect replied, "No. No, indeed. I want you to take this contract at a low price. I know how much the job is worth. You take this job at"—mentioning a ridiculous price such as architects of that kind are accustomed to offer. "You take this job at that price and you will get the cream of the building work in this town."

The price offered was one at which there would have been a loss of $100,000. The builder told the architect so. It didn't phase the architect. He unblushingly avowed that it didn't make any difference if the loss was $200,-000; it would pay the builder just the same. In fact, the greater the loss the greater the glory.

The builder was not that kind of a person—meaning that the argument did not appeal to him. The "gentleman's agreement" was not broken by him, nor, as far as I ever learned, by a single one of the builders who helped during the next year or more in the work of rebuilding the city.

The architect's game was to induce some builder—a general contractor, of course—to take the contract at a loss with the false hope that the builder would profit in the long run. If he had taken the job it would have been his last with my architectural hero, unless he wanted to make some more reputation. Whether there would be someone else—some other architect or owner—on whom the builder could "make up" was a matter of no consequence to Mr. Architect. Having got this contract out of the fire, he would find some other gullible one for the next, and so on.

So, when I read the words in the publication referred to, about everything being in combinations and gentlemen's agreements, it set me thinking of the man who tried to break a "gentleman's agreement."

It also set me to thinking of an occasion when the builders, for once at least in their lives, did what they ought to do all the time. They should stand for a profit on their work.

Interesting Report on Elevator Traffic

For the past three or four years the Building Owners' and Managers' Association of Seattle has taken a count of elevator traffic every six months. This practice was begun at the time when the association fought the passage of an ordinance to compel the installation of elevator safety devices. Mr. James D. Shaw, the secretary, has prepared the following resumé of the elevator traffic report which was read at the last monthly meeting:

Four hundred and eight thousand persons per day is a conservative estimate of the elevator passenger traffic in Seattle.

Office buildings alone provide free elevator service for 204,000 passengers per day, or more than twenty-four persons for each office served,· as shown from a count taken in thirty buildings. In addition, department stores, hotels, apartment houses, public buildings, wholesale houses, etc., furnish constant elevator service and undoubtedly their combined traffic more than equals that in office buildings. From reports furnished by the City Utilities Department, the Puget Sound Traction, Light and Power Company on their lines, during 1916, carried 88,417,069 passengers, an average of 241,576 per day, or 160,000 less rides daily for surface transportation than for vertical transportation furnished by building operators.

The general public, who use free elevator transportation, does not appreciate the service rendered, the many miles traveled by elevators during the day, and the number of trips made by each car. The L. C. Smith building elevators travel 162 miles every day, and its tower elevator alone travels 47½ miles per day.

The safety factor in elevator transportation is not appreciated by those availing themselves of this service, as provided in office buildings. Neither is it realized that vertical passenger traffic is the largest and safest in the world. Notwithstanding the movement of such large crowds of people, fewer accidents occur in transporting passengers vertically than on any other form of conveyance, in spite of the fact that the number of passengers thus served far exceeds that of any other common carrier.

* * *

Be Prepared to Wage War Against Fire

"WE are wide open to a land attack by Germany, and only a few realize it; most of us fondly imagine because the broad Atlantic separates us from the trench warfare in Europe, we only have to fear attack by sea, but an attack by organized incendiarism might reduce us to a condition little short of impotence in a single night.

"And the enemy probably knows better than most of us how utterly susceptible we are to this kind of attack. In all of the talk about our needs for preparedness hardly a word has been heard about our needs for defense against fire, an enemy against which we have been waging a stale-mate fight for years, and one which can well-nigh overwhelm us if supported by the organized incendiary cohorts of an enemy power bent on our dismemberment."

"Automatic sprinklers are the best defense against incendiary attacks," said Mr. I. G. Hoagland, secretary of the National Automatic Sprinkler Association, before the Credit Men's Association at Savannah, Georgia, on April 20th. He told of an instance in France where attempts of enemy incendiaries to burn a French cotton mill were frustrated by automatic sprinklers, and of others in South Africa where they saved buildings owned by Germans from destruction by fires started by English rioters. The police were impotent; fire brigades overwhelmed, their hose cut and fires burning everywhere. One store in Capetown was fired at seven different points, but the sprinklers put them out.

Mr. Hoagland declares that in the United States and Canada sprinkler protection has been in use for thirty-five years, and so successfully that more than 30,000 fires have been controlled, which has conserved the material wealth of the nation as much as $3,500,000,000 in property saved from fire, in preservation of losses from business interruption, and in reduction of the cost of insurance, from 40 to 90 per cent—to say nothing of the lives—on which it is impossible to set a price—that have been saved.

*   *   *

The Architect in War Times

MR. BURT FENNER, architect, has written a letter to the profession, detailing his experience at the front and describing some of the possibilities that exist in the military life for the man with architectural training. Mr. Fenner says in part:

"Military surveying is done by pacing and compass bearings primarily. I am not going into intersection and resection, contouring, slopes, clinometer and slopeboard work, but you start with a sketch-board in one hand, a compass in the other, a pencil between your teeth, and a scale any place. I shall never forget when I was first dropped in a field with hills, ravines, a stream running through it with patches of cultivated fields and a winding road at one side, and my Captain said, 'I'll send for you at four; 5 per cent accuracy will do.' When I remarked that I could do more accurate work with instruments and longer time he replied, 'In war, 100 per cent accuracy and two hours late and we're all dead. Go to it.'

"Any architect or draughtsman should be able, after some practice, to make road and position sketches; it takes, of course, some little time to learn all military indications, and what is of great importance about visibility problems, arriving at positions without being seen, and occupying artillery positions defiladed from the enemy, all from observance of the contour lines on maps. However, to proceed to my work, I managed to successfully lay out the camps, though attending drills, and company work as far as possible. I had not a single evening or Sunday free as the others did. Owing, I suppose, to my familiarity with the camp-sites, I was then relieved from my company and made first sergeant in charge of headquarters, war college, field artillery, hospitals and band. I was ordered to go to quartermaster stores and draw tentage, had one hundred and one things charged to me, and was given two squads of regulars, and four war-college negroes as a command, and four one and one-half ton motor trucks.

"Now as to what an architect can do for his country: First of all his training should give him proficiency in two particular things; military topography, which is of the utmost importance in reconnaissance, and outpost work. Geological surveys are practically one inch to the mile. We shall always need innumerable sketches three inches to the mile or greater, and need them every day as we proceed or fall back. The sketches I made were one inch equals 100 yards.

"The second branch is engineering, which includes buildings, barracks, warehouses, earth and concrete works, and lines of communication. The other branch—field works—includes demolitions. This takes in field defenses bridges, clearances, and pontoon work, all of which is relevant to our profession. A practical problem to be solved on the ground. That is our every-day work, is it not? Instead of making plans for circulation, we must block it, and find vistas for our fire but not for that of the enemy.

"One of the greatest assets the architect has in war is imagination. It is laid down by the authorities that 'War is an art and not a science.' Tactics is logic, tempered with imagination. Strategy is imagination tempered with common sense. I believe no profession develops these qualities as does ours. Who were the great military engineers of history? Michael Angelo, Leonardo da Vinci, Benvenuto Cellini, and many others of the world's great architects.

"It will be seen that the architect has the adaptability to make himself a very important factor in the military scheme of things. And if the war, now under way, should develop into the long and tedious struggle that some of the military experts predict, we have no doubt that new fields of military usefulness will suggest themselves, fields in which the trained capabilities of the practical architect will enable him to be of particular and unique service to his country."

* * *

Advantages of Using Hydrated Lime in Concrete*

THE use of a small proportion of hydrated lime mixed with the cement in concrete improves the structural and working qualities of the concrete and sufficiently reduces the cost of handling it to nearly or quite eliminate any additional expense and to secure a better structure with quicker and easier working conditions.

While the solid contents of the concrete can be easily specified and their exact proportions maintained, it is much more difficult to regulate accurately or uniformly the quantity of water used in mixing, especially since the general desire of the designer is to reduce the proportion to a minimum, while the builder is likely to increase it to a considerable extent in the hope of promoting the rapidity of mixing and the facility of distribution through chutes and filling small or obstructed forms.

An excess of water is likely to reduce the strength of the concrete, sometimes to a very great amount, and may cause honeycombing through the segregation of the aggregate in the forms. It may also cause classification of the fine and coarse particles and the formation of laitance on top.

Sometimes an excess of water may cause chutes to choke up through the accumulation of solids and the flowing away of liquid. When concrete is mixed too wet it is likely to develop interior and surface imperfections that may require cutting out or repairs at considerable expense to the constructor and the ultimate injury of the work.

When hydrated lime, the most plastic of building materials, is wet, the impalpable powder loses its granular character and is converted into a smooth paste, which lubricates the aggregate in the concrete and helps to give the latter homogeneity, density, strength, water-tightness, and a smooth, uniform exterior surface. Besides this, it greatly facilitates the handling and placing by increasing the mobility and plasticity of the wet concrete. It enables the mason to do more and better work.

The addition of a small percentage of hydrated lime to concrete enables it to flow down chutes without segregation and to be spouted at a smaller angle than is possible for even the wettest concrete not containing the lime. It can also be dumped out of wheelbarrows and carts without digging, as it is easily handled with a consistency firm enough to produce the greatest density and strength and keep the aggregate suspended in the mass.

Concrete mixed with hydrated lime has been spouted at the St. Louis filter plant to a distance of 400 feet on an incline of 1 on 5 or a little more than 11 degrees. When hydrated lime is not used, concrete is usually spouted at an angle of about 27 degrees, corresponding to a rise of 1 on 2.

Although it is recorded that hydrated lime concrete has been spouted at a smaller angle than 11 degrees, it may be assumed for purposes of comparison to be spouted at an angle of 15 degrees, which reduces the necessary height of tower 24 feet for every 100 feet of run that would be required for con-

*Abstract of article by Bela Nagy, chief engineer Hydrated Lime Bureau.

crete spouted at an angle of 27 degrees. In the case of large work this means that fewer towers and mixing plants can be installed for the same results.

The labor required for placing and spading hydrate of lime concrete is considerably reduced and in case of complicated construction such as that on some of the bridges for the Indianapolis-Frankfort R. R., this saving is reported to be as much as 50 per cent.

Some contractors use hydrate of lime where it is not specified and consider it to their advantage to add 5 per cent of hydrate of lime by weight to the amount of the cement used, paying for it out of their own pockets.

* * *

Greatest Real Estate Era in History Near

By VALENTINE SURGNOR*

I HAVE been asked by many members of our organization and by many other real estate men as to the probable effect upon the real estate business that will be exerted by the war. I think American entrance into the war will prove a tremendous stimulant to practically all lines of business, and to none more significantly than the realty business.

My reasons why? They are plain enough. The government has voted an initial war credit of $7,000,000,000. That is the greatest single government credit in the history of the world. What does it mean?

It means the dispensing of that huge sum of money in all avenues and arteries of trade in this country. Yes, even the three billions that we shall lend to the Allies, because that money will unquestionably be used in stabilizing financial balances in the United States, consequent upon the huge purchases made of us during the past three years or so and, as a consequence, we shall have our own government behind the obligations which have been entered into by foreign powers to our manufacturers and producers. That means, of course, from the business viewpoint that there will be no crash due to panicky financial conditions, and will serve to imbue our whole industrial, financial and commercial fabric with renewed confidence.

But more than the mere stabilizing effect, the raising of this huge sum and its distribution will mean stimulated business activity. My own opinion is that within a few weeks we shall see an activity that is almost feverish.

We shall see all industrial lines worked to their fullest capacity. We shall see high wages, speeded-up production, increased farm yields, with price restrictions but fair and even high prices to the farmers; in short, we shall witness a period of the greatest business and industrial activity that this country has ever known.

We shall see millions—yes, billions—of dollars, previously hoarded, come out from their hiding places and placed in government securities. This, when distributed, will mean the appreciation of other securities, because it will mean business expansion. We shall see less "blue-sky" and "get-rich-quick" schemes succeeding, because the people are patriotic and will put their money into government bonds at lower rates, to help their country and, with the stimulation that the spending of this money will afford, will be able, later, to receive good interest rates upon sound investments, including sound real estate investments, of course.

The influence of all this upon the realty market is plain enough. Factory sites will be in acute demand. Homes for workmen will be in lively call. Homes of the better grade, for men who have made an unusual amount of money out of the expanded condition of trade, will be in considerable demand. Store sites, especially in the neighborhood of new or expanded industrial centers, will command good prices and a good market.

*President of the Chicago Real Estate Board.

Why Not Sail the Danger Zone in Protected Fleets?

MR. F. W. FITZPATRICK, consulting architect, formerly of Washington but now of Omaha, suggests a way of fighting· the submarine peril that must, until somebody tells why it won't work, appeal powerfully to the intelligence.

His suggestion is that cargo vessels be sent out in protected fleets.

Vessels now sail alone, and may meet their doom alone. The murderous pirate submarine, which shoots from ambush, picks them off at will, meeting them thus alone. Men are drowned, men—and women and children, too—are left in small boats far out on the stormy deep, and if they do get to port it is usually after bitter hardship. That is because the murdered vessels sail alone.

Suppose, instead of sailing alone, they sailed in fleets, with warships and swift small craft to guard and scout. Would a submarine tackle such an array, with every vessel in the fleet armed and every gunner on the watch for periscopes? If it did, would it get away? It might get one vessel, or two; but one of the others would surely get the submarine, and the others could take aboard the crew of the stricken vessel.

It sounds reasonable, practicable. Why not try it?

Here is the way Mr. Fitzpatrick sets it forth:

"Why sit down and howl pitifully about the U boats? Why not do something? The one idea that seems to obsess us is to build vessels fast enough to replace the destroyed shipping! Surely a most woeful confession of inefficiency, of childish simplicity! Why is so little done in real defense against the 'peril'?

"Our land warriors—for WE are now the allies—have found it expedient to resort·to ancient armor to protect themselves from the ultra-modern weapons of this war, but for some utterly inexplicable reason our naval experts have not deemed it wise or expedient or seemly to resort likewise to a very ancient marine device of defense, the only one that really can be of any use against the U boat and that will insure the minimum of maritime losses.

"Why let one poor, forlorn ship after another go out alone to possible, nay, probable doom? For every sailing, every course is known to the directors of the U boat activities.

"The flotilla, the armada, the 'convoyed' fleet of old is the one only real protection for our or any other sea trade these perilous times.

"Don't let vessels go singly, however well armed; make them wait until ten or a dozen are ready, or have regular sailing dates, when a powerful convoy, a couple of warships and a lot of scouts and speedy craft can escort them across. With so many eyes awatch, so many guns ready, the U boat that will show its periscope in the vicinity of such a fleet is indeed a valorous craft. At worst, one boat might be picked off. Certainly no such havoc as is being wreaked today would be possible. The slight delay in sailing is a negligible objection.

"Storms may scatter such a flotilla. That's one of the possibilities that confront those who go down into the sea, but we have a long season ahead of the year's best sailing weather, so that now's the time to do the shipping and to do it intelligently and not just sit down and lament anent the 'U boat peril.'"

Owner, Architect and Decorator Should Co-operate

ONE of the most interesting and significant features in American life today is the exceptionally widespread and growing interest in the country or suburban home. With this awakening there has never been a more concerted effort on part of developers, architects, builders, and decorators to co-operate in securing the best possible houses for those who are seeking them in ever increasing numbers.

Remember that it is economy in the end to select the best architect that you know, and let him take up your ideal, and plan for you a house that will not only meet the needs of your family but one that fully expresses your own individuality and theirs.

The architect will not only plan the structure but will also give the inspiration for its interior.

Always keep before you the fact that the relation of the architect to the interior decoration is vital, for the structure, its form, lines and scales are the keynotes to all correct decoration.

Too often this is entirely ignored, forgotten, or neglected, and by not observing this relation the architect's ideals are destroyed, and the best efforts of the decorator lost.

There can be no decoration worth the name unless the architect and decorator have the same ideals and work in closest harmony with the owner to secure the best possible results.

An owner who has very little knowledge of architecture or decoration may handicap both architect and decorator by intrusive personal sentiment, rather than by co-operation aid them in carrying out a well arranged scheme for interior.

Unless you really know, do not insist upon some impossible plan, arrangement or color, if you expect desirable results on the whole. Your architect has already led you through a maze of detail, or advised on all the uncertain things that make or mar your home.

The woodwork, so fine a part of every house, has been carefully selected, and you have assisted in decisions concerning the finish, for no doubt you own many choice pieces of furniture which must harmonize with same. Specially designed hardware and lighting fixtures are in place, and the many other essentially architectural features of the very foundation of the interior decorations are complete.

Who has not seen beautiful exteriors without the slightest relation to the interior, after that has gone through the so-called process of decoration. Simply because the owner or decorator neglected to take the inspiration given to them by architect upon completion of building.

A technical knowledge of interior decoration is not an essential necessity, if a woman really possesses that exceptional gift and guide, "good taste," and is willing to be advised by those who do know, and by their skill and experience guided.

· She can learn to recognize suitability, simplicity and proportion, and apply her knowledge to her needs and that of her family, remembering always that it is the personality of the mistress that the home expresses.

A man may plan, build, and decorate a beautiful house, but it is the woman's work to make of it a home.

Two things are essentially the foundation for her interior decoration plans.

First that the house should be a haven of rest.

Then endeavor to make it the very best place in all the world, for each member of the family; it should be the place where the highest ideals of life are formed, shaped and nourished, and therein expressed.

Good taste, comfort, simplicity studied, you can not make many errors in your decorations.

When all these things are settled and decided, floors, ceilings and wood-work finished, you may then begin to plan your wall coverings.

Walls should always be treated in a conventional way, for the wall is the background of the room and must be flat in treatment, and again, restful in tone.

What allurements are found in the "newest" wall papers, windows are filled with them, and there is a tendency on the part of a new home builder "to shop and select wall papers," and one who knows the dangers of such selections as she may make just because they are "new" and "beautiful," would love to write a page or two on the "pit-falls in selections of paper for the decoration of walls."

One is so apt to forget that they are to be lived with, in some cases, a very great while, owing to high cost and quality chosen. O, how often we have wanted to tear them all off and start over again, but we can't.

The most beautiful walls are plain and this is often obtained by painting. While black and white papers and fantastic colored designs interwoven, are decidedly fascinating, and amazing effects obtained, the great majority of home lovers can not afford the novelty of the scheme necessary to be worked out in every detail of room furnishings; the same can be said of mauve, and similar fads, so attractive as to be tempting, and many attempt them who really can not afford to do so—the regrets come later.

Above all else, your walls must be beautiful in themselves. In short, walls, windows, rugs before pictures and furniture.

Too often furniture is the first consideration, until the house becomes a sort of "sample shop" affair in type and arrangement; ideals lost sight of; plan gone; architectural beauty of rooms destroyed by furniture, just for furniture's sake.

The owner sees an attractive piece and buys it, though it has no refer-ence in form or color to the general scheme of her home—the result is a jumble of mission, fine old mahogany, craftsman, or wicker furniture.

Every object purchased in the house should be considered for its use-fulness and comfort. No matter how good your house is so far as the architecture is concerned, you have it in your power to completely kill all artistic effects by ill-chosen furniture and furnishings.—Realty.

* * *

Spouting Concrete 700 Feet

Ellis Soper of the Cuban-Portland Cement Company, Mariel, Cuba, writes that by the aid of a steel tower 250 feet high some concrete foundations were poured 700 feet away. On account of the hot sun it was found that the use of a small percentage of hydrated lime was very beneficial in aiding the flow of the concrete. Making proper allowance for the relative elevations of the chute and the forms the inclination of the latter was found to be about 17 or 18 degrees.

It is probable, on account of the great height, that the chutes were not easily accessible for cleaning or for the acceleration of the flow and that the flow was continuous and unimpeded. In any event, the horizontal distance spouted was nearly or quite a record and the height of the tower approaches the limit of economy and safety.

Has the Pike's Peak of War Prices Been Reached?

EVERY large modern war has caused a rise of prices in the belligerent countries. Often the effects have extended to countries far removed from the area of conflict. The greatest of all wars—the present one—has effected the greatest of price changes, and had it not been for government price fixing in the belligerent countries the rises in prices would have been even more extreme.

In America we are concerned at present over the question as to the probable fall or rise of prices during the present year. Much construction work is being held up until material prices drop and labor ceases to be scarce. Has the Pike's Peak of war prices been surmounted, and are we about to descend into the valley beyond? An answer to this question will be of great importance to many engineers and contractors.

All economists are agreed that prices rise when there is increase in the metal money and "credit money" seeking exchange for "goods," or when there is decrease in the quantity of "goods" seeking exchange for money. In war times both these conditions prevail, for "credit money" increases through government action, and the production of "goods" seeking exchange decreases through the removal of industrial works to the battlefields. In America we have had the greatest gold flood during the last two years in all our history. Even more important in raising prices has been the flood of "credit money." Abnormally small crops and congestion of railways have reduced the available quantity of "goods," and have thus aided the general rise of prices in this country.

A review of these facts is essential before prognosticating as to the future course of prices. It is also necessary to consider what psychological effects the high prices of the present will have upon producers and investors. To begin with, we may be certain that the glittering, golden bait of dollar corn and two-dollar wheat will cause most farmers to swallow the "bait, hook, line and sinker," and to come back so eagerly for more that the bait will presently begin to be withdrawn. In other words, there is no doubt that the year 1917 will be a year of unprecedented planting of almost every kind of crop, and, barring adverse climatic conditions, this will be a "banner year" for foodstuff production. This alone would tend to produce a general lowering of the price level during 1917, but there will be other potent forces working toward a drop.

When England notified American manufacturers of shells and shrapnel that they must finish all deliveries by the end of March, and that no further contracts for such munitions will be made, the economist's ear heard the clang of the gong that announces this to be the last lap of the war—and this without regard to who will be the victor. Immediately there followed such significant incidents as the discharge of 1800 men working for the Baldwin Locomotive Company on munitions, and the announced reduction in the dividend rate of the Dupont Powder Company.

Hard upon the heels of these incidents came the definite statement from government officials in England that imports would be greatly reduced, both as a matter of necessary economy and because the British Empire has at last so organized its industries as to need little outside assistance. This points unmistakably to a very marked reduction in the shipment of American goods to Europe, entirely aside from any forced curtailment as a result of submarine warfare.

So now we face simultaneously an increased production of foodstuffs in America and a decreased demand abroad for many of our goods. The congestion of our railways will rapidly decrease—is already decreasing—so that a further drop in prices will follow from this change.

Still, all the metal money that America now holds will remain, and will probably increase for a .time. Will this condition not serve to hold up prices? Metal money forms only one-fifth of the total "real money" normally in "circulation," for bank "credits" based on metal money are many fold the volume of metal money and serve every purpose of exchange. Let there be started a well-marked fall of prices—as from the curtailment of foreign demand for goods—and "credit money" automatically begins to shrink in volume. This merely means that manufacturers and merchants, seeking a declining market, hesitate to engage in so large a volume of production and storage of "goods" as formerly. They thus cease themselves to "demand" so many "goods' from one another and from the producers of "raw materials." The circle of reduced "demand" rapidly widens, some laborers are discharged, and " demand"—i. e., money in search of goods— decreases in geometric proportion.

Many signs already point distinctly toward a period of declining prices in America. Even our own entrance into the war is unlikely to change materially the general trend of price reduction.

Will a marked fall in prices affect civil engineers and contractors unfavorably? We think not. Indeed, we look for a favorable effect. Most civil engineers are employed on public works or works of a semi-public nature, like railways and other "public utilities." Capital for works of these sorts is usually raised by the sale of bonds. But the high rates of interest that have prevailed since the war began have often deterred both public officials and the managers of "public utilities" from entering upon large construction programs. Higher interest rates always accompany a general rise of prices. With a fall in prices, lower interest rates will occur, and this alone will stimulate the marketing of bonds for public and semi-public enterprises. A further stimulus will be the lower prices for materials.

If the drop in prices were consequent upon a great shock to credits in general—a "panic"—of course there would be no reason for expecting a revival of public or semi-public construction work. In fact, a great decrease in such work would result. But we are neither entering upon nor emerging from a "panic." General confidence is not shaken, capital is abundant and will be available at low interest rates. Profits in many industries have been large, and capitalists are eager for continued action—a chance to "sit in" at the great game. All conditions co-exist, we believe, for a progressively prosperous time for civil engineers and contractors—Engineering and Contracting.

* * *

Dangerous Optimism

The young and inexperienced contractor is very likely to think that if he can figure a profit of 15 per cent above the cost of all labor and material he is very safe and prosperous. Perhaps he will make money on some contracts with this margin, but the time will surely come when accident. delayed payment, strikes, a rise in prices, and various contingencies will wipe out all the margin and far more, and lucky he is if it does not entirely ruin him. This is particularly the case with a capable foreman accustomed only to earning wages but who knows the cost of labor and material. A small profit looks relatively large to him and he is prone to invest his savings in a contract taken far below the proper price. If he can carry through at all he may feel that he has made money because by working twice as hard as usual he has secured fair or even extra wages, although in reality he has been up against a losing proposition. Such men perennially replacing those that have failed pour out year after year their capital on the altar of low contract prices and serve to perpetually keep prices below their proper level and maintain an unhealthy competition.—*Contracting*.

A Letter from the Front

EDITOR The Architect and Engineer of California:—
Dear Sir:—You probably remember a number of months ago we sent you copy of a letter written to us by R. R. Christien, who was on your mailing list as an architect in Santa Ana, Cal., but who, in reality, was fighting with the British Army somewhere in France. You published this article and we, ourselves, sent him a box of cigarettes.

Attached is a copy of a letter he has written us, and which he has asked us to show to you. This appears to us to be very good reading.

Yours very truly, WHITE BROTHERS, C. H. WHITE, Manager.

*   *   *

France, April 29, 1917.

Messrs. White Brothers, San Francisco, Cal.

Dear Sirs:—It is many months since that box of cigarettes so kindly sent and so gladly received, left your hands and began its pilgrimage across the continent and ocean to where I was then billeted. It will surprise you as much as it did me, to know that it was over six months or thereabouts in crossing. I am at a loss to understand it, for letters from California have reached my hands regularly in less than four weeks, save in the case of one, which made the acquaintance of salt water, thanks to a U boat, but after being carefully fished up again, dried by the British postoffice officials, was forwarded to me none the worse for immersion.

At any rate, I hope you will not regard it as too late for me to write and thank you on behalf of all those who shared them and to say how welcome they were. Most "Tommies" start the day with a cigarette, have one in preference to breakfast (sometimes), go over the parapet and stick the Germans with one between their lips, are wounded and carried off on a stretcher still smoking, and spend all their spare time in the hospital seeing how many they can get rid of.

Many thanks for sending me that number of The California Architect and Engineer. It was good to see that while Europe is being laid waste through the mad despair of the Huns, California had begun to build faster than ever. Since he was good enough to publish that note I sent you (I little thought I should see it there), will you kindly let the editor see this one, as I may not be able to write him?

America's coming into the war a few weeks ago, has made my ten years' sojourn there extremely useful. I have become a sort of walking American Encyclopædia, full of facts about her enormous resources and her fighting qualities once she takes off her coat. Incidentally I have been boosting California; her natural charms and her potential business prospects. I do not think I shall ever forget her, and certainly if I come out of this miserable war alive, I shall hope to return there once more.

You are probably so fed up with the war news that I hesitate to refer to the conflict, but, as you will know, the Germans have had no successes this year; their military power is declining, they are falling back steadily. They have had a chance to say that their first retreat from the Somme was strategic instead of being due, as was actually the case, to the incessant artillery bombardment we gave them all last winter, when our communiques stated "Nothing but artillery activity." But the fight this month (their heavy losses in men and guns), shows the pressure of the British Army is reaching its culminating strength, as well as on the front, where the French proved themselves superior to German tactics.

The individual is simply lost amid the millions arrayed against each other. The struggle now raging is proving what Kitchener once said, that "Generals win battles, but armies win wars." Now that America has come into the war, any remote possibility that Germany might stalemate us into a patched-up peace is gone forever. Perhaps the hammering of her armies may be so successful this year—we started our offensive five months earlier this year—that she will sue for peace rather than face another winter. All the signs point that way at present. In the air she is beaten. One rarely sees a German aviator behind our lines. If ours are brought down, it is invariably far behind the German lines, and such cases are largely due to the fact that our airmen fly low, so low as often to rake the German trenches with their machine guns, while the German aviator soars aloft, thousands of feet up, too far up to be of any military value, hence his success against women and children.

On sea they have failed, save in a slight measure of unavoidable success with submarines against unarmed boats—one saw that last week when those two British patrol boats tackled six German destroyers, rammed one and torpedoed another. Think of ramming boats in the 20th century! It takes me back to the days of Nelson, when men swarmed across the rigging and fought with any weapon handy.

On land we are superior to them in artillery. They come into our lines prisoners, more like idiots than men; dazed, nerve-shattered wrecks. For the first time in the

- war the German people (as well as their army) have become war weary. When that symptom appears among a proud and haughty nation like theirs, the end cannot be very far off.

. And now, as a crowning blow, an irremediable disaster, they have forced America to put on one side, her long suffering patience and neutrality!

I am sorry that I cannot say more about my personal doings,—we are not allowed to say much, but you can imagine. I have seen the fitful glare cast by the artillery far along the horizon; heard their incessant noise, their culmination before an attack, and then a deadly silence amid the early morning, and far behind the line though we may be, we knew that our chaps were climbing out of the trenches and crossing "No Man's" Land. A few hours later, a day maybe, the convoys of ambulance speeding back to the rear, tell their own tale.. One accepts it as a matter of course—he becomes surprised at the unemotional interest he displays. But one thing I have never ceased to wonder at, the cheery smile, the unfailing optimism, the inevitable jest and wit that wounded Tommies display. Once I saw twenty London buses on active service in France, loaded outside and inside with wounded on their way to Blighty, but however seriously they may have been wounded, and many were, they shouted cheery greetings to any passing, waved their hands to any jolie mademoiselle in sight, sang snatches of song as though all was part of the game. You know you cannot beat chaps like that, though I belong to the same nation.

Well, this letter has spun itself out longer than I intended, so let me conclude once more with many, many thanks for those delightful cigarettes.

With kind regards believe me, Yours sincerely, (Signed) R. R. CHRISTIEN.

Don't Blame the Cement

EVERY once in awhile someone who has attempted some concrete work complains because the results of his efforts are unsatisfactory. Usually the cement is blamed. The concrete does not harden properly and the home worker or other user thinks the fault lay with the cement.

Anyone who has seen the workings of a modern cement plant will be convinced that portland cement is a carefully manufactured material. It is made and sold on a guarantee to fill certain specifications. These specifications are the result of years of study and have proved that if cement is up to their standard it is rarely or never to blame for any trouble one may have with concrete work. Anyone can readily see that if portland cement did not possess a certain standard of quality the manufacturers could not long stay in business. Naturally, therefore, they endeavor to turn out a product that meets the requirements of specifications in every way.

Throughout the process of cement manufacture, samples are taken at regular and frequent intervals, these samples being tested in a laboratory by experts to prove that the product meets requirements. With these facts in mind, the concrete worker should be convinced that unsatisfactory results of his labors are not due to poor cement.

Almost invariably the sand, pebbles or broken stone used in concrete mixtures might be more carefully selected, prepared, or be of better quality. The concrete user naturally tries to secure sand and pebbles near where he is doing his work. This is especially true in case of small jobs. A gravel bank is near by and he makes this serve the purpose. He forgets that not all sand and not all pebbles are suited to concrete work just as they are taken from the bank. Frequently they contain large quantities of loam, clay or other foreign materials. Sometimes this is distributed throughout the bulk and in other cases is in the form of a coating on the particles.

Bank-run material is not separated into coarse and fine particles (sand and pebbles). The concrete worker takes them just as they come from the gravel bank without any special preparation and dumps them in his concrete mixture. If there is any kind of dirt or other foreign material in them, it goes into the concrete. It is rarely true that sand and pebbles as found in the ordinary gravel bank are correctly proportioned for the best results in concrete. Usually there is a great deal more sand than there should be and to get strength and density it always pays to screen the bank-run mixture, separating sand from pebbles and then to remix the two in definite proportions.

THE

Architect and Engineer

OF CALIFORNIA

Founded in 1905 by E. M. C. WHITNEY

A. I. WHITNEY - - - *Manager*
T. C. KIERULFF - - - *Legal Points*
FREDERICK W. JONES - - *Editor*

Published Monthly in the interests of the
Architects, Structural Engineers, Contract-
ors and the Allied Trades of the Pacific
Coast by the Architect and Engineer.

BUSINESS OFFICE AND EDITORIAL ROOMS
627-629 Foxcroft Building, San Francisco
Telephone Douglas 1828

The publishers disclaim any responsibility for statements
made in the advertisements of this magazine.

TERMS OF SUBSCRIPTION

(Including postage) to all parts of the United States $1.50
per annum; to Canada 50c additional; to all Foreign points
$1 additional.

VOL. XLIX. JUNE, 1917 No. 3.

Americans have a habit of quitting work and crowding around when an accident occurs. The case in point is the world's "accident" in Europe.

LET'S BUILD WHILE WE FIGHT

We are in danger of losing our heads and stopping work while the conflict is on. This would be a serious happening, but happily every American can help to prevent it without adding to the noise and confusion of going to war. The only thing necessary is to go quietly on in attending to our own business.

While our naval and military forces are hastening to the front to destroy agencies and obstacles that seek to impede our growth, it is essential that we redouble our constructive efforts at home.

We can both build and fight and we ought to seize upon this advantage as the greatest opportunity created by the war.

Let both public and private useful building construction proceed. Production and handling of building materials and public and private construction work are fundamental industries of the country. Any tendency to suspend or postpone building projects is inconsistent with maintaining our prosperity. The country is prosperous. Building investors should not hesitate to go ahead with their plans. Railroads should spare no effort to supply the building industry with the cars needed to transport materials. Government, state, county ' and municipal authorities should encourage the continuance of all kinds of building. Road and street improvements in particular should go on unabated. Bad roads and streets are factors of first importance in the present high cost of foodstuffs. Never before was the improvement of highways so essential.

The lumber, brick. cement, lime, sand, gravel, stone, and other building materials industries are basic. Neither government regulations nor railroad restrictions should be unnec-

'essarily imposed to interfere with them. If any action is taken which results in the prostration of so fundamentally important industries, there is real danger of a surplus of unemployed labor, a surplus of railroad cars and a crippling of business that will seriously embarrass the Government in financing the war. Let us build while we fight!

A reader of The Architect and Engineer wishes to know why the schools of San Francisco are

BETTER VENTILA- not equipped with
TION WANTED up-to-date ventilat-
IN OUR SCHOOLS ing apparatus. Ac-
cording to our correspondent, the last school building to be ventilated is the Girls' High School, and the equipment here is said not to give satisfaction due to faulty inspection. It seems that in many of the new schools the original plans called for ventilation systems, but in order to keep the cost within the appropriation the equipment was cut out at the last minute. So it happens that a number of our new schools are ventilated only in respect to the toilets. The class rooms have no fresh air going into them except through open windows, and on a cold day an open window will create a draught that invariably means a cold for the pupil who sits near it. The average size of a school room is 22 by 30 feet, and the average number of pupils to a room is 45. One need not be a physician to realize the necessity of constant fresh air in circulation if those 45 young people are to retain their health. It would seem as if the city could better afford to cut down on some other item of expense and leave the ventilating apparatus alone. The principal cost of good ventilation is motor power to run the fan and proper inspection. If the city could afford to spend $56,000 for a plant in the new City Hall, it ought to be able to spend a small proportion of that sum in each of our school houses, for the future of San Francisco depends quite as much upon the health of our boys and girls as upon their education.

The Editor of Concrete Age writes that in a publishing experience of twenty-five years he has
THE TIME TO never known a time
ADVERTISE when trade paper advertising was so important, so practical, and so certain of fixed results as at present. "For when the war ends," he says, "the advertising done now will have a double value, first in producing new customers while your competitor is 'off duty' (making war munitions, perhaps), and second in the increased demand for your goods which is sure to follow the declaration of peace.

"Advertise now, as you never did before, and reap results one hundred fold. There can be no question about this investment, for the returns are absolutely certain."

Giving Away Plans and Specifications

Architects are human like everybody else. They are willing to contribute to charity when the appeal is deserving. But they are not practicing their profession altogether for their health. Therefore, when a layman appeals to the profession for a set of plans or blue-prints and specifications, even though they may originally have been prepared for another client, the architect is entitled to compensation. Read how a San Jose architect was approached by a contractor who wished to "purchase" the architect's plans for a trifling sum:

Editor The Architect and Engineer of California:
I am sending you, enclosed, a copy of some correspondence lately received by me.
I have left the names and addresses blank, but the letters are on file in my office. This correspondence seems to me to have a certain humorous value and is an example of how Architecture is frequently practiced. If it is of any value to you, I should like to see it printed, with any comment you may choose to make.
Yours truly,
WARREN SKILLINGS.

LETTER NO. 1—THE REQUEST

Dear Sir:
I stopped at your office on Monday at the suggestion of Mr. .... whose home you were the architect for, in order to get from you a copy of the blue prints for his house. I did this at Mr. .... suggestion and with his full knowledge and consent.
Will you kindly forward me blue prints of the house and detail. I shall be very glad to pay for said blue-printing. The card on your door mentioned that you would be back Wednesday, hence I am writing.
Thanking you in advance, I beg to remain,
Sincerely,
....

LETTER NO. 2—THE ARCHITECT'S
ANSWER

Dear Sir:

Your letter of the 22nd inst. received. I am glad you like the house.

It is not customary to use the plans made for one client in building a house for another client, but in this case, as you have received his consent and are to build in another locality, I have no objection.

The plans and specifications of a house are instruments of service and as such are the property of the architect.

It is customary when more than one building is constructed from the same set of plans to charge a fee for the second building, according to the circumstances.

I will send you three sets of plans and specifications, and one set of the detailed drawings, for the sum of $75, and if you should require any further services I will make four visits of supervision, from time to time, as you require them, for the additional sum of $50.

Yours truly,

....

LETTER NO. 3—SOMETHING FOR NOTHING

Dear Sir:

Your letter relative to the plans of Mr. ...... house received. My business is building, consequently no supervision or assistance of that kind is needed at any time.

The blue prints I asked for of you are not for any particular client, but to show generally and to work up business and also for my personal use.

I am going to build a new home for myself and like the exterior of Mr. ......, home extremely well and the interior quite well also. Both exterior and interior, however, I would make some changes in and I would use the basic outline and idea of the ...... place and change both inside and out to suit our particular requirements. I will have my own draughtsman make the changes, naturally. Under these conditions you can readily see it would be unnecessary and unwise to pay $75 for the blue prints I asked of you.

The courtesy that I am asking of you is one that I myself frequently confer on others, and have found it good business, as it costs nothing, makes a friend, and sometimes actually produces new business.

If with this explanation you feel disposed to change your mind, I shall be very glad to receive the blue prints from you and pay for the same as per my previous letter.

Thanking you in advance for any courtesies extended, I beg to remain,

Sincerely,

....

American Institute of Architects

(ORGANIZED 1857)

OFFICERS FOR 1916-17

PRESIDENT.....JOHN LAWRENCE MAURAN, St. Louis
FIRST VICE-PRESIDENT......C. GRANT LA FARGE, New York
SECOND VICE-PRESIDENT....W. R. B. WILLCOX, Seattle, Wash.
SECRETARY....W. STANLEY PARKER, Boston, Mass.
TREASURER..........D. EVERETT WAID, New York

San Francisco Chapter

PRESIDENT...................EDGAR A. MATHEWS
VICE-PRESIDENT.........SYLVAIN SCHNAITTACHER
SECRETARY AND TREASURER.........MORRIS BRUCE
TRUSTEES...................... { W. B. FAVILLE
                           { G. A. WRIGHT

Southern California Chapter

PRESIDENT................ ..J. E. ALLISON
VICE-PRESIDENT.................J. J. BACKUS
SECRETARY ....A. R. WALKER
TREASURER.................AUGUST WACKERBARTH

Board of Directors
ROBT. D. FARQUHAR   PERCY A. EISEN
S. B. MARSTON

Portland, Ore., Chapter

PRESIDENT..................JOSEPH JACOBBERGER
VICE-PRESIDENT.................J. A. FOUILHOUX
SECRETARY....................W. C. KNIGHTON
TREASURER.....................FOLGER JOHNSON
TRUSTEES................., { ION LEWIS
                       { M. H. WHITEHOUSE

Washington State Chapter

PRESIDENT.............CHARLES H. BEBE, Seattle
1ST VICE-PRES....DANIEL R. HUNTINGTON, Seattle
2D VICE-PRESIDENT.........GEORGE GOVE, Tacoma
3D VICE-PRESIDENT........L. L. RAND, Spokane
SECRETARY.............JOSEPH S. COTE, Seattle
TREASURER............ELLSWORTH STOREY, Seattle
                     { JAMES STEPHEN, Seattle
COUNCIL.............. { JAMES H. SCHACK, Seattle
                     { CHARLES H. ALDEN, Seattle

California State Board of Architecture

NORTHERN DISTRICT.

PRESIDENT....................EDGAR A. MATHEWS
SECRETARY-TREASURER.....SYLVAIN SCHNAITTACHER
Members
JOHN BAKEWELL, JR.   J. CATHER NEWSOM

SOUTHERN DISTRICT.

PRESIDENT...................JOHN P. KREMPEL
SECRETARY-TREASURER.........FRED H. ROEHRIG
                   { OCTAVIUS MORGAN
MEMBERS................... { SUMNER P. HUNT
                   { WM. S. HEBBARD

San Francisco Architectural Club

OFFICERS FOR 1917

PRESIDENT ....CHAS. PETER WEEKS
VICE-PRESIDENT ....A. WILLIAMS
SECRETARY ....JOHN F. BEUTTLER
TREASURER ....WILLIAM HELM

San Francisco Society of Architects

PRESIDENT...............CHARLES PETER WEEKS
VICE-PRESIDENT............GEORGE W. KELHAM
SECRETARY AND TREASURER.....WARREN C. PERRY
                   { ERNEST COXHEAD
DIRECTORS................ { FREDERICK H. MEYER

Engineers and Architects Association of Los Angeles

PRESIDENT....................A. H. KOEBIG, SR.
FIRST VICE-PRESIDENT......!........A. S. BENT
SECOND VICE-PRESIDENT...........IRA J. FRANCIS
Directors
J. J. BACKUS, GEO. P. ROBINSON, ALBERT C. MARTIN, H. L. SMITH.

Washington State Society of Architects

PRESIDENT...................A. WARREN GOULD
SECRETARY....................WM. J. JONES
TREASURER...................J. L. MCCAULEY
                   { HARRY H. JAMES
                   { WM. J. JONES
TRUSTEES................... { ALFRED BREITUNG
                   { J. L. MCCAULEY
                   { G. F. ROWE

San Diego Architectural Association

PRESIDENT...................CHARLES CRESSEY
VICE-PRESIDENT.........W. TEMPLETON JOHNSON
SECRETARY...................ROBT. HALLEY, JR.
TREASURER...................G. A. HAUSSEN

San Joaquin Valley Ass'n of Architects

PRESIDENT....................W. J. WRIGHT
VICE-PRESIDENT..................E. B. BROWN
SECRETARY-TREASURER...........FRANK V. MAYO

With the Architects
Building Reports and Personal Mention of Interest to the Profession

School Work for Spokane Architects

Messrs. Ellis & Wells, Hyde building, Spokane, Wash., have been busily engaged the past few months on school work. Among their jobs is the new six-room school building for Almira, Lincoln county, costing about $18,000; new parochial school at Union Park, Spokane, $25,000; Francis Willard school, Spokane, $20,000; Grandview, Washington, school building, $25,000. They also prepared plans for the 50-room hotel to be erected by Thompson & Shrock at Almira, Wash., to cost $40,000, and a two-story lodge room to be erected adjoining the hotel at a cost of $10,000. Plans have been completed for the Citizens' State Bank at Tekoa, Wash., costing $10,000.

Messrs. Whitehouse & Price, architects, Hutton building, have a busy season mapped out. The commissions they have include the David Bemis school, Spokane, $25,000; Colfax, Wash., high school, $25,000; and Libby, Mont., high school, $37,000. They also have plans out for alterations in the Gray Manufacturing building, Spokane, to cost $20,000.

Have Joined the Colors

Among the San Francisco architects who have joined the colors are Mr. John Davis Hatch, who is well known as a designer of Masonic Temples throughout the State, and Mr. F. Holberg Reimers of Berkeley. Mr. Hatch has joined the Coast Artillery, National Guard and Mr. Reimers the Officers' Reserve Corps. Mr. Chas. T. Phillips, consulting engineer, with offices in the Pacific building, has enrolled in the Engineers' Corps. Another recruit to the Officers' Reserve Corps is Mr. W. W. Thurston, formerly of Lilly & Thurston, and for the past two years San Francisco representative of the Kinnear Manufacturing Company. Mr. Walter D. Reed, formerly of Dickey & Reed, and later Meyer & Reed, has also gone to the front with the Officers' Reserve Corps.

Four-Story Apartments

A contract has been let to Messrs. Cameron & Disston of San Francisco for the erection of a four-story Class C store and apartment house at Polk and Post streets, San Francisco, for Messrs. Trowbridge and Perkins. The building will cost $100,000. Mr. E. E. Young is the architect.

San Jose Residence Work

Mr. Frank D. Wolfe, Auzerais building, San Jose, has completed plans for a $4,000 Frank Lloyd Wright house for Mr. George T. McLaughlin. Mr. Wolfe has also made plans for a two-story plaster residence to be built at Hollister for Dr. J. H. Tibbitts.

Mr. William Binder is preparing plans for an $18,000 country house to be built for a client near Gilroy.

Mr. Chas. S. McKenzie has let a contract for the erection of a $30,000 apartment house at Third and Julian streets, San Jose, for Mr. Mitchell Phillips.

Competition for Odd Fellows' Orphanage

An architectural competition by invitation has been authorized by the State Odd Fellows for an orphanage building to be erected on North Twenty-fourth street, San Jose. The orphanage at Gilroy is to be abandoned. A building to cost from $60,000 to $80,000 is planned. Among the architects who will be invited to participate in the competition are Mr. William Binder and Mr. Frank D. Wolfe of San Jose and Mr. J. H. Boehrer of Oakland, all members of the Odd Fellows fraternity.

Berkeley Business Block

Mr. James W. Plachek of Berkeley has completed plans and contracts have been let for a three-story reinforced concrete store and hotel building to be erected at University and Shattuck avenues, Berkeley. This is the principal business corner of the college town and the new structure will be a welcome improvement to that corner. The building will cost in the neighborhood of $40,000.

Two-Story Addition

Plans have been completed and contracts let by Messrs. Ward & Blohme, San Francisco, for a two-story Class C addition to the two-story building at 55 Union street, San Francisco, the property of Mr. Wm. T. Sesnon. The lessees are the Cudahy Packing Company.

Hotel Addition

Plans have been completed by Mr. C. H. Skidmore, New Call building, San Francisco, for a four-story reinforced concrete addition to the Niagara Hotel on Howard street, near Fourth, San Francisco.

Personals

During his absence at the front, Mr. Wm. A. Newman, Hewes building, San Francisco, will take charge of the architectural work of Mr. John Davis Hatch. This includes the Masonic Temple at Vallejo, now under construction, and a $40,000 building for the Masonic Hall Association at Modesto.

Mr. Wm. A. Newman has recently returned from Honolulu, where a contract was signed for the construction of a $60,000 Christian Science Church.

* * *

Mr. W. E. Dennison of the Steiger Terra Cotta & Pottery Works is in the East attending a meeting of the National Terra Cotta convention. Mr. Dennison is undecided whether or not he will rebuild the Steiger plant recently burned in South San Francisco. He has spent 20 years' active service in developing the industry and today terra cotta is one of the most popular building materials manufactured.

* * *

Professor C. R. Richards, professor of mechanical engineering and head of the department since 1911, has been appointed dean of the College of Engineering and director of the Engineering Experiment Station of the University of Illinois, to succeed Dr. W. F. M. Goss, who has resigned to become president of the Railway Car Manufacturers' Association of New York.

* * *

Mr. R. J. Huntington, who has been San Francisco manager of the Otis Elevator Company for a number of years, is now manager for the same company at Portland, Oregon, with headquarters at 482 Burnside street, that city. The Pacific Coast business of the Otis Elevator Company is now in charge of Mr. G. B. Grosvenor, with headquarters in San Francisco.

* * *

Mr. Gottlieb B. Maguey, A. I. A., announces the removal of his offices from 22 New York Life building to 607 Metropolitan Bank building, Minneapolis, Minn. Catalogues and samples of building material will be appreciated from the trade.

* * *

Messrs. I.. C. Steiger and M. M. Miner, both formerly connected with the Steiger Terra Cotta & Pottery Works of San Francisco, whose plant was recently destroyed by fire, and Mr. M. E. Empena have taken an option on the old Antioch (Cal.) Pottery Works.

* * *

Mr. Smith O'Brien, formerly of the architectural firm of Meyer & O'Brien, has moved from the Humboldt Bank building to suite 318 Bankers Investment building, San Francisco.

Mr. Paul C. Pape recently returned to Los Angeles after having spent some time in New York with Mr. J. M. Annechini, proprietor of the Marcel French restaurant, 215½ West Fourth street, investigating the high-class cafes of the metropolis. It is Mr. Annechini's intention to erect a cafe building in Los Angeles.

More About New Engineers Club

As noted in the May Architect and Engineer, an Engineers' Club has been formed in Oakland, Cal., the object of which is to assist the Oakland Chamber of Commerce in solving engineering problems that affect the betterment and future welfare of the East Bay Cities, and to promote goodfellowship among the members of the profession. The club has already a membership of over fifty, and hopes to increase this number to 100 in the near future. A committee has been formed consisting of Mr. Thomas J. Allen, engineer of the Realty Syndicate Company; Mr. E. M. Boggs, chief engineer of the Key System, and Mr. W. D. Bunker, general manager of the Judson Iron Works, to act as a preparedness in conjunction with Governor Stephens' Council of Defense. The officers of the club are: Mr. Harlan D. Miller, president; Mr. R. S. Chew, vice-president; Mr. J. A. Britton, Jr., secretary, and Mr. R. W. Myers, Mr. A. Vander Naillen, Jr., Mr. E. S. Blake and Mr. H. N. Mosher, directors.

San Francisco Society of Architects

A meeting of the San Francisco Society of Architects was held in the Palace Hotel after luncheon on Wednesday, May 9th. Members present were:

Charles Peter Weeks (President)	Lewis P. Hobart
George W. Kelham (Vice-President)	Ernest A. Coxhead
	Charles S. Kaiser
Warren Charles Perry (Secretary-Treasurer)	Louis C. Mullgardt
	John Reid, Jr.
	Loring P. Rixford
John Bakewell, Jr.	John Galen Howard
J. Harry Blohme	(with Messrs. Paul F.
Arthur Brown, Jr.	Denivelle and B. E.
Henry H. Gutterson	Holden as guests)

The meeting having been called for the purpose of nominating officers for the coming year, the following names were proposed and seconded:

```
For President...............George W. Kelham
For Vice-President...............John Reid, Jr.
For Secretary-Treasurer....Warren Charles Perry
For Director (1)..........Charles Peter Weeks
For Director (2)............{ Charles S. Kaiser
                           { Arthur Brown, Jr.
```

Oroville High School

Messrs. N. W. Sexton & Company, Merchants National Bank building, San Francisco, have completed plans for a new Union High School building to be erected at Oroville, Butte county. A bond issue of $60,000 has been authorized. Construction will be reinforced concrete and hollow tile.

University of Idaho Buildings

Mr. C. Richardson, architect, Moscow, Idaho, has come right to the front in his profession during the two years he has lived there. Mr. Richardson was with Cutter & Malmgren of Spokane for years. The work he has on hand includes improvements for the University of Idaho, Moscow, calling for the erection of a three-story wing to the administration building, 53x82 feet, to cost $75,000; a central heating plant for the University consisting of two new boilers and extension trunks, to cost $7,000; also $30,000 to be spent on farm buildings and other improvements for the agricultural department. Another commission is a new wing, 64x64 feet, three stories in height, to be added to the State Normal school, Lewiston, to cost about $30,000, and remodeling the administration building of this school, at a cost of $10,000.

Lewiston Architects Busy

Mr. R. S. Loring, architect, Lewiston, Idaho, has plans for a new office building for doctors to be erected on Main street near the depot. This will be a one-story brick building with basement. He has also under construction an addition to the warehouse of the Lewiston Mercantile Company, a one-story concrete structure, to cost $16,000.

Mr. J. H. Nave, architect, Lewiston, has completed plans for an additional class room to the Lewiston Orchards school, which will include a boiler and fuel room, improvement to cost $5,000. Mr. Nave also has plans completed for a new school building at Leftridge, to cost $10,000.

Los Angeles Mercantile Building

Mr. W. J. Dodd and Mr. Wm. Richards, 609 Breckman building, Los Angeles, and Mr. A. C. Martin, associate, are preparing preliminary plans and estimates for a Class "A" reinforced concrete mercantile building to be erected at the northwest corner of Seventh and Hill streets, on the Dillon property, for Shirley Ward and associates. The building will be 115x150 feet and is being designed for 12 stores and basement, the city building ordinance having been amended to permit the erection of reinforced concrete buildings 150 feet in height.

Community Mausoleum

Mr. A. F. Rosenheim, 1118 Van Nuys building, Los Angeles, has been commissioned to prepare plans for a reinforced concrete "community mausoleum." The estimated cost is $250,000.

Mr. Rosenheim is also preparing plans for extensive alterations and additions to the two-story brick residence at 1120 Westchester Place.

Government Appoints Architects

The United States Government has named three San Francisco architects to serve without remuneration as an advisory board in connection with the preparation of plans for federal buildings on the Pacific Coast.

Mr. Walter D. Bliss has been appointed chairman of the committee, with Mr. George William Kelham and Mr. William Mooser as the other two members. Work at the various navy yards, coaling stations, radio stations and naval training stations, including those located at Puget Sound, Mare Island, Goat Island, San Diego, Pearl Harbor, Hawaii and in the Philippines will come under the observation of this committee.

Coast Architects to Address Educators

Mr. John J. Donovan, architect for the city of Oakland, has been invited to give an address at the annual meeting of the National Education Association to be held in Portland, Ore., July 11-12. His subject will be "The Relations Between Boards of Education, Their Superintendents and the Architect."

In the discussion of the subject of school house standardization, addresses will be made by Mr. Edgar Blair, architect of Seattle, and Mr. F. A. Naramore, school architect of Portland, Ore.

Addition to Sugar Refinery

Plans have been completed by Mr. Wm. H. Crim, Jr., 425 Kearny street, San Francisco, for doubling the present plant of the California and Hawaiian Sugar Refinery at Crockett. A number of different buildings will be constructed, the main one a seven-story steel and brick structure. There will also be an immense smoke stack, 175 feet high and constructed of reinforced concrete.

Built San Francisco Postoffice

A press dispatch from Milwaukee says that Mr. Henry Ferge, 64 years old, one of the foremost building contractors in the country, died June 4. Among the buildings erected under his management was the San Francisco postoffice.

Changes to Flood Building

Plans are in the hands of Mr. Morris Bruce for extensive alterations to the interior of the James Flood building, the improvements to be made as soon as the Southern Pacific Company vacates the premises in the fall.

May and June, 1905, Copies Wanted

The publishers will pay 25 cents per copy for above copies of The Architect and Engineer.

Mr. Reed Designing Bank

Messrs. Reed & Corlett of Oakland have prepared plans for the reconstruction of the Bank of Concord, which was damaged by fire recently. Through an error it was stated in the May number that Mr. G. A. Applegarth was doing the work. Mr. Applegarth designed the original building.

Fresno Architect Busy

Mr. Ernest J. Kump reports considerable new work under way in his office. He is making the plans for a group of high school buildings at Coalinga for which a bond issue of $85,000 has been authorized, and he is also preparing plans for a sixteen-room grammar school building at Los Banos to cost $60,000.

Hollow Tile Clubhouse

Messrs. Winter & Nicholson, 705 Marsh-Strong building, have been awarded the contract for the erection of the clubhouse to be built at Santa Barbara for the Santa Barbara Club. The structure will cost between $95,000 and $100,000. The architect is Mr. Bertram Goodhue, 2 W Forty-seventh street, New York.

Prune Growers Office Building

The prune growers of Santa Clara county, as well as the state organization, will make their headquarters in a new office building to be erected at San Antonio and Market streets, San Jose, from plans being prepared by Messrs. Binder & Curtis of that city.

Piedmont Residence

Mr. Wm. E. Milwain, Albany Block, Oakland, has prepared plans for a two-story basement and attic frame residence in the Colonial style to be erected on Sierra avenue, Piedmont, for Mr. A. W. Clark, at a cost of approximately $20,000.

Berkeley Fraternity House

Plans have been prepared by Messrs. Richardson & Burrell for a two-story and basement Class C fraternity house to be built in Piedmont Place for the Delta Kappa Epsilon. About $25,000 will be expended on the work.

'Residence Alterations

Mr. G. A. Applegarth has made plans for alterations and additions costing $30,-000 or more, to the Pacific avenue home of Mr. George Newhall. The house is to be converted into modern apartments. Mr. George A. Bos has the contract.

$18,000 Residence

Mr. John H. Thomas, First National Bank building, Berkeley, is preparing plans for a three-story and basement residence to be built in Piedmont for Mrs. I. H. Crosby. The improvements will cost in excess of $18,000.

Nevada Building Is Active

"There is an unusually large amount of building going on in Reno and nearby districts at the present time," said Mr. Fred J. DeLongchamps, local architect, in discussing general industrial conditions in Nevada.

"Some very large buildings are being put up, contracts have been let for many more and I am drawing plans for others which will add very materially to the communities in which they are located when completed.

"Reno is receiving its share of new construction work. In addition to many fine residences now in the course of construction two apartment houses are being built, the Overland hotel expects to add a fourth story and work will start in the near future on the new Baptist church."

Plans have been drawn for the new cell house for the state prison. The cells will be made of concrete and will be 100 in number. The cell house will be made of stone from the prison quarry.

Bank and Loft Building

Mr. Edward T. Foulkes has completed plans and let contracts for the construction of a new bank building at Alameda. Mr. Foulkes has also let a contract to Messrs. Carnahan & Mulford to build a two-story Class C loft building on Sacramento street, San Francisco, for Mr. George A. Webster. Building will cost approximately $35,000.

Six-Story Office Building

Mr. Frederick H. Meyer, Bankers Investment building, San Francisco, is completing plans for a six-story Class "C" physicians' and dentists' building to be erected on the southeast corner of Sutter and Mason streets, San Francisco, for Mr. W. F. Perkins. The building will cost $100,000.

Addition to Factory

A two-story brick addition to the Workman Packing Company's plant on Seventh street, San Francisco, is to be built from plans by Mr. Smith O'Brien, who has moved his offices from the Humboldt Bank building to the Bankers Investment building, San Francisco.

Class C Garage

Mr. Mathew O'Brien, Foxcroft building, San Francisco, has completed plans for a one-story and mezzanine floor Class C garage and automobile show room building to be constructed on Golden Gate avenue, near Steiner street, San Francisco, at an estimated cost of $15,000. Mrs. Annie Shea is the owner.

Electrical Department

Proposed New Illumination Effects

By W. D'A. RYAN, in Journal of Electricity

(The West has ever played the leading role in evolution of artistic lighting design. In 1905 there was installed in Los Angeles the first ornamental electric street lighting system, which consisted of a seven-light standard, thirteen and one-half feet in height. This served to advertise Los Angeles the world over. Since then development has been rapid. Two new systems, described below, are proposed for Los Angeles and San Francisco by the author, who is the well-known designer of the beautiful lighting effects for the Panama-Pacific International Exposition.)

Proposed Ornamental Luminous Arc Standard for Broadway Lighting Effect in Los Angeles.

Proposed Two-Light Ornamental Standard for San Francisco Triangle Business District.

N Los Angeles it is proposed to use two designs of lighting standards alternating in pairs. This will add to the decorative feature and will furnish an additional element of advertising value. The designs are, respectively, the Rose standard and the Spanish Renaissance, both of which are particularly appropriate to Los Angeles. These were executed by Mr. J. W. Gosling, who has been associated with the writer for a number of years, and he also designed the major portion of the lighting standards and units used at the (San Francisco) Panama-Pacific International Exposition. The Los Angeles standards, without question, represent Mr. Gosling's best effort in this particular field.

The system recommended represents the most advanced practice in modern street illumination. The lighting will be lively without excessive lutrinsic brilliancy. The arcs will be at an approximate elevation of 25 feet., where they will not interfere with the window lighting or sign lighting either by simultaneous contrast or otherwise, but will soften the general effect. They will add dignity and beauty to the streets by day as well as by night, and the apparent broadening of the streets and sidewalks as compared with the present effect of the globe cluster lights will be most marked. Not only will Los Angeles have a well lighted street surface, but owing to the high co-efficient of reflection of the buildings, the facade and sky line lighting will be unusual. We have aimed to combine modern flood lighting and utilitarian results with a slight suggestion of the Carnival. The soft tone of the glassware specified will be much less insistent than the present white glassware.

In San Francisco, the business section, bounded by Market, Powell, Sutter and Kearny streets, with a block extension on Kearny, is to be known as the Triangle District.

Nearly nine thousand feet of streets are to be lighted in this district with approximately fifteen thousand feet of abutting property. There are to be a total of two hundred and fifty-six lamps. It is recommended that there shall be two 6.6 ampere luminous arc lamps on each standard. These lamps are to be equipped with San Francisco gold carrara glassware.

The definite design of the standard will be determined at a later date. For estimating purposes a suggested design is given which shows the distance to the arc to be 22 feet. This measurement should be maintained.

On the lighting plan certain locations are designated where lamps are to burn all night. All other lamps are to be extinguished at midnight. The present electrolier locations have been chosen in order to utilize the existing laterals. These laterals are one inch pipe and a special cable ⅞ inch in diameter.

A New Fire Hazard

A new form of fire peril is coming into prominence as a cause of much destruction and its fires are so directly associated with carelessness that it seems advisable to issue a special warning to property owners, agents and tenants.

Because of their convenience, small electric devices such as pressing irons, curling irons, toasters, electric pads or blankets, electric plate warmers and electric sterilizers or heaters are now to be found in every community.

If these were used with proper care the danger would be negligible, but unfortunately many of their users do not realize the peril of leaving them in circuit when not in use. In such cases these devices tend to become overheated, whereupon they are likely to set fire to anything combustible with which they are in contact.

Most of these fires are small, but the aggregate loss as well as the loss to the individual is large, and a number of recent instances have shown extensive damage, as in the case of the $350,000 fire in the Boston residence of ex-Governor Draper, which was traced to an electric plate warmer in the butler's pantry.

Fires of this class furnish a peril to life, being most frequent in dwellings and breaking out often at night. A characteristic example is that in which an electric pressing iron is left upon the ironing board with the current turned on and then forgotten. In such a case the fire may not occur until hours later. The burning of the residence of John Wanamaker a few years ago was due to this cause.

That this form of hazard is already assuming large proportions appears from the statistics. For example, the Actuarial Bureau of the National Board of Fire Underwriters in one day reported approximately 100 fires from this cause out of a total of 2,000 losses in the day's reports, and it is estimated that small electrical devices are causing 30,000 fires a year.

It is safe to say that most of these fires are entirely preventable and are due to carelessness.—Realty.

Cantonment Work at the Presidio

During the past month the government entered into contracts with the G. M. Gest Company and the Barrett Roofing Company of Boston for the construction of $1,600,000 worth of work at the Presidio, San Francisco. The Gest Company will put up the buildings and the Barrett Company will be in charge of the road and sewer work. Both contracts were let without advertising for bids, and naturally the San Francisco contractors are much perturbed over the award. The buildings are to house the Coast division of the United States Army.

Why You Should Specify KOHLER Sinks

KOHLER Sinks have same quality distinctions that make KOHLER Bath Tubs and Lavatories first choice for the well-planned home.

The designs have the hygienic features that are characteristic of all

"It's in the Kohler Enamel"

KOHLER WARE

always of one quality—the highest

KOHLER Sinks are made for right and left-hand corners and for open wall spaces. They have right, left and double sloping drainboards, and are made with and without aprons.

The whiteness of the enamel is notable in all KOHLER products, each of which has our permanent trade-mark—a guarantee of its high quality.

Architects who specify KOHLER WARE get no complaints from their clients.

KOHLER CO., Founded 1873 Kohler, Wis.

Boston   New York   Philadelphia   Atlanta   Pittsburgh   Detroit   Chicago   Indianapolis
St. Paul   St. Louis   Houston   San Francisco   Los Angeles   Seattle   London

★ The KOHLER permanent trade-mark in faint blue appears on end of sink shown by star.

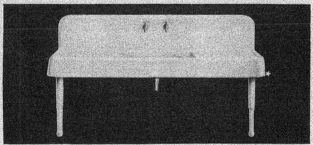

K-100-A

CONTRACTOR AND BUILDER

Public Versus Private Work

A CONSIDERABLE difference exists between public and private work. In letting private contracts two courses are open—either the selection of a single contractor and giving him the work on percentage without competition or the inviting of competitive bids and then awarding the contract to the responsible low- man. There can be no question as to the right of an architect to award a contract without competition if his client so wills. When, however, bids are taken, then a co-operative arrangement is entered into by which the contractors pool their time, experience and money in sub-mitting estimates, with the job as the stake. If they lose out on prices, they cannot comp'ain. If their figures are the lowest they naturally expect to be given the contract. The question of whether the low bidders are capable and responsible should have been considered before their time, experience and money were used. Any other course is like accepting a man as a member of a club, taking his initiation fee and dues and then denying him the club privileges. His eligibility should have been decided in advance of his acceptance as a member. The practice with some architects of throwing the doors wide open in the bidding and then awarding the contract to a "favorite", or "turning down" the low bidder on grounds of his irresponsibility has caused much dissatisfaction. This has resulted in the East in the "Nelson" method of choosing bidders and awarding contracts by which the unsuccessful bidders receive pay for their time lost in estimating.

The San Francisco contractors, while not yet insisting upon this radical innovation, still maintain that they have rights which must be recognized and protected and at a special meeting of the General Contractors' Association held April 19th, 1917, the following resolutions were adopted:

"Whereas members of this Association have from time to time reported that, after having placed bids on certain private work, they have found themselves discriminated against in the awarding of the contract, the award being made to others than the low, regular bidder; and

"Whereas an adequate estimate of quantities on a building involves a substantial outlay by the bidder of time and money amounting to from one-fifth to one-half of one per cent of the ultimate cost of the building and in addition involves a knowledge of methods and val-ues that represent the major result of his entire business experience and constitutes in reality his stock in trade; and

"Whereas in competitive bidding, the only prize is the job, as represented by the plans and specifications submitted, to gain which the bidders willingly hazard time, money and experience as aforesaid; and

"Whereas in private work it is always possible to select satisfactory individual bidders in sufficient number to insure adequate competition and to exclude from the privilege of bidding any and all to whom, for any reason, there should be any hesitancy on the part of the owner, architect or engineer in awarding the contract, if he were found to be the low bidder; and

"Whereas to receive from a person a thing of value under conditions that render it possible or unlikely that he will receive compensation therefor is dishonorable and dishonest; now therefore be it

"Resolved that the General Contractors' Association of San Francisco condemns the practice referred to in the opening paragraph hereof and hereby declares that where competitive bids are invited, all such bids shall be based on the same conditions, all bids considered in the competition shall be opened at the time and place of which each bidder shall be notified with the privilege of representation thereat, and that the original low bidder, in accordance with plans and specifications submitted, is entitled to and shall be accorded first considera-tion in the final award of contract; and

"Be it further resolved that this Association use its influence to promote this principle and to require its members to abide thereby and to refuse to place bids with owners, architects or engineers who will not agree to the principles embodied herein."

* * *

In the matter of contracts for public work a different state of affairs should exist. Private contracts should be eliminated, for in this "free and equal" country, Uncle Sam should know no favorites. To select a man who has "influence at court" is a "monarchial" procedure inconsistent with a republic's democratic principles. Consequently, the announcement that con-struction jobs at the Presidio of San Francisco, involving millions, had been awarded to C. M. Gest & Company of New York and Barrett Roofing Company of Boston (reputed to be affiliated con-cerns) without competition, on a per-

centage basis, has caused a wave of indignation to roll over the Pacific Coast and the beating of the surf against the official shores will be heard quite clearly, we believe, by our somnolent representatives at Washington before this incident may be considered closed. Why, when this section is so rich in competent firms engaged in building and street construction, should Eastern concerns be sent three thousand miles on a rush job, when the assembling of equipment alone will take some three weeks' time and the added delay of local organization for the work must still further prevent rapid progress? San Francisco (like all California) is pre-eminently loyal and has been one of the first to respond with money and services to our Country's demands and it is with a feeling that we have been,"thrown down" without reason or justice that has caused us to voice a vigorous protest against this summary action.

In the time it has taken the Eastern construction company to assemble its plant in San Francisco and perfect its organization, the government could have advertised ten days for bids, let contracts here to the low bidders and the work could have been well under way now. Furthermore, if the government entertained any doubt as to the ability of San Francisco firms to handle $1,600,000 worth of work, it could have divided the work into eight or ten contracts

which would have permitted the construction of buildings in units.

It seems to us to have been a very bad piece of politics and it should not be allowed to go without rigid investigation. The people of this Coast, our building interests in particular, are entitled to an explanation and the blame should be put where it belongs.

Offers Uncle Sam Patent Process for Generating Gas

The office and factory of the Union Gas Electric Company, manufacturers and distributors of the Fish gas system, have been moved to 50-54 8th St., San Francisco.

Mr. George L. Fish, head of the company, has been East the past three weeks, stopping at Washington, D. C., where he offered the United States government his process for generating gas and electricity and thereby eliminating storage batteries, motors and dynamos on submarines and other vessels in use by the government in war times.

The California Union Gas Electric Company has been incorporated in Sacramento with a working capital of $100,-000. This organization will handle the Business of the Union Gas Electric Company in all territory outside of San Francisco. Messrs. H. Jorgenson, formerly of the National City Bank of New York, and A. H. Blackiston, also of New York, are now identified with the subsidiary corporation.

The Building Situation

Building operations throughout the country continue with but little abatement, the first quarter of this year showing a loss of only a fraction of one per cent as compared with 1916, while 1916 displayed a great gain over 1915. Hoggson Brothers, the New York and Chicago builders, announce that they started active operations in April on five buildings for banks alone in different sections.

The impression is gaining strength that while present costs of materials entering into the construction of buildings appear to be high, the prospects are for prices to go to still higher levels. The American Architect points out that inasmuch as a dollar will buy only three-fourths as much of any commodity as it would three years ago, the cost of building is in practically the same ratio to former costs.

"It is possible to enumerate one reason after another in favor of the contention that present prices are low—not high," declares that paper. "If owners can be made to see that the really pertinent comparisons of costs are with the future rather than the past, building cannot fail to take on greater activity. Viewed in this light, present prices for building materials actually appear to be bargain prices."

Authorities for the most part seem agreed that the chances for building material prices to take a drop are quite remote, whether hostilities continue for some time or whether peace should come within the near future. It is argued that the after-war demand on our industrial resources will be infinitely greater than they have been. France has just recently closed a contract involving two hundred million francs, most of which sum is to be spent in America for building materials to be used in the reconstruction of important buildings in cities in the vicinity of Verdun, the Argonne and the heights of the Meuse.

The danger of a cessation of building activities does not lie so much in the impression that prices are too high as it does in an attempt to carry the economy idea to harmful lengths. Nothing could be more injurious than indiscriminate delaying of plans for building. This would create an industrial situation that would be far-reaching in its evil effects.

The government is actually carrying on a campaign against the holding up of industrial activities, Howard E. Coffin, of the advisory commission of the Council of National Defense, declaring that "waste is bad, but an indiscriminating economy is worse. Unemployment and closed factories brought about through fitful and ill-advised campaigns for public and private economy, will prove a veritable foundation of quicksand for the serious work we have on hand. We need prosperity in war time even more than when we are at peace. Business depressions always are bad, but doubly so when we have a fight on our hands. The declaration of war can have no real evil effect on business. What bad effects are apparent are purely psychological and largely of our own foolish making. For our markets are the same in April as they are in March. We need more business, not less. There is real danger in hysteria. Indiscriminate economy would be ruinous. Now is the time to open the throttle."

Two years ago the prospective builder was urged to "Build Now" to secure the advantage of low prices and to give employment to idle labor. Today he is urged to "Build Now" so as to keep skilled labor employed, to keep the wheels of industrial activity going, and to take advantage of present prices, lest he be forced to pay even more if he delays.

Big Government Contract

The Turner Construction Company has obtained a contract for the erection of two large reinforced concrete storage buildings at the Brooklyn Navy Yard, the total cost of which will be approximately $2,000,000. This is one of the first important government contracts to be awarded, and is the forerunner of a mass of important government work.

Factories Require Abundance of Light

Mr. W. Fred Locke, Jr., of Lockwood, Greene & Company, Boston, Mass., writes in the Industrial Building issue of the American Architect:

"Any one who has followed the changes in modern industrial methods is familiar with the new attitude of the up-to-date factory manager in regard to fire-proof construction. No longer is it merely a question of getting the most advantageous insurance rate; it is a question of life itself. The manufacturer now says, "a disastrous fire in my plant would practically put me out of business. Fire insurance would never repay me for the loss of business, loss of prestige, least of all for the certain loss of skilled operators. The struggle to rebuild and to re-equip a new plant, to train a new force of employees, to get back lost business in these days of strenuous competition, would require an outlay of capital and efforts which would be beyond my resources.

"An abundance of daylight is now an accepted essential in factories. In fact, any added expense that may be necessary within reasonable limits to procure a full measure of natural light will be justified. Well-lighted workrooms unquestionably make for good health, relieve eye strain, tone up a working corps, insure a better product with less weight and reduce the hazard of accidents."

Manufacturers' Inquiries

The president of the society was recently asked the following question by the advertising manager of a large manufacturing concern, says the Monthly Bulletin of the Illinois Society of Architects: "Why do not architects answer letters of inquiry from manufacturers?" The answer was the statement that

"Every architect receives on an average of twenty letters per day, not accompanied by either a return post card or a stamped envelope, asking for information when there is work on the boards. Assuming that every architect was busy the entire time, it would mean that every architect would be expected to answer, say 20 letters of inquiry per day, or 6,000 per year, and as no letter can be written at a less cost than about 20 cents, counting postage, stationery, time and overhead, every architect would be expected to spend the sum of $1,200 per year in answering these inquiries if they were answered." Is further comment necessary?

California Leading

California is leading the states in the amount of concrete construction placed under contract, so far having awarded the following work:

Concrete roads, 1,047,720 square yards; streets, 113,120 square yards; alleys, 7,575 square yards; total, 1,168,415 square yards.

Mr. John H. Powers Busy

Mr. John H. Powers, architect, 460 Montgomery street, San Francisco, has the following work under way:

A great number of improvements at Winehaven, Cal., for the California Wine Association, including ten bungalows, a reinforced concrete wine storage cellar 150 feet wide by 230 feet long, containing about 2,000,000 gallons of wine storage capacity.

A nine-room residence for Mr. John R. Cahill on Lyon street near Jackson, San Francisco. The plans contemplate a stucco exterior colored a blue stone gray, the walls being crowned by a red terra cotta tile cornice, the same feature being used over other openings.

Two other improvements held in abeyance at present are a two-story addition to a class "A" building on Townsend street and an apartment in Hyde street.

California Architects Should Get in Line

The Architectural League of New York announces that it has enrolled a food battalion which will cultivate a forty-acre farm at Forest Hills Garden. The battalion is made up of 100 architects and employees, who have promised to give a week of their vacation to the work. The proceeds will be divided between war charities and volunteers.

Economy Range Boiler Cover Free

Architects planning homes find it advisable to allow for a few inches additional space in the range boiler closets to permit the application of an insulating jacket to cover the boiler.

These covers take up but little room—being manufactured in three thicknesses, one, two and three inches, the most efficient type being the three inches thick —and the saving they make in fuel or current soon more than pays for the cover itself.

And it is not only the saving in money which appeals to the modern housewife, but also the solid comfort these range boiler covers give by not permitting the hot water to cool down rapidly in the boiler. There is always hot water on tap at minimum fuel cost when one of these jackets covers the range boiler.

Probably the most widely-known and generally used covers of this type is the "Economy" Range Boiler Cover, sold by the H. W. Johns-Manville Company at Second and Howard streets, San Francisco. This company has an interesting leaflet describing the "Economy" Range Boiler Cover which will be sent to architects, engineers and home-owners upon request.

New Corporation Formed

Messrs. M. V. Van Fleet and Geo. H. Freear, for a number of years representing the Armstrong Cork and Insulation Company, and David E. Kennedy, Inc., respectively, announce that they have formed a corporation for the distribution of all the materials formerly handled by them independently and that hereafter all their business will be carried on under the firm name of Van Fleet-Freear Company, San Francisco.

The new firm extends a cordial greeting to its clientele and solicits their continued patronage.

Factory and Residence

Mr. A. B. Benton, 114 North Spring street, Los Angeles, has been commissioned to prepare plans for a two-story factory building and about thirty dwellings to be erected at Walnut Creek, Contra Costa county, Cal., for the Contra Costa Company, glove manufacturers. Those active in the Glove Company are Mr. E. B. Bull, Mr. Wendell Phillips and Mr. J. W. Phillips, all of Oakland, Cal. Mr. Bull is now in the East gathering data for incorporation in the new works.

Cotton Warehouse

The engineering department of the Santa Fe Railway Company, Kerckhoff building is preparing plans for a one-story cotton warehouse to be erected for the railway company in San Francisco. It will be 174x400 feet.

CARMEN-JOHNSON BUILDING, SAN FRANCISCO
PAINTED WITH GOLDEN STATE BRICK AND CEMENT COATING

Golden State Brick and Cement Coating

The accompanying photograph shows the Carmen-Johnson building at Sansome and Sacramento streets, San Francisco, after being painted with two coats of Golden State brick and cement coating, manufactured in San Francisco by R. N. Nason & Company. This is a waterproofing paint that may be applied to either a cement or brick surface, and is guaranteed to keep out the moisture, prevent cracks and preserve the material to which it is applied. The coating is manufactured in any desired color.

Japanese a Poor Substitute for American Oak

Efforts of the American oak flooring manufacturers to discourage the use of Japanese oak on the Pacific Coast seem designed to be realized, according to advices from lumber dealers who are posted on the situation.

Mr. C. H. White, manager of White Bros., one of the largest hardwood lumber dealers on the Coast, says:

"Japanese oak is a soft, easily worked wood, and is therefore desired by some furniture manufacturers on that account, as well as on account of its cheapness. It, however, is not a high class oak by any means, being too soft and showing very little figure. Moreover, when it grows old it becomes dingy and dirty looking, exactly opposite to the action of the American oak which, as you know, improves and grows richer with age.

"The cheapness of Japanese oak has recommended it and it is estimated that twelve to fifteen million feet a year have been used on the Pacific Coast alone. At the present time, however, there is no Japanese oak in the market on account of a lack of shipping facilities, and Pacific Coast manufacturers are turning again to the use of American oak.

"The Japs have done a lot of damage to Eastern lumbermen and Pacific Coast lumbermen inasmuch as they started a yard here in San Francisco of their own, selling Japanese oak to the smallest consumer at practically the same price they would sell, as wholesalers, to the dealers here. Naturally they got all the business and this action on their part irritated the San Francisco dealers so much that for the last several years, they have been using every effort they could to combat the Japanese oak and birch, and with very gratifying results."

To Be Model Town

A model town, patterned after W. A. Clark's town of Clarkdale six miles eastward, is to be built adjoining the townsite of Jerome, in Yavapai county, Arizona. The site is on a hogback, high upon the mountain. No surface rights will be sold, but long-term leases will be granted. A number of residences and business blocks will be built for rent. Most of the United Verde Extension copper mine will be housed in the new town. The Extension Company will build a similar town at a proposed new smelter, the site of which has not yet been selected.

The United Verde Extension mine, which will support the new town, has been shipping 12 or 15 cars of ore daily, and still is holding up to that production. The profits of the mine are about $400,-000 monthly.

Crane Company's Hot Water Heating Plant Described Before Illinois Chapter

"Hot Water Heating Under Forced Circulation, as Installed in the Crane Plant," was the subject of an illustrated address presented by Mr. S. H. McCreary of the Crane Company, at the March meeting of the Illinois Chapter, March 12. The talk followed a chapter dinner at the Chicago Engineers' Club.

The speaker was introduced by President F. W. Powers. Mr. McCreary stated that the total cost of the new Crane Company plant would approximate $10,-000,000 of which $1,000,000 would represent the cost of heating equipment. The entire plant comprises 50 buildings covering an area of 50 acres and the company has an additional 160 acres adjoining its plant for possible future extensions.

No less than 300,000 square feet of heating surface are now in service, arranged on six circuits in tunnel systems, aggregating a total length of 4,978 feet. The heating system contains 5,332 gallons of water and Mr. McCreary stated that the average drop in temperature of the water in making the circuit of the system is 16 degrees. He stated that one day during the past winter, when the temperature outdoors was 10 degrees F. below zero, the outgoing temperature of the water was 187 degrees and the incoming temperature 152 degrees, giving a drop of 35 degrees.

At the conclusion of Mr. McCreary's address and upon his request, President Powers gave a description of the system of temperature control installed in connection with the heating plant.

E. C. Dehn Gets Dahlstrom Account

The Dahlstrom Metallic Door Co., formerly represented by M. G. West Co., has appointed E. C. Dehn, Hearst building, as its San Francisco representative. Besides this important agency, Mr. Dehn represents the International Casement Window Co. (making English and French casement windows); the Watson Mfg. Co.'s line of

metal furniture; Western Blind and Screen Co. of Los Angeles (schools excepted); American Metal Weather Strip Co., Grand Rapids, Mich., and Draper Shade Co.'s line, "Draper Fabric," on Hartshorn shade rollers.

Yes — We are doing our bit to defeat the menace

For **M & G** machinery is VITAL to the industries that are VITAL to our Government.

In the mines—*of whatever nature--*powder works, or chemical works, and industrial plants of all kinds, from sugar mills to tanneries—

M & G machinery will be found working to defeat autocracy.

For without Pulleys, Bearings, Shafting, Gears, Sprockets, Elevating, Conveying and Transmission Machinery, PRODUCTION along every line would CEASE, and all the bravery in the world would avail NOTHING.

Hotel Orlando, Decatur, Illinois, Holmes & Flinn, Chicago, Architects.
All Sheet Metal Work of ARMCO Iron.

Leading Architects Specify

The Iron That's Made To Last

As a result of years of observation of its behavior in service, modern architects are more and more regularly including in their specifications—*"All sheet metal work and metal lath of Armco Iron."*

This is the purest, most even and most carefully made of irons. It is the material chosen by men who look to the future.

The trade mark ARMCO carries the assurance that iron bearing that mark is manufactured by The American Rolling Mill Company with the skill, intelligence and fidelity associated with its products, and hence can be depended upon to possess in the highest degree the merit claimed for it.

THE AMERICAN ROLLING MILL COMPANY

Licensed Manufacturers under Patents granted to the International Metal Products Company

MIDDLETOWN, OHIO

ARMCO Iron Sheets, Plates, Roofing, Metal Lath and other building products

Pacific Coast Sales Office — Monadnock Building, San Francisco; other Branch Offices in New York, Chicago, Pittsburgh, Cleveland, Detroit, St. Louis, Cincinnati, Atlanta, and Washington, D. C. An Ample Stock of Armco Iron is Carried at San Francisco.

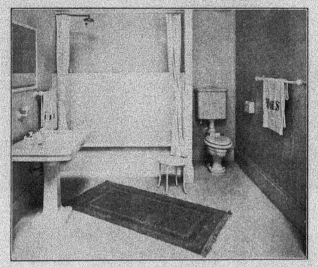

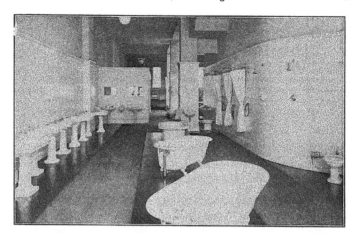

SHOWING PART OF DISPLAY ROOM, HOLBROOK, MERRILL & STETSON

Holbrook, Merrill & Stetson Establish Uptown Display Room in San Francisco

AN ENTERPRISE likely to be appreciated by architects and prospective builders is the establishment of an uptown display room bv Holbrook, Merrill & Stetson, one of San Francisco's pioneer plumbing supply houses. Ground floor space has been taken in the Holbrook building on the north side of Sutter street, between Sansome and Montgomery streets, San Francisco, and no expense has been spared in fitting up the place so as to display to the very best advantage the company's varied line of plumbing fixtures. Here the architect may see the fixtures under actual water pressure, and to further assist him in the selection of suitable equipment a number of separate bath rooms have

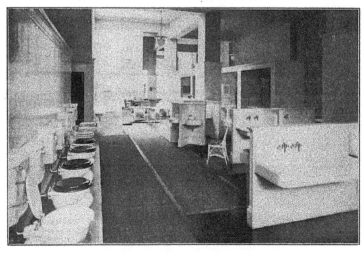

TOILET AND LAVATORY DISPLAY, HOLBROOK, MERRILL & STETSON

When writing to Advertisers please mention this magazine.

been built with tub, shower, lavatory and toilet completely installed. The architect is thus enabled to bring his client and show him just what he is going to have in his own building or home. All this is so much more satisfactory than the old method of selecting one's fixtures from an uninteresting catalogue. The very latest things are shown in plumbing advancement, including built-in tubs, foot baths, showers with overhead, side and needle spray, and lavatories with combination fittings which regulate the water to any desired temperature. Moderate priced as well as the more expensive fixtures are displayed. Mr. W. H. Burt, for many years identified with Holbrook, Merrill & Stetson, is in charge and is prepared to give architects and others interested the benefit of his wide experience by way of advice or suggestion.

Navy to Build Here

Mr. Walter Bliss, who is to act with Messrs. George W. Kelham and William Mooser as an architectural board in charge of new construction work on the Pacific Coast for the United States Navy, recently returned from Washington, D. C., where he went to confer with Government authorities. Just how much work there will be the Government has not yet fully determined. It is planned, however, to do considerable building at Mare Island at once and all structures to be erected there will be permanent. Several buildings are also to be built at the Presidio.

Have Fine Screen Exhibit

Messrs. Simpson & Stewart, 565 Sixteenth street, Oakland, announce the completion of an attractive display at the Building Material Exhibit, 770 O'Farrell street, San Francisco. The line includes window shades, Hipolito screen doors, rolling screens and metal screens, also silicate blackboards.

A representative of the firm is in charge of the exhibit and he will be pleased to supply information to architects and owners at all times. Messrs. Simpson & Stew-

art are putting out a casement window adjuster which will be handled by various hardware stores throughout the State.

The firm was recently awarded a contract for supplying all the screens in the Alameda County Infirmary, also some nine or ten big State jobs, including the Fresno Normal School.

Review of Recent Books

SANDSTONE QUARRYING IN THE UNITED STATES. Bulletin 124 of the Bureau of Mines, Department of the Interior. By Oliver Bowles, quarry technologist.

This is said to be the only publication at present in the English language which takes up the subject of sandstone quarrying and deals with it exhaustively.

It is the aim of this bulletin to point out in a general way the location of workable sandstone deposits in the United States, and to outline the most efficient and economical methods of quarrying and preparing the rock for structural and other purposes.

The bulletin deals with the varieties, composition and physical properties of sandstone and the various uses for which it is adapted and contains a detailed discussion of the method of quarrying, including prospecting, stripping, channeling, drilling, wedging, blasting, and hoisting. The purpose is, not only to describe the methods, but to point out the advantages and disadvantages, and the conditions under which each method or machine will render the most efficient service. Many points are brought out, therefore, which should be of assistance to quarry operators. The process of shaping a stone into building blocks, curbing, flagging, grindstones, and other forms, is described in some detail.

The following facts, developed in this bulletin, demand special attention on the part of architects and builders: First, that well-cemented sandstone is one of the most durable and attractive of all building materials. Second, that attractive sandstone of good quality is to be found in nearly every state in the Union. And third, that sandstone to the value of only about $1,600,000 is sold annually for building purposes in the United States. The United States has passed the pioneer stage in building, and consequently the erection of structures combining both permanence and attractiveness, should, at this stage of our history, be a national aim, and ideal conditions can be attained in a large measure by selecting for building purposes the finer grades of sandstone with which the country is so richly endowed.

THE LIVABLE HOUSE. By Aymar Embury II, architect. Moffat, Yard & Co., New York. $2.50 net.

In this book Mr. Embury has made a distinctly valuable contribution to the literature available to prospective home-builders. The work concerns itself primarily with the problem of the small suburban residence, and the author discusses this problem with conciseness and

great breadth of view, considering the architectural aspect of the problem from both the client's and the architect's standpoint. Many other aspects of the home-building program, social, financial, sanitary and the like, are treated with thoroughness and lucidity. The numerous illustrations, which are a chief feature of the book, are as noteworthy for the wide variety of styles presented as for the excellence and interest of the subjects.

Literature Received

Summary of Judge Killits's Decision on Peaceful Picketing in the Home Telephone Company Case.

Nonpareil Cork Machinery Insulation, published by Armstrong Cork & Insulation Company, Pittsburgh, Pa.

"The Mexican People and Their Detractors," by Fernando Gonzalez Roa, published by Latin-American News Association, 1400 Broadway, N. Y.

Journal of the Western Society of Engineers, published in Chicago.

Some Fundamental Considerations Affecting the Food Supply of the United States, by Thos. F. Hunt, University Press, Berkeley, Cal.

Farmers' Short Courses, University State Farm, Davis, commencing September 24, to November 2, 1917.

GENERAL BULLETIN REGARDING ELECTRICAL BIDS TO THE ARCHITECTS OF SAN FRANCISCO

Many efforts have been made in the past to impress upon the persons and firms to whom electrical contractors submitted bids for electrical work that such bids represented considerable expense and labor and should be treated as confidential, but for some unknown reason we find that this is not the case.

In line with our past efforts, we find that the only remedy for the situation is to submit our bids to the architect or owner direct at some particular date, time and place. In order that this matter may not be unwieldy to the architect or owner, we have limited such bids to $500 or over, or, in other words, all electrical work costing $500 or over the bids shall be given direct to the architect or owner and none other.

Commencing Monday, June 11, 1917, no electrical contractor member will submit any bid for electrical work the cost of which is $500 or over except direct to the architect or owner or his representative, who shall set a date, time and place for the receipt of such bids and at which time and place such bids shall be opened. The contract for the electrical work shall be awarded to one of the contractors whose bid has been received at such time and place. (Signed)

ELECTRICAL CONTRACTORS AND DEALERS OF SAN FRANCISCO.

For Employees' Safety

The State Industrial Accident Commission has issued a call to the Northern and Southern California Chapters, A. I. A., and to the different building trades organizations to delegate representatives to attend a series of meetings for the purpose of formulating plans for the protection of working-men on buildings in course of construction. Meetings will be held both in San Francisco and Los Angeles.

Announcement

M. V. VAN FLEET and GEO. H. FREEAR, representing the Armstrong Cork & Insulation Company, and DAVID E. KENNEDY, Inc., announce that they have formed a corporation for the distribution of all the materials formerly handled by them independently and that hereafter all their business will be carried on under the firm name of Van Fleet - Freear Company.

The new firm extends a cordial greeting to its clientele and solicits their continued patronage.

VAN FLEET-FREEAR COMPANY,
120 JESSIE STREET, SAN FRANCISCO, CAL.

When writing to Advertisers please mention this magazine.

When writing to Advertisers please mention this magazine.

When writing to Advertisers please mention this magazine.

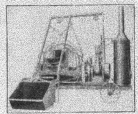

When writing to Advertisers please mention this magazine.

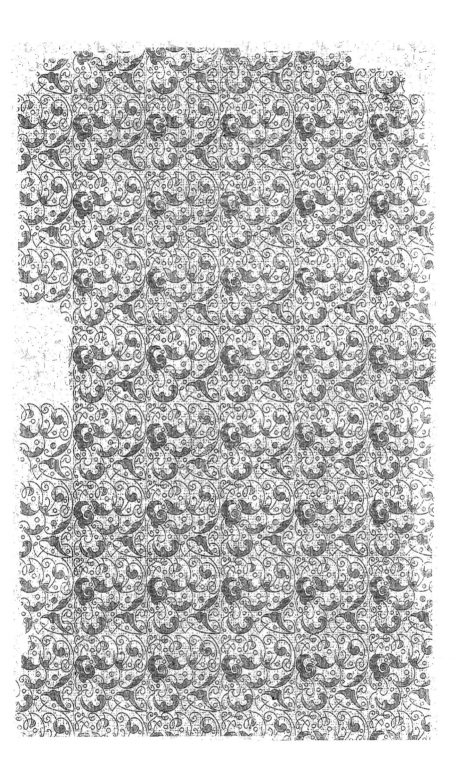

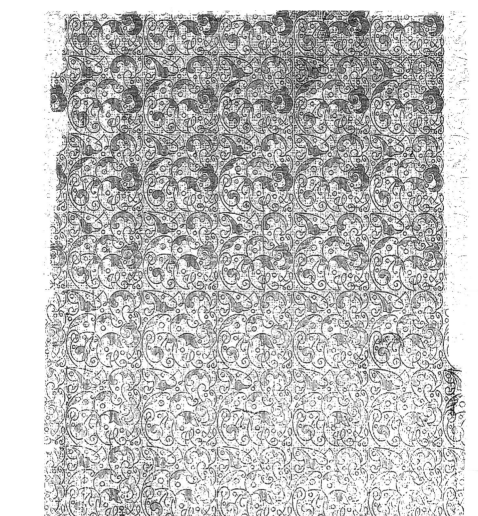